THE LETTERS OF SEAMUS HEANEY

Seamus Heaney (1939–2013) was born in County Derry in Northern Ireland. *Death of a Naturalist*, his first collection of poems, appeared in 1966, and was followed by books of poetry, criticism and translation which established him as the leading poet of his generation. In 1995 he was awarded the Nobel Prize in Literature.

Christopher Reid is the author of many books of poems, including *A Scattering* (winner of the Costa Book of the Year Award 2009), *The Song of Lunch*, and, most recently, *Toys / Tricks / Traps* (2023). He was editor of the *Letters of Ted Hughes* (2007).

by the same author

poetry

DEATH OF A NATURALIST
DOOR INTO THE DARK
WINTERING OUT
NORTH
FIELD WORK
SELECTED POEMS 1965–1975
STATION ISLAND
SWEENEY ASTRAY
SWEENEY'S FLIGHT
(with photographs by Rachel Giese)
THE HAW LANTERN
NEW SELECTED POEMS 1966–1987
SEEING THINGS
LAMENTS BY JAN KOCHANOWSKI
(translated with Stanisław Barańczak)
THE SPIRIT LEVEL
OPENED GROUND: POEMS 1966–1996
BEOWULF
ELECTRIC LIGHT
DISTRICT AND CIRCLE
THE TESTAMENT OF CRESSEID & SEVEN FABLES
HUMAN CHAIN
NEW SELECTED POEMS 1988–2013
AENEID BOOK VI
100 POEMS
THE RATTLE BAG
(edited with Ted Hughes)
THE SCHOOL BAG
(edited with Ted Hughes)
THE TRANSLATIONS OF SEAMUS HEANEY
(edited by Marco Sonzogni)

prose

PREOCCUPATIONS: SELECTED PROSE 1968–78
THE GOVERNMENT OF THE TONGUE
THE REDRESS OF POETRY: OXFORD LECTURES
FINDERS KEEPERS: SELECTED PROSE 1971–2001
STEPPING STONES
(with Dennis O'Driscoll)

plays

THE CURE AT TROY
THE BURIAL AT THEBES

The Letters of

SEAMUS HEANEY

Selected and edited by

CHRISTOPHER REID

faber

First published in 2023
by Faber & Faber Ltd
The Bindery, 51 Hatton Garden
London EC1N 8HN
This paperback edition first published in 2024

Typeset by Sam Matthews
Printed in Poland

A CIP record for this book
is available from the British Library

ISBN 978-0-571-34109-2

Printed and bound in the EU on FSC® certified paper in line with our continuing commitment to ethical business practices, sustainability and the environment.
For further information see faber.co.uk/environmental-policy

10 9 8 7 6 5 4 3 2 1

Contents

List of Illustrations

John Hume, Seamus Deane, Brian Friel and SH, St Columb's College, Derry, 1987.
Reproduced courtesy of the Heaney family (photographer unknown).

John Montague, SH and Liam O'Flynn, Gate Theatre, Dublin, 1989.
Reproduced courtesy of the Heaney family (photographer unknown).

SH, Helen Vendler and Czesław Miłosz, 1990s.
Reproduced courtesy of the Heaney family (photographer unknown).

Derek Walcott, Ted Hughes and SH, Stratford, 1992.
Reproduced courtesy of the Heaney family (photographer unknown).

Michael, Catherine, SH, Marie and Christopher, Nobel Prize ceremony, 1995.
© Eric Roxfelt/Associated Press.

Tom Sleigh, SH and Sven Birkerts.
Reproduced courtesy of the Heaney family.

Paul Muldoon, 1986.
© Jean Hanff Korelitz. Reproduced by permission.

Barrie Cooke.
Reproduced by permission of Julia Cooke.

SH and Carol Hughes, memorial service for Ted Hughes, 1999.
Photo by Tim Graham/Hulton Archive/Getty Images.

Dennis O'Driscoll and SH, Lannan Foundation in Santa Fe, New Mexico, 2003.
Reproduced courtesy of the Heaney family.

SH and Karl Miller, National Library of Ireland, Dublin, 2010.
© Andrew O'Hagan. Reproduced by permission.

Introduction

Compiling this book has brought me many gratifications, not the least of which has been the chance to hear Seamus Heaney's voice again. Of course, in the ten years since his death, the globally disseminated and instantly recognisable Heaney *public* voice – speaking his poems into studio microphones, addressing audiences in lecture halls, answering the questions of interviewers – has not ceased to be accessible by way of electronic media. Perhaps no poet of our time has left such an abundant record. More than that, the impression given is that what has been offered for public consumption, to feed the curiosity generated by an outstanding body of published work, the poetry above all, contains within it an uncommonly generous helping of the personal. The recorded poems are not so much declaimed as confided to the listener; the lectures were never so tightly scripted as not to allow room for spontaneity and a teacherly transparency; and the answers supplied in interview seem to be retrieved from depths of self-interrogation that lend them a unique trustworthiness.

When all this is available, plentifully, as supplement to a poetic *oeuvre* that needs no apology in the first place, what of value can publication of the private letters add to the picture? Don't we already know enough?

Consider *Stepping Stones* (2008) which, of all the works published in Heaney's own lifetime, comes closest to full autobiographical disclosure. Growing out of interviews conducted over a number of years between Heaney and his younger friend, the poet Dennis O'Driscoll, remarkable for its Proustian richness of recall and air of candour as it takes the reader through the steps and stages of a well-documented career, it would appear to satisfy most reasonable needs. But does it? Designed to serve as a book of record, its publication quickly brought Heaney misgivings of his own. In a letter to the American essayist Sven Birkerts of 1 January 2009, he confesses: 'Something faltered in me around Christmas '07 when I had big doubts about the wisdom of having committed *Stepping Stones*; and then I think the fact that I had cadenced myself towards a conclusion in the last chapter of that book, allied to the fact that I'd let myself in for co-operation on that 70th birthday TV documentary – which felt a lot like a "summing up" exercise – all combined to induce a not so subliminal sense of an ending.' To his old Belfast friend Michael Longley, on 11 July 2011, he describes the book flatly as being 'meant to keep biographers at bay'.

If that was the case, he must have had some sort of holding action in mind, necessary to the defence of the very sources of his poetry. In a number of letters to the literary scholar Michael Parker that are included here, he is blunt about his dread of too intimate an encroachment. Writing on 2 November 1985, after learning that Parker had pursued his researches to the extent of seeking out and speaking to members of the Heaney family, he warned him: 'There are whole areas of one's life that one wants to keep free of the gaze of print – not that there is anything to cover up but that there is a sort of emotional robbery in the uncovering'; and on 12 July 1988 he was even more emphatic:

> As you will recall, there has always been a very significant distinction in my mind between your researches for a thesis and your plans for a book. The data you collected so impressively is actually part of the lining of my memory. The people you interviewed – with a few exceptions – are not literary acquaintances but presences in the life of my first affections. The places you photographed and hope to map are actually now images that inhere as much in what I wrote as in what I remember. For this reason, the shock of intrusion, which I felt when I heard of your initial visit to my family, has been dramatically renewed with the news of the Macmillan project. For example, the Moyola sandbed. That place I marked so that you could see it. If any photograph appeared, or map that gave access, I would be devastated. It is one of the most intimate and precious of the places I know on earth, one of the few places where I am not haunted or hounded by the 'mask' of S.H. It would be a robbery and I would have the cruel knowledge that I had led the robber to the hidden treasure and even explicated its value.

Heaney's repetition of the word 'robbery' is telling: already by the time of the letters quoted above he was a conspicuous figure in the literary world of Ireland and beyond, exciting the broadest range of feelings in his readers and critics, from adulation to downright hostility, and he could not but be aware of it. This would have been a challenge to a writer who from the outset drew naturally and deeply on his personal experience, whether in the relatively unguarded poems of *Death of a Naturalist*, his first book, or in subsequent volumes where the personal was apt to be subjected to degrees of mythic transformation. Finding different ways by which to effect these transformations accounts, it seems to me, for the sense of continual self-renewal that his career gives us, especially at the early stages. The writing of *Wintering Out*, Heaney's third volume, where personal and domestic matters are addressed, or tested, through a sort of linguistic archaeology, appears from his own reports to have been especially thrilling, confirming him – at a moment of deracination, as he and his family moved from Northern Ireland to make their home in the Republic – in his poetic vocation. *Sweeney Astray*, his translation of the Old Irish text *Buile Shuibhne*, begun around this time, concerns the plight of a more spectacularly displaced individual, who even so may be taken for the provisional spiritual disguise of a poet whose name happens to rhyme with his. *North*, hard on the heels of *Wintering Out*, shows Heaney turning his attention back to home territory, enabled to do so with startling force when the sacrificial Iron Age burials that the Danish archaeologist P. V. Glob had written about in *The Bog People* came to his notice, affording him a working metaphor – controversial as it proved to be – for the Troubles.

Among Heaney's early correspondents, three stand out: Seamus Deane, his friend from St Columb's College, the Catholic boys' school in Derry; the Belfast Protestant Michael Longley; and Charles Monteith, born in Lisburn, Co. Antrim, who had made his career as a London publisher and was now Heaney's editor at Faber and Faber. With the first two, both poets, Heaney enjoyed relations that his letters indicate were characterised by both true camaraderie and a laddish, bantering habit which could sometimes show a competitive edge. The relationship with Monteith, his senior and, in effect, his patron, was more straightforward; and it is Monteith above all in whom Heaney confides, the letters to him being those that trace most clearly the poet's brisk professional debut and subsequent rapid progress, as well as his occasional detours and dead ends. Those to Deane and Longley, however, have no less a value; and perhaps they will have an even greater one for readers well acquainted with the poetry for whom Heaney's off-duty high spirits, comic flair and tendency to pranks and naughtiness may be surprising news. In the last, he was abetted by another northern compadre, the singer and television director David Hammond. The 1968 reading tour titled *Room to Rhyme*, which Heaney, Hammond and Longley – one Catholic, two Protestants – undertook together, was promoted by the Arts Council of Northern Ireland and had a serious, quasi-evangelical purpose in asserting the possibility of cultural pluralism even as widespread sectarian strife was beginning to appear unavoidable; but it was also a matter of three boyos on the lash, with all the scampishness that implied. Heaney's occasional bawdy letters and postcards to Hammond, some verging on what would now be regarded as political incorrectness, some diving with glee straight into it, are an expression of the need to let off steam felt by a writer otherwise driven by an unremitting sense of duty and accountability. The undated 1976 postcard to Hammond is included here as a token of this strain.

If my selection of letters has a principal theme, it is Heaney's obligation to duty. From the start, it manifests itself in a variety of ways. One of these was the sense of himself as a teacher that Heaney seems never to have lost. After graduating from Queen's University Belfast in 1961, with a first class honours degree, he took a diploma course at St Joseph's College of Education before going on to teach at St Thomas's Secondary Intermediate School in Ballymurphy, Belfast. Then he returned to St Joseph's as a lecturer, which is where we find him at the start of this book. For much of the rest of his life teaching supplied him with an income, and even at the period immediately following his move to Co. Wicklow in the Republic in the early 1970s, when he hoped to make a go of survival as a freelance, he was trying to persuade Charles Monteith and others at Faber and Faber to commission educational books from him. Although none materialised, perhaps this is not to be regretted as Heaney's strong teaching impulse was duly channelled elsewhere, into the more broadly ranging and appealing magazine articles and lectures that came to be gathered up in his 1980 prose collection, *Preoccupations*. The academy proper, however, soon reclaimed him: first with a job, teaching teachers once more, at Carysfort College in Dublin; then with the initially temporary appointment at Harvard that led to his long association, in a variety of posts, with the university.

America's importance to Heaney cannot be overstated. His first academic job there had been in 1970–1, at the University of California, Berkeley, and, from the bedazzled letters he wrote to friends back home, it seems to have granted him a vision of horizons far wider than any available to a young writer in the stifling, conflicted Northern Ireland of those days. American freedoms of the flower power age were something he could be both amused by and sceptical of, but the more down-to-earth and nurturing connection was with a convivial group of colleagues in Berkeley's Irish Studies programme, including Thomas Flanagan, later the author of the epic novel of the 1798 Irish rebellion, *The Year of the French*, and Robert Tracy, who was not just an Irish specialist but also a translator from the Russian of Osip Mandelstam's poems. Flanagan, in particular, went on to be one of a number of friends, older than Heaney, who were close to his heart on a level that may fairly be described as avuncular or elder-brotherly – Ted Hughes, Robert Lowell (for the brief time that was possible between their first meeting and Lowell's death in 1977), Czesław Miłosz, Helen Vendler and Bernard McCabe being others. Certainly, each of them met a strong need in the younger man, whether for example, advice, encouragement or vindication, and his letters to them are singularly affectionate and grateful.

As well as offering him a congenial academic home from home, that first year in Berkeley introduced Heaney to the possibility of earning extra income from readings at other campuses and cultural institutions. So began a lifelong routine of personal appearances on the podium, whether reading his poems or delivering lectures and speeches, that grew ever more time-consuming and exhausting as the years passed and demand for him expanded to worldwide proportions, but that his tenacious sense of duty forbade him to give up. 'Duty-dancing' is his repeated term for the urge that had him perpetually flying between Europe and the USA, or across the American continent, and, if not exactly providing another class of home from home, planes and airports could at least serve as unlikely writing dens – far from the intrusions of phone and fax machine – from which an increasing number of his personal letters were dashed off. Haste, however, did not mean superficial attention, and readers of this book are likely to marvel at the care that Heaney brought to each item of correspondence: pitched accurately to the sensibility of the individual receiving it, and seeming to well, phrase by phrase, from the same inexhaustible lexical source that supplied his poems. If duty drove Heaney's correspondence as it did his public life, he was careful not to show it, and while many a letter in this book starts with a wail of self-blame for replying late, or some other perceived sin of omission, he more than makes amends with the unwithheld intimacy of what he then goes on to write.

Fame brought with it incessant calls on Heaney's time and mind. Scholarly acquaintances gave him their books to read, thesis writers assailed him with queries, strangers sent unpublished poems with requests for his advice or endorsement, administrators hoped to co-opt him for civic projects – and he is both humorously and plaintively eloquent about the wear and tear on him that all this involved. Duty, however, prevailed, to the extent that in a letter to Thomas Flanagan (20 May 1997) he could berate himself for taking a vacation while being unable to stop 'thinking of the mail piling up at home and the faxes gulping and slithering into one's life and the requests for recommendations and introductions lurking . . . A feeling' – he adds – 'that sunlight and silence and free time on a Tuesday morning on a Greek island is an affront to the workers of the world.' Comically stated, the sentiment is nonetheless sincere. For most of the latter half of his life, in obedience to a self-imposed ethic, he was heroically put-upon. The wonder is that he could meet the never-ending impositions on him with a courtesy that seldom failed, or that just occasionally became an elaborate, defensive courtliness. Frustration and anger could be fired off privately, as readers will discover, but the responsible public man never flagged.

Letter writing was not always, or even largely, a chore, of course, and the joy I mentioned at the top of this introduction – that of hearing Heaney's voice again – would be a lesser thing were it not for the pleasure he unmistakably takes in it. The writer's delight in his own fertile rhetoric, meant to communicate delight to an immediate correspondent, can now delight us as latter-day listeners-in. The verbal aptness and playfulness; the sense of an uncommonly capacious vocabulary being within hand's reach for the plucking of the *mot juste*, often a surprising and revelatory one; the metaphors that spring into place so nimbly and freshly; the jokes, excellent and not so excellent; the truly scholarly range of literary reference – Yeats, Wordsworth, Hopkins and Frost being favourite suppliers – are all at the service of pleasure. Those who knew Heaney personally, as I did, first as his editor at Faber in the 1990s, then as a friend, will confirm that there was nothing forced in any of this, and that Heaney's everyday conversation, face to face or on the phone, naturally shared the same qualities. For which reason, I made the pleasure principle one of my constant touchstones as I went about choosing letters for this book.

Selection from an epistolary output as vast as Heaney's has inevitably involved both rewards and regrets. I cannot count the number of letters I have read, nor, it must be admitted, the number I may not have read, either because of my ignorance of their existence or because I was not allowed to see them. I am not displeased that the present book opens where it does: with the poet crouched and ready to sprint, waiting to hear whether his first collection will be accepted for publication, tentatively confident but in no position to know what a long, arduous, complex and challenging course he has ahead of him. That makes, I think, for a satisfying shape; but what of the letters he wrote before December 1964? What of those of his childhood? We can be sure he wrote them, thanks to a particularly lovely poem that went into his final collection, *Human Chain*. In 'The Conway Stewart', Heaney describes, with the tender, animating closeness of inspection that he above all poets brought to descriptions of inanimate objects, the acquisition of his first pen:

'Medium', 14-carat nib,
Three gold bands in the clip-on screw-top,
In the mottled barrel a spatulate, thin

Pump-action lever
The shopkeeper
Demonstrated,

The nib uncapped,
Treating it to its first deep snorkel
In a newly opened ink-bottle,

Guttery, snottery,
Letting it rest then at an angle
To ingest,

Giving us time
To look together and away
From our parting, due that evening,

To my longhand
'Dear'
To them, next day.

One could hardly not yearn to see the letters home that this gorgeously evoked implement enabled him to write! Yet when I appealed to Heaney's surviving siblings at the outset of my researches they were unable to show me any. Another omission that readers could not fail to notice is that of letters to living members of the immediate Heaney family: Seamus's widow, Marie, and his children, Michael, Christopher and Catherine. From the start, it was made clear to me that their privacy in this regard was to be inviolable, and I have had no difficulty in respecting their wish, not least because in all other ways they have been generously supportive, prompt in answering requests for information and a constant source of encouragement. Most especially, it was they who commissioned me to put this book together, and I could not have asked for a greater gift than their trust in me when they did so.

A Note on the Text

At some stage it must have occurred to Seamus Heaney that his letters would be published: first, in a selection like this one, and then, perhaps many years later, in some scholarly, monumental, multi-volume 'Complete Letters' that, even with such a title, would be likely to omit a fair amount of stray or throwaway material. Precisely when this thought struck him, supposing it did, is not for me to guess; the letters themselves present, year by year, a continuity that betrays no obvious gear-change; and even when Heaney writes to the most worldly-eminent of his later correspondents there is no evidence that his address to them is tilted, however slightly, towards any hypothetical reader of the future. His epistolary manner varies from individual to individual and circumstance to circumstance – sometimes utterly spontaneous and open, sometimes a lot more politic or guarded – but the sense is always that he is writing to the moment, whether freely or concentratedly, with his faculties duly attuned and no other consideration interfering.

However much I should have liked, as editor of this volume, not to hide the many verbal casualties of such dedication to the immediate moment – the typos, the spelling errors, the dropped words and forgotten punctuation marks, all the minor accidents of improvisation or haste – the reader's need for a clean, unfussy text had to be borne in mind, and the disciplines of a publisher's house style brought to bear. Heaney himself would have understood the necessity, and in any case the air of impromptu effusion, where it matters, easily takes care of itself, transcending any amount of textual tidying-up.

As a veteran of the published word, Heaney was used to dialogue with his editor, and indeed welcomed it warmly as I discovered when I worked with him on such books as *The Spirit Level* and *The Redress of Poetry*; but that dialogue is now silenced, leaving the editor to make some arbitrary and uncontested decisions of his own. A degree of compromise between house style and personal style had to be achieved. To this end, misspelt words and names have generally, though not always, been corrected without comment. The same goes for some of the more jarring or confusing instances of aberrant punctuation. The occasional inadvertently omitted word has been restored inside square brackets, but those brackets have been kept to a minimum and I have done all I could to avoid the '[*sic*]' that follows on the heels of some minor solecism, with its (to my ear) note of haughty pedantry. House style ordains that titles of books be presented in italics, and those of poems and prose essays between inverted commas, and this was plainly a reasonable thing to impose given not just Heaney's inconsistent treatment of titles but also the professional acceptance of such practices. Another assumption was that underlined words should be italicised, except when standing at the head of a list, while double underlinings were kept as such. Ampersands, or the plus signs that often stood for ampersands when Heaney was writing quickly, have all been replaced by 'and'.

Some of Heaney's verbal idiosyncrasies have, however, been allowed to remain: for instance, the hyphens in 'to-day' and 'to-morrow', which are frowned on in the Faber rule book, and the words ending '-ize' and '-ization', which he generally favoured against '-ise' and '-isation' in his collections of poems. My rule of thumb has been that any semantic divergence from house style must be honoured, particularly in the prose of a poet so sensitive to, and stimulated by, the etymology, or archaeology, of words. A habit of speech or writing learned in the schoolroom and devotedly maintained for the whole of a life says something quietly significant about the person concerned.

Footnoting brought particular challenges as well. When I compiled the book that appeared as *Letters of Ted Hughes* (2007), I resolved to annotate as sparely as I could, to give the letters, already a drastic reduction from Hughes's enormous output, all the uncrowded space they demanded, and this seemed to suffice. With Seamus Heaney, however, such an economy was not possible. Heaney matches Hughes in epistolary copiousness and again I have had to cut back severely to make a book of publishable proportions; but Heaney's way of life was utterly different, and the sheer outward-facing busyness of it – its international extent and ever-increasing populousness – called for equally busy footnotes. More than that, Heaney carried a great wealth of absorbed reading around in his head and his letters are naturally strewn with quotations and literary allusions, many of which – those that didn't escape me – I thought should be identified. So, one way or another, the footnotes have multiplied and put on weight, though not, I trust, to the extent of overwhelming the texts they are meant to serve.

Heaney was by and large careful to put at the head of his letters both the dates of their composition – day, month, year – and the addresses from which they were written. Where he neglected to do so, but circumstantial details permit, square brackets indicate reasonable editorial supposition. In his travels he sometimes gave his Dublin address instead of, or in addition to, the one he was actually writing from, and in such cases square brackets are again employed to regularise and clarify. Postcards have, where possible, been dated by their postmarks. Faxes, which from the early 1990s Heaney favoured for their rapid delivery, are sometimes doubly dated, by him and by the automatically printed band along the top, which on occasion provides the only clue.

From the earliest days of the period covered here, Heaney wrote letters both by hand and on a succession of typewriters; later, iBooks and their electronic progeny became welcome tools, while the fax machine, excoriated by Heaney as it sometimes was for inundating him with unwanted correspondence from the world beyond, was gladly exploited when the exchange went the other way. The choice between manuscript or typescript depended, it would seem, largely on mood or circumstance, and there is no reason to assume that handwriting was reserved for intimate letters or that typing necessarily indicated a more serious purpose. Heaney's handwriting presents few puzzles to the reader who has got his or her eye in, though an unconventional choice of word could sometimes stop me in my tracks: 'retrievals', for instance, in his morale-boosting letter to the painter Barrie Cooke of 26 May 1985, kept me nonplussed for a while until I was helped by other statements of his to understand the special sense that was intended there. I may, admittedly, have been too quick or presumptuous in my deciphering of other less legible words or phrases, and if this is the case future scholars will no doubt put the matter straight.

No attempt has been made in my footnotes to identify systematically those letters that were typed by some hand other than Heaney's own, either from dictation or a manuscript draft, and while I occasionally wondered if it might be of interest to certain readers, I decided that the amount of editorial conjecture this would have entailed was disproportionate to whatever might be gained. This is a book, in the first place, for the lover of Heaney's poems who hopes to understand more about them and their author from the sometimes deliberate, sometimes incidental, light his letters shine on them. As such, it is designed to set discussions going, not to be the last word.

I am grateful to readers of the hardback edition of this book who have drawn my attention to errors, imprecisions, misinterpretations and other defects in my notes there; this edition seeks to put such matters right. My thanks, therefore, to Michael Cullinan, Greg Delanty, Stephen Enniss, John Wilson Foster, Jim McGreevy, Michael McKee, Janet Montefiore, George O'Brien, Robin Taylor and Mark Wormald.

Editorial Annotations

GC greetings card
MS manuscript
PC postcard
TS typescript
m.d. misdated
< > indicates marginalia: an insertion, addition or correction by SH
[ ] indicates an editorial insertion

Cynthia Hadzi, Carl Hahn, Katie Haines, Charles Hall, Brendan Hamill, David Hanly, Chris Hardy, Maurice Harmon, David Harsent, Simon Harsent, Niall Hartnett, Robert Hass, Cynthia Haven, the late Stratis Haviaras, Kristin Headlam, Dan Heaney, Jonathan Hennessey-Brown, Magdalena Heydel, Michael D. Higgins, Sophia Hillan, Brenda Hillman, Rosemary Hobsbaum, Angi Holden, Rupert Hopkins, John Horgan, Adam Horovitz, Susan Hoskings, Philip Hoy, Carol Hughes, J. S. Hurst, Jerzy Illg, Helen Ivory, Jerzy Jarniewicz, Ann Henning Jocelyn, Dillon Johnston, the late Brian Johnstone, Gabriel Josipovici, Des Kavanagh, Paul Keegan, the late Edmund Keeley, Mary Kelleher, Pauline Kelleher, John Kelly, Tim Kendall, Saima Khan, Declan Kiberd, Frances Kiely, Frank Kiely, Pauline Kiernan, the late Thomas Kilroy, John Kinsella, the late Thomas Kinsella, Karl Kirchwey, Adam Kirsch, August Kleinzahler, Stephen Knight, Agnieszka Kosińska, Vera Kreilkamp, Grigory Kruzhkov, Nick Laird, Desmond Lally, Premesh Lalu, Aoine Landweer-Cooke, Hermione Lee, the late Maurice Leitch, George Lensing, Brian Leyden, Grevel Lindop, Jazmine Linklater, Edna Longley, Michael Longley, Pura López Colomé, Adam Low, John Lucas, Elizabeth Lunday, Camille Lynch, Thomas Lynch, Sean Lysaght, Alan Lysander, Morag MacInnes, Peter Mackay, Bernard MacLaverty, Dolina Maclennan, Niall MacMonagle, Alasdair Macrae, Elise Macrae, Anne Madden, the late Derek Mahon, Bill Manhire, Fred Marchant, Neil Martin, Tony Martin, Belinda Matthews, the late Derwent May, Ben Mazer, R. John McBratney, Cathal McCabe, Chris McCabe, the late Jane McCabe, Thomas McCarthy, Brian McCormick, Fiona McCrae, Jim McCue, Peter McDonald, Tara McEvoy, Madeline McGahern, Iggy McGovern, Frank McGuinness, Jamie McKendrick, Michael McKimm, Mel McMahon, Andrew McNeillie, Jean McNicol, John Mee, Paula Meehan, Janetta Mellet, Askold Melnyczuk, Michael Meredith, Bruce Meyer, Katharine Ogden Michaels, Jane Miller, Anthony Milosz, John Minihan, John Mole, David Morley, Blake Morrison, Andrew Motion, Gina Moxley, Paul Muldoon, Paddy Mullarkey, Gerry Murphy, Sigrid Nama, Vicki Nash, Lucy Newlyn, Joan Newmann, Kathleen Newmann, Nuala Ní Dhomhnaill, Kate Noakes, Mary Noonan, Colm Ó Baoille, Edna O'Brien, George O'Brien, Sean O'Brien, Conor O'Callaghan, Shivaun O'Casey, Heather O'Donoghue, Hughie O'Donoghue, Eoghan Ó Driscoll, Andrew O'Hagan, Brenda O'Hanlon, Andrew O'Mahoney, Anne O'Malley, the late Jane O'Malley, Tim O'Neill, Frank Ormsby, Fran O'Rourke,

Cathal Ó Searcaigh, Alice Oswald, Fintan O'Toole, Barra Ó Tuama, Michael Packman, Jay Parini, Michael Parker, Don Paterson, Glenn Patterson, Giti Paulin, Tom Paulin, Madeleine Paxman, Robert Perkins, Katherine Pierpoint, Robert Pinsky, the late Valentina Polukhina, Katrina Porteous, Craig Raine, Camille Ralphs, Yvonne Reddick, Clare Reihill, Adrian Rice, Christopher Ricks, Maurice Riordan, Sue Roberts, Robin Robertson, Peter Robinson, Seán Rocks, Padraig Rooney, Martin Rosenbaum, Gibbons Ruark, Michał Rusinek, Noel Russell, Declan Ryan, James Ryan, Richard Ryan, Peter Sacks, Ann Saddlemyer, Chrys Salt, Eva Salzman, Fiona Sampson, Michael Schmidt, Ronald Schuchard, the late Peter Scupham, Sudeep Sen, Renata Senktas, Andrew Shields, Frank Shovlin, Steve Silberman, the late Charles Simic, Peter Sirr, Ann Pasternak Slater, Tom Sleigh, the late Anthony Smith, Tracy K. Smith, Elzbieta Smolenska, Gerard Smyth, Piotr Sommer, Alicia E. Stallings, Julian Stannard, the late Anne Stevenson, Stephen Stuart-Smith, Bill Swainson, the late Matthew Sweeney, Rosemary Sweeney, George Szirtes, Barry Tebb, Philip Terry, M. Wynn Thomas, Luke Thompson, Ben Thomson, Róisín Tierney, Richard Tillinghast, Colm Tóibín, Claire Tomalin, Angela Topping, Rebecca Tracy, the late Robert Tracy, Monica Tranströmer, the late Shaun Traynor, Joe Treasure, James Underwood, Helen Vendler, Erica Wagner, William Waldegrave, Chris Wallace-Crabbe, Gerry Wardle, Marina Warner, Elizabeth Wassell, David Wheatley, Aidan White, David Whiting, David Whittaker, David Williams, Jonathan Williams, Samantha Williams, Rab Wilson, Joseph Woods, Mark Wormald, Duncan Wu, Adam Wyeth, Enda Wyley, Eunice Yeates, Jane Yeh, the late Adam Zagajewski, Krzysztof Zagórski, Natalia Zagórska-Thomas, and Jakob Ziguras.

And of course I am glad to acknowledge the indispensable contribution made to this book by the librarians, archivists and curators of collections, both private and public, where Seamus Heaney's letters are conserved. I have met nothing but courtesy, eagerness to help, diligence and patience, sometimes well beyond the limits of duty, from staff at the institutions I have dealt with in my pursuit of letters. No less than the individuals named above, official custodians of Seamus Heaney's literary remains evidently share a high sense of obligation to his memory and I have benefitted more than I can say from the assistance of the following:

Avice-Claire McGovern, Mary Broderick, James Byrne, James Harte,

Gearóid Ó Luing, Sandra McDermott, Katherine McSharry, and others, at the National Library of Ireland;

Selina Collard and Sarah Poutch at the James Joyce Library, University College Dublin;

Maeve Gebruers and Liam O'Connor at the Irish Traditional Music Archive, Dublin;

Emer Brogan, John Fitzgerald, Crónán Ó Doibhlin and Emer Twomey at the Boole Library, University College Cork;

Samantha McCombe at the Linen Hall Library, Belfast;

Kelly Copeland at the Public Record Office of Northern Ireland;

Matthew Hendry at the Arts Council of Northern Ireland;

Jayne Dunlop at the Library for Arts, Humanities and Social Sciences, Ulster University Business School, Coleraine;

Cathy Brown at the Seamus Heaney HomePlace, Bellaghy;

Hilary Copeland at the John Hewitt Society;

Ulrike Hogg, Colin McIlroy and Suzy Pope at the National Library of Scotland;

Stephen Willis at the Centre for Research Collections, Edinburgh University Library;

Rowan Grout and Sam Maddra at Archives and Special Collections, Glasgow University Library;

Helen Melody and Richard Price at the British Library;

Lorraine Marriner and Chris McCabe at the Poetry Library, Southbank Centre, London;

Robert Brown and Jane Kirby at the Archive, Faber and Faber, London;

Joseph Heffernan at Arts Council England;

Nika Narkeviciute at the Victoria and Albert Museum, London;

Ruaidhrí Dowling at the Irish Embassy, London;

Liam Austin, Frank Bowles and John Wells at Cambridge University Library;

Oliver House and Sam Lindley at the Weston Library, Bodleian Libraries, Oxford;

Michael Riordan at The Queen's College, Oxford;

Petra Hofmann at St John's College, Oxford;

Christine Faunch at Heritage Collections, University of Exeter;

Peter Dixie at Hull History Centre;

Drummond Bone, Jeff Cowton, Catherine Foster and Michael McGregor at the Wordsworth Trust, Grasmere;

Margaret R. Dakin at Archives and Special Collections, Amherst College;

Jennifer Meehan and Kathleen Shoemaker at the Stuart A. Rose Manuscript, Archives and Rare Book Library, Robert W. Woodruff Library, Emory University, Atlanta;

Andrew Isidoro at the John J. Burns Library, Boston College;

Mary Walker Graham at the Woodberry Poetry Room, Harvard University;

Mary Haegert, Thomas A. Lingner and Leslie A. Morris at the Houghton Library, Harvard University;

Sara Gunesekara at the Shields Library, University of California, Davis;

Rebecca Aldi and Natalia Sciarini at the Beinecke Rare Book and Manuscript Library, Yale University;

Dean M. Rogers at Special Collections, Vassar College Libraries;

Stephen Enniss and Richard B. Watson at the Harry Ransom Center, University of Texas at Austin;

Mary Dunn at the William J. Clinton Presidential Library, Little Rock, Arizona;

Meredith Mann at the Brooke Russell Astor Reading Room for Rare Books and Manuscripts, New York Public Library;

Lara Szypszak and Lewis Wyman at the Library of Congress, Washington DC;

Judith Gantley at the Princess Grace Irish Library, Monaco;

Daniel Biedrzycki, Anna Romaniuk and Michał Szymański at Biblioteka Narodowa, Warsaw;

Urszula Klatka at the Special Collection Department, Jagiellonian Library, Kraków.

Sources of Texts

In addition to any other information, the source of the original text is given at the head of each letter. Where those texts are in private ownership, the surname of the owner, whether a living person or a person's estate, is generally provided. The list below is an index to the institutions, libraries and archives, that hold the rest of the letters in this book.

Amherst: Archives and Special Collections, Robert Frost Library, Amherst College, Amherst, Massachusetts

Beinecke: Beinecke Rare Book and Manuscript Library, Yale University, New Haven, Connecticut

BL: British Library, London

Bodleian: Bodleian Library, Oxford

Boston: Boston University, Boston, Massachusetts

Cambridge: Cambridge University Library, Cambridge

Cork: Boole Library, University College Cork, Cork

Davis: University of California, Davis, Davis, California

Emory: Stuart A. Rose Manuscript, Archives and Rare Book Library, Emory University, Atlanta, Georgia

Faber: Archive of Faber and Faber Ltd, London

Galway: James Hardiman Library, National University of Ireland Galway, Galway

Glasgow: University of Glasgow Library, Glasgow

Harry Ransom: Harry Ransom Center, University of Texas, Austin, Texas

Harvard: Houghton Library, Harvard University, Cambridge, Massachusetts

HomePlace: Seamus Heaney HomePlace, Bellaghy

Hull: Hull History Centre, Hull

ITMA: Irish Traditional Music Archive / Taisce Cheol Dúchais Éireann, Dublin

Linen Hall: Linen Hall Library, Belfast

LOC: Library of Congress, Washington DC

NCAD: National College of Art and Design, Dublin

New Hampshire: University of New Hampshire, Durham, New Hampshire

NLI: National Library of Ireland, Dublin

NLS: National Library of Scotland, Edinburgh

NYPL: Manuscripts and Archives Division, New York Public Library, New York

Pembroke: Pembroke College, Cambridge

PNL: Polish National Library/Biblioteka Narodowa, Warsaw

Pratt: E. J. Pratt Library, Victoria University, University of Toronto

Princeton: Princeton University Library, Princeton, New Jersey

PRONI: Public Record Office of Northern Ireland, Belfast

UCD: James Joyce Library, University College Dublin, Dublin

Vassar: Archives and Special Collections Library, Vassar College, Dutchess County, New York

THE LETTERS OF SEAMUS HEANEY

1964

Towards the end of this year, we find Seamus Heaney – hereafter, 'SH' – in possession of what he thought might be enough poems to make up his first published collection. He had already received a good number of acceptances from literary magazines and newspapers both north and south of the Irish border and his name was getting known. Recommending magazines in the Republic where his friend and fellow Northerner Seamus Deane might send his own poems, he shows his experience in the field. At this moment, he was waiting to hear if the poems he had submitted, under the title *Advancements of Learning*, to Dolmen Press in Dublin would be accepted for publication.

To Seamus Deane

MS Emory

9 December 1964 St Joseph's Training College, Belfast 11

Dear Seamus,

Christmas had better be a time of good will if you are not to stop reading just about here. My neglect of your last letter and your first son amounts to an insult; my accumulating guilt feelings grow into a neurosis. Perhaps it is not too late to make amends.

I was delighted when I heard about Conor (?) Fitzgerald – my corresponding pen was impotent but I wrote a short secret poem (which I feared later was sentimental, so did not send it to you – maybe I will sometime). Marion and you have certainly taken life by the scruff of the neck and I trust it is as rewarding as I imagine it must be. All three of you have my accumulated good wishes – and envy.

And congratulations again on your fellowship. I was speaking to Butter about a week ago – as usual he was vague but conveyed the necessary information – that you were doing well and had obtained a Peterhouse? (no?) research fellowship. I am delighted and confident that is merely the first rung of [a] new ladder of honours.

Now to minor matters. I got engaged a fortnight ago to Marie Devlin and hope to be married next August. We are very happy and believe that we can remain so for a lifetime. I don't imagine you knew Marie – she was at St Mary's TC and has been teaching in Co. Down this last three years. I met her two years ago and knew from the beginning that she was the girl to hunt – but now she is not so much a quarry, more a way of life.

I have wasted the whole time since leaving Queen's (apart from finding Marie). I have not written a chapter of a thesis – I am not yet engaged upon one. With the help of God and the engagement I'll get stuck into something from the New Year onwards. I'd like to do something on 'The Repressed Hero in Modern Irish Writing' but nobody in Queen's is interested.

I will not consider the three years a complete fiasco if one venture which I have in hand at the moment succeeds. I have thirty poems with the Dolmen Press in Dublin. They say they like them but have come to no final decision about publication so far. If they happened to take them – which is extremely doubtful – I should slam into an MA on Irish literature and in two years' time try for a spell in some American university as lecturer in this field. Then I should like to come back to the Training College or an Irish university. However, there are too many 'ifs' involved here and more than likely I shall drift lazily and discontentedly towards unqualified senility in the lackadaisical philistine womb of St Joseph's. Enough said about St Joseph's. Last year I worked, this year it has affected me so successfully that I too am happy to freelance fuzzily in half my lectures. Which is not good enough.

Are you doing any writing yourself now? I think you asked me for some addresses in the last letter so that was hopeful. The best places in this country at the moment are:

Poetry Ireland
23 Upper Mount Street,
Dublin 2.

This comes out twice yearly and is devoted almost entirely to new poetry.

The *Dubliner*,
Haccombe Parva,
Killiney,
Co. Dublin.

A quarterly containing short stories, critical articles on literature, painting and theatre, and a good proportion of poetry.

The *Kilkenny Magazine*,
c/o Kilkenny Literary Society,
35 High Street,
Kilkenny.

Same as the *Dubliner*.

Besides these, the only other place where you could wish to appear is the *Irish Times*, Westmoreland Street, Dublin. It prints poems nearly every Saturday and pays more than any of the others.

If you are coming home at Christmas, be sure and let me know. We have a phone in Bellaghy – 257 – and I have a Volkswagen for which I am still £300 in debt but which will get me around for another year or two. So if I can do any runs for you or call to see you, write or ring.

Until then, regards to Marion and the baby, apologies and congratulations again and good luck.

With every best wish,
Seamus Heaney

PS I trust the address is correct.

SH had been appointed Lecturer in English at St Joseph's after a short spell as a schoolteacher.

Seamus Deane (1940–2021) was one of SH's oldest friends, having attended St Columb's College at the same time, he as a day boy, SH as a boarder. Deane had then gone on to take both a BA and an MA in English at Queen's University Belfast, before a research fellowship enabled him to study for a PhD at Pembroke College (not Peterhouse), Cambridge. Like SH, he was also writing poems. Conor Fitzgerald was indeed the name of Deane's first child, born in May.

The English scholar Peter Butter (1921–99) taught at Queen's.

Marie Devlin (b.1940) was second of the six daughters born to Tommy (1906–90) and Eileen (1908–85) Devlin, who farmed in Ardboe in Co. Tyrone. She and SH had met at a dinner at Queen's two years previously.

Dolmen Press had been founded by Liam and Josephine Miller in 1951, specifically to publish the work of Irish poets. In the brief letter that Liam Miller (1924–87) sent SH on 5 February 1965, he wrote: 'I return your manuscript herewith and will be very glad to hear from you at a later date. If you are in Dublin some time perhaps you would like to telephone me and we might meet.' By then, however, SH had already been invited to submit poems to the London publishers Faber and Faber.

1965

Professionally, the two most significant events this year for SH were the unsought invitation that came from London publishers Faber and Faber to submit a collection of poems for consideration, and the agreement to publish that swiftly followed. In his personal life, the most significant was his marriage to Marie Devlin.

To Charles Monteith

TS Faber

2 February 1965 — St Joseph's Training College, Belfast 11

Dear Mr Monteith,

Thank you for your most encouraging letter of 15th January. It gave me new confidence to find that people who were neither friends nor rivals took an interest in my work and I look forward to submitting a collection for your consideration.

I have no objections to your making photostat copies of the poems.

I remain,
Yours sincerely,
Seamus Heaney

Charles Monteith (1921–95), born and brought up in Co. Antrim, had been Director at Faber since 1954. One of his achievements as editor of the poetry list had been to overcome his initial caution and, heeding T. S. Eliot's encouragement, to publish Ted Hughes's (1930–98) *The Hawk in the Rain* (1957). Monteith wrote to SH after seeing 'Digging', 'Storm on the Island' and 'Scaffolding' in the 4 December 1964 *New Statesman*, of which Karl Miller (1931–2014) was Literary Editor. The poet Edward Lucie-Smith (b.1933) subsequently showed Monteith more of SH's work.

To Seamus Deane

MS Emory

[undated] — St Joseph's Training College, Belfast 11

Dear Seamus,

I had begun twice and your card was what I deserved. Apologies once again for everything, including the notepaper. I am supervising an examination here at the moment.

I return the poems – reluctantly in the case of 'Lost and Won', 'Heat-Tossed Night' and 'Abandoned Treasure'. I agree that 'Lost and Won' is a big attempt and think that you have succeeded in the most difficult area – sustaining a large open rhythm without formulating it into any monotonous pattern of beats. The orchestration of the images is magnificent, the sense of quest as pervasive and urgent as in 'Childe Harold'. I see what you mean when you said [it] is a bow-wow without a bite – but the genre in which you are working is rhetorical rather than witty and the orotund quality I think comes off. There are some places where a word fills out a cadence impressively but I feel is a large gesture rather than an explosion of insight – e.g. 'contagiously' at line four (it could be argued about), 'persuasively coaxing and cajoling', 'noiselessly hummed' – but this is putting a first draft through the mill rather severely.

The love-poems are probably the most achieved. You have a rich vein of metaphor that is disciplined by an almost Donnish sense of form. But again, I think it is in [the] throbbing quality of the rhythm that you are most individual.

On paper lined and with a ruled margin – very likely St Joseph's College issue – this interrupted letter was not sent for another six months: see letter to Deane of [4th?] August, below.

To Charles Monteith   MS Faber

18 May 1965   St Joseph's Training College, Belfast 11

Dear Mr Monteith,

I enclose a selection of poems for your consideration. You have already seen a few of these in the batch which you obtained in December. I hope this group is a bit stronger.

I remain,
Yours sincerely,
Seamus Heaney

This selection of poems, which now bore the title *Death of a Naturalist*, was arranged differently from the typescript submitted to Dolmen and contained new work. It was read and commented on not only by Monteith but also by a junior editor at Faber, Mary-Kay Wilmers (b.1938). Of SH's revised submission, she reports that 'a large batch of childish folklore has been weeded out and replaced by a number of new poems which, though they have their weaknesses, show far

Reputation of Some Thinkers of the French Enlightenment in England between 1789 and 1824'.

To Charles Monteith

MS Faber

24 August 1965 Barna, Co. Galway

Dear Mr Monteith,

I always seem to write to you from Galway – we've been here since last Friday, battening on cottage-renting friends, and should have written long ago to thank you for your hospitality all the time we were in London. You helped to make it the most memorable fortnight we have ever spent. Though I'm sure Carol and Rosemary are glad to see the heels of the inefficient Irish layabout who had to get his typing and layout done at a moment's notice and who interrupted one of the most hectic weeks at Faber's (*The Story of Malaysia* and all that).

We return to the North and will be of no fixed abode until the building society showers its blessings (with interest). As soon as we get a home address, we'll let you know.

By the way, after a futile incubation period, the only title I can find for the nameless poem is 'On the Embankment'. Would this do?

Thank you again. I hope you enjoy your holiday as we did ours.

Sincerely,

Seamus and Marie Heaney

Barna was where the Heaneys were holidaying after their honeymoon, with college friends of Marie's.

The Story of Malaysia was the title of a book by Harry Miller (1923–98) that Faber published in 1965.

'On the Embankment' had become 'Twice Shy' by the time it was included in *Death of a Naturalist*.

1966

Death of a Naturalist was published in May, first in the UK, to wide critical acclaim and excellent sales, and then in the USA. Back home, the Heaneys moved to a larger house in Belfast, 37 Beechill Park South, and SH was appointed to a lectureship at Queen's University. Having had his own pamphlet, *Eleven Poems*, published the year before, SH was now editorially and administratively involved with the production of pamphlets for the Belfast Festival, which was organised from Queen's.

To Seamus Deane

MS Emory

30 January 1966 37 Beechill Park South, Belfast 8

Dear Deansie,

(Since you seem to recall Quinn with something akin to affection), as you surmised only someone as smug as myself would have taken your delightful, welcome letter as my due. Well done. And only someone as basically decent (as you, that is) would excuse my delay in acknowledging, if not replying to, it. However, it gives me great pleasure. And all the associations that that phrase entails.

I grow old. Marie, yes, is, yes, expecting a baby in June. So you can start your poem anytime. None of your bloody impromptu effusions, something of a Pindaric or at least a villanelle. And you, I take it, are expecting your doctorate. I will have my verses, dedicatory, hortatory, celebratory, ready. I was delighted to hear you had completed a first draft. In my own minor, off-hand and amateurish, sly fashion, I too have been tickling the arse of the monster research, completing some days ago the first chapter of a dissertation on the works of another potato-centred poet – Patrick Kavanagh. That bloke in the last *Delta* – J. M. Newton – is fairly up the creek about K. but don't tell him so until the thesis is examined, which should be in roughly three years' time.

Talking of Patrick Kavanagh, Marie has dubbed me 'the laureate of the root vegetable'. And I was glad that you saw 'Follower' – I'm not sure whether you're not right about the 'tail-flick of meaning' in the last stanza. I felt that it was perhaps not condensed enough, but I do not think that it is so sudden or arbitrary as to be illegitimate: does the last verse not give the dimension of metaphor to something which was necessary background knowledge for the assertion in the last verse? (I should *say* that to make sense.) Does it not illuminate retrospectively? (What about that then?) Nevertheless, I enclose bashlessly (opposite of bashful?) a copy of the pamphlet and when you look on the back cover, tremble, and get together about twelve poems and forward to the above address, to I, the editorial board. Incidentally 'For the Commander of *The Eliza*' has appeared in no magazine. So if you would like it for the *Cambridge Review*, all's well. I have been unusually in demand during the last two months: *Encounter* and the *Dublin Magazine* have solicited poems and all I have written of late has been with them for some weeks now so no decent poems are at hand – Possibly the latest one I've managed is all right, I don't know, but I'm sending it anyhow. If you're not happy about either, wait and pray. Enough of poems.

We hope to get to London some time before Easter and would love to visit you, if not stay over. I don't know when the book is due – 'Spring' can cover a multitude – but we are going to blow our enormous publisher's advance of £25 on a trip to London when it comes out. We now have an extra furnished bedroom, incidentally, at least we have acquired a second-hand double-bed which covers half of the bare boards, so if ever you're in Ireland, please make arrangements to spend one night in Belfast. But bring your own carry-cot, if it's before June. How did you get on in Paris? And how did you afford it? Don't answer that.

Suddenly my patter halts. I have fathomed the pit of patter. I grow less fit and fatter. Am I fit to be a father? The farther this fares, the more futile it feels. And so to end. And why not? The observed of all observers, quite quite down. Enough said, smiling fondly at his pretty wife, as Tierney would have said. Well, well.

I must apologize for not conducting the whole letter in this vein. I look forward to your humble reply. Love to Marion and Conor.

Carry on.

Yours ever,

Heaney.

'Dear Deansie . . . Quinn': Deane recalled a fellow student at St Columb's, John Joseph Quinn, who boarded in the same digs as SH and strongly disliked him. The feeling was returned and SH may have bestowed on him the nickname 'Quinsy'.

SH's 'first chapter of a dissertation' on the poet Patrick Kavanagh (1904–67), from rural Co. Monaghan, survives and is in private hands. *Delta* was a thrice-yearly literary magazine coming out of Cambridge University; it had been founded by the English poet Peter Redgrove (1932–2003) while he was a student there. A later editor was the poet and teacher Philip Hobsbaum (1932–2005), who from 1963 to 1966 hosted and presided over meetings of the young Northern Irish poets – SH, Deane and Michael Longley (b.1939), among them – who came to be known as The Group, or the Belfast Group. An earlier coterie of Hobsbaum's in London had also called itself The Group, and it was one of its members, Edward Lucie-Smith, who at the instigation of Hobsbaum had supplied Charles Monteith with examples of SH's work (see letter to Monteith of 2 February 1965).

'when you look on the back cover, tremble': SH's *Eleven Poems* carried an announcement that the Festival series would include a pamphlet of Deane's.

'For the Commander of *The Eliza*', from *Death of a Naturalist*, was taken by the *Cambridge Review* for its 7 May 1966 number, as was 'The Peninsula', which SH held back to be published in *Door into the Dark* (1969).

Fr Eamon Tierney was a mathematics teacher at St Columb's.

To Seamus Deane TS Emory

24 March 1966 37 Beechill Park South, Belfast 8

Dear Deansie,

By Christ, and by-y-y Christ! How did you manage this lot? I think the poems are excellent and must say they strike me as rich and unstarved, unurban, unscreaming. My favourites are 'The Roads You Walked', 'Against All Non Socialist Lovers' (though I'm not so keen on the title), 'Alone and Together', and (though I'm a bit at sea as to the old implications here) 'Come You from Wittgenstein?'

But I like every one of them and hope to have a good natter (as the wee man from Oxford said to me) next week: Marie and I are going to London to-morrow (Friday) (I fancy myself as a bit of a Keats with all these parentheses in my letters) because I have an interview in connection with the Gregory Award on Saturday. I am shortlisted with five other young British creative writers and have a 4 in 6 chance of raising a hundred quid or so. They are paying my expenses over but I thought Marie should take the chance to get out of the country while the going is still good – ish. So we are being quite irresponsible and giving our bank manager the shits but he won't get them until the damage has been done: we are staying until Thursday morning next. Wherefore, rejoice, because I hope to go down to see you all either on Sunday or Tuesday. Can you ring here (Belfast 649298) to-morrow evening about half past six and we'll see how when and where. Yes, I have got the phone in.

I am delighted about the brain drain. In fact, I am envious of your coming semesters, your comely sophomores, your pacific summers. It's hard to whack a place that's liberal and experimental where they regard, one hopes, drunkenness as eccentricity and unpunctuality and inefficiency as the hallmark of individuality. It's good to have the whole thing more or less fixed up at this stage: and I hope they pay you far too much.

What poems did I send you besides 'The Peninsula' (I think it is a good enough one now that I've lived with it a while)? Because I've just written what I consider my best for a long time and if you could fit it in instead of the other wee ones (I imagine they must have been wee ones) I'd be delighted – presuming, of course, that you agree that the enclosed is good enough. Does the title need the following: *Note. Despite heavy preventive legislation, cockfights – or 'battles' – are still held on Easter Monday in many places in Ireland*?

Hoping to hear your old croak to-morrow.

Sincerely,

Seamus

SH had now formally invited Deane to send poems for a Belfast Festival pamphlet.

The 'wee man from Oxford' remains unidentified, but was possibly a representative of Oxford University Press.

SH was one of three applicants to receive a 1966 Eric Gregory Award; Robin Fulton (now known as Robin Fulton Macpherson) (b.1937) and Hugo Williams (b.1942) were the others. Gregory Awards go to young poets of perceived promise. (See letter to Charles Monteith of 7 April 1966.)

'brain drain': a phrase much in vogue at the time and applicable to the situation of Deane, who was on the point of leaving to teach at the University of California, Berkeley.

'*Note*': a slightly different phrasing of these words formed the epigraph to the poem 'Triptych for the Easter Battlers', printed in the *New Statesman* of 23 December 1966 but never included by SH in any collection.

To Charles Monteith

MS Faber

7 April 1966 — 37 Beechill Park South, Belfast 8

Dear Charles,

Many thanks for your letter: I just can't believe it. Surely this must be a poet's dream – to have a publisher who finds another publisher.

My sincere thanks for your endeavours on my behalf.

I should have written before this to tell you how we enjoyed our evening with you and Rosemary. Marie was saying how Fabers were to us more of a family than a firm – you added so much to our stay.

I hope to get to London soon again. Anyhow, give my regards to Rosemary and Mary K. and believe me deeply grateful.

Sincerely,

Seamus

The first US edition of *Death of a Naturalist* was brought out, a month after the UK one, by Oxford University Press.

'Rosemary' was Rosemary Goad (1928–2021), an editor at Faber, who went on to become the firm's first female director.

To Charles Monteith

TS Faber

21 April 1966 37 Beechill Park South, Belfast 8

Dear Charles,

I've just received the first six copies of *Death of a Naturalist* and I am absolutely thrilled and delighted: I think it's delightfully produced and I just cannot quite realize that I am really in the Faber list. Nevertheless, it seems the time to thank you and everyone else at Russell Square for much encouragement and interest over the last eighteen months and I can only hope the reception it gets repays this in some small way.

It has been quite a day: I did an interview for a lectureship at Queen's – which was quite an event in any week – and when I got home there was a phone-call from the college telling me that there was a parcel from Fabers. I put two and two together quicker than ever before, I can tell you.

Marie sends her regards – and give mine to Rosemary and Mary K.

With every good wish,

Seamus

Monteith had also sent a copy of the newly published book to Ted Hughes, who in May wrote back with measured praise: 'Thank you for the Seamus Heaney book. He has a very warm and real and attractive poetic personality. CHURNING DAY, AT A POTATO DIGGING, COW IN CALF, TROUT, GRAVITIES, SYNGE ON ARAN, are my favourites. Healthy as a fish, as Seamus here says, when they come off. At his best, a real artist. The other pieces seem to me still very much University pieces, though it's churlish to say that, considering how good his best is and how young he is.' It is striking that Hughes seems to have had reservations about poems, such as 'Digging', 'Follower', and the title poem itself, that now stand among SH's most widely admired.

A lectureship at Queen's had fallen vacant upon Philip Hobsbaum's departure to teach in Glasgow. As the following letter reports, SH's application for the job was successful.

To Seamus Deane

TS Emory

10 May 1966 — 37 Beechill Park South, Belfast 8

Dear Seamus,

Delighted with all communications which have arrived here from Cambridge in the last few days. Your present is something we value all the more because, despite its aesthetic qualities, we just did not have a decent sized casserole. But not wishing to take away from the present, I am truly stunned with pleasure at your breakthrough with *Encounter*. With three in there, I'd say next step is a collection of thirty or so and a suitable title. Congratulations: let's do an Irish takeover on English poetry.

I hope you'll excuse this hurried note and expect something more like a letter from me when the pamphlet is nearly out – which should be in about three weeks. I got the Dannie Abse etc. Again my thanks. God, I nearly forgot. Yes, I got the job in Queen's, got word a week ago. Lecturing on modern poetry mostly, tutorials with 4th and 1st year Honours plus a bag of first arts stuff. More anon.

Do you fancy the new paper? It's a present from Marie's sister. Just arrived to-day. I'm in a furious hurry and should have written long-hand. Excuse the typing and give my love (honourable as ever) to Marion and Conor.

With good wishes, and may you be dead and in heaven a fortnight before the divil finds out.

Seamus

Encounter was the mandarin and, for much of its existence, highly respected literary and cultural magazine, founded in 1953 by the British poet Stephen Spender (1909–95) and American journalist Irving Kristol (1920–2009). At this moment, Spender was its literary editor.

'Excuse the typing': a larger than usual number of typos and botches have been corrected here.

To Brian Friel

MS NLI

13 May 1966 — 37 Beechill Park South, Belfast 8

Dear Brian,

Thank you for your congratulations on *Death of a Naturalist* – but the congratulations should have been coming in the other direction. I was delighted when *Philadelphia* had such deserved success and read *The Gold in the Sea* with pleasure – the best kind – I kept saying about many of the scenes, situations, characters, 'Why didn't I think of that myself?' Call us if you're in town here any time; and thank you again.

Seamus Heaney

Philadelphia, Here I Come! became the first international success of Irish dramatist Brian Friel (1929–2015) when, after receiving its first performance at the Gaiety Theatre in Dublin in 1964, it transferred to Broadway in 1966; its plot concerns the move of the central character, Gar O'Donnell, from Ireland to the USA. *The Gold in the Sea* (1966) is a book of short stories by Friel.

SH's rhetorical question, 'Why didn't I think of that myself?' already, at this early stage of what was to become one of his deepest friendships, suggests the intuition that he and Friel were exploring, by different means in their respective arts, shared ground. This was to be confirmed when he read the script of Friel's play *Volunteers* (see letter of 21 October 1974).

To John Hewitt

MS PRONI

18 May 1966 — 37 Beechill Park South, Belfast 8

Dear John,

Many thanks for your letter. I am delighted that you like the book and grateful that a poet is reviewing it for the *Telegraph*. I look forward to the review with impatience.

Thank you also for the Coventry off-print and the inscribed copies of the poems you so kindly sent me last year. I suspect you have almost fallen in love with Coventry – has it anything to do with your namesake from the eighteenth century?

I am forwarding under a separate cover some of the other Festival pamphlets which are still appearing. I was wondering if you'd be interested in reprinting 'Conacre', with an introduction by you – or me – or none – as one of the series next year. They intend to keep it going and

I was asked to think about contributors. Or would you like to print a selection of the later poems? We hope to include work by more established, full-grown poets next year – Kinsella, Montague and Murphy, if possible. I'll understand if you prefer to hold on to your work for a full collection later on, but thought I'd mention the thought to you.

Thank you again for your encouraging interest. I hope we meet soon again.

With every good wish,
Sincerely,
Seamus

The poet John Hewitt (1907–87) was, by his own description, 'an Irishman of planter stock, by profession an art gallery man, politically a man of the left'. He was a moving force behind what came to be known as 'Ulster Regionalism', asserting the importance to the arts of local rootedness. At this stage of his career, however, he was running an art gallery in Coventry, where he had moved after being thwarted of a promotion he had expected in Belfast.

James Hewitt, 1st Viscount Lifford (1712–89), a lawyer who became Lord Chancellor of Ireland, was the son of a Coventry draper.

'Conacre' was a long poem by John Hewitt first published in 1941; his *Collected Poems 1932–1967* appeared in 1968. In the event, Hewitt's 1967 Festival pamphlet was a selection of new work under the title *Tesserae* (see letter of 3 September 1966). Neither Thomas Kinsella (1928–2021) nor John Montague (1929–2016) nor Richard Murphy (1927–2018) had Festival pamphlets of their own.

To Peter Crawley

MS Faber

18 May 1966

37 Beechill Park South, Belfast 8

Dear Mr Crawley,

There is a gallery here which carries a stock of second-hand Irish books and is building up quite a good clientele of interested customers. I mentioned *Death of a Naturalist* to them and they said – half in joke, half in earnest – that they'd sell signed copies at a guinea each. Personally, I do not want to do this, but I feel if you approached them they'd be prepared to retail the book in the normal way. Would it be worth a try?

With good wishes,
Sincerely,
Seamus Heaney

Peter Crawley was Sales Director at Faber. The establishment that had caught SH's opportunistic eye was the Bell Gallery on Alfred Street, Belfast. The first edition of *Death of a Naturalist* was priced at 18/-, three shillings less than a guinea.

To Seamus Deane

TS Emory

30 May 1966 — 37 Beechill Park South, Belfast 8

Dear Jeem,

Here are the proofs of what I had put in to be printed: I was going to add the *Encounter* stuff but since that's been shot down, have you anything else to bung in here? I have some which I did not include, but perhaps now you might like to pick a couple of them: 'Green and Brown'; 'A Complaint Against Dying'; 'Only the Familiar'; 'Come You from Wittgenstein'; and 'For Edith Sitwell'. I don't seem to have 'After the Soldiers', which you mentioned. I think three or four more would be in order, if they are at hand. If not, a couple of what you would like most to see printed of the ones you would prefer not to print, if you know what I mean. With regard to the *Encounter* poems, I like 'Blind Man's Bluff' most, then 'Return', then 'On the Mimicry' etc. In the latter while I respond to the symbolism – you explained it – I find the very luxuriance of the sounds is distracting and possibly a bit too much: agglutinate, exfoliate, organically eviscerate all in three lines is too much for me. And I think that a word like blafard is dulled and made to look extravagant rather than explosive when it is linked to two other adjectives. The second stanza of that one is my favourite. 'Blind Man's Bluff' is conceived and delivered much more cleanly, much more inwardly, I think. I have also got 'Separated by Weather' which I find overloaded also with exotic electronic-type language – but I'm such a rural traditional orthodox that you'd better not listen to me – John Clare's my hero at the moment, so enough said.

[. . .]

I am full of sympathy and envy with regard to the thesis. I wish to hell I *knew* something: you are a man of learning now, for God's sake. Publication would fly your flag for life and I hope it comes off.

Marie sends her love and give mine to Marion and Conor. Thank you also for the Cambridge Review: it came out just in time. The book was on sale 19th. The reviews are better than I expected to put it mildly: did you see Ricks in the *New Statesman* of Friday?

Sting in tail: CAN YOU RETURN THESE PROOFS WITH ADDENDA BY TOMORROW. I'm supposed to be correcting them myself, so I'd be obliged if you could give them the old immediate attention and all and all.

With good wishes,
Seamus

SH's typing here is obviously hasty, so a number of distracting errors have been corrected.

Christopher Ricks (b.1933) was at this time teaching English literature at Worcester College, Oxford. He began his *New Statesman* review assertively: 'Literary gentlemen who remain unstirred by Seamus Heaney's poems will simply be announcing that they are unable to give up the habit of disillusionment with recent poetry. The power and precision of his best poems are a delight, and as a first collection *Death of a Naturalist* is outstanding.' He then went on to demonstrate how certain poems gained their specific power.

To Michael and Edna Longley

MS Emory

[6 July?] 1966 37 Beechill Park South, Belfast 8

Dear Michael and Edna,

I have been deeply upset since Monday night, not because of anything you said, but because it was only then I realized what I had done, or rather had not done, in the article. Until I have talked this out of myself, in your presence, as it were, I won't be able to give my attention to anything. I prefer to write, rather than call or phone, because in a conversation it might sound as if I was making excuses; I don't think excuses are in question: it is more an examination of conscience.

First of all, I was simply ashamed of myself: why I did not make the article an offensive for all that was good here, in art and people, I just don't know. As you say, I was not evangelical (although I think the experience of the last two days has changed that for ever). I believe I regarded your friendship and poetry, Derek's, Colin's, Harry's etc. as something private and precious in the way one's marriage is. It was 'ours', it had nothing to do with journalism and public pictures of Belfast. Somehow, the weekend I was doing the article, it never even crossed my mind that I should concentrate on this reality that I knew

– I was not serious in my attitude to the thing at all; it was more a case of getting it over with, and my whole attention was focussed (by events and phone calls from Miller) on the political side. My attitude on the arts side must have been 'Who is the kind of person that thrives on this kind of publicity?' and I believe I regarded the whole thing as irrelevant rather than central. It may have been the uneasy haste plus the pressure of other work to be done that blinded me, it may (more likely) have been my complete thoughtlessness about redressing wrongs and neglect suffered by my friends. Curiously, I think that if [I] had not been as friendly with everyone concerned I would have been more solicitous for them. Obviously, I am hurt to have hurt other people, but the most distressing feature of the whole business was the blind that was drawn in my own mind. One's self-regard can only be shattered by oneself. My reaction has been to try to forget it but the issues are too great and the wrong done too irrevocable.

I hope a letter is not too melodramatic: it is not so much in the hope of redressing any hurt as to allay my own embarrassment and guilt. As usual your attitude has been gracious and gentle in the face of yet another let-down. I simply hope this will give me back my power of speech, if not my complacency, when I meet you on the happy occasion – of which I am beginning to despair, to say nothing of Marie.

I don't know what this all sounds like and I won't read it again in case I don't send it.

Love,
Seamus

PS If you can endure a pat phrase that has just leaped to mind, I think until now I have enjoyed the luxuries of friendship without being aware of the full responsibilities.

The letter is actually headed 'Wednesday morning', no more than that, but is dated speculatively here on the grounds that 6 July was the first Wednesday after publication of the article that had offended the Longleys (see below).

Michael and Edna Longley had first met SH at a supper given by Philip Hobsbaum and his wife Hannah. They themselves had met in Dublin where, having gained a degree in Classics at Trinity College, Michael taught at a Protestant school in Blackrock. In September 1963, Edna (b.1940) moved to Belfast to take up a Junior Lectureship at Queen's University. Michael joined her there in 1964, initially teaching at his old school, the Royal Belfast Academical Institution. They were married in September 1964, in Edna's home town, Dalkey, Co. Dublin, and SH and Marie Heaney were among their wedding guests. Michael Longley believes that it was at SH's request that he and Edna were invited to join The Group.

The Longleys had taken SH to task over a piece about Belfast, its political and cultural situation, that SH had written for the *New Statesman* of 1 July: in their view, while skilfully evoking the uncomfortable mood of the city, he had given an inadequate account of the artistic awakening that was taking place there and that was exemplified by the likes of Derek Mahon (1941–2020), who had just published his first pamphlet of poems, the painter Colin Middleton (1910–83), and the English poet, editor and publisher, at this time active in Belfast, Harry Chambers (1937–2012).

To Charles Monteith

MS Faber

3 August 1966 — 37 Beechill Park South, Belfast 8

Dear Charles,

As usual, I should have written long ago but what with my marking GCE papers and Marie having and tending a baby, things have got out of hand entirely.

Marie had a baby boy – Michael, now – on July 8th and what better excuse for a celebration of all the good fortune that came our way this year – my bachelor cronies of yesteryear were almost in residence and intoxicated here for a week. Both Marie and the baby have made great strides of growth and rehabilitation since then.

I got word this week that one of my poems is in the final five selected to be read at the Cheltenham Festival on October 8th. So fingers are crossed again.

The book is selling well in Belfast – and I hope that unexpected but fantastic boost on *The Critics* gets rid of some more in England.

We may well see you before October – but Michael, small as he is, constitutes an anchor just now.

Please give our best wishes to Rosemary and Mary K. – and John McGahern, when you see him. And I do hope we can meet you in London some time soon.

Sincerely,
Seamus

The Heaneys' first child, Michael, was born on 8 July.

The poem in contention for the Cheltenham Festival of Literature's Poetry Prize was 'The Outlaw' (*Door into the Dark*, 1969).

The Critics was an arts programme broadcast on the BBC Third Programme.

The Irish novelist John McGahern (1934–2006) had also been taken on to the Faber list by Monteith.

To Seamus Deane

MS Emory

13 August 1966 37 Beechill Park South, Belfast 8

Dear Seamus,

When I got your letter with final instructions about what to include and proofs (early in June), the Festival Office had already printed out of impatience a misprinted and under-nourished collection. I was so angry and embarrassed by the whole business that I did not immediately send the pamphlet off in triumph, and the next thing I was up to the neck in GCE, late pregnancy and early fatherhood (since July 8th). I had not been at Festival Offices since June until this morning. All this, of course, is no excuse for you or consolation for you that your final selection was overruled. But believe me, the printing went ahead without any consultation of your interests with me.

The result of the Fatherhood stakes is a boy whom we've called Michael, who is comparatively well-behaved, long-lipped and big-nosed. So far, he has had nothing to say.

Could you let me know if you'll be in Cambridge until 29th as I'd like to make a bid to see you both – or three – if you're not going to be in Ireland.

Yours in confusion and apology,

Seamus

To John Hewitt

MS PRONI

3 September 1966 37 Beechill Park South, Belfast 8

Dear John,

I was delighted to get your letter and the cuttings – as a matter of fact I have taken a cuttings subscription, but had not been posted the notice in *The Times*. As you say, it had a good reception, and is going well for they are shortly going to reprint. I am also grateful that you are agreeable to bring out a pamphlet and am glad that you have given such a choice. On second thoughts, maybe a pamphlet like this, in a series, is not the place to reprint work so I'd be happy to go with either of your first suggestions – the batch written since your going to England or the Glens of Antrim sequence. I'd leave the choice to you, unless, as they say, you're in swithers, in which case I'll ask the other editors what they think.

Your review in the *Telegraph* was the fullest and most intimately concerned that the book had – a poet's attention is the most valuable and his approval the most necessary in establishing one's confidence. You fairly hit the nail on the head about development, too. I'm waiting and trusting, though I have some things which I don't believe I could have done a year ago.

I have to read a poem at the final judging in the Cheltenham Festival, so I hope to be in England in the week ending October 8th. If I can arrange a suitable itinerary, maybe I could drop in on you for a couple of hours some day for a chat. At the moment I'm not too clear when and how I'll be travelling, but if there's a possibility of a firm arrangement, I'll let you know. This is rather a self-invitation, I'm afraid, but there it is.

Since I last wrote, Marie has had a baby boy (Michael) and a new rhythm of life has been established, a stressed rhythm but a good one.

With all good wishes,
Seamus

To John L. Sweeney — MS UCD

3 October 1966 — 37 Beechill Park South, Belfast 8

Dear Jack,

Many thanks for your letter which was the first indication I'd had that *Death of a Naturalist* had been published over there – and you were quite right about the cards. Actually, I have initials that are priestly enough – Heaney S. J. – but I've never written a book on marriage. I am truly grateful for your good offices in this case, though I imagine the Library of Congress is even more so. And there is a sad footnote – the Seamus Heaney in question was killed over there in a car accident some time ago and the newspaper reports caused some consternation among distant friends of mine then.

I am curious about the reception the book will have in America – the technique so traditional and the subject matter so remote – but the main thing is that it is available. I can't help thinking of a remark by a friend, when I told him that it was going to appear. 'Publishing poetry in the USA', he said, 'must be like dropping a feather over the Grand Canyon and waiting for the echo.'

Thank you again for your good wishes and for risking your job in the interests of poetry and bibliography – not to say the reputation of the dead.

Good luck, and regards to Máire.

Seamus

John Lincoln Sweeney (1906–86) was an American scholar and art collector, based at Harvard University. The Heaneys had been guests of him and his wife, the Irish folklorist Máire MacNeill (1904–87), on 24 August the previous year, after which SH had written to tell them: 'We have spent the morning purring in the afterglow of your hospitality.'

1967

As an ex-schoolteacher, who had taught trainee teachers and was now a teaching member of a university faculty, SH had soundly based pedagogical views. How these might have been elaborated for public airing is suggested in his letter to Charles Monteith of 28 October. Although he himself describes it as 'tentative and incomplete', the proposal he sketches there would seem to indicate an original and maturely considered approach to the teaching of literature.

To Charles Monteith

MS Faber

4 January 1967 [m.d. 1966] 37 Beechill Park South, Belfast 8

Dear Charles,

I have just heard (indirectly) that Michael Longley has submitted his collection to Fabers. While I have little taste for pushing myself into affairs that are no concern of mine, I feel I would be failing myself (not Longley, who knows nothing of this letter) if I did not take the opportunity of saying to you personally that I believe him to be a genuine poet, and would base my opinion on, for example, the mythological poems and those on Dr Johnson. I am taking this most uncharacteristic step because of a friendship with him that has not affected the fibre of my own poems, but has given me a sense of vocation and a feeling of poetic community in this unpoetic town. I have little doubt that he will keep writing and developing for years.

Obviously this will not enter into Faber's deliberations and decisions: what I am saying, I suppose, is that it is time Longley was published and I am possibly abusing your friendship by saying it in a not irrelevant quarter. Anyhow, I have done.

[. . .]

Did I tell you we called the baby Michael? He is unaccountably placid, hardly ever cries, and produced his first tooth without any tearful preliminaries. Something superstitious in me keeps whispering that the success of the book and baby must augur a fall of some kind. God forbid. Give our love to Rosemary. And pardon my word in your ear. Good luck.

Sincerely,
Seamus

Longley was, with SH, one of the young poets who participated in Philip Hobsbaum's discussion group at Queen's (see note to SH's letter to Seamus Deane of 30 January 1966). In the event, Longley's first full collection of poems, *No Continuing City*, was published in 1969 by Macmillan.

SH dates this '1966': a mistake of the kind that SH was prone to fall into at the start of any new year; here, the true date is plain.

To Seán Ó Riada

MS Cork

5 January 1967

Department of English,
Queen's University, Belfast

Dear Sean,

That story about 'the music of the spirits' kept floating around in my head till I tried to exorcise it in a poem. I would dedicate it formally to you except that you would most likely be confused with the 'he' in the poem. But it's all yours.

I hope you enjoyed your time up here and look forward to meeting you some time again. My phone no. at home is 649298, if you're ever in the vicinity.

Good luck,
Sincerely,
Seamus Heaney

SH had met Seán Ó Riada (1931–71), Irish composer and arranger of traditional airs, whose orchestral piece *Mise Éire*, based on his soundtrack to the nationalistic film of the same name, was then highly popular, at the Belfast Festival the previous year; the poem SH wrote for him is 'The Given Note' (*Door into the Dark*). On the typescript presented to Ó Riada, SH adds: 'For Sean O Riada [*sic*], whose story deserved a better poem.' Preserved with this in the Cork University Library is a note in Ó Riada's hand on a scrap of lined paper: 'On Playing Port na bPúcaí at Belfast Festival' – 'Port na bPúcaí' ('Tune of the Fairies') being an ancient air from the Blaskets for which Ó Riada had devised a harmonic setting.

To Charles Monteith MS Faber

28 October 1967 37 Beechill Park South, Belfast 8

Dear Charles,

Finally I've had a couple of days to think more or less systematically about the textbook idea: and I was in the middle of typing samples for each section this afternoon when the baby pounded the typewriter to peace, if not pieces. The ribbon refuses to run: but rather than wait until it's fixed or changed, I thought I'd best enclose the section (though it's not complete as it stands) and outline the shape and part content of other sections. So far I am only concerned with material, and organizing principles in each section. When I've got that all typed out, I'll have to think about whether there should be

a) discussion, in print, by me, of the samples in each section
b) discussion of one sample and questions on the rest in each section
c) an introduction to each section, roughly indicating areas of interest in the writings grouped together therein – and no discussion of, or questions on, individual samples.

But this may, obviously, be jumping the gun: perhaps when the following scheme is considered, it won't be what you'd wanted at all:

Introduction: Allusion to general study of poetry as finished product; little enough attention paid to psychology of composition, processes of imaginative reduction of experience. This latter approach specially relevant in Colleges of Education where student's subsequent life as teacher of English (or any other subject) will involve a sympathy and understanding of his pupils' imaginative effort and achievement.

Section I – Sample enclosed.

Section II – Poetry which arises to some extent from poet's reading to be set beside that reading: e.g. –

i) Account of Cleopatra's barge etc. from North's *Plutarch* set beside Shakespeare's 'The barge she sat in . . .'
ii) Vasari's Life of Andrea del Sarto and Browning's poem.
iii) Mayhew's full account of the 'ruin' of the prostitute referred to in Philip Larkin's 'Deceptions' and that poem.

Section III – Displaying how poetry arises out of a penumbra of preoccupations, rather than a singleminded intention and readymade technique: how different areas of poet's experience and his aesthetic convictions merge in the poem: e.g. –

i) Dorothy Wordsworth's account of the 'daffodils' walk; extract from Preface describing the process of 'recollecting in tranquillity'; 'Daffodils' by Wordsworth.
ii) Yeats's description of hearing tinkle of water in Strand; his pronouncements on rhythm; 'Lake Isle of Innisfree' / or something more complex from Yeats.
iii) Opening (?) of Lancelot Andrewes sermon referring to the Magi (A cold coming they had of it etc.); Eliot's reference in *Use of Poetry and Use of Criticism* to seeing old white horse etc.; his statement about the way in which a poet's most disparate experiences relate themselves; 'Journey of the Magi'.

Section IV – The Poet's Revisions: a selection of manuscript revisions, from poets, living and dead.

Section V – Translations? The same poem translated by different *poets*.

This is obviously very tentative and incomplete but it may give you something to work on. Perhaps we'll be able to get to closer grips with detail if you come over for the Festival.

Karl Miller – or rather Derwent May – has taken five poems from me so you'll be getting a look at some new shapes and hearing new noises from me. I'm wondering what you'll think of them.

Anyhow, Charles, I'm looking forward to meeting you soon in Belfast – as is Marie. Give my love to Mary K. and Rosemary.

Sincerely,
Seamus

'Section I – Sample enclosed' is not to be found in the Faber archive.

Derwent May (1930–2020) was Literary Editor of the BBC's weekly magazine, the *Listener*, to which Karl Miller, who had published SH in the *New Statesman*, had moved to be Editor.

1968

In May of this year, SH, Michael Longley and the folk singer, radio producer and documentary film-maker David Hammond (1928–2008) – like Longley, a Protestant – joined forces in a week-long tour across Northern Ireland. Conducted under the banner *Room to Rhyme* – a phrase from an old mummers' play – their performances are now remembered as an optimistic and high-spirited expression of cultural pluralism before the calamity of the Troubles.

For himself, SH was now working towards his second volume of poems, *Door into the Dark*, which would appear in 1969.

To Harry Chambers

TS Hull

[Late February 1968]

Department of English,
Queen's University, Belfast

Dear Harry,

Many thanks for the *Phoenixes*; I am dashing off a note immediately because if I linger it won't happen for three weeks. I think it's a fine issue, actually, the only really weak spot being 'Plantation' which I have gone off in a big way. Jimmy Simmons's apologia was a good idea and I must say the first two poems are some of the best of his I've seen.

I am sorry not to have let you know earlier that Marie had a baby son a fortnight ago. He was well overdue so they induced labour and the whole thing was surprisingly over in less than three hours. She and he are well and we've called him Christopher Ronan. Ronan is an Irish saint's name whose feastday happened to occur on his birthday.

As far as I know, Edna is quite OK now. I was up over a week ago and she was blooming and quite obliviously involved in Rebecca. It's probably hard for you to imagine Edna doing baby talk to a bare-assed infant on its back in the middle of the floor, but it seems to me as good an indication of mental and bodily vigour as one could expect. Longley is not writing yet, and is a bit depressed about that but one good thing has happened in the shape of Tarling's pamphlet which is really a lovely job. Did you hear that he and David Hammond and I are doing a week's tour of schools and giving nightly readings at various centres in the north during the first week in May? Big Ken Jamison has got the Arts Council to sponsor it, so we stand to make a few quid, as well as having the odd ball of malt.

Of course I'll do something in Didsbury College. I think it would be best to think in terms of lunchtime on the 8th but we can finalize that closer to the day. Also if you sent me a couple of dozen PHS I could probably dispose of them in the University.

I haven't written much of late, I fear, and some of it's corny – no point in beating about the bush with 'transitional'. There's a shortie which I'll stick over the page which seems to me to work. Give my love to Muriel and my good wishes to Glyn Hughes and *Phoenix* generally; and I'm looking forward to seeing you again in June. Muck spreading once more, I hope. Good luck to you anyhow.

Seamus

Harry Chambers was by this time the widely liked editor of the magazine *Phoenix*, as well as of a series of poetry pamphlets – later, of books. He taught at Didsbury College of Further Education, but through a previous teaching job in Belfast he had become friends with SH, Michael Longley and other young Belfast poets. SH's poem 'The Plantation' was included in *Phoenix*'s Spring 1968 number.

Christopher Heaney was born on 9 February, which helps to place, however imprecisely, this undated letter.

Edwin (Ted) Tarling (1938–2004) was a jazz musician and, with his Sonus Press, a publisher of hand-printed editions.

Kenneth Jamison (1931–2016) was Director of the Arts Council of Northern Ireland.

'a couple of dozen PHS': presumably, *Phoenixes*.

The 'shortie' remains unidentified.

Glyn Hughes (1933–2011) was a writer of poetry, fiction, and elegiac treatments of Northern English subjects; his *Love on the Moor* (1968) was a *Phoenix* poetry pamphlet. SH evidently admired him enough to recommend him to Charles Monteith at Faber (see letter to Monteith of 19 May 1969).

To James Simmons

TS Emory

6 April 1968

Department of English,
Queen's University, Belfast

Dear Jimmy,

I hope this will be in time. I just wrote it two days ago and am not sure that I shouldn't keep it a week or so to find out how it wears on me. But it's a piety as much as a poem – for an old character who taught me many rustic rhymes, and could have no better resting place than the *Honest Ulsterman*.

I hope things are going well for you.

Sincerely,

Seamus

James Simmons (1933–2001), Protestant Northern Irish poet and songwriter, had recently founded the *Honest Ulsterman*, which for the next few decades, under his own editorship, then that of Frank Ormsby (b.1947), was to prove itself Northern Ireland's pre-eminent literary journal. The poem offered here by SH, and accepted by Simmons, was 'The Forge', which pays tribute to the blacksmith of Bellaghy, Barney Devlin (1920–2016). A line from the poem, 'All I know is a door into the dark', would give SH the title for his second collection.

To Charles Monteith

TS Faber

9 April 1968

Department of English,
Queen's University, Belfast

Dear Charles,

I should have written to you long ago but I wanted to accompany my letter with this manuscript. It is a kind of peace offering (to the gods or somebody), for the good luck of the award. I am not submitting *Doors into the Dark* officially at the moment, but I would like you to have a look at it so that we can talk about it on the 25th. There are some poems which I have in reserve, and there are some in the manuscript over which I would place a fairly large question mark. What do you think of 'The Plantation' and 'Reclining Eve' for example? Or 'Triptych for E.B.'?

Marie and I look forward very much to meeting you and Rosemary again. We were half wondering whether I should not decline the Geoffrey Faber Award because of the Maugham Manna. Do you think I should wonder any more about that?

With all good wishes, sincerely,

Seamus

On 2 April, Monteith had telegrammed SH 'TORRENTIAL CONGRATULATIONS FROM EVERYBODY HERE' on the news that he had been given a Somerset Maugham Award; the 'Maugham Manna' was the sum of £500. Despite his politic doubts, SH accepted the Geoffrey Faber Memorial Prize as well.

'I am not submitting': it is interesting to note this early instance of SH's custom of showing unfinished manuscripts to his Faber editor, for advice or confirmation, before a complete collection would be more formally submitted months later. '*Doors into the Dark*' is not a slip but the actual working title. Of the poems mentioned here, 'The Plantation' was eventually included, while 'Reclining Eve' and 'Triptych for the Easter Battlers' were not.

To Charles Monteith

MS Faber

10 May 1968 37 Beechill Park South, Belfast 8

Dear Charles,

Late, or later than usual! But what a memorable time we had on 25th of April. Marie and I cannot hope to return the hospitality and goodwill of the party and the dinner. All we can say is Thank you again.

The only excuse I can offer for this tardy letter is the fact that we spent last week doing a highly successful tour of the North here, and ended up at Dungannon on Monday last speaking into the small hours of the morning on 'Marriage in Irish Literature'. The latter was all booze and blather, I'm afraid, but the poetry and song drew good audiences and genuine response in the previous week.

I had the photographs from Rosemary earlier in the week – I think you are the most photogenic of the lot of us – my expression moves from disdain to inane with little between. But it's good to have them.

It was a great time in London again and our gratitude is unbounded.

Sincerely,
Seamus

To Paul Muldoon

MS Emory

30 May 1968 37 Beechill Park South, Belfast 8

Dear Paul,

Forgive my exact delay of a month in writing to you. I like these poems very much and I think you don't need anyone to tell you 'where you're going wrong'. I think you're a poet and will go where you decide. And thank you for the Somerset Maugham poem, which I hope you won't mind me keeping.

I am also keeping three others which I think are excellent – 'Stillborn', 'Snail' and 'Skeffington's Daughter'. I am guest editor of the next issue of *Threshold* and hope to use some or all of these in it. Could you tell me the background to 'Skeffington's D.' which comes across very powerfully? And have you any more poems?

Sincerely,

Seamus Heaney

The sixteen-year-old Paul Muldoon (b.1951) was still a pupil of St Patrick's College, Armagh, when he sent some of his poems to SH for comment. 'Stillborn' became 'Behold the Lamb', and 'Snail' became 'Thrush', when they were included, with 'Skeffington's Daughter', in Muldoon's first book, *New Weather* (1973). In the book, an epigraph explains that Skeffington's Daughter was the name of a sixteenth-century instrument of torture.

SH had contributed poems to the magazine *Threshold* the previous year, and was now, for the one and only time, acting as its guest editor. For his issue, which appeared in the summer of 1969, he took 'Snail' and 'Stillborn', plus a third, 'Poem at Eighteen'.

To Charles Monteith

TS Faber

9 July 1968

Department of English,
Queen's University, Belfast

Dear Charles,

I fear I'm playing truant again from my correspondence: and I know you wanted the landscape poems finally for the end of June but I couldn't possibly get the things finalized during the exam rush. Is it too late to add one ('Bann Clay') and substitute new versions of 'Whinlands' and 'Shoreline'? I think 'Bann Clay', if you like it enough to include it, should now come between 'Shoreline' and 'Bogland'. I also enclose three others. 'Cana Revisited' is two years old and I thought it might come between 'Mother' and 'Elegy'; 'Gone' is new and a bit of the same again, I fear, but would it work immediately after 'Night Piece'? 'American Dream' is a literal report of a dream which I felt was too violent to write down until the assassination of Martin Luther King, the riots and then the second Kennedy assassination.

'Loch' should be spelt 'Lough' as you suggest; and I would not be unhappy with a note about eels. I'll try to concoct something during the week and bring it to Dorchester. I am going to the Hardy Festival for six days or so and will be leaving Waterloo at 8-30 on Saturday morning. Perhaps I'll give you a ring at Fabers before the end of the week to see if I could meet you for a while down there.

How would you feel about changing the title of the book to *Door into the Dark*? I'm beginning to feel that the singular noun is crisper.

Anyhow, perhaps I'll see you soon. And I'm going to sign the contract now and convince myself that there [is] nothing more to be done to the blessed MS.

With every good wish,
Sincerely,
Seamus

Two PSes – i) I'm not sure whether to include the American Dream, you see.

ii) Can you add a dedication to Bogland – 'for T. P. Flanagan'. He's a painter whose vision of the moss might have brought on the poem.

This letter came towards the end of the series of letters between SH and Monteith in which the contents of SH's second collection were discussed, certain poems being removed, while others were added, and the shifting sequence of poems gradually settled. SH overcame his qualms about 'American Dream', which was given the new title 'Dream'; no 'note about eels' was after all thought necessary for 'Lifting', part 5 of 'A Lough Neagh Sequence'; and the improved title of the book was agreed.

The 'PSes' are handwritten. Enniskillen-born T. P. (Terence Philip) Flanagan (1929–2011) was a friend of SH's, a landscape painter and teacher of art.

To John Montague — MS Cork

[Late 1968?] 37 Beechill Park South, Belfast 8

[. . .]

We did not, in the end, make Paris. We had a week in Dingle and an interview with the bank manager, and that was that. We had a night's boozing last week with Brian O'Donnell, a real dolmen round my drinking, a dark permanence. He was brooding kindly about you. Apparently, they missed you at the Claddagh launching – I could not make it myself – O'Donnell spent a night 'in one of Paddy Falloon's flashy bedrooms, on top of the clothes'.

I was wondering lately if you like Michael Longley's poetry well enough to mention it for consideration to MacGibbon and Kee. He has a collection, the best part of which has not been published anywhere so far, and it has been rejected three times in the last six months – Oxford, Cape and Faber, so I cannot do anything for him there. He is at the moment understandably discouraged, though not shaken in his dedication or belief in his talent. I only mention this because I remember you liked his poems and because, unsolicited, you did a similar good turn for me. And nobody would be angrier than Longley, if he knew what I was up to. Of course, I shall understand completely if you prefer not to commit yourself. It's only a thought.

If you're at home here round Christmas, I hope you'll get in touch.

Sincerely,
Seamus

An undated letter, placed here speculatively. The first few paragraphs, omitted here, discuss proofs of a publication which I have not been able to identify but which may have been notes intended to accompany the LP that is mentioned below but was not in the event used.

Born in New York, brought up in rural Co. Tyrone, and currently living in Paris, John Montague had had his second collection, *The Chosen Light*, published in 1967 by the London firm of MacGibbon and Kee. He and SH had first met socially a couple of years before, at the home of Pearse (1918–2004) and Mary (1918–2006) O'Malley, who ran the Lyric Theatre in Belfast, and in 1968 the two poets had come together professionally to record poems for an LP, *The Northern Muse* (Claddagh Records, 1968).

In his remarks about Brian O'Donnell – who remains unidentified – SH alludes to a poem from *The Chosen Light*, 'Like Dolmens Round My Childhood, the Old People', with its concluding line, 'Into that dark permanence of ancient forms'; Paddy Falloon (1911–2003), businessman, restorer of derelict houses and a man of restless energy, was noted for his wit and hospitality.

1969

Publication of *Door into the Dark* was the high point of this year, but already SH was mining the seam that would yield the poems of *Wintering Out* (see letter of 19 May to Charles Monteith). For a while, too, as the letter of 12 March to John Oliver indicates, he remained hopeful that his ideas for a pedagogical book might still appeal to Faber and Faber; the project, however, was never taken up.

To Charles Monteith

MS Faber

17 January 1969 16 Ashley Avenue, Belfast 9

Dear Charles,

I've had so many letters and cards from you since I last wrote that my sense of failure on the correspondence front mounts again. Thank you for your good wishes at Christmas and your confabulations with Eric White over the reading in March. I've written to Sir William Jenkins and await the outcome. Also, I was surprised and delighted to get the proofs of *Door into the Dark* so promptly: it was a good idea to repeat the print and layout of *D. of N.*, and I'm just curious now how the cover will look. You haven't decided on a publication date yet? Longley's book is coming out in May, I think, and I was wondering if it wouldn't be better to stagger the two of us by six weeks or so at least. I tend to run away from the notion, which the reviewers might create, of a Northern Ireland 'School'. It's a variety, but not much else.

BBC Television are going to do a half-hour – or twenty minutes, I'm not sure – film on my astounding life and works for a series that's going out all over in April–May. Originally, it was to be studio readings and interviews but Roger Owen, the producer, has decided to make my slot nearly all film of the rooted native in his green glades. It should help the book along anyhow. I'm also engaged to do a twenty-minute film/ commentary for a religious type programme called *Viewpoint* which I intend to make mostly poems also.

Polly has been up to her welcome nepotism once again – this time in Virginia. I'm going over to give a talk on something or other to a literary club in Richmond for which they intend to offer $600 – enough to pay my fare and give me a margin. I'll be staying with Polly and Andy in New York for a few days – the thing is on Sunday 23rd February – and I was wondering if OUP might arrange a reading to provide something more than pocket money. Is there anyone I could write to? If they haven't sold the poems, perhaps they would buy the poet. I'd like to furnish a couple of bedrooms on the trip, but that's hardly likely.

[. . .]

PS We had a marvellous reading by Ted Hughes just after the Festival and he and Ass?ya (I don't know quite the girl's name) spent a memorable evening with Marie and myself. Quiet and relaxed; and blessed with a sprinkle of poteen.

New address: the Heaneys had moved from Beechill Park South to the more bohemian and congenial Ashley Avenue (see *Stepping Stones*) in 1968.

Eric Walter White (1905–86) was the dynamically active Literature Director of the Arts Council in London from 1966 to 1971; 'Sir William Jenkins' looks like a garbling of Hugh Jenkins (1908–2004), Labour politician who was involved with the Arts Council.

Roger Owen's film of SH – in which 'Seamus Heaney, the young Irish poet, reads and talks about his own work and its background' – was part of the BBC series *Something to Say*. It was broadcast on 11 May 1969.

Marie Heaney's sister Polly was married to the businessman Adrian ('Andy') Garnett (1930–2014). The trip to New York and Richmond would afford SH his first, appetising taste of the USA.

The previous year, Ted Hughes, accompanied by his lover Assia Wevill (née Gutmann) (1927–69), had given public readings in Dublin and Belfast, both of which SH had attended.

To John Oliver

MS Faber

12 March 1969 16 Ashley Avenue, Belfast 9

Dear Mr Oliver,

First of all, I'm sorry for the delay in replying to your letter – but it went to my old address. I thought that my new address had been circulated at Fabers: it's at the top of the page anyhow.

I am deeply guilty about the overdue poetry book. But pregnancies, house-moving and decoration and various other commitments knocked my schedule about rather last year. I can promise the MS by the end of June. The subtitle of the book would be 'A Poetry Work-Book' – so that it's not aimed to *tell* people *how* they should teach. It rather allows people to approach poetry from the point of view of the practitioner: to show how some poems came about, to let people see, and to hope they move from *sight* to insight. I'll append a few extracts from a provisional introduction. It is suited to training colleges, sixth forms, creative writing courses etc. It would never be a GCE set text, but I am sure that a number of colleges of education would take it for one of *their* set texts.

I was talking to a couple of people in the inspectorate here and they feel that the book of Irish verse has little chance of becoming a set text; but they felt that it *could* have a fairly general sale in the secondary intermediate schools here (i.e. the North – secondary modern in England). So on a quick reaction, I'd say we needn't settle for the school library type of edition just yet.

One thing we might talk about (and I'll be in London from Wednesday till Friday of next week and will ring you up) is whether we should include *only* poetry. BBC Schools do a very popular couple of programmes here every year called just 'Irish Writing'. I compiled the stuff for this year and may be doing next year's. I'll bring the pamphlet and teacher's notes so that you can have a look.

I'm sorry for the haste now, but I want you to have a minimal reply for Friday.

Hope we can meet next week.

Sincerely,

Seamus Heaney

John Oliver (1921–70) was Faber's Educational Manager.

To Paul Muldoon

MS Emory

[Spring 1969?]

16 Ashley Avenue, Belfast 9

Dear Paul,

I've just put together the twenty-second issue of *Threshold* and I've used three of your poems – a miserable cheque will arrive sooner or later – 'Still Born', 'Snail' and the Procrustes bed one. I think they are probably the best work in the magazine, and this is no flattery and is not meant to be more than gratitude for having come upon your work.

Somebody told me that you were for Maynooth so this may reach you there. I know you'll be involved in all kinds of new intellectual strategies but hope you keep writing and would be glad to see what you do when you feel like letting it into the light. You *must* show your work to Father Peter Connolly (and give him my regards). Also, Dr Brendan Devlin (French) is a very good friend of ours so convey our best wishes to him – he is a Tyrone man too who has published an interesting Irish allegorical type book.

Door Into the Dark comes out next September and includes the guitar poem. *Threshold* should be out before the end of October and I'll forward a copy as soon as it appears. Perhaps we'll meet some time during the year. Good luck for now.

Sincerely,
Seamus Heaney

Could you drop me a card by return including a brief (very brief) biographical note or if it's inconvenient I'll just write that you are from Tyrone, young and that this is your first published work (? is it?).

The 'Procrustes bed' poem was 'Poem at Eighteen', which did not qualify for inclusion in *New Weather*.

Muldoon had for a while intended to study at Maynooth, where most students studied for the priesthood but which was now taking secular students; he had been accepted there by Tomás (later Cardinal) Ó Fiaich (1923–90) on the strength of his translations from the Irish. Fr Peter Connolly (1927–87) was Professor of English at St Patrick's College, Maynooth; Dr (now Monsignor) Brendan Devlin (b.1931) was Professor of Modern Languages there and author of the novel *Néal Maidine agus Tine Oíche* (1964).

To Rosemary Goad

MS Faber

28 April 1969 — 16 Ashley Avenue, Belfast 9

[. . .] We're still short of water after the explosions and I'm almost certain that the last flat wheel I got (it was flat when I went out yesterday morning) was the work of Protestant saboteurs. You're lucky to be out of it. [. . .]

Although SH had joined a protest march against the Royal Ulster Constabulary the year before and, as a Catholic, was acutely sensitive to the sectarian divisions in Northern Ireland that would culminate in long years of bombing and bloodshed, he seldom in his letters mentions the impact on him personally. This is a rare instance.

To Charles Monteith

MS Faber

19 May 1969 16 Ashley Avenue, Belfast 9

Dear Charles,

Your book arrived at the most exciting moment of my writing life and it was a delight to see it – my own haven't got here yet. But in the last week, beginning on Monday 12th, I wrote twenty-three poems nearly all of which I believe I'll be keeping. How would *Blood on a Bush* sound for a title? My one fear is that this is a huge self-deception so I don't want to let you see them yet. They are new for me, but half-promised by 'Dream' and, in another way, 'Bogland'. Anyhow, that's the news.

I only half-expected that Glyn Hughes's poems would make it, but they are genuine, which is a lot, and I mentioned him for this reason. But he should have no trouble finding a publisher.

Perhaps I'll get to see you in London some time before or around publication day. And when these new poems sort themselves out I'll let you have them – on a personal basis, for a start. (Not that Faber and Faber Ltd are ever impersonal.) Until then, every good wish from Marie and myself.

Sincerely,
Seamus

'Your book': i.e. the early copy of *Door into the Dark* sent by Monteith as a personal courtesy, as opposed to the half-dozen contractually due to the author ('my own').

The exceptional outpouring of twenty-three poems suggests SH's own excitement at the thematic and stylistic advances that were to be revealed in his next book, *Wintering Out* (1972). In *Stepping Stones*, SH recalls the moment as a 'dam-burst . . . a visitation, an onset, and, as such, powerfully confirming. This, you felt, was "it". You had been initiated into the order of the inspired.'

To John Hewitt

MS PRONI

18 June 1969 16 Ashley Avenue, Belfast 9

Dear John,

A couple of days ago I read Hawthorne's introduction to *The Scarlet Letter* where he talks of authors who 'indulge themselves in such confidential depths of revelation as could fittingly be addressed, only and exclusively, to the one heart and mind of perfect sympathy, as if the printed book, thrown at large on the wide world, were certain to find out the divided segment of the writer's own nature and complete his circle of existence by bringing him into communion with it'. I think Hawthorne was a bit sceptical about the possibility, but after your two letters, first after the television programme which I should have replied to long since, and now, about the book, I am convinced I am one of the lucky authors who has found an ideal audience. The sincerity and solidity of the Hewitts' response and the kindness that is, we feel, parental (our parents cannot say what they feel about literature) – these things are as reassuring to me as geology is to architecture. I always know that your praise is not a compliment but a communication and am sensible that a gracious patter of gratitude to you only scratches the surface of what I feel. My good luck in all spheres of life makes my Irish Catholic consciousness apprehensive that, as my mother would say, 'something is going to happen', but all that occurs is the returning tide of kindness which no one could predict for himself. The calm rooting of your friendship has been one of the bonuses of declaring for poetry. I'll write again before the 12th – I'm up to the oxters (how *do* you spell it?) in exams just now. Regards to Roberta. With good wishes and thanks,

Seamus

To Michael and Edna Longley

TS Emory

30 July 1969

Sorde-l'Abbaye, par Peyrehorade,
Landes, France

Chers Amis,

Swallows shit from the rafters all around me; our landlord sprays the vines out at the back; Marie and Helen indulge in the ancient French pastime of tan-tan; and Michael and Christopher pursue the bewildered ducks in the yard. After a fortnight we have all more or less established our ways of life; mine, characteristically – I hear you cry – covered in shit.

I am writing in a big shed/garage/playroom that is part of the farmhouse opening on to the village street with one of those big arched double doors, opening also into the yard at the back and the house itself. And there really are swallows nesting above me. I've meditated on a swallow's flight in various stages of vinous concentration. The yard is marvellous for the kids. There are cows and pigs and hens and ducks and geese and cats and a dog. Not to mention a hayloft with steps up to it and a tractor. Behind that again is the vineyard. In the house we have a big living room, kitchen and bathroom à la moderne and two very adequate bedrooms upstairs. Lots of what you might call rural artefacts in evidence all round: Elizabeth David type utensils inside; more, perhaps, reminiscent of the Archers outside.

The village has about six hundred people – a secretive assembly of Basque berets, straw hats, gutty slippers and widow's weeds. The women spend most of their time just behind the shutters and the men are mostly arsing about with fishing rods. Not to be outdone, I've bought a very simple but astonishingly long and wobbly rod myself. No cracks please. So far without results. I also bought a sweety bag full of maggots for bait and left them out in the shed at the back. When I opened the bag four days later, out burst a few hundred big strapping bluebottles. Guess what Hobsbaum would say.

We've been to the beach at Biarritz a couple of times, to a bullfight at one of the local fetes; we've eaten out a couple of nights; and been on the wine of the country since we arrived. We take the kids to the river, go once a week to a marvellous market in Peyrehorade and generally laze through the day. The cost of living is nearly twice as much as at home – wine being the only cheap thing you can get – but we eat big shafts of bread and the fruit and vegetables are so [seductive? attractive?] that you never think of expense; the dark day of reckoning will be in the dolorous depths of Ashley Avenue.

We set off for Spain – via Fatima in Portugal where I've got this nun aunt (guess what Liam Barbour would say) on Sunday; hoping to see Anne Devlin in Madrid and then to go east to the province of Castellón where we have been told you can rent a country house like this cheaply. The kids travel very well, apart from a few sharp protests at bedtime. But no sickness, thank goodness. If they behave as well in the hotter climate of Spain and if the money goes further in that Papish paradise, we contemplate arriving back in mid-September. But it could be much sooner.

I've written a little verse interlude about the death of Henry Munro since I came – it's for Stuart Evans's series; supposed to be a radio play but really three hundred lines of heroic couplets divided between Munro and General Nugent, the commander in chief of the militia who hanged him. I'm trying now to do a book review on George Mackay Brown's beautiful book about the Orkneys and Conor Cruise O'Brien's entertaining introduction to Ireland – but I can't get the damned thing under way at all. Apart from that, nothing doing. How are the mills of your own muse grinding? And how are the reviews of the book going, I wonder. I don't want to know until I go home. I have really forgotten totally about the business. When I go back, you'll be squaring up for the fray yourself. *Noli timere, frater.*

Since we're off on Sunday and don't know where we'll be, it'll probably be September before I hear and see youse. I hope you're enjoying yourselves and that Michael especially is preparing for the strict disciplines imposed by a year at grass. As they say at the end of French letters (ha ha) I embrace you cordially and so do Marie and Helen. The boys embrace Rebecca. Good luck for now.

Sincerely,
Seamus

PS I trust Barry forwarded the Frost book.

PPS I'm teaching myself Spanish from a French primer.

Accompanied by Marie's sister Helen (b.1952), the Heaneys had gone to France in order to fulfil the terms of SH's Somerset Maugham Award, the sole stipulation of which was that the recipient should use the cash that came with it to travel and broaden experience. In *Stepping Stones*, SH remembers this as a time of creative confidence: 'I got terrific strength throughout that summer from the sheer familiarity of the farmyard in Sorde-l'Abbaye . . . I was writing every day in an old barn in the *gîte* and felt guaranteed in my work.'

'I've meditated on a swallow's flight': see the first line of Yeats's 'Coole Park, 1929'.

In the fourth and fifth paragraphs, a crescent-shaped tear in the margin, like a large bite, has made certain words either invisible or only partially legible; many of them, however, may be guessed, the one exception being where 'ctive' is all that remains of what could be either 'seductive' or 'attractive' – or some other word that has not occurred to me.

The 'verse interlude' was broadcast as a radio play, with the title *Munro*, by BBC Northern Ireland on 14 January 1970. Henry Munro (1758–98) was executed for his actions as rebel leader in the cause of a United Ireland.

A joint review by SH of *An Orkney Tapestry* by George Mackay Brown (whom he spells 'MacKay Browne' in this letter) and *Conor Cruise O'Brien Introduces Ireland* was written for the *Listener* of 21 August.

'*Noli timere, frater*': Latin for 'Don't be afraid' (or, 'No fear'?), 'brother' – Michael Longley's *No Continuing City* being about to face the critics; the phrase, originally in the plural, '*Nolite timere*', and addressed by Christ to his disciples, is from the Vulgate Bible, Matthew 14:27.

After leaving his teaching job, Longley had taken himself off to a remote cottage in Co. Wicklow intending to write, but, as he reports, 'the Muse did not come with me', and the following year he was relieved to be offered a job at the Arts Council of Northern Ireland.

The postscripts are handwritten.

To John and Madeleine Montague   TS Cork

8 September 1969   'The Laurels', Sessia, Coagh,
Co. Tyrone

Dear John and Madeleine,

Just a postcard, as it were, to thank you for what was the most delightful and memorable week of the summer for us; you made things so easy and your generosity was so abundant and thoughtful that we can only hope that some day we will be in a position to be hosts to you as well. The drive to Honfleur was delightful and we fell in love with the town of Honfleur itself. Budding Francophiles.

A Protestant vigilante was shot in Belfast last night and it seems that fear is abroad in Belfast again. We haven't been there yet since we came straight to Ardboe here with Helen and we're going off to see my parents now. When we get a taste of the situation in 'the city' we'll write again.

I was a bit surprised – and I'm sure you were – to see seven poems including 'Idyll' in the *Listener*. I can't understand why Miller did this because I had not submitted them officially to him and was wanting to hold on to a number of them for elsewhere – you could overdo the *Listener*. I lent him the Ms in the same way as I lent it to you – as a friend interested in the stuff – and there was an understanding that after I came back he might take some of them. He must have seized an editorial opportunity with NI in the news. Probably there will be a letter when I get to Belfast. But it means that there's no chance of 'Idyll' for *Threshold*. When you come in November we may be able to substitute something.

Thank you for everything. And sorry about our over-demonstrative bitching session in the small hours of Friday morning. Love to you both.

Seamus

On the journey home from their holiday in the south, the Heaneys had stopped in Paris where John Montague and his French wife had given them hospitality.

The poems that Karl Miller had piratically scooped for the 4 September issue of the *Listener* were 'Serenades', 'Midnight', 'Navvy', 'First Calf', 'Medallion', 'Icon' and 'Idyll'.

1970

SH's first spell of teaching at the University of California, Berkeley, in 1970–1, proved an eye-opening and life-changing experience. Through a chance encounter in 1969 with the Yeats scholar Thomas F. Parkinson (1920–92), he had been invited to spend a year as visiting lecturer at the university. 'Exactly what I was looking for,' SH says in *Stepping Stones*, 'so no hesitations whatsoever about accepting.' He took his family with him.

The chattiness and exuberance of letters written from Berkeley to friends back home reflect his delighted apprehension of new freedoms and readiness for potential discoveries.

To John Montague

TS Cork

11 January 1970 16 Ashley Avenue, Belfast 9

Dear John,

Glad to hear from you and to receive 'Omagh Hospital' which is unchangeable, I think – firm and beautiful, and a real companion piece for the banshee lyric. Nothing but good 'poretery' this weather!

I'm sending you 'Bye-Child' for a reaction really. I'm thinking of a scandal of about fourteen years ago when the authorities found this youngster in a henhouse in Co. Down, four or five years of age, unable to speak and suffering from malnutrition and all kinds of deficiencies. It has been in my mind for a long time and the loneliness and remoteness of the thing, the emptiness, got mixed up in my head with those ghostly movements of the astronauts on the moon. And I was prepared to let the rhythm wander: I think the thing as it stands is odd but I'm afraid it might just be gobbledegook. It's either a very good one or no good at all.

[. . .]

SH and Montague were now in the habit of showing each other and commenting on their work-in-progress. Montague's 'Omagh Hospital' would go on to be incorporated in 'The Leaping Fire', the second section of his 1972 volume *The Rough Field*, as would 'A Hollow Note', his 'banshee lyric'.

'Bye-Child' would be included in *Wintering Out*: the last lines evoke the child's 'gaping wordless proof / Of lunar distances / Travelled beyond love.'

To Harry Chambers

MS Hull

28 January 1970

Harry – 'Wedding Day' was copied from an earlier draft but there's only a couple of corrections so would this copy (overleaf) suffice?
Donald Davie simmers.
Do you think the deletion in 'High Street' is wise?
'Tweed' came out of the Stroud visit.
'Bye-Child' is the latest. Shaky?
How are you both?
Seamus

Written down the right-hand margin of a poem with the title 'Icon', from a sheaf that also included 'Limbo', 'Wedding Day', 'The Last Mummer', 'High Street, Belfast, 1786', 'Tweed', 'Dawn' and 'Bye-Child', offered to Chambers for his editorial consideration. 'High Street, Belfast, 1786' was eventually the subtitle for 'Linen Town', from which two scene-setting stanzas were deleted – visibly so on SH's typescript – before it appeared in *Wintering Out*. 'Tweed', now with the title 'The Wool Trade', and all the rest, except 'Icon', would be collected in the same volume, though several, 'Bye-Child' among them, were still to undergo significant revision. Chambers took only 'Wedding Day' for the Summer 1970 edition of *Phoenix*. 'Donald Davie simmers' appears to carry some private reference.

To Karl and Jane Miller

MS Emory

[September 1970]

Flat 1, 2444 Carleton Street, Berkeley, CA 94707

Dear Karl and Jane,

In some way the colour problem has insinuated itself already and I've permitted myself the affectation of brown ink. Anyway, we've arrived safe and sound and are just beginning to get over the exhaustion – Marie is even now singing the little exiles to sleep in the next room of the Carleton Hotel and – oops – one of them has just mutinied and is at my elbow. They survived and revived on what turned out to be a 24-hour journey very well, although we did carry them sleeping from the airport in Los Angeles to the motel. It was 10 o'clock, local time, when we got there – 22 hours after that rude awakening in Limerston Street. We cannot thank you enough for cushioning us on our way – again – and we'll certainly always recall our departure with pleasure because of your hospitality.

We were out to dinner the first night with the Flanagans (actually, they're not Irish but he's an Anglo-Irish specialist) who helped us to find an excellent flat with a garden – address as above – and we're moving in on Wednesday. It's 6 minutes' walk (just off Telegraph Avenue) from the Campus so we may see some action. I imagine it's like living on the peace-line in Belfast. By the way, any chance of the *Listener* sending that article by the Scotsman?

We feel we're going to like this place very much. I'm teaching just Tuesdays and Thursdays this term – so I may send the *Listener* some sort of local colour, first impressions, views, whatever when I gather them. OK? And if you don't want them, no matter. Thanks again. Love,

Seamus and Marie

This undated letter, despatched shortly after the arrival of SH and his family in Berkeley, gives the address of their first home there. Limerston Street is where Karl Miller and his wife Jane (b.1932) lived.

American scholar and novelist Thomas Flanagan (1928–2002), of Irish descent, was Professor of English at Berkeley, where he taught both English and Irish Literature; he and his wife Jean visited Ireland frequently. At this time, he was yet to publish *The Year of the French* (1979), the novel for which he is best known and which deals with events around the Irish insurgency of 1798. In *Stepping Stones*, SH describes Flanagan as 'a sort of literary foster father' and adds, 'It would be no exaggeration to say that he reoriented my thinking.'

'we may see some action': Berkeley had been an incubator of student revolt in the late 1960s. In the paragraph from *Stepping Stones* already quoted, SH says, 'I had a curiosity about the whole Beat scene, and at that time the Bay area was as hot politically as it was poetically.'

'Views', a piece by SH about living in Berkeley, appeared in the *Listener*, Karl Miller's magazine, at the end of the year.

To Michael and Edna Longley

TS Emory

22 September 1970

[Flat 1, 2444 Carleton Street,
Berkeley, CA 94707]

Dear Michael and Edna,

I'm smoking a cigar and coffee is brewing on the stove – not the cooker, see, stove – and no students have so far troubled the idyll. It was great to get your letter which in uncharacteristic fashion I am answering immediately. Something about the air here has me writing letters more promptly than ever before.

Actually, the house we live in is in a cul-de-sac. It's the end of a long street that cuts across all the main avenues of the town. The last one, the last intersection or crossroads (ha, ha) is with Telegraph Avenue, a tourist attraction that draws them from all over the States. It's the astonishing King's Road of Berkeley, running into the University just as Royal Avenue and Donegall Place runs into the City Hall. We are situated at about the *Irish News* office in Donegall Street; Telegraph is two spits away from us and the walk straight down into the campus takes about eight minutes through one of the most fantastic scenes you can imagine. Hippies, drop-outs, freak-outs, addicts, Black Panthers, Hare Krishna American kids with shaved heads, begging bowls and clothes made out of old lace curtains, it seems to me. They're chanting 'Hare Krishna' all the time but the most familiar chant is, 'Got any spare change?' There's an overpowering reek of joss sticks and incense floating out of the gear shops and book shops and herb shops (notice on sunblind of herb shop – 'All hail to the one cosmic mind'). Everywhere there are posters inviting you to 'personal exploration groups'. 'Lose your mind and come to your senses.' The feelies, in fact, are all around. Boy, if only I had the neck . . . It's lotus land for the moment, the sun always shining, peaches hanging at our kitchen window, a banana plant in the garden; there's an elysian atmosphere these mornings when I go down to the campus, with hippies in hillbilly outfits – your blue-bibbed overall and flowery print – lounging about on the steps, playing a flute in the sunshine, or wandering around blowing blues on a mouth organ (I knew my day would come), guitar music and song coming out from the shade of the Student Union steps. A damsel with a dulcimer (Appalachian mountain dulcimer) is always a-picking a toon, a black with a bongo, and Heaney with a haircut a bit sheepishly taking it all in. I hope the students don't spoil it – I've got two courses to teach this term. I do a course of my own devising with first years Tuesdays and Thursdays from 12 until 2 – practical criticism plus a few First Arts texts; and a survey of Eng. Lit. from Wordsworth to Yeats on the same days from 3 to 5. And that's the teaching load. A graduate student to mark the work for the first class. There's bound to be a snag.

Glad to hear the awards turned out (and I won't say anything about them) and that ole man Chambers is cotton-pickin' again. What I would really like to be in Belfast for now, though, is the Great L-Plate Story, learning with Longers, a serial in *perpetuum mobile*, the clutch is stuck, help. I've written to Les, well it's easy to see . . . I want a reading. Must put your name down on any circuit that I sneak into. Love to Becky and Edna. And all the Allens. Marie is heeled up like a pink cart in the garden trying to get all brown and the boys are playing aeroplanes in the undergrowth. There's a grand garden we have the use of here, like the hothouse in Botanic Gardens at the moment. I'm in the study as far from the light as possible. I'll enclose, by the way, a poem I stumbled on thanks to the decor above me. What do you think? And hey, if Ballard remembered to keep a George Best print for me, could you forward it and I'll send you a cheque when you bill me for post, etc. All power to the people. Love, Seamus and Marie.

Numerous mistyped words and names, the result of heedlessness or excitement, have been corrected here.

'the Great L-Plate Story': Michael Longley had been obliged by his new job at the Arts Council of Northern Ireland, which involved travel to far-flung places, to learn to drive.

'I've written to Les': Lester Conner (1920–2005) was an Irish specialist teaching at Chestnut Hill College in Philadelphia, and the author, after many years of work on it, of *A Yeats Dictionary: Persons and Places in the Poetry of W. B. Yeats* (1998).

Botanic Gardens is in Belfast. The recklessly talented and glamorous Northern Irish footballer George Best (1946–2005) was at the peak of his career at this time.

To Rosemary Goad

TS Faber

23 September 1970

Flat 1, 2444 Carleton Street, Berkeley, CA 94704

My Dear Rosemary,

It's about time I apologized for suddenly bursting in on your unsuspecting schedule the day before we left and thanked you for all your good work in the booking business. As it turned out, we stayed with Karl Miller, sat up chatting until twelve o'clock, only half-slept with the excitement and were on the go again at 5.15 a.m. Naturally the plane didn't leave Stansted until one o'clock which left us, to cut a long story short, arriving in Los Angeles at 5 a.m. our time, but only 9 p.m. by their reading. By their reading again, the kids wakened in the motel at a quarter to six the next morning and we knew we had really arrived because they could switch on the early morning television and be content until their stunned parents came round to their new situation. I think we've finally realized that we're in California for the year, and thank goodness, it gives us great pleasure.

Berkeley swings like a swing-boat, has all the colour of the fairground and as much incense burning as a high altar in the Vatican. When I walk home from the campus I can almost hear the joss sticks frizzling in every apartment. The fragrant follies of lotos land. The sun has never clouded once since we arrived and Marie unpinks assiduously. The flat, which we found on the second day, is ideal, far better than we ever anticipated, with a garden for, as Philip Larkin would call them, the nippers; and two bedrooms; and a study; and, no excuse now, two bathrooms. The kitchen is better decorated and better appointed than the one we have at home. And we're just six blocks from the campus and ten yards off Telegraph Avenue, the greatest tourist attraction this side of Haight Ashbury. The herb shop has a text on the sunblind 'All hail to the one cosmic mind'. They say 'Hare Krishna' instead of thanks. They're in blue bibbed dungarees and foundationless swaddling clothes. And of course I had to have my hair cut the day I left. You'll notice that about an Irishman: the turning points of his life are marked by a haircut and a new suit – First Communion, graduation, marriage and then somebody shaves him and gets him a new brown outfit so that he looks well in the coffin. 'He's very like himself', as they say at the wakes. Anyhow, new suits and haircuts have about as much chance here as a snowball in hell.

We're lapping it up and already have met nice people that I want to give a Faber book to. The man who looked after us when we arrived (a New Yorker in the English department called, naturally, Tom Flanagan) confessed to having read a couple of Hughes's crow things with some shock and respect so could you ever make me up a wee parcel – or get somebody else to do it – of: 2 Crow Poems; 1 *Dance the Dance* by Tom MacIntyre; and 2 of John McGahern's stories when they come out. Can you send them air mail and attack my account with it. I realize John McGahern's book may not be out yet, so let that wait, if necessary.

Marie sends her love and I do too. We'll keep in touch,

Love,

Seamus

The publication this year of Ted Hughes's *Crow: From the Life and Songs of the Crow* was an immediate and widespread sensation, thrilling some readers, appalling others. *Dance the Dance*, a book of short stories by Tom MacIntyre (1931–2019), Irish author better known as a playwright, and John McGahern's book of short stories, *Nightlines*, were published by Faber in the same year.

To Peter Crawley

MS Faber

26 September 1970

Department of English,
University of California, Berkeley

Dear Peter,

A belated thank you for those royalties you forwarded! It raised the standard of our farewell parties and lowered the pressure in the bank account. And we've landed here to try to recuperate three months of neglected correspondence. Somehow this summer was a time when NOTHING got done.

One of the neglected corners of my correspondence that I've just attended to raised another thing that I've always been intending to mention to you but never thinking of it at the right time. But now that I'm in America, the matter of the American publication of *D. of N.* and *D. into D.* is on my mind seriously, for the very first time. I've just been paying a bill for six copies of *D. of N.* that Oxford sent as publicity copies to Polly Devlin at *Vogue* when I went to New York over a year ago. With the exception of a letter from Whitney Blake, who has now left to go to Yale UP, this bill in its repeated arrival at 16 Ashley Avenue, Belfast, constitutes the total correspondence I've had with my American publisher. I never even knew when they released *Door into the Dark* and I had to buy the American editions of each book myself, in bookshops. So I've permitted myself the first grump of my career in the world of books – and paid the bill.

It does raise the whole question of American publication, however. As I say, I've never given it a thought before except to be grateful that Fabers found somebody to issue *Death of a Naturalist* in America. Oxford, I know, issued it indeed, but I doubt if they sell it. And from my sniffing and sampling in the excellent bookshops of New York and Berkeley, I can see why. It's impossible to find.

What exactly is the position? I know Fabers sell the copies to Oxford, and I'm sure the whole thing has been explained to me before, but how

and blue mail, I'm ever delighted to open the box downstairs to find the Hammond hand. I met the postman yesterday and he eyed [me] with some curiosity and said laconically, 'So you're the Irishman' – the various titles seem to have confused him; but what the hell was he talking about – he's a Chicano himself. Did you ever have a tequila? You should try one some time.

Well, have you hanged the craythirs in Downpatrick? A day you'll remember, feth. Now that you're in the way of civic duties I should write and put up your name for the Board of Management of the Dundonald Hospital. There cometh after me one mightier than I . . . Happy birthday, posthumously. Did Andy Crockart tell you the joke I put on his postcard about Conor C. O'Brien? O'Brien worked with Val Iremonger in External Affairs in the fifties when the *Irish Catholic* newspaper was very worried about having him and his freethinking ways in the civil service at all. They were always checking on him. One day O'Brien had his hat on to go to lunch and the phone rang. Iremonger took it and said (hand over mouthpiece) 'Christ, it's the *Irish Catholic* again. What will I do with him?' 'Offer him five pounds for his horse,' says O'Brien. The source of all this is Tom Flanagan, a New Yorker whom you may have met in Dublin. Anglo-Irish scholar, friend of Kiely and co. and a nice man to have around. He's trying to get a lecture for Horgan on this side of the country and has succeeded I think so the senator threatens to arrive. I had a tragi-comic letter about the car. The comedy was Horgan's slight pomposity about the condition it was in, the tragedy the fact that in four months or so I'll have chalked up a hire fee of five pounds. What more, I suppose, can an Irish Catholic expect for his horse.

I've had two weeks of teaching now and a lot of dining out with various members of the department who are afraid that we're lonely and don't realize they're setting themselves up for a party on the eve of our departure. And I've been writing like a whore. I've done two short stories, but don't tell anybody. And the *New Yorker* accepted a poem – called 'Home', about home. Maybe you remember it. This morning I got John McGahern's new book called *Nightlines* from Fabers but haven't read it yet. I think my stories were sired by reading some by a man called Leonard Michaels – they're published by Corgi or Panther in paperback in England (lurid cover) and by ~~Cape~~ <Weidenfeld, I think now> in hardback. Called *Going Places*. Some of them are very funny

– if you get the book start with 'City Boy'. Lenny is a very pleasant guy himself who takes us out for a drive about once a fortnight.

I've lost thirteen pounds through dieting and walking but there's plenty of wobble left, as the bishop etc. People know we've no car so offer to drive us all around. A couple that we met at a reception in the English Department are going to take us to the vineyards to-morrow to see the grape harvest. (I suppose they're pratie gathering at home.)
[. . .]
Many thanks for the big contract – Everyman one hasn't arrived yet but I'll return the million dollar deal to John Boyd and ask him did he not make a mistake. I'm glad you like the Everyman – if you let me know the real deadline, I will certainly lengthen it out. I've also started on the idea I mentioned to you about the cockfights as the image of Ulster but again not a word in case it doesn't come off. Do you know of any literature on cockfighting? Has George Thompson got anything, do you think? I wish I'd asked my father about the jargon and what they say about the cocks and shout at them. All this activity on the writing front makes me think that there's something freakish and futile about it but I'm hopeful that something will survive. Sooner or later I'll let you see what comes of it.
[. . .]

Downshire Road in Belfast was where David Hammond and his wife Eileen lived.

'hanged the craythirs in Downpatrick': presumably a facetious reference – Hammond being a Protestant – to the hanging of three Franciscan priests by Protestants in Downpatrick, Co. Down, in 1575.

Andy Crockart was a producer at Ulster Television; Conor Cruise O'Brien (1917–2008) worked in various departments of the Irish civil service while maintaining a career as historian and writer; Valentin Iremonger (1918–91) was an Irish poet as well as a diplomat. O'Brien's quip alludes to the old Penal Law that, if a Protestant offered a Catholic £5 for his horse, the Catholic was bound to accept it.

'a friend of Kiely': i.e. of the novelist Benedict Kiely (1919–2007).

The short stories mentioned here and in the following letter to Seamus Deane have tantalisingly vanished.

Leonard Michaels (1933–2003) was both a writer of fiction and, at this time, a Professor of English at Berkeley; *Going Places* (1969) is the book that made his name.

A 'pratie' is a potato.

The 'big contract': presumably for SH's radio play, *Munro*, the text of which was printed in the Northern Irish magazine *Everyman*. John Boyd (1912–2002) was a playwright and producer at BBC Northern Ireland, with which Hammond was professionally associated.

SH had already published, in 1966, his poem 'Triptych for the Easter Battlers', with its descriptions of 'birds fed up like kings of the yard . . . gathered and starved into condition' and 'airborne cocks, buoyant on their own blood', so he appears now to be seeking yet another way of developing the theme. Hammond, who was deeply versed in Irish customs and lore, would have been the man to ask, but the idea seems not to have got off the ground.

George B. Thompson (1925–2021) was director of the Ulster Folk Museum.

To Seamus Deane

TS Emory

15 November 1970

Flat 1, 2444 Carleton Street, Berkeley, CA 94707

A Sheamuis, A stóirín,

[. . .]

Well, we love Berkeley, we have not once regretted coming, we congratulate ourselves continuously; I've never worked as hard at teaching and never enjoyed it so much; I've never before experienced a sense of intellectual community and enjoyed meeting the informed and unstuffy. It's great for the year, it unsettles me prospectively for the rest of my thirties which was what I hoped it might do. It has given me a glimmer of ambition (unlocalized but glimmering, glimmering) and dislodged the Northern clay from my obstinate root. I run to rhapsody but irony has held the field too long.

[. . .]

I've written short short stories – three – since I came and I'd like your opinion of them as soon as I can get through with typing. But that's between ourselves. They mightn't even be readable and I've shown them to nobody here. Enclosed is the one real poem I've done since coming here – would you fancy it for *Atlantis*? Robin Skelton at *Malahat* took four other free ones the other day so I'm down on the stock again. And the *New Yorker* has taken a twelve-line effort ($50, bejazus) which they may publish sooner or later.

I hope we can write a few letters during the year – or to put it honestly, I must break the habit of laziness and immorality in personal relationships – all good will and no goods – and hone the edge of the Derry literature of the future. Good luck to you all. How are the lads and lassie? Marie sends love to Marion and concurs in all the predictions about clothes, climate and shoes. Our boys, incidentally, are not at any school yet. And to-day, to end on a savoury note, Christopher reaffirmed the rural traditions of the family by breaking into a nice round ringworm. And there are no cows' scratching posts in Berkeley. I wonder if that was ever said about Berkeley before.

Love, all power to the people,

Seamus

'*A Sheamuis, a stóirín*': SH occasionally addressed Catholic friends in Irish; *a stóirín* is an endearment meaning something like 'sweetheart' or 'love'.

Several paragraphs, some conveying gossip of a remote and elusive kind about individuals presumably connected with Berkeley, others containing material already covered in letters printed above, have been omitted.

The 'one real poem' was 'Westering', then titled 'Easy Rider', which Deane accepted for the 1971 issue of the magazine *Atlantis*, founded by him and Derek Mahon.

1971

SH's job at Berkeley continued until the late summer of 1971, after which he and the family returned to Belfast, where he resumed his teaching at Queen's. The busy, lucrative, but exhausting schedule of reading tours that was to be such a large feature of his periods of employment in the USA in years to come seems to have established itself at this early time.

To Michael Longley

TS Emory

26 April 1971

Department of English,
University of California, Berkeley

Dear Michael,

The correspondence does seem to have sunk deep in the bog of unfulfilled intentions: I've just been re-reading your letter of January 8th and biting my tied tongue to think that we never sent off one scrape to you – even after the good news of Boy Longley. Our love and welcome to him and Edna: how does it feel to have another foreskin in the house? Or have you made him one of the chosen, like myself? He is good news and he has a good nest in the family tree: we look forward to seeing him; which should be some time after August 15. That's that piece of essential information disposed of anyway.

Another welcome and gratitude: Edna's review of *Door into the Dark* was deep and heartwarming and a confirmation of some of the things I've been slipping towards here – the elements as self, secret rather than public poems, a return to *D. of N.* territory though not the manner: there's so much in that old terrain that for so many reasons went untouched. I think *Door into the Dark* was a necessary self-conscious brake, bulwark, whatever you want to call it. Whatever it was, it was almost never vulnerable. I want more and more to risk the open self, or to find a manner of saying that blends discipline and disarms disciplinarians, if you know what I mean. Something like Shakespeare's later blank verse might do, though even Shakespeare, at this stage, mmm . . . Perhaps a few poems would show better what I mean. Let me know what you think some time.

'Caravan' is a great success: a complete fidelity to the Longley voice but a new drift and a relaxation after those couplets – although mind you I liked the Explosion poem a lot – I saw it in the *New Statesman*. But the 'Caravan' voice can include more roughage and can wind its way into human tentativeness of resolution in a way that the more heraldic notation couldn't. I look forward to what I too sensed in the very ease of the thing – more. Have you the guts of another collection? I've been throwing things out as often as I've been adding to my putative third. Which, by the way, I hope to call *No Man's Land*. I think.

I am hellishly busy here and will be until August 5. I've taken on a Summer Course so that our fares will be easier; and I'm now three weeks into the summer or rather spring quarter, teaching 'An Introduction to Modern British and American Literature' and a writing class with 42 people! Disastrous for the ego of most of them, stupid, illiterate, long-haired, hippie, Blake-ridden, Ginsberg-gullible, assholes (assholes or cunts, I hear you cry). Seriously though, it is an exhausting assignment with a lot of anxious and eager kids all wanting to hear they're the greatest thing since, say, Charles Olson. In the two and a half weeks between winter and spring quarters, I was on a reading beano in Michigan: about seventeen appointments but I should have cleared about $1000 in the end. I saw Les and Des and Maurice in the course of the proceedings, reading at their venues, although I had to fly for hours in all directions out of Michigan. I also read at the Poetry Centre in New York with (for God's sake) Max Frisch, the dramatist. An odd occasion. It was totally exhausting but rewarding. I stayed in Ann Arbor most of the time and saw much of Frances and Tom MacIntyre who was there for the term. Then I came back here on March 31 and started teaching on April Fool's Day. I'm just about catching up with sleep and work – and correspondence. It meant that I've had no break since January 7th; I'll have ten days or so in June and then hard at it until homesville.

How are things at the Arts Council? I think of you in those open-plan offices doing the only sane administration in all Ulster. I've given up politics, I think. I'm beginning to think of our ever-loving community as a good starting point for personal redemption, but little else. How does the master-plan for Come to Ulster proceed, if at all?

Is the Group still grouping? Is the *Honest Ulsterman* still pecking away? Thank you for the Dugdale, McLaverty etc. Norman's book had a good deal of him there and was, you may say, satisfactory. Tell me what you want from America, besides withdrawal from Vietnam, an end to air pollution and big-business corporations.

All our love to your growing family and my apologies for a short letter but it's now or never and half a loaf . . . Pick a dingleberry for me. Lift up your hearts. The saviour of Ulster can be expected August 15.

Sláinte,
Seamus

'Boy Longley': Michael and Edna's son Daniel was born on 20 March.

Edna Longley's review of *Door into the Dark* had appeared in *Phoenix*: in it, she commended the book as superior to *Death of a Naturalist*, being a 'taut and unified whole' and 'a universal exploration of the dark, rich places in the human psyche'.

'Caravan' and 'Kindertotenlieder' (the 'Explosion poem') are in Longley's 1973 collection, *An Exploded View*, which was dedicated jointly to SH, Derek Mahon and James Simmons.

'Les and Des and Maurice': Lester Conner; D. E. S. (Desmond) Maxwell (1925–2009), a Derry-born Protestant expatriate academic, who taught for many years at York University, Toronto, and whose many publications included *A Critical History of Modern Irish Drama 1891–1980* and a book on Brian Friel; and Maurice Elliott (1937–2016), an English expatriate also teaching at York University.

Max Frisch (1911–91), Swiss dramatist and novelist, was at the height of his international reputation at this time.

Norman Dugdale (1921–95), whose professional career was in the civil service, was associated with The Group; his first book of poems, *A Prospect of the West*, came out in 1970. For 'McLaverty', see letter to Michael Longley of 8 February 1975.

To Charles Monteith

MS Faber

5 May 1971

Department of English,
University of California, Berkeley

Dear Charles,

The new Glob (lovely name) book came yesterday and I see you've moved to Queen Square so I thought I better first-foot you right away. We're surviving happily in Berkeley, although I'm still busy and will be until the middle of the summer. We fly home, defiantly, on Friday 13th of August.

I've written and rewritten a good bit here, advancing and retiring towards a collection. I've a feeling that I want what I have off my hands and yet I'm wanting it to fly away coherent and whole as a book. Perhaps I'll be able to let you see something soon – it would be too late now to appear around Christmas, I suppose. But I'm thinking of calling it *Wintering*; or maybe *No Man's Land*.

I've sent four poems to Liam Miller for a 'Poem Card' which I believe will be some sort of broadsheet. I trust this is in order.

The news from the North hasn't improved over the year, has it? Conor Cruise O'Brien is here at the moment as Regent's Lecturer, and we sway between visions of limbo and apocalypse. It's irretrievably the former, I fear. No man's land.

Marie and the boys still thrive in the Bay Area's kindly weathers. All our love to you and all the friends (disposed in open-plan offices now?) at Fabers. We look forward to seeing you again in a few weeks.

Sincerely,
Seamus

The first UK edition of *The Bog People* by P. V. Glob (1911–85) was published by Faber and Faber in 1969. The immediate influence on SH's poetic development of this hauntingly illustrated book, an archaeological and anthropological account of Iron Age bodies exhumed from the peat bogs of Denmark, cannot be exaggerated. 'The Tollund Man' and 'Nerthus', in *Wintering Out*, and more poems on the theme in *North*, three years later, were the first fruit of SH's abiding fascination.

To Michael Longley

MS Emory

[14 June 1971]

c/o Gary Snyder, West Gulch,
Ballyscullion, Big Sur

Dear Michael,

Do you remember writing like this in your wee copying-out book? Poertry was the last thing in your head then, I bet ye. I am not drunk but just hung-over and reading your translation in the *Irish Times* which comes to me on Mondays (having been posted on Saturdays) has put me on your wavelenght again. It is impossible to think and write like this so I will stop, having taken you on yet another trip down memory lane. (Ha! ha!)

Your verse dialogue is really excellent – great pace, great style, great energy coming up out of its 'hibernatory sleep' – the way your Aran bit shows its back among the waves of sense is marvellous. (I wish to Christ I hadn't started this monkeying about with the *script* for I can't help noticing every letter I write now.) You both could hit a rabbit punch with it – in the world of action as well as the world of poetry. I really think it could be at once epoch-making, defining the whole decade we've been through, and it could be a best-seller. Flog on. This is the kind of stuff that exhilarates, it's so fucking well written (and deep, deep) I kid you not. Those lines ride into the head like the Magnificent Seven all drawing at once and holing seven silver dollars in the air. I'm delighted to know such poets.

But you're a right bastard for writing that love poem for two days before the package arrived I did a wee tight dingleberry about herself in the bath which I will forward with others for imprimatur. And you've learned Swedish since, hmm. Captain Steel has nice steel in it.

I'm not going off my head, just writing in the middle of Michael-and-Christopher's posse which is riding shotgun on my headache. All this cowboy imagery! Ah yes, the west has gone to his head – his cheques have stage-coaches on them and his bank is Wells Fargo, for Chrissake.

All hail to the family. I will return to my people after two moons. We will sup heap fire-water. God bless.

Seamus

The salutation and first paragraph are in an infantile copperplate, with heavily curlicued capitals; in the same spirit, 'Poertry' and 'wavelenght' are spelt thus.

Longley and Derek Mahon had planned a 'verse dialogue' commenting on immediate political events; Mahon soon withdrew and elements of Longley's own side of the exchange went into his poem 'Letters', in *An Exploded View*. SH's jibe about learning Swedish refers to Longley's 'Songs from the Swedish', a version of a poem by Lars Forssell (1928–2007).

SH adds, as postscript, section III of his poem 'Summer Home', titled 'Bathing'.

To James Simmons

TS Emory

[September? 1971]

Dear Jimmy, I've read *Energy to Burn*
And your image floats before me, man and shade –
Ghost laurels shape up for your funeral urn,
A ring of truth comes off the life you've made.

So I'm involved, at one o'clock a.m.
In a short note of gratitude and praise:
Your excellence won't blame the odd weak rhyme
From one more drawn to sagas than to lays?

I've written also to Sir Bernard Miles
To half-say no to an Ulster Poetry Circus
For I believe that all our different styles,
Angles, vanities, small lies – what makes us

And what marks us as performers
Is always a bit cramped at quartered sessions.
Before a crowd of hippies and reformers
I'd trim the sails of postures and of passions

Because of you boys, not because of them.
Either we'd have to fit into some pattern
Or undercut, like an unstitching hem,
The effect of the ensemble. What in

Hell's name am I talking about?
You'll know, I know, who stand well on your own.
I just don't want to be parading out
With the team. I want a solo run

And a drop kick to rattle the small net
Lined by Alvarez, Hamilton and Thwaite.
'Slick rustic' and 'flat bottomed', 'Tribe of Ted' –
The skitters use a tackle that I hate

Though up till now I've kept my wee mouth shut.
A bit embarrassed by a young success
My stance was, of necessity, up-tight –
Yet I must learn to call a shite a shite.

O reputation! I do possess, they say,
A slippy rind of manners; but my pith
Is kind and sometimes hurt. My own true way
Runs secretly towards the bog of myth

But it seems to me that yours goes bravely through
The corner-boys, the watchers at the curtain,
Dignitaries, men at desks and bars, all who
Snigger, nag, obstruct the rare and certain.

A joy, gift, skill for letting in the light,
A scalpel for wounds and secrets: your mark

A healing one. You suffer for, and by it.
Your door still opened outward from the dark.

I'm a solemn bugger when it comes to print –
Ah 'fake concern', 'tight-arsed' and 'Liberal-tongued' –
For the light touch is hard with spuds and lint.
Yet my best poems I almost feel I've dunged.

Still, a light formality has been useful.
'The environment and the written word'
May vent more of the pent and make us full.
In the meantime I remain the 'booming' bard,

And send much love to Laura and the clan.
I don't think we'll get up *en famille*
In the near future – The American
News must keep a little longer. See ya.

Seamus

James Simmons's collection, *Energy to Burn*, was published in 1971; the invitation from Sir Bernard Miles (1907–91), actor, director and founder of the Mermaid Theatre in London, was to *Poetry International*, the festival held at the Mermaid in 1972; so this undated verse letter must have been written some time in between. Reference to '"verse epistles" I wrote last weekend' in SH's letter to Karl Miller of 30 September argues for its position here.

'Alvarez, Hamilton and Thwaite': Al Alvarez (1929–2019), who at this time was known publicly as A. Alvarez, Ian Hamilton (1938–2001) and Anthony Thwaite (1930–2021); all three poets were with some justice regarded by SH as representative of an English faction hostile to, or suspicious of, his work. Alvarez was an influential reviewer, mainly for the *Observer*; Hamilton was from 1962 to 1972 editor of the *Review*, a magazine noted for its merciless critical pronouncements; Thwaite wrote occasional reviews and presented programmes about poetry on BBC radio. Their shared attitude towards SH may be summed up by the opening paragraph in Thwaite's *New Statesman* review of *Door into the Dark*: 'It's impossible to fault the clean language, sensuous delight, concise and modest statements; and I'm sure it's all completely authentic. But I'm equally sure that the appeal of Heaney's work is of an exotic sort, to people who can't tell wheat from barley or a gudgeon from a pike. His poems are of a different, neater order from those of Ted Hughes, but I think he must be counted as one of what someone has called the Tribe of Ted . . .'

Simmons's reply to SH, also undated, also in quatrains, pleads the case for a group appearance. 'If Miles took only one it would be you,' he writes, adding a few lines later: 'I'm afraid / if I don't take these terms I'll have to wait.' In the event, a group reading took place.

To Thomas Flanagan

TS Amherst

24 September 1971

A Letter to Tom Flanagan

Men die at hand. In blasted street and home
The gelignite's a common sound effect.
As the man said when Celtic won, 'The Pope of Rome
's a happy man to-night.' His flock suspect

In their deepest heart of hearts the heretic
Has come at last to heel and to the stake.
We sense a tremble of change but want no truck
With the actual firing. We're on the make

As ever. Long sucking the hind tit
Cold as a witch's, and as hard to swallow
Leaves us fork-tongued on the partition bit.
The liberal papist note sounds hollow

When amplified and mixed in with the bangs
That shake our hearts and windows day and night
(It's hard here not to rhyme on 'labour pangs'
And diagnose a rebirth in our plight

Yet that would be to ignore other symptoms.
Last night you didn't need a stethoscope
To hear the eructation of Orange drums
Allergic equally to Pearse and Pope.)

On all sides little platoons are mustering
And we who clapped for Conor on Burke's state-
smanship are holed up with a pestering
Drouth for words at once both gaff and bait

To lure the tribal shoal to epigram
And order. I believe any of us
Could cut a line through enmity and sham
Given the right line, *aere perennius*.

I saw you angry once, the night you tumbled
To machinations in an upper sphere:

Your principles, and your friend, were humbled
By cruder men, emboldened by crude fear,

So you would know what some internees felt like
That day in August. And our golden age
Of Belfast Pamphlet and of Wexford pike
Is hearthstone to the cold spark of that rage.

You too are swung by the long tail of race.
Your grandfather, in that photo, as a boy
With Yankee uniform and a blank face,
Fenians his comrades and a drum his toy,

Stares at the approach of civil war
Hooded and real as the photographer.
But enough. There's a clear head where you are
And that national safety valve – laughter

Pace the old *Dublin Opinion*.
The killings are absurd and don't add up.
It isn't possible we're in on
The birth of a nation? I better stop.

Seamus

SH dates this verse epistle, which may have come with a covering note that is no longer attached to it, beneath the final stanza and his signature. Writing to Flanagan as to an American with Irish Catholic antecedents, he calls on tropes familiar to all and sundry, while adding details that must depend on private knowledge between the two of them; the first seven stanzas of this were adapted slightly to form part II of the poem 'Whatever You Say Say Nothing', in *North*.

The Anglo-Irish politician, orator and writer Edmund Burke (1729–97) was a figure of lifelong fascination to Conor Cruise O'Brien.

'*aere perennius*' alludes to the boast of the Latin poet Horace, '*Exegi monumentum aere perennius*' ('I have raised a monument more lasting than bronze') (*Odes*, Book III, 30); 'Wexford pike' to the rebellion of 1798, fought out in Co. Wexford, and the subject of the novel, *The Year of the French*, that Flanagan was to publish in 1979.

The *Dublin Opinion* was an Irish satirical magazine that flourished between 1922 and 1968.

To Michael Foley

TS

[Autumn 1971]

Letter to an Editor

Michael, you know I'm an expert with the spade
and get official backing for each action;
then stand back, for this folk-museum blade
can choose to lop off handshake or erection.

I warn you, your wee fly bedsitter-king
sweats in the palm of this Rachman of the arts
who comes with fake concern and a Claddagh ring
to evict him from the reek of his own farts.

(God but this *HU* stuff, so sweet and sour,
is easy going as the turnip snedder –
I'd say at least twelve quatrains to the hour,
including tea-breaks, which gives us a newsletter,

eight times a day, going at minimum rate.
There's a vocation lost, but what's the use?
I should have read, I realize too late,
not *The Great Hunger* but *Collected Pruse*.)

Now didn't you learn it all from Kavanagh,
the slapdash truth and the well-meaning lie?
Distrust your solemn man. Go for the ba.
And ironically don't care – spit in their eye.

Your prose style, I must say, is excellent,
fit instrument for cheek-slash and death-blow
but is all that courage at the sticking point
screwed up by the real thing or some dildo?

Official gadflies are co-opted. Then beware.
You too might lunge and find your angry stick
is dunlopillo. Who do you think you are?
Rare Ben Jonson? Swift? Dryden? Or Ulick?

We both know the Big Study and Pre Par,
the half-day syndrome and the day-boy lunch.

It would be a pity to spoil things as they are
with a clip on the ear or rabbit punch,

so instead I write to say I am fed up
finding myself too much in gossip columns.
Show proper respect, you editorial dope.
You're dealing with a prefect from St Columb's.

Printed in the November/December 1971 issue of the *Honest Ulsterman*, which Michael Foley co-edited with Frank Ormsby, this appears to have been prompted by a review of James Simmons's *Energy to Burn*, in an earlier issue of the magazine (29, 1971), in which Foley had dubbed SH, Michael Longley and Derek Mahon the 'tight-assed trio'. The 'Letter' was printed again many years later, in an article for the *Irish Times* of 15 April 2019, in which Foley, who had previously regarded SH's work as 'everything that poetry should not be, a rejection of the urban world for pastoral nostalgia, a cautious upholding of all the Irish pieties (especially the Holy Trinity of nation, church and family), and an avoidance of anything emotionally disturbing or intellectually challenging', explains how he came to revise his estimation.

To Karl Miller

MS Emory

30 September 1971 16 Ashley Avenue, Belfast 9

Dear Karl,

I look forward to seeing you some time next week: Marie and I hope to be in London from Monday until Thursday. I'm reading at the Queen Elizabeth Hall in a poetry circus on Wednesday night.

In the meantime, I'm enclosing a gather-up of verses that I took out of a group of 'verse epistles' I wrote to people last weekend. I'm not sure that I should publish them: and if I did, it would be as a piece of straight journalism – in the *Views* section, if anywhere. Anyhow, I'd be glad to hear what you think; and to take things up from where I left you, in that Benedictine dressing gown, at 5 a.m. . . .

Good luck,
Sincerely,
Seamus

Karl Miller printed 'Whatever You Say, Say Nothing: Seamus Heaney Gives His View on the Irish Thing' in the *Listener*'s 14 October number. The final section of this, under the title (or dedication) 'For David Hammond and Michael Longley', appears ahead of the contents list in *Wintering Out*, while the entire poem is included in *North*.

To Charles Monteith   MS Faber

24 November 1971   16 Ashley Avenue, Belfast 9

Dear Charles,

I've been more than unmannerly in not answering your letters; somehow, since I came back visitors, old contacts, new thoughts, decisions to be taken about career etc. have left me floating in an almost solipsistic frame of mind. My apologies. Your kindness and attention deserve much more of me.

First of all, the terms suggested for the contract seem fine so please go ahead with that.

As to the Ulster book, it's more and more coming into my mind as various assays and essays of an autobiographical nature, strung together with prose poems and verse. Not all the autobiography would be as pious and celebratory as the *Listener* piece, which was originally strung together around poems read on the programme, but the note of Eden would be there to sustain the entry of the serpent in the form of religious, political and cultural divisions, and how they enter, at a secret, subtle level, into the consciousness of the growing child. To make the thing worthwhile, I feel it should go to at least 100 pages, ideally 200 – but knowing my tight-mouthed way when I sit down at a desk, I'd better not promise too much. All I do in fact know is that a pressure to get out of me many aspects of growing up which I think are aspects of the communal psychology – this pressure has been building and will out. It's almost a moral need to unscrew the sump of the soul and begin clean again.

I hope this is of some use. I'll give you a more formal proposal in the next couple of weeks but Marie tells me that you were ringing to-day and I want to respond right away.

I feel I must get out of Belfast: too many ties and obligations to get a silence for writing.

More anon.

Sincerely,
Seamus

SH's essay, 'A Poet's Childhood', had appeared in the *Listener* on 11 November, excerpted from the radio broadcast he had given that week in the series of programmes for schools under the title *People at Work*. If an 'Ulster Book' exactly matching the one proposed in this letter never materialised, elements of it may be discerned in part I of *Preoccupations*, SH's first collection of prose writings, published in 1980.

1972

The return from Berkeley to Belfast in 1971 had prompted SH to take stock of his relations with a city that he was finding increasingly uncongenial to live in and to think about his own future as a writer more ambitiously. The impulses behind his move, with wife and two children, to the Republic of Ireland, and the steps by which he achieved it, are discussed fully in *Stepping Stones*; but if a single statement in that book were taken to sum up his motives, it might be: 'I'd breathed and walked free in California, so when I got back I envied people here who'd managed to go it alone on the home ground.'

The example of recently acquired friends, the artist Barrie Cooke (1931–2014) and his wife, the Dutch ceramicist Sonja Landweer (1933–2019), who were living self-sufficiently in Co. Kilkenny, encouraged the Heaneys to think about moving there; but then an offer from the Canadian scholar of Irish literature Ann Saddlemyer (b.1932), of the use of a gate lodge she owned in Co. Wicklow, came their way.

To Ann Saddlemyer

MS Pratt

24 January 1972 16 Ashley Avenue, Belfast 9

Dear Ann,

Many thanks for your letter: I had forgotten that I had sent couriers towards Toronto, and, as D. H. Lawrence might have put it, I am full of little prickly gushers of excitement . . .

The thing is, I am half-decided to leave teaching at the end of this year, just to see how far it would be possible to live as a writer, I mean live with one's own imagination as well as by one's pen. God knows, with a wife and two children and a caution born in the bone, the move is being made in no grand theatrical 'casting the trammels of security and bourgeoisie' spirit. But I do feel something like confidence or energy rising, and guess that I should risk a renewal of sorts now. But there is nothing definite.

What I would be interested in, then, would be a chance to rent the house from, say, mid- or late September 1972 until, preferably, the end of June, 1973. It sounds a dream of a place and I think if we could work an arrangement something like this, and not too expensive – at least not high tourist terms – I'd give in my notice in a couple of months.

I'm writing this between tutorials, and they've started to arrive now. So I'll stop curtly – the main point is that I would like to explore this possibility of a lease from season to season, for next year. Here's hoping!

Until I hear from you,
Sincerely,
Seamus H.

PS This is obviously after the tutorial. You can see I'm very interested: it usually takes three months and a reminder to get a note out of me.

If you can envisage letting the house for the best part of a year, the only difficulty I can envisage, on my side, is a financial one. And I think it's well that it *should* be a difficulty, because I am supposed to be taking my life into my own hands. Nevertheless, I would optimistically expect to average £60 a month, free-lance, and could not realistically think of much more than £20 of that for rent. Perhaps, if the thing looks possible, I could pay you a lump sum for the whole lease before the end of the year; which we could negotiate. That might be more satisfactory all round.

Perhaps it would be possible for us to take a trip down to see the place soon, if any arrangement looks possible? I pray that you have no sabbatical next year and no graduate already lined up.

There will be no need to remind you, Ann, of the sensitive acoustics of Ireland – so until we know something definite, I'd as soon keep this confidential. I'm thinking of the arrival of Michael Longley in Canada in February. I don't know if he'll be seeing you or not, but still . . .

I live in the shadow of the glen until I hear from you.

Sláinte,
Seamus

By this stage of her career, Ann Saddlemyer had published studies of Lady Gregory (1852–1932) and John Millington Synge (1871–1909). Saddlemyer and SH had met at Queen's University the previous year, when she gave a lecture during celebrations of the centenary of Synge's birth. 1971 was also the year when she purchased Glanmore Cottage, which is close by Glanmore Castle, the home of the Synge family, from the Yeats scholar A. Norman Jeffares (1920–2005). SH may have heard of the possibility of renting it through mutual friends – the 'couriers' mentioned here – and this letter is a prompt response to Saddlemyer's first one to him, dated 15 January.

To Charles Monteith TS Faber

9 February 1972 16 Ashley Avenue, Belfast 9

Dear Charles,

This is literally the fifth time I have written a version of this letter. The first was a week after that delightful lunch with you and Bill Webb when I left for the plane and crossed the channel like a rubicund ruminant – my belated thanks again.

I had written a couple of poems then and wanted to put them to the collection; but more came and I revised and reshuffled; and I wrote letters and sealed envelopes; and let it lie, and broke the seal and changed everything. However, I think this is where the vision emerges from the revisions which a moment had reversed.

I dearly want these new ones to go in; and the contents page to be revised as enclosed. I realize you may have started to do something with the manuscript but even if it entails expense on my behalf, can we please

1) take out 'Astray' and 'The Island';
2) change the dedications page to take in the verses from the *Listener* piece – perhaps they should be in italics?
3) reshuffle the ones you have to align with the new contents.

I have borne in mind the final look of the poems on the page as much as possible; so I hope that the long ones will open in a single spread, with as little turning over as possible. As far as I can calculate 'Bye Child' will be the first one to break at the foot of the right-hand page: I'm beginning to get pernickety, by God.

Anahorish and Broagh are places, townlands, that our farm ran into; Toome, as you know, is on the Bann. I think they fill out the preoccupations of 'Gifts of Rain' and 'The Wool Trade'. 'Nerthus' came from a photograph in the ever-inviting *Bog People*. Glob will soon be looking for royalties. Talking of which, do we need permission for the epigraph from Joyce in 'Wool Trade'?

Things worsen here, I think; I look forward to seeing you if not at the Mermaid, then at Lindy Guinness's the following Friday. I hope to get the week off in between but I'm not yet sure of that.

Tell Rosemary that I don't know what photograph the Mermaid people used as I haven't seen the programme, but there's a Mrs Pomeroy at the theatre who would know all about it.

I'll finish before I start revising again. Tell me if you don't like any of this stuff.

Sincerely,
Seamus

W. L. (Bill) Webb (1928–2019) was literary editor at the *Guardian* for many years.

The most significant of SH's requests were heeded, but the design of the book, which followed the format established by *Death of a Naturalist* and confirmed by *Door into the Dark*, made it impossible for all two-page poems to fall on a single spread.

'Lindy Guinness': aka Lindy Hamilton-Temple-Blackwood, Marchioness of Dufferin and Ava (1941–2020), painter, and befriender of artists and writers.

To Ann Saddlemyer

MS Pratt

6 March 1972 — 16 Ashley Avenue, Belfast 9

Dear Ann,

Between one thing and another, it wasn't until yesterday that we managed to get as far as the Devil's Glen – or rather Glanmore – and I must say we were delighted with the house. Straight away (I hope it's not too late) I want to confirm that we'd move in in mid-September, or earlier, if it's free. I'm going to give my notice here soon.

What we thought we might do, if this is all right by you, would be to spend a week there in the Easter vacation – beginning on March 27 – just to get the feel of it, to let the kids get a sense of the place, and to allow ourselves to find out about schools, shops etc. – to explore the rhythms of the place, as it were. We'll treat this as a tourist season letting, by the way, and count it into the rent.

Marie would be glad to redecorate the small bedroom, and in fact we'd probably be happy to freshen up paint and cut down weeds etc., as long as we felt we weren't taking over a place we didn't own. We can consult by letter or post card anyhow, if things like that arise.

It's a very attractive house: the upstairs study/sitting room and the big downstairs room with the open fire are so inviting! If you couldn't write yonder, where on earth could you?

By the way, Bob Tracy is in Dublin from Berkeley and I think he'd be interested in negotiating for a few weeks during the summer. I told him to write to you anyhow – he's a Synge editor also, I believe.

We'll write when we go (if you have no objections) at the end of the month. As I say, this is just to say yes, please – from September until the following June. I'll know better later whether a renewal would work for us after that.

Pardon the rush, but after three days in Dublin, much seems to be crowding on me.

God bless and thank you for everything,

Love,
Seamus

SH had inspected Glanmore Cottage in the company of Robert Tracy (1928–2020) and his wife Rebecca. Tracy taught English and Celtic Studies at Berkeley: besides his work as an editor of Synge, he made translations from the early work of Osip Mandelstam (1891–1938), Russian poet and victim of Stalin, which were published in the volume *Stone* (1981) and which came to be a major enthusiasm of SH's.

To Karl Miller

MS Emory

8 March 1972 16 Ashley Avenue, Belfast 9

Dear Karl,

As usual, that was a happy weekend we had with you: our love to Jane and the children.

These are a few poems that haven't seen the light of day. I don't know if they'll make much sense divorced from the context that I hope to place them in in the book. 'Traditions' and 'Bog Oak' explore, I suppose, the particular dissociation of sensibility that occurred with the Elizabethan conquest and plantation of Ireland: loss of language, loss of a native literary tradition. But do, or undo, them as you will. Think of them as a Patrick's Day card.

Sláinte,
Seamus

'Traditions' and 'Bog Oak' were taken immediately and printed together with 'Oracle', 'Cairn-maker' and 'Nerthus' – all poems destined for Part One of *Wintering Out* – in the *Listener* of 23 March.

To Barrie Cooke and Sonja Landweer TS Pembroke

19 March 1972 16 Ashley Avenue, Belfast 9

Dear Barrie and Sonja,

Last week I told the head of department that I would be resigning at the end of this academic year. Since we met, we found a house to rent for the year – beginning in September – near Ashford in Co. Wicklow, in the hills, a two-storey stone place that has had a bathroom added in the last couple of years. We are going down there to try it for a week, beginning next Monday, so maybe we'll go and see you some day – or you come and see us and it.

'Cairn-Maker' will be in the *Listener* next week, I think; and the enclosed is a kind of 'grace before freedom', gathering its energy in some way from that sacramental moment near the pigeon wood. As I wrote it, I began to realize that to go freelance could ideally release energies as exhilarating and subversive as those that must rise in a guerilla fighter when he joins up. Anyhow, it's meant as gratitude to my instructors who led to the decision – in the main, yourselves and Ted Hughes. Your confidence in us engendered confidence in ourselves and it is strange how the secret will to change burgeoned after that morning's walk at Luggala and then, more irresistibly, in your kitchen on the Saturday night when we ate the pike. The first supper! We would have liked to be near you in Kilkenny and may still be, in the end; but I felt I'd like to be nearer airports and radio stations to begin with, and this house came as an offer, by post, from Ann Saddlemyer in Toronto, at the psychological moment. We hope to let the Belfast house, to begin with.

This is just to offer you our gratitude for your nurture towards the decision, to tell you the news and to ask pardon for not going the whole hog and buying a stake in Kilkenny. We'll see more of one another next year anyhow and we must work together on some things. I've a child's story to show you for a start. We [look] forward to seeing you again.

Love,
Seamus

The poem sent with this letter was 'The Island', which has some of the manner of the poems that would appear in *Wintering Out* but was never included in any of SH's published collections. The Island was the name of Cooke and

Landweer's house in Thomastown, Co Kilkenny.
The 'child's story' was 'Ronan and the Riverman' – see letter to Charles Monteith of 23 October 1974.

To Ted Hughes

TS Emory

19 March 1972 16 Ashley Avenue, Belfast 9

Dear Ted,

A few days ago I told the people at Queen's University that I would be resigning at the end of this academic year, so I thought I would tell you too because your encouragement was one of the first things to bring the decision out of daydream into possibility. We have rented a two-storey stone house in the Wicklow hills, about 25 miles south of Dublin, not too far from Wicklow town and we go there in September. The address will be Glanmore Cottage, Ashford, Co. Wicklow so if you're going to be in the region any time after then, call and see us.

Barrie Cooke was anxious that we settle – buy a house, in fact – near them in Thomastown, and we spent a couple of months on the verge of that. But the house wasn't altogether right and we couldn't afford to buy yet. But again Barrie and Sonja put a confidence into us to get off our dithering arses.

The enclosed poem is just a 'grace before freedom', so to speak. I began to feel like a guerrilla-writer, which may be excessive, but the feeling of risk and possibility is in the air all round us here. In a perverse way I'm sorry to leave Belfast at the moment of truth.

Anyhow, this is just to say thanks for bolstering my confidence in myself and to wish you and yours good luck. Marie sends her love.

Sincerely,
Seamus Heaney

This is the earliest surviving letter from SH to Ted Hughes: an earlier letter, evidently in the nature of fan mail, has not been traced. The two poets had first met at a teachers' conference in 1967, and later, on the occasion reported to Charles Monteith in SH's letter of 17 January 1969. A marked feature of Hughes's own career was his deliberate and canny avoidance, after a brief spell of school teaching, of conventional waged employment, and he had strongly encouraged SH in his bid to cut free.

Barrie Cooke was also a friend of Hughes's and often accompanied him on fishing expeditions in Ireland.

The 'enclosed poem' was presumably 'The Island' – see footnote to the letter above.

To Louis and Deborah Simpson ᴛs LOC

7 April 1972 [Glanmore Cottage, Ashford, Co. Wicklow]

Dear Louis and Deborah,

The above address is a fake: we're actually in Co. Wicklow, in a cottage in the hills – near the Devil's Glen – twenty-five miles outside Dublin. I came here with Marie and the boys and a case full of guilt and unanswered letters. I'm going through them ruefully.

I should have written to you long ago. The enclosed cheque came into my hands finally a couple of weeks ago, and your excellent despatch of Green Shield stamps arrived like latter-day manna in the deserts of the Queen's English Department. Thanks for that, even at this late date.

How are you? Marie and I are going to be here (Glanmore Cottage, Glanmore, Ashford, Co. Wicklow) after next September. I've taken the academic bull by its salaried horn and resigned from the end of the year. We'll be wintering out here to begin with. It has its exhilarations but we realize exactly what kind of risks it involves – we're neither of us simple lifers at heart, but we felt the tide in our affairs was running towards this kind of surfing and ooops . . . we've done it, or nearly.

We'll be back in Belfast in a few days. The explosions continue but there's a bit more hope in the air. All the same, it would be nice to stay here, watching rabbits and bluetits and hawthorn buds outside the window, playing a silent piano . . .

Hope we meet again some time. Marie sends her love.

Sincerely,
Seamus

'The above address is a fake': written on 16 Ashley Avenue headed paper.

The previous November, SH had invited the Jamaica-born US poet Louis Simpson (1923–2012) to read to the English Society at QUB, and the 'enclosed cheque' is presumably payment, while the gift of Green Shield stamps – promotionally issued to shoppers and used to purchase a limited range of goods – would have been of no value to the Simpsons back home.

To his letter of invitation to Simpson, SH had added as postscript: 'There's no shooting in our area. So far.'

To Charles Monteith

TS Faber

9 April 1972 16 Ashley Avenue, Belfast 9

Dear Charles,

I want to put these poems between 'Broagh' and 'The Wool Trade' in the book – they really belong to the whole first sequence, moving in and out of the theme of language and Ulster and identity. If they wait two or three more years for a book, they'll be orphaned. They belong in *Wintering Out*. I know this may wreck a relationship but it will help the volume.

I am really sorry to keep this up, but this is the end. Absolutely. I just feel these must go in – Marie is a bit worried about harassing you again, and to tell the truth, so am I. But I mustn't appear to be. Can you help? Again?

I'm going off for a week's filming on Lough Erne to-morrow with David Hammond, another schools broadcast. And then it's back to bombsville. The whole thing is possibly driving me into this exaggerated sense of the urgency of a poem: but I actually think, or hope, that some of the stuff in *Wintering Out* could re-define things for at least a few people here, on both sides. My God, I'm getting messianic in my old age.

Charles, I really hope you can do something about this.

Sincerely,
Seamus

PS Bruce Berlind wrote last week offering me a Visiting Chair (no less) for a semester in 1974 and I've accepted. It's quite a Faber outpost, Colgate.

PPS Order of poems: ORACLE
BACKWARD LOOK
TRADITIONS
A NEW SONG
THE OTHER SIDE

And just to go the whole hog, what about dividing the book into Sections I and II, Section II beginning at 'Wedding Day'.

Also, I agree with you about changing Paul's title. *New Weather* has got that open ring of possibility about it.

And Bill Webb, by the way, has followed up the suggestion he made that day about doing a piece on being an 'Irish' poet for the *Guardian*.

Sláinte

S.

'a week's filming on Lough Erne': the documentary made there was titled *The Loughsiders* and broadcast later in 1972.

Bruce Berlind (1926–2014) was chair of the English faculty of Colgate University, where he played host to numerous visiting writers, both Irish and British.

SH's essay, 'The Trade of an Irish Poet', printed in Webb's paper, the *Manchester Guardian*, on 25 May, forms the third part of 'Belfast' in *Preoccupations*.

To Brian Friel

MS NLI

10 April 1972 c/o BBC Flotilla, Kesh Marina

Dear Brian,

As a man who lost his bollards, not to mention his mahogany rail, you'll sympathize: I care of Skipper Hammond on the raging deep for a week.

I'm sorry to have missed the amphibious exercises on the Shannon. First of all, we had fixed up Wicklow. And then our phone was cut off: this time I literally forgot to pay it.

Your piece in the *TLS* had as much to say to poets as playwrights. I thought it was beautifully clear-headed and pointed. At the heart of 'being a writer' but not at all literary.

Hope to see you soon. Yo ho ho and a bottle of rum. Cast off,

Seamus

The address given by SH is plainly facetious: see letter to Monteith of 9 April.

In his article for the *Times Literary Supplement*, titled 'Plays Peasant and Unpeasant', Friel had argued for the creation of native, non-metropolitan, non-cosmopolitan Irish drama, distinct not just from the English tradition but from that of Sheridan, Goldsmith, Wilde and Shaw as well.

To Barrie Cooke

MS Pembroke

17 July 1972

Bradley Court, Wotton-under-Edge,
Gloucestershire

Dear Barrie,

I don't know how you will like these lines, or indeed, if they will satisfy Mr Merrill. I intended to get to Kilkenny for a talk and second look at the bones, but was so busy and fraught that I didn't manage it.

However, I am very pleased with what came in the end; and the prefatory note should explain how the images multiplied. I like *v* and *vi* especially: even though they are not invested with too much bone as such, it seems to me that they lick their way into preoccupations shared in some way by both of us.

I have been in England now for two weeks. I was teaching a course at York until last Thursday and then came down here to Marie's sister – who lives in a magnificent mansion with her director-husband. Tomorrow we return to Belfast for six weeks and then to Wicklow. I hope we see you soon.

And again, I hope these lines don't let you down. Love to Sonja and Ainne.

Seamus

Bradley Court was the Elizabethan manor in Gloucestershire where SH's in-laws Polly Devlin and Andy Garnett lived.

The 'lines' SH is sending sound like the poem 'Bone Dreams', later to appear in *North*; bones were also a theme of Cooke's watercolour paintings and drawings at this time.

Cooke's daughter is called Aoine.

To Rosemary Goad

MS Faber

21 July [1972]

Dear Rosemary,

Back to porridge and gunfire. It was great to see you again last week, and we both felt that we had rather overindulged in the proof-copies, but still enjoy having them. Thank you very much.

Fay's photographs are terrific: the only one I don't so much go for is 1154-5-37a, which I feel turns me into a lascivious and almost bankrupt restaurateur who might be called Mario – but actually it's good too. My favourite is 1152-5-1a, and then 1155-4-29 and 1153-7-3a. So there: how about 1152-5-1a? Just testing.

I've had a circular from the Poetry Society saying that nation-wide poetry readings are envisaged in National Bookweek (November 4–11). Charles guessed that *Wintering Out* would be published in November so I'm wondering if it would be possible to arrange with Michael Mackenzie a reading to mark publication, and publish during that week? It's a thought: a second thought: in Dublin? Too much.

Sincerely,
Seamus

'Back to porridge and gunfire': the Heaneys had returned temporarily to Northern Ireland, as Glanmore Cottage was to be let to Robert and Rebecca Tracy for the summer.

Fay Godwin (1931–2005) had been hired by Faber to photograph SH for publicity purposes: in keeping with the spirit of *Wintering Out*, the shots were posed outdoors.

Michael Mackenzie was an official at the Poetry Society in London.

To Ann Saddlemyer

MS Pratt

7 August 1972 [The Laurels, Sessiagh, Coagh, Co. Tyrone]

Dear Ann,

In fact, we are in Co. Tyrone, at Marie's home place, on the shores of Lough Neagh, and have not been living in Belfast for the past four weeks. So I was delighted to get your note, and kind offer of tenancy before September. I think, thanks to your kindness, we'll try to move in sometime during the last week (24–31) so that, as you guessed, the children can get settled in before school.

I gave a lecture to primary school teachers in Maynooth two weeks ago and met the principal of the Dominican primary school in Wicklow which, I understand, is a very good one. So the boys are fixed up for there. Not, mind you, that they are desperate to get started in a new place.

We called to see the Tracys who were very happy in Glanmore and were surprised also to hear that the Flanagans were going. It's quite a Berkeley pad by now.

Thanks for the invitation to attempt something for *Modern Drama*: maybe before Christmas . . .

I enclose a cheque as earnest of our goodwill from September 1st. I don't know if there will be any difficulty about changing it, but if there is, return it and I'll get a money order. And I suppose Glanmore Cottage will be the address when you write again!

With gratitude and love,
Seamus

To John Hewitt

MS PRONI

29 August 1972

Glanmore Cottage, Ashford,
Co. Wicklow

Dear John,

We've landed anyhow with a dresser and a table, into the relics of oul dacency: this was once a forester's house on the Synge estate. We're just waiting to see how the youngsters will take to the school next week.

In the meantime, I want to remind you about the anthology, *Soundings*, which I am editing for Blackstaff Press. I have to deliver a MS to James Gracey by the end of September so if you have some new work I'd be delighted if you could submit something. We'll be able to pay a civil fee since we're subsidized from Belfast and Dublin. The idea is that this should be hitherto unpublished work but I wouldn't be too worried about that: whatever work from the last few months you want to put in a collection to be subtitled 'New work from Ireland' . . .

Come down and see us here when you get settled. I don't know if you have moved into Stockman's Lane yet so I'll send this c/o Terry F. And I'll write again when I get more rhythm and routine into my days, and more clothes out of cases into drawers.

Love to Roberta,

Sincerely,
Seamus

Blackstaff Press was a new venture, founded the previous year, in Newtownards, Co. Down, by Jim and Diane Gracey. In the event, *Soundings '72*, the second in a series subtitled *An Annual Anthology of New Irish Poetry*, included Hewitt's poem 'The Distances'.

To Ann Saddlemyer

MS Pratt

30 August 1972

Glanmore Cottage, Ashford,
Co. Wicklow

Dear Ann,

Thank you for your letter and my apologies about the cheque. I'm glad you have done it in your time, because it's a regular habit of mine. God send that I don't forget it this time.

Well, we arrived on Monday at midnight and to-day we're almost unpacked. The weather is dry and warm so it makes us feel happy to be here – we went swimming at the Silver Strand, just beyond Wicklow, this afternoon.

The house is now painted and at this moment Mick Gregan is down cutting hedges round the garden. Still no car-park – I was talking to Janet and Gareth at the Sligo summer school who were asking about it – but it makes absolutely no difference to us. In fact I rather like the rambling leafage instead. We park our VW Beetle very easily outside the gate.

We brought a dresser and an old scrubbed deal table of our own – just to fully savour the 'cottage' world, and we've taken down one of the beds in the spare room and put your polished table in there. We are thinking of having an open shelf unit made to fit between the kitchen and bathroom doors, for storing spices, jars etc. – we can use it again as a bookshelf. The little cupboard isn't sufficient to our impedimenta.

I've become a man of letters by writing half-a-dozen of them to-day. But I look forward to other enterprises. When my new book comes out in November I'll send you a copy – and incidentally, the *Irish Press* and *Irish Times* carried stories recently that 'Heaney quits Queen's for Poetry'. O la la

Anyhow, we'll be here.

Love, Seamus

Saddlemyer recalls that this was not the only time SH forgot to pay the rent: see the speculation about 'something Freudian' in his letter to her of 16 May 1973.

Mick Gregan, from nearby Ballynahinch, regularly tidied and did odd jobs about the property.

Janet (1928–2000) and Gareth Dunleavy (1923–2004) were American colleagues of Saddlemyer's, also Irish specialists.

To Charles Monteith

MS Faber

31 August 1972

Glanmore Cottage, Ashford,
Co. Wicklow

Dear Charles,

As you see, we've moved and at last I'm in a house where I can sit down and think. I apologize for the delay in answering your letter, but since I saw you in early July we have not been back in Belfast and we've been living, *en famille*, with other *familles*, which doesn't induce the contemplative, studious or even attentive mood. However, there can be no excuses for the next year: a man of letters has to write them.

We have no phone yet but it's coming. In the meantime, if there's a chance of your being in Dublin in the middle of the month, you can leave a message for us at Wicklow 4143 – Mr and Mrs Chapman, who live about 200 yards up the road. I could collect you to spend a while in this part of the world. This is a forester's cottage, relics of oul dacency, on the erstwhile Synge estate.

I enclose an initial sketch of the kind of thing I would include in the Anglo-Irish anthology, with a few notes. And I still envisage having the final gathering made by the new year.

My typewriter (and I hope there's nothing ominous in this) cracked up en route from Belfast, so the hand-grown script is all I can produce just now.

With every good wish,
Sincerely,
Seamus

On the Idea of an Irish Poetic Tradition

Discussion of the topic has been more or less conditioned by the existence of two languages, two social groupings, some would say two literatures: the Irish and English languages, the Irish Catholic 'Gael' and the Anglo-Irish 'Ascendancy', writing in the 'Irish Mode' and the 'Colonial Mode'. The anthology would include

i) A general historical essay, such as the first chapter from Thomas Flanagan's *The Irish Novelists 1800–1850*

ii) Significant historic introductions:
e.g. Charlotte Brooke's introduction to *Reliques of Ancient Poetry* 1789
Douglas Hyde's introduction to *Beside the Fire*
John Montague's introduction to *Faber Book of Irish Verse*

iii) Essays pertinent to the theme by seminal writers:
e.g. Samuel Ferguson
W. B. Yeats on Ferguson, on Popular Poetry, on Young Ireland, on his 'ancestral stair'
Thomas MacDonagh on 'The Irish Mode' from *Literature in Ireland*
Daniel Corkery on 'Anglo-Irish Literature' from *Synge and A-I Literature* and/or perhaps 'The Courts of Poetry' from *The Hidden Ireland*
Patrick Kavanagh on 'The Irish Tradition', 'Nationalism and Literature' from *Collected Pruse*
Thomas Kinsella on Tradition from *Davis, Mangan, Ferguson* (Dolmen)

iv) A commissioned essay from Michael Longley (he has already dealt with this in a paper to the Yeats Summer School) on the relation of the Northern Protestant sensibility – MacNeice, Rodgers, Hewitt – to the idea of an 'Irish' tradition

v) A scattering of relevant poems
e.g. Yeats: 'To Ireland in the Coming Times'
'Irish poets, learn your trade'
Hewitt: 'Ireland'
'Once alien here . . .'
Longley: 'Irish Poetry'
Heaney: 'Traditions'

vi) A critical 'afterword' or final essay by the editor

This is a rough outline of the kind of thing I envisage. The nineteenth century – Ferguson, Mangan etc. – needs some researching, but the stuff is there.

The shape of the book would be a revelation of a presumption that there are two traditions – Native Irish and Ascendancy – and a plea that the idea must be widened, if 'Irish Tradition' is to mean anything, to include the Northern Planter voice.

Outlining ideas for another prose book that never happened, this letter is included here to show the breadth, depth and judiciousness of SH's current thinking about what might constitute an Irish literary 'tradition', in the singular. He expands on and qualifies his thoughts on the subject in his next two, longer letters to Monteith, both of 10 October.

To Brian Friel

MS NLI

29 September 1972

Glanmore Cottage, Ashford,
Co. Wicklow

Dear Brian,

Yesterday I received what I first thought was a solicitor's letter but it turned out to be an invitation to the Hennessy Awards presentation on Thursday week. I see you have been through the mill as one of the judges and was wondering if you were coming down for the presentation. If so, would you like to come the day before, or better still come out that night or next morning to see the place here?

Also, I am 'presenter' of a new fortnightly books programme on Radio Eireann called *Imprint* – the first one goes out on Monday at 8 p.m. and is a bit heavy, I fear, not to say incoherent when I am wired and earphoned to Edna O'Brien in a London studio – but we're recording for the second programme 2.30/4.30 that Thursday. Is there anything booky we could talk about for 8 or 10 minutes – like judging the awards, or writing a masterpiece – or would you fancy reviewing anything currently appearing or due to appear? There's a new history of the B Specials, for instance . . .

So far so good in the thrilling world of the full-time writing recluse. We're glad we made the move. How did you manage on the Bann?

Our love to Anne and the family.

Ahoy and *sláinte*,
Seamus

In *Stepping Stones*, SH counts his commission from Raidió Teilifís Éireann to present the books programme *Imprint* as part of the 'back-up I had from the start', enabling him to sustain his new freelance life.

The B-Specials, or Ulster Special Constabulary, were a form of auxiliary police force, mainly Protestant and resented by Catholics.

Anne – which SH spells 'Ann' – is Friel's wife.

To John Montague

MS Cork

5 October 1972

Glanmore Cottage, Ashford,
Co. Wicklow

Dear John,

Moving south is one thing but green ink?

Anyhow. I'm doing this *Imprint* programme every other Monday evening and called with Dolmen about getting new books. They tell me *Rough Field* is due around October 26 and gave me an unbound proof copy.

In many ways, I am as excited by it as you must be yourself: it is so close to the grain of my own sensibility (a tilt off, naturally) and I have lived with 'the emerging order of the poem' so long that this delivery elicits sympathetic satisfactions in myself. It's a powerful achievement which I'm grateful for, 'getting in' so much more than the bag apron. And the epilogue reads like a scenario where the last mummer will lie down at last. I hope it gets the gratitude and acclaim that it deserves.

I'd like to do something about it on this programme – the one to go out on October 30th. The only snag is that the producer wants to record this, if possible, on this day week, 12th October. I can easily do a piece myself, including illustrations off the record, but would you like to be interviewed? I'm sure we can arrange a studio link-up with Cork, and if you'd like this, could you let me know right away?

Any chance of a copy of 'Primal Gaeltacht'? I'd like to quote from it, as an approach to the Rough Field of Garvaghy.

Again, a salute to you and it, and good luck. Love to Evelyn from both of us.

Sincerely,
Seamus

PS What about a *G-yard in Queens*!

Montague's 1972 collection *The Rough Field* takes its title from Garvaghy, the village in Co. Tyrone where he spent much of his childhood, the name being an anglicisation of Garbhachadh ('rough field'). His essay, 'A Primal Gaeltacht' (printed in the *Irish Times* in 1970), argued that, because 'the Irish language is a kind of primal Gaeltacht' and 'anyone brought up in it has already absorbed a great deal of the language', the 'racial aspect of a poet's inheritance must be unconscious'.

Montague's poem 'A Graveyard in Queens' would be included in his subsequent collection *A Slow Dance* (1975). The proposed radio discussion went ahead.

To Charles Monteith

MS Faber

10 October 1972

Glanmore Cottage, Ashford,
Co. Wicklow

Dear Charles,

My apologies for the delay: for once I can say honestly I have been very busy.

[. . .]

I should say that I have two purposes in thinking about this book. One is to provide a text that I – and others – would find useful in the seminar room. But more centrally and obliquely, I would like it to be a statement about the idea of an Irish tradition in poetry. Since I talked to you first, I've mentioned it to a couple of other people, and was taken aback when one said that it would have the effect, ultimately, of strengthening a view that in some way I fundamentally wish to at least qualify, i.e. that Anglo-Irish poetry is a self-contained literature. To put it in another way, a tenable view of these Anglo-Irish courses is that they fence off a field of English literature and cultivate it as a nationalist patch. And that is true, and yet Irish writers are at an interesting tilt off the English tradition.

So while I was all for hurtling through a job of putting school-texts together, I am now thinking of the thing much more carefully – especially in relation to where such a book would place me. Ideally, what I would like to do would be to publish simultaneously a book of essays, mostly on Irish poetry. Pre-Yeats, Yeats, and post-Yeats including Clarke, Kavanagh, Kinsella, Murphy, Montague and the Northerners. Obviously, again a tricky enterprise, but both from my own point of view and from a publisher's, I think much more satisfactory. At the beginning of the book of essays would be a long essay on the idea of a tradition, drawing its references from material in the anthology. And there would be a couple of essays on Irish poems, available in translation and by now almost co-opted as part of English literature – such as *The Midnight Court*. I'm saying, in a roundabout way, that I'd like to wait for a year or so before delivering the ms.

I enclose another reason for the delay. This is exactly half of a version of the Middle Irish poetic romance *Buile Shuibhne* – Mad Sweeney, the Frenzy of Sweeney – whatever you like to call it. I started this five weeks ago and became obsessed: I would love to publish it, if you like it, again with an introduction and notes. For many reasons:

1) It 'bloods' me to speak on Irish as well as English literary matters in the proposed books.
2) Sweeney was a king in Dal Araidhe – Antrim and Down way. The text is full of place names – Rasharkin, Moira, Mournes, Bush (of B'mills fame), Dunseverick, and various others – that gives Ulstermen of all sides a stake in the earlier literature.
3) Sweeney is both fallen establishment and implacable underdog, a voice to lament for all Ulster. Lear and Poor Tom.
4) He was ill done-by by Flann O'Brien in *At Swim-Two-Birds* – made into a comic device. I see him as a much more elegiac, if not tragic, figure, and would want to take this up in the introduction.
5) There are a number of very beautiful poems, intrinsically valuable, and deeply rooted in the poetic domain I inhabit myself.

I have been working on this and will continue to do so for the next six weeks or so; so I *have* to revise my submission date for the other book. It just came over me when I landed here, and I want to finish it now, or I'm likely never to.

So far, you are the only person to see this, besides Marie. I don't want any grapevines to be buzzing, especially since I think Montague feels he owns Sweeney. (By the way, if it's not an immoral piece of literary espionage, would you check how much of it John translated for the FBIV, – I'm curious). I'd like to know how you feel about it. The only full translation that I know of is a deadly Victorian prose crib (that I work from) published parallel to the Irish by J. G. O'Keeffe for the Early Irish Texts Society in 1913. I've pencilled in O'Keeffe's Section Numbers, so that you will see this is not altogether a consecutive narrative that you've got. You'll also see that it's a first draft, and I'd be glad if you could let me have it back – or take a photo-copy – when you are finished with it.

This letter is more of a confusion than a clarification in response to your letter. As I see it, the anthology would be a slow, steady seller, selling more as years went by. But Sweeney only comes once in a lifetime. Perhaps I'll see you next month?

Sincerely,
Seamus

PS Some of the poems are pedestrian and repetitive, and I had thought of doing only the high points – e.g. 19, 21, 23, 27, 40, 45, etc. – but on the whole, I think a full assault is the only worthwhile thing.

I would have to consult with a scholar, if publication were in the air, about the place names. I'm inconsistent in this text, because I discovered things as I worked; for example, that Magh Rath was MOIRA!

PPS This is the solution to a riddle I set up for Rosemary.
I hope it interests you.
S

PS[2] I've two lectures on Yeats (delivered to the Sligo summer school) which give me a basis for the book of essays. I'd obviously like to do something on *Buile Shuibhne* as well.

You can see Wicklow has gone to my writing head.

The omitted first part of this letter concerns SH's estimate ('perhaps pessimistic') of likely sales for the book initially under discussion, and acceptance of the terms proposed by Faber.

Montague's *Faber Book of Irish Verse*, not to be published for another two years, contains passages from *Buile Shuibhne* in his own translation.

To Charles Monteith

MS Faber

10 October 1972

Glanmore Cottage, Ashford,
Co. Wicklow

Dear Charles,

When it comes to visions and revisions, I can outdo *Prufrock*. I have posted you a first reply to your letter earlier, including half of the Sweeney text. I want to revise my general remarks on page 2 and 3. The idea of a book of essays has been in my head and will probably continue to be there, but I grabbed at it to steady the unease that Seamus Deane (contemporary of mine, lecturer at UCD) set up with his remarks about the proposed anthology. On second thoughts – and I suppose I had to write the letter to get to this – I think a long introduction and an afterword, or last essay – covering post-Yeatsian poets – would 'place' the material neatly and exonerate me from necessarily sharing the views of Daniel Corkery or Hewitt. So the anthology is all I'm proposing. Forget those improbable essays. All the better if they come. But if you could think of Easter as a delivery date – Sweeney and poems and other things multiply around me.

I haven't touched the autobiography, formally, in prose, but it's working in other ways. I'm well established in a cluster of poems, all exfoliating from a central consciousness – another Glob spirit – a 'queen' found in a bog on Lord Moira's estate in the late 18th century. She dreams things, in her peaty bower. Hopefully, she re-dreams a myth for a new Ireland. You know that C19 Fenian song 'Will you come to the Bower': I think the name of her dreams might be 'Come to the Bower'. With a fallen Ulster king and an inhumed queen of bog, I'm certainly going obliquely at our troubles. But obliquity can stand a good few strains. I think MacNeice's 'Sunlight on the Garden' is as much an *ave* to Auschwitz as it is a *vale* to a love. Why don't you commission me to write a book on Irish bogs?

It looks as if things will work out fine for the year. I'm doing a fortnightly books programme on Radio Eireann up to Christmas, that gets £50 a month, and after Christmas, I'm teaching a day a week in UCD. What with reviews and other piece-meal helps from royalties and advances, I'm easy in my mind. And the kids like the school.

Rosemary said in a letter that you might possibly get over on 20th November: I'm very grateful to you for co-operating with the Abbey people. I think it should be worthwhile, and I really feel like doing a reading that night, convincing myself of the worth of the book, if not anyone else.

Anyhow, let the Anglo-Irish anthology appear apace – if you feel the sales would warrant it. I was probably too gloomy about that. But prefer to be so.

Sincerely,
Seamus

To Karl Miller

TS Emory

8 November 1972

Glanmore Cottage, Ashford,
Co. Wicklow

Dear Karl,

I've intended to write ever since we moved here in the last week of August. This is a small gate-lodge on the edge of what was once the Synge estate – the forester lived in it. There are woods quite close, roses on the gable, bracken and briars crawling all around, and altogether it's like living in a Georgian poem. We're very glad we made the move. The children go to school in Wicklow town, about five miles away, and like it – if they had been unhappy, it would have affected us all.

Also, I think we'll survive happily enough in the freelance world. I'm presenting a books programme on Radio Eireann once a fortnight – a kind of *Now Read On* – and do the occasional reading and review. Certainly it is good to be out of Belfast. I was up there again last weekend and for the first time I was literally afraid to drive in the streets. I think the atmosphere is darkening – a mixture of exhaustion and new threats of Protestant militancy. I also found that Paisley's newspaper, the *Protestant Telegraph*, had given me a boot in the back early in September, saying that I was a well-known papist propagandist and had gone to my spiritual home in the popish republic. I was retrospectively upset because they mentioned my address in the thing. But it's nothing compared with what C. C. O'Brien must put up with.

I'm enclosing a poem that George MacBeth is using on the 50th anniversary poetry programme next Monday. Derwent wrote to me for something so I'm sending him a copy also. I'm writing easily enough, but I want to hold on to what comes and feed on it for a while: I think this 'Bog Queen' might gather other poems around her. And I'm in no hurry to publish too much till *Wintering Out* has been seen.

Fabers are sponsoring a reception in the Peacock Theatre – a small theatre in the Abbey building – on publication day, and I'm doing a reading there that night at 8 o'clock. I told them to send you an invitation, but I don't expect you could get over. However, I don't have to tell you how grateful I am for the way you have encouraged and published me.

I don't know when I'll get to London, but in the meantime, all our good wishes to you and the family. I should say that Marie is pregnant and expects the new arrival on my birthday, 13th April. Narcissism can't go much further.

Sincerely,
Seamus

George MacBeth (1932–92), a poet himself, edited and presented the BBC radio programme *The Poet's Voice*. 'Bog Queen' another Glob-inspired poem, would have given listeners a first glimpse, even before the publication of *Wintering Out*, of the new matter and manner of SH's verse, most fully exposed in *North*, which was not to be published for another three years.

To Ted Hughes

MS Emory

6 December 1972

Glanmore Cottage, Ashford,
Co. Wicklow

Dear Ted,

Your letter meant a lot to me and I meant to write long ago: now that we've cut out of Belfast and the university, it is really a confirmation to have you responding so warmly to the book. I have a sense of excitement about some things that are surfacing but little enough sense of perspective. Enclosed are poems written in the last few months and I was wondering if Olwyn would be interested in them: they are all bog-elegies of sorts, and though I realize there may not be enough to warrant a printing, I'd still like you to have a look at them. 'Dark Rosaleen' sets out from a report of the death of Eoghan Rua O'Suilleabhain, an Irish poet who wrote a lot of *aislings*, dream-visions of the maiden Ireland: he died, according to one story, of a relapse during his fever, brought on by masturbating. Clerical exemplum, perhaps, but inviting and extensive when you think of all those centuries of honeymoons in the hand.

I'll be in London Thursday next and Friday and will maybe ring Olwyn. Until I see you again, good luck and my gratitude for such a nurturing letter.

Sincerely,

Seamus

In his undated letter to which this is a reply, Ted Hughes had spoken of the 'intense pleasure' that *Wintering Out* had given him, predicting 'great things ahead', but warning SH of the perils of a seeming progress that left 'too much behind'.

Olwyn Hughes (1928–2016) was Ted's sister: her Rainbow Press, which produced limited editions of high quality and matching expense, did indeed publish *Bog Poems*, a selection of items from *North*, but not until 1975, the year of *North* itself.

While ostensibly a love song, 'Róisín Dubh', composed in the sixteenth century, carries a strong political or nationalistic charge; the Dublin poet James Clarence Mangan (1803–49) made a celebrated translation of it, under the title 'Dark Rosaleen'; Eoghan Rua Ó Súilleabháin (1748–84), is regarded as one of the last great Gaelic poets; an 'aisling' is a type of vision poem, developed during the seventeenth and eighteenth centuries in Irish-language poetry, in which Ireland takes the form of a woman who comes to the poet in his dream.

SH's own 'My Dark Rosaleen' remains uncollected.

To Ann Saddlemyer

MS Pratt

[December? 1972]

Glanmore Cottage, Ashford,
Co. Wicklow

Dear Ann,

I can't believe that Christmas is almost upon us: it's as if we'd been living here always.

I enclose a copy of the book which came out on November 20th. We had a reading and reception in the Peacock Theatre and the week was generally a celebration, but I'm settling back to sober, un-hung-over mornings in the Cranford room; watching the rose-hips and haws, and the autumn on Devil's Glen wood.

I also enclose another instalment towards rent and a receipt for the year's rates (£22.69 altogether) which I paid to a very civil collector. I thought it was the neatest procedure, rather than have him go through postings and letterings of all kinds.

Did I tell you that Marie is expecting Heaney number 3 in April? That Mr Shannon appears intermittently with designs on the wall and hopes for a car park. That the phone people in Dublin may one day turn on the phone. That Glanmore Cottage is a grand place to write in, the Racedown of Wicklow.

With all good wishes for Christmas and our continued gratitude that we can be here.

Sincerely,
Seamus

'Cranford room': when first writing to SH about Glanmore, Saddlemyer had described the upstairs sitting room as 'straight out of *Cranford*' – alluding to Elizabeth Gaskell's novel. The name stuck and it became SH's favourite place to write in.

Tommy Shannon was a local builder.

Racedown, in Dorset, was where Wordsworth lived and wrote some of his earliest poems from 1795 to 1797.

1973

SH's statements to the Northern Irish writer Brendan Hamill (b.1945) in his letter of 8 January, may constitute his frankest declaration, albeit in a private letter, of a political position. His voice and his views were becoming more publicly audible as well: in broadcasts commissioned by David Hammond for BBC Schools, and on the weekly programme about books for Raidió Teilifís Éireann. He was increasingly in demand as a book reviewer, too. Less conspicuously, he took on committee work for the Irish Arts Council. These activities, necessary for the maintenance of a freelance life, may have threatened to sap his creative energies, but poems of the quality of 'Punishment', 'Bone Dreams', 'The Grauballe Man' and 'Mossbawn: Sunlight' continued to appear in Irish, British and American magazines.

To Brendan Hamill

MS Hamill

8 January 1973

Glanmore Cottage, Ashford,
Co. Wicklow

Dear Brendan,

Thanks for your letter which does go to the heart of the questions: whatever I say in this letter should be supplemented by a review of the Russian poet Mandelstam to appear in the next *Hibernia*.

I think the poets generally have evaded 'hard' comment on issues like the Derry massacre, but I don't think they have been 'evasive about the NI crisis'. I can speak best for myself and I've no doubt the others will do this also.

I think you have to read any poem in the context of the poet's whole work, and the relation of that work to the society he inhabits. Northern Ireland always has been an especially neurotic and oblique place. You don't have to make noises against the establishment if your name is Seamus, for example; it's just taken for granted. In my first two books I had a few poems which were 'political' in the northern context, in that they assumed that Ulster was part of the Irish experience, not part of the British. One – 'Docker' – not very world-shaking as a poem in itself, did insist on the submerged violence; one – 'Requiem for the Croppies'

– was an image of resistance resurrecting itself. Others like 'At a Potato Digging' and 'Bogland' arose out of an apprehension of the Irish past being part of my – and most Irish Catholics' – psyche. So I would begin by saying that from the beginning I was writing from a perspective that was at odds with the prevailing 'Ulster is British' atmosphere. I was not, however, very politically conscious *as a poet*. I began to write with a desire to make poems adequate to my personal experience and to my sense of the English language. Ted Hughes was as important to me as an influence as Paddy Kavanagh. England was as much an audience as Ireland. If I had a 'poetic' or an 'aesthetic', it was a romantic/symbolist one, derived from a reading of English literature at University, and in particular from the dominant Eliotesque assumptions that a poem was a poem, cut free from author and audience, an object rather than a statement. This was strengthened by the Joycean/Yeatsian tradition in this country of regarding the word itself as somehow magical; turning the act of writing into an act of consecration where the bread and wine of daily life is consecrated into the host of language, the holy wafer of art. (If you look at poems like 'The Diviner', 'Personal Helicon', 'The Given Note', even 'Digging', you have portraits or metaphors of the artist and the artistic act as I apprehended it.)

All in all, I think that I unconsciously assumed that the poet was apolitical and priestlike; what seemed political – the poems on history etc. – were really celebrations of a cultural deposit. Politics, to put it another way, were almost indistinguishable from history with me.

This may be what you refer to as 'the otherness', 'an unlocated thing at an almost mystical level', that you detect in poems arising out of the present situation. Even as the violence proceeded, I still sought ways of keeping within the style and landscape of my earlier poetry; still waited for poems to accrue round seminal images; refused to allow the will to direct the motion of the imagination; tried to be non-partisan and to comprehend all that was happening within the terms of history and myth – so you have poems like 'High Street, Belfast'; 'Tinder'; 'Traditions'; 'The Other Side'; and 'The Tollund Man' in *Wintering Out*. I would have liked to do a really big poem on Bloody Sunday at the time but couldn't manage it. I wrote a song that Luke Kelly was going to use, but it wasn't good enough, or durable enough to let out (Phil Coulter's recent song about Derry is a warning!).

Yet I suppose the real difficulty is one of basic moral confusion. By upbringing and education, and by experience of life in the north, one is destined to be partisan. Yet an intense fidelity to one's own tribe can only lead to a continuous cycle of revenge – that's what we have anyway, but to embrace it as a deliberate view of life and to celebrate it as the truth goes against the grain of Christian/humanist feelings.

Or does it just go against the grain of liberalism? As you can see from what I have written already, I am not satisfied that the way I have responded so far is the whole story. Perhaps the poetry hasn't been personal *enough*. Certainly with internment being condoned by almost everybody, there should be a voice of freedom issuing from the poets. But the voice can't be *summoned* – a poem is a different utterance from a newspaper leader.

Perhaps the real answer to your enquiries is that you treat as finished and done with work that is still in the making. There is no reason to suppose that the writer will leave exploration of the last few years once the political scene appears to calm down. The important thing is that work adequate to the terrors and wrongs should appear sooner or later. But it doesn't need to appear as public poetry; nor as liberal poetry. A personal, partisan 'venting the pent' is probably the sure way towards the real thing. I certainly don't regard what I have done as a complete statement; but because of the nature of poetry and poetic composition, I can't promise a full report by a certain date.

All in all, I have been involved with uncertainties – within the culture, within myself – but I think my voice is firming up.

Maybe I'll see you inside the next six weeks at Coleraine. I am bewildered to think of those fellows from St Thomas's being shot: how does a poet deal with that? Were they victims or heroes? Both, I suppose. Martyrs? For what gods?

Write again if you want to pursue anything.

Sincerely,
Seamus Heaney

PS I must send you a few recent poems and you send me some of yours.

The Belfast poet Brendan Hamill, who had been a pupil of SH's at St Thomas's, had written challenging him to clarify his position in respect of Northern Ireland's political divide.

By 'Derry massacre', SH means the events of Bloody Sunday, 30 January 1972, when unarmed civilians in Derry's Bogside neighbourhood were shot dead by British troops while taking part in a protest march against the internment of political prisoners.

'The Road to Derry', the song that SH wrote – to the air of 'The Boys of

Mullaghbawn' – for Luke Kelly (1940–84), folk singer and founding member of the Dubliners, was never actually performed by him. Phil Coulter (b.1942) is a musician, song writer and record producer from Derry; while working with the Dubliners, he wrote 'The Town I Loved So Well', about Derry, for Kelly to sing.

'those fellows from St Thomas's': SH has in mind the shooting, in April 1972, of two Catholic civilians, Gerry and John Conway, outside St Thomas's School in Belfast, by soldiers in plain clothes.

To Ann Saddlemyer

TS Pratt

28 March 1973

Glanmore Cottage, Ashford,
Co. Wicklow

Dear Ann,

Decisions, decisions have been occurring: Marie expects the ba in three weeks and it seems to concentrate the mind wonderfully. I was to go to California in July and stay there until Christmas; then to proceed for the Spring semester of 1974 to Colgate University in NY state. For various reasons – I'm writing well here, the move with the whole family for 4 months would be too much, and so on – I have decided not to go to Berkeley and wrote to them this morning to say as much. That means, of course, that I will be staying in Ireland, and I'm wondering now what to do about housing here. I don't intend to go back to Belfast – I'll have to decide whether to sell my house there but I don't think I can yet afford to buy a house in Wicklow, much as I would like to do that. So – you can see it coming – I'm wondering if you intend to be in Ireland in the autumn and if not, if it would be possible for us to rent Glanmore Cottage until Christmas? I am certain that if I rooted into the pile of letters which grows in the upper room I could piece all the information I want from your previous correspondence, but if I write it will give you time to think about your decision. You will be coming over in the summer, I know, and you may have arrangements made to rent the cottage anyhow; and you'll probably want to live here yourself when you come – now, realizing all that, I want to ask if we can rent the cottage over the summer and through until the end of December. It would, of course, be entirely possible for us to move away in the summer, and it would also be understood that you would be due a realistic summer rent if we were to stay.

Basically, I suppose I am asking when and if you need us out of this dear spot.

Mr Shannon has made a neat job of the car park at the front and has curved a sturdy stone wall from the little gate across the middle of what was once the lawn, as far as the pump house. And he has also straightened and re-hung the outer gates. The weather has been magnificent and the sense of spring and well-being burgeons in us. How could one want to go to California?

I enclose some renteen; and keep promising myself to send you a copy of the work I've done here this year. I will too. We'll let you know about the baby when it comes. *Sláinte*,

Seamus

Because Saddlemyer had expected SH to be teaching at Colgate, she had arranged to let Glanmore Cottage to others over the summer.

The Heaneys' daughter Catherine Ann, 'the ba', was born later than predicted (see next letter).

'renteen': SH turning the English word into an Irish diminutive.

To Ann Saddlemyer

MS Pratt

16 May 1973

Glanmore Cottage, Ashford,
Co. Wicklow

Dear Ann,

Thanks for your letter of April 9; and sorry once again for not including that money: something Freudian in that neglect, no doubt.

Anyhow, stirring times since your letter. Marie has had a baby daughter that came twelve days late on April 25th. Both are doing well, and we called her Catherine Ann. Since April 25 we have been away from here until Monday last, 14th. Marie went to her parents in Co. Tyrone for the company and moral support after getting out of hospital in Dún Laoghaire; and then I had to go to England for a week of readings until Friday last, so she stayed on rather than face the trials of *three* in Glanmore on her own. However, here we are again and all is working in green May – ferns and leaves and grasses, as you can imagine, all around us; and the Chapmans and the Johnsons being kind as ever.

We don't really know what we are going to do. I'd love to get a house round here and settle within striking distance of Dublin but really property is out of the question; the little thatched cottage that faces you as you come up from Ashford in the V opposite the post office was sold a couple of months ago for £8000. Yet we don't want to go back to Belfast; and then there is the indecision about what I want to do myself – the freelancing has worked out well enough this year. And last week I won the Denis Devlin award for *Wintering Out* – £350 and very welcome too.

Confidentially, I must tell you that a group called the American-Irish Foundation is going to announce early in June that I have got a grant called the Writer-in-Residence Grant – worth 7000 dollars, the only requirement being that I live in Ireland for 10 months. So I'd like to confirm that we'd be interested in staying here from September until at least Christmas. I still don't know what will happen then – I had arranged to go [to] Colgate in NY state for the spring semester and haven't decided what will happen now with the ten-month residence requirement. It depends on the Foundation to some extent also. If they grant me permission, I'll probably absent myself from this country for two and a half months. But that's in a state of flux at the moment.

Anyhow, the main point is that we'll clear the decks here for July 1st. We have a rather nice dresser, deal table and chest in the living room which we'll leave, if it's all right with you. It gives a nice country feeling to the room. We moved the china cabinet into the downstairs bedroom and I think that for the sake of stylistic harmony in the living room, we'll leave it there for the Hoenigers. The 'Cranford' room upstairs is now my study and fairly strewn with books and papers but that we will restore to its antique and mellow charm of yesteryear. Also, we'll clear drawers and wardrobes. But we might leave kitchen utensils, and kitchen storage that we improvised. I think it would be useful to anyone staying.

I'm not sure what we'll do over the summer. Ideally, I'd like to get a place in Dublin but as soon as we have plans I'll let you know.

In the meantime, our continuing gratitude and good wishes.

Sincerely,
Seamus

'the Chapmans and the Johnsons': David and Evelyn Chapman were a farming couple who lived up the road and were relied on for care of the spare key and other kindnesses; the Johnsons were neighbours as well.

Dublin. I have a roof-rack and the same VW so I think you could all pile in and pile up. It would be very simple for me and would give me great pleasure to translate you to Dublin. So if you dropped a card with the expected arrival time of the flight I'll try to be there.

Last week I got news that I won the Denis Devlin award (£350) for *Wintering Out*. It is a delight to the Wicklow bank manager and myself, but my paranoia in the environs of McDaidsville is growing.

This is not so much a letter as an inept signal of love and guilt to you all. We look forward to talking to you again and I hope that I can ferry you from Shannon.

Love,
Seamus

'I would love to meet you at Shannon': meeting friends at airports was a kindness SH long continued to take pleasure in.

'McDaidsville': McDaid's is a pub in Dublin, where Montague could often be found.

To Charles Monteith

PC Faber

[October 1973]

Thanks, as ever, for the hospitality – and the handling of the reading – last Thursday. I got back on Friday afternoon and came gradually to domestic earth after a boggy high in Jutland. I think more and more that I'd like to do a book on the bog – Irish bog with salutations to Jutland. I joked about it before but now it's a rising obsession that I should strike before it's cold. I know you couldn't say if Fabers would be interested until the thing takes shape, but perhaps you could say if they would *not* be. It would be a kind of imaginative exploration – part myth-making, part travel book, part catalogue of bog finds, part praise of the landscape itself. Necessarily illustrated with photographs, I think.

Anyway, I want to get Sweeney to you in the next six months, and get another sizeable enterprise under way.

With every good wish,
Sincerely,
Seamus

Written on two postcards, marked by Monteith as received on 29 October: the cards, from the Silkeborg Museum in Denmark, show the human figures exhumed from peat bogs that SH had first learned about from P. V. Glob (see letter to Monteith of 5 May 1971) and that were his current poetic obsession. The pretext for SH's visit to Denmark was a reading in Copenhagen, but he took the opportunity to visit both the museum and the sites where the bodies were discovered.

Having immediately replied that 'the idea of a Bog Book is an absolutely splendid one', a few days later Monteith was ready to offer SH a contract.

To Ciaran Carson

MS Emory

1 November 1973

Glanmore Cottage, Ashford,
Co. Wicklow

Dear Ciaran,

Belated thanks for your excellent pamphlet: an exfoliation, the real thing, La Tène spontaneity, insular illuminations. I really take great pleasure from your poems – and had been thinking of asking you for more for *Soundings* and then thought maybe not again this year, but as the last minute – deadline 10th November – approaches – I do want to ask you to submit as many as you care to for consideration. What about 'Well of Saints', 'Gaeltacht', 'Colmcille's Return' – published, I know – plus any others you like to muster?

If you feel like it, I'd be obliged if you could deal with this almost by return. I'd like to have them by next Wednesday. Sorry to hassle you – and please yourself about it – but glad to have got round to greeting *The Insular Celts*, however inadequately. Call sometime when you're in this direction. Glendalough is only 8 miles away . . .

Sláinte,
Seamus

PS I'm talking about Sweeney at festival, on afternoon of 13th November. But you're probably caught in the fine meshes of work at that time.

By 'La Tène', SH is evoking the culture of the Late Iron Age, which in Ireland produced artefacts, principally metalwork, characterised by particularly free and lovely ornamentation.

The Insular Celts was the title of the first (1973) pamphlet of poems by Ciaran Carson (1948–2019), whom SH had taught at Queen's University and who was now working for the Arts Council of Northern Ireland.

To Ted Hughes

MS Emory

2 November 1973

Glanmore Cottage, Ashford,
Co. Wicklow

Dear Ted,

I don't know if you have departed yet for Ireland or whether your plans still hold: an idea has struck me, however, that you may or may not want to take up.

I have compiled a series of ten programmes (BBC) for schools in Northern Ireland, and in the poetry programme – which is fundamentally about naming things – I have 'Full Moon and Little Frieda'. Rather than have an actor do it, I think it would be ideal if you read it yourself. There are a few other poems in the broadcast you might want to do if you were to come to the studio – a list of names for the hare – from George Ewart Evans's *The Leaping Hare* – and D. H. Lawrence's short poem 'Discord in Childhood'. (And Muir's 'Horses' – the rhymed one) I thought if you were here, we might get a studio in RTÉ in Dublin and record some stuff down the line to Belfast. It's only a thought: the producer is David Hammond whom I think you met when you were in Belfast. Anyhow, even [if] you don't feel like interrupting your freedom with commitments, I hope you'll call if you're in the vicinity. We're only an hour south of Dublin.

I enclose another lump of bog-fruit.

Love to Carol.

Sláinte,
Seamus

Of the poems mentioned, 'The Names of the Hare' (in SH's version of the Middle English original) was later included by Hughes and SH in their anthology *The Rattle Bag*, as were 'The Horses' (unrhymed) by Orkney poet Edwin Muir (1887–1959), and many poems by D. H. Lawrence, but not 'Discord in Childhood'.

The Leaping Hare by George Ewart Evans (1909–88) and David Thomson (1914–88), an account of the hare in nature, folklore and literature, had only just been published.

1974

The process by which the various sections of SH's fourth collection, *North* (1975), came together to form a unity, apparently taking the poet himself by surprise, deserves close academic study, but his letters of this year offer at least a glimpse. Coincidental with that process was SH's realisation that his friend Brian Friel, the leading Irish playwright of his day, and he were engaged in comparable attempts to express, in metaphorical or mythic terms, the more submerged forces driving contemporary political events (see the unfinished letter to Friel of 21 October).

To John Montague — MS Cork

23 January 1974 [m.d. 1973] Glanmore Cottage, Ashford, Co. Wicklow

Dear John,

Sorry you couldn't manage the link-up for the Muldoon Arts Programme. We had an interview that I recorded with MacDiarmid, plus Paddy Moloney on *Chieftains 4* and Deane on *Crow* recording. Time, in the end, prevented what I had envisaged at the end – a discussion – including Deane and yourself – on 'the parish and the universe', hung on the re-print of *Collected Pruse*. But I know the kind of disruption a trip to Dublin involves.

I am just, I hope, lifting out of a despondent, sluggish, lazy, uncoordinated, un-energetic couple of months. I'm not writing and I'm not sure what I'm doing here or what I'm going to do. I seem to have lost touch with whatever sense of purpose and confidence I had last year – and to be spending my time doing itty-bitty broadcasts and articles. But the last couple of days have seen a resurgence – witness even this letter. I think it would be therapeutic to take another race at the *Sweeney*, so I would welcome any responses you feel worth communicating on that score. I had thought we might get down to see you before March but I doubt it now. I have to do a couple of weekend recordings for Hammond, and really it takes a day or two to get back into smooth domestic running after an expedition like that. Somehow three children are a lot more than two. So maybe you could put Sweeney in a registered envelope some time.

My typewriter is broken, so I enclose as fair a copy as I can of a poem that came last month. I don't know what to make of it – is it alive? It's certainly *meant*.

Toronto lifts and lays my heart all at once. I've written to say yes to *Temple*, and that I do look forward to. I'm also trying to fix a few readings in Michigan, on the approach, with Hammond to soften the blow. But I've had no final word. If you come towards Dublin, let us know.

How are Evelyn and Una? Catherine Ann sings the last word of each line in 'Baa Baa Black Sheep'. And Michael has started telling jokes. 'What do Sea-monsters eat?' 'Fish and ships.' Also, I got an old churn staff the other day and Christopher put it into his 'news' at school. The teacher wrote on the board, 'Christopher's daddy is going to make his own butter'!

Did you hear that Mahon is now features editor with *Vogue*? The scamp.

Sincerely,

Seamus

The placing of this letter is a confident guess. SH heads it '23 January 1973', and some of the events he refers to – the issue of *Chieftains* 4, the reprint of Kavanagh's *Collected Pruse* – were of that year. But Catherine Ann would still have been in her mother's womb and Derek Mahon did not work at *Vogue* until 1974, and so, late in the month as it may be, I have taken this to be another example of SH's new-year absent-mindedness.

Hugh MacDiarmid (1892–1978): poet, Scottish Nationalist, and driving force behind the revival of literature in Scots.

Chieftains 4: latest album by the Chieftains, the Irish band founded and led by multi-instrumentalist Paddy Moloney (1938–2021).

Claddagh Records had put out an LP of Ted Hughes reading from his 1971 volume of poems, *Crow*.

SH's report on the progress of his translation of the twelfth-century Irish tale *Buile Shuibhne*, to be published in 1983 as *Sweeney Astray*, and his invitation to comment on it, look like an appeasing gesture.

The 'poem that came last month' was 'Exposure'.

Evelyn (née Robson) was Montague's second wife; Oonagh – rendered phonetically by SH – his daughter.

'Mahon is now features editor with *Vogue*': in interview, Mahon admitted, 'It was a big mistake, but I did it for a year.'

To Charles Monteith MS Faber

9 May 1974

Glanmore Cottage, Ashford,
Co. Wicklow

Dear Charles,

Many thanks for the Glob book – it's a lovely thing to handle and look at, even before you begin reading it. I've just done a review of it for the *Listener*, in fact.

America went off very well – beginning with a splendid reading in the New School in New York, continuing through Ann Arbor, various Michigan campuses, Toronto, Philadelphia and back to New York, where I met W. S. Merwin and James Wright, among others, at a memorable all-Sunday literary brunch. I was away for three weeks and enjoyed it as a holiday – the readings were well spread out – but like a holiday, it cost more than I anticipated. The last place I read, by the way, was at Bard College, courtesy of Richard Murphy – they were caught in a freak fall of Easter snow!

Marie went to Spain for a week when I got back – not in a huff, but as a pre-arranged part of the bargain. But now we're settled again and I've done a lot of reviewing work in the last couple of weeks: and hope to get into Sweeney soon. Also, I'll be doing a 15-minute BBC film on Wordsworth, in the Lake District – you may have seen a similar series last year, with Margaret Drabble on the Brontës, etc. – so I may be in London to arrange for that soon. If so, I'll drop in; but I'll certainly be over for Poetry International on June 7th, so one way or another, we should meet soon.

Also, in June, I'm joining a dig in Co. Mayo where they've found the outline – stone walls, burials, foundations – of a stone age settlement down under the peat! The first chapter of a bog book, maybe. 'Every layer they strip / Seems camped on before.'

With every good wish,

Sincerely,

Seamus

The new 'Glob book' was P. V. Glob's *The Mound People: Danish Bronze-Age Man Preserved*: SH's review of it appeared in the *Listener* of 6 June, under the heading 'Summoning Lazarus'.

W. S. Merwin (1927–2019) and James Wright (1927–80) were both US poets and recent Pulitzer Prize winners, Merwin for *The Carrier of Ladders* (1971), Wright for his *Collected Poems* (1972).

The Anglo-Irish poet Richard Murphy was also published by Faber: after making his home in Galway for many years and earning a living by taking tourists out to sea in a working boat which he had renovated, he was now writer-in-residence at Bard College in New York state – one of many such postings by which he subsisted.

The BBC film went out as *William Wordsworth Lived Here: Seamus Heaney at Dove Cottage.*

'joining a dig': in August, SH and Marie Heaney were shown around Céide Fields, a Stone Age site in Co. Mayo, by the archaeologist who had unearthed it, Seamus Caulfield (b.1939). Below the bog, there was found to have been a farming system more than 5,000 years old, exactly like the one above it. The quotation is from SH's own poem 'Bogland'.

To Jill Thomas

MS Faber

11 October 1974

Glanmore Cottage, Ashford,
Co. Wicklow

Dear Jill,

Uncharacteristically, I'm writing within minutes of getting your letter because if I don't now, it may be weeks: and I'm so pleased to hear from you.

I don't think there's the least contradiction between being a nurse and a poet: both involve sensitivity in action. Could you say there's a difference between being sensitive and being exquisite? The tougher the outlook the better: cruel to be kind, and all that. It's understanding that counts, the care and the acuteness lying in wait behind our professionalism or patter or defences or whatever. Listen to me preaching! Yeats was tough, Frost was tough (do you know Frost's poems 'Home Burial', or 'Out, Out' – and what about Yeats's 'Second Coming' or 'Leda and the Swan'? Boom, boom, as Basil Brush says) and Alexander Pope wasn't exactly a wilting flower – nor Donne etc. etc. . . .

I think 'Woman – Aged 67' is powerful and does work. I only wonder if you need to say 'cancer cat' – the cancer is such a powerful word that it overpowers the powerful image. If you just said 'the cat / —— ——' [two indecipherable words: hung purring?] it would perhaps be more predatory – the kitten image prepares us for it as a metaphor for malignant flourishing growth.

I do like 'Mountain and Cloud' – very like 'Act of Union' indeed. In general, I feel about it and the other two that their poise and finality is just slightly blurred by too many adjectives – I am writing honestly because these are poems, not embarrassments, and I don't want to substitute dainty evasions for poet-to-poet responses – so:

Mountain and Cloud:

1) I can see the 'nebulous' is attractive – etymologically, especially. But with it, and 'dissolving' inside three lines, it's maybe overdone. What about 'I climb in my own way'? It will shorten the line, of course, and upset the visual pattern of the stanza.
2) 'wallow lethargically' I feel is just a wee bit too 'wallowy' – I wonder if 'wallow' is too ponderous, too flabby and physical for a cloud – it certainly is for you! What about a verb like 'moon' – wrong, of course, for a cloud, but it has that aimless drift about it.
3) I would leave out the 'And' to make a new sentence, and a firm rhythmic closure in the last 3 lines.

Night Duty: lovely poem: spider image is the strength!

1) Maybe I'm even tougher than you – or just afraid of words like 'silken' – what about 'thread of duty'?
2) 'Gather the lines of care' is lovely and rich.
3) I feel that one of these three adjectives could be lost: 'trusting', 'unknown, dreaming'.

Night: Sorry. I would leave out the first two couplets – and then what a compact, marvellous poem it is. The first two couplets strike me as a kind of limbering up, lifting those old dumb-bells, 'tide', 'earth', 'space' – heavy!

It is a pleasure to write about these, Jill. I know you won't mind – and will disregard my ear for your own. You must. They're yours, not mine. All I'm doing is trying to make them what I'd write.

It was a delight for me to talk to you in the pub. When I get back to Shropshire I hope we'll meet again.

Sincerely,
Seamus Heaney

Jill Thomas has not been identified; this letter to her was found, unaccountably, in the Faber archive.

To Brian Friel

TS NLI

12 October 1974

Glanmore Cottage, Ashford,
Co. Wicklow

Dear Brian,

Cautious as I am not to enter the realms of brock or slabber – not to say the maudlin – I still have to risk it: it's half eleven and I've just put in one of the most excited days of my time. *Volunteers* played on every stop in me: no grace and discretion involved at all, just the old *duende* (get out your Penguin Lorca now). Maybe it is partly the subject matter, maybe it's because we're both in the same territory – and how much so you'll find out from some of the poems I enclose – but chiefly it's because of the fullness and control and the lovely seamless web of realism, symbolism, psychic and dramatic double-takes that the play involves. It's the real thing – a poetic drama, I'd say, and God I hope its buoyancy in the theatre will not mean that its big undertow is missed. The breaking of that jug! I've only read it the once, but I've been stirred within myself to such an extent that I've typed out the guts of a book. The communal generator is kicking into life. I feel that Friday night wildness – honest to God.

The first performance of Brian Friel's *Volunteers*, which is about IRA prisoners put to work on an archaeological site, and which may have chimed in SH's mind with his recent experience at Céide Fields, was to receive its first production at the Abbey Theatre, Dublin, in March 1975.

Two copies of this significant, if frustratingly curtailed, declaration survive among the Friel papers in the National Library, the second with alternative phrasing penned below the typed text. An unsubstantiated guess is that what started as a letter was never either completed or mailed, but was given to Friel personally by SH – too wary or bashful to drive the thoughts he was beginning to articulate to a conclusion – but other interpretations are certainly possible.

To Charles Monteith

TS Faber

23 October 1974

Glanmore Cottage, Ashford,
Co. Wicklow

Dear Charles,

It was magnificently encouraging to have your response to the book coming over so loud and clear on Monday morning: a sure enough test of any enthusiasm, I'd say, to muster it at ten o'clock at that time of the week. And I'm extremely grateful for your suggestions about royalties.

The niggles have started already, but I also feel they're nearly over. I've not talked to anybody else about this – nobody else has seen the ms. apart from Marie and Fabers – but here are a number of question marks first and I'd be grateful for your opinion:

1) I enclose two new pages for Parts I and II – the only difference is that these now have epigraphs. I find them attractive enough and appropriate enough, but do you think they risk the portentous? Always a touch of the reflected glory bit in a T. S. Eliot epigraph. Anyhow.
2) I also enclose a sequence of prose bits – prose-poems? – which I did in a fast burst last May and June. Perhaps significantly when I was axing material for *North*, these dropped out of the final selection. Yet I still have an affection for them. Yet I think if I put them in Section II they will clutter it and make it reminiscent of *Death of a Naturalist* country. I think they're out but I'd like you to see them. Maybe a pamphlet there.
3) I enclose as well a possible second epigraph for 'Singing School': a delicious bit in its own right, and maybe exactly right in the context – especially since 'Singing School' is Yeats's own phrase. But again, is it weighing the thing? I think not in this case.

The other things have to do with re-arrangements and revisions.

1) I cannot remember which of the dedicatory poems comes first in your ms, but if we *are* going to use the Eliot epigraph to Part I, then I think 'The Seed Cutters' should immediately precede it and therefore come second.
2) Can you please insert the date *1966* at the end of the first poem, 'Antaeus'. It happens to date from then, and also this gives more point to the answering poem at the end of the section.
3) I've added a few lines to the 'Summer 1969' piece (Part 4 of 'Singing School') and I enclose a new sheet of this. Incidentally, in the new bit there's a reference to that Goya painting – black, as they call it – which has two characters

> like tinkers beating hell out of one another in a quagmire. I used the word 'holmgang' which I heard in Denmark last year – prepared to risk the Old Norse thing, and then discovered it was in the two-volume Oxford Dictionary. But I was curious about berserk – Marie said she thought it was African, but I'm damned if it doesn't mean: 'a wild Norse warrior who fought on the battlefield with a frenzied fury known as the *berserker rage*'. *North* has to be right!

And since I'm in the way of sending out stuff, I thought I'd let you or the children's editor or whoever look at a story I did for the kids three years ago. It's maybe not stripped enough, maybe a bit obvious – I'd need responses from that specialized department – but if it was promising, what I had in mind was to do another eleven with Ronan as a central figure, and the months of the year as the structural principle, and call it something like *Ronan's Bedtime Calendar*: in which he has a kind of dream encounter each month with a spirit of place or season. In May it would be a flower-woman queen of the May, in October a corn-dollie presence, in November a severed head, a turnip man spectre; in December, the last mummer. The enclosed might fit in about June. But you get the idea, even if what is here enclosed doesn't get to the mark. What I'd try to do would be to publish one a month in the *Education Times* here – and/or with some educational magazine in Britain, and then collect them. Maybe *Vogue* – no use having relations in the trade unless you use them.

[. . .]

Seamus

In reply to SH's offering of *North* and his subsequent 'niggles' about it, Monteith said he thought it would be unwise to include the prose poems, which would 'upset the general feel and texture of the book as a whole and would tend to disturb that extraordinary and impressive unity which it's got'. One such, however, remained in the published book: 'The Unacknowledged Legislator's Dream', the first item in Part II. A pamphlet of SH's 'prose poems', *Stations*, preceded the publication of *North* by three months in 1975; eight of its poems were subsequently printed together as 'Autobiographical Borings' in the *Irish Times* on 8 July.

The 'Eliot epigraph', which SH had taken from part III of *Little Gidding* and which ran all the way from 'This is the use of memory' to 'transfigured, in another pattern', was dropped. In a letter to Lorna Simmonds, in the production department at Faber, dated 30 January 1975, SH writes: 'Delete the Eliot piece on page 11 and the Yeats bit on page 55 – I think they are both heavy-handed, only interferences with the reader's response, really.'

The Ronan story, 'Ronan and the Riverman', was passed to Faber's Children's Books Editor, Phyllis Hunt (1927–2006), but nothing came of SH's scheme for a whole calendar of stories – perhaps because its proposed design resembled too closely that of Ted Hughes's book of poems for children, *Season Songs*, published by Faber in 1975.

The final, omitted paragraph, explaining how the elements of *North* came together, is more or less duplicated by SH in the letter to Thomas Flanagan that follows.

To Thomas Flanagan

TS Amherst

25 October 1974

Glanmore Cottage, Ashford,
Co. Wicklow

Dear Tom,

After a strange fortnight – and a good jag of the Paddy in Ashford – with O'Riada (and what a falling-off was there) going full blast in the corner – the only possible society (after oneself, *pace* Wilde) is yourself. You would know I was from the north with that many qualifications in the first sentence.

The strangeness had to do with 'that sweet mood in which the affections lead us on' to novels, poems or decisions. On Saturday week last I got a copy of Brian Friel's new play that's to go on in the Abbey next March. It's called *Volunteers* and set on an archaeological dig in perhaps Dublin – certainly in Ireland – with internees on parole as the diggers. But one of the main 'characters' or symbols or props is a Scandinavian skeleton called Leif. Bones, bodies, politics, the ground – the whole nexus of the thing totally complemented the bits of things I've been doing myself in the last couple of years: it was as if we'd been tunnelling out of our different solitary confinements and connected at the same exit. Anyway, I was high enough to type out a brutally selected bunch of poems from the last couple of years and found that they connected also to make a book called *North* – Viking image, vicious Ireland – that all of a sudden has been accepted, blurbed, and scheduled for next June. I'd never put the things together. They were piecemeal in my head, belonging to the same root but never actually typed out and 'viewed'. Well, I've done the deed. It's a pitch towards *Responsibilities* of a sort of beginning not so much in dreams as in the brute ordinariness of what has happened to us – us, the family afflicted by a father bewildered by this word poet, and us, the crowd driven to kill one another with a certain aplomb, insouciance, whatever. (Paddy is your only man for a letter.)

Anyhow, to-day I was excising the excesses – not altogether – from the blurb that Fabers proposed, and it came to me that although I'd mentioned to you that I would suggest to them that they should do *The Irish Novelists* in the Faber paperback series, I had not actually got my ass together, as Marie says, to do so. So I remedied the thing this evening, and I just want to let you know that it's with them, with a suggestion that they should think of including it in their list. In case they're sharp enough to follow it up, I thought you'd better have time to have second thoughts or to have a deal up your sleeve for them.

And, high as I was, I was launched by your opening remarks on Carleton to splutter out the enclosed which will stand as a kind of epigraph, I hope, to Section II of *North*. The inverted commas are what Kavanagh called 'the secret sign' between us – coming from the second page of your first chapter on the poor scholar. And the Sussex reference is an oblique criticism of the Thirties melodrama of MacNeice in his *Postscript to Iceland*. Anyhow. *Quibus rebus dictis . . .*

How is *Late Summer*? Not that I'm putting any *geasa* on you to answer. This is sheer exuberance on my part. All I mean is that the excitement and apprehension about that self-delighting, self-affrighting foray has not at all abated in me. What a good occasion – occasions – those were in Ballinamuck and environs. Not to mention the readings, both on the night of my excessive drinking and insolence in asking you to house the Kilroy party, and that other totally memorable night between the four of us.

I suppose you're destined to be a father-figure of sorts to me. Blooming awful. Why don't you come here and be Yeats to all the urgent and undirected energy? Tell Cronin what to do (Anthony, that is), get Ben to write a masterpiece besides himself, socialize the structuralism in Deane, take Donoghue and wring rhetoric's neck, get Conor back to grips with the papish imagination and to hell with his nostalgia for pre-republican Ireland, put an intellectual thrill into the Anglo-Irish department in UCD. *Pardon, old father . . .*

I better put this into an envelope and not re-read it in the morning or I'll funk it. Joan Keefe is on my mind but *Soundings* is to come out in a couple of weeks with a poem of hers in it so I'll write to her then. Give our love to Jean and the girls. Ask Lennie if he is ever going to write the children's book we talked about three years ago because if he isn't, I could maybe make a couple of hundred quid by doing it here (and now – Liam Nolan has left that programme to join the sports department of RTÉ – great).

Most appositely, Catherine Ann has started to cry out – and her cry 'Distracts my thought'. Or distracts me from distraction. If I get into the right mood or company in New York in early December I'll try to ring you. *Sláinte*.

Seamus

PS You've no errands east in December yourself? Kinsella and I are to read in Pittsburgh, Pa, on Wednesday 4th. Good luck. S.

'a good jag of the Paddy': the whiskey of that name.

'a pitch towards *Responsibilities*': SH alludes to Yeats's 1914 volume, *Responsibilities and Other Poems*, which marked a turning-point in the poet's sense of vocation.

Flanagan's *The Irish Novelists: 1800–1850* was published by Columbia University Press in 1958; Faber did not take it up. It had been crucial in reviving interest in William Carleton (1794–1869), author of *Traits and Stories of the Irish Peasantry* (1830), whose combative ghost, incidentally, SH encounters in section II of *Station Island*.

The 'enclosed': presumably, 'The Unacknowledged Legislator's Dream'.

Late Summer may be the provisional title of some work in progress; *geasa* is the plural of *geas*, Irish for 'taboo', which in its plural form means a curse that stops something from happening.

'What a good occasion . . . in Ballinamuck and environs': SH had accompanied Flanagan on excursions to the scene of the Battle of Ballinamuck, fought in 1798 and described by Flanagan in *The Year of the French*.

Anthony Cronin (1928–2016) was a poet and notable presence in literary Dublin; 'Ben' is Benedict Kiely; Denis Donoghue (1928–2021) was an influential literary critic, born in the Republic of Ireland, brought up in Co. Down, latterly teaching in the USA; 'Conor' must be Conor Cruise O'Brien.

Joan Keefe (1932–2013) was a mutual friend, associated with the Celtic Studies programme at Berkeley.

To Charles Monteith

MS Faber

30 October 1974

[. . .] I am stunned by that 10,000 print order and hope that your trust is completely justified. I still feel slight aftershock about the book itself: it all came together so quickly, just like a poem. I'm still wondering about the prose-poem stuff and still haven't showed the thing to anybody else. I'm inclined now to feel that they should go in, but one to a page. As I say, my only unease is not to do with the merits of the things *per se* but with their effect on the compactness of the collection. They are relevant, of course, but would eleven of them sag the thing? [. . .]

1975

Busier than ever, professionally and socially, SH saw two contrasting works published this year: *Stations*, his pamphlet of prose poems, never reissued in its own right, though nine items from it are preserved in *Opened Ground: Poems 1966–1996*; and *North*, which as soon as it appeared received extremes of both acclaim and disparagement, and which, however regarded, has established itself as central to SH's *oeuvre*.

Appointment to a lectureship at the Carysfort College of Education in Dublin afforded financial security. Less conspicuous work as both Arts Council committee member and behind-the-scenes mover, shaker and fixer also continued.

To Michael Hartnett

TS NLI

11 January 1975

Glanmore Cottage, Ashford,
Co. Wicklow

Dear Michael,

You'll have been calling me all the shites in the world for not answering your letter of last month but until yesterday I had nothing to say except a pious hope that something would be done some time. In spite of your fury to hear that the Arts Council does not recognize 'the existence of individual writers', your putting it that way indicates that you are well and painfully aware that this has been deliberate policy until now. However, I think we are on the verge of bursting that one. Sean O'Tuama and myself and others, including J. B. Keane, have been hammering at a policy for literature and drama over the last year. The hold-ups have been exasperating, chiefly budgetary, but as you can guess, the representatives of other interests – music, visual arts – are all jockeying for their cut of a very meagre budgetary cake. However, it now looks as if the council may pass our recommendation that some kind of bursary scheme for individual writers should be initiated; and if all goes well at the meeting next month, we hope the thing would be in operation by Easter. You will realize that I am now writing to you in a confidential and personal capacity, not as a member of that council; but I would obviously press your claims very hard when the matter would come up, and have already indicated your predicament to O'Tuama and Keane, who would also be sympathetic. The thing is, of course, that all of this will have to be ratified – it is by no means formally fixed, and within the whole council it's a matter of our stealthily laying hands on funds for our purposes; and when it has been ratified, it will have to [be] advertised and applications invited from Irish writers generally. And we'll have to appoint external judges and ensure that the thing is seen to be more than a private flow of public funds between the council and mysteriously chosen beneficiaries. But all of that said, I am glad to be able to answer your letter with a good hope of financial benefits being available to individual writers within the next six months. I appreciate your writing to me as you did; and I know to some extent the desperate sense of being in full imaginative flow yet dammed by work, lack of time and lack of money. I liked immensely the corn-woman poem in the *Irish Press* some time back. I would like to be able to send you an immense cheque, but the best I can do at the moment is to give you this hard news and, I hope, hope of real benefit before long.

Sláinte, Seamus

1975 was the year in which the Limerick-born poet Michael Hartnett (1941–99), with a couple of volumes already to his name, published *A Farewell to English*, in which he announced that from now on he would write poems exclusively in Irish. The book includes his poem 'The Oat Woman'.

Seán Ó Tuama (1926–2006): Cork-born, Irish-writing poet, scholar and teacher (see letter to Louis de Paor, 1 August 1997); John B. Keane (1928–2002): playwright and novelist from Listowel, Co. Kerry.

To Michael Longley

TS Emory

[8 February 1975]

Glanmore Cottage, Ashford,
Co. Wicklow

Dear Michael,

I intended to snatch an hour for lunch last Wednesday – I was in Letterkenny last Tuesday – Hammond drove me up from Belfast and as you probably heard, I was to collect Joe Burke's motor in Ballymena and drive it over the border, but Joe had other ideas. Anyhow, the whole expedition ended in a depressed mood for to begin with I arrived in Letterkenny a fortnight early, thus wasting two days; then I called to see Tommy Devlin who was/is in hospital in Magherafelt after an operation for kidney stones, and he was shaken and in pain; and I went down home and found my mother in low form, not ill but lonely now that my sister Ann is away in Canada. So I spent until the last possible minute in Co. Derry and rushed straight to the train. I must say it was rather odd to be hurrying to the station with yourself and Muldoon upstairs in Bedford House and not to have the time to stop and ponder, if not legislate for, the state of poetry and politics. Anyway, the result of it all was the third sonnet in the sequence I enclose.

I am in a seemingly unbreakable lethargy, but not a fulfilling one, for I keep saying to myself what I should be doing. Income tax should be cleared up. Sweeney should be got to hell off my hands. Money-making projects should be initiated. Poems are wished for. I have this notion that only a wilful act of making – sonneteering, shouldering the burden of set forms – will stir the pool.

North is to come out now in the last week of June. Next thing Montague will be saying I copied the title from him. Jesus. He is tedious. He only lost his dignity by that letter about Edna. It's not so much a case of who does he think he is as whom does he think he's addressing. Anyway, I'll be glad to be shot of that whole blockage of 'crisis' verse, and to have the boggers laid out in state. Back to the pure.

Christopher will be seven to-morrow. I'll be thirty-six in April. The only thing is to dig in for a long Yeatsian development. Or a Hewitt holding action. What do you think of the Kavanagh bit, in the cold of print, by the way? It's a bit fussy here and there where it does its wee practical criticism bit, but it will do.

How are you doing? The job botheration has slackened a bit, I hope. I hear from Hammond that the tour of the trad. men was a magnificent success, Aughnacloy and other tensions notwithstanding. It may sound incorrigibly old-fashioned and arrogant, but only the authority of the pure stuff, rooming to rhyme or out of the blue, can redeem us and them. Get the sidereal images circling, boy. These last years have been an immense lunacy. And we've all been sucked towards it. Poetry has to be peremptory – peremptory strikes, and other lyrics, a new sequence by Seamus Heaney – 'He copied the prose poem form from me,' Mr Montague said, 'as did Mallarmé, Zbigniew Herbert, T. S. Eliot, Elizabeth Bishop, Derek Mahon and Charles Baudelaire.' 'I admit he has what it takes' (Michael Longley). 'The sense of humour has got in at last' (James Simmons). 'Zap!' (Clive James). 'Hm'm' (R. S. Thomas). 'Major poets are rare as the phoenix . . .' (C. B. Cox).

How is Edna now that she must be, in McLaverty parlance, in full sail? I can assure you that the third grows preciouser and preciouser. Captain Ann is a real joy, and one also given to peremptory, pre-emptive striking.

As Maxwell would say, that'll do now. My granny was Doherty.

Sláinte,
Seamus

PS I had thought of unloading the prose poems for an *HU* pamphlet. But now I'm inclined to use these enclosed as the guts of it. What do you think?

PPS You don't fancy a run to Donegal – to Letterkenny – on Tuesday 18th? I could come to Belfast on 1:10 train, we could lunch in Dunadry, stay the night in L'kenny, and be back for the 11:30 train next morning. It's only a thought: justifiable as an Arts Council liaison on literature. I'm supposed to address them, by the way, on 'The Poet and Society'. You might want to join the 'discussion' (ha, ha, I don't think) and oblige.

It's only a thought. Otherwise, there is the express bus thru Monaghan, direct to the venue and back.

Grow in pure mind, but out of what begin? Och aye.

S.

Bedford House in Belfast was where the Arts Council of Northern Ireland had its headquarters.

'third sonnet . . . sonneteering, shouldering the burden of set forms': SH's sequence of 'Glanmore Sonnets' seems to have been written, or begun, around this time, though the first printing of any of them was not until the end of the following year.

John Montague's 'letter about Edna' had been printed in the *Irish Times* of 31 January: in it, he had taken issue with a piece about 'Recent Northern Irish Poetry' by Edna Longley that had appeared in the same paper. 'I marvel again', Montague wrote, 'to see how kindly she is to a northern songster like Simmons, whereas she usually feels obliged to ritually trounce Mr Kinsella and the Dolmen Press whenever they show their Southern heads.' Then, as a side-swipe, he characterised Longley as 'a charming example of the effect of partition on the intellect'.

'the Kavanagh bit': SH had written on Patrick Kavanagh for the January 1975 issue of Ian Hamilton's magazine, the *New Review*.

'Aughnacloy and other tensions' refers to the incident in March 1974 when two members of the Provisional IRA were blown up while laying a landmine on Aughnacloy Road, Dungannon.

'in McLaverty parlance, in full sail': as Michael McLaverty (1904–92), Northern Irish novelist and short story writer, also headmaster of St Thomas Secondary School where SH had his first teaching job, might have described Edna Longley's advanced pregnancy; her daughter Sarah was born in April.

'Captain Ann' was Catherine Ann – also, occasionally, 'the Captain'.

SH's postscripts are handwritten on a second sheet, previously used for a shopping list. The final remark plays on Yeats's 'Grew in pure mind but out of what began?' ('The Circus Animals' Desertion').

To Robert Lowell

TS Harry Ransom

28 February 1975

Glanmore Cottage, Ashford,
Co. Wicklow

Dear Robert,

Before he left for Borneo – great opener – Barrie Cooke told me that he had written to you to see if you'd be willing to do a reading in Kilkenny in the last week of August, in connection with their Arts Festival down there. I was to follow this invitation up long ago – I'm to be chairman at their readings – but unfortunately I've been very sluggish about it. You may have written to him already but he's been away now for over a month, and I don't know what's happening. I'm writing to-day to Ted Hughes and George Mackay Brown and Spender and a couple of others to see if they'd be willing to face the journey also, so I thought I'd better let you know the way the committee envisaged the thing: it would be a fee of £50 plus travelling expenses, and you could stay in a hotel or with Barrie and Sonja, who have a big house with a walled garden and peacocks – I hope to stay with them myself for that week.

Anyhow, this is to fulfil my promise to repeat the invitation and to say that it would be a pleasure to meet you again and an honour to chair your reading. I enjoyed the hurtle to the airport a couple of months ago – and I hear that Belfast enjoyed you too.

The Kilkenny reading, by the way, would be in a room in Kyteler's Inn, although no 'insolent fiend' is expected: they're a very lively, civilized crowd altogether.

Maybe we'll meet then.

With every good wish,
Sincerely,
Seamus Heaney

SH had first met the US poet Robert Lowell (1917–77), of all his near-contemporaries the one with the most marked influence on him, in 1972, at a party given in London by Sonia Orwell (1918–80) to celebrate Lowell's marriage to Lady Caroline Blackwood (1931–96).

In 1324, Dame Alice Kyteler, of Kilkenny, was condemned as a witch. Part of the case against her was that she was familiar with an 'insolent fiend' – as Yeats called him in 'Nineteen Hundred and Nineteen' – by the name of Robert Artison.

To Terence Brown

MS T. Brown

3 March 1975

Glanmore Cottage, Ashford,
Co. Wicklow

Dear Terence,

'At present I am living in Vermont' – it must be nice to be in old Frost's footsteps – I never knew you had gone off, but I'm sure you're liking it. We found California a terrific enhancement, hamburgers, television and all.

Of course, I've no objection to your using the piece. I only hope it was coherent and (a close second) that it was half-true at least. I was in the middle of mythologizing the bog-men into north-men. I have a collection called *North* coming in June, including that funeral poem from the *Irish Times* which I'm delighted you saw and liked: Gunnar, at the end, is from *Njal's Saga*. Anyhow.

After years of resisting the notion of a 'northern school' or 'movement', I now believe it to be a reality. I even believe the thing can grow, that poetry as a significant action in the mind of the whole country – or the whole mind of the country? – has a chance. Poetry still has or has retrieved some *mana*, north and south.

I wish you all good luck with the book – Seamus Deane did a nice piece in *Imprint*, by the way, on *Time Was Away* – a book which I regret I have not got yet. But it has won golden opinions. Bog on!

Regards to you and yours. It's been a great February.

Sláinte,
Seamus

PS I'm full of good will towards America just now – I got word on Saturday that I'm to get something called the E. M. Forster Award from the National Institute of Arts and Letters (confidential until announced in May) – a grant of a couple of thousand bucks for travel in the US – I didn't even know it existed.

In fact, I'll try to use it for petrol in Ashford. As they say in Belfast, it's despert.

S.

Terence Brown (b.1944), after lecturing at Trinity College, Dublin, was now teaching in the Department of English at the University of Vermont. Robert Frost spent the summer and autumn months of his final decades on a Vermont farm.

'that funeral poem': 'Funeral Rites' had been in the *Irish Times* on 9 November the previous year.

SH not only got around to reading *Time Was Away: The World of Louis MacNeice* (1974), by Terence Brown and Alec Reid, but he reviewed it, together with another book by Brown on MacNeice, in the *Guardian* a few months later.

The E. M. Forster Award, administered by the American Academy of Arts and Letters, is given annually to an Irish or British writer to fund travel in the USA.

To John Montague

MS Cork

15 April 1975

Glanmore Cottage, Ashford,
Co. Wicklow

John,

Ye hoor ye, you didn't come over at Easter.

Marie's father is out of hospital, debilitated, with an arrested cirrhosis of the liver – but on the mend: it was unfortunate I had to rush from Cork so suddenly that afternoon. As you said, we could have harrowed a few of the scores we ploughed the previous night: for now, let me just direct your attention to Robert Frost's 'For Once, Then, Something'.

The poems you sent me hold: 'Courtyard in Winter' is definitive Montague – the only thing that I'm uneasy about is the literary gesture – is it visually right? – of 'Mallarmé swans'. I know it is a poem of deliberate ritualistic movement, and maintains itself by rhetorical push, but I resist that one flourish. But it's a niggle – there is a grandeur about the cold masonry of the thing itself which does not fail.

'Small Secrets' and 'Song for Synge' – delicious: the latter could be out of 'the little monasteries'! 'Homes', 'Scenes', 'Sawmill, Limekiln', 'Almost a Song' – also drops of the pure – naming these things is the love act . . . And 'Dowager' deals nicely with strains of the impure: exhilarating as Montague in full cry. I'm just not as sure of 'Windharp', because of the definitiveness of the first line – 'The sound of Ireland' – what about 'sounds'? The plural takes it out of twilight into 'a bright day'.

North should be with you in a couple of months. I'm sending a few of those 'Sonnets from Glanmore' – I know you disliked that nomenclature – and I refuse to revise the penultimate line of 'Glanmore Twilight (1)' just because your windharp echoes it. It was done last May if it's any consolation to you.

I remember your house with pleasure – you're all nicely situated there. My hope now is to go to Berkeley next year for a quarter on my own and bring back the guts of a deposit. I've been offered a lectureship – endowed by one Beckmann – that nets $10,000 in 2½ months and I think I'll take it. We badly need a lump sum.

In the meantime, still no hard news of the magazine. Longley's Literature Committee meets to-morrow, and he's going to propose a co-operative venture: turn *Soundings* into a biennial literary miscellany. It could be all right.

Our regard to Evelyn and Una – those were memorable pancakes!

Sláinte,

Seamus

SH's spelling for 'cirrhosis' here is 'scirrosis'.

Frost's poem 'For Once, Then, Something' may be read as a commentary on the nature of vision (in a double sense) and truth.

The poems cited in the third and fourth paragraph are all in Montague's collection *A Slow Dance* (1975), where the 'Mallarmé swans, trapped in ice' remain. *The Little Monasteries* is the title of a book of poems translated from the Irish by Frank O'Connor (1903–66). SH borrows 'naming these things is the love act' from Patrick Kavanagh's poem 'The Hospital'.

The third of the 'Glanmore Sonnets', though lacking a title as it appears in *Field Work*, has a twilight setting, and its penultimate line, 'Outside a rustling and twig-combing breeze', might just about be thought to echo the scraped tree branches and combed and stroked landscape of Montague's 'Windharp'.

'the guts of a deposit': enough money to start paying for a mortgage.

To Charles Monteith

MS Faber

15 April 1975

Glanmore Cottage, Ashford,
Co. Wicklow

[. . .]

Since we met, I've been offered what they call the Beckmann Professorship in Berkeley – it's an endowed stint of 10 weeks, worth 10 grand (dollars) – so I hope to go to California to take it up this time next year. And maybe we'll get the deposit for a house rustled up out of that. Somebody must be praying for me, as my mother would say. I am deeply grateful for the powers of upper air that seem to take an interest in me.

You may remember, by the way, you sent me R. S. Thomas's address so that I could invite him to Kilkenny. He wrote to say he'd come and then by the next post reneged on it: in the meantime he'd received a letter from John Montague attacking him for never sufficiently acknowledging his debt to Patrick Kavanagh, and as he put it, if Montague's letter 'is a reflection of even a section of Irish literary life, I decline to come among it'. Thank you for the address, all the same – it let me have a ringside seat at yet another Montague cockpit. Amazing, isn't it?

[. . .]

In a letter of 29 March 1975 to R. S. Thomas – anglophone Welsh poet, vicar in the Church in Wales, and outspoken Welsh nationalist – Montague had truculently accused him of 'reworking' Kavanagh's *The Great Hunger* in certain early poems of his own. Writing to SH on 9 April to announce his withdrawal from the Kilkenny Festival, Thomas declared: 'Apart from its ill-nature, his [Montague's] letter shows considerable confusion over the question of echoes, influences and such like.'

To John McGahern

MS Galway

4 May 1975

Glanmore Cottage, Ashford,
Co. Wicklow

Dear John,

The number of times I've told myself to sit down and write: anyhow, I can hardly now believe it to be two months since I got your letter.

We're still in Wicklow. We came here not altogether on impulse and not altogether on a clear-cut decision. When I came back from California in 1971 some of the clay round the tap-root had loosened, and also some kind of confidence had grown in me. I was ready to risk myself at sea with myself – and thought I could carry the family through it all right. We got an offer of this cottage at a very respectably low rent and we just walked out of Belfast in August 1972, in a kind of fog, as Kavanagh would have said.

Partly I wanted to be rid of the enervating social footwork entailed in the role of papist-writer-makes-good-and-in-danger-of-co-option-by-Unionist-establishment; partly I felt I was never going to encounter my shallownesses and small possibilities if I stayed swathed in Queen's and the swaddling bands of the 'Belfast literary scene'; partly I enjoyed the grandeur of walking out. Anyway, we never regretted the move.

However, we didn't sell the Belfast house and we didn't buy this one. We're still in transition, and it is just beginning to be a sort of disabling condition. Michael will be 9 in July, Christopher is 7 and Catherine Ann – our Irish citizen – is 2. We have to think about secondary schools, and – occasionally – their teenage life. This place was and is literally idyllic but I think in the next few years, we'd be better to set up in the Dublin area. So we hope to deal for a house about this time next year. I'll sell the Belfast outfit and I'm to go to California (Berkeley again) for 10 weeks after Easter 1976. I hope to come back with at least £3,000. (Marie and the kids stay here.) It may be wishful thinking, but we may be able to deal for something, say round Dún Laoghaire.

I've a book coming out in a month's time, the second part of which carries the poems that deal more or less directly with the North. I remember you not liking some of them, but as far as I'm concerned, publication of them is one way of exorcising this pressure to 'say something about the north'. It has cleared my head already.

As far as my own work is concerned, I'm a bit spent and floundering at the minute; and content enough to wait. But I'm discontent at not doing anything else. I've farted about from broadcast to broadcast to occasional reviews, and spent days this year in a torpor of aspiration without action, and the 'self-yeast of spirit a dull dough sours'. Still, the month of May here would lift anybody's heart.

Are you going to be over in Leitrim this summer? If you are to be in or through Dublin, we'd be delighted if Madeline and yourself would call out. I'd be happy to collect you in the car at Dún Laoghaire or North Wall if you were coming by boat: for salutation instead of 'leavetaking'.

'The beginning of an Idea' is marvellous, I think. I'm sorry that Gill and Macmillan have reneged on the anthology – budgets again – and apologise for the unmannerly delay in returning the Mss. I'll put them in a bigger envelope.

Are you working yourself? And is the Newcastle job/position right to write in? (If there are, indeed, conditions necessary other than one's appetite for it.)

Obviously, I should have written long ago.

With every good wish to both of you,

Seamus

McGahern was married to the American photographer Madeline Green, whose name SH more often than not spells 'Madeleine', as he does here. McGahern was Northern Arts Fellow at Newcastle University from 1974 to 1976. 'The Beginning of an Idea' is the title of a short story by him, perhaps his most overtly Chekhovian; it was first published in the *New Review* in August 1974. *The Leavetaking* was the title of his most recent novel, published the previous year.

SH's quotation from Gerard Manley Hopkins's sonnet, 'I wake and feel the fell of dark, not day' – strictly, 'Selfyeast of spirit a dull dough sours' – would, if taken literally, imply some graver spiritual predicament than 'farting about'.

Gill and Macmillan are Dublin publishers.

To Michael Hartnett

MS NLI

15 June 1975

Glanmore Cottage, Ashford,
Co. Wicklow

Dear Michael,

I knew already that you like *North*, but I have to turn thanks for your telling me into thanksgiving that such open-handed praise and generosity can happen. That such good things should be said about the book is enhancing, but that you should have said them is a cause for rejoicing. I know that both of us envisage the poetic enterprise as something larger than a personal achievement or vindication and it is powerfully enabling to know that one's poems have passed into your sensibility and so into some larger continuum of the imagination.

Go raibh míle maith agat arís. Agus arís eile.

Seamus

'*Go raibh . . . eile*': 'A thousand thanks to you again. And again.'

To Michael Longley

MS Emory

17 June 1975

Glanmore Cottage, Ashford,
Co. Wicklow

Dear Michael,

That was the week that was: I went through it on a kind of exhausted high, beginning on Friday week in Derry with a 7 a.m. session in Friel's with young Deane; then out with the brothers in Bellaghy until 4 on Saturday; a catch-up of sorts on Sunday and then the boozy slide through Monday, Tuesday, Wednesday and Thursday evening home here. And then to Kilkenny for a reading on Friday. I'm only coming to.

Tuesday exhausted me in all kinds of ways: the signing session in the University bookshop for a start, talking minute by minute to people you half-knew. But that was nothing to the Museum, before and after the reading, and then the hotel. I wanted the people I knew and liked to be there but there were too many in the end to establish any kind of peace. However, it was a good night, I think; and I'm glad I didn't go over to your place – you probably had a better inquest without me anyhow.

Naturally, I'm gratified and appeased by the reviews so far – if only because the book has conquered the Dublin resistance, or begrudgers. Leaving aside the grandiloquence, as far as I can see the pressure of feeling got through to people – they seemed to need to *write* with some feeling themselves.

I am curious – nothing more – about what else is to come in the reviewing line; and in a hiatus in the poetic life, feeling quite emptied out. The three years in Glanmore seem to be closing themselves down quietly, and I am thinking about jobs, houses, schools – all the comforting urgencies that were a matter of indifference to me since I came here. I'll never regret the time I've had here, and the knowledge that it must come to an end in a year or so saddens me. Deliberate steps backward can be spaces for run-ups to leaps forward: I've grown in confidence, personally and poetically, through the experience.

I also meant what I said about gratitude in the museum that evening. It required a lot of tact and empathy for you and others in Belfast to keep the welcome in your hearts for me after my deliberate absenting of myself, and I am aware of a sustenance even in the solitude. But I am also aware that all of us have established by our work in the last decade a kind of continuum in the imagination of the people, north, south, from Connemara to Camden, and I believe that our separate enterprises from now on can only deepen and strengthen and amplify what was so well begun.

Which brings me to *Man Lying on a Wall*: you always had style, but this is a book with a style. It is so abundant and fluent, so delicate locally and tough generally, that I find it difficult to pick out individual poems. It's like a big plasm of Longleyism: if you cut it anywhere, it joins up, all mucus and membrane. I still have not a distance from it as a collection to sense contours and see shape, but I do have a strong sense of release, exuberance and insouciance, 'crying what I do is me, for this I came'.

Finally, ye hure ye, a problem. Between ourselves (between ourselves! ha, ha!) I have been approached to take a nice lucrative post (£5,000-ish p.a.) in Carysfort College of Education – for young ladies – starting in September. I haven't made up my mind, but if I do take it, I'll be reneging on the Mahon tour, or else we be to fit it into their Christmas holidays. When did we say we'd move anyhow? I'm saying this now so that you can work out contingency plans – although it might never happen.

Give my love to Edna and the children. Edward McGuire was asking for you, by the way; he thinks you're a nice man and, of course, I agreed.

Good luck to you, [illegible]
Seamus

Michael Longley had been among the large number attending the launch of *North* at the Ulster Museum, Belfast: 'a rather reverential occasion,' Longley remembers, with 'a fine reading, as always.'

'I am curious – nothing more – about what else is to come in the reviewing line': it was to include, in sharp contrast to overwhelming praise from the English press, two items in the *Honest Ulsterman* that he may have sensed were on their way: a scathing review by Ciaran Carson, who rebuked SH as 'the laureate of violence – a mythmaker, an anthropologist of ritual killing', and Edna Longley's unconvinced '"Inner Émigré" or "Artful Voyeur"? Seamus Heaney's *North*.'

SH must have seen a typescript of Longley's 1976 volume, *Man Lying on a Wall.*

Carysfort College of Education is in Blackrock, south Dublin. SH started there in the autumn, making the daily journey between Glanmore Cottage and Carysfort initially for a few days a week. He was grateful, also, for flexible terms of employment that allowed him leave to teach at Berkeley the following spring.

'crying what I do is me . . .': from Hopkins's 'As Kingfishers Catch Fire'.

Edward McGuire (1932–86) was the painter whose portrait of SH had adorned the back cover of the Faber paperback of *Wintering Out*.

To Robert Lowell

TS Harry Ransom

6 September 1975

Glanmore Cottage, Ashford,
Co. Wicklow

Dear Robert,

After that special and memorable time, I feel it not only proper but necessary to direct salutations towards you again: this time last week we were cloudy in that bar in Kilkenny. And while it is probably needless to say my gratitude for all the talk and the confirmation through and in the talk, I'm saying it anyhow. This is just to let you know that on Sunday 21st next, at around ten o'clock in the evening, there's a recording of a talk I did for the Third Programme being broadcast which I'd like you to hear if you can. It's a shortened version of a lecture I did for the Royal Society of Literature last year, an attempt at a mini-*Prelude*. It's a bit po-faced and narcissistic but there's a strong grain of truth in it also. I hope.

I'm enclosing also a poem I did a few months ago that came out of a visit to Cooke's in 1972, before we had left Belfast, when Barrie and Sonja were urging me to cut away from the academic life – if you could call what we had in Belfast academic life. I think it's more sure-footed than those too metrical and melodious sonnets that I now regret having given you.

Elgy's piece wasn't too bad in the end. Good, even. And the people at Radio Eireann were huffed that I hadn't made a recording/interview with you. I said that it wasn't possible in the domestic circumstances of the Cookery, so they said that if you wanted to come to Dublin at their expense at any time, that would be all right, and we could do it in a studio. So there the matter rests. I only mention it in case you ever feel like another weekend in the Dublin area – we could do a half-hour or forty-five-minute piece to be broadcast here when *The Day* appears, for example. But as far as I'm concerned, it's entirely up to yourself.

I don't suppose you got as far as Antibes: it was as much as I could do to make it back to Ashford. But I've finally got back in front of the desk, even if I haven't yet got into my stride.

All our love to yourself and Caroline and the children.

Seamus

PS I *should* have taken the Kent address – I'm sending this via Fabers.

S.

'special and memorable time': Lowell had not only agreed to read at the Kilkenny Festival, but he stayed on for several days.

The lecture, later broadcast, that SH recommends was 'Feeling into Words'.

'Elgy': the *Irish Times* journalist, Elgy Gillespie (b.1950), whose piece 'Robert Lowell in Kilkenny' had appeared in the paper on 4 September.

To Brian Friel

TS NLI

24 November 1975

Glanmore Cottage, Ashford,
Co. Wicklow

Dear Brian,

It was as good as a retreat to see yous. Friday with the head was a small price for Thursday with the high. On the other hand, I felt that Saturday night was just a bit uneasy – especially that time I was getting the exam on Deane as intellect versus Deane as poet. A body couldn't be half careful enough . . .

You made me feel I should be writing, which is all to the good. But really I can't see much by way of a feeding drip gathering up until the housing question is cleared and probably until the Berkeley excursion is over. However, I enclose one ('The Badgers') that I did about a month ago and the other one is a new version of something that I worked at but didn't work out a couple of years ago. Do you think the latter is publishable, given that Kinsella and Montague – and, yes, Sean Lucy – have been over the ground already? Alas for the perfect and aristocratic simplicity.

Talking of that: the touches that worried me were very much local effects – things small as (top of page 4) 'Dressed in cord jacket, bow-tie, greasy velour hat. I never knew much about his background except that . . .' – I'd be happier without that – it seems to caricature what is characterized in the run of adjectives just before that. Then 'I had a fairytale image . . .' is too self-conscious for me, though I realize he may be setting himself up self-consciously there. Then, top of page 5 – my inclination is to run – for some kind of naturalness, even though it's shorter on information – from 'And then there was Gracie, my mistress. A Yorkshire woman . . . She never asked for marriage' – and then I'd put in after 'adequate for her' 'Would have attempted to reform me . . . than her impulses.' Well, there it is. Rewriting another man's is a snip compared with the other.

I'd love a music as granite as Falcarragh and Gweebarra, a door into the light. *Faith Healer* is beautifully blocked in, nice architectonic. Reposed on itself. There be the unleavened elements.

All our love to all of you.

Seamus

'The Badgers' is in *Field Work*; the second poem is probably 'In Memoriam: Sean O'Riada', in the same volume.

Sean Lucy (1930–2001), whom SH spells 'Lucey', was a poet and colleague of John Montague's in the English Department at University College, Cork.

Friel's play *Faith Healer*, which consists of narrative monologues for three actors, was not performed until 1979. From the published text, he seems to have ignored SH's editorial suggestions.

To Michael Longley

PC Emory

[1975] [Postmarked 'Cookstown']

There was a young man from the Munchies Whose language would surely affront yez, It was fuck yez Hell roast yez Yez fuckin whores' ghosts yez, Yez bollocks, yez bastards, yez cunts yez. Yez are all right anyway.

R. Lowell

The postmark here is largely a blur: 'Cookstown' can be inferred from it, but the date is wholly illegible. Nonetheless, the year – pencilled in by an Emory archivist – seems right, being that of SH's friendliest encounter with Robert Lowell.

'Munchies': the Montiaghs, pronounced as SH writes it, is a townland in Co. Antrim, touching the south-east corner of Lough Neagh.

The image on the other side of the card is of Dante Gabriel Rossetti's *Beata Beatrix*.

1976

SH returned to teach at Berkeley, this time as Beckmann Professor, and gave as his Beckmann Lecture an account of the work of three contemporary British poets: Philip Larkin (1922–85), Ted Hughes and Geoffrey Hill (1932–2016). The text of this was printed, first, in the Spring 1977 issue of the magazine *Critical Inquiry*, under the title 'Now and in England', and then, as 'Englands of the Mind', in SH's first volume of prose, *Preoccupations* (1980).

Meanwhile, he maintained his connection with Barrie Cooke and the Kilkenny Arts Festival, inviting and hosting a more international round-up than the previous year's. Guests for 1976 included the Breton French poet Eugène Guillevic (1907–97), Judith Herzberg (b.1934) from the Netherlands, and the Gaelic-writing Scot Sorley MacLean (1911–96).

Finding a house to buy in Dublin was also heavily on his mind until the autumn, when the purchase of 191 Strand Road, Merrion, Dublin, SH's home for the rest of his life, was achieved.

To Paul Muldoon

TS Emory

6 February 1976

Glanmore Cottage, Ashford,
Co. Wicklow

Dear Paul,

It was a restoration to see you and encounter [you] in some kind of renewed way last week. And on second thoughts, perhaps there was too much melodrama in my bewilderment about the Hammond's behaviour – he was self-reproachful the next morning, and said (what I didn't know) that it was your first time in the house. Anyhow, it was a good night for us.

I didn't say in time, then or now, how beautiful and absolute I feel the poems in *Mules*. At once cut in ice and compacted with flowers, 'modern' in their solitude and 'traditional' in their intimations, art of love and scepticism. And of amplitude and intellect. Some day I'd hope to try to extend metaphorical casts at the stuff into an article – for I think I could rectify some mis- and incomprehensions – and that in spite of a contrary twisted declaration to you that night about not understanding.

I hope we meet before I go to Berkeley at the end of March. Meanwhile, I append the second dribble of thaw after the *North*ern frost. Love to you and Ann Marie.

Sincerely,
Seamus

'It was a restoration . . .': does SH mean to suggest recovery of his spirits after the critical battering that *North* received from some of his old Northern Irish associates?

'Ann Marie' was Anne-Marie Conway, Muldoon's wife.

Typed below the letter: an early, shorter version of 'The Harvest Bow'.

To Charles Monteith

TS Faber

23 February 1976

Glanmore Cottage, Ashford,
Co. Wicklow

Dear Charles,

Marie and I got over to London for the weekend but did not arrive until lateish Friday evening and were much afoot until we left on Sunday – so I did not think there was much point in trying to arrange a meeting. The ICA went well enough, I think – though a little tense for me with the full pantheon of Ulster poetry in the stalls – Hewitt, Montague, Muldoon, Foley, Ormsby – but the one consolation was that the night was a sell-out (of the seats, I mean). Anyhow. I should say also that this is a new typewriter and I'm not altogether at ease with it yet.

I'm not sure whether this is a personal or an official letter but since the distinction has never applied in the Faber context, I suppose it is just an ordinary one. It's a request for a favour, if possible. I'm wondering if I could have an advance of the royalties that should be accruing to *North*? This afternoon I saw a house in Dún Laoghaire – Georgian terrace, over basement, iron railings etc., you know the kind of thing – which is for auction on March 10. There is no guarantee that I'll get it, of course, for my price limit must be around £22,000, or rather, my loan limit is round 11–12 thousand. So what I'm suddenly trying to do is to assemble as large a deposit as I possibly can. I've got rid of the Belfast house and will probably clear about £6,000 on that; I've another couple tucked away out of the E. M. Foster award, and the rest is silence. The auctioneers said that they expected the property to go between 20–25, but as you know, anything could happen. However, if there was the chance that we could make it, I wouldn't like to lose it for the sake of a thousand or two at this moment. Property is likely to rise again here, and I am off to Berkeley for two and a half months on March 28 so I have this sudden urge to settle something before I go. We have been looking around constantly this past two months, and this is the first one that looks and feels like us – it's not, in other words, a case of impulse buying. It would also mean a lot, I think, to Marie if the house was there during my absence: something to work at and look forward to.

Do you think there is any chance of raising a four-figure sum from Harlow? A thing I noticed there is that the income tax are removing their cut at source – which I'll have to get cleared, since I am tax-free on that score here. I wonder if it were doled out as advance royalties could that be got around at the moment? Obviously, I'll be claiming back what has been deducted already once I get into my fiscal stride here. I don't know what sum to mention, but if the thing is at all possible, obviously I'd like as much as possible and would leave that to your good offices and good will.

If you could help here, you know how much it would mean to us, and I am therefore joining the ranks of the begging letters. Apart from everything else, there would be a room for the Faber representative within three minutes' walk of Kingstown Pier.

Anyway, Charles, I know if you can do anything you will, so although I am hopeful, I realize there may be hurdles to hold the thing up. I'm just high with anticipation about the auction.

If you have read this far, I thank you, as they say, in anticipation.

With every good wish,
Sincerely,
Seamus

'ICA': the Institute of Contemporary Arts in London.

Harlow, in Essex, is where Faber's accounts department is situated. Following SH's plea, Monteith sent an internal memo asking that royalties due to SH at the end of April be paid in full; even so, at the auction itself, the bidding exceeded SH's funds (see letters to John Montague of 12 July and to Brian Friel of 13 July 1976).

To Barrie Cooke

TS AND MS Pembroke

19 March 1976

Dear Barrie,

I suggest you try again:

[. . .]

Gradually, I see a line-up that is coherent – the idea of cultural cross-fertilization, sometimes in one language (Mackay Brown writing in English, living imaginatively off Norse deposits), sometimes in two (Crichton Smith), sometimes by translation (Davie, from Polish and Russian, tho' he would do his own poems too: and he's obsessed about English/American tensions and relationships). Then you have your last evening – French poet, Guillevic's – I'll do a few translations, and read others.

Therefore, you could well incorporate Máirtín Ó Díreáin – a man and poet of great dignity, strength and grace, a sure fire success 'on the night'. He paraphrases in English himself.

Also, perhaps, Hartnett/Lorca and a young Dublin poet Michael Smith who has translated Machado. (Both together for a Spanish/Irish evening?)

Food for thought.
Sorry, hurry.
Great Saint Patrick's Day.
Are you sending catalogue notes?
Sincerely,
The young man from the Munchies.

In the omitted passage, SH supplies Cooke with postal addresses for the Scottish poets George Mackay Brown and Iain Crichton Smith (1928–98), James Simmons, Seamus Deane, Eugène Guillevic, and the English poet Donald Davie (1922–95); the implication seems to be that Cooke had fallen short of his responsibilities as organiser of the Kilkenny Festival and been slow to send out invitations to participants. In the margin by Davie's name, SH writes, 'Lowell thinks a lot of this man – he taught at Trinity once. I like the idea of him. Very good man – occasionally v. good poet – has translated Pasternak in his time.'

Máirtín Ó Díreáin (1910–88), a native of the Aran Islands, wrote in Gaelic, but his poems also show a wider European influence.

Michael Hartnett's translation into English of Lorca's *Romancero Gitano* had appeared in 1973; the Dublin poet Michael Smith (1942–2014) translated not only Antonio Machado but many other important Spanish poets as well.

To Paul Muldoon PC Emory

[12? April 1976] [Postmarked 'Berkeley']

I thought this might look well on your bedroom wall, or wherever.

Berkeley is as Elysian as ever, and there are roughly 3,000 poets in the Bay Area. Bewildering. The bookshops are crammed with small press publications, there are readings everywhere and I can't bring myself to believe in any of it.

I hear your St Patrick's Night programme was excellent: I'm sorry we were travelling that day and missed it. All the best to you and Anne-Marie.

Seamus

The postcard reproduces a movie poster showing a pensive Constance Talmadge in Lewis J. Selznick's *Good Night, Paul.*

To David Hammond TS Emory

13 May 1976 68 Tamalpaid Road, Berkeley 94708

[. . .]

In Berkeley I stayed between the Flanagans and the Dillons (from Dublin) for two weeks and then got this place. It belongs to a retired professor and wife who have gone to New York for two months. A big mansion, with an acre of gardens. Earlier tonight a skunk walked over the terrace and during the day there's a squirrel and a blue-jay. Not to mention two lemon trees, an orange tree and an artichoke plant. I wish somebody could share it with me: the only bit of crack I've had has been the visit of the Chieftains to SF last week. I went over to a concert on Tuesday night, lay out in their hotel and spent the Wednesday with them. We ended up here in the afternoon and it was a pleasure to see them stripping down to their white farmer's bellies and facing into the bourbon on the rocks. A great success, as the man said.

Otherwise, I am teaching steadily, dining relentlessly with kindly faculty members who treat my bachelor status as a kind of pitiable outcast condition (fools and meddlers) and fending off the temptations.

I've read about twenty books of poems in manuscript by new and old friends, fended off about twenty more, and have only been into San Francisco twice. I suddenly realize that the trip is nearly over and I've been rushing and sweating since I landed. And to-morrow, for Christ's sake, I have to mark 20 essays. And I still have to write the public lecture for Monday next. Which reminds me, in an oblique way, how did *Standing Stones* work out? I've a cheek to even mention it.

I had offers from three places for jobs since I landed: Princeton, Columbia and Ann Arbor, but it's out of the question. I have this idea of settling quietly for the next three or four years and tilling the garden of my verses, not to mention working over the virgin territory of Carysfort. I also intimated to them that I would be interested in the headship, but it's by no means certain that I'd get it. Brian Cosgrove from UCD has applied, and Kilroy too. But at this moment, I don't give a shite.

I had a card from Friel to-day: 'Come home with your shield or on it': how can you follow that?

[. . .]

'a skunk walked over the terrace . . . I wish somebody could share it with me': very likely the 'intent and glamorous, / Ordinary, mysterious' creature in SH's unconventional love poem, 'The Skunk'.

'Come home with your shield or on it': according to Plutarch, the injunction of Spartan mothers to their sons as they went off to fight.

To David Hammond

PC Emory

[1976] [Postmarked 'Berkeley']

The minute I saw him I thought of you. My life at the massage parlour changed the minute you walked in the door. It has become a bye-word with us, your first words, remember? 'How far would ye go for fifty bob?' We've had times. I miss your guitar: I hope I didn't damage it irrevocably.

Sadie

Undatable, thanks to the postmark, which makes only 1976 clear.

David Hammond is described in *Stepping Stones* as, among other things, 'a free spirit, up to all kinds of pranks and carry-on', and the exchange of practical jokes between him and SH was an enduring element of their friendship. The image on the other side of the written message is taken from an advertisement for 'Dr Pierce's Medical Adviser', and shows a muscular male figure wearing only a leopard-skin loin cloth, holding a stout club and surrounded by an array of patent medicines. The card, with its openly readable message, is addressed to Hammond at his place of work, the BBC in Belfast.

To Brian Friel

MS NLI

3 July 1976

Glanmore Cottage, Ashford,
Co. Wicklow

Dear Brian,

Thank you both for a good day and night: the good form you remarked in me was generated on the spot!

The Hammond man came to Bellaghy on Thursday morning and we killed the day with him until train-time at 5:30 – after a day of wobbly intercourse between Flanagan and the rustic community. Good will on both sides but 'He's awful quiet' etc. spoken in earshot of the enigma himself.

I'm not going to get settled here for a day or two. This housing bother upsets everything.

I'll see you soon, I hope. Love to Anne. And thanks again.

Seamus

Written shortly after SH's return from Berkeley, after which the small scale of Glanmore Cottage seems to have been felt as irksome.

To John Montague

MS Cork

12 July 1976

Glanmore Cottage, Ashford,
Co. Wicklow

Dear John,

It's pure coincidence that the twelfth should start the juices running, or is it? I'm back from Berkeley, incredibly, a month. I spent two weeks on exams, a week north, and last week frantically to-ing and fro-ing to Dublin about a house in Sandymount. Which I funked in the end, at the auction. I'm in a furious mess over the housing question. This place is a hell-hole because of lack of space. Five of us straining for elbow room, like Mahon's mushrooms. The launderette in Wicklow has closed down, so Marie washes for four of us and herself in the bath.

Hardy ould stuff. As to the life of the mind . . . it's locked, until her bridegroom brings her to a house . . . I don't know whether to try in Dublin or here. There's a fine stone establishment coming on the market up the road from us – behind the windowed wall you can see from our place – and something in me stirs at the possibility of living in the green otherwhere of Glanmore and travelling to work. But the schools for the boys in the next ten years would be the Brothers at either Bray or Wicklow and *je me demande*. Then there is the absence of any context of civility whatsoever, the isolation involved for Marie, the long trek to the slightest commitment in Dublin . . . I am inclined one way and another, day by day. To live within walking distance of Carysfort would be a great conservation of energy, and the schools situation would be better, we might get to the pictures or to a play sometimes . . . Yet we'd be walking out of an enhancing corner of the land, deliberately. Something will have to be done soon, despite the mortgage. *Ochone*.

I was glad to hear from you in Berkeley, which was its sunlit self. I had very little leisure there, landing a day before classes started, leaving (with exams marked) on the last day, and meanwhile making a trip east for 6 days and two darts to LA and Sta Barbara. I got a few quid for a deposit, but little real satisfaction in the hurry. Nevertheless, just to be in that honed-up world of academic chat was exhilarating. Parkinson was to come to Ireland in August but has reneged: he's a bit more tremulous as a result of the illness, certainly, but physically, he seems to be all right. Bob Tracy is manfully and impressively dug into Mandelstam – and you'll be seeing him, and translations, soon, so he'll report on the Heaney presence, no doubt. I had an excellent day in SF with a few Chieftains – Moloney, Potts and Keane – and ended up at my house in Berkeley, which was an excellent stroke: I was in Mark Schorer's mansion in the hills north of campus. It has a little railway up the side of the slope, and it gave me great pleasure to elevate the hungover remnants, electrically, toward whiskey and vodka among the orange-trees of the garden. They did a mighty concert.

I did very little except teach, dine, mark, read, sleep, walk. Some verses, but I couldn't settle to it. All has been in transition this last year – the leaving-of-Belfast adventure has come home to roost, and I have to commit myself to a permanent base or basis, and the simple choice and the financial prospects seem to daunt me abnormally. I feel like Gulliver with the Lilliputian net pegged over his head.

[. . .]

12 July, often referred to simply as 'the Twelfth', is a day of celebration and parading for Ulster Protestant Loyalists, or 'Orangemen' – neither SH's own kind nor Montague's.

'like Mahon's mushrooms': see Derek Mahon's poem 'A Disused Shed in Co. Wexford'.

'the Brothers': i.e. Christian Brothers, educational order within the Catholic Church.

To Brian Friel

TS NLI

13 July 1976

Glanmore Cottage, Ashford,
Co. Wicklow

[. . .]
I bid for a house in Sandymount last Thursday but funked it after £27,000 – I hadn't a loan arranged and the thing went for £28,500. I'm just as well without it, I think, because it would have needed a few thousand spent and if I'd gone on even another one or two grand, I could not have spent a penny on it. Despite a hankering to lie out in the farmhouse, it's coming in on me more and more that Dublin would be so much handier. I'm thinking now even of living, if possible, within walking distance of work – so that it could be treated as a distraction to one's life, rather than occupying a central role, involving an expedition of hours and a corresponding waste of energy. I can think about nothing else – and with the kids on holiday here and Marie out at the course in Dublin, the mind is driven to pondering conflicting claims. I get into blind furies because of the impossibility of silence and study here: the summer is my only time just now, and it's utterly shot to bits. They're up round me here at this minute. Anyway, soon, I hope, a move will be initiated.
[. . .]

To Ted Hughes

TS Emory

22 July 1976

Glanmore Cottage, Ashford,
Co. Wicklow

Dear Ted,

This very conjugal notepaper was a present from friends in Berkeley – I was there for the spring quarter – and since our address is likely to be changing in the next couple of months I am possessed of an unusual impetus to write letters. I am to go to Totleigh Barton from September 10 until September 15, and I was hoping that you might be at home then so that we could meet, maybe the day before or after the course – or maybe the place is near enough to connect during the proceedings. John McGahern is the other tutor so I am looking forward to it.

[. . .]

I got the American edition of *Season Songs* which is a beauty, lovely amplitudes and weathers in the poems, the colds of them taking me most. The wind that blew through Poor Tom's hawthorn is still raising gooseflesh.

And talking of the poems, I included the 'Leaves' one in a BBC schools broadcast, with others from the Early Irish, Bashō, Eskimo, Elizabeth Bishop's 'Giant Snail' and a couple of American Indian invocations: I'm wondering just now if you'd like to read your own and a couple of the others – or suggest an actor in their rep. who would have the feel for them? I hope to record that script when I'm over in September also.

My good wishes to Carol; and I hope you keep as buoyantly and abundantly at work as ever.

Sláinte,

Seamus

The 'conjugal notepaper', used also in a number of the previous letters of 1976, is headed 'Seamus and Marie Heaney', with address underneath, in an 'Irish' typeface.

Totleigh Barton, in North Devon and not far from Hughes's home, is one of the centres of the Arvon Foundation, which hosts week-long writing courses.

'Poor Tom's hawthorn': see Act III, Scene 4 of *King Lear*.

To Brian Friel

MS NLI

29 November 1976 — 191 Strand Road, Dublin 4

A Bhriain,

I should have written before – I'm without a phone here and will be for a couple of weeks, unless at Carysfort (887336) – but between the moving and the motions (Mahon over Saturday for D. Devlin award, Longley, Muldoon etc. on rampage; then I read with Mahon in Cork last night, surfing the Montague undertow) I'm only getting to it now. It was a great pleasure to have you on the London jaunt, and I hope you got your freedom on Thursday and Friday. I felt after it that the rush and push of Tuesday and Wednesday was really only a preparation – a body should have stayed and kicked about more. But it was impossible for me. Anyway, I'm proud of ye.

Mahon was in very good form and conducted himself. Montague conducted himself too, but he struck me this time as a bit of a gipe. He was going [on] about a party in O'Tuama's in a way that was half silly preening, half stupid ould flyness. A good enough weekend, and it was worth it, just to clear the air and fix the distance. I believe Mahon is in with a good chance for a writer-in-residence at Coleraine.

The house is a great success – the heart lifts, even if the body shivers. I'm disinclined to turn on the electric heaters all over the place. One initial bad thing is that we have a burst pipe somewhere, so no hot water. We hope to get that fixed soon, and then the Raeburn cooker has to go in. By Christmas, we should be in production. We still haven't fully moved, but are colonizing a few rooms. *Deo gratias* anyway. I feel it will be a reposing and enabling ground. Say a prayer for me . . .

McGahern is coming to Carysfort next Tuesday, so that's another event.

There's room here anyway, and it would be a restoration to see you some time. I'll have to go up to see my mother next weekend – she's in hospital, under traction – disoriented, I'm sure. But I'd likely go on the bus. If there's a chance of a connection, we'll make one then. Meanwhile, good luck, and love to Anne.

Sincerely,
Seamus

'191 Strand Road': as SH reported to Charles Monteith in a letter of 15 October, the Heaneys had 'got the house at auction, just at our limit of £28,500'.

'gipe': more commonly 'gype', meaning an awkward or loutish person.

Derek Mahon was to spend a year as writer-in-residence at the New University of Ulster in Coleraine, 1978–9.

1977

In the middle of the year, SH was able to tell Brian Friel: 'There are a couple of free months ahead, and the financial situation all round is not as disastrous as I had fantasized.' The note of precarious improvisation is audible, but evidently a workable *modus vivendi*, with the salaried job at Carysfort College allowing a measure of freedom to write and to cultivate a public profile, was now established. The house on Strand Road was hospitably open to visitors from far and wide, while Glanmore Cottage, relinquished as a home for the time being, was celebrated in a limited edition of the sequence 'Glanmore Sonnets'.

To John L. Sweeney

MS UCD

15 March 1977 — 191 Strand Road, Dublin 4

Dear Jack,

How do you *thole* people who never answer your letters? You are very good to write again: I'd been feeling so guilty over a request I got a couple of years ago for the script of a documentary on literary magazines from the north. The fact of the matter was that there was no physical script, no typescript; the piece was a jig-saw of photocopied quotations and scribbled links, all last-minute work. And the job of tidying and typing never got done. Unprofessional, sadly; and in the end unmannerly not to reply.

I have left Glanmore, and moved to Sandymount Strand Road, having taken a teaching post at Carysfort College of Education. It means that life is busier, but I hope that sooner or later I will establish routines to give a part of my day every day to my own work and the rest to other matters. I've always had a very ragged and impulsive working schedule, but I believe that if the enterprise is to be sustained, a deliberate approach to one's time and energy is called for.

I haven't written a lot since *North* and no book is in the offing. I enclose a short love poem that I'm fond of, and hope that before the end of the summer Marie and I will see you and Máire again. Our memories of our visits with you are heartening and restorative.

With every good wish,

Sincerely,

Seamus

PS The green pen is accidental, but since it's Patrick's Day soon, I thought I might as well go through with it!

S.

The radio script that Jack Sweeney appears to have requested is unidentified.

The poem SH encloses, in manuscript and dated 'Patrick's Day, March 1977', is 'Homecomings', later included in *Field Work*.

To Ted Hughes

MS Emory

22 May 1977 191 Strand Road, Dublin 4

Dear Ted,

I've read *Gaudete* twice and was deeply pleasured by it each time. Since there's nothing else like it, there's no ready-made lingo for saying what it does, but I feel the shape of the story was a plough that got deep into the ground of your gift and opened it marvellously. The abundance of the thing from line to line is a blessing: I had to say something about it on Irish radio, and I mentioned *Leaves of Grass* – not that it's the proper comparison in other ways – but in this magnificent opulent epiphany of a sensibility and an unmatched energy, I thought the allusion was just right. What you were saying at – I think – Loughborough, about writing headlong, without the brakes of nicety, has paid off. And the whole 'Epilogue' sequence sings in context – songs of a man who has come through. It did me good to read it.

I thought I might have got over to Charles Monteith's do last Wednesday but we're up to the ass in exams here and anyway, Westminster School, whom I was relying on for expenses, didn't come through.

Maybe I'll get over for a few days during the summer: it would be good if we could break the back of the anthology before it gets on our backs. Are you happy with the terms Monteith offered? I haven't done anything about that side of things, and won't, until I hear from you.

Sláinte,

Seamus

The comparison of Hughes's *Gaudete* – which the author himself once described as 'a collision between a debased demonish spirit-power . . . and the sterile gentility of a Southern English village' – with Whitman's *Leaves of Grass* suggests the measure of SH's bewilderment. More to the point is his implicit invocation of D. H. Lawrence, who, in his book of poems *Look! We have Come Through* (1917), first liberated himself from strict form and so may be said to have written 'headlong, without the brakes of nicety'.

The anthology mentioned in the final paragraph is what five years later was published as *The Rattle Bag*.

To Brian Friel

MS NLI

6 July 1977 — 191 Strand Road, Dublin 4

Dear Brian,

Sorry to have missed you en route to London. That weekend we were in Aberystwyth: I had to do a trick on the Friday and Saturday for the Extra-Mural Department of the University so we all travelled by car and ferry: had a good break. It was a busy month of June – the exams continually, but interspersed with visiting Americans and a terrific five-day trip to Rotterdam. Her ladyship came with me at half-fare and we really got great pleasure out of the thing. The Dutch were very decent hosts and delivered $250 for a 20-minute stint (at Poetry International) so we were hardly out of pocket at all. But all being well, the summer should settle from now on and a bit of reading and composure set in. I'm going to get the hair cut this afternoon – and taking the boys, the first time they've been to a barber's. *O tempora, o mores.*

The election will have pleased you: I got a sense of hope for the first time when I saw them all to-day on the *Irish Times*, nest-featherers and chest-beaters, chancers and bouncers. One result is that Máire C. O'B. rang me to sponsor Conor for the Senate. I told her I was sponsoring Gus Martin – which I was – and would leave it to his lordship. But he's using the name all the same. I've suddenly got a violent dislike for the man – I thought he was engaging in an educational venture but I think now it's really egotistical and, well, west British. But there I am. (De Paor also asked me to sponsor him, and again, I had to leave it to himself. I don't know whether he'll use me or not.) Rent-a-poet at last!

I saw the angelic doctor on Monday – he was at the exam board with me – and we had a depressed drink. He was in the doldrums over some class of a row at home: temporary and in the nature of things – but he was in one of those downspins. The builders are still in the house; and Conor is back from a holiday on Aran, talking about 'seducting girls' . . .

I find it hard to believe Hammond ever got set off for Florence. I advised him to overdraw and have an easy time. Not that he would need much of that class of encouragement. He seems to have had a hellish rush of work just before leaving but no doubt all was in order as he piped them aboard on Saturday morning.

I'm up to the ass in unanswered letters myself but have a chance to get at them now. For the first time since I joined Carysfort, I feel some sense of pay-off. There are a couple of free months ahead, and the financial situation all round is not as disastrous as I had fantasized. This last prompted by the recovery of £725 this morning which a shite of an auctioneer had retained since last August after I reneged on the house in Monkstown – it cost £90 to get it back, but it was sweet.

We hope to see *Equus* on Friday night – I've been at nothing since the MacIntyre debacle. I'd like to see *Brief Lives* too, but I'm not sure I'll make that.

I also have a half-notion of taking a few days to myself in London, just going to a couple of Shakespeare plays and seeing a friend or two – like Karl Miller, whom I haven't really talked to for years. Marie wants me to so she can get on the pad again herself with a clear conscience. Surely, surely.

I had in my head to go to see youse after August 10 – the day I lecture at Sligo. But what I'd really enjoy would be a sudden skip up before that: I won't promise anything, however, because a while at the desk is deeply called for; never mind what might result, the old peace dropping slow would be a bonus in itself.

I look forward to seeing you, sooner or later. I hope the summer is restorative and that we have the opportunity to wrest a few days' summit conference from it. Our love to Anne and the family.

Slaynt,

Seamus

PS Does London last week bode well for *Triptych*?

PPS Kilroy got the doctor's job at UCD for next year – and I heard from Monteith that McGahern's father died a few weeks ago. I wrote him a note yesterday.

The other thing is that I had the right arm in a sling all last week

– and it's still bandaged. I burned it from the elbow down with boiling coffee. Never help in the kitchen! S

Poetry International is Rotterdam's annual poetry festival.

In the Irish general election of this year, Fianna Fáil, led by Jack Lynch, was voted in by an unforeseen landslide. 'Maíre C. O'B' was Conor Cruise O'Brien's wife, better known as Máire Mhac an tSaoi (1922–2021), Irish-language poet and scholar; Augustine ('Gus') Martin (1935–95) was an Anglo-Irish scholar and member of the Seanad Éireann from 1973 to 1981; Liam de Paor (1926–98) was the author of, among other works, *Divided Ulster* (1970), an account of the Troubles, and a member of the Labour Party.

The 'angelic doctor' must be Seamus Deane.

Equus by British playwright Peter Shaffer (1926–2016) was running at the Gate Theatre in Dublin; *Brief Lives* was a one-man show with a script adapted from the gossipy potted biographies of John Aubrey (1626–97), Aubrey himself being played by the British actor Roy Dotrice (1923–2017).

'MacIntyre debacle': perhaps a reference to Tom MacIntyre's play, *Find the Lady*, which had premiered at the Abbey Theatre in May – or even to his *Jack Be Nimble*, of the year before.

To Thomas Flanagan MS Amherst

18 October 1977 191 Strand Road, Dublin 4

Dear Tom,

I should have been buckling to this page long ago – 'brute beauty and valour . . .' – but the Strand Road Hotel is still making a few demands. Last week we had Shirley Samuels, erstwhile Berkeley writing student (*Fuck!* says Mrs Heaney), the Cooke family, John McGahern and Marie's sister and children from England (*Fuck!* says Mr Heaney). Anyhow, the house is silent for an hour or two – I thought it was, the electrician has just arrived. We had to have the whole place rewired in the last three weeks, just to add to the confusion. Here's how: Tradesman A was engaged to sand the boards in the bedroom and put a gloss on them. In the course of his work, he fused the electricity. Tradesman B called in emergency. He reveals dangerous and decayed system of wires all over the place. Tradesman C called in to overhaul system. Walls ripped open, floorboards up, carpets torn away (all the stuff off the downstairs rooms). Result – what was to be a £50 job turns into £500. *Eheu*, as the Latin poet would put it.

My trip to Stony Brook reassured me about your move. I had an extremely hospitable, quiet time with the Simpsons, who are much looking forward to your arrival. I got a better sense both of the campus and the environs and both improved with knowing. I was there from Monday 26 until Friday 30 September; did office hours in the morning, an interview with Louis for the University TV, a lecture to an undergraduate group and a reading which, luckily, was not anti-climactic. Louis is a magnificently crisp manager on these occasions, clocking you in and out with all the scrupulous meanness (towards the system) of a shop-steward, then turning princely in his own palace. Levine repeated the invitation to come for a semester, so who knows but we may have a reunion on your side in a couple of years' time.

I also met Jack Thompson and was glad to – that week I was preparing a memorial address on Robert Lowell that I gave in London on October 5, from the pulpit of St Luke's Church. I was both honoured and uneasy to be asked to do it – what with Alvarez and Ted Hughes and William Empson and other hounds of heaven in the congregation – so the finished piece inclined to the marmoreal (as you will shortly see in the *TLS*). I think I was asked by Caroline because she and the great man had been here for a night on the Tuesday before he died in New York. It was a happy enough occasion – I guess because Marie and I have maintained the half-fiction that they were settled man and wife and therefore in our company they simulated a security between themselves that became real enough for those few hours. Anyhow, it was one of those confirming moments, and I felt I was fully fledged in the friendship – no longer diffident – *et alors*, the end. Marie and I were shaken and sorry. And now Caroline is back in Castletown, boozing and depressed and astray, ringing us regularly, hunting for company which we are too busy to give.

[. . .]

'brute beauty and valour': see 'The Windhover' by Gerard Manley Hopkins.

'*Eheu*': 'Alas', as in Horace's '*Eheu fugaces, Postume, Postume, / labuntur anni . . .*'

Flanagan was about to leave Berkeley to take up a post at the State University of New York, Stony Brook; Louis Simpson, a mutual friend, taught there.

'scrupulous meanness': James Joyce's own description of his prose style in *Dubliners*.

John ('Jack') Thomson (1918–2002), who had been a friend of Robert Lowell's since college days, also taught at Stony Brook.

Robert Lowell had died on 12 September, on his way to rejoin his ex-wife, the novelist and literary critic Elizabeth Hardwick (1916–2007), in the USA, only a few days after dining at the Heaneys' in Dublin.

To Michael Longley

MS Emory

15 November 1977 191 Strand Road, Dublin 4

[. . .]

Enclosed is the Lowell piece and a poem that came quickly after the news of his death. I should have sent it to you before this, and thanked you for the rich garden and haggard and graveyard of verses you let me have six weeks ago. My favourite pieces were 'Wreaths', 'Monologues', the sonnets and (especially) 'The Linen Industry' – but the whole web of the work is rich and sure, a great sense of repose and fluency. I have so much rebuked the lyric in myself that I have been shy of such riches, but there is a tide in the affairs of verse too, and I find myself surrendering to this new work of yours with much pleasure. It is indeed important that we are all working – something of the old capillary action between the tap roots is under way again perhaps.

[. . .]

'Wreaths', 'Mayo Monologues' and 'The Linen Industry' are all in Longley's 1979 volume *The Echo Gate*. A haggard is an enclosed area, adjacent to a farmyard, where crops are stored.

To Seamus Deane

MS Emory

3 December 1977 191 Strand Road, Dublin 4

Dear Seamus,

The house is quiet – Marie and the kids are in Kilkenny – and I've just come back into it after being over in London. Your letter was here and lifted the lagging spirit enormously. *Retarius* may be wrong, *retiarius*? Anyway, he was the net-wielder in the arena; I always thought Owen Kelly (remember him as Caliban in the college?) was cut out to be one.

I am delighted that the mortal frame is no longer such a rack for you. It was awful news, fear-bringing, sorrow-raising, but I rejoice that your grace and guts sustain and retain you. We all wince away from imagining the pains of others, but the pain and the terror both must have been like axes at your tree of life. What a durable stump you are. It must have been a black nightmare in the first weeks, physically, psychologically, financially. The fucking money-fears are so cruel as well as all the rest. I am at the moment *in medias* of *res* like that, over £2,000 overdrawn and the water rising. What was it Ralph Hodgson said about 'stand and stare'?

Your good words about the Lowell poem have given me a rush of confidence. I think it should have the first stanza lopped: the remark was made by Pasternak, anyhow, and it seems there that it is Lowell's. It's strangely abstract to have been done in the grip of the feeling, but anyhow.

I see myself doing far too much hack work, dissipating energy, rushing, neglecting the silence or neglecting to fence it off and graze in it deliberately. But I hope to create order soon. I cancelled a proposed trip to Australia, and a possible summer school in BU. The ideal would be to live on one's salary and go on such jaunts as rewards to one's self for work completed. But at my back I always hear the Bank of Ireland hurrying near.

I was in Coleraine last week because Derek Mahon asked me and I didn't want him to think me distant by putting it off, though God knows I could have done without it. But he seemed in the financial and domestic horrors too. Unfortunately, he was very drunk in the course of his confessions, and had had a row with Doreen that morning. He's writer-in-residence at the New University, and they've got a house in Portstewart. Two children now. He's not cut out for the *paterfamilias* stuff (not that I can be smug about my lad-of-the-chimney-corner status) and the lack of security seems to have him rattled at the moment. The consequent bibulous dolor meant that I did not get out to confessions in Muff, but went down to Bellaghy a day early. I was sorry to miss Brian, and have not been in touch since the night Martin spoiled here.

[. . .]

Long poem! You're right not to let it out until you are well established in labour. Nest on it and it grows under you better. Contemplate it like a revenge. Pursue the verse-form, exhilarate, indulge: all your energy will come with you, and it is capable of the *enormous*. You have the gift for astonishing and you should not even slightly hold yourself back. If humanly possible, keep the three months clear for writing. Yes, Daddy, I hear you cry.

[. . .]

Owen Kelly: immortalised in the opening lines of 'The Real Names', a poem written by SH many years later and included in *Electric Light* (2001): 'Enter Owen Kelly, loping and gowling, / His underlip and lower jaw ill-set, / A mad turn in his eye, his shot-putter's / Neck and shoulders still a schoolboy's.'

It was W. H. Davies (1871–1940), who wrote the more frequently quoted lines, 'What is this life if, full of care, / We have no time to stand and stare'; but SH may conceivably have had in mind these lines from the poem 'The Song of Honour' by Davies's contemporary Ralph Hodgson (1871–1962): 'I stood and stared; the sky was lit, / The sky was stars all over it, / I stood, I knew not why, / Without a wish, without a will, / I stood upon that silent hill / And stared into the sky until / My eyes were blind with stars and still / I stared into the sky.'

The 'Lowell poem' was 'Elegy', written soon after Robert Lowell's death and included in *Field Work* two years later: its first three lines, 'The way we are living, / timorous or bold / will have been our life', could derive from Pasternak, who had a marked penchant for aphorisms about life, but I have not been able to trace them to any unambiguous source.

Doreen Mahon (née Douglas) had been married to Derek since 1972 and, though long separated, was still married to him at her death in 2010.

'Muff': in Donegal, where Brian and Anne Friel lived and where the 'confessions' were unlikely to have been of a religious nature.

1978

In addition to the volume of new poems that in 1979 would appear as *Field Work*, the retrospective labour involved in the planning and preparation of two separate selections of his poetry – *Selected Poems 1965–1975* for Faber, and *Poems 1965–1975* for his recently acquired US publisher, Farrar, Straus and Giroux – as well as of *Preoccupations: Selected Prose 1968–1978* (all three books to be published in 1980) suggests SH's arrival at a point from which he could survey and summarise his already substantial achievements with a measure of satisfaction. As for the future, he had a new temporary lecturing job at Harvard University to look forward to: one that would enlarge his scope perhaps more than he could predict, fixing him in the role of travelling, lecturing, poetry-reciting and pomp-attending public figure that would consume more and more of his time and energy.

To Michael Longley — MS Emory

4 January 1978 — 191 Strand Road, Dublin 4

Dear Michael,

Rotten with the cold, enervated by Christmas and the New Year, unwriting, doomed to lectures that I have not written and broadcasts that I have no stomach for, what else is there but to write to you?

It was a pity to miss you in December, but one is so caught up, one had better get off the hook. I heard one of the broadcasts – very sexy, with Cummings and Rodgers. I could hear the horn in your microphone work.

How is Mahon? I dropped him a note before Christmas and half-expected that he might make a motion in this direction. It was unfortunate that our afternoon there shambled into confusion, because it began so hospitably and auspiciously. I really should convey official gratitude and congratulations to you for the way things were set up.

Marie is howling about downstairs. Life is wonderful: remember the time our servants did it for us?

I am stiff and dull as to verse. Cannot even muster the energy to type out things I have revised. Say a prayer for me. Too laden with fucking things I should never have taken on: like 'The Sense of Place' – it seemed like a good idea at the time, but it's only a time waster and a scrabble for stuff to fill 60 minutes.

Sorry to whinge and sprawl. I just wanted to say Happy New Year and wish you ease and abundance and more linen trade than ever in the next twelve months. Love to the family. Maybe see you next week.

Sláinte,
Seamus

'The Sense of Place', a public lecture given at the Ulster Museum, offers a survey of Irish poets – Kavanagh, Montague and others – and their relationship to the home landscape: 'a good idea at the time' and good enough to be included in SH's first book of prose writings, *Preoccupations* (1980).

'more linen trade than ever': see SH's letter to Longley of 15 November 1977.

To Robert Fitzgerald

MS Harvard

12 May 1978 191 Strand Road, Dublin 4

Dear Robert,

That telegram with the Harvard Invitation was one of the most enlivening things that has happened to me. Gradually the gift and honour of the thing has seeped in and I have to say how richly thankful I am to you for your good offices on my behalf. What I anticipate with special pleasure is the time: it's the first occasion when the teaching consists only of writing classes, so the preparation and correction loads are so much lighter. I may even get established in labour at my own work.

I like the idea of the workshop for advanced students and then a more regulated, reading-and-writing course. I found in Berkeley that my writing class was where I *really* got to grips with the poems of the past – Wyatt and Ralegh's 'Three things there are . . .' in the field of the sonnet, for example, with students who would have disdained a course on Renaissance Poetry. Anyhow, I look forward to working things out.

I am writing today to Monroe Engel and to the Chairman to confirm things officially.

When the end-of-term hurly-burly settles here, I must send you some new poems. In the meantime, *gaudeo*. And it is proper, I think, that I should make a sign of my gratitude with the enclosed which has just been got out by Faber (privately, of course). Thank you again. I look forward to my time in Cambridge.

Sincerely,
Seamus

Robert Fitzgerald (1910–85), a poet celebrated mainly for his translations from the Classics, was Boylston Professor of Rhetoric and Oratory at Harvard University, a post that SH himself would occupy later; Monroe Engel (1921–2014), novelist, was also a member of Harvard's English Department, teaching creative writing.

'*gaudeo*': 'I rejoice'.

The item enclosed 'privately' was probably *Robert Lowell: A Memorial Address and an Elegy*, newly published by Faber in a limited edition.

To Michael Longley

MS Emory

24 May 1978 [London]

Dear Michael –

Actually, I'm in London. The only time I seem to have to get into myself and my letters is when I'm afoot.

'Home Ground' I like a lot: what about switching townland names for initials – those who know S.H. and P.M. will know Mossbawn and Keenaghan, or Broagh, to be precise. But I see the difficulty of calling another poem 'Broagh'.

Those moon-rocks ripening are beautiful.

I'm translating (!) a canto of the *Inferno* by the well-known Florentine Catholic. End of 32, most of 33: no prizes for guessing who figures there. In a way, it merges with the elegies for Sean Armstrong and Louis O'Neill – and matches what's happening in H Block.

The Arts Council day was good and I think just about right in the balance between good rhetoric, good intentions and hard decisions. And, my dear man, my remarks about eptitude and its opposite were all ironical and playful – you are the least inept man I know, and I'm surprised that you do not know this yourself. But then, like myself, you are so unselfconscious . . . ye cunt ye.

Derek rang and said he would like to come down and I hope he does. I feel that I should slough off a whole straight life here for a few days and re-enter the young poet's life and dally in Belfast and Coleraine for a week, just drinking and talking. And I still may do it – though I spoil my chances on the home front by being so much away like this. I did a good lecture on Yeats in the University of Surrey last night and I have to go to St Andrews to-morrow.

And that ends it for the summer.

I hope we meet soon. When I get the Italian *completo* I'll send it to you.

I heard, by the way, of a loyalist who referred to Micheál Mac Liammóir as a 'fenian pouf': dead on, eh.

Love to Edna and the weans.

Seamus

Actually, I'm in London: written on 191 Strand Road headed paper.

'Home Ground' is a poem in two parts, the first dedicated to SH, the second to John Montague; the latter ends on the line, 'There the moon-rocks ripen in your hand.'

The cantos from Dante's *Inferno* that SH was working on gave him the poem 'Ugolino', which comes at the end of *Field Work*. In it, Ugolino is punished horribly – buried up to his neck in ice and gnawing at the head of his enemy, buried next to him – for his treachery. (Two months later, Charles Monteith wrote to SH: 'The more I re-read "Ugolino" the more impressed by it I am; and I'll be delighted – and excited – if you do decide to tackle the whole *Inferno*' – a publisher's wild hope destined to be disappointed.) The elegies SH mentions are 'A Postcard from North Antrim' and 'Casualty', which are also in *Field Work*. The 'dirty protests' at Maze Prison's H Block, where members of the IRA and INLA were incarcerated, were current.

'The Arts Council day': a joint meeting of the Belfast and Dublin Arts Councils, SH being on the board of the latter, when for the first time, in a spirit of optimism, the possibilities of cross-border co-operation were discussed.

The Yeats lecture, 'Yeats as an Example?', was to be included in *Preoccupations*.

Micheál Mac Liammóir (1899–1978) was a British actor, impresario and writer, who changed his name from Alfred Willmore and adopted Dublin as his home; his romantic partnership with the producer Hilton Edwards (1903–82) was unconcealed and generally tolerated, the two of them being known about town as 'The Boys'.

To Seamus Deane

MS Emory

24 May 1978 [London]

Dear Seamus,

This is ridiculous. I'm in London, staying a day with Karl Miller, between a lecture last night in Surrey University and a reading to-morrow in Edinburgh: but it seems that these times in the silence of another person's home and in the oasis of time pulled out of Dublin's hurry are the only times when I sit down and take stock. And I've taken stock often of the need to write but have waited until that mythic moment when I could do a 'proper' letter and then, naturally, did fuck all.

The six months since I wrote have been the usual hurly-burly. Too much activity, too little time in the study. Then as well as the afflictions I brought upon myself there was the flu which kept me in bed for three weeks (abscesses on the teeth forbye!) and which got me off the fags as a side effect. Not a *toitín* since January 12 – but I smoke about five cigars a day. Anyway.

How is the form and the frame and the family? I bet you'd like to stay in that kindly sunlit arena with all the people whom I have not written to – Flanagans and Tracys and Parkinsons, to name but a few. I think Marie has written to the latters, but can you tell Bob T. that I can certainly fix him up in suburban semi-detached country – Dundrum or Stillorgan – still, for July.

Tom Kilroy tells me that a severe reprimand was delivered because the 'Group' was not meeting here, and I must say it is deserved. I regret not having seen more of the Professor during his stay. We did try to pack a lot in one night about six weeks ago when B.F. was in town, but the usual hurry of alcohol all round kept the proceedings more hilarious than heuristic. Then I went off for what was to be a healing or at least a quiet weekend with B.F. and D. Hammond a fortnight ago – up to Kincasslagh, all boys out together – and that turned into a pub crawl too. A certain amount of ecstasy, naturally, but again, enlightenment thin on the ground. There seems to be nothing for it but the study and sedentary toil.

Brian has been in flat form, I think, and the whole absence after his mother's death and, of course, Anne's mother's death, has been undermining him a bit. And then *Faith Healer* is still hanging, and the new play (which I have not seen) he seems to be uncertain of.

30th May in Dublin

Somebody came into the house at that point and here I am in Paddy's land again. I came home through the North on Sunday because a nun/aunt (a nonantity?) of mine is home on holidays and I had to see her. So that kept the disruption going, and yesterday when I landed back I had the thin-lipped company of Richard Murphy in the house all day. He was up to do a review (with me too) of McGahern's new book of stories called *Getting Through* which he (Murphy) characterized exactly enough as being about the failure of marriages and the success of funerals. It all went out on TV last night.

8th June 1978

That letter never got finished: as you see from the notepaper, exam time has come round again and now it will be Gus's turn to have the Carysfort mixed grill and *Oloroso* – or is it *Amontillado*? I'm supervising and slightly hung over so I thought I'd try a cure by thinking of you.

Derek Mahon is staying with us at the moment. He was in Gransha a few weeks ago drying out and has been off the stuff ever since; and now he proposes to spend the summer being sober and indolent in the houses of friends. He's been with us for a week and when he leaves, he's proceeding to the house of Eamon Grennan, then to Tyrone Power, then to the exacting McGahern. I must say it's a pleasure to have him about – the crack is good and the disposition sunny – except when he thinks on the debts incurred in his gin-before-breakfast period.

Through him I met last Monday the man who is surely the most poetic of Irish poets: Desmond O'Grady, passing through Dublin and Leland Bardwell (I think) on his way back to his island in the Cyclades, and looking like one of Odysseus' mariners. He has an actor's voice and a MacIntyre gift for souping up every utterance towards the condition of poetry or something and is apparently the most dangerous man to have as an overnight guest. He goes in for what Mahon would call the 'dying art' of wrecking the house. 'A man who could fuck up the last supper', it is said. Why am I talking about him? I suppose because we just missed having him to stay overnight and I'm releasing the tension.

Yesterday we heard from the Tracys and the Parkinsons: Marie, as I said, had written belatedly. So Berkeley arose again like a fragrant accusation and I decided I had to get the pages away to-day.

Did I say already about Harvard? We're going to be there for the February/May semester next year. Teaching two writing classes, so I felt I should not pass that up. Apparently, however, the housing is very dear and Caroline Lowell tells me that her daughter had her arm broken (deliberately) in one of the schools, so the prospect, while being 'sticking out', is not altogether what you might call 'dead on'. Anyway, if you know of anybody who needs a £200 a month house in Dublin just then, tell them to apply here.

[. . .]

'*toitín*': Irish for 'cigarette'.

After some years teaching at Berkeley, Deane was about to return to Ireland.

Friel's 'new play' could be *Aristocrats*, on which he is known to have been working at this period and which eventually opened at the Abbey Theatre in March 1979.

The 'nun/aunt' was Patrick Heaney's youngest sister, Jane (1915–2003), who as 'Sister Martina' joined an enclosed order in Drogheda.

The Irish poet Eamon Grennan (b.1941), who taught in the USA but returned occasionally to Ireland, had known Mahon since his student days.

'Tyrone Power' obviously does not refer to the US film star, noted for his swashbuckling roles, who had died in 1958, but may be SH and Deane's private nickname for John Montague, brought up in Co. Tyrone.

Desmond O'Grady (1935–2014), poet and translator, had lived for long periods away from Ireland – France, Italy, the USA, Greece – and was renowned for his cosmopolitan leanings and the breadth of his erudition; Leland Bardwell (1922–2016) was a poet and novelist, and the author, in her later years, of a candid memoir with the title *A Restless Life* (2008).

To Charles Monteith

MS Faber

12 August 1978 — 191 Strand Road, Dublin 4

Dear Charles,

So much to get over. I cannot properly account for my hesitation over the *Selected Poems* and my dilatoriness in settling the selection itself. I'll try to put some shape here on the mumblings of our telephone conversation – I was then more embarrassed than articulate about the thing, I'm afraid.

Any book that I've done heretofore has come together more or less organically, as a natural extension of the one before, and all the backpedalling and hesitations have occurred before the MS goes in. The *Selected*, as you know, arose in my own mind more for the American audience than for the one here – I always had this notion that in spite of the issue of each volume by Oxford the poetry did not really have a presence or a profile on the US poetry bookshelf, as it were, and I thought and still think that a selected volume – going perhaps under a title other than *Selected Poems*? – could by now change that. The Faber *Selected* arose naturally and uncritically from the idea of the American one.

When I began to hover on the verges of an actual choice of poems, I found some deeply, dully registering unease. Apart from the dithering about which verses would go, which would stay, I gradually found myself thinking that to do a selected at this stage on this side of the Atlantic was premature, even if it were still OK for US. I think that whereas a *Selected* in an American list could be seen in some way as almost a first book over there, a serious address to the American readers, in the Faber list such a book is my declaration of having reached the end of a period, a certain plateau, of having perceived the shape of the achievement so far and having decided upon the artistic outline that others are to perceive. I have perhaps almost got to that point with the first four books, but I feel that the tact of publication – the four books are available here, still settling in others' heads as well as my own – and the timing require that a fifth book come available here before the selections from the first four. It's as much superstition as anything else: to do a selected before the next new book is like taking all the eggs out of the nest and trusting that the empty straw will automatically fill – not even a delph egg in sight!

I'm still perhaps not making much sense at explaining myself but anyhow I propose again that Farrar Straus do a *Selected*, perhaps under a new title; then Faber and Farrar do the *Easter Water* (if that's what it's to be called) and *then* Faber do a *Selected*?

I'll get the choice of poems fixed up before the end of the month. [. . .]

'delph egg': a ceramic egg is sometimes placed in a nesting box to encourage chickens to lay or to keep a broody hen distracted.

To Valda Trevlyn Grieve ms NLS

14 September 1978 191 Strand Road, Dublin 4

Dear Valda,

Yesterday I had hoped to be at Langholm but many things conspired against me and I am sorry that my sympathy has to be carried on the page.

Chris's death left us all feeling weaker, as if a source had been closed off, so I can only imagine how you must feel, after the snapping of those strong and long and tender bonds. I am honoured to have known you both and cherish the memory of that heartwarming visit to you last September. I hope that if I get to Scotland soon again it will be all right to visit again: until then, my love and hopes for your good survival of this unhappy time.

If you can pick up RTÉ – Irish radio – you may wish to hear a little tribute I did to MacDiarmid, going out Monday 18 at 7:45 p.m. It scraped the surface of his greatness, at least.

Affectionately,

Seamus Heaney

Valda Trevlyn Grieve (1906–89) was the wife of Christopher Murray Grieve, known to the wider world as Hugh MacDiarmid; Langholm, in Dumfries and Galloway, Scotland, was where he was both born and buried.

To Charles Monteith

MS Faber

19 October 1978 191 Strand Road, Dublin 4

Dear Charles,

It's almost exactly four years since I sent you *North*: I hope *Umber* moves a quarter as well. It has not got the obsessive intensity of the bog poems about it but I am pleased with the love poems and the voice I got going in the longer elegies. Anyhow, it's the book that has come at this time.

The title I just settled on. I had a long list but this one has been selected by the unconscious ear. Even though it is again a single word title, I feel that the weather and weight of the word is very different; that the monosyllabic bluntness of *North* was proper to the chisellings in that text, whereas the more relaxed and assuaging vowels of *Umber* catch the warmer and kindlier notes in the new book.

[. . .]

The prose is gathering, and it's now a matter of rewriting two of the lectures. I was thinking of calling it *The Makings of a Music* which is the title of a lecture in the thing on Wordsworth. I enclose a putative contents for the finished thing, and would hope to let you have a MS by Christmas. It could be done earlier if you thought it would be worth issuing at the same time as *UMBER*. Everything is ready except the title-essay – a matter of typing and rewriting – and a revision of 'The Sense of Place'.

Anyhow, Charles, I hope we continue to deliver the goods between us as well as we have done heretofore, and better. I look forward to seeing you, even for a short time – or a short one – on November 23 or 24. Marie sends her love.

Sincerely,

Seamus

The book offered to Faber as *Umber* eventually – and to its advantage – acquired the title *Field Work*. The paragraphs omitted here show SH fussing about with dictionary definitions in an attempt to show the multiple resonances of the word 'umber', one meaning of which is 'the shadow of the pointer on a sun-dial'.

To Karl Miller

MS Emory

20 October 1978 191 Strand Road, Dublin 4

Dear Karl,

For better or worse I have submitted this collection of poems to Faber, to be published in a year's time under the title *UMBER*. Maybe that will change – I've had a lot of bother settling on it, and may yet again unsettle it.

The MS I sent to Faber has 'for Karl Miller' on the dedication page and I hope this was not presumptuous. For 'a multitude of causes', as Wordsworth says, I'd like the book to be yours: your trust in what I have done from the beginning has been vital and vitalizing, and your encouragement over a number of the poems in *Umber* was restorative and confirming. But let me not grow too homiletic. It's the least I could do for a friend.

There are many typing errors to irritate your editorial eye – and it strikes me that you would be the best person to read the proofs when and if they arrive – but I hope you'll get a quiet pleasure from the stuff. It's by no means as tight and obsessive as *North* but I like to think that there's more of my personality relaxing in it. Anyhow.

Our love to the family. Marie and I are going to Cambridge on Friday 24 November so we might be able to say hello in London on our way to or fro.

With every good wish,
Sincerely,
Seamus

PS It was strange that you rang last Tuesday – I was gathering the poems and thinking of you – but I thought it better not to declare my hand on the phone. Cautious wee papist.

S.

Field Work carries the dedication 'for Karl and Jane Miller'.

1979

SH went to Harvard University in Cambridge, Massachusetts, as visiting lecturer for the spring semester, and his family went with him. Harvard and Cambridge were to furnish him with some of the most important friendships of his life: notably, with Helen Vendler (b.1933), then a professor of English at Harvard, later A. Kingsley Porter University Professor there; and Bernard McCabe (1923–2006), Professor of English at nearby Tufts University, and his wife Jane.

Almost immediately on arrival at Harvard, he found himself in demand as a guest reader and lecturer at other US universities – a demand that never relented in all the years that followed. At the same time, the New York firm of Farrar, Straus and Giroux embraced him as his US publishers.

To Robert Giroux

MS NYPL

1 February 1979

20 Crescent Street, Cambridge,
MA 02138

Dear Mr Giroux,

The copy of Robert Lowell's *Oresteia* was waiting here when I landed last week. Thank you for sending it.

Needless to say, I am honoured that your house is going to publish *Field Work* and I hope that it turns out to do some credit to – or at least not to discredit – your list. I'm writing to Pat Strachan about the notes etc.

With every good wish,
Sincerely,
Seamus Heaney

Robert Giroux (1914–2008) had joined Farrar, Straus and Company in 1955 as Editor-in-Chief, before becoming a partner in Farrar, Straus and Giroux in 1964; Pat Strachan edited the firm's poetry list.

To Robert Fitzgerald

MS Harvard

8 February 1979 [m.d. 1978] [In transit]

Dear Robert,

The address is a feigning, as your Elizabethan might have it. I'm aboard an aeroplane for Cincinnati for the first of the readings, blocking the holes in the wounded calendar of the next few months.

But I've gone through the selection of students for the two groups and just had my first meeting with the K6 – advanced – outfit, and a heavy weight of hours – or ours? – has lifted. I had 34 postulants altogether for the two courses, most of whom appeared in hopes of K6. But now I have done the deed, and taken on twelve in each section, and since noon to-day when I posted the list for J6 I've felt at ease more than before. Not that I was uneasy, just tense. The real menace lifted on Thursday last when the children came home from the Agassiz school as relieved and pleased as Marie and I were. They are content and that means a relieved life for the parents, as you must only know a hundred times more than we do. So.

I introduced the bold O'Grady on Monday night at the Lamont and have seen him a couple of times. Not the worst, as they say in their hyperbolic way in Dublin. Marie had a cautious approach because of reports she heard of devastations when he was, as it were, *in* his *poculis*, but half-thawed when faced with the decent warmth of the man. Though she shares our hesitations in face of the rhetoric. I had only met him, tentatively, in Dublin, but now I do like the man. There's an eagerness and away far back in him, perhaps, an appeal. Like the rest of us, I hear you say.

Your daughter came to say she would like to audit one of the classes and I had a too flurried exchange with her – I did not want the other students to sense that they were being headed off – but I do look forward to having a talk with her and to her sustaining presence in the group. For God's sake, I didn't even get her name . . .

We've met Elizabeth Bishop twice, once at Helen Vendler's last Sunday when Helen was entertaining H. Moss, and last night at Alice's, at a birthday party for Elizabeth herself. So we feel quite swirled in the bath of honour. And I think of your good offices and thank you, I hope not superfluously, again.

One of the wounds – on April 9 – says I have to be in Hartford,

Conn. If we don't encounter before that, perhaps we might do so around that time. Meanwhile, I have begun to write in 106 Pusey, almost a new experience, because since the MS of *Field Work* (coming, coming) I'd not relaxed or released. *Gaudeamus.*

Our love to Penny and yourself.

Seamus

Rather late in the year for SH to be heading his letters '1978'.

'The address is a feigning': written on paper headed with a Crescent Street address, where SH and his family had their lodgings a few blocks north of Harvard University.

Agassiz is a district of Cambridge, still called that, although Agassiz School has been renamed, the Swiss-American biologist Louis Agassiz (1807–73) being now in disgrace for his promotion of eugenics.

For SH's earlier, unmodified opinion of Desmond O'Grady, see letter to Seamus Deane of 24 May 1978. The Lamont Library serves Harvard students of the humanities and social sciences.

'*in* his *poculis*': SH's cod Latin for 'in his cups'.

The poet Elizabeth Bishop (1911–79), admired by SH, had taught a poetry course at Harvard from 1970 to 1977; Alice Methfessel (1943–2009) was her partner. Howard Moss (1922–87), a poet too, was poetry editor at the *New Yorker*, with which Bishop had had a close association throughout her career.

Pusey: another of Harvard's libraries.

'*Gaudeamus*': genuine Latin for 'let us rejoice'.

To Charles Monteith

PC Faber

6 March 1979

[Postmarked 'New Orleans LA 701']

Oysters Rockefeller
Pompano Pontchartrain
Baked Alaska.
Wish you were here!
Seamus and Marie

The card, a promotional one from Antoine's restaurant in New Orleans, shows diners raising toasts in red wine; Pompano Pontchartrain was a fish and crabmeat dish special to the restaurant. 'Oysters' is the first poem in *Field Work*, which was shortly to be published.

To Ted Hughes

MS Emory

24 May 1979

20 Crescent Street, Cambridge,
MA 02138

Dear Ted,

At last I've got started – four days in the poetry room of the Lamont – and I hope to keep going on the anthology matter for about eight days solid. In the meantime, Derek Mahon arrives from Ireland and various less enhancing irritants are due. *But*, I'll be in Dublin, to mark exams, from June 10 to June 24 and I can mark them anywhere, so I'm hoping we can meet for a talk for a couple of days and hammer the job inside a month after that. Can you ring me at Dublin 696791 soon after I arrive so that we can talk? If you can come over to Barrie's between 17/24 – or I can go over to you – it might be a great help. But I don't want to fix or suggest dates now, since I'm slightly in the clutches of my college – examiners' meetings with the university, external examiners, all that delirium of the weak . . . I'm making copies of each poem I choose, one copy, which can be re-copied – and I'm not duplicating your poets. I hope to have a decent heap by June 10.

These months have been fiscally rewarding but depleting in other ways. Harvard poetry-writers are exacting and vain, which leaves me flat and empty, but there has been a good breaking up of the guarded ground of the heart: mostly by having it worn and trampled.

I am ashamed not to have told you how important and, as ever, nurturing, your good words about the latest poems were to me. Since I opened *Lupercal* in the Belfast Public Library in November 1962, the lifeline to Hughesville has been in its emergent differing ways a confirmation.

Give my love to Carol, and think of a connection – a day or two, possibly in London/Devon/Dublin/Kilkenny between June 10 and June 24. I go back to USA for a month then.

Seamus

PS I'll have a big house on Long Island all July. Are you coming over? That wd do as well, if you cd stay. S.

'At last I've got started': on choosing poems for the anthology, *The Rattle Bag*, that Faber had commissioned from Hughes and SH. It would be published in 1982.

'over to Barrie's': because Hughes visited Ireland often, to fish with Barrie Cooke.

'all that delirium of the weak': see 'All that delirium of the brave' in Yeats's 'September 1913'.

Lupercal, Hughes's second book of poems, was published in 1960; Carol was Hughes's wife.

To Thomas Flanagan

MS Amherst

29 June 1979

33 Gnarled Hollow Road, East Setauket, Long Island, NY 01733

Dear Tom,

My second morning in this fragrant clime and the pace is settling to a quieter one than I've known for months. I feel the system calming and am grateful: the house and trees and grass are all kindly influences. Wordsworth might have spoken of powers and intercourse . . . At any rate, I'm at your desk in the study which will remain inclined to be pilot house and engine room, as long as I have anything to do with it. And presently I shall assay, for the first time, the electric typewriter.

We got here by hired car (Hertz) at enormous expense – neither Avis nor Budget had cars, and the drop-off rates are exorbitant with Hertz – but it was all worth it, since we still had a lot of junk to carry away from Cambridge. I was sorry to leave because, in a way, I had only settled there a couple of weeks before I went to Dublin: it is a very liveable region and I'd like to go back some time. To the frugal oyster and the opulent library.

I am looking forward to July in this place – it couldn't be better, from the point of view of silence, space and friendly spirits – and then I hope we'll meet for a while before you return. We should be in Dublin early August.

[. . .]

Pull no tug-of-war . . . Sustain all references to literary success and make notes on begrudgers. Your tuxedo will be here – though it has not yet arrived.

Sláinte – and love to the arriving ladies.

Seamus

The 'fragrant clime' was home of Flanagan himself, who had let SH use it while he was in Dublin.

'Wordsworth might have spoken . . .': SH seems to have in mind lines from *The Prelude*:

There are in our existence spots of time
Which with distinct pre-eminence retain
A fructifying virtue, whence, depressed
By trivial occupations and the round
Of ordinary intercourse, our minds –
Especially the imaginative power –
Are nourished, and invisibly repaired.

Enclosed with this letter was a typescript of the poem 'Near Anahorish', with this note in SH's hand: 'Tom – My first assay on your typewriter. This is the poem about Louis and that much pummelled progenitor of mine. Seamus.' 'Near Anahorish' was to undergo some expansion before it appeared in *Station Island* as 'Making Strange'. The Louis in question was Louis Simpson, now a teaching colleague of Flanagan's.

'literary success . . . begrudgers': Flanagan's *The Year of the French*, a novel on the epic scale dealing with Irish history but written by a non-Irishman, was just out.

To Elizabeth Bishop

MS Vassar

12 July 1979

33 Gnarled Hollow Road, East
Setauket, Long Island, NY 01733

Dear Elizabeth,

Tucked in the middle of this stuff you'll find a poem dedicated to you which is not good enough but has one or two images which we probably share. I hope you and Alice get some pleasure from it: it's really a *billet-doux*.

I've an idea that some day I might do a collection called 'Giveaways' and these poems, or some of them, would be included. Each one would be dedicated to, and have some internal connection with what they used to call in Berkeley 'a real human being'.

I've done a number of these since coming to America, and the 'Villanelle', 'Hank of Wool' and 'Late Offerings' since coming here.

I have to be in Vermont on July 23 so I may call you about then – I'd love to come up but I doubt if I can make it. All our love to you and Alice,

Seamus

[Postscript at the head of the letter:] Marie spends much time on her back in the sun. It's beginning to show. On her.

S.

The dedicated poem was 'A Hank of Wool', which appeared in the *Times Literary Supplement* on 7 March 1980 but was not included by SH in any subsequent volume: in it, he describes holding wool for Bishop while she wound it into a ball – a service that seems to imply an unspoken connection between them. Bishop's death a few months later allowed him to add 'i.m. Elizabeth Bishop' below the title.

On the reverse of a postcard showing Gentile Bellini's *A Turkish Artist*, which SH sent later in the month, he apologises for not being able to pay a visit after all: 'I've just looked at the map and realized that the Burlington/Sabine Farm trip is quite complicated and that my time is going faster and faster.' The original 'Sabine Farm', country estate of the Latin poet Horace, was a gift from his patron, Maecenas.

To Christopher Ricks

MS Boston

13 November 1979 191 Strand Road, Dublin 4

Dear Christopher,

On October 15, publication day of *Field Work*, I had a terrific reading in Trinity in Dublin and as I left the hall somebody gave me 'The Meal, the Mouth, the Book'. I went to bed exultant, feeling trusted. The piece moved, exhilarated me. I could feel the sport in your own writing and the grace after the meal you made of the thing . . . *Gratias ago*. Marie once told me that my mind has all the manoeuvrability of a combine harvester, so I rejoice that a wit as lambent as your own can be bothered to stay so happily near it. And I must plead my sluggish shunting ways as an excuse for not writing sooner.

My love to your otter and cub. Till we meet again.

Seamus

Christopher Ricks was at this time teaching English Literature at the University of Cambridge. Praising *Field Work* in the *London Review of Books*, he had written: 'Seamus Heaney offers "Oysters" ("Alive and violated") as his opening. Opened at once are the oyster, the mouth, the meal and the book.'

'*Gratias ago*': 'thank you'.

To Brian Friel

MS NLI

26 November 1979 191 Strand Road, Dublin 4

Dear Brian,

I read it on Friday evening, and lay with the flu all weekend, woozy with images out of it – the sweet smell, the army moving over the ground, the quickfire between Jimmy and Hugh – those sounds and sights have a dream power to them; and the name/map/translation scenes are beautifully managed, and the ending is a triumph. The lines of your statement are perfectly drawn – or discovered – and the cultural, artistic and political declarations cohere, are congruent. The dare of the Irish through English is a hell of a coup. Do you remember the oleograph of the penal altar in the snow, with redcoats on the horizon? That deep-laid thing comes to life in it and finds itself in cahoots with remembered quotations by Yeats – of Carleton – 'people half-sprung from the earth etc.' It is all working at the haunting level. Hugh, Owen, Sarah, Yolland are sure fire, and Manus is a difficult mastery. Jimmy, of course, is irresistible.

I'm still in bed – it's Monday – and hope to read the second time through before I get back on the conveyor belt to-morrow, for I'll probably not get a chance at it again before I see you on December 7. (I look forward less and less to Belfast visits – Des Wilson has put me on *faoi gheasa* for Ballymurphy.) The translation to the stage will make *Translations* a thing of great panache as well as half-disguised passion. Why should they funk it in NIAC? Mind you, the 'sharp resentment', as the man said, could be said to be implicit . . . Wonderful what a checkpoint on your own roads does for the imagination. *Gaudeo. Gaudemus. Gaudeamus.*

I spoke to D. Hammond this afternoon – he too was in bed, but suffering from excesses of last week. Eileen, he said, rebuked him with talking to 'actresses' in the Europa Hotel. And then, did you see the remarks about the 'grubby' state of things under the surface down here?

Love to Anne; trust *Translations* – I think it's going to be a powerful exciting 'event' as well as the deeply conceived work that it is. Will that play of yours send out . . .? See you.

Seamus

Friel's *Translations* would receive its first performance at the Guildhall in Derry the following year. One of the play's ingenuities is indeed what SH here terms the 'dare of the Irish through English': i.e. while an Anglophone audience is allowed to understand the Irish-speaking characters, the English characters onstage are excluded from understanding.

'penal altar': i.e. one set up for the clandestine celebration of the Mass at the time of the Penal Laws in Ireland.

Yeats wrote, in one of his comments on William Carleton: 'He was but half articulate, half emerged from Mother Earth like one of Milton's lions . . .'

Fr Des Wilson (1925–2019), Belfast priest of Republican sympathies, had founded the Springhill Community House as a centre for the promotion of education, in Ballymurphy, Belfast.

'*faoi gheasa*': under a spell.

'Will that play of yours send out . . .': see Yeats's poem 'The Man and the Echo'.

To Paul Muldoon

MS Emory

26 November 1979 191 Strand Road, Dublin 4

Dear Paul,

At the risk of some mutual admiring, I think it's your best book – a very relaxed confident arc to the feeling and form, sure of its ground. The *Immram* is a fantastic coup. I can hardly believe it. 'Promises, Promises', 'Grief', 'Come into my Parlour', 'Bran', 'Whim', 'Why Brownlee Left' are among my favourites, but there is not one poem I don't have an affection for. And there's 'Cuba'.

Is there any chance of using a good big selection of these in *Ploughshares*, which I'm editing in Boston, to appear early in the new year? A more or less Irish issue. I don't think it would matter if they had appeared here – only US published material would be taboo. Is it too much to expect that the *Immram* might be a possible entry? The *Ploughshares* is a decent enough home.

I'm in bed with the flu! *Sláinte.*

Seamus

Muldoon had shown SH a typescript of his third collection, *Why Brownlee Left*, due out the following year.

Founded in Cambridge, Massachusetts, the literary magazine *Ploughshares* twice a year invites a guest editor to select the contents.

To Michael McLaverty

MS Linen Hall

27 November 1979 191 Strand Road, Dublin 4

Dear Michael,

I am ashamed to be so dilatory in answering your abundant and moving correspondence of last month. I was sorry to hear that you had to go into hospital again, but if the buoyancy and generosity of your letters was anything to go by, it didn't seem to take a flinch out of you.

Yes, *Field Work* got a decent response: I had half-expected the backlash to come this time – as it is bound to come some time – and was gratified when it seemed to pass. But the assent to the work will bring about a dissent, so it's well to have had the advice 'to go your own way' dinned in years ago. I think I have a feel of the shape of what I'm doing, and have a couple of eggs in the nest again – a book of essays and lectures called *The Makings of a Music* and a translation of the Middle Irish Sweeney material, which I might call *Sweeney Astray*.

I'm glad that Lough Beg houses spirits dear to both of us – I always feel around New Ferry, on the Derry side, about Church Island there, a sense of the first fishermen in the Bann valley. A strong yet benign sense of primeval habitation, or rather traces of presence. There's something kindly yet dolorous in the air of the place that soothes and steadies.

I have to go to Trench House in a week or so to speak about Francis Ledwidge – God only knows what possessed me to name him as a subject – more pathos than achievement there – but maybe we'll manage to meet either on the Thursday or the Friday morning. I have to do something in Ballymurphy for Des Wilson, I think on Thursday night. Marie and the children had hoped to come up, but we've decided not – it would mean two days off school. They all send their love, as I do too, to you and Molly. May you sell another 20,000 copies by Christmas!

Seamus

In a radio programme celebrating Michael McLaverty's literary achievements (see letter to Michael Longley of 8 February 1975), SH recalled his first interview with his future head, in which 'Classes weren't mentioned. Quotation followed quotation, poet after poet was praised and appraised; image after image was invoked with delight . . . This was Michael McLaverty's way of revealing what an English teacher should be.' McLaverty's 1932 novel *Call My Brother Back* had been successfully republished this year.

Francis Ledwidge (1887–1917), Irish poet, was killed north of Ypres while serving with the Royal Inniskilling Fusiliers. SH's poem about him, 'In Memoriam Francis Ledwidge', had appeared in print the year before this; his essay on him, 'Poet of the Walking Wounded', would be printed in the *Irish Times* in 1992.

Trench House was a teacher training college in Belfast.

1980

With the publication and critical success of *Field Work* behind him, SH's main creative project of this year was the long, ambitiously different, self-confronting poem in twelve episodes, 'Station Island', which is at the heart of his collection of the same name (1984). Meanwhile, adding to his ever-growing portfolio of public commitments, he rashly took on the judging of the newly set-up Arvon/*Observer* Poetry Competition, together with three senior British poets, Ted Hughes, Philip Larkin and Charles Causley (1917–2003). It appears that all four were dismayed to find what a toll on their time this was, and how unsatisfactory the process.

1980 was also the year in which SH's first prose book, *Preoccupations: Selected Prose, 1968–1978*, was published.

To James Simmons

MS Emory

11 January 1980 — 191 Strand Road, Dublin 4

Dear Jimmy,

Constantly writing. You're a credit. Many thanks for the poems – I'm certain I'll use 'The Baggage and the Toff' which is a beauty and my favourite in the group. Also 'Mr Cordelia', 'The First Goodbye Letter' and 'The Honeymoon' – all of them constantly singing. I don't respond as fully to the quatrain poems, dainty tho' they be, and while the honesty of 'The Second Time Around' carries its force a long way, I don't think it lifts as well as the other ones.

I'd prefer to come the week before Patrick's Day, because teaching practice supervision will be in full swing around the 18th and I'll have to be afoot in the schools. What to talk about? Ledwidge is too too thin: I did a lecture on him at St Joseph's College of Education before Christmas and it caused me more bother than anything. What about doing something 'On translating Sweeney'? I re-worked most of the verse last summer and hope to hammer it to a conclusion soon. I'd let you have different versions of a couple of the poems ahead of time and I'd talk generally about finding a language. Come to think of it, 'finding a language' might be a better title, for Dermot Devlin, of the Irish Department there, also wanted me to submit to inquisition by his

MA people – as to why I wasn't writing in Irish! Could we combine the groups? One way or another, I'd like to connect. (It was at a seminar like that that Blake Morrison got the earlier 'Casualty' version – he was in Karl Miller's class a couple of years ago at London University.)

Of course, Cal – sorry, Jimmy – I exaggerate the literary jealousy. And so does James Fenton. But I hope there is an element of good crack in 'An Afterwards' as well as a perception of that fierce jealousy the spouse has for the writing. But I don't know quite what you mean about lyric occasions – 'Oysters' is impatient with a too sedate laying down of memories, but on the other hand, the touchstones within the memory for good are bound to be more or less 'lyric occasions'. One man's self-deception may be another man's commitment.

Maybe you'd be interested in one or two lines of the enclosed interview – and I hope you might like 'The Road to Lough Derg', although it blathers on at a great rate. And do you think there's anything to the short ones? I did them all in a day last weekend, very odd and rare: I pine for the fluent visitations.

Love to Imelda – and if you have M. Foley's address, send it some time. Is that Ormeau Road in Belfast you're living in?

Cheers and *sláinte* – or is it *slaynt*?

Seamus

On 5 January, SH had written to Simmons asking for contributions to his 'trans-atlantic' issue of the *Ploughshares*; in return, Simmons had invited SH to read to students at the New University of Ulster, Coleraine, where he was now teaching.

In his *Field Work* poem 'In Memoriam Francis Ledwidge', SH writes, 'I think of you in your Tommy's uniform, / A haunted Catholic face, pallid and brave', before going on to express doubts about his poetic achievement, regretting that it missed 'the twilit note your flutes should sound', and measuring him beside the greater British war poets: 'You were not keyed or pitched like those true-blue ones, / Though all of you consort now underground.'

Dermot Devlin, aka Diarmaid Ó Doibhlin (1942–2017), was an Irish-language scholar who lectured at St Mary's College, Belfast, and at the University of Ulster, Coleraine; he also wrote poetry.

Blake Morrison (b.1950), British poet, novelist and memoirist, was to write one of the earliest monographs on SH: *Seamus Heaney* (1982).

The self-punitive vehemence of 'An Afterwards', in *Field Work*, actually goes some way beyond 'good crack'.

What SH here calls 'The Road to Lough Derg' became an early section of the poem-in-progress 'Station Island'.

To Pat Strachan TS NYPL

24 February 1980 191 Strand Road, Dublin 4

Dear Pat,

Thank you for keeping me posted with all those reviews – even Alvarez, never mind the quality, feel the width – and for getting the signed copy of Derek's book to me.

As you know, it takes something in earnest to get me into letter-writing mood and the present stimulus is a letter I got this morning from Charles Monteith where he tells me that Fabers have more or less stonewalled (not his way of putting it) on the idea of any change in the British *Selected* when it appears in the US. I had spoken to him when I was in London three weeks ago, and understood that no final decision had been taken. I liked the idea of a larger *Selected* from FSG and in the meantime wrote suggesting that your edition might carry the whole of *North* – since that volume has the strongest (or had, or has the longest) reputation over there. So I wonder if you might not consider doing a Farrar edition of it separately? Unless, that is, you are still out of sympathy or unagreed to carrying the Faber *Selected* as it stands. I realize that for a new arrival on your list to come like Oliver Twist asking for more is enough to bring out the beadle in your editorial board, but I have a hunch that *North* could hold its own by now, if only as a textbook in the Anglo-Irish studies courses. I would be grateful, at any rate, if you could think seriously of it.

I changed the title of the prose book to *Preoccupations* which I think is better and truer – giving, among other things, the impression of a man with one or two things to cud on over and over. Marie says that my mind has all the manoeuvrability of a combine harvester.

And I think I'll be over for a three-week reading tour next February/March. My agent is intent on PROMOTING. I am not unhappy with three weeks out of the classroom. And so it may all happen.

With kindest wishes from Marie and myself,

Love, Seamus

To Pat Strachan

MS NYPL

6 March 1980 191 Strand Road, Dublin 4

[. . .]

I like your copy very well. In fact, I prefer it. Ahem.

As to the 'quarrel with ourselves' bit – I was half-quoting Yeats there, and since I cannot exactly remember where the lines come from I cannot check them. He said something like 'Out of the quarrel with others we make rhetoric, poetry out of the quarrel with ourselves.' So perhaps the idea should not be attributed to me in the blurb, or else it should be introduced with 'As he writes, echoing Yeats, in one of . . .'

I think the piece is very good: true about the subjects, flattering about the writer. It's about time Marie knew I was 'passionate, cultivated and authentic'. Yippee. I'm flushed with good feelings to think Farrar are doing it and the *Selected*. And *North*? That was in another letter . . . Thanks again.

With affection,
Seamus

Strachan had been improving SH's first draft for the jacket copy of *Preoccupations*. Yeats's aphorism concerning 'quarrels', slightly misremembered by SH, is from 'Anima Hominis' (1918), and the jacket copy duly alludes to it.

To Brian Friel

MS NLI

31 March 1980 [In transit]

Dear Brian,

I'm on EI 166, for London. Went off a day early because I was fit for nothing else. I was sorry to renege again, but felt scattered and without self-possession on Friday anyhow and was glad to sit for B. Cooke. He started to draw me around 10:00 a.m. and suddenly got the hots for a portrait. I stayed until yesterday/Sunday afternoon and the job is nearly done. Good work in the making, I think. More of a farmer this time than a Maguire Aran-knit.

[. . .]

I'm going to lie about to-night, I hope, just walk round Soho on my own. I'm wondering whether to contact Cahal Mór to-morrow. Wish you were here.

Love to Ann, regrets again.
Seamus

Written on 191 Strand Road headed paper. The discrepancy between the address given at the head of the letter and the actual place of writing is plain enough, but as SH's habit of writing letters on aeroplanes grew he became just as likely to put the flight number – in this case, the service between Dublin and London – as his address.

Barrie Cooke's 1980 portrait in oils of SH is here compared with the Edward McGuire one that adorns the back of *Wintering Out*.

The omitted paragraph reports on a noisy and boring dinner party.

'Cahal Mór': private nickname for Charles Monteith; 'King Cahal Mór of the Wine-Red Hand' features in James Clarence Mangan's poem 'A Vision of Connaght in the Thirteenth Century'.

To Paul Muldoon

MS Emory

19 June 1980 191 Strand Road, Dublin 4

Dear Paul,

Herewith *Ploughshares* and I am delighted to have been able to carry your poems in it. When O'Malley sends the dollars, I'll send you some of them too.

I am a bit embarrassed that four contributions – from M. Longley, J. Hewitt, T. Kilroy and an American called Alfred Alcorn – seem to have disappeared into the desks of the US co-editors. They were in a batch I sent out in February and until the copies arrived I had no idea they were missing from the final line-up – done in Cambridge. It is not a question of their having been edited out – more of a balls-up. A pity they are not in with the rest.

Thank you for your note about Mary. It was a relief for her in the end and she was ready to go. The survivors, the older ones, have realigned well enough since then.

If you are coming to Dublin, get in touch. Now that the summer is starting, there's more room for causerie. I hope that I might get some work done, but feel far from sources. A bit ossified. Rise, roll, carol and creation not on the agenda.

I hope you get some pleasure from the magazine.

Sincere,
Seamus

Peter O'Malley co-founded both the magazine *Ploughshares* and the Plough and Stars bar on Massachusetts Avenue, Cambridge, Massachusetts, which has continued to attract writers and musicians, predominantly Irish, among its clientele.

Mary Heaney (1902–80), SH's aunt, had lived with his family and exerted a powerful influence on him during his childhood (see *Stepping Stones*); she is the subject of such poems as 'Field of Vision' and 'Mossbawn: Sunlight'.

'Rise, roll, carol and creation': from Gerard Manley Hopkins's poem 'To R.B.'.

To Brian Friel TS NLI

4 July 1980 191 Strand Road, Dublin 4

Dear Brian,

I am sorry to have been so long in getting anything to you for the *Translations* programme, and now that I have this bit trimmed I have lost faith in it. I am like the spent clet I mean celt (a clet is a clit in Ballymena?) anyhow for the last week has been social and wasteful though not too drunken or unpleasant, just constant servicing. To bed late and up tired, with consequent doldrum and abrasiveness. Och och. I just love whinging about it.

The Sweeney stuff I thought might do because of the counterpoint voices, the antiphonal thing, and the misunderstandings or misfirings between the two voices. But now that it's done I'm not so sure. The bird metaphor – all right in context – is maybe a bit heavy when the piece is orphaned, and it would probably take too much scene-setting. Look at it anyhow and see what you think. Do not take it if your instinct don't approve. I was thinking even of 'Anahorish' and 'Broagh' in *Wintering Out* but they are probably too much in line with the other stuff you have selected already.

Also enclosed another madness, envisaged as a possible last scene of 'Lough Derg'. I was asked to contribute to a Joyce symposium for 1982 and that set it off. He does not come through properly – but then how can I do a genius? And there may be a dangerous breach of tact in allowing oneself to meet the man at all. The first page is all right. Maybe he should only say about four words. Anyway, just to give you a look.

[. . .]

I saw Deane and Monteith – the latter giving the former hope but no contract yet. But there seems to be possibility. Deano in great shape.

Call from Hammond whom you have seen since I have – he sounded alienated from himself and his activities again. Belfast is sore on all of them, I think.

I'm not going to see you for a couple of weeks at least, I regret to say. But you'll probably have company anyway, it's the time for it. Love to Anne and family.

Seamus

Enclosed: passage from *Sweeney Astray* concerning the meeting of Sweeney and Eorann, taken largely from §§31 and 32. In the event, two of SH's translations, though not from *Sweeney*, were printed in the programme for *Translations* alongside the original Irish.

'another madness': what became Section XII of 'Station Island', where Joyce is given many more than four words of dialogue.

Although Seamus Deane was never taken on to the Faber poetry list, his *Celtic Revivals: Essays in Modern Irish Literature*, which may be the volume being considered by Charles Monteith, was published by the firm five years later.

To Donald Davie

MS Beinecke

17 August 1980 191 Strand Road, Dublin 4

Dear Donald,

You have come and gone – I had hoped to meet and talk when you were en route from Sligo, but the shifting sands of these holidays have kept me struggling and moving so it didn't happen and what would have been a late greeting and gratitude for 'Summer Lightning' may now be too late.

The poem was a surprise and an honour. Then a pleasure and a challenge. Again, I was on the move in England three weeks ago when I came on it (when I got back to Dublin ten days ago, Blake Morrison had forwarded a copy to me) and its force and commitment almost knocked me off my indolent perch. I've been wobbling and wasting the summer, feeling unfocused and dry, and the charge of reading it left me both excited and tongue-tied. I haven't yet got my hands on the Ronsard, but your thought of me as an addressee and what you say (and the affection with which you say it) at the end move me and leave me richly indebted.

Strange that Sisson's Dante should figure – at the moment when *Quarto* were about to publish the review I'd just done – of it and

Holmes's OUP introduction. The plainness is there all right, but there was something about the diction and word-order, something subtly off-key for me, not quite plain-spoken, that muffled the thing for me. It's a thrillingly serious piece of work, but it is the seriousness of the enterprise that thrills me, more than the workings of the thing, page by page. I found it difficult to review, partly because I was tongue-tied by praise thrown towards my Ugolino effort by reviewers who meant the praise to be dirt in Sisson's eye, and partly because Edna Longley had hammered a brutal job on his *Exactions* and I felt that I would be viewed as one of the Longley outriders, though in fact Edna has [been] busy with her knife at my own tree of life.

At the moment, I am lying out in Connemara with Marie and the three children. I had hoped to work in July and August but because I made no plans for an escape from Dublin, no fixed holiday bolt-hole, I've been more or less on the run and have let time slip away. I've been fiddling at bits of a sequence that might be coaxed into a book-length poem, though perhaps 'coerced' is more the word than 'coaxed'. And voices sing in my ear that this may be all folly. But when I get back to Dublin and get settled into the unsettling business of being head of the English Department at Carysfort College once more, I'll let you see some of the bits. There's a Dantesque element in the plan, if not in the execution!

I hope this reaches you sooner rather than later. My best wishes to Doreen and my warmest gratitude to you. 'Inconsiderate, blunt, low-spirited?' I wouldn't be without that considerate, careful, high-spirited speech, your cordial inspiration; you sing 'as if you had a sword upstairs'!

Sláinte!

Seamus

Donald Davie, English poet and academic, had addressed SH directly in his poem 'Summer Lightning', published two years later in the *Times Literary Supplement*, where Blake Morrison was an editor, and eventually in Davie's 1982 volume *The Battered Wife, and Other Poems*. The poem, a rueful meditation on the cost of lifelong service to poetry, contains the lines:

'I am opinionated and embittered,
Inconsiderate, gruff, low-spirited,
Pleased and displeased at once, huffy and raw . . .
So there you have me, Heaney . . .'

The Divine Comedy, in a translation by the poet C. H. Sisson (1914–2003), a literary ally of Davie's, had been published earlier in the year, and SH's review of both it and George Holmes's *Dante* were in the August number of the British magazine *Quarto*, then edited by the poet Craig Raine (b.1944). Edna Longley had reviewed Sisson's *Exactions*, a volume of his own poems, for the same magazine.

'my own tree of life': see 'the blind / swipe of the pruner and his knife / busy about the tree of life', from Robert Lowell's 'Waking Early Sunday Morning'.

'bits of a sequence': 'Station Island', which may indeed be described as 'Dantesque'.

'a sword upstairs': see Yeats's 'When I was young, / I had not given a penny for a song / Did not the poet sing it with such airs / That one believed he had a sword upstairs' ('All Things Can Tempt Me').

To Pat Strachan MS NYPL

23 September 1980

[. . .]

I'm a bit nervous, I must say, about how *Poems* and *Preoccupations* are going to splash down. It was all part of a publication plan I conceived eight or nine years ago – to have so much done by 40! – and I was determined to go through with it. But a few jitters are starting, partly, I suppose, because all of the stuff is relatively old and one has no longer the slight excitement and curiosity that hovers over the unaired material. Still. The main thing is to have it available and whatever the press reaction, I'm sure there's an audience there to come to it gradually.

[. . .]

To John Montague MS Cork

3 November 1980 191 Strand Road, Dublin 4

Dear John,

It appeared on the feast of all hallows – and hallowed us all. I was moved and delighted by what you wrote. It was generous, sportive, confirming – with a refreshing glint here and there to keep a man on his toes. You're probably right about the reviews – but I cannot see the book except as I first foresaw it – a solid lump in the middle with two small *bings* at each end. (Did you have [a] bing? A bing of spuds/turnips.)

The 'ghosts' are not as numerous as I could wish, but I'll hope they keep flickering up. At the moment, I feel assailed by a great blunt force pressing in from the thousands of unrealized poems in the competition. Ted rang last night to say there were now about 35,000 in. Which means we have to read about 15/20 thousand in the next four weeks. My scanning mechanism has been well tuned by it all, but there's something deeply disturbing about pushing aside cry after inchoate cry, in pursuit of excellence.

I'm writing this at nine in the morning, on my way to the college. If I don't do it now, it may not get done – and on this occasion, a card might be carrying consistency to the point of excess. Thanks again for the *élan* you supplied on Saturday. My love to your three graces.

Sláinte,
Seamus

Montague had written to declare his admiration for *Field Work*.

A 'bing' is a heap, usually of potatoes in storage.

The competition mentioned was the first Arvon Foundation Poetry Competition (see introductory paragraph to 1980).

To Monroe Engel — MS Harvard

10 December 1980

Dear Monroe,

Thank you for your letter. And thank you for your help behind the chairman in the whole business. It all shifted quite suddenly. Until this term, nothing in me answered the thought of change: I was still securing the life we took on here a few years ago. But all of a sudden, the answer rose from inside – inside Marie too, I should say, because her support rather than assent was crucial – and the excitement started once the possibility of the half-year appointment on the five-year basis came up. I hope and trust it will work out well for the university and for ourselves.

These days I am being pushed to the side of my own life by a monstrous heap of poetry: I am one of the judges for the Arvon Poetry Competition – basically a fund-raising venture for a Foundation that runs creative writing courses in Britain, a brain-child of Ted Hughes's – and I am just finishing the reading of 35,000 poems. Long and short.

Obscene and sentimental. All human life was there. So everything else has been given less attention than it deserved.

I enclose, however, possible entries for the course catalogue. Reshape, re-phrase, shorten, extend them, if you feel they should conform better to the house style. I took the title 'The Practice of Poetry' in case a title is needed: I do realize that the courses had different names before – 'Advanced Poetry Writing' (?) and something else – and I'll be very happy to work with these titles again. (I thought that the 'practice' word would allow the focus of the course to widen naturally to include the reading of work other than the student's own.)

The teaching schedule I had in Spring '79 worked well: it was Tuesday/Thursday, morning and afternoon, two two-hour sessions, I think, and if that were possible again, I'd welcome it. It leaves a long weekend – and as I hope to nip back to Dublin once or twice on the cheap weekend flights, this would be a useful layout. (Incidentally, I intend to do no readings at all during the semester: I hope to hug my time to myself more than was possible in '79.) If this arrangement is not available, I'll leave it to your own decision and discretion.

Marie joins me in sending her warmest wishes to you and Brenda. It's good to know we'll be meeting again.

Happy Christmas.

Seamus

SH had been invited to return to Harvard, where the novelist Monroe Engel taught in the English Department, on a new, five-year contract.

'pushed to the side of my own life': not the only time SH seems to have found allusion to Philip Larkin's 'Something is pushing them / To the side of their own lives' ('Afternoons') irresistibly apt.

'a brain-child of Ted Hughes's': more exactly, of the English poets John Moat (1936–2014) and John Fairfax (1930–2009), although Hughes was a strong and active supporter of the enterprise.

1981

The Field Day Theatre Company had been set up in 1980 by Brian Friel and the Northern Irish actor Stephen Rea (b.1946), its immediate purpose being to put on a production of Friel's play *Translations* at the Guildhall in Derry. The possibility of a broader, literary and political purpose for the theatre company was soon conceived and, along with Seamus Deane, David Hammond and the poet and critic Tom Paulin (b.1949), SH was appointed a director in 1981. Thus, all the original directors were from north of the border; Thomas Kilroy (b.1934, in Co. Kilkenny), joined later. SH's involvement in the decisions and actions of Field Day was to deepen over the next few years.

In response to the growth of his other commitments and activities, some of which took him abroad for periods of time, SH resigned from his job at Carysfort College where he had been promoted to head of the English Department. The offer of a teaching post at Harvard, limited to the spring semester, had made that decision easier (see letter to Michael Longley of 4 February).

To Karl Miller — MS Emory

2 January 1981 — 191 Strand Road, Dublin 4

We're late with the Christmas poem/card, though you have seen it already. So I enclose a new one, a strange thing only an hour old at the moment, but one which I think I'll continue to like. If you like it, keep it for the *London Review*. Among other things, it is a kind of retort to Alvarez, who made much sport of not being able to find 'loaning' in a dictionary. [. . .]

Miller was now editing the *London Review of Books*, which he had founded in 1979, in emulation of the *New York Review of Books*. The poem SH offers here was the one actually titled 'The Loaning', and Miller did keep it, placing it in his magazine the following month. Perhaps an extra taunt to Alvarez, who in a review of *Field Work* in the *NYRB* (6 March 1980) had cast cold water on SH's achievement in general, was the summoning, in a poem that deals with a child's experience of the local and bucolic, of Dante's name.

To David Hammond

MS Emory

3 January 1981 191 Strand Road, Dublin 4

Dear David,

I've had three days in the study, without going out anywhere and without interruption – Dan and Mary didn't come and Des and Norah Anne postponed until this evening – and I don't know myself. It's quite hard to settle back in, even though you say to yourself it's what you most want, because with being busy you get so keyed to attending outwards, aiming yourself away at what's around you rather that lining up towards what's at your own centre – you're so keyed that way that to relax and trust the relaxing is almost a hallucinatory experience. What I mean to say in simpler language is this: now that I'm at work like this, writing letters, thinking about people, with a bit of time, a bit of pleasure in the poems, I just don't want it to end, don't want to go to England, or back to work, or out of the house. Nevertheless, as in Ben's story of the MC, nevertheless, we're moving on Monday. We'll probably go north that evening and leave the children in The Wood, then Marie and I will cross to London Tuesday morning. Unless I have to go on Monday – I was talking to Ted on the phone on Wednesday and he is having uneasy feelings about our final judgement, as I am, and since nothing is announced to anyone, we think it might be worth while having another hour or two of meditation on the stuff together.

I was sorry I got into a muddle and hurry last Monday, but in the end I thought I should skite up to Muff, even though I hadn't felt up to it earlier in the day. I was glad I did. Had a good quiet chat and set out early next morning, via Bellaghy and Ardboe to here. I should have been writing business letters and marking essays since, but instead I pored back into the poems and wrote and fixed up a couple – which I enclose: you see your God the Father image found a home of sorts. I'm fond of 'The Loaning' which came yesterday.

Meanwhile, if you're coming down, stay here. There'll be a key in the Berrys. And you'll be near your work and can make up your piece before you go out in the morning. I hope 1981 is a more settled year for you anyhow. Regards to the rest. Seamus

'Ben's story of the MC': Benedict Kiely is the likely source of this forgotten item.
'our final judgement': concerning the Arvon competition.

To Desmond Kavanagh

PC Kavanagh

8 [?] January 1981

Complete the following:
'____ ___ , Paddy.'
Then, post your entry to: Gristlegrippers Ltd.
The Lay-by
S.W.1.

Desmond Kavanagh (b.1939), familiarly addressed by SH as Des, had been a contemporary of his at St Columb's, and a boarder too, and he remained a lifelong friend. Most of SH's communications with him were on postcards, dozens sent over the years, many satirical or facetious. The photograph on the obverse of this one is of a bookie at Epsom races, seen from below, shouting to be heard.

To Michael Longley

TS Emory

[4? February 1981]

Our Lady of Mercy College,
Carysfort Park, Blackrock, Co. Dublin

Dear Big Lad,

The new year has almost become the old year and everything is streaming away and still I didn't get down to writing the letter. I've just started all of a sudden here at the plant, between classes. I should have let you know that I was using 'The Linen Workers' on a programme that went out on Radio 4 last Sunday – called *With Great Pleasure*, but nothing's perfect – but at the same time, I knew you would be embarrassed to be on the same programme with Frost and Yeats and Shakespeare so in an unconscious way I was probably sparing your feelings.

As usual I am feeling that most of my life is busy and useless, that the time is being frittered yet somehow the frittering is inevitable. The Arvon business, for example, was a great wound in the last year, and a mistake – the results you will find disturbing, I have no doubt – the first prize was an impossible thing to do justice to, and the decisions we came to, with wobbles and reluctances, are no triumph. But the biggest unease I have is the TV programme which we were contracted to do for Bragg – 15th February. Trying to be honest but inevitably blathering and fudging it. Hughes is himself on it, interesting, and C. Causley is very C. Causley.

The college here is a clammy hold and a fairly demanding one. I made a mistake also in taking on the headship of the department – and now I may be making another. I have decided and agreed to do a three and half month stint each year at Harvard; so will be resigning at the end of the academic year. The Harvard decision came quite suddenly at the end of November. I have been here six years, and have more or less secured a life for the kids and for Marie. But I have an unease about the big hoods of domestic and professional routine settling too firmly or comfortably. In one way, of course, I believe in them absolutely – life, stupid life, as Henry James so exquisitely puts it – but on the other hand, I have warning fears that whatever freedom the self might have had or tried to have is atrophying and the way to alert it to itself again is to be at risk. I want a bit of solitude, to try to settle under and down into the first levels again.

I have been refusing lots of readings, and I think it is imperative to continue to do so. The bard of the Irish soul bit will have to blow over: the thing to do is to get the head down and keep it down for a few years. The whole hoisting of the name is by now a real menace. So I'll be on my own in Harvard for the spring semester next year, late January to late April or early May. Marie is in favour of it and it was as much her decision as mine. The salary will work out at about three-quarters of what I get here, but I think the drop is worth it for the sake of the time bought during the rest of the year. And in a way the separated life could be good for Marie and myself: not that there is any strain in being together but again, the refreshment of being on your own is not to be underestimated after sixteen years of the conjugals. That's the theory anyhow.

[. . .]

Amicus tuus,
Seamus

'here at the plant': i.e. at his place of work.

With Great Pleasure was an occasional BBC Radio 4 programme on which invited guests chose favourite pieces of literature to be read.

'*Amicus tuus*': your friend.

Enclosed with this was a typescript of 'The Railway Children', inscribed 'for Michael and Edna' and dated.

To Derek Mahon

MS Emory

17 February 1981 191 Strand Road, Dublin 4

[. . .]

Next year I'm going to take on a half-year appointment at Harvard – go for a semester on my own, clan stays here. It may be a mistake, money drops, absence, etc. – but more time and elbow room. I took the decision with brio, am living with it with caution.

[. . .]

To Anne Stevenson

MS Cambridge

[Undated] 191 Strand Road, Dublin 4

Dear Anne,

Thank you for the praise and the strength of your question. 'Laying on of hands' may have been as otiose as it was religiose and I don't know whether I am seduced by sonority into unreality: but as it happens, I've just had the enclosed photocopied – a copy of an address to the MLA last Christmas (1979) and I thought it might be a substitute for the letter I should be writing. Also I enclose a copy of a poem that sprang from the visit with Michael, Paul and Noëlle to Kilpeck – and the Síle na Gig. It is a lame exchange and a late one for your kind and generous gift of the Percy *Reliques*. Forgive me for my usual boorish lethargy in not dropping a note.

Aaagh! Arvon! *Ochone.* Your *TLS* letter such a pure clear voice in the murk. It *was* fund-raising. But it raised – and will raise more – hackles and dust.

That was a lovely moment at Hay. I remember especially crossing the road to the pub! And the boys with their soda machine. Hope the poems keep visiting you.

Love to you both from both of us.

Seamus

In a letter to SH of 28 January 1981, the poet Anne Stevenson (1933–2000) had written, apropos of *Preoccupations*, of her 'uneasiness' with an assumption she had discerned in the book to do with 'the sanctity of poetry': 'You speak of a "laying on of hands", which seems to suggest a kind of episcopacy of poets.' She went on to point out the danger of a 'college of self-ordained poets, because it substitutes language for godhead', suggesting that 'the taking of the "word" for the Word is an error easily made in a faithless time'.

Parrying, SH sends her his 'Current Unstated Assumptions about Poetry', from the Summer 1981 issue of *Critical Inquiry*, the transcript of a statement he had made at the Modern Language Association's 1979 convention. In it, he had proposed Robert Lowell as the exemplary creator of a poetry that, refusing to be merely 'a passive activity within the life of a society, or at best an activity parallel with that life', stood in opposition to 'current assumptions that the poetic enterprise is too pure or too exquisite to survive the impurities and coarseness of the historical moment'. And he had gone on to argue as follows:

> I take it that the one central, current and indispensable assumption that still goes without saying is that poetry has a binding force, a religious claim upon the poet, and I take it that his ambitions will not be merely aesthetic, his activity not merely therapeutic or histrionic. I also assume that the poet still has in some sense a tribal role, that Matthew Arnold's scholar gypsy flying from contact with our feverish strange disease of modern life is not an image for the proper exercise of the imagination.

The poem additionally enclosed was 'The Figures at Kilpeck', which in *Station Island* came to be called 'Sheelagh na Gig'.

To Charles Monteith — MS Faber

29 May 1981 — 191 Strand Road, Dublin 4

Dear Charles,

Excuse the vivid ink – I'm down to the last pen in the house.

That was a memorable weekend in Oxford – from the first enlargement of finding myself in that legendary suite of rooms to the peace of Sunday morning. The reading, the signing and the dinner – to say nothing of the evening service – were all special occasions with their different delights and satisfactions and tremors, but over all I am thankful for your consideration and welcome all through. The Craig Raine lunch turned out to involve James Fenton and Ian McEwan, as well as a decrepit Michael Longley, just back after a sousing at the Lumb Bank Arvon Centre.

I regret I did not get to Fabers en route through London – but I thank you for sending on the Haffenden interviews, which I read through with curiosity and pleasure. The tussle with Philip is particularly good, I think. However, I renewed contact with Derek Mahon and saw Tom Kilroy's Chekhov – a marvellous play about nineteenth-century Ireland – the right play that should have been written then, but how good that Chekhov and Tom fill the gap even now.

However, the best news of last week is that between Wednesday and Saturday I was in Devon with Ted and we assembled a first shape for the *Book of Verse for Younger People*. It came to about 690 poems, 385 of which were in copyright. Too big a book and too high a copyright quota, I guess. Now we are in the process of cutting back.

We have copies of all the poems – in photo-copy – and each of us has a list of the putative contents, so the second job of cutting down is in train now. However, the book is on the way, and if we *could* make it as big as possible, I think that would eventually pay off in a big way. A kind of anthology-stopper of an anthology.

Ted has the material over there. Meanwhile, prepare the accounts department for a pay-out of £3/4000 for reprinting fees . . .

P. D. James has been in touch and we're going to meet before the departure for France, which is on June 16. Meanwhile, back to the exam papers.

Again, my gratitude for the hospitable time at All Souls.

Sincerely,

Seamus

Monteith was a Fellow of All Souls College, Oxford, where SH had stayed at his invitation. The poets Craig Raine, who had recently been appointed Poetry Editor at Faber, and James Fenton (b.1949) both lived in Oxford at this time, as did the novelist Ian McEwan (b.1948).

Lumb Bank, in Heptonstall, West Yorkshire, once owned by Ted Hughes, was now one of the Arvon Foundation's centres for creative writing courses.

Faber had recently published *Viewpoints*, a book of interviews that John Haffenden (b.1945), academic, biographer and editor, had conducted with poets – Philip Larkin among them.

A Voice from the Trees, Thomas Kilroy's adaptation of Chekhov's *The Seagull* was on at the Royal Court in London. Here and elsewhere, SH writes 'Chekov'.

P. D. James (1920–2014), writer of detective novels, was, like Raine, Haffenden and Kilroy, published by Faber.

To John Montague

MS Cork

11 June 1981

Dear John,

How's times? I'm in the middle of marking a question on *The Deserted Village* – hence pen – and towards the end of a massacre of exams, all piled into a short concentrated spurt since we are leaving to take a holiday in France on Tuesday. We go to the Dordogne for two weeks, then two weeks down further into Hautes-Pyrénées (both Gîtes de France houses) and then we cross into Spain for another fortnight with Marie's sister.

Twelve years since we met in Paris! Yet they have not been altogether wasted. Things have been shored against the ruin, but, by God, the northern ruin has much advanced since then. I was up in Bellaghy two weeks ago and the 'polarization' – I hate the word – is at its height. Non-Provo people pulling in behind the hunger-strike feeling because of Thatcher and RUC and the whole intransigence and hard-faced righteousness. Francis Hughes's funeral was an enormous affair, a kind of Pope's visit crowd, a big emotional charge all round.

Five minutes ago I didn't know I was going to write this. And now I must get back to the scripts. But my best to you and Evelyn and the girls for the summer. Hope you get working and get relaxed. We'll be back in August and I hope to see you sooner or later after that.

Yours on election night,

Seamus

Written on eye-catching Rebel's Rest, Tennessee, notepaper, but presumably in some other place – either at Carysfort College or Strand Road.

Francis Hughes (1956–81), interned as a member of the Provisional IRA, had died in the Maze Prison as the result of a hunger strike; he was a native of Bellaghy.

To Brian Friel — TS NLI

2 July 1981

A Thaisce,

I don't know about it – it may not be the thing at all, but it landed very fluently the other night, one bit after the other, and at the time I was lit up, with it and what I was taking at the time. Even if you like it, it's probably too long – perhaps I, II, III, and V? I had been reading Hingley's *Eleven Stories*, in particular the triad where the schoolmaster, the vet and the landowner reappear: 'A Hard Case', 'Gooseberries' and 'Concerning Love', and that got the opening lines of the second section going. My vet, needless to say, is pure invention – or is it impure?

At the same time I have been deep in Mandelstam and have completed a piece that runs to 25 pages in longhand for Karl Miller at the *London*

Review. It had been long promised – since the widow died last December – and I was terrified that I might not be able to get the gears to grip for it but thank God it moved with conviction and I was able to plough a deep enough score. Now I have to type the damned thing out.

This Dordogne area – which we have to leave the day after to-morrow, wedding day to you – was tremendous. I got a lot out of the caves, very rich to see the engraved horses and bison, and the uvular entry in was a reminder to trust the old secretive charge in oneself to the very end. Then medieval towns all about and the castles, the woods of oak and the river itself – did me good. And to crown it, I had an attic to myself in this house. If things go half as well at the next above address, I'll have got much more out of the summer than I dared to hope for.

How is Field Day? Botheration? But it will be worth it – there was the Abbey and the early Gate and now there's this – nothing else significant, to my knowledge. It is *not* expense of spirit in waste. ('Hens cackling and sunlight – it's all I remember,' she has just called in: we have hens and cocks and goslings shitting about the step and the *bean a' tighe* is a wee fresh-faced woman with broken veins, a navy-blue overall and low shoes and rolled down ankle-socks. Who wants St Tropez when you can have this.) I'll be keeping the lines in in case Chekhov bites again. All our love to you both – and the reduced – or is it 'gaining a son' – family. Seamus

SH gives the address of his next holiday place at the top of the letter, but doesn't record where he wrote this.

'*A Thaisce*': an endearment, literally 'My Treasure'.

Ronald Hingley's edition of *Eleven Stories* by Chekhov had been published in 1975. There is a poem by SH, not included in any of his main collections, only in his 1990 limited edition *The Tree Clock*, which has the title 'Among the Whins' and the subtitle 'From Chekhov's "Donegal Notebook"'. Friel's adaptation of Chekhov's *Three Sisters* was a Field Day production, opening at Derry's Guildhall on 8 September 1981.

'Osip and Nadezhda', SH's review of a number of books by and about Osip Mandelstam, was for the 20 August–2 September issue of the *London Review of Books*.

The caves at Les Eyzies, in the Dordogne, fit the description SH gives here.

'*bean a' tighe*': 'woman of the house'.

'in case Chekhov bites again': in *Stepping Stones*, answering a question of Dennis O'Driscoll's about the impossibility 'not to feel something like guilt', SH sheds light on his poem 'Chekhov on Sakhalin', written at this time of H-block hunger strikes and general sectarian strife: 'If I had followed the logic of the Chekhov poem, I'd have gone to the prison, seen what was happening to the people on the hunger strike and written an account of it, "not tract, not thesis".'

To David Hammond

MS Emory

7 July 1981

Chez M. Auguste Falliero, Caussade Rivière, 65700 Maubourget

Dear David,

Glad to get your letter with the good news of Catherine's success – *je l'embrasse pour félicitations* – and to know that Sadie's card got to the BBC. It was Christopher's idea that she should send it.

Meanwhile, we have left the riches of the Périgord for the quiet maize-fields and shimmering hillside vineyards of rural Gascony. The house here is much more spacious/elegant – I have colonized a real American-spacious garage, appointed with a sofa, a stack of perfectly cut logs, a loft full of bric-a-brac and walls of old stone, a floor area twice as big as our house in Dublin – and we have a pond with bulrushes at the end of a tree-hung garden. We're going in for indolence here, which we need after a busy but enriching – and slightly impoverishing – time in Dordogne. The surroundings there were unexpectedly better than I could have hoped for. I got a lot out of the caves, the medieval towns and made the pilgrimage – at least, I went on my own – to Rocamadour, a penitential place full of steps up the cliff-face, which has been in business since the twelfth century. (Catherine has just rushed in in consternation, having seen a snake!) As well as the travelling and the eating in restaurants, which was hoggish and enjoyable, I got time to do a really worth-while piece on Mandelstam for Karl Miller's *Review of Books*. It had been weighing on me since the new year when I took it on, but my fear was that I would not rise to the occasion. In the end I got a lot out of doing it, and while I was at it, the flow carried in a Chekhov poem which may work for Brian's *Three Sisters* programme. I also wrote to Tim O'Neill to send me some Boyne/Drogheda material for the third script, but nothing has come from him so far: his mother had been taken to hospital just before I left so there may have been trouble for him in the meantime.

You'll be at the Braid Valley business when this arrives. I hope all goes well and that the fuck-up over the rearranging of filming at the end of the summer has not put you into too uneasy a position. Mexico goes ahead, and Marie is coming with me. I have a sense of enormous self-indulgence, but a sense of starting again, with the Harvard arrangement looming.

If you're in Dublin, ring the McCabes. They seem to be having a good enough time – at least they've met Ben and John O'Doherty – and I'm sure they yearn to pick up the threads that we left so happily unravelled after *Faith Healer* last August.

Have one for me with Brian when you get to Donegal and give all our love to all your ones. Michael is 15 to-morrow . . .

Sláinte,

Seamus

'Catherine's successes': Catherine is Hammond's eldest daughter.

'Sadie's card', sent from France, was a spoof certificate, pretending to have been issued by the Centre d'Insémination Artificielle, and with a drawing of a plump, coyly blushing bumpkin in place of a stud animal's photo.

Rocamadour is known for its old religious buildings, one of which houses a Black Madonna, possibly of the fourth century and believed to effect miraculous cures.

The poem of SH's that appeared in the *Three Sisters* programme was 'Chekhov on Sakhalin'.

Tim O'Neill (b.1947) is an Irish calligrapher and writer about calligraphy with whom SH later came to collaborate on the translation of Old Irish poems.

'Mexico goes ahead': see following letter, to Homero Aridjis.

SH's Cambridge friends, Bernard and Jane McCabe, were house-sitting for the Heaneys.

To Homero Aridjis

MS Aridjis

1 September 1981 191 Strand Road, Dublin 4

Dear Homero,

It was the best fortnight in our lives and I cannot thank you enough for the opportunity you gave us to share in the whole experience. Morelia was one long climax and it was a cause of great satisfaction to all of us that the official artistic events of the evenings were as triumphantly successful as the social occasions in the afternoons and afterwards in the nights.

The culture of the country, the energy of the hospitality, the care of the Fonapas girls, the magnificence of Villa Montana, the personal hospitality, the official welcome, the whole sense of occasion, the constant note of celebration, the good poetic company, how powerful it all was! In memory, it remains as warm and alive as ever! To meet Borges then, and to have the driver and interpreter in Mexico: it was like a dream come true, yet I have a gold coin in my pocket to prove that it was no dream. You deserve all the credit for putting things into action: and for letting us see the Dance of the Old Men, the masks, the copper-beating, the Comensales . . . Our love to Betty and you, and our everlasting gratitude. We'll keep in touch!

Seamus

In August, SH had been a guest at the First Morelia International Poetry Festival in Mexico, organised by the poet and novelist Homero Aridjis (b.1940) and his wife (also his translator) Betty Ferber. The starry guest list included – in addition to the Argentinian Jorge Luis Borges (1899–1986) – João Cabral de Melo Neto (1920–99) from Brazil, Andrei Voznesensky (1933–2010) from the USSR, Vasko Popa (1922–91) from Yugoslavia, Tadeusz Różewicz (1921–2014) from Poland, Tomas Tranströmer (1931–2015) from Sweden, Günter Grass (1927–2015) from West Germany, and numerous others. The gold coin, a *centenario*, was payment for a television interview. The final festival dinner was held at the restaurant Los Comensales.

To Derek Mahon

TS Emory

22 September 1981 191 Strand Road, Dublin 4

Dear Derek,

I had some difficulty with it myself, and what I enclose may be too worked over. Part of the difficulty was that I wasn't finally sure of the tone – whether impersonal unsigned publisher's voice or personal statement. I have written what I feel is the truth about the book in 108 words – and if you want to use it or dump it doesn't make a difference either way for the book remains triumphant.* Did you ever hear Niall Montgomery's story about some Dublin shite who was listening to the talk about the magnificence of *Ulysses* sometime in the 1930s? 'Joyce?' he says. 'Jimmy Joyce? Jesus Christ, sure I knew him!' Jesus Christ, sure we all knew Mahon.

I'm feeling odd and faintly convalescent these last ten days, my first time to settle at home after the peregrinations of the summer and my first taste of four months' free time. There's a sense of occasion and privilege but I can't get a grip on myself or my hopes. Just sitting dopey and fiddling, with a heap of letters to answer and a reluctance to commit myself to them before I open some vein that promises poetic life. But maybe we'll get going after this.

I'll be glad to heave to with Montague and hope we have some time for a talk in November. As usual I've tackled myself with too much in too short a time but as O. Wilde said, time is waste of money. Here's hoping for positive results from New York in the meantime.

I've got to the stage where the kids are telling me dirty school jokes:

they've just asked me did I hear about the short-sighted castrator? He got the sack.

Love to Doreen and the tomboys.

Seamus

* After this, I separated two strains and wrote two different things. They're all yours, to throw away or keep.

PS The Ovid sequence is a lovely and fluent addition – especially the opening triads of the *Ovid at Tomis* poem; pure, pure excitement there.

S.

In answer to a request for a back-cover endorsement for Mahon's OUP collection, *The Hunt by Night* (1982). Typed on a separate sheet, the 'two different things' are headed 'Publisherly' and 'Personally'; in the event, Mahon's own blending of the two was used. At the foot of this sheet, 'Damned right, sir!' appears in Mahon's hand.

Niall Montgomery (1915–87) – both of whose names SH mistypes – was a Dubliner, an architect and a Joyce expert.

To Pat Strachan

TS NYPL

23 September 1981 191 Strand Road, Dublin 4

[. . .]

I enclose a MS, as you see. Derek Mahon's *The Hunt by Night* will be done in Britain by Oxford University Press, who published four previous volumes, the most recent being *Poems 1962–1978*, an interim new and selected kind of book which consolidated his first-rate achievement up till that. Oxford also did these books in the USA but this time he has reserved the right to find his own US publisher and when I was talking to him earlier this year I offered to put the new book your way when it was ready. I did so because I think he is the best in my own generation and is now writing at the top of his bent. There is a tremendous technical elan and a real imaginative territory which he has created for himself. He is the 'freest' of the Northern poets here, indelibly printed by the Protestant markings of a Belfast youth but stylish as hell in defiance of it. I always think of him as the Stephen Dedalus of Protestant Ulster, though he might not want that label. But anyway, you can see for yourself and decide what you think. As he said in the letter that accompanied the MS to me, 'FSG have got their Irish poet

after all' – not that he yearns to be slotted in that ethnic group either. I just think he deserves the best house he can get.
[. . .]

For all SH's advocacy, FSG decided not to take Mahon on to their list.

To Edna Longley   MS Longley

14 October 1981

Dear Edna,

Many thanks for sending us *A Language Not Betrayed*. It is unexpectedly abundant with toughness and hard critical delights, tremendously readable. I've not got through all of it, but I'm brought up short by the weight of the intelligence and the dimensions of the literary scanning device E.T. had. All those tired sentences about his 'literary hackwork' are blown to hell by your book. It's a real revelation, and the introduction clears the right paths into the field. There must have been a long hard slog of assembly and excision involved but it was all worth it. Your selflessness in his service makes you a true heir: can't you imagine his gratitude if he were to get the book for review?

Such evidence of industry goes through me like a rebuke. I have resigned from Carysfort and am treading water before the Harvard exit in January, yet have no sense of doing anything worthwhile. And these free months are what I have hankered for for years. Half-heartedly, I'm thinking of returning to Sweeney and getting him to fuck into print. Clear the desk, if you can't supply it . . .

Will we see you at the Simmons nuptials? One way or another, I hope we'll have a talk before Christmas, but in the meantime, congratulations on the work. A real contribution and confirmation.

Love,
Seamus

A Language Not to be Betrayed: Selected Prose of Edward Thomas is the full title of Edna Longley's book, which chooses from the vast output, in a wide range of genres that included reviewing, by which Thomas earned a living before he turned to poetry. Longley believes Thomas exerted a greater influence on SH's own poems than has generally been recognised; SH himself refers appreciatively to Longley's 'comprehension of Edward Thomas' in the Foreword to his first prose book, *Preoccupations* (1980).

1982

SH was at Harvard for the spring semester.

Publication in June of *The Penguin Book of Contemporary British Poetry*, edited by Blake Morrison and Andrew Motion, in which SH himself was placed prominently as senior and presiding figure, eventually roused him to issue a public statement of dissociation from the British context. In a business letter to Morrison, written after the anthology's appearance, SH says nothing about the matter, waiting till the following year before sending 'An Open Letter', in which he declares his position bluntly, to both editors.

The Rattle Bag, an anthology based on very different criteria, was published in the same year.

To Dennis O'Driscoll

MS Emory

22 January 1982 — 191 Strand Road, Dublin 4

[. . .]

Kist reading I'd like to be at – in those premises, especially. I hope the publication shifts along speedily anyhow, and that it releases you into new freedoms. Don't mind what the local tweezers might nip at: your own world is so rich and true that begrudging cannot – must not – breach it.

Thank Julie for sending on the review: indeed, thank you for awakening a part of me that slumbered – I went and wrote to Les Murray a year or two late, but still, a letter. I got to like the *Funeral Boys* better when I settled to it. In fact, the poem is wonderful in many ways and places – the grail image, the characters, the set nature pieces go well. It's pure Les. What more do we need? Maybe, less insistent opinions of Les. Still.

[. . .]

Dennis O'Driscoll (1954–2012), poet, essayist, civil servant and – in due course – the interlocutor who helped SH's *Stepping Stones* into being, was about to see his first book of poems, *Kist*, published by Dolmen Press. He was married to the American poet Julie O'Callaghan (b.1954).

Les Murray (1938–2019), Australian poet, who in those days styled himself

Les A. Murray, brought out his verse novel *The Boys Who Stole the Funeral* in 1979. Regrettably, SH's letter to him has not been traced.

To Rand Brandes

MS Emory

[February[?] 1982]

Adams House #I.12, Harvard University, Cambridge, MA 02138

Dear Randy,

Two weeks in, and I'm just getting settled. I am doing two lectures a week on modern poetry and am a mass of anxieties each week until they are done. Sorry to be slow off the mark.

Ted did all the Lawrence, if I recollect correctly. I did the Hardy, and he added 'Bags of Meat' and 'The Garden Seat'. He did the Blake, I did the Wordsworth. He did the Shakespeare, I did the Ralegh. But 'doing' meant making an initial list, or a heap of copies, and then we'd both skid through the list/heap and agree together. It was not a very organized enterprise, since we were essentially assembling a lucky-bag of goodies and there was no pedagogical or didactic end immediately in view. We had permission to be whimsical and personal, and were eager to put in off-the-beaten-path poems. It was very *happy* work, an excuse to meet and eat and talk about poems, a way of ploughing up the old furrows opened by our early reading. I seem to remember Ted suggesting that the anthology should contain in one volume lots of things that we came upon with a sense of discovery and by accident. And I suppose there was an unspoken slightly counter-cultural push in using so much Blake and Lawrence – since the mainstream sixth-form educational system don't lay so much emphasis on them – or on Clare. We were conscious that Donne/Herbert/Milton/Augustans/Romantics/Victorians were usually taken care of by the system and were half-consciously adding on, extending, opting for more emotionally direct, rumbustious pieces.

I'll certainly drop Ted a note to praise you and press him to answer. But. You know. Well . . . Mention my name and our hog-life. Our Carolina corn-spirits. But he's drowned in letters since he became Laureate. I think it best to write c/o Faber – unless somebody gave you his home address. My pact is that I don't divulge it.

Much love to all Emorians. Seamus

'Two weeks in': i.e. into SH's first spring semester at Harvard.

Rand Brandes (b.1956), who went on to be SH's bibliographer, was at this time a graduate student at Emory University and working on his dissertation *The Myth of the Fall in the Poetry of D. H. Lawrence and Ted Hughes*. Having met SH the year before, he had written to enquire which of the Lawrence poems in *The Rattle Bag* had been chosen by Hughes, and which by SH. The 'hog-life' and 'corn-spirits' refer to a party thrown by Ronald Schuchard (b.1940), who taught at Emory, and his wife Marsha Keith Schuchard (b.1940), which both SH and Brandes had attended and at which, in characteristic style, a whole roast hog had been the centrepiece.

To Michael Longley PC Emory

24 February 1982 [Postmarked 'Boston MA 021']

So far so good. The students are omnivorous, Ashberyian, disdainful in their way of anything too well written. I am housed monastically in an apartment with a red leather sofa, and eat meals in a student refectory. Does it make the heart young? No. Good wishes to all of you.

Seamus

On the back: Ingres's *The Bather* (1808) in the Fogg Art Museum, Harvard University.

To Desmond Kavanagh PC Kavanagh

18 May 1982 [Postmarked (semi-legibly) 'Boston']

Hello Auntie Bridie!

It's a shame I didn't write earlier but you see how I was kept occupied! God, the Orris men would fairly enjoy themselves over here. See you soon.

S.

'Auntie Bridie', who is invoked in many a postcard sent by SH to Kavanagh, sprang into being from a schoolboy joke that the two had once shared. This card shows a sequence of photographs by Eadweard Muybridge (1830–1904): *Two Women Disrobing*. I am unable to identify the 'Orris men'.

To Charles Monteith MS Faber

26 July 1982 191 Strand Road, Dublin 4

Dear Charles,

Marie very much enjoyed her lunch with you and Rosemary and John – and as for Catherine, well, her gift for taking pleasure in these occasions is already very highly developed and it was lovely that she was part of it all. Thank you for arranging it, nay, for cooking it.

The Yeats idea (with a long introduction, and the book to be substantial, prose, drama perhaps, and poems) I presume to be agreed in principle and would prefer to hold off on contractual sign-ups until the thing is in some kind of shape.

And the Professorship – much as I would like to be sponsored by you and John, and the very fact that you both thought of it means much to me, I think that I must not engage myself for it yet. I'd like to lay down two or three more works, which I feel responsible towards until they are finished, before venturing out into the ring. I do not mean the ring of the election, but the ring of the lecturer's spotlight. I feel that if I can complete certain tasks in the next five years or so, I shall be in a better position, psychologically and critically, to deliver the kind of statements that I feel the position calls for – though I do realize that it would be possible to get through the lectures without feeling the need to make them 'statements' . . . Sorry.

I must get on now to another bloody 'statement' – more a piece of uplift, a kind of foundation garment for the drooping spirits of those who assemble in Dublin this week for the annual conference of the World Reading Association – educational psychologists, testers and such. I have to give the opening address. Like you know what, it is 'full of quotations'.

With good wishes,
Sincerely,
Seamus

The 'Yeats idea', in the form sketched here, was not pursued, though a more straightforward selection of poems, *W. B. Yeats: Poems Selected by Seamus Heaney*, first appeared from Faber in 2000, a revision of an earlier selection for Field Day.

It is interesting that the Chair of Poetry at Oxford, which SH was to accept in 1989 (see various letters of that year) was something he was already training his sights on.

The *International* Reading Association, now International Literacy Association, is an American institution and holds its conferences in the USA.

To Blake Morrison

MS Morrison

24 August 1982 191 Strand Road, Dublin 4

Dear Blake,

Very glad to hear from you: it was my place to have been in touch long ago and I was keeping telling myself I'd get ready to write *the* letter about the book and the reaction etc. etc. John Carey's review seemed to be charged with an energy in excess of its occasion, and was very vehement, unfairly and punitively so. He simplified your record of my record on the political side of things and attacked a target of his own making. But the fact of the reviewing matter is that extreme reactions finally work inversely: the book surfaces against the put-down as surely as it goes down a bit against the big puff. Also, the Irish papers had not read the book; they were picking up the whiff of a row and that animated them. The joyousness with which people sympathized at the 'attack' on the book, the pleasure with which I asked them if they had read it . . . I consider myself honoured and lucky to have you as the commentator and the book is true and very enabling for me. As a matter of fact, the thing I have been most anxiously involved with since late 1979 – anxious because it has been slow to come and voices cry in my ear that this may be all folly – is a shot at a long poem, vaguely Dantesque, involving confrontations with various people/parts of myself, and the questions plied are those of fidelity/infidelity, community/self, a kind of search for end-of-'Casualty' freedom. It's set on Lough Derg, a place of pilgrimage, fasting, walking round in circles . . . But at any rate, what I think I'm at and what you get at in the book complement each other happily and this seems to say fully enough that you worked along the grain of things intimately and truly. I would like you to see a bit of the Lough Derg business, but until I have the bulk of it set up – or set down – I am shy of circulating it. But I hope we can meet at the end of September, when I'll be over for a couple of days. If you are free on September 30, maybe we could have lunch or drink or dinner. I'll be over the day before for a TV spectacular with Ted Hughes.

[. . .]

I look forward to seeing you in September.

Sincerely,

Seamus

Blake Morrison was at this time working on the books pages of the *Observer*. He had written to SH asking him to review certain books; in a paragraph omitted here SH gives reasons for turning the request down. Morrison's own monograph, *Seamus Heaney*, the first full account of SH's career to date, had come out earlier in the year. John Carey (b.1934), Merton Professor of English Literature at Oxford, an admirer of SH ever since *Death of a Naturalist*, had reviewed the book disparagingly.

The poem SH describes is 'Station Island'.

To Piotr Sommer

MS Sommer

25 August 1982 191 Strand Road, Dublin 4

Dear Piotr Sommer,

Thank you for your letter and for the many translations, which I have seen over the years, in different magazines. I have to apologize to you for not writing when you previously wrote to me, a failure which had more to do with my own lethargy and inefficiency than with any reluctance to be in contact with a translator. In fact, I am honoured to have been chosen (so copiously) for the anthology and am very conscious of the debt of gratitude to you. The translation of poetry is as exacting and difficult as it is rewarding, and it was shameful of me not to have answered your letter the last time. I have to plead guilty – by nature.

Broagh – from the Irish language *bruach* meaning a bank, riverbank – is the name of a small townland (that word itself having nothing to do with towns, but denoting a small defined district within a parish, in the countryside). It is situated on the northern bank of the River Moyola, a mile or so south-east of the village of Castledawson. The farm I grew up on was in two parcels of land, one called Mossbawn, in the townland of Tamniaran, and the other in Broagh. Three of our fields were actually on the riverbank, and the names we used for them (within the family) were 'the long rigs', 'the riverbank' and 'the half-acre'. The poem, as well as taking pleasure in naming the place, has a second but not necessarily obvious function for me, insofar as it weaves words from Irish (*Broagh*, with its characteristic Gaelic *gh* sound, *rigs* which is Scottish in origin and almost certainly came over to Ireland with the seventeenth-century plantation, and *docken* which is an Anglo-Saxon plural of *dock*, the broad-leafed weed) – Irish, Scottish and English heritages implicit in the local words. Though the English cannot pronounce the *gh* sound.

Gunnar is a figure in the Icelandic saga called *Njal's Saga*. His death is recounted in §77 of the Penguin edition – he was surrounded by enemies in his house and fought to the death with his bow and arrows. Then after his death, people on two occasions had a vision of him in his burial mound, the second occasion being narrated like this:

> One night, Skarp-Hedin and Hogni were standing outside, to the south of Gunnar's burial mound. The moonlight was bright but fitful. Suddenly it seemed to them that the mound was open; Gunnar had turned round to face the moon. There seemed to be four lights inside the mound, illuminating the whole chamber. They could see that Gunnar was happy; his face was exultant. He chanted a verse so loudly that they could have heard it clearly from much farther away . . . (*N.S.* trans. Magnus Magnusson and Hermann Pálsson, Penguin, 1972, p. 17)

And after the verse:

> 'There is great significance in such a portent,' said Skarp-Hedin, 'when Gunnar himself appears before our eyes and says that he would rather die than yield to his enemies; and that was his last message to us.' (p. 174)

However, while the explicit meaning of Gunnar's apparition in the saga seems to imply revenge, there is a great beauty and peacefulness about the scene itself, which seems to carry in its very atmosphere the possibility of peace and forgiveness. I think I probably used the image in the poem to concede the likelihood of the cycle of violence continuing, yet to express a longing for a possible repose and forgiveness. I realize this probably exceeds the amount of information you need, but the actual story of Gunnar is thrilling itself, and I cannot not let you have the moment of climax in the death-fight, when he is in the house with his woman Hallgerd, and his bow-string breaks:

> He said to Hallgerd, 'Let me have two locks of your hair and help my mother plait them into a bow-string for me.'

'Does anything depend on it?' asked Hallgerd.

'My life depends on it,' replied Gunnar, 'for they will never overcome me as long as I can use my bow.'

'In that case,' said Hallgerd, 'I shall remind you of the slap you once gave me. I do not care in the least whether you hold out a long time or not.'

'To each his own way of earning fame,' said Gunnar. 'You shall not be asked again.'

Great stuff! Anyhow, I am glad to have finally broken the corresponding ice with you, and delighted to be published in a Polish anthology. Polish poetry in translation has meant much to me, and earlier this year in Harvard I had the pleasure of attending Miłosz's lectures, and hearing him read.

With every good wish,

Sincerely,

Seamus Heaney

The Polish poet and magazine editor Piotr Sommer (b.1948) was the first of SH's translators into Polish, and one of the earliest in any language to translate his work. 'Broagh' is a poem from *Wintering Out*; Gunnar's name occurs in the political poem 'Funeral Rites', in *North*, where SH imagines 'those under the hill // disposed like Gunnar / who lay beautiful / inside his burial mound, / though dead by violence // and unavenged.'

Czesław Miłosz (1911–2004), Lithuanian-born Polish poet who had emigrated to the USA, had taken US citizenship and currently taught at Berkeley, eventually became a fatherly friend and figure of reverence to SH. For all his importance to him, SH persistently spells Miłosz's name without the stroke through the 'l'.

To Derek Mahon MS Emory

7 September 1982 191 Strand Road, Dublin 4

Dear Derek,

What do you think of this thing? The first five and a half stanzas are part of a six-stanza Christmas card I did four or five years ago and I suddenly put the other fittings on a couple of days ago. As you would say – and as I thought to myself in your exact formulation – 'it's very Christmassy'. If it's up to your scratch, feel free to hold it for the seasonal issue. If you feel it would discredit both of us, you're wrong, but tell me.

Meanwhile, what's happening? I'll be over at the end of the month and would like to see you. I'm hotelled by the BBC but that shouldn't be a bother – some time around 29/30 I hope we can all meet.

I'm simulating work by working on the Sweeney manuscript that is now ten years old. I'll have to get rid of it soon, if only to pretend to some 'achievement' before I return to the gilded young in Massachusetts 02138.

Love to Doreen and the burgeoning sons. Michael is now an indolent and sexual sixteen years old. And bad at exams forbye. Looking forward to the book.

Seamus

At this period, Mahon was working at the *New Statesman* in London. The typescript poem offered for his editorial consideration, 'An Ulster Twilight', was almost identical to the one included in *Station Island*. Mahon accepted it and it appeared in the *NS*'s issue for 23 and 30 December.

To Brian Friel

MS NLI

27 September 1982 191 Strand Road, Dublin 4

Dear Brian,

A week later: delighted that all swam along so well last week and that the reviews were so positive. The production was held very briskly together by Joe and Stephen flew through it like a bird. The more the anxiety of hoping it would go well recedes, the more the buoyancy of the thing insists itself into the memory. Thanks again for the hospitality and, in retrospect, apologies for keeping you up late on the night before one of the most anxious days of your year. I hope Belfast lifts off to-night.

A long talk with S. Deane on way back about what we might deliver to Field Day did not yield very much. It seems that if we are to do our thing, it should be a literary/publication kind of input. The idea of handing in a play seems risky for all and should not, anyhow, just come from a sense of obligation. Indeed, *could* not.

Anyhow, I thought I'd let you know the kind of things we canvassed as genuine possibilities. These should not be regarded as proposals yet but more as my briefing 'the onlie begetter', so that you can have a few thoughts before the meeting.

I thought of a *Field Day Review* – perhaps even the title extended to

FDR of Books – an annual or biennial publication. A forum for critical discussion at the Deane/Paulin level of selected books significant in or for Ireland. To be anchored on longish review articles – e.g. at the moment, Cronin's book on Anglo-Irish literature, the re-issue of *Black List #H*, the recent Banville. The point of it being that without setting out to preach or take a line, it could provide a lung through which certain airs could breathe naturally. It would also provide a service to Irish letters generally. It would not be against publishing poems and stories, but perhaps its main thrust should be in the critical/reviewing/essays-on-current-crises area.

The unease is the commitment to constant work on it. Deane's thought was an anthology to start with, or some kind of book. If the *Duanaire* had not been done, to do something like that. As we kicked this around, he evolved a large notion about a big 'Cabinet of Irish Writing', from C18 to present. But this would be a two-/three-year editing job. I thought, incidentally, of some time doing Tom Flanagan's unpublished essays on Tone, Davis, Mitchell, George Moore, Somerville and Ross: but that could not be a first step.

I also fluttered the idea, soon brought to earth, of a book for schools. No? Walk in with the *Field Day Book of Verse for Schools*? Or not just verse? A notion only.

I don't think a literary magazine, with the usual poems and stories, by the usuals, would have the new edge we hope for.

Another thing that flitted across my mind: is there anything like Alec McCowen's *Gospel according to Mark* possible for us? A shortened *Inferno*? To be called *Hell Open*. Oh hell.

I'm rushing off to-morrow to do the BBC pre-publication programme for the anthology (which I've asked Fabers to forward). Then it's on with the motley on the campuses, then the Cheltenham Festival, and back here around October 19th. A balls-up, in a way.

Much love to Anne and again, thanks for the welcome. Tell Noel I'll be available to drive T. Paulin from Dublin on the weekend of 24th. I'll be available surely. The cord pulled happily. Pull away till I see you.

Adh Mór,
Seamus

Friel's play *The Communication Cord* had enjoyed an autumn tour by Field Day.

'Cronin's book' was *Heritage Now: Irish Literature in the English Language* (1982), by the poet and literary all-rounder Anthony Cronin; Francis Stuart

(1902–2000) was the author of the novel *Black List, Section H* (1971), which had been long out of print, largely because of Stuart's notoriety as an unrepentant Nazi sympathiser; John Banville (b.1945) had just published his novel *The Newton Letter*.

Seán Ó Tuama and Thomas Kinsella's anthology, *An Duanaire, 1600–1900: Poems of the Dispossessed*, had appeared the year before.

The 'Cabinet of Irish Writing' sounds like a first hint of the *Field Day Anthology of Irish Writing*, eventually published in 1989.

The British actor Alec McCowen (1925–2017), whom SH here calls 'Alex McCowan', had devised and toured widely with his theatrical presentation of *St Mark's Gospel*, in which he performed the entire text solo.

'*Adh Mór*': Good luck.

To Ted Hughes

TS Emory

28 October 1982 [191 Strand Road, Dublin 4]

Dear Ted,

I have this compulsion to take notepaper from hotels: a trace element of the younger impulse to piss in the hand-basin when drunk. Anyway, it's the nearest to hand.

There may be something among these three that you [and] Leonard can use. The *Beowulf* bit comes from a sample I did a year or so ago when I thought I might face a commission to translate the whole thing. But after less than a hundred lines I felt I was not hitting the right swing and that the bitty movement and the pert alliterations were just too without inner rhythm, neither hammer nor oar, so it has stalled.

The basilica piece is a section from the Lough Derg pilgrimage sequence that seems to go on its own, and the other is a little flutter above a strange accident I heard about in Antrim where one whiff of the silage gas killed a man who went up to inspect it. (I'm beginning to write, by Christ, as if I were doing one long poetry reading.) Anyway, I hope Leonard will find one of them usable.

I'm in a kind of uneasy turmoil at the moment. First of all, to-day news has broken about a rich (£8000 (Irish) approx.) American award – the Bennett Award, from *Hudson Review* – which I have been given, and it's all over the newspapers and was on the radio this morning so the whole bloody country is in possession. It's a wonderful unlooked-for bonus but of course it is strangely unnerving. I feel I should give half of it to my poorer brothers and half of it to some good literary cause. Luxurious uneases, I suppose, after all.

But the other thing that is disturbing is a submerged sense of crisis about this whole cultural/political profile, brought into focus by a new Penguin *Contemporary British Poetry* where I figure as a kind of pride-of-place goodie. I know in one sense the British banner means nothing, but in another sense I have a feeling of *mauvaise foi* or whatever because I have bonded myself firmly into the Irish dimensions here. I have a notion of writing an open letter to the editors (B. Morrison and A. Motion, for God's sake) and yet that parade goes against my usual instinct to keep the head down in these areas. But maybe it is time to open the discourse beyond the brutalities of IRA, UVF, British Army, Paisley, and so on. I stayed clear of the hunger-strike propaganda here last year but now if I am not careful I shall get entangled with a triumphalist Falklandia image which is equally subtly propagandist and misrepresentative.

The weekend was wonderful and full. There was something rejuvenating about reading those poems in Mary's house, in that company. It fed the dwindling hump.

And thanks for the otter news. Soon we'll have to go Jerpointing but before that we have to go to see the families in the north. Things are in danger there again: there was a report last night of a man who had his hand cut off by a hacksaw in Larne: he fled, and the police found the hand and the saw behind in the flat. It is said to be non-sectarian, but it is not without its symptomatic dimensions.

Much love to Carol. Hope we meet again soon.

Seamus

On notepaper snaffled from the Four Seasons Hotel, San Antonio, Texas, but presumably sent from 191 Strand Road.

'Leonard': Leonard Baskin (1922–2000), US printmaker and sculptor, whose images helped Hughes to conceive the character of Crow, and with whom Hughes occasionally collaborated, notably in such publications as his *Cave-Birds*, *Under the North Star* and *Flowers and Insects*. Baskin published numerous titles through his own Gehenna Press, but nothing by SH. The poems enclosed with this letter, for Baskin to consider, were 'Grief in North Antrim' ('The sunlit basalt spondee of Fair Head . . .'), 'A Ship of Death' (section from *Beowulf* beginning 'Scyld was still a strong man when his time came') and 'In a Basilica' ('I knelt inside *basilica*. I knelt / in its mother-of-pearl sounds . . .').

'*mauvaise foi*': SH writes *mauvais fois*.

'I have a notion of writing an open letter': an early version of this letter, in verse, was addressed to Blake Morrison on 31 March the following year.

'triumphalist Falklandia image': because of Britain's victory in the Falklands War of 1982 and the jingo spirit this had stirred nationally.

To Charles Monteith

TS Faber

29 October 1982 191 Strand Road, Dublin 4

Dear Charles,

Times are critical again here and it may be in response to the distresses and crises of the moment that I find myself in a sort of small turmoil. A couple of things on the private front first: by now you may have heard that another award has come my way, this time from the *Hudson Review*, a mighty offering of $12,000, previously awarded to V. S. Naipaul, Andrei Sinyavsky, and either Nicolás or Jorge Guillén – I always get them mixed up. Such a thing always puts one oddly on the line, feeling a mixture of guilt and responsibility, to whom or on behalf of whom it is hard to say, but let's say to those less gilded with 'success'. A second little crisis is my pride-of-place and exemplary status in *Contemporary British Poetry* – given that I have had an Irish passport for years and have bonded myself to some extent into an understated (I trust) but not undetermined Irish constituency. And having survived some pressures on the Provo propaganda front – especially during the hunger strike last year – I feel vaguely assumed into a triumphalist Britisher machine just now. I realize, of course, that Blake and Andrew are not involved in any devious political action and I also realize that these anxieties are to do with my own definition within this island. But that definition becomes more and more important as the situation here becomes more and more rent – at least the northern situation.

Which brings me to my real reason for writing. I feel that I should publish *Sweeney* – at least initially – on this side of the Irish Sea, neither north nor south, as it were, but in the fifth province. The concept of the fifth province, of those with a disposition rather than a position, those disposed to an idea of cultural redefinition without necessarily asserting their predisposition in stark political terms – a procedure which has so far yielded little – this concept has been espoused by Field Day, the company of which I am a director, along with Brian Friel, Stephen Rea, Seamus Deane, David Hammond and Tom Paulin. So far the work of the group has been really in Stephen and Brian's hands, producing the last three plays of Brian's. But we are committed to further action, and publications are a possibility. None of them know that I am writing this letter.

I feel, however, that they would all be delighted if I were to offer *Sweeney* as a first Field Day publication and I wish to ask you to consider earnestly and quickly, freeing me to offer it to them. Not necessarily for ever. But from the beginning I had some idea that a mad king from Rasharkin who loses his head at Moira and goes through traumatic experiences in Bushmills and South Armagh, who feels at home on Slemish but who ends up in Carlow, who is driven mad by violence between northern dynasties and who retreats into peace and paranoia among the trees everywhere from Mourne to Galtee – I had some idea that he was a salutary figure for the contemporary imagination in this country, north and south. And suddenly now I feel that the obvious thing and the best gesture and the authentic event would be to publish the text here in the first place. I should also say that I have always had a slight unease about its appearance next, after *Field Work*, on the Faber list, insofar as it would seem to ask for a certain kind of attention and significance that it may not intend. I did it as a service, to have it available here in the first place. Anyhow, come to think of it, I don't think we have signed a contract; but contracts are not what I feel bound by but rather the trust between all parties that precedes and survives contracts.

May I feel free to offer the text – not yet quite ready – to Field Day for first publication, for a definite number of hardback and paperback copies? I don't know how many, say one thousand hardback and two or three paperback, and then, if Faber is interested, Faber to do a paperback edition in a couple of years? In the meantime, I should hope that the Lough Derg poem would form the core of a book which I would expect to submit inside six months.

As I say, this is a proposal which none of the other directors of Field Day knows about, and if it meets with your agreement and the agreement of the Faber board, I should be grateful if it were kept as confidential as possible until the book would be nearing publication.

The lavish Dolmen limited edition *à la Táin* now seems out of date – though I'm sure it would not have been unacceptable as a double publication ten years ago. Can we think of what I propose as simply moving with the times, tenderly and responsibly? I hope so.

I have written this very quickly because if I stop to consider I will hesitate and not write frankly enough.

There we are then. I hope to God the *Rattle Bag* is getting a lift and that all goes well with you. Marie – and Catherine – send their love.

Sincerely,
Seamus

PS It is, of course, possible that FD may not be as interested as I have assumed – though I know they are searching for a role which *I* think *Sweeney* would fill. But I wish to be able to give them first option. S.

Sweeney Astray duly appeared as a Field Day publication a year later; the Faber edition had to wait till 1984.

'*à la Táin*': Thomas Kinsella's translation of the Irish epic had been published in a handsome edition, with illustrations by Louis le Brocquy (1916–2012), by Dolmen in 1969.

To Brian Friel MS NLI

5 November 1982

Dear Brian,

Can you take a look at this? It was a valedictory lecture at Carysfort, but I might trim it and, on page 10, add a couple of paragraphs *de re Britannica* in the north, how one has to withdraw from the mono-cultural prescriptiveness implicit in 'British' as fastidiously and steadfastly as one refuses the monocular vision of *fíor*-Gaeldom. Then I wondered if it might do as the John Malone Memorial Lecture – Hammond wants me to do the first one – and then – would it have any chance as a pamphlet? Be absolutely frank in your response, for Christ's sake.

I enjoyed yesterday immensely. In haste,

Seamus

PS It probably has not enough punch for a pamphlet.

Attached to this was a typescript, with many manual crossings-out and revisions, of the lecture 'Among School Children, Carysfort, May 7, 1981', which never became a Field Day pamphlet, but was published as *Among Schoolchildren*, printer unspecified, in 1984.

'*fíor*': 'true', or *echt*.

1983

Again, SH was at Harvard for the spring semester; later in the year, engagements to teach and read took him to the West Coast. As for his relations with Britain (or 'the land of the Britons' as he sometimes referred to it in letters to friends), it appears from his correspondence with both Blake Morrison, for whom he wrote book reviews, and Craig Raine, his editor at Faber – see the letter of 8 August – that a crisis in his own feelings of allegiance, albeit not concerning them personally, was to be weathered.

To Brian Friel

MS NLI

19 February 1983

Adams House #I.12, Harvard University, Cambridge, MA 02138

Dear Brian,

I'm writing this in a laundrette: even worse than playing scrabble at home.

[. . .]

After three weeks I've got settled and am in some kind of unfussy state of control. As you may remember, I went first for a week to Ann Arbor and then arrived here spent after a hectic bout of teaching, eating, drinking and reading. Then when I landed I got a note from the IRS. And the gable broke off one of my back teeth. And I was bleak to start with . . . Anyway, I think it was getting a shape put on my pamphlet that heartened me. Then I saw two nice women accountants in Boston and they sorted out the tax people. (It was a false alarm.) Then Mahon arrived and was on my hands all last week. So gradually things are getting settled.

Anyway, here's a revised version. Mahon was very insistent that I should make it more strictly obedient to metre and rhyme-scheme. For two reasons. One artistic – you should stick to the rules of the game, a position I half believe only, but when he offered the other reason, namely that the piece cannot afford to be unbuttoned since it will be heavily leant on, I took his point. He wanted me to drop the yarn about the drawers. I still like it as a contrary, local bit of blather. What do you think?

In the end I suppose the piece refuses to get stuck into the IRA/UDR/BRIT dirt-energies. In the end, they're all anti-artistic constituencies and Field Day has to maintain a superb artistic red-socked imaginative infallibility. It has to run the Inquisition from an extra-national point of vantage.

What about publishing it after it appears as a pamphlet? I know Miller will be mad to have it for *LRB*, but I am not sure what will be the better procedure: to have him print it there as a piece, with the rubric saying where it's printed and what it's part of and where the pamphlets are available, or just to make sure he has three reviewed.

I'll talk to you this weekend – Meanwhile, the drier's stopped, the warm heat's driving me out. Love to Anne. See you.

Seamus

SH was staying in Adams House, one of the university's residential houses, occupied mainly by undergraduates. He had been revising *An Open Letter*, for its publication by Field Day in September. The other two Field Day pamphlets were prose items: Seamus Deane's *Civilians and Barbarians* and Tom Paulin's *A New Look at the Language Question*.

Whatever the gist of 'the yarn about the drawers', SH took Mahon's advice and it was removed.

IRS: Internal Revenue Service.

IRA/UDR/BRIT: Irish Republican Army/Ulster Defence Regiment/British.

To Blake Morrison

MS (LETTER) AND TS (POEM) Morrison

31 March 1983 — 191 Strand Road, Dublin 4

Dear Blake,

Thanks for sending the copy of the basilica poem – some other citizen sent me a copy of the *Private Eye* and both were waiting when I got back here last Friday for the mid-term.

I have to apologize again for not delivering Neruda but in the meantime I enclose copies of the lines in response to the nomenclature. It is, of course, a kind of public gesture but it springs from a genuine sense of crisis about the whole thing. I've a reluctance to raise the subject but a sense of abdication if I leave it alone. The exercise is finally purgative for me and may prove a salutary irritant all round. At the same time, I don't want it to be a sectarian *anti-Brit* tract: so I'm relying on tone and our friendship to carry the day. I enclose a copy for Andrew too.

I'd be grateful if you kept it close to your chest for a few weeks. Between ourselves, it may come out as a pamphlet here and if that is to be so, I'd like it to spring unexpectedly into notice.

Meanwhile, the Chilean will be my next concern. I'm reading the *Memoirs* – what a horny bastard he was, among other things.

Craig is hard at me to come over in June and if I do, I hope we'll meet again.

Sincerely,
Seamus

AN OPEN LETTER

What is the source of our first suffering? It lies in the fact that we hesitated to speak . . . It was born in the moment when we accumulated silent things within us.

Gaston Bachelard

1
Addressed to: The Editors,
The new *Penguin* of British verse,
Harmondsworth, Middlesex. Dear Sirs,
  My anxious muse,
Roused on her bed among the furze,
  Has to refuse

2
Your adjective. It makes her blush.
It brings her out in a hot flush.
Before this she was called 'British'
  And acquiesced
But this time it's like the third wish,
  The crucial test.

3
For weeks and months I've messed about,
Unclear, embarrassed and in doubt,
Footered, havered, spraughled, wrought
  Like Shauneen Keogh,
Wondering should I write it out
  Or let it go.

4
Anything for a quiet life.
Play possum and pretend you're deaf.
When awkward facts nag like the wife
            Look blank, go dumb.
To greet the smiler with the knife
            Smile back at him.

5
And what price then, self-preservation?
Your silence is an abdication.
Your Prince of Denmark hesitation
            You'll expiate
In Act Five, in desperation –
            Too much, too late.

6
To think the title *Opened Ground*
Was the first title in your mind!
To think of where the phrase was found
            Makes it far worse!
To be supplanted in the end
            By *British* verse.

7
'Under a common flag,' said Larkin.
'Different history,' said Haughton.
Our own fastidious John Jordan
            Raised an eyebrow:
How British were the Ulstermen?
            He'd like to know.

8
Answer: as far as we are part
Of some new commonwealth of art,
Salute the independent heart
            And equally
Doff and flourish in your court
            Of poesie.

9
(I'll stick to *I*. Forget the *we*.
As Livy said, *pro se quisque*.
And Horace was exemplary
            At Philippi:
He threw away his shield to be
            A naked *I*.)

10
Yet doubts, admittedly, arise
When somebody who publishes
In *LRB* and *TLS*,
            The *Listener* –
In other words, whose audience is,
            Via Faber,

11
A British one, is characterized
As British. But don't be surprised
If I demur, for, be advised
            My passport's green.
No glass of ours was ever raised
            To toast *The Queen*.

12
You'll understand I draw the line
At being robbed of what is mine,
My *patria*, my deep design
            To be at home
In my own place and dwell within
            Its proper name –

13
Traumatic Ireland, where I live
So sceptical of all I love,
Where politics have slipped a glove
            On mind and hand
And numbed their rapture as they rove
            The opened ground

24
Exhaustion underlies the scene.
In Harmondsworth, on Stephen's Green,
The slogans have all ceased to mean
Or almost ceased –
Ulster is British is a tune
Not quite deceased

25
In Ulster, though on 'the mainland' –
My trope for it's 'the other island' –
Ulster is part of Paddyland,
And Londonderry
Is far away as New England
Or County Kerry.

26
So let's not raise a big hubbub.
Steer between Scylla and Charyb
A middle way that's neither glib
Nor apocalyptic,
Suggested by the poet Holub
In his Aesopic

27
Story set in a picture-house.
During a film, this man cuts loose
When a beaver's called a mongoose
By the narrator –
Who, after all, was just a voice
Dubbed in later

28
On footage of some beaver dam,
Some old-style, B-feature flim-flam.
Anyhow, as the creature swam
And built and gnawed,
This man breaks out into a spasm
Of constant, loud

29
And unembarrassed protestation.
Names were not for negotiation.
Right names were the first foundation
	For telling truth.
The audience, all irritation,
	Cries 'Shut your mouth!

30
'Does he have to spoil our evening out?
Who is this self-promoting lout?
Is it an epileptic bout?
	Mongoose? Who cares?
Get the manager. Get him out.
	To hell with beavers!'

31
Need I go on? I hate to bite
Hands that pushed me to the limelight
In the Penguin book, I regret
	The awkwardness.
But British, no, the name's not right.
	Yours truly. Seamus

The covering letter is on Harvard notepaper, but also headed with SH's Dublin address.

The satirical London magazine *Private Eye* had printed lines from 'Station Island' in its column 'Pseuds' Corner', of which the poet Christopher Logue (1926–2011) was compiler.

'An Open Letter': included in this selection with some hesitancy because, while nominally addressed to Blake Morrison and Andrew Motion as the editors of *The Penguin Book of Contemporary British Poetry*, its primary purpose was to make a public declaration, and it seems to me that this ambivalence is reflected – for all Derek Mahon's advice, reported by SH to Brian Friel in his letter of 19 February – in the awkwardness not just of its manner but of much of its versification too. SH also supplied notes: one apologises for replacing *Poetry* with *Verse* in the title of the book which had prompted his outcry – 'a result', he admits, 'of the constrictions of rhyme'; another refers to reviews of that book by Philip Larkin, Hugh Haughton and John Jordan; a third, to Donald Davie's essay in *Critical Inquiry* (vol. 9, no. 1, 1982), 'Poet: Patriot: Interpreter'; and a fourth, to Miroslav Holub's poem 'On the Necessity of Truth'.

The text received by Morrison differs here and there from what was printed when it was brought out by Field Day. See letter to Morrison of 10 August.

To Derek and Doreen Mahon

PC Emory

5 June 1983 [Postmarked 'Clochán Liath' (Dungloe)]

The car in the field is true enough, anyway. We're up in Donegal for a week – the only holiday we're likely to get this year. I hope Greece was a great event for you all and that the return to London has been effected. I might get over with Tom (*Year of the French*) Flanagan for a couple of days in early August and will contact you if we make it to London. (Dorset is what he wants to see.) Meanwhile, looking forward to *Hunt by Night*. Love from all of us. Seamus

PS Your man on the stamp once described by Kavanagh as a 'fake tramp, with his donkey tied to a lamppost outside the Bailey'.

An Clochán Liath is a town in the Gaeltacht.

The postcard shows an idealistically sunny pastoral scene of sheep (and a car) in a field.

Thomas Flanagan's novel *The Year of the French* had been published and received with immediate acclaim in 1979.

The 'man on the stamp' is Pádraic Ó Conaire (1882–1928), most of whose books were written in Irish. The Bailey is a Dublin pub that Patrick Kavanagh frequented.

To Tom Paulin

MS Emory

15 June 1983 191 Strand Road, Dublin 4

Dear Tom,

Congratulations on the book – which I look forward to seeing – and my apologies for not being with you at the launching. I had no idea that it was going to be a prelude to the cassette reading. And I hope you don't mind my not turning up for that – I'm afraid I am mad at myself for not taking the opportunity Craig gave me to re-record my tape for that series, which I cannot bear to listen to. And so all celebrations connected with the damned thing make me turn tail. But it is a great pleasure to share the tape with you and I look forward to hearing your side of it. (Fabers haven't sent me one yet.)

That was a very rushed event at Dunadry, and uneasy too because of that sense of pressure. I was sorry in a way that the argument or statements of purpose Seamus D. was looking for did not have time to get formulated, but I was grateful that you felt you could approve of the open letter and that you picked up the cultural gesture in the Burns stanza. I have revised the thing again in a few places and will send on the new one when it's copied. I also have to write to Blake again – I've added a stanza addressed personally to him, which, when I thought of it, was a bad omission in the first place, given his immense commitment to the work I've done through the work he has done. But I'm afraid the neurosis of trying to get something said on the well-known complex subject made me insensitive to other decencies that were to be preserved.

I don't know what's happening about the play. I liked the Fugards a lot – there's a breath of air in them that is our air, a kind of clarity and concern as well as a hard-bitten emotional accuracy. But I agree that *The Island* is going to be seen as a Provo espousal if we do it, and I wonder if the other one is not just a bit too locally placed not to be on the edge of boredom for our audiences. By the way, do you know Lowell's *Agamemnon*? A bit of a liberty, a butchery I suspect, but it has tremendous direct lines.

Enjoy yourself, and trust in the force of your book. I think you have the channels well opened! *Sláinte*,

Seamus

In the early 1980s, Faber brought out a series of poetry cassettes, two poets per cassette; SH shared his with Tom Paulin, whose new collection of poems, *Liberty Tree*, was published in 1983.

The 'event at Dunadry' was a Field Day Company meeting which took place at the Dunadry Hotel – not, as usually happened, at the home of either SH or Brian Friel – and was unsatisfactorily rushed.

The 'cultural gesture' that Paulin picked up was that SH's decision to employ the 'Burns stanza', which was Protestant in origin, should forestall any complaint that the 'Open Letter' was merely Nationalist in spirit.

The Island (1973), by the South African playwright Athol Fugard (b.1932) in collaboration with John Kani (b.1943) and Winston Ntshona (1941–2018), is set in a prison cell and – interestingly, considering the versions both SH and Paulin made of it – incorporates a performance of Sophocles's *Antigone* in shortened form. The other play SH had been reading is likely to have been Fugard, Kani and Ntshona's *Sizwe Banzi Is Dead* (1972), which has on occasion been presented in repertory with *The Island*. Powerful and politically resonant as both plays are, Field Day did not take them on.

Robert Lowell had translated the whole of Aeschylus's *Oresteia*, of which *Agamemnon* is the first part.

To Joseph Brodsky

MS Beinecke

20 June 1983

Adams House #I.12, Harvard University, Cambridge, MA 02138

Dear Joseph,

Jonathan Aaron told me on Friday that your mother had died. A pang of unexpected shock occurred – I had never taken into account that your parents were still behind you all that time. Stupidly, I had assumed that your spiritual state – Yeats's 'finished man among his enemies' stage? – of solitude and beyond-ness was some sort of absolute condition. I am sorry to hear of your loss and hope it can be ridden out without too much distress.

Sincerely,
Seamus

SH had first met Joseph Brodsky (1940–96), the exiled Russian poet now living in the USA, at the 1972 International Poetry Festival in London. Brodsky, who had taught at various US colleges, was by this time something of a poetry superstar, and SH, whose public pronouncements on him include an article rejoicing in the 1987 award to him of the Nobel Prize in Literature and a eulogy written after his unexpectedly early death, confessed to being exhilarated by his company. Sadly, from the point of view of this book, the friendship seems to have been a matter more of merry lunches and late-night conversations than of illuminating letters.

Jonathan Aaron (b.1941) is a US poet and one of the translators of Brodsky's poems into English.

To Craig Raine

MS Faber

8 August 1983

191 Strand Road, Dublin 4

Dear Craig,

Thanks for sending back the Maxton MS.

Farrar Straus are indeed bringing out the Sweeney and I regret that I did not clarify this in the meantime. I assure you it was not in any spirit of stealing a march or moving behind backs: when I reconsider, I realize that it was done in a kind of sleep-walk, and always, I suppose, I assumed that Farrar and Faber were in constant contact and that Pat Strachan/Roger Straus would not proceed unless all the formalities were being observed. A certain anxiety has hung over the Field Day venture for me, it being a first-time, one-off venture and I simply had not got Fabers on my mind in the context of the Sweeney book.

I have not yet signed the formal contract with Farrar so if Fabers wish to re-negotiate that, I am happy to have them do so, as an earnest of my good faith in the matter – though now that I find myself in New York as often, maybe oftener, than I find myself in London, what has been 'the normal way' of doing things, i.e. Fabers selling the book to Farrar, seems to have become subtly abnormal.

I should be very sorry if this turned into a crisis of trust between me and Fabers. It was negligence on my part and, perhaps, some submerged notion that *Sweeney Astray* was not a MS that was going to cause all that much excitement in Queen Square, that brought about the present situation.

I have just got back from three weeks of poetry workshops in California. Never worked as hard in my life, so am taking a holiday in France for the next couple of weeks. Will be back here by September 1st.

Sincerely,
Seamus

SH had asked Craig Raine to consider a manuscript by the Irish poet Hugh Maxton (aka W. J. McCormack; b.1947) for publication by Faber, and Raine had turned it down.

The publication of *Sweeney Astray* by Field Day in November 1983 was followed by editions from Farrar, Straus and Giroux in May and Faber in October 1984.

To Blake Morrison MS Morrison

10 August 1983 [Normandy]

Dear Blake,

I am writing this at a hotel window overlooking the Seine, in Normandy, on the first morning of a two-week holiday. The family are still in their beds and the mists are not yet lifted.

I was in California until 29th July and then was hosting visitors for the first week of August in Dublin. Consequently, I am carrying a small bag of unanswered letters by sea and road, holiday or no holiday . . .

When I get back, I'll send you a revised 'Open Letter'. Your note earlier in the spring was a salutary reminder of what, in my anxiety about other things, I had forgotten, namely that our private friendship should be given its weight as well as the public issues. I've tried in a couple of places to give the thing more personal intonations – beginning with 'Blake and Andrew' in line one – and hope that it won't seem an unseemly thing. It should appear as a pamphlet here early next month.

In America, I had a look at that new Neruda collection, and it didn't seem anything very exciting. So, if you haven't committed the Synge letters to anybody, I'd be happy to have a go at them. Or, failing that, if Miłosz's *Witness of Poetry* (last year's Nobel lectures) is going, I'd like a shot at that.

I'll be in Dublin now until next January, and am hoping to keep the head low, have refused many readings, but will probably be across in London at least once before Christmas. At which time I'll certainly be in touch.

But now the *petit-déjeuner*; and if you're ever near Les Andelys stay here, at Hôtel Chaîne d'Or. Lovely setting, on the water. Barges and all that. And Monet's gardens, at Giverny, about 15–20 miles south.

Take care.

Seamus

SH did indeed review Ann Saddlemyer's edition of *The Collected Letters of John Millington Synge: Volume One*, in a piece that would not be printed in the *Observer* until January 1984.

To Barrie Cooke

MS Pembroke

30 August 1983

Dear Barrie,

That exchange on Saturday night was confirming and generative. I'd love to get the Murdoch and Wilder quotations, which were unexpected and authoritative and deeply helpful.

Meanwhile, to-day, and probably helped by the exposure to your own open and half-determined (I mean in the *determinist* sense) elk-images, and thoroughly *given* boat image, I wrote another poem (*Sweeney and the Scribes*) in a sequence that has just opened and that I want to keep open and opening.

I am so rigid that in order to make Sweeney my persona, my puritan self had to feel that it had earned the right – by a rigid translation – to make free with his possessions, which were/are, to some extent, mine.

Anyhow, *cher ami*, at this late hour, I typed out these new tremors for an earnest of the nurture in your studio. Maybe being tired is the way to be open? See you. Seamus

PS In exchange for your quotations, this one from Gaston Bachelard:

> 'What is the source of our first suffering? It lies in the fact that we hesitated to speak . . . It was born in the moment when we accumulated silent things within us.'

PPS Much love to the ever-lovelier Aoine.

The 'sequence that has just opened' makes up the third and final section of *Station Island.*

Aoine is the daughter of Cooke and Sonja Landweer.

To Paul Durcan MS NLI

19 September 1983 191 Strand Road, Dublin 4

Dear Paul,

Your letter means a lot and I am grateful for your thought in writing it and the corroboration it gives.

Obviously, as you divine, the thing was not as simple and populist as it looks. I had a sense of disrupting innocent enough complacencies and connivances, within the English and Ulster situation, but for inner cleanliness (poetry as Andrews Liver Salts) I felt I had to say in public the old-fashioned nationalist thing: I could not go on amphibiously because it was not so much amphibiousness as a sort of skulk. Good nature masking failure of nerve, all that. I am well aware too how ungrateful it may sound to the London literati and how old-fashioned to the neo-unionist imaginations of the north. Still, it did me good and the good is sweetened by the knowledge of your approval. Love to Nessa.

Seamus

The Irish poet Paul Durcan (b.1944) recalls that he and SH first met some time in the 1970s, possibly in Cork, and that their friendship deepened and warmed as the years passed.

To Blake Morrison

MS Morrison

20 September 1983 191 Strand Road, Dublin 4

[. . .]

And to let you have this copy of the pamphlet. I was moved by your gracious handling of the thing in the *Guardian* and I am now, of course, in the post-coital tristesse, asking why I ever bothered. Nevertheless, I feel the exercise has clarified and appeased something.

And I have been writing – a kind of rich outburst, long longed for, which also kept me from the Synge. A pay-off and refraction of the Sweeney translation, a persona sequence. Will let you see them before long. [. . .]

'gracious handling': Morrison had been quoted by the *Guardian* in its account of the *Penguin Book of Contemporary British Poetry* debacle.

To David Thomson

MS NLS

27 September 1983 191 Strand Road, Dublin 4

Dear David,

Yesterday I spent all day getting out of myself in the Camden Town book: a real writer's book, all the more so because of the way it eschews 'writing'. It is clear of all intent to woo and denies itself any appeal other than the direct and wholly personal transmission of a world – the world of a sensibility as well as the world of those streets. What is so triumphant and original and what must have been unnerving in the writing of it is [the] way in which an artistic work is wrested from the realm of history and chance. The diary form was clearly a risk but the right risk because of the way it releases the flow – the book's experimental stroke is completely instrumental in opening its emotional veins. You will pardon these immodest abstractions, I hope, because I think that beyond the immediate rewards of the portraits of characters and incidents (that funeral, for example, and those children in the Bermudas) and beyond the intrinsic delights of the daily entries, there is a new sort of achievement, one which is implicit in the methods of *Woodbrook* but which wins through in a less *given* subject here. And how marvellously you deal with the 'writing block' – to make that the subject of the writing is indicative of the resource and the honesty of the thing. It is pure work and I was thrilled to find Marie and myself floating up in its clear-water memories. And how truly the vernal presence of M. is rendered – your M., I mean. P. Kavanagh once talked about what he regarded as an impossible but proper ambition for himself as a poet: to play a true note on a slack string. He meant, I think, that a true writer is always aware of any technical trickery he may practise, however justifiably, and that this sense of rigging his material will rob him of some of his pride in the work. It seems to me that the purity and directness of *In Camden Town* has brought reader and writer to a condition of honesty that is both salutary and challenging – for both.

Much love to you all from all of us.

Seamus

It is the sadness and trust and the durable intelligence that bathes the whole caste and setting that is the immediate pleasure of course. I've gone on too much about the artistic puzzles and resolutions that were a special compulsion for me. S.

David Thomson, memoirist, social historian and employee of the BBC, was most celebrated as author of *Woodbrook* (1974), his account of working, when young, as a tutor in a big house in Co. Roscommon. His *In Camden Town* (1983) also addresses Irish themes, investigating as it does the history of the large Irish population of the London borough.

'children in the Bermudas': Thomson quotes a newspaper report of 1851 concerning the transportation to the Bermudas of pauper children from the borough of St Pancras.

'your M.': Thomson's wife Martina Mayne (1925–2013), who had been an actress and was now an art therapist.

For Kavanagh's 'true note on a slack string', see the posthumous compilation of his prose writings, *A Poet's Country* (2002).

To Roger Garfitt

MS Garfitt

29 September 1983 — 191 Strand Road, Dublin 4

Dear Roger,

Long long ago I should have written. Your friends and Frances' have been giving me the news and you have both been in our thoughts here. And at times like this I wish we all could say 'in our prayers' but if the old catechism's definition can be extended to a communing with 'whatever means the good', you have been in them too. For Frances to have been stricken brings us so deeply back into our first places of solidarity and refuge. Please give her all our love and hope, and both of you, know we rejoice in your wedding. You are wedded to so much that the verb and the noun have been raised to awesome powers of beauty and strength.

Your book is true and in flight from the spurious: I admire especially 'Blue' and 'Rosehill', the second pulling off a difficult balance of inwardness and outwardness, a true sequence that does generate out of its elements and keeps within the one field of emotional force. 'The Doppel Gang . . .' has a good feel of release and supply, and the title poem has very pure lyric life, in that 'tarmac over flints' and those 'blue-blacks of tar' – strange how the energy transmits at certain points, without intervention.

I wish I could agree to a couple or three days in Northumberland with you, for many reasons, not least the pleasure of renewing the good life of talk and sympathy we have known. But I regret that I have bound myself to a term of the least movement possible. Each spring I go to Harvard, for the months from February till end of May, so that I am away from home, and buccaneering for four months. Last year I spoiled the autumn by too much toing and froing, and already this autumn I am breaking up the time with three outings: and since the proposed event would in reality involve the guts of a week away from home and the gutting of the writing for a fortnight, I have to apologize and decline, for the moment. The idea, as you outline it, has possibilities all right: but, among other things, I am fairly into a stride of work and I am in terror of losing it.

Much love to Frances and you: Marie joins me in all good wishes,

love,
Seamus

Roger Garfitt (b.1944) had sent SH a copy of his Northern House pamphlet, *The Broken Road*, and invited him to be guest reader at a writing weekend in Northumberland. Garfitt was married to the poet – also admired as a reader of other people's poetry – Frances Horovitz (1938–83), who had developed cancer and was to die of it a few days after this letter was sent.

'whatever means the good': see Louis MacNeice's 'Meeting Point'.

'What next . . .?': see the refrain to Yeats's poem 'What then?'

To Pat Strachan

MS NYPL

26 October 1983 191 Strand Road, Dublin 4

[. . .]

The whole unexpected Faber intervention in the Sweeney business took the spring out of my step in relation to the edition going forward in your care; and at the same time, I got into a swing of writing in September that kept me absent from the world of duties but happily absorbed in poems in a way that had not occurred in years: a sequence of lyrics which use Sweeney as a mouthpiece and which I hope will go together to make *Station Island* a biggish book, at least physically. I am enclosing a scarred copy of the MS – just to let you get the feel of the thing. I've cut out five sections of the 'Station Island' poem, which I thought was too cumbersome as it stood; the original first section came to feel too programmatic and scene-setting, the British army section too coat-trailing, and so on. Anyway, take a read at it some time at your leisure and let me know what you feel.

[. . .]

To Charles Monteith

MS Faber

1 November 1983 191 Strand Road, Dublin 4

Dear Charles,

The expedition through London and Bristol was speedy and fraught – by Monday afternoon, when I got back to London, it was 4:00 p.m. and I had to be at Heathrow by 7:00 p.m. and I hadn't the energy to go to Fabers, where I had hoped I might see you.

Thank you for your letters, and forgive me for not being in touch to rejoice about the Golding prize – we were delighted for him, of course, but in a way we think of it as your prize too. Enjoy what W.B. called 'the bounty of Sweden' – a far cry from the golf-club at Cushendall, but we'll raise a glass to you there, and make it clear that it was through the Bounty of Queen Square that Field Day are doing the book. Enclosed a copy for you and five others, signed but not dedicated to anyone in particular.

The *River* and *Quoof* make a powerful package: I was delighted to get them and read them with benign jealousy. Tremendous riches, an unabashed quality in each book that's very thrilling.

Meanwhile, I dropped off the MS of *Station Island* with Frank. I cut the title poem by 5 sections in the end, but I think it's still long enough and all the better for the surgery.

The main development, however, which I wish to try out with you before we go any further, comes from an idea I had, which I tried out on Ted and he jumped at it. Which is that we do – and really do it, a MS before the end of '84 – a follow-up to *The Rattle Bag*, called *The School Bag* (or is that one word, *The Schoolbag*)? Which would be a furrow ploughed down the field of the main tradition, the book that was assumed by the *RB*, the one which does Wyatt, Shakespeare's Sonnets, Dryden, Tennyson, Pound, Eliot – a tour of the monuments, a big compendium again, but obviously a cheaper event, since the copyright will be much less. At least, I think it should be less.

I guess there are three reasons for proposing this.

1) We enjoy seeing each other and working at the texts, and miss the excuse for meeting.
2) We are both, half-secretly, uneasy that the *Rattle Bag* seems to license a departure from the main achievements of English poetry, and feel a slight educational responsibility to stand up for the great tradition.
3) We think it would be a seller.

If you think this is a good idea, I propose that the advance on the royalties should take the form of paid tickets, London–Dublin, Dublin–London, for four or five sessions. And that we should all meet to talk it over before January 25, so that I'll have an excuse to go across and meet you, having been remiss on this last trip. Well, more harried than remiss, to tell the truth.

Anyhow, whether or not *The School Bag* is on, I hope you enjoy *Sweeney*. Marie sends her love, and Catherine insists on being mentioned to you too. So there y' are!   Fondly,

Seamus

The award of the Nobel Prize in Literature to William Golding (1911–93), whose novels Faber had published ever since Charles Monteith had spotted the MS of his first, *Lord of the Flies* (1954), after numerous rejections elsewhere, had recently been announced.

The launch of *Sweeney Astray* took place at Cushendall Golf Club.

River by Ted Hughes and *Quoof* by Paul Muldoon were newly published.

'Frank' was the Faber editor Frank Pike (b.1936).

To Craig Raine

TS Faber

6 December 1983

Dear Craig,

Many thanks for your letter, with its suggestions and queries, all useful and welcome. My only hope is that the contents of this package don't prove too daunting. I'll try to gloss it all here in some order.

1. New contents page: I've added the titles of the enclosed poems, and removed a couple of the Sweeney ones. I've also removed 'Sweeney' from the title of some of those poems. OK? <Also take out 'Names of the Hare.'>

2. The new poems: I had held back these because I felt the first section should not be too long, but now that I am piling in more sections to the title poem, I think the right policy is to pack it all in. Otherwise these things will never see the light of day. Whaddya say?

3. New sections of *Station Island*: old sections, actually. I took them out in a mood of impatience with the sheer dogged ongoing length of the thing, but on reflection, they give a thematic helping hand and the cumulative burden of sheer 'subject matter' is probably important too in this poem. So can you readjust the manuscript as outlined and see if anything happens to your reading of it in the new form? The last section is a bit off the wall, but I think it should be. The 'mug' lyric I see as a bridge between the symbolic discovery of the bugle in what is now Section X and the rhapsody of XII. I also have revised the basilica section (IV). The shit factor here is that my friends who sent it to *Private Eye* will be too delighted; but it was a bit highly larded with the murmurous litany and the trope of kneeling in the sound of the basilica, well, I don't know. What you say?

4. The sketch for a blurb: Too long but it will give you something to go on. I think the 'growth of a poet's mind' phrase is probably right. Anyhow, I'd welcome a chance to look at what you come up with in the end.

5. Dedications: Dedication page: for Brian Friel
Individual poems: 'Chekhov on S.': for Derek Mahon
'Widgeon': for Paul Muldoon
'King of the Ditchbacks': for John Montague

6. Revisions. And here you just rang me on the electrical phone.

'Lights come on' – I thought the two *ons* gave the one after another illumination a little drama of repetition.

'like effigies' – Right. Cut. Redo:

We lay beneath in silence.
No birds came, but I waited

'Dirt-veined flints' – Make them 'Clay-scabbed flints.'

'Camaraderie of rookeries'. I see what you mean but the effect was quite uncalculated and so I am loth to change it.

'Sile na Gig' or Sheelagh: Cut the third section.
I'll also have to do something about the pale thug in the fork 'in the beech'. But that's it for the moment. *

Acknowledgements: Are they necessary? If I start on them, there'll be a plethora of things and I am bound to forget some of the places where they appeared or reappeared. I'm always getting into trouble with the editors whose publications I seem to have slighted. Also there are three or four pamphlet and limited edition appearances that I know will begin to be hunted out by dealers if I broadcast them and I hate the shits getting the prices inflated. But I can do them, I can do them . . .

I'll think about the big anthology, nervously.

The John of the Cross poem is *Cantar del alma que se huelga de conoscer a Dios por fe*, so there!

NOTES: now we'll have to add – Oh, shit, I'll do the whole notes again. The numbers have changed of *SI* sections and I have to put in extra information for VI – Kavanagh's *Lough Derg* was published in 1941.

Love to Lea and the lovelies. Have you a copy of your own book in MS or do you want to wait?

Sincerely,
Seamus

* I'll be sending a slightly revised monk/kaleidoscope section soon.

Written in response to Raine's detailed editorial queries and suggestions concerning the text of *Station Island*, now with Faber and bound for publication the following year. Raine's own new collection, *Rich*, had just been published.

Li (pronounced Lea) is how Ann Pasternak Slater (b.1944), Raine's wife, is known to her family and friends.

1984

SH's contract with Harvard changed upon his appointment as Boylston Professor of Rhetoric and Oratory. Among his many well-liked and respected Harvard colleagues, it was Helen Vendler, who arrived at the university in 1981 and was now a professor in the English Department, who became his closest friend. More than that, having written notable critical books on poets including Yeats, Wallace Stevens, George Herbert and Keats, she showed herself to be SH's foremost champion with the publication, in 1998, of her monograph *Seamus Heaney*.

After a squally episode with Faber, in which SH's horror at the prospect of a barn-storming publicity tour involving helicopter journeys between venues led to the helicopters being cancelled, *Station Island* was published on 15 October.

A few days later, SH's mother died.

To Helen Vendler

MS Harvard

23 May 1984

Adams House #I.12, Harvard University, Cambridge, MA 02138

Dear Helen,

Welcome back. And sorry to add to what will certainly be a heap of door-stopping correspondence.

Enclosed is the Phi Beta Kappa effort, a bit dainty, a bit occasional, but with some personal as well as occasional life, I hope.

The third section is about the Irish alphabet, which was still in use in the fifties when I learned Irish at St Columb's College – i.e. Coláiste Cholmcil a' Doire nuair a bhí mé óg, and that sort of thing.

[. . .]

The 'Phi Beta Kappa effort' is 'Alphabets', which came to occupy the opening pages of *The Haw Lantern* (1987). Helen Vendler had invited SH to officiate as Phi Beta Kappa Poet at the ceremony of conferral of the honour on undergraduates who had been elected to the Harvard Alpha and Radcliffe Iota chapters; she had not expected him to write a new poem for the occasion, but SH presented her with worksheets of this one, later revised.

Coláiste Cholmcil a' Doire nuair a bhí mé óg: at St Columb's College in Derry when I was young.

To John Montague MS Cork

21 June 1984 191 Strand Road, Dublin 4

Dear John,

On the night of the longest day I am conscious again of the longest delay in writing to you. My dream-self has been in touch with you but what good is that unless it got to you? Anyhow, this is not so much the right letter as a greeting to open the channel of thanks: for a just and honest review of *Sweeney*, and for the intimate truths of *The Dead Kingdom*. I was flat on my back with the flu when the launching of your book took place one Thursday in late March – or early April – raging at the waste and inanition of my mid-term break in bed. Marie had collapsed for the first part of my week at home and then I caved in – *forbye*.

There is a courage of going through with a style and a record in *The Dead Kingdom* which I salute, and I can hardly separate my recognition of the truth-to-life from the brought-to-art in the writing. I am walking into my own intimacies as I read through the pages but I still recognize the otherness of 'The Well Dreams' and am without resistance to 'The Silver Flask' section. The tenderness and exactitude come very near, and 'The Music Box' still gets in close. I suppose in the end we all cave in to a desire for the thing that strikes home, and I feel myself the right and vulnerable reader for a lot of the book.

I got back from Harvard ten days ago, after a term that was all go. The arrangement began as a release but is turning into a way of life, and a way of life that happily is working. Michael, for God's sake, is doing his Leaving Certificate and will be at UCD, all being well, in October . . . We/they give birth astride of the grave . . .

My good wishes to Evelyn and the young. Give us a call some time.

Sincerely *agus le grád*,

Seamus

In his review of *Sweeney Astray* for the Belfast magazine *Fortnight*, Montague wrote of SH's having 'striven manfully to remind us of an early Irish masterpiece', but regretted that his lack of 'the crucial gift or wound of a grafted tongue' told against him: a roundabout way, it would seem, of saying that SH's Irish was not up to the task.

Montague's *The Dead Kingdom* was published in 1984.

'astride of the grave . . .': see Samuel Beckett's (1906–89) *Waiting for Godot* (1953); Montague was a friend of Beckett.

'*agus le grád*': 'and with love'.

To Ted Hughes MS Hughes

21 June [1984]

Dear Ted,

The plan was that I would spend a lot of time in Harvard at my desk just writing letters and atoning for the neglect and stupor of last autumn but, of course, America being the conveyor-belt that it is and me being the torpid swamp-creature that I am, I never got round to doing what the oneiric self kept thinking about. So this is only a short and breach-holding greeting to you and Carol, in the time of the sea-trout, a kind of late-night leap to keep the line flicking. Harvard was the usual mixture of solitude and social punishment: the latter unsolicited but not unembraced and not unresented, the former not prolonged enough, merely suffered between scenes, off-stage. I was delighted to find *River* again, just before I left: it restored me to the joy of the first place where your poetry touched me. You will have to forgive me for blabbing it – but the way your poems backfire and resume the energies of their predecessors wakens the love of poetry in me like nobody else's. Anyhow, much love to you and Carol from Marie and me. Are you coming over at all? Seamus

This transcription is from the draft for a fax, given by SH to Carol Hughes, Hughes's widow, in September 2003. *River*, Hughes's book of poems about fishing – and much more – was published in 1983.

To Desmond and Mary Kavanagh PC Kavanagh

9 August 1984

This man did so much damage to the national psyche of Scotland I could find no suitable postcard on display anywhere in the nation. Still, wish you were here to enjoy a good time in Edinburgh. See y' all. Seamus and Marie

Written in Scotland, posted in Ireland. The image is of an old woodcut portrait of John Knox ('Ioannes Cnoxus') (*c.*1514–72) from the Scottish National Portrait Gallery.

To Ted Hughes

ms Emory

23 August 1984 191 Strand Road, Dublin 4

Dear Ted,

Months have passed without my moving to write but with many moments of irritation at myself for not writing. But I've just come back from the Yeats School in Sligo and on the long drive through the lakes and tumps of the midlands, I got the determination focused enough to get started. The last time we were to meet was at the Faber *School Bag* event, but I was so in pain with a condition called 'dry socket' – often experienced imaginatively but never in the gums – that I scratched at the last minute. Then I went on to Cambridge, Mass. in the same afflicted condition and before I knew, was running to stand still on the moving stair of American activity. Somehow, when I get into the rhythm of the term over there, scuttling between students and readings and visiting poets and visiting Irish, running from hospitalities and unsolicited manuscripts, maintaining some sense of the residual self by resentment and exhaustion, I never get round to doing the thing that I thought I would most enjoy doing – writing from a distance to friends one takes too much for granted at closer quarters.

Anyhow, I've been back since the middle of June and been dispersed again in the usual summer rites of entertainment, conferences and more – though individually welcome – Americans. I was in Grasmere at the end of July at the Wordsworth conference where I did a lecture and Marie and Catherine came with me. We went on for a day to Hadrian's Wall, spent a night in an attractive Northumbrian town called Hexham and took photographs of ourselves on the banks of Otterburn. This last gave me unexpected simple pleasure, since 'The Battle of Otterburn' was the first poem I read on my first day at grammar school.

The summer has also been fraught by the whole vulgarity of Faber's 'promotion' for *Station Island* and *Sweeney*. I agreed a year ago that I would do some readings with Craig when the books came out, but they went ahead, without consultation, to arrange the tour, engage and publicize the helicopter, and then, a couple of weeks ago, Desmond Clarke, their new publicity person, affirmed his desire to make the firm 'the Mills and Boon of poetry publishers'. I feel co-opted into something that I deplore but I do not wish to start complaining in public because that only creates more burble; so I wrote to Matthew a couple of weeks ago, putting strongly on record my disapproval of the way the whole thing was conducted. I felt better after that, but still groan at the thought of whistle-stopping with the bandwagon in October. It was my own fault for agreeing to do the readings in the first place, but some dignity might have been retained if they had not startled the ugly 'publicity' razzmatazz, treated the thing as they have done heretofore as a 'launching' rather than a 'promotion'. They are doing damage to themselves as a firm, but I regret to say that I am going to be one of the walking wounded very soon myself.

Sorley MacLean was over in Sligo to read Yeats, but with bardic unself-consciousness read mostly from his own Gaelic and his own translations and then, with equal indifference to Noraid, southern embarrassment and revisionary historians, blasted politically into 'Easter 1916', and carried it all off splendidly. He is also reported to have been shown round a holy well on the shores of Lough Gill, a place over-appointed with plaster virgins and technicolour plaster Stations of the Cross, and to have summed up all his reactions with two long-drawn-out, free Presbyterian 'Well, wells.'

Barrie is coming to-morrow to stay for four nights. He has work included in a big international exhibition here – a promotion, indeed – called *Rosc* and we'll all be jostling in the odious pretence that official receptions and enforced gregariousness are enjoyable ways of spending an evening. Tom Flanagan, who was with me a couple of years ago on the Hardy outing, is also around, so the summer continues.

What a whoosh of life there is in *What Is the Truth*. I got it when we were in England and was light-hearted with wonder at the supply and invention and easy rumbustious capacity of it all. Too much there for me to recall it all but I took special pleasure in the hen and the encounter with the fox and the cow-consort and the donkey poem – but it's the overall keeping-going, the improvisation and the reliability of the inspiration that lifts the heart. To have all that up your sleeve after pouring out the *River* poems – it's awesome and glorious.

Much love from all of us here to you and Carol: maybe we'll contrive to see you at some stage between now and the return to Cambridge in January. Meanwhile, keep at it!

Seamus

'The Battle of Otterburn' evoked fondly here is more likely to have been the Scottish ballad than the Old English poem called by the same name.

Desmond Clarke (1945–2017) was Faber's Sales and Marketing Director; his devising of the helicopter tour and his 'Mills and Boon' pronouncement were characteristic of his ebullient, sometimes iconoclastic, efforts to refresh the firm's public image.

What Is the Truth? (1984) is one of Hughes's books for children.

To Roger Garfitt

MS Garfitt

16 September 1984 191 Strand Road, Dublin 4

Dear Roger,

Your letter was a generous telling of good news and I appreciate the care and trust implicit in it. I am very glad that your life begins anew with Tessa and to hear of the nurture you are all finding in the house and district where you live. Rededications can be immensely fortified by re- (and dis-) locations. When Marie and I went to Wicklow, we started again. It was like a second marriage, and the cottage and countryside where we lived were party to it. Remembering the place has always involved remembering a mood and a weather of feeling, which is how your own life now seems to be occurring. Our fondest wishes go to you both, and we look forward to seeing you here. Your first weekend is the tail end of the odious Faber/helicopter event (tho' the helicopter may have to go . . .) so I don't expect I'll be fit for much then. But telephone us when you land and call us so we can arrange a more serious engagement for the following weekend.

Marie and I were at Hadrian's Wall this summer and I wrote a poem about Coventina – so then the whole abundance of the Chesters Museum poem swam into our ken in *Snow Light, Water Light* (I had heard it last year but forgotten) and wakened a wonderful fluent sense of communion. The whole book is very pure – there's something rinsed and absolutely without 'writing' in the writing, spiritual repose secluded in the simplest of the physical. The Japanese disciplines of the other book are the proper ones for what was going on. I thank you for sending them and look forward to a talk next month. Forgive my brevity – but the priority is to get this off to you while the mood is alive. You know what a procrastinating fucker I can be about letters.

Fondly,

Seamus

Garfitt had moved with his partner, the poet Tessa Lund, and her son to a new house in Herefordshire. They had planned to call on the Heaneys in the course of a holiday in Ireland, but the death of SH's mother prevented it.

Snow Light, Water Light (1983) was a pamphlet of poems Frances Horovitz had written from Hadrian's Wall, published by Bloodaxe Books; *Rowlstone Haiku* (1982), a pamphlet (published by Five Seasons) she and Garfitt had written together.

To Blake Morrison

MS Morrison

19 September 1984 191 Strand Road, Dublin 4

Dear Blake,

Dark Glasses arrived in the post a couple of hours ago and I have read most of it. And I'm writing immediately in case I don't write at all – the usual thing is that I delude myself into thinking a moment will come when I can write the 'real' letter.

It is a rich and tender and coherent book. The landscapes are wonderfully full of their different weathers – from the otherness and frugal, haunting tones of the Poland in 'The Inquisitor', through the lush familiar of chestnut parks to all the different verities of London. The way you have found of drifting the stored sensations of a personal memory across the recognitions of a sceptical and observant adult mind, and then crossing that with intimate stealths of sex and self – it makes for a special Morrison signature. Though, of course, I am still a sucker for the pure gifts of 'A Child in Winter'.

The good thing is the way your thematic concerns – 'loyalties and lies' – are bred into and out of your material and images and intonations. 'The Inquisitor' I will read again, but the feeling at this early moment is that it is well held by the pitch and insinuation of the writing itself. Full of local delights, of course, but the big overall test of holding the disparate material is passed by the steadfastness of technique, yes, but maybe more by the emotional charge which the different parts of the narrative are plugged into. I'm not saying this very well: to put it another way, for all the 'narrative' elements – which are intrinsically interesting – there is a constant hooded personal presence in the poem, a 'third' walking between reader and writing.

It's a true book, not just a miscellany of pieces. And the long one is a real heft of achievement. I'm delighted for you and hope it gets the greetings and send-off it deserves.

Fondest wishes,
Seamus

Dark Glasses was Morrison's first collection of poems.

To Ted Hughes

MS Emory

8 October 1984 191 Strand Road, Dublin 4

Dear Ted,

Aye indeed. Chief woes and world sorrows powerfully dragged up and out in that one, terrific opulence and slaked need, so direct and at the same time laden with inwardness. Thanks for sending it and for the good things you say in your letter. The old definition of work – 'to move a certain mass through a certain distance' – is what I feel applies to the 'Station Island' sequence and I'm glad you feel it opens in. Certainly, there was enough dull-browed butting at the ordinary.

I'm writing this sudden uncharacteristic response because I happened to be bogging into the heap on the desk this morning and am grateful for the chance to put off dealing with the long-neglected, evaded and unwanted envelopes that I am too ready to keep evading and neglecting. But I also just want to shift 'The Stone Verdict' in your direction because of the 'unspoken' theme. And I'll include a few others that drifted up lately.

Matthew Evans, to whom I wrote a pretty stern note some time ago, says that the Helicopter is cancelled. But the damage is done. And now Craig has begun to warble about Clive James 'doing a piece on the tour'. *Hein*! How wise you are to stay in Devon. Love to Carol. And thanks again for the encouragement over the book: I suspect I'm going to need it all.

Seamus

PS I funked *Antigone*. Couldn't face it without some purchase on the Greek. The cribs had ideas and paraphrases and all that, but they were cobwebby for me. I could not get my ear or nostril or tongue to any source I could rely on. So Tom Paulin did a quick and excellent swoop on it and it's touring at the moment, with a Mahon *Molière*.

Hughes had written a letter praising *Station Island* – 'I get the feeling your real kingdom is in there' – in the course of which he confessed to have been 'startled to meet Part II of "The Loaning"', perhaps suggesting that the item prompting SH's awed remarks in his first paragraph was 'For the Duration' (later included in *Wolfwatching*, 1989), also a poem about a child listening to adult talk.

Clive James (1939–2019), Australian journalist and TV personality, did not after all write about the tour.

'I funked *Antigone*': only *pro tem*, as the idea was restimulated and brought to fulfilment in 2004. Paulin's version of the Sophocles play, to which he gave the title *The Riot Act*, and Mahon's *High Time*, his translation of Molière's *L'École des maris*, were presented by Field Day at the Guildhall in Derry on 19 September 1984.

To Philip Hobsbaum

MS Glasgow

8 October 1984 191 Strand Road, Dublin 4

Dear Philip,

Your long letter was a great warm pleasure, and the thought of a dedication from you in the Lowell context is an honour and a balm of affection for both Marie and myself. Both you and he, at different times and in different ways, transmitted good trusting energies into my too tentative self and it is a proper personal triangle that is established by the dedication. I shall cherish it.

Again to Glasgow and, I suspect, no chance for the proper ease and atmosphere 'to chew the fat', as Holden Caulfield said. The whole 'promotion' that Fabers are doing is whistle-stop politician stuff. It was all put in motion, without any consultation with me, when I was in America, and I came back this summer to learn of the aerobatic tour and the bookshop walkabout. I have quashed the helicopter factor, but not before all the ballyhoo has been in the papers and the damage done. But anyhow, I am to be in Glasgow with Craig Raine on Wednesday week, and have no idea where we are reading, or what the arrangements will be. We'll be taken care of by the Faber 'minders', I suppose, necessarily, because the whole event has been in their hands from the beginning. If I see you there, it will be a pleasure, but what way the aftermath of the reading will pan out, we must wait and see. Among other things, we have to proceed early next morning to Belfast for another jamboree at Queen's and the university bookshop, so I don't want to go hung-over into that old arena.

I asked Fabers to send you a copy of the book and I hope you like it. The title sequence was work almost in the scientific sense of 'moving a certain mass through a certain distance' and while there was a slow obstinate burn – almost opposition rather than inspiration – there were very few flashes of that high pleasure that can be a reward (sometimes specious, OK) in itself. The bit I most enjoyed doing, and did fast, was the third section. But what's done is done and I hope some of it pleases you.

Philip – the usual case. I left off and now am going off in half an hour to London. Forgive the hash, but better this than nothing.

Love to you both from both of us.

Seamus

Hobsbaum's *A Reader's Guide to Robert Lowell* (1988) bears the dedication 'For Seamus and Marie Heaney, his friends in Ireland'. After leaving Belfast in 1966, Hobsbaum taught at Glasgow University until his retirement.

To Sorley MacLean

MS NLS

24 October 1984 — 191 Strand Road, Dublin 4

Dear Sorley,

In other circumstances, I would not have missed the launching of the Hallaig film, but my mother died last week and things have been knocked about inside me and around me, and I just don't think I'd be ready for the outing. But this is just to say what an honour I consider it, to have been allowed to speak about you and share the screen with you: I'll be there in spirit, and hope that before long we'll meet again, maybe on your home ground. Marie joins me in sending our love and congratulations to you on this good occasion, and our good wishes to your wife and family.

Le grá,

Seamus

Sorley MacLean, as a Gaelic writer, published under the Gaelic form of his name, Somhairle MacGill-Eain. SH admired his poetry and felt close to the man (see letter to Ted Hughes of 23 August 1984). In *Stepping Stones*, he explains how, lacking Scots Gaelic, he was yet able to make his own translation of MacLean's poem 'Hallaig', which gave its title to Timothy Neat's film, 'partly because I have enough Irish to go word for word into the Gaelic, partly because I have the cadences of it in my ear from hearing the poet read it, and partly because I know the kind of place the poem evokes . . .'

'*le grá*': 'with love'.

To Julie Barber

MS NLI

26 October 1984 — The Wood, Bellaghy, Co. Derry

Dear Julie,

Many thanks to you personally for your letter, and to the Field

Day Company for their lovely wreath. It was a good waft of sweetness at a sad time.

Love,
Seamus

Julie Barber was manager of the Field Day Company; SH's reply to her kind gesture came from the family home, where his mother had lived for the past thirty years.

To Ted Hughes

MS Emory

29 October 1984 The Wood, Bellaghy, Co. Derry

Dear Ted,

Up here for a few days, just to be in the way. My sister – 43 and unmarried – and my father are on their own in the house, and although the brothers and in-laws are close by and in and out, they still need an alibi from the silence. He has more fortified and codified procedures for conduct than she has, but is maybe more adrift.

Anyhow, we were all at the bedside when she died, easily, on Thursday night week – with the exception of my brother in Canada. A massive stroke on Tuesday. But all kinds of uncertainties about how long and how soon, until about 9:00 p.m. that evening, when she rapidly declined. But with the two-day warning and the gathered household, there was a good sense of completion about it.

It was unfortunate the way it all got into entanglement with Desmond Clarke's enterprise. But after that week with Craig, I must say I find something very trustworthy in him (Craig) – not that I did not trust him, but before the prolonged familiarity of the tour, I would have kept him familiarly at bay. But there's a real geology in him, which I was delighted to find. Why am I saying it – I suppose because of my withholdings after he took the Faber job. Tho' I still think they've crossed some Rubicon as a publishing firm.

Many thanks to you and Carol for being there on that Monday. It was a great send-off. Hope we'll all meet again in January.

Seamus

To Thomas Flanagan

MS Amherst

14 December 1984 191 Strand Road, Dublin 4

Dear Tom,

Winter is icumen in: flu and furies in the home, booklaunchings and the usual crowd in town – last night I was at Newman House for the launch of three new books by the fresh-faced Richard Kearney. The rough-faced Mac Réamoinn embraced me and I had beard rash when I got home.

Away from it all in Frielsville last weekend, however, your name came up again at a Field Day meeting as a possible contributor to a possible series of books. I have been urging them to follow *Sweeney* and the pamphlets with another book, and so I have taken the liberty of going ahead here to ask you, formally, if you would be interested in putting together the essays which have appeared in various places over the last few years – I'm thinking of Mitchell, Tone, Davis as the core, with Moore and Somerville and Ross, and there may be others suitable, such as Joyce and Irish history – would you be interested in having them appear as a Field Day book? Next year, Hutchinsons are publishing the first six pamphlets in England as a book, but the project I am thinking of would be in Ireland – with possible co-publication elsewhere, if you would want that.

I know this is a bother to you but all I'd be interested in now would be a yes, with a sketchy list of contents, or a no, let's leave it.

Here included also is a copy* of the latest effusions. Much love to Jean and yourself from all of us.

Seamus

* Hardbacks not available yet. Par for the course.

PS The oyster with the pebble-bunion had to be evicted: foul airs began to waft from its stunted form . . .

One of the 'three new books' by the philosopher Richard Kearney (b.1954) was a Field Day publication: *Myth and Motherland*. Seán Mac Réamoinn (1921–2007), was a journalist, broadcaster and noted wit.

Despite SH's energetic encouragement, Field Day published nothing by Thomas Flanagan.

The noxious 'oyster' resists diagnosis from this distance.

1985

Teaching duties at Harvard and constant demands for personal appearances from other US campuses were unrelenting. While SH's administrative mail increased proportionately, the connection to home through such private correspondents as Barrie Cooke (see the two letters below) was not just a solace for him but the means by which he kept engaged with events that mattered.

Academic and critical attention to his work was increasing as well, and here, it seems, his instinct was to be open to enquiries, even when, as in the case of Michael Parker's approach to him (see letter to Michael Parker of 8 August 1985), things got off to an awkward start, before turning businesslike and, in short time, cordial.

To George O'Brien

MS O'Brien

2 March 1985

Adams House #I.12, Harvard
University, Cambridge, MA 02138

Dear George,

Forgive the hold-up. I was at home last weekend and am wobbling and rushing since, socially and pedagogically, making up time and surviving jet lag. I have coined a name for what I do – I jet-sit rather than jet-set.

Lester Conner pinned me for Wednesday May 1, en route to Washington (he's at Chestnut Hill College in Philadelphia). Folger has me Thursday night and Friday morning, maybe even for lunchtime. To be eaten, to be divided, to be drunk . . . I'd like to feather your cap except that I recognize the irony in your invitation . . . And you'll recognize that by Friday I'll be a frazzled, frizzled item, a worn-out Triton, a punctured Michelin man, a posthumous Paddy, a waft of aftermath. But if you still think you can arrange with Folger to carry the remains to Georgetown on Friday afternoon, I'd like to honour our friendship and do some wee turn – tho' I don't think I could face a full-scale reading on Friday night. Keep that free for all of us/them. If a class discussion or an O'Brien-led seminar or an informal O'Brien-hosted teatime were to be arranged – even a teatime

where a few staves would be uttered – that would be fine. And not to worry about fees/budgets, unless they drip and are available. It could be a 'friendly'.
[. . .]

The Irish writer and scholar George O'Brien (b.1945), recently appointed Professor of English at Georgetown University, Washington, had had fleeting dealings with SH before this date. Seeing that SH was booked to appear at the Folger Shakespeare Library, O'Brien had taken the opportunity to invite him to Georgetown, where he duly came and read, not his own work, but selections from *The Rattle Bag*.

To Barrie Cooke

MS Pembroke

4 March 1985

Adams House #I.12, Harvard University, Cambridge, MA 02138

Dear Man,

Can't tell you how good it was to get your good letter to-day. And wish I could take more time to answer. When I'm here, I gradually become an instrument, and have a deliberate, haughty intention to be as good a lecturer and attender to students as any academic on the campus. But I harden. I dry. I need the voices of my best secret life and life-support. I need to hear fellow-anxieties and intuitions. And the simple sentence that told me you were working was the best one. No need for you to worry, fuck you, about consolidation. If, in your fifties, you can use that verb 'work' in the slightest verifiable way, forget it. Repeat it. Test it.

I'll be home on March 23; call; and enjoy this portrait of artistic life, real? life, stupid life. And give my love to Sonja.

See you,
Seamus

The 'portrait of artistic life' is a crude pen drawing at the foot of the page, of a small fish, with 'LIFE IS UNJUST' in a speech bubble, about to be swallowed by a larger fish, with 'LIFE HAS SOME JUSTICE' coming out of its mouth, about to be swallowed in turn by the largest fish, which declares, 'LIFE IS JUST'. Cooke, who was mad about fishing, also specialised in painting fish.

To Peter Balakian

MS Balakian

22 March 1985

En route – The Tara Lounge, Kennedy Airport

Dear Peter,

Forgive me for the bad delay in answering your letter and my seeming indifference to all you have been sending over the year. I'm afraid I go into a kind of torpor at home and am caught in a kind of idiotic rush when I am at Harvard: I find myself answering letters in the lost hours in airports, away from phones, students and the whole pressure of the open life.

The Appletree Press clearly does good work but I have nothing to print at the moment, and have already overdone the private press thing: one part of me delights in the physical fact of lovely books, another part of me rages at the rip-off factor which begins once they enter the market. My prices in the book-trade are inflated and various sharks have been charging ridiculous prices for early books and I have begun to hate the thought of the catalogues marking *Death of a Naturalist* at $100 – or more.

So, I'd prefer not to do anything just now.

I'm giving two lectures a week this year on the main poets Hardy → Lowell, and feel it a great strain. There are 200 undergraduates in the class, but in fact each event might as well be a public lecture, since the senior colleagues drop in, and the auditors include many writers and spies from the area. But, as my friend Brian Friel says, everything is a test.

I'm going home in a couple of hours, for mid-term, and look forward very much to seeing the family. Give my love to yours – and to Terence and the mighty Michael H. Tell him he was right not to go to Annaghmakerrig: and see if he can pronounce it.

Much more should be written, but the pile of unanswered letters beside me beckons. Every good wish to you and for your work.

Sincerely,
Seamus

On Aer Lingus notepaper.

Peter Balakian (b.1951), US poet and scholar, then teaching at Colgate University, had had pamphlets of his own published by the Press of Appletree Alley, Lewisburg, Pennsylvania.

Annaghmakerrig is the home of the Tyrone Guthrie Centre, in Co. Monaghan, which offers residencies to writers and artists.

To Collette Lucy

18 May 1985

Dear Collette Lucy,
One of my favourite poems is 'Cuchulain Comforted' by W. B. Yeats. Written a few days before his death, it is a mysterious and difficult poem, but one which seems to fulfil Yeats's stated ambition 'to hold in a single thought reality and justice'. It presents a confrontation between heroism and cowardice, between violence and resignation, between life and death, and communicates a deep sense of peace and understanding.

Sincerely,
Seamus Heaney

This letter was SH's contribution to an anthology of poems, *Lifelines: Letters from Famous People about Their Favourite Poems*, edited by Joann Bradish and Niall MacMonagle; children from Wesley College, Dublin, wrote the letters that elicited such responses as this one.

To Barrie Cooke

MS Pembroke

26 May 1985

Adams House #I.12, Harvard University, Cambridge, MA 02138

Dear Barrie,

In the last two days I have written thirty-two letters – none of them a real letter, of course, but all of them a weight that was lying on my mind even as the accursed envelopes lay week by week on my desk. The trouble is, I have about thirty-two more to write: I could ignore them but if I do the sense of worthlessness and hauntedness grows in me, inertia grows and, fuck it, I'm going to get rid of them before I board the plane on Thursday. In the middle of all this, and haunted also by income tax considerations – accounts to be made up, money to be paid back, thousands *aagh* – it is a pleasure to address myself to the woes of another! But I envy you, all that backlog of work, crows and jingles and nudes, Provence and Lapland and elks: the catalogue of retrievals is like a poem itself and I am going to enjoy the show and be at home in time for it – I only hope you don't cave in to caution and start culling it. You should let all stream out from your gifted hand. Flow on. You're a Lawrentian by conviction, so let it be the pouring out of the coffers. And yippee for *Sweenee*. Tom MacIntyre, I believe, is doing a play for the Abbey on him. All goes in one direction. (Meanwhile, I'm looking at Sophocles' *Philoctetes* – have you read that?)

Philoctetes. It concerns your decision. Because of his suppurating wound, Philoctetes was put ashore, marooned on Lemnos with his great golden bow, while the Greeks sailed on to Troy. And got holed up for 10 years. Then Greeks discover (seer tells them) they will take the city by having *Phil.* and his bow: he will lead the sack of Troy. *So*, Odysseus and Neoptolemus are sent off to Lemnos to lure Philoctetes back. But Philoctetes' rage against those who deserted him is Kinsella-like. He won't go back to help them. So Odysseus schemes and lies. But Neoptolemus cannot bear to see the wounded man deceived and uncovers schemes, and so on and so on. It is about the artist and his relation to society. His right to his wound, his solitude, his resentment. Yet society's right (?) to his gift, his bow, his commitment to the group. *But* – we must beware, since it was written by a civic Greek, yet one who was probably near ninety and wise at the time. Wise always, for that matter.

Of course you have no suppurating wound. At least it does not smell like that to others. But you have, as it were, the island. You have the bow. And you have given, you are related, you belong to me *comme peintre* – in the late sixties, it was your painting I knew and it was a resource, a little tingle and weather. So you belong to everybody in the same way; your art is a public possession, maybe not a public *service*, but a gift to the group. So the *selfishness* you speak of is relative, debatable, and an imposed notion. You have kept free, fought free, held the line. The inner dynamics of the domestic world I cannot quite speak about. This is another factor, a harder one for the outsider to speak about. I suspect you and Sonja are so expert at goading each other now that you do it unintentionally – as Marie and I do. I somehow feel that the curve of your destiny does not incline you to be head of that department. I also can appreciate the anxiety about yielding up the dough. Could you offer to try it for two years? No, you probably couldn't, because you do not want to yield the time. You'd be full of recrimination if you were in Dublin three days a week. But if you could get it cut down to two days, a day and a half? That would not cut in on you so much. But, but, but. I am not one to recommend moral decisions upon others – rather, I ask myself, is this like his *wyrd*, his fate, his true curve of nature, the grain of his nature and habit? And it's no this time for you. I think you were right.

Sorry to blab so much. See you. Seamus

Tom MacIntyre's 1985 play was *Rise Up Lovely Sweeney*.

SH's interest in Sophocles's *Philoctetes* bore fruit five years later with Field Day's production of *The Cure at Troy*, the ambitious political purpose of which is already adumbrated in the second paragraph of this letter.

To Michael Longley

MS Emory

16 July 1985 191 Strand Road, Dublin 4

Dear Michael,

Your letter was heartening. I was sorry to be so long with the review, but it was all go in the States and then when I got back I was off balance in the usual way and I did it swiftly and pleasurably in the end. They wanted 800 words but afterwards I was sorry I didn't make a meal of it. All the time, though, I was glad enough to deliver what they had asked for.

I had hoped to lounge about during next week's conference but just last Friday the Soviet Embassy spoke in dark-jowled English down the phone and offered Marie and me our tickets and keep for 10 days in Moscow, departing on Wednesday 24. We hesitated but then it seemed madness not to take the chance. So that means we'll either have to set out late on Monday night or very early on Tuesday, because on Tuesday we have to go to see Catherine in the Gaeltacht in Ballyvourney, a hell of a long journey in itself. And then we have to get from there to Shannon, so as to be ready for Aeroflot early on Wednesday.

Maybe we could meet at lunchtime on Monday? I'll likely get to Belfast on Monday morning and will call you some time around noon to see what's what.

Meanwhile, Odysseus's strung bow led me on to his shot through the axes, so my mother becomes a flighted arrow. Not so rich and sweet as a white butterfly, but equally peregrine. Enclosed . . .

See you soon. Love from us here to yous there.

Seamus

SH's review of Longley's *Selected Poems 1963–1983* was in Ireland's *Sunday Tribune* of 23 June 1985.

'10 days in Moscow': at the invitation of Yevgeny Yevtushenko (1932–2017), SH was to visit the USSR to attend a Festival of Youth and Students, to read in Moscow and to travel to other parts of the country.

'Catherine in the Gaeltacht': it is common practice for Irish schoolchildren to spend some weeks in the Gaeltacht, the Irish-speaking parts of Ireland, living with families and acquiring greater fluency in the Irish language.

'Odysseus's strung bow': SH's review of Longley had appeared under the heading 'Bowstring, Harpstring'; 'White Butterfly' is an especially tender poem in the book reviewed.

A typescript of 'A Quick Note', much the same as 'Two Quick Notes', only not divided into two sections as it is in *The Haw Lantern*, follows in the Emory file.

To Paul Durcan

MS NLI

16 July 1985 191 Strand Road, Dublin 4

Dear Paul,

Shamefaced, late as ever. The gift of the poem is so rich that I was waiting until I'd got the right time and silence to reply. Forgive the bad delay: as usual we have been to-ing and froing and toed and froed upon.

Lovely wisdom poetry and pleasure poetry washing into each other like an imaginative vale of Avoca: the picture behind the poem is a lovely floodlight but the phantasmagoria of the dream and the drift of the truth out of the dream is the triumph. And phoenix. And ashes. The felicities are one sort of gift – 'a thin smiling tail the length of a clothesline' – 'as if the dusk was a touch on his brow' – those kind of lines are absolute and heart-lifting – but it is the overall sense of being in the presence of true and reliable human custody that makes the thing such a powerful statement as well as a sweet vision. Marie and I are proud and moved, and Marie is especially ensnared in delight because of the common love of the picture and the talk you both had about it.

The poet Mahon is on his way here some time this week, so maybe we'll meet when he walks among us. Otherwise, it will be a couple of weeks more since, suddenly, Marie and I have been invited to Moscow, going off next Wednesday, for 10 days. Your story of Belgrade – or was it in Macedonia – airport rises to haunt me when I think of putting ourselves, without a word of Russian, into the care of Aeroflot. But still. It's a great opportunity.

Part of the reason for my bad delay is that I've been writing myself, on and off, and when I'm like that I go lazy on all other fronts, however imperative. I enclose a couple of the things that got done. The arrow piece is my mother's soul as Odysseus's arrow going through the axeheads.

Much love for the big gift.

Seamus

Durcan's poem 'The Rape of Europa' (included in his 1987 volume *Going Home to Russia*) takes its cue from Titian's painting of that name and is dedicated to SH and Marie Heaney.

To Michael Parker

MS Parker

8 August 1985 191 Strand Road, Dublin 4

Dear Mr Parker,

My apologies for not answering your letters before now, and for not thanking you for the good photographs.

My family in Co. Derry had told me of your visit and they spoke well of you and of the time you spent there. They were also grateful for the photographs.

It should be possible for us to meet for a drink in Dublin some time after August 31. If you telephone 697569 a couple of days before you leave Courtown, we'll fix up a meeting-place and mutually suitable time.

I am curious about the nature of your research, and would certainly wish to know what parts of it may be destined for book publication. I admire the thoroughness of your background work in the north but must say that I prefer my family and the more personal hinterland of my life to remain private. There is quite enough of me and about me in print, I think, without going into the domestic and intimate details. It would be dishonest of me not to tell you that I was not a little irked when I heard you had visited The Wood – I would have thought that that should have been a matter of my decision as well as yours. However, as I say, I know it was done from the best of motives and that you left the best of impressions, so it's all water under the bridge by now.

Until September, every good wish.

Seamus Heaney

Researching for the book that would, in 1993, appear as *Seamus Heaney: The Making of the Poet*, Michael Parker (b.1949), on sabbatical from his job as Head of English at Holy Cross Sixth Form College in Bury, Lancashire, had on his own initiative paid a call on The Wood, where SH's father was still living; he was greeted there by Patrick Heaney, who summoned SH's brother Hugh (1942–2021) and sister Ann (b.1941); Parker then took the photographs for which SH thanks him here.

Parker and SH met for the first time on 2 September 1985.

To Mary Fogarty

MS NLI

14 August 1985 191 Strand Road, Dublin 4

Dear Mary Fogarty,

The problem is not in my readiness to participate but in my uncertainty about whether I could come up with a poem that would satisfy you – and me. Let's leave it for a couple of weeks and if something comes into focus or promise I'll let you know definitely. There would be no need for a fee. If I could hit the note correctly for the sake of the poem and the sake of Amnesty, that would be more than enough of a reward.

Sincerely,

Seamus Heaney

To Mary Fogarty

MS NLI

14 August 1985 191 Strand Road, Dublin 4

Dear Mary Fogarty,

Since I wrote to you this morning, I got moving on the notion of conscience and this strange enough but I think good enough poem emerged with the pleasure and surprise of the genuine article. If it pleases you then I am very happy that you should have it.

This is all very sudden and it may be that I'll want to revise the thing. But for the moment I send it for your consideration. I must apologize for its being in longhand but my typewriter jammed on me yesterday.

Yours sincerely,

Seamus Heaney

Head of the Irish branch of the human rights organisation Amnesty International, Mary Fogarty had written to SH asking for a poem to celebrate Human Rights Day. The one that he produced so quickly was the first version of 'The Republic of Conscience', which he later revised and included in *The Haw Lantern*, and which appears to be an early – perhaps the earliest – example of the parabolic method he cultivated deliberately in that book. In its revised state, the three-line stanza form is retained, while the initial four sections are reduced to three, differently ordered, and numerous small but telling improvements are to be noted here and there.

To Helen Vendler

MS Harvard

3 October 1985 — 191 Strand Road, Dublin 4

Dear Helen,

My cup overflows. The path you picked through *Station Island* gave me a firmer trust in what is going on in the book and what I have been doing since. I loved the way you talked about the Sweeney poems, the ivy phrase, the rich young man; but especially when you locate 'the space of writing' and talk about that bewilderment of the 'self-born'. The things said there are so true and enabling in themselves but they do apply with great accuracy to this creature and I was proud to be the occasion of your words. They also prompted me to try to salvage and re-do a piece out of a discarded 'canto' which I enclose as 'From the Frontier of Writing' – how it will hold up I am not sure, but it is one of a series which I'll let you see some time, all reports from imaginary countries – 'From the Republic of Conscience', 'From the Land of the Unspoken', 'From the Canton of Exhaustion', and so on. They are more 'modern', in the way you descry in the Sweeney stuff, more detached but not deserting the old terrain.

But your review. You must know how irrigated the writer in me feels when I read such praise. I metamorphose from the pot-bellied sluggard into a trampolining *victor ludorum*. I want to do better. I believe in the note I might one day get right and get farther with. I know/knew there was something doughy and dutiful about the verse here and there in 'SI' – the sequence – but I sullenly went for that kind of writing and I hope I'll not cave in to do it again.

Though, in a way, these enclosed sonnets are a bit of a retreat into an earlier mode. But no apologies, really, for this, since I think they are working their passage OK. (I've pulled out the Robert Fitzgerald one to make it his own).

As I said, the Harvard book is a thriller to read. The number of grain-splitting truths about poets and poetry in the introduction: 'Pound is all nominal phrases; Lowell is all syntax.' Writers finding 'an uninhibited place in the Zodiac of poetry'. All those perceptions, and then the way you manage to cover the historical-survey-here's-what's-been-happening bit without seeming to be doing a survey – it's a terrific outstripping of the conventional introduction which nevertheless does all that the convention expects.

The black contingent are well chosen and earn their ground; and your selection from Ammons, O'Hara, Strand, Charles Wright and Goldbarth brought me into a new conviction about them. The Ashbery section is bound to settle a lot of uncertain responses into the deepest of all assents – he really comes up very richly. The whole book wakens me up to the pleasures and almost too-taken-for-granted achievements. How do you do all that you do? (Not much Frostian sound of sense in that sentence!)

My apologies for not posting this letter of last June until now. I kept thinking I was going to add to it. And my too hasty thanks to you for the argosies you keep launching over the flood. Love from us all,

Seamus

Perhaps the most vital service that Vendler provided SH – one that was established early in their friendship and would continue – was as reader of, and trusted commentator on, drafts of his poems. The 'enclosed sonnets' were the elegiac and memorialising sequence 'Clearances'; 'In Memoriam: Robert Fitzgerald' was placed separately from the others when they all came to be published in *The Haw Lantern*.

SH was grateful, too, for Vendler's public validation of his work. She had reviewed *Station Island* for the *New Yorker*, and, far from finding the collection 'doughy', had declared her opinion that 'Heaney's voice . . . is of a suppleness almost equal to consciousness itself'.

Vendler's anthology, *The Harvard Book of Contemporary American Poetry*, had appeared earlier in the year.

To Piotr Sommer

MS Sommer

28 October 1985 — 191 Strand Road, Dublin 4

Dear Piotr,

This is shameful: not to have written to you even to say that the excellent anthology arrived long ago and that I was not only delighted to be included and grateful for your dedicated work, but that I was especially proud to have poems in the Polish language, which seems to me one of the richest in poetry these days. At any rate, I get more corroboration and more sense of encountering wisdom in the works of Miłosz, Herbert, and Zagajewski – to mention only three whose work

I have been reading lately – than I get from most contemporary poetry in English. It is an odd paradox that I keep invoking Polish poetry as my yardstick and example of what is the best in the world, and then I shamefully ignore the chance to keep in touch with my best friend and advocate in the Polish language.

[. . .]

I am also sending, under a separate cover, a copy of a book I published in a limited edition here last Christmas. Chiefly because of a poem called 'The Mud Vision' which I think I might use as the title poem of a new collection – in a year or so. But I feel that it might strike an answering response in a Polish imagination. It's entirely a fantasy about an apparition – not of the Blessed Virgin but of a great flower of mud, spinning in the sky. It excites and terrifies and somehow verifies the people while it's there, but then, when it disappears, they discredit it and allow the commentators and newsmen and media pundits to explain it away as illusion. I had in mind a sort of allegory for the failed vision of a separate, coherent, resistant and convinced culture in Ireland itself . . . But I should not go *explaining* the damned thing ahead of your reading.

Fundamentally, Piotr, this letter is to apologize for my bad manners in neglecting our correspondence, to thank you for your commitment and hard work on behalf of all our poetries and to hope that sooner or later we'll meet, here or in Poland. The British Council would sponsor me there, but I'd prefer not to travel under that flag, even if I necessarily am occasionally printed under it! I go back to Harvard at the end of January, for a few months.

Every good wish.

Seamus

The 1984 limited edition volume SH sent was *Hailstones*, published by Gallery Books.

To Michael Parker

MS Parker

[2 November 1985] 191 Strand Road, Dublin 4

Dear Michael,

Many thanks for all your letters. This is first in answer to your recent one, with the questions.

The sonnets are to appear as a limited edition called *Clearances* from

Cornamona Press, situated in Amsterdam and in Ireland. I don't know when – maybe in a few months – or how much – maybe very expensive. Some of them will be in the next issue of the *Honest Ulsterman*, including the potato-slicing one.

As to the critical documents book you mentioned, I am not inclined to hinder you but I am not disposed to cheer it on. If you go ahead with it, I think it should be confined to material in the public domain. I should be loth at this stage to give any prior assent to the publication of your researches into the biographical matter and background stuff you are assembling with the help of friends and relatives – this is all very well as a project for archives but it seems to threaten one's privacy and resource as a writer if one thinks of it published. There are whole areas of one's life that one wants to keep free of the gaze of print – not that there is anything to cover up but that there is a sort of emotional robbery in the uncovering. (I apologize for sounding like Princess Anne with all those 'ones', but I mean that this is as much a general principle as a personal feeling.)

[. . .]

I must have read the Montague *Poisoned Lands* round about 1962/3 also. 'The Water Carrier' was the poem of his that touched me – the shape of 'Mid-Term Break' was suggested or informed by it.

I read *Sailing to an Island* and *Battle of Aughrim* as they appeared. I hope I can send you a poem called 'At St Enda's Settlement on Aran' which I think reflects Murphy-speak. It was never published.

I read Roethke when *The Far Field* appeared and then I reviewed the *Collected* when it appeared. The things I liked were 'Meditation at Oyster River' and those long sectioned late Whitmanesque things; plus, of course, the greenhouse poems. I don't know that I was influenced: corroborated in a sense that the charges in a place could be a proper inspiration for poems, helped to trust a frank celebratory kind of writing, made to feel that illiterate, inchoate memory-place-feeling-stuff was as important as 'thought'. (But all this that I'm saying is a reconstruction.)

Marie did a four-year teacher-training course at St Mary's College, 1958–1962, concentrating on English/Speech and Drama. She was teaching all the years until the late sixties in a secondary modern school, St Colmcille's at Crossgar in Co. Down.

Terry Flanagan's family and Marie and myself and baby/babies used to go for the occasional weekend to McFadden's Hotel in Gortahork in

Donegal. I remember we were there one Hallowe'en, probably 1968/9. I think I did the 'Bogland' poem independently, but the whole feeling of shared pleasure in the landscape, the bleakness and bareness, was a shared one. Terry, however, was very much a visual, painterly reactor: I don't think he had much politico-historico-interest in it as an image. Apart from anything else, we went to Donegal as much for rascality and booze and a bit of a break-out as we did for any 'creative' jag. I think one of Terry's bogland paintings is in the Ulster Museum. He lives at 35 Marlborough Park North, Belfast 9, and he may have his own memories of all this. He's an extremely articulate man and would certainly be worth talking to if you go to Belfast.

PD was a student organization, on the whole. I was in at a number of their meetings in late 1969, but was not formally attached. These were large Student Union assemblies. Heady and boisterous but with a sense of moment. I was not a leader of the Newry march. There were thousands at it. My involvement with the Civil Rights was marginal in that I held no office or card or membership, but was real enough in that some marches – I think 3 in all – gave a sensation of participation in active politics – its satisfactions and ashy aftermath. I've not written about it. [. . .]

Thank you for all the poems – and forgive the suggestion that in 'Juliet' – which I like a lot – you might think about cutting the last stanza? It's so airy and merry up until that point that the slightly insistent wisdom comes on too strong, I think.

Forgive this speeded-up ending. I'm rushing, for God's sake, to another bloody festival – Newcastle-upon-Tyne – but at least I'll be back here to-morrow. One night stand!

Best wishes to Aleksandra and her new care and the girls and to yourself and your work.

I should tell you also, I guess, that Marie's mother died on the Monday after I saw you. We were in Paris and had to rush back for the funeral. It was a sort of release for her – she was losing her memory and was 78.

Every good wish,
Seamus

The date of John Montague's *Poisoned Lands* is 1961; it includes the poem 'The Water Carrier', which, in its sharp, vivid and unsentimental recall of a rural childhood experience, could be described as 'Heaneyesque' if it were not that it predated SH's own poems in this vein. A few years later, a line from 'The Water Carrier' – 'That heavy greenness fostered by water' – was used by SH as the epigraph to his poem 'Fosterling', in *Seeing Things* (1991), where it appears without attribution, perhaps because it was readily recognisable.

Richard Murphy's *Sailing to an Island* was published in 1963, his *The Battle of Aughrim* in 1968.

'PD': the People's Democracy movement was concerned with the civil rights of Northern Ireland's Catholic community. As here, SH is careful, when asked about it in *Stepping Stones*, not to overstate his active participation.

Marie Heaney's mother, Eileen Devlin, died on 14 October 1985.

To Paul Muldoon

MS Emory

4 November 1985 191 Strand Road, Dublin 4

Dear Paul,

Reading the resourceful and flourishing 'Salvador' in the *TLS* gave me the necessary push to write to you about something that has been at the back of my mind for a while. I suppose this is more in the nature of a confidential consultation rather than a formal enquiry. Anyway, I thought I should raise it with you.

You may remember that when you first told me about your Faber anthology, I had mentioned that the notion had been in my head, to do something similar. I still harbour the notion and specifically I would like to do it as a Field Day publication, partly to offset the heavy ideological/cultural discourse with more fluent and artistic matter, partly to make a contribution to the enterprise beyond my own writings in *The Open Letter* and the *Sweeney*. The one thing that hampers me, besides natural sloth and a reluctance to get embroiled in the who's in, what's out kind of business, is an unwillingness to seem to be in competition with your book. Obviously, the Faber anthology will have appeared before long and, I suppose, the Kinsella Oxford anthology also, so if and when this other one came out, it would be at the back of the field. But even before I set my sights on really doing the thing, I would want to clear this point with you. I realize that you have no desire to hold monopolies on anthologies and that the audience for the Faber one is likely to buy all the anthologies that come on the market rather than choose between them. But a scruple of courtesy impels me to let you know that I may be going ahead. The thing is, I would prefer to do some of the work *before* I see yours, so that the coincidences and differences, whatever they might be, would be innocent/independent. What I have in mind is nothing very definitive, a selection of various poets since around 1960 with headnotes written as short definite essays. It may never happen, of course, so until such time as it does get under way, I'd be grateful if we could keep this exchange between ourselves. I'll be seeing you in a couple of weeks at the Kavanagh-fest, but if you're in this area in the meantime, give us a call.

Fondest wishes,
Seamus

By the time *The Field Day Anthology of Irish Writing* appeared in 1991, it had grown to be a very different thing from either Muldoon's *Faber Book of Contemporary Irish Poetry* (1986) or the anthology cautiously envisaged here.

To Tom Paulin

MS Emory

10 November 1985 — 191 Strand Road, Dublin 4

Dear Tom,

I read the play on the way down this evening on the train to Dublin. It really wakens up terrifically when Herby and Austin get at it and when the Chief comes into the action. He (Chief) is done with real affection, as is Herby. I enjoy the Bimbo send-up and the whole sharp caricature of Bimbo/India, but I wonder if the first act goes on a bit long in establishing them and their modes and attitudes.

The mixture of the sinister and the callous and the campish is a good one. But over all I am in awe of your boldness and ease with dialogue. It really rips along and has some good cruel laughs. I wonder what the drama heavies will have to say.

[. . .]

Love to you all. Seamus

Paulin's dramatic satire on Ulster politics, *The Hillsborough Script*, was written with production by Field Day in mind, but it was not taken up by the 'drama heavies' – principally, Brian Friel and Stephen Rea – and appeared merely in print in 1987.

To Alasdair Macrae MS Macrae

29 November 1985 191 Strand Road, Dublin 4

Dear Alasdair,

The piece on *Station Island* is very sympathetic and closely read. You come in to the shape and criss-cross of the thing in a way that could not be bettered – and you give a very heartening assent. I am proud to have you say and see those things, and I apologize for being such a gobshite and not reading the piece *in situ*. Caution has become such second nature that it exercises itself now in spite of me – I knew there would be nothing to worry about in the piece but it must have looked as if I were evading reading it. But *blah*, *blah*, *blah* – thanks for the lift!

And for the great time with you both. From the moment I stood up at the counter of the Railway Hotel with Elise to the moment of departure at Edinburgh, it was the happiest of times. Your house is a welcome in itself, and when you are both added in, the thing is womby with security and home-heat. I also enjoyed the actual reading in Stirling more than my condition warranted: Monday night having been a mighty apotheosis. Once again, the chimes at midnight.

It would be a great pleasure to hear them chime in summer, and I'll certainly bear in mind your good invitation and advice. Marie appreciates the custodianship you promise, and I have a notion we'll be afflicting you *en route*. But knowing us, we're unlikely to have clear plans until a few days before departure.

Much love to you both. Maybe we'll see you on this side? *Oui?*

Sláinte!

Seamus

Alasdair Macrae (b.1939) was teaching in the English Studies Department of Stirling University, where he specialised in Irish and American poetry. He had first met SH at the Yeats Summer School in 1983. His essay on *Station Island* was collected in Masaru Sekine's *Irish Writers and Society at Large* (1985), no. 22 in the series *Irish Literary Studies*.

The 'great time' was had at the celebrations for Norman MacCaig's (1910–96) seventieth birthday, which involved a reading at the Queen's Hall, Edinburgh, where SH was among the many performers, then a private lunch the following day, and finally a solo reading at Stirling University.

To Ted Hughes

MS Emory

3 December 1985 [The Wood, Bellaghy, Co. Derry]

Dear Ted,

In Co. Derry, at home with my father and sister for a couple of days, more or less in retreat – and Philip dies. Very strange and distancing, to be here in the more or less bookless first place as that presence leaves. And then, coming home from my brother's place last night, flailing along at 50 mph, a badger comes right out under the car: suddenly yet in slow motion somehow. I can still feel the clunk under the chassis, and feel oddness this morning. It's the first time I've killed anything other than insects in a car: the destructiveness of the implement came home to me, all the same.

I just caught the very last minute of Kingsley Amis's remarks on *Newsnight* and then your own remarks printed out and reported in. Certainly, unlike Joshua Reynolds's pictures, Philip's poems did not fade yesterday. His solitude grew worthier in them, and the perfections hardened. He had no childhood poems and yet the *oeuvre* is foetally crouched now round some far protected core. Probably he had to put up a lot of emotional earthworks to repel the inroads of Amis and co.

It was a hateful way to report his death, to insinuate somehow that he was laureate in exile, as one of the channels did. I felt that it put a pressure upon you that was uselessly hampering, but no doubt you'll be hounded for memorial tributes and just get through with them. Somehow, the knowledge that what you say is already a 'quote' gags you at an original point. The fact is, I think, that Philip's death leaves a certain gang without their redemptive voice and I wouldn't be surprised to find a lot of us under the lash of their bereft tongues in the next few weeks. I don't know what exactly or who exactly I mean, it's just an instinct that his death has signalled an end of more than himself and that the recognition of that will cause backlashes of a petulant sort. Up and at 'em, I suppose; or equally, who cares?

Your letter about the anthology unnerves me. Fabers are about to carry (I think) Helen Vendler's *Harvard Book of Modern American Verse*. They have on stock Heath-Stubbs' and somebody else's *Twentieth Century Verse*. And I suppose they still carry an updated Michael Roberts *FB Modern Verse*. I would like the refreshment of meeting and making up another heap but I still incline to the notion of a schoolbag. If we were to do a twentieth-century schoolbag? But then that's almost covered in the *Rattle Bag* . . . I would not jump with joy at the prospect of another anthology with 2/3 poems each by all the biggies, with four Faber names on the editorial page, and a whole Faber publicity drive to flog it. On the other hand, if we could write ourselves a policy document, some description of an anthology with its own angle and justification, which would not just be a roll-call and yet would cover the central names . . . The fact is that I'd *feel* surer about what I feel about it if we talked. And I very much regret not getting to see you during the summer. [...]

The kitchen here is filling with siblings and South Derry vowels so my focus on this is failing. I hope to write again more clearly about the anthology business – something that could be done by a fortnight's intense labour would be the thing. My wariness has to do with becoming (too much) part of a 'drive' by Desmond, fuel for boastfulness about great sales etc., so that one's endeavour becomes co-opted into a sort of media mania.

Much love to Carol. I wish we could all meet for a feast some time before I go to Harvard again, but I can't see it happening. Up to the tree house with you, then.

Sláinte!

Seamus

Philip Larkin died on 2 December 1986. Kingsley Amis (1922–95), novelist and poet, had been a friend of Larkin's since they were undergraduates together at St John's College, Oxford, and their ensuing correspondence, apart from being often very funny, shows how the two writers egged each other on to ever more scurrilous confidential utterances. Both Hughes and SH were to find themselves targets of Larkin's mockery when his letters were published in 1992.

If Larkin had been 'laureate in exile', Hughes was Britain's actual Poet Laureate.

1986

An indication of SH's now firmly established status at Harvard was the commission to write a poem celebrating the university's 350th year, to be recited by him in front of an audience of 20,000; 'Villanelle for an Anniversary' was what he produced for the occasion. There was a smaller audience for the less purely ceremonial T. S. Eliot Memorial Lectures that he delivered at the University of Kent at Canterbury in the autumn, addressing, among other topics, the poetic examples of W. H. Auden, Robert Lowell and Sylvia Plath. These lectures would be at the heart of his 1988 collection of critical writings, *The Government of the Tongue*.

Patrick Heaney, SH's father, died on 17 October.

To Michael Parker

MS Parker

23 January 1986 — 191 Strand Road, Dublin 4

Michael –

I'm off in half an hour – your letter came at breakfast time – but I thought I'd better answer swiftly rather than late.

Ann Heaney at The Wood could get you the dates of birth, probably. I have no way of doing so now.

I am not prepared to do the writing about my mother or my aunt.

Very few poems began as prose journal entries. 'The Seed Cutters' in *North* is the only one I remember as having its genesis immediately in prose. Lerner gave me pleasure in the practice of practical criticism, praised an essay of mine in my first year at Queen's, which 'corroborated' me, albeit early on and anonymously. I read *The Green Fool* in the original edition in the reference section of Belfast Library, in the early sixties. I would have read *The Hidden Ireland* a little in St Columb's. In 1964? '63? I gave a lecture – small affair – on Corkery, as part of the early activities of the QUB Festival. A sort of lunchtime event. But I read *HI* for that, and other Corkery material. I don't think the *WG* had any impact on me.

Sorry to have to rush.

Seamus

Laurence Lerner (1925–2016), South African-born poet and literary critic, taught at Queen's while SH was there.

The Green Fool (1938) is Patrick Kavanagh's memoir of his rural, Co. Monaghan childhood; *The Hidden Ireland* (1925) is a study by Daniel Corkery (1878–1964) of eighteenth-century Irish-language poetry; *WG* looks like *The White Goddess* (1948) by Robert Graves (1895–1985), formative adolescent reading for Ted Hughes, but evidently not for SH.

To John Montague — MS Cork

Holy Saturday [29 March 1986] — [Aer Lingus flight] EI 117

Dear John,

'Hearth Song' sang this morning. I was moved and helped to find it, so unexpected, at breakfast, and me ready to leave again. I phoned but could not raise an answer. Maybe yous are away for the holiday weekend. At any rate, it was a heartsome follow-up to what I felt was a good public phalanx of the imaginative estate, last Thursday. The actual poem is so tender and so solid at the same time . . . actual and imagined, at the secret back of the hearth and in the usual circle fornenst it. *Gaudeo. Gratias ago.*

This is not much of a place to start the correspondence: I'm on the outside edge of a crowd of rugby players from Solihull who are flying Aer Lingus to Boston. The meditative man in me is much assailed by the joviality, as W.B. would have scornfully termed it, of these simple Britons. And then there's the hovering presence of two men from Ardboe, from a firm called Forbes Kitchens Ltd. One is a son of John Forbes, the *late* alcoholic who entered Tommy Devlin's pub, full, at 3:30 p.m. on Ash Wednesday years ago and announced: 'There was a lot of pressure from weemin in our house for me to give up the drink for Lent, but *I didn't cave in.*' Anyhow, Forbes *fils* and partner are travelling west to market a spinning wheel; they have recreated, reproduced, in working order, your actual 'mellow-the-moonlight-young-Eileen-is-spinning' model, in kit-form. From the shores of Lough Neagh, backed (they are sly about this) by British subsidies, the antique emblem rides again. 'Jasus, Seamus, there's a wild mark-up on this stuff when it crosses the Atlantic. Two hundred per cent. This ould thing's goin' to cost $500.' Soft craythurs, making the poor mouth. More power to them.

I'm buoyant but in cramped conditions. I hope I'll get down to writing again when the term cools off and the May month flaps its glad green wings. In the meantime, from Flight EI 117, and from a flushed and honoured dedicatee, fare well. Spin on . . . Love to all the ladies of 25 Grattan Hill.

Seamus

'Hearth Song', later to be included in Montague's *Mount Eagle* (1989), is 'for Seamus Heaney'. Whether by accident or design, 'The Spinning Wheel', the song which SH alludes to in the next paragraph, is apt in the context, having a hearth-side setting.

The spinning motif continues as SH alludes to Hardy's poem 'Afterwards', where 'the May month flaps its glad green leaves like wings, / Delicate-filmed as new-spun silk'.

To Thomas Kilroy — MS Galway

Holy Saturday [29 March 1986] [Aer Lingus flight] EI 117

Tom –

I hope ye all had a good night – Good Friday, good God! I was sorry I could not stay, but at the same time, there is a perverse pleasure in *having* to rise and go.

This is just to say, at this elevated distance – 2 hours out, God knows how many miles up – that *Double Cross* made me proud and delighted. To go to the theatre in Ireland and not to have to make allowances, intellectual or technical – this in itself is a matter of rejoicing. But to have the unrealized spaces opened up, to have such confidence in giving oneself over to an intelligence sporting itself fornenst you – I mean one on the stage . . . It was and is a special occasion. I speak gratefully for myself, I speak with slavering redeemed pleasure for Field Day.

Much love to Julie and yourself. Keep that prose moving.

Seamus

Kilroy's play *Double Cross*, in which he dramatises the contrasting political profiles of two mid-twentieth-century Irishmen, William Joyce (1906–46), the pro-Nazi wartime broadcaster nicknamed 'Lord Haw-Haw', and Winston Churchill's henchman Brendan Bracken (1901–58), had just been put on by Field Day at the Guildhall, Derry. The play opened in Derry before touring Ireland and then transferring to the Royal Court in London.

To Seamus Deane

MS Emory

10 June 1986 Akademie der Künste, 1000 Berlin 21

Dulcis Wag,

The academy of the cunts – in an extended sense, though even that qualification gets me in, as it were deeper – is no doubt where you have long ago consigned me. When I could not deliver the translations before May 1, I simply averted my eyes, suppressed my promise, and skulked. My alibi was hurry among students, the toils and sweats of office, the screen of distance, the usual reliance on the tolerance of friends. But I cannot bare to face thee, I mean bear to, on Friday without apologizing.

The problem is/was, time to do the translations. Let me promise (faugh, you say) to have a bunch of stanzas by August 1. My problem is a miscellany of unfinished tasks and deadlines, no one of them insuperable but each of them requiring a few days. But the few days are hard to find. There was Kavanagh's Clonmany, now there is the Künste Colloquium, then at the weekend the Field Day Fallout, then a week after that the Rotterdam Roister . . .

The pang of failure was sharpened for me when I got my hands on the *History*. That put the delighters and the frighteners into me at once, the latter because of the awesome clarities, condensations and sheer breadth of reading, the former because of the exhilarations and convictions of the writing itself. Needless to say, much pride and relish taken in the poetry section, and great admiration for the stamina and courage of the whole contemporary section. But the Toland/Swift/Burke chapter also was a good jag, and the survey of the early Irish stuff should have been printed by Kinsella in his great Kin-sell of an anthology. Wonderful blunt instrument, those initial 170/80 pages of his . . .

Tell Carpenter my apologies too. Tho' you are the one most abused by my laziness and procrastination . . . Meanwhile, The Hun awaits his reading and his seminar; and then the trip back to Dublin, and the trip North to Yanks-and-Banks night . . .

Dessy Irwin and Hugh Bredin came to the Kavanagh launch in Ballyliffin. Bredin played piano, Irwin sang 'Lovely Derry on B. of F.' *Lacrimae rerum!*

Seamus

'Dulcis Wag': alluding to 'sweet wag', Falstaff's ingratiating address to the

Prince in Act One of *Henry IV, Part 1*.

SH had promised translations of Early Irish poetry for the *Field Day Anthology*, which Deane was co-editing with the scholar Andrew Carpenter, of University College Dublin.

'*History*': Deane's *A Short History of Irish Literature*, published in 1986 by Hutchinson.

Dessy Irwin and Hugh Bredin were both at St Columb's at the same time as SH and Deane; 'Lovely Derry on the Banks of the Foyle' is a tear-jerking song.

To Bernard and Jane McCabe — MS NLI

5 July 1986 — 191 Strand Road, Dublin 4

Dear Friends,

I would like to dedicate the next book to you both, for reasons which I know I need not spell out – but which include poetic judgement and poetic support. I enclose a draft MS, something we can consult on, mull over, pull from, cull from, and look for a title for. So far, I've only got *Hard Water* – which I quite like. It may also need re-ordering, lengthening etc. But this is the rough shape. I hope you like it: it comes to you with much love.

Seamus

The Haw Lantern is dedicated to the McCabes, who had rapidly grown to be close Cambridge friends since SH began his teaching at Harvard. In the memorial address SH gave for Bernard on 6 April 2006, he described his friend as 'a cultivated and educative companion, a guide to be trusted whether you were going into a gallery or a good restaurant'. And he went on: 'Bernard also helped me to trust my own vocation as a poet. He helped me to sort out what I felt about my own work. His responses to new poems were always honest and accurate. His ear was so perfectly pitched and deeply attuned to the rightness of music that he couldn't fail to hear the false note in anything.'

To Helen Vendler — MS Harvard

20 July 1986 — Castello di Gargonza, Monte San Savino, nearer Arezzo, near Siena

Dear Helen,

It is a stone village, a little walled city, rather, with its tower and its church and its gate. Flagged alleys, stone staircases, beams in the roof, irons, braces and bolts, chimney breasts, sooty hearth-backs, red tiles, red wine, melons, olives, and Italian vowels everywhere.

We've been on the road for almost two weeks already: Marie and Catherine and myself. There was a week or so in England to begin with – the York degree took us north, to a completely satisfactory drift among Anglo-Saxon churches, moors, Cistercian Abbeys, fish and chip villages, pubs where all the horse brasses of the world seem to have secreted themselves, and restaurants where *nouvelle cuisine* would still seem to mean a complete replacement of the cooking equipment. Then south for a couple of days to the Lincoln area, where we visited Tennyson's birthplace, out in the sad rainy and still previous fields around Somersby. The ghostly silt, as Larkin calls it, still undispersed. Then on down to Cambridge, to do a turn at a British Council International School; then to London where we saw Karl and Jane Miller, Helen (Devlin) and Michael, and the crew at Fabers. Fabers was the last encounter and it was with some formal sense of climax, closure and commencement once again that I handed over a MS, of the book to come, entitled *The Shape of Things*. I had been toying with *Hard Water* and *Alphabets* but Jane McCabe came up with the 'S. of T.', from 'The Ballad of the Bullets' and even though it is a somewhat overbearing title, and even though the bullet poem is not one I'd want to point up too much, I still think it has a clinch and plumbness to it that is right.

The McCabes came to York for the doctoring and did the Lincoln circuit also. And they have an apartment around the paved corners from us here. We travelled to Pisa and spent two nights in a Renaissance beauty called Pienza, all perfect cools of *duomo* and courtyard, yellow stone, more walled and massy promontories, alleyways, murals, carved arms, and liver – the speciality of the region. Then a wonderful day in Orvieto where I thought of Jorie Graham in the Signorelli chapel but was more entranced myself by the stone carving on the columns of the façade of the cathedral. From the creation of light to the last enfolding at the judgement, all in delicate hard and unmistakable images, up and up the front of the place.

Result is that we were exhausted with sights and relishings when we got here forty-eight hours ago, and have lolled in a kind of suspended siesta, reading, dozing, doing absolutely nothing that is strenuous or noisy. The quiet of the place is its true gift. There are probably another dozen houses, all let out to holidayers like ourselves, but the sense of privacy remains. It is a place without shops, bars, cars – the latter are parked outside the walls. A small citadel. The spirit roosts in fortified conditions.

I hope to get to Urbino. I would love to go on my own but since the McCabes are half-hirers of the car and since people in these conditions are instinctively on the alert against somebody stealing a pleasure-march on the group, I suspect we'll either not go at all, or go and be too communal. Siena, Arezzo, San Sepolcro, Montepulciano – all these are on the list.

There is much to be getting on with, however. Around August 20, I have to do a lecture in Aberdeen at a conference focused somehow on Regional Writing. A dolorous topic, in the end. But I hope I can say something generally interesting to myself: I have a title which derives from the old BBC Radio Meteorological Service: 'The Regional Forecast'. Then there's Penny Laurans's English Institute in Cambridge, and the seminars and after that, back to get ready for four Eliot Memorial Lectures in October.

But I look forward to seeing you in August. My diary says we are having lunch at our house in Dublin on the Sunday that Sligo ends and then that we're Wicklowing on the Monday. But all that is still fluid and workable and reworkable, if you need to reshape your time. We can finalize the SF book then, but in the meantime, I hope I'll be able to get a MS of the new collection (which you know bit by bit already) to Sligo, to await . . .

Catherine and Marie send their love. Catherine is a bit out of it and pines, I think, for her friends and for Carlo. Christopher is in Spain. Michael is with Florence Tamburro in Cambridge. Did he ever telephone? He's probably staying clear of all his father's friends, and good luck to him. Hope you're having a good summer too, Love, Seamus

PS I eventually got my D. Thomas piece in the *NR*.
PPS Home on August 1.

The 'book to come' shed the title *The Shape of Things*, to emerge as *The Haw Lantern*.

'At Luca Signorelli's Resurrection of the Body' is a poem by Jorie Graham (b.1950), a poet highly regarded by Vendler.

Penelope Laurans taught in the English Department at Yale.

SH's Eliot Memorial Lectures, a set of four, were delivered in October 1986, at the University of Kent at Canterbury and with T. S. Eliot's widow, Valerie (1926–2012), in the audience. They would be included in *The Government of the Tongue* (1988), which takes its title from the introductory lecture.

Carlo was the Heaneys' dog, a border collie.

SH had reviewed the *Collected Letters* of Dylan Thomas for the *New Republic*.

To Bernard and Jane McCabe

MS J. McCabe

6 August 1986 — 191 Strand Road, Dublin 4

Dear Bernard and Jane,

And another happy McCabe birthday is saluted . . .

When I got home on Saturday evening, after stand-by up-grading to executive class, Heidsieck champagne and Irish salmon, all was well. Then I had a phone call from Co. Derry (where I am now) to say that my father was in hospital. He'd had an operation last Thursday, to by-pass the pancreas. Jaundice had developed, they found a tumour on the pancreas, but the procedure nowadays is to bypass the organ rather than to operate.

He's 76, he's weak and withdrawn – the latter condition having increased gradually and inexorably since my mother's death. But the prognosis is that he will recover from the operation, come out better than he went in to hospital, and then, well, months, plus or minus, until the next jaundice. Everybody is in sane possession of the facts and of themselves – and quoting his own recipe for getting through life: 'a bit of common sense and a bit of manners'.

This is just to put you in possession of the news. All is well. No panics or alarms.

It was a great time, which continues to glow.

Wish I had a card for yous.

Love,
Seamus

Patrick Heaney had not long to live: he died on 17 October.

1987

SH had committed himself to teaching for the full academic year of 1987–8, and the strain of this, to which a fatiguing schedule of guest lectures and poetry readings was added, became an increasingly recurrent theme of his letters.

To Michael and Aleksandra Parker — MS Parker

6 January 1987 [m.d. 1986]   191 Strand Road, Dublin 4

Dear Michael and Aleksandra,

Forgive me for not writing before now to thank you for your very true letter of sympathy – and your Christmas card. This being the last official day of the season of good will, I am relying on it in you.

I go off in a couple of weeks again, full of some anxieties about the teaching, the usual pangs about leaving the family and the occasional lift of excitement at the prospect of American energy and bachelor quarters. It has been a crucial autumn, with the absence at home being felt by us all, but especially – naturally – by Ann, who is left most alone. But I'm afraid I did very little writing, or reading. Just seemed to wobble from pillar to post, at the beck and call of circumstances.

[. . .]

Another misdated January letter: the Parkers had sent their condolences on learning of the death of Patrick Heaney.

To Jonathan Williams — MS Jonathan Williams

6 January 1987   191 Strand Road, Dublin 4

Dear Jonathan,

This is what occurred. On the other hand, there is the first section of the title poem in *Field Work* and the Glanmore Sonnet in the same collection beginning 'I used to lie with an ear to the line . . .' And 'The Railway Children . . .'

But if the enclosed is not *too* short, I'd incline to it. It's about the right length for a DART read. Won't give people a crick in the neck.

Anyhow, there y' are.

Sincerely,
Seamus

Jonathan Williams, Welsh literary agent working in Dublin, had instigated and organised the posting of poems in carriages of the city's DART (Dublin Area Rapid Transit) rail system. Asked for a contribution, SH offered, in preference to his better-known railway poems, 'Dublin 4', a four-liner whose title alludes to the district in which he lived, the DART line running close to the back of his house. Williams included it in his 1994 anthology *Between the Lines*, but SH himself never put it into a book.

To Paul Muldoon

MS Emory

9 January 1987 — 191 Strand Road, Dublin 4

Dear Paul,

The season of goodwill is officially over but I'll have to ask you to stretch it a day or two to include me in – I've been meaning to write since we met in Canterbury, and then your Middagh Street poems came and I was to read them to the point where I would have great responses to make, but of course it all flowed on and past, without my sitting down to the blank sheet . . . Thanks for your card at Christmas, and for the ever-generous remarks about early days to Alan J. in *The Times*. We have been lucky in all being around together, or nearly together, at nearly the same time, and the abundance of '7 Middagh' is multiplied when it is seen and heard in relation to all the tensions – now turned into cliché and *blah blah* – of the last couple of decades. The nimbleness and unexpectedness of the data/imagery married to the art/life/politics frame keeps the latter in its place. The merriment of the invention and the strictness of the attitude are well tightened and tuned up.

Wystan, Carson and Louis are my favourites – Carson is wonderfully unreeled at the line endings and the rhymes – but I still like Salvador, it being the first one I saw and the one that clued me in to what you might be up to. Wonderful defiance in the whole performance.

I've not done a stroke of work this year. Bits and pieces of lectures and reviews but no settled focus or indeed drive. Partly it was the unsettling effect of the Eliot Lectures as they loomed over September and October, then it was the aftermath in the family of my father's going. And then just the constant hurly-burly of the house and home, here. Besides which, I have an immense gift for indolence, snoring like the bog-eel in the dirty loanin'.

How's the back? Marie was very conscious not only of the pleasure of seeing Canterbury with you that morning, but also of the pain you were in as you lugged the case around. I hope it has cleared by now: maybe you sent it to Deane, who has been on the mat, flat, with back trouble for over a week now.

Anyways. My love to Jean and you for the New Year. Keep in touch, and keep the channels open. I'm off in two weeks.

Seamus

'7 Middagh Street', the long poem which concludes Muldoon's 1987 volume *Meeting the British*, was inspired by the curious fact that this Brooklyn address was at one time shared by a disparate group of writers and artists that included W. H. Auden, Carson McCullers, Louis MacNeice, Salvador Dalí and Gypsy Rose Lee.

To Julie Barber

TS NLI

23 January 1987 — 191 Strand Road, Dublin 4

Dear Julie,

I promised to write about the Frank McGuinness play and so here goes. You will forgive the typing errors in advance, I hope, and the hurry of a man on the verge of take-off . . .

The Carthaginians seem workable to me: the first decision being, I assume, whether we accept the play or get again into the Rudkin syndrome, then I would be for accepting the play. It is worrying at a theme and trying by dramatic means to get to grips with a condition of mind and a certain 'spirit of the age'. The mode of the piece seems to me to derive somewhat from Frank McGuinness's experience of improvisatory theatre, for children in schools and in other experimental conditions, and I kept wondering as I read it (quickly, I grant) if it mightn't be made a little less repetitive, or emphatic. Mind you, the music is going to make a considerable difference and the setting (set, I mean). The crack is good in places and the jokes here and there are sudden and true (sado-marriage?) but I hope it is not just my sedateness that makes me feel that Dido's almost immediate need to declare a plaque for his balls is a kind of premature ejaculation, and that an audience might justly feel itself being got at. The dramatic rightness of Dido's gay masquerade I do not question, nor the tolerability of the balls-plaque *per se*; I just wonder if the latter is (so to speak) placed right. But this is a detail and if it comes to details there are many that one could niggle about. What I most wonder about is whether the first scene does not promise a kind of play which the rest does not deliver? I mean, the business with the bird and the child/grave and so on is thematically necessary, you have to establish those identifying rites/obsessions straight away, but I wonder if it does not go at this task a bit portentously. The dirty jokes are meant to defuse the heavy atmosphere, I know, but there again I feel that the audience is getting strong contradictory signals very soon. But then, this is just a reaction by a non-theatre guy to a script . . . I like the Listeners scene and the play within the play and think the piece could be given with a real punch. It is full of quotations, knowingly, and fly for itself. I think it would be necessary to direct it very tightly, to pace it smart and to keep any indulgent arty mood very spare. Love,

Seamus

Carthaginians, the play by Frank McGuinness (b.1953) that SH is considering here, was produced, though not by Field Day, in Dublin the following year.

'Rudkin syndrome': Field Day had commissioned the play *The Saxon Shore* from the British dramatist David Rudkin (b.1936) and then refused to produce it.

In his haste, SH writes 'experiental', while presumably intending instead 'experimental'.

To Bernard McCabe

MS J. McCabe

13 April 1987

Adams House #I.12, Harvard University, Cambridge, MA 02138

Cher Ami –

Letter received. Mutual jubilation in dedication of *Lantern*. Yous = soft-eyed calves. Me = big-eyed (sorry), wide-eyed pre-reflective stare. Mutual gazings. Grazings, even, as we become cows of the rain, steers of the hailstones, bulls of the alphabet. All of which goes to prove that I went to the Plough and the Stars for the late-night birthday drink and am now blabbing buoyantly of the pursy, pouchy comforts of the dark pints.

I look forward very happily to meeting both of you in London, and *après ça*, the deluge in Dublin.

Before that, a prehistory of pleasure in Cambridge. Geoffrey Summerfield – he of *Voices*, John Clare *et al.*, a *goode felawe* – will be here that weekend.

Anyhow. The books stand open and the heart unbarred.

Love,
Seamus

The letter is headed 'Adams Happiness' – rather than 'Adams House' – and the date looks more like 1989 than 1987, but this is plainly written in response to thanks from McCabe for the dedication of *The Haw Lantern*; 'Hailstones' and 'Alphabets' are two poems in the book.

To Dennis O'Driscoll   MS Emory

17 June 1987   191 Strand Road, Dublin 4

Dear Dennis,

To-morrow I'm off to Brussels and then I wobble through the land of the Britons, Oxford, Cheltenham, Norwich, London, all in the cause of self- and book-promotion. Always I say I won't be doing it, always I end up on the road. But at least it's being done stealthily, in a Raineless, 'copterless sky.

Many thanks for *Hidden Extras*. And I am delighted that the crowd turned out to greet and gratulate. My own favourites, on a first read through, are the ones where the old life is newly apprehended – 'At Killykeen', 'Two Silences', 'Disturbing My Mother', 'Thurles'; then the ones where a new life is suddenly always there in an old way – 'Day and Night'; 'G-Plan Angst'; and then the ones where your own angle of vision is so truly and sadly played on no-life or life-that-was or life-as-it-alas-is – 'Man Going to the Office', 'Stillborn', 'Republican Sympathies', and 'Brief Lives'.

There is something uncomforted but non-vindictive in your gaze, and something wonderfully stretched between intimacy and abstraction, which is all your own and which I find steadying and deepening its note. Although I do indeed find the emotional impact of the family/loss poems the strongest, I know that a style cannot be raised from accidental sorrows and gifts like those, and do respect the push to naturalize the more European, or Middle-European modes. It's all full of good imaginative example.

I enclose the Herbert piece at last and thank you for sending the *PR* piece. I'd have been a little easier on *Tremor*. That 'Ode to Softness', no? Anyways, thanks for everything. I hope the *Extras* get a good lift in the reviews, and that you and Julie have a summer beyond all those 'Republican Sympathies'. Love from all of us.

Seamus

'a Raineless, 'copterless sky': see letter to Ted Hughes of 23 August 1984.

'easier on *Tremor*': the *Selected Poems* of Polish poet Adam Zagajewski (1945–2021), which O'Driscoll had reviewed in *Poetry Review*. O'Driscoll's own book of poems, *Hidden Extras*, was about to be published by the UK press Anvil.

To Paul Muldoon

MS Emory

22 June 1987 191 Strand Road, Dublin 4

Dear Paul,

I am sorry to have been made instrumental in such an ill-disposed and unfair assault on your book. Any pleasure I might have taken in Carey's exaggerated praise is cauterized by his excessive spitefulness against what you have done. Anyhow, it's a nice trick to be meeting in such good circumstances on Wednesday when once more the 'diversity' *blah, blah* of *etc. etc.*

Love,

Seamus

As the *Sunday Times*'s lead book reviewer, John Carey had reviewed *The Haw Lantern* and Muldoon's *Meeting the British*, both newly published, side by side, remarking that to compare SH to Muldoon was like putting a Derby winner next to a pantomime horse (see letter of 16 May 1988 to Carey himself).

The 'meeting in good circumstances' refers to SH's imminent trip to the University of East Anglia, where Muldoon, teaching Creative Writing there after leaving his job with the BBC, had invited him to read to students.

To Joseph Brodsky

MS Beinecke

[*c*.8 July 1987] 191 Strand Road, Dublin 4

Dear Joseph,

Welcome. The Heaneys are all at the above address, *en famille*, with a couple of Marie's sisters. We've had a 21st birthday lunch for

Michael, and if you felt like coming to join us for indolent crepuscular *causerie*, or a walk on the Strand, please do. Call anyhow, I am in high jubilant mood to think you are on our island! Love, Seamus and Marie

To David Hammond

MS Emory

11 July 1987

c/o McCabes, Tanza Road, London NW3

Dear David,

When you rang again on Wednesday afternoon, with the re-proposal on the Yeats film, I had been dozing on the bed and was without much nimbleness or relish at your proposal. At last I am well slept and decisive – I did nothing all day yesterday but sit about the McCabes' flat, doze, go out and drink soft pints of bitter, fart, day-dream, eat an Indian meal, fart again and sleep for eight hours again last night. Now the birds are singing in the garden, it's nine in the morning and it's all clear. The thing is: my plan. I had forgotten the plan. Which is: to land back from Harvard in the summer of 1988, absolutely free of the deadline, the commitment, the promised review, the anthology selection, whatever. To try to have my year off to myself, to do nothing in, if necessary. Madness to take on a major contribution like Yeats. Even if one 'only wrote the script', it's a major psychic/public link in. I've written to Garvey to scupper it. And, *cher ami*, I'd rather not commit myself with you.

Friel's play was terrific, I thought. Wonderfully written and acted. Very sure. You felt safe from the first scene. Well cast, I thought, too. Even Brian seemed not dissatisfied – although two of the reviews to date are dissatisfied. *Times* and *Independent* against it. *Financial Times* and *Guardian* for it. Anyhow, I'm seeing him and Anne to-night, after bringing Marie and Catherine to *High Society*. Also will see S. Rea. And Dolours (I suppose).

Going on the Thames boats to Greenwich to-morrow, with Catherine. Looking forward to it. Will be in touch next week – when I have Michael Durkan on the premises all week, hoking through 'my papers'. Groan. Love,

Seamus

PS Dropped a note to Eileen too.

Sent from the flat to which Bernard and Jane McCabe had moved upon his retirement from Tufts.

For all the reluctance voiced here, SH did participate in the 1989 TV programme 'W. B. Yeats: Cast a Cold Eye', broadcast to mark the half-century since Yeats's death.

Brian Friel's new play, an adaptation of the Turgenev novel *Fathers and Sons*, had premiered at the National Theatre in London; the Cole Porter musical *High Society* was running at the Victoria Palace Theatre.

Stephen Rea was married to Dolours Price (1951–2013), who in 1973, as a member of the Provisional IRA, had been found guilty of car bombings in London and served a prison sentence in the course of which she went on a protracted hunger strike.

Michael J. Durkan was the author, with Rand Brandes, of two standard works: *Seamus Heaney: A Reference Guide* (1996) and *Seamus Heaney: A Bibliography 1959–2003* (2008).

To Michael Longley

MS Emory

20 July 1987 191 Strand Road, Dublin 4

Dear Michael,

Too bad. Somebody came up to me in the middle of the hurly-burly at the Cottesloe Theatre – Friday June 26 – and told me he was in hospital and gave me an address. But I was back to Dublin the next morning and then on to the Gate, and David Keir and all that. What a stun. It breaches the memory seals all right, and I'm glad you got to the Limavady obsequies. If you know the brother's address – indeed his name – I'd be grateful if you could stick it on a card. He was really opulent. 'I recognize the face of the crucified Jesus.' No joke. And what a joker. All that tenderness and mockery and exactness really brought me alive. Really a crater in the middle of the road.

[. . .]

I am delighted by your warm words about the *Haw Lantern*. I like the book myself but I had no anticipation of the loud ballyhoo profile factor which was in store. I saw it as a little pleasure trip, a skiff pushed out for relish. The *Irish Times* profile, the *Observer*, and the *Guardian* were all done without consultation. And of course the Carey review was bad news, really unnerving to be instrumental in the Noodlum-hunt. I was lucky to be able to see the lad at Norwich where he conducted himself with that natural princeliness that is so endearing in him. Other elements are there too, I know, but he's a brick, as they say. Unfortunately, I cannot do the wedding. Hangdog confession: I am going to Japan for 10 days at the end of August. Marie and I and Catherine and Christopher head off on August 13, for a whole fucking year, and inside a week I'm away to Tokyo. Then, however, a quiet spell in a nice big house in Cambridge, farting and scratching and sweating and moaning. Teaching too, of course.

Dear old Hewitt. Beloved Barbour. What it takes to get us writing letters.

Love,
Seamus

The individual whose death SH laments here was Liam Barbour (d.1987), formerly a Presbyterian minister in Belfast, latterly teaching in London. A brilliant and charismatic figure, much admired by the Longleys at whose wedding he had officiated, he had been, in Michael Longley's words, 'too louche, outspoken and ecumenical for the Irish Presbyterian Assembly' and was sacked by them.

John Hewitt had also died, on 22 June.

To Dorothy Walker — MS NCAD

2 August 1987 — 191 Strand Road, Dublin 4

My Dear Dorothy,

The time at home has not been misspent – as if time at home ever could be misspent. Anyhow, much filing of publications and ordering of bookshelves occurred when my bibliographer – *my* bibliographer, what! – descended. Then I went on to face into the Augean stable of my 'papers' and found, among other things, the enclosed scribbles and fiddles towards 'January God'. I cannot honestly get them into any ultimate order, so I've separated what is the true path towards the poem that was ultimately printed from the odd by-ways and wobbles. Since you have always stuck up for the poem, I thought you should have the swaddling clothes it came in.

Now. I hope you'll not mind me also, on Marie's behalf, sending you the Moore. What happened was this: in Cheltenham, when we were over for the *Haw Lantern* launch, Alan Hancox – bookseller, festival organizer, host to the visiting poet and wife – presented us with C. Day Lewis's copy of the *Melodies*. Dublin bound, silk endpapers, C19 edition. It would be greed and improper reticence if we were to hold on to your book, which was on a kind of permanent loan, I realize.

Now. We're on countdown to exit. Screaming pitch in the domestic breast. We need to think about seeing you, all the same – *so* – give us a call when you get back. Our plans are about as firm as a basket of eels: it will be all wobble and rush until August 12.

Love to all.

Seamus

Dorothy Walker (1929–2002) was an influential Irish art critic, an advocate in particular for modernist and abstract art.

The poem 'January God' was printed as a broadsheet in 1972, but never included by SH in any subsequent collection.

To Thomas Flanagan

MS Amherst

6 August 1987 — 191 Strand Road, Dublin 4

Dear Tom,

At last, a letter not written in an aeroplane or at an airport. In one week's time Marie, Christopher, Catherine and I take off for Cambridge, MA 02138 – we'll be at 10 Kirkland Place, don't yet have the phone number. The house is spacious, gracious and about five minutes', nay three minutes' walk from the Faculty Club. Four bedrooms, four figures rent, but what the hell? Seventeen years ago we lived in – relatively – comfortable and opulent circs in Berkeley, so why not now? You both must come up, there's a spare room, lots of roaming space – *à la* Gnarled Hollow – downstairs, and every opportunity for amorous or rancorous or even blood-spilling doings between at least two sets of spouses, without interference or embarrassment.

[. . .]

Meanwhile, B. Friel has done a version of *Fathers and Sons* for the National Theatre in London. We went over three weeks ago for the first night bash and enjoyed the play and the bash tremendously. Turgenev, as far as many of the Brit. reviews were concerned, was not sufficiently obeyed, but this judgement was (often) based on a simple expectation that the death of Bazarov be done on stage, which the wily dweller by Swilly refused to do. It was a sure and amicable piece of adaptation, and we were all proud to be part of the action, in our attendant way. As we are with *ToT*.

I hope FSG sent you a proof of the American edition of *Haw Lantern*.

I enclose a British paper edition, because I have only a paper one to spare at hand, and because you will be able to see how much better the American cover is when they send you the hardback. Love to Jean and you, and the scattered brood.

Seamus

The ellipsis indicates not editorial excision but where a page, or more, of the original is missing.

'*ToT*': *Tenants of Time*, Flanagan's second novel, also with an Irish historical setting, about to be published in 1988.

To Bernard McCabe

MS J. McCabe

4 September 1987 [Postmarked 'Boston MA 021']

Astronomical
mysteries contemplated
pissing during frost.

My jetlagged contribution to the pestilential form. But at least it's shorter than a sestina. Love, S.

A 'pestilential form' it may be, but SH had earlier this very year written a haiku of quiet gravity, which, under the title '1.1.87', would go on to be included in *Seeing Things* (1991). His sestina 'Two Lorries' (*The Spirit Level*, 1996) was presumably yet to be written.

To Stanisław Barańczak

MS Barańczak

17 September 1987 10 Kirkland Place, Cambridge, MA 0213

Dear Stanisław,

Forgive me for not being in touch with you before this. When I arrived here in August, your translation of the Herbert article awaited me and I was prouder of that than of most MSS of my own! I hope that the message got to you that the Wilfred Owen quotation about 'the eternal reciprocity of tears' comes from his poem 'Insensibility'. (For some reason, I have a nagging feeling I may have said it was from 'Greater Love' when I spoke to your secretary . . .)

Meanwhile, I have received and read with assent, with relish and great profit *A Fugitive from Utopia*. I love the steady gaze you turn upon the whole *oeuvre*, and then the precise attention you give to each facet of the subject. The inheritance/disinheritance theme, plus the irony/metaphor focus – they both constitute wonderful working instruments, tongs which allow you to turn over and examine the minutiae as well as the mastering shapes of the poems. I especially value the uninsistent but unremitting exposure that 'poetry' and 'life' have a distinct but not dissoluble relationship. And the last chapter rises to a moving act of faith and definition of the poetry we can believe in and still need.

Even though we have not met in any thorough way, I have to say that your presence here is a fortifying one and I hope that you and Anna will be able to come to our house, maybe just the four of us, and, if you like, the children. Our daughter Catherine (14) and son Christopher (19) are with us for the year. Our home phone is 547 1887. But I'll try to get in touch with you next week.

No escape. I enclose a copy of the latest slim volume; it has my first 'Eastern European' poems (?), especially 'Frontier of Writing', 'Republic of Conscience', 'Land of the Unspoken', etc. No need, please, to reply or to think of anything to say about the stuff. I'd just like you to have it.

Sincerely, Seamus H.

The Polish poet, scholar and translator Stanisław Barańczak (1946–2014) had left Poland after the declaration there, in 1981, of martial law, and he was now a lecturer at Harvard. *Fugitive from Utopia* (1987) is subtitled *On the Poetry of Zbigniew Herbert.*

To Czesław Miłosz

MS Beinecke

17 October 1987 Iowa House Hotel, Iowa City, IA

Dear Czesław,

Sorry not to be able to stay to hear your poetry reading and perhaps to have an opportunity to speak with you again. Our meeting yesterday was a great pleasure – and pride – for me.

You probably have some idea of how important your work has been for great numbers of people; I can only speak for myself, through the veil of translation. Nevertheless, the tone and substance of your poetry ploughs a deep furrow in me. During the last eight or nine years, the register of your music as much as the level, wide, unfooled gaze of your vision has been like a sanctuary for me: reliable, confirming but not too comforting.

I apologize for this outburst of face-to-face praise. But I feel emboldened because of all I have found and been fortified by in your poems. Mandelstam (*Conversation about Dante*) writes that 'when Ugolino begins to speak, it is all cello and rancid honey'. Something of that voluptuousness and hurt is what I have loved in Miłosz.

The Haw Lantern is indebted to 'The World' in its first poem, 'Alphabets'; and generally indebted in 'The Mud Vision'.

I hope we meet again. If you come ever to Boston or Dublin, I'd like you to meet my wife. Meanwhile, I must rush to the airport in Cedar Rapids – and hope this gets to you this afternoon. Sincerely,

Seamus Heaney

This boyishly enthusiastic note seems to mark the first meeting in the flesh between SH and the Polish poet Czesław Miłosz, long resident in the USA and an American citizen since 1970; the two were guests at a celebration of the twentieth anniversary of the University of Iowa's International Writing Program. Sent from a hotel on the campus, unusually for SH it is not on appropriated notepaper and the heading, simply 'Iowa House', is in his own hand.

In the translation of Osip Mandelstam's *Conversation about Dante* by Clarence Brown and Robert Hughes, the Ugolino episode is described as being 'enveloped in the dense and heavy timbre of a cello like rancid, poisoned honey'.

To David Hammond

MS Emory

11 December 1987 [In transit]

Dear David,

Remember the photograph you took in that desolate airport lounge, in upstate New York – Rochester? Albany? Syracuse? – after the Berlind refrigerator raids and the McGahern madnesses – well, you should be here, now, to take what Big Patsy would have called 'a comrade' for it. I'm in Salt Lake City airport, awaiting a delayed Boston flight, gazing at the snow-capped Rockies. It's strange, the way things have developed, so that what was once the domain of magnificent romance becomes the humdrum of a slightly impatient, stressed, schedule-haunted, fat-bellied man. I rebuke myself for being in the land of Mormon, in the big sky of the west, and only being able to worry about the undone and overdue tasks of my life. On my way here yesterday (4¼ hour flight) I wrote fourteen letters and recommendations. I have as many more to do on the way back, and then when I land, more testimonials and blurbs. My desk is full of books (pre-publication proofs of big novels by Tom Flanagan and my colleague Monroe Engel) that I am meant to puff. I am also nowadays on appointments committees and have the work of fourteen poets to read – all applicants for a post, the shortlist already culled from an original intake of 120.

Sorry to moan. It's just spilling out. The year is going well, really, but it is inordinately, inexorably, minute by minute, unexpected visitor by visitor, telephone call by telephone call – busy. Deane-o, Dermot Devlin (NUU, Magherafelt), Joanna Mackle, Polly and Andy, etc. etc., in the house and on the agenda. Backlogs of reviews, lectures, and festschrifts. The chance to sit at a desk has almost disappeared from my life.

For example, I am the victim of shit like this overleaf, by every mail. Not that it [is] all Irish-oriented: most of it is 'poetry'. But it creates an enormous rage in me at times, a feeling I've allowed myself to be pushed to the edge of my own life. (We're boarding.)

This last 24 hours I've been the guest of a poet called Mark Strand. It was easy enough. One class at 11 in the morning, a lunch, a snooze in the afternoon, a reee-ding, a party, a sleep and a good fee. But it involved crossing the whole continent. Although it is convenient enough by plane, there is something affronting about the speed and wobble of it all.

The payoff – I hope it will feel like that when it arrives – will be the 18 months at home. Harvard are going to give me a half-year's salary, so it will be a sabbatical. I look forward to it, as a last chance to get started to write again. In the meantime, I have the Richard Ellmann memorial lectures to do in Emory in April. I don't see when I'll get them started even. Every weekend between now and then is buggered. I'm even going to California in March to do a frigging Field Day benefit. Bob Muse, a lawyer here in Boston, has a daughter who is a judge in Sacramento, and she *offered* to raise thousands. I did not feel I could refuse. Fuck it, all the same. Or, as I'm told the Mormons say at moments of stress, HECKY DARN!

[. . .]

Well, imagine me now, above the Donald Campbell testing grounds, elated by Delta Airlines but not altogether by my spirits . . . Much love to Eileen and all the children, and all our best to you for Christmas.

Seamus

PS I'm over the Salt Lake. All water. But not the Gweebarra.

The poet Mark Strand (1934–2014) was at this date teaching at the University of Utah, Salt Lake City.

Three paragraphs of catch-up gossip and optimistic looking into the future have been omitted.

1988

In April, in the midst of his academic duties at Harvard, SH delivered the inaugural Richard Ellmann Lectures at Emory University, Atlanta, Georgia. Reportedly, he had been chosen by Ellmann himself, from his death-bed. Ellmann (1918–87), who had taught at Emory, was a noted Irish scholar, author of monumental biographies of James Joyce (1959) and Oscar Wilde (1984), and he had donated his extensive Yeats library to the university. The title of SH's first lecture was 'The Place of Writing: W. B. Yeats and Thoor Ballylee'.

After completion of his first full Harvard year, he returned to Ireland, but not exactly the fruitful peace and quiet he had promised himself. The three-volume *Field Day Anthology of Irish Writing*, of which he was a contributing editor, was in progress, and there were numerous other distractions.

One tangibly beneficial achievement, however, was the purchase from Ann Saddlemyer of Glanmore Cottage (see letter to Ann Saddlemyer of 10 September).

To Helen Vendler

MS Harvard

1 February 1988

English Department, Warren House,
Harvard University, Cambridge,
MA 02138

Dear Helen,

Overwhelmed is an overused word but it doesn't overstate my feeling of gratitude when I opened the proof. So many things caught and so many others raised. The whole quotation marks/punctuation marks drama is one I shall now leave to Fabers. I screech at the thought of discussions by phone with them about individual occasions: I myself have been inconsistent, Nancy has made the occasional revision, and their typesetter or copy-editor may have been at work too.

I am particularly grateful for the 'persuasive'/'lucid' drone to be corrected; I have the bad somnolent habit of filling in with such verbal pacifiers, and without your awakenings I should end up with a prose made up entirely of dozing repetitions.

'Steeped in luck', truly. I hope that you didn't mind my extending the company of pre-publication readers and toning down the pitch of my salute to them. Bernard and Frank did read a couple of things – Bernard did raise nice points on the Auden front, and Frank zoomed in on a couple of matters of fact. Just as you helped me to get free of the dog-licking implications in the Walcott piece, Frank had found a tom-tom earlier – blood beating from Africa and all that. Groan. And all that was in *Parnassus*.

I look forward to our lunch next Monday; and am sorry I missed the *ad hoc*. No doubt, however, there'll be a follow-up to all that soon. This is simply to give an inadequate squeak of pleasure and gratitude.

Love,
Seamus

PS Infant chirps gone; chorister's after-echo now in its place.

S.

Warren House is the site of Harvard's Department of English and American Literature and Language.

'opened the proof': of *The Government of the Tongue*, SH's book of essays and lectures, which Vendler had read and commented on in helpful detail.

'Bernard and Frank' were Bernard McCabe and Frank Bidart (b.1939), poet, professor of English at Wellesley College, in Massachusetts, and editor of Robert Lowell's *Collected Poems*.

The 'Walcott piece' is the 'The Murmur of Malvern', originally written for the magazine *Parnassus* and then included in *The Government of the Tongue*, the contents of which Vendler had read and offered notes on in advance of publication. The St Lucian poet and playwright Derek Walcott (1930–2017) was awarded the Nobel Prize in Literature in 1992, five years after Joseph Brodsky and three years before SH; the three poets were not only personal friends but came to be regarded, by certain commentators, as constituting a sort of poetry pantheon or A-list.

To John Carey

TS Carey

16 May 1988

English Department, Warren House,
Harvard University, Cambridge,
MA 02138

Dear John,

Ever since that evening of the *Sunday Times* event, I have been feeling very turned around. The circumstances were awkward and I fear I did not handle them as surely as I might have.

A couple of weeks before the dinner, I was upset to learn that I had been part of an advertisement – myself and Edna O'Brien actually – of the 'come and eat with the Irish at the banquet' sort. I never actually saw it, but it caused me to approach the honours with a sort of ill-grace. Then there was the whole bloody turmoil of the Belfast/Gibraltar/Stalker/Birmingham Six business. And there was also the pebble in the shoe caused by the Muldoon tie-up. At any rate, when I woke up the next day, I felt somehow that the whole text – which one part of me felt 'responsibly' forced into – was not 'me' at all.

I write not to wheedle about it but to apologize for not saying more capaciously, on the occasion, how much the particular terms of your praise meant to me then. I have been so blessed that I fear to run too eagerly towards the next blessing – and can look like an ingrate in the process. *Basta!*

Sincerely,
Seamus Heaney

SH was guest of honour at a banquet held by the *Sunday Times*. He attended it in spite of his strong dislike of the way the paper, under its proprietor Rupert Murdoch (b.1931) and editor Andrew Neil (b.1949), had covered recent political events in Ireland and elsewhere.

At the banquet, Carey gave a speech in praise of SH. The 'pebble in the shoe' signifies SH's lasting irritation at Carey's joint review of *The Haw Lantern* and Paul Muldoon's *Meeting the British* the previous year (see letter to Paul Muldoon of 22 June 1987).

To Michael Parker

MS Parker

12 July 1988

Department of English and
American Literature and Language,
Harvard University

Dear Michael,

Many thanks for sending the photographs and for keeping me up with your proceedings. I was at home in Dublin for a week in June, at the International Writers Conference; but I returned to the States for three final weeks and am only back in earnest since July 5.

[. . .]

Maybe it was because I was going at such a lick, or because Michael H. never forwarded any mail, but for whatever reason, it had not registered with me that you were so far advanced with book plans. I must say, I find the prospect unnerving and would indeed welcome a chance to see the text.

As you will recall, there has always been a very significant distinction in my mind between your researches for a thesis and your plans for a book. The data you collected so impressively is actually part of the lining of my memory. The people you interviewed – with a few exceptions – are not literary acquaintances but presences in the life of my first affections. The places you photographed and hope to map are actually now images that inhere as much in what I wrote as in what I remember. For this reason, the shock of intrusion, which I felt when I heard of your initial visit to my family, has been dramatically renewed with the news of the Macmillan project. For example, the Moyola sandbed. That place I marked so that you could *see* it. If any photograph appeared, or map that gave access, I would be devastated. It is one of the most intimate and precious of the places I know on earth, one of the few places where I am not haunted or hounded by the 'mask' of S.H. It would be a robbery and I would have the cruel knowledge that I had led the robber to the hidden treasure and even explicated its value.

So not only would I not mind glancing over the chapters, I desperately desire to do so. I feel this text which you propose is radically different from critical explication – about which I feel I should keep a strict 'hands off' policy; it actually interferes with the way I possess my own generative ground and memories; is therefore potentially disabling to me in what I could still write. And I feel it a matter of the highest risk.

I thought I should let you know all this, that went through me like a volt of shock, rage and self-rebuke, when I read your letter of June 21.

Sincerely,
Seamus

'first affections': in his continued guardedness, expressed here so fiercely, SH summons to his cause, as the highest and most pertinent authority, Wordsworth in his 'Ode: Intimations of Immortality from Recollections of Early Childhood'.

To Seamus Deane — MS Emory

Friday evening [5 August 1988] 191 Strand Road, Dublin 4

Dear Pal and Editor,

I am abandoning my effort for the anthology – only for a week. I have got 20 foolscap pages of the introduction, in longhand.

Consummatum est, except for three pages, maybe two, which I must insert to cover the majesty *blah blah* of the achievement in the twenties. *Tower. Blah blah. Stair*/stare *etcet* . . .

My trouble is the unwritten lecture I am to have written for next Wednesday in Sligo. But I go to Galway Arts Festival, and all that that entails, on Sunday. And Hammond arrives to-morrow. And this is my – our? – wedding anniversary . . . so, I have to-morrow morning to do Sligo-slop.

I promise. Lash me if it's not in by end of month. I cannot get back to it until August 22. I'll finish a week after that.

I'll show you the longhand in Derry. Honest.

Hope France was good and that you survive this last procrastination.

Big Daddy.

Letter headed simply 'Friday evening', but datable by SH's mention of his wedding anniversary.

As General Editor of the three-volume *Field Day Anthology of Irish Writing*, Deane had the job of rounding up the contributions of numerous 'contributing editors', SH among them.

'Sligo-slop': SH's lecture for the Yeats Summer School was on Yeats's 1899 collection, *The Wind among the Reeds*.

To Ann Saddlemyer

MS Saddlemyer

10 September 1988

Glanmore Cottage, Ashford,
Co. Wicklow

My Dear Ann,

This is my first night in the cottage. I am here on my own, at ten in the softly raining night, and intend to stay for three or four days. The silence, the accumulated previousness of life here and the big voltage of munificence you directed into our lives – it's all very much with me, and I felt the proper way to set the house in order – spiritually – was to write to you.

[. . .]

I also, in the headiness of the first return, had the idea that we would re-do, architecturally and all that flash, the kitchen and bathroom. But it won't be for a while. And as I sit here, in the original space, with the bolts and latches and steps down and sturdy sink and chilly iron windows of the two rooms in question, I have a great affection for all their starkness and pristine, functional originality. Madame Heaney may not find the primal conditions as irresistible, but she too is susceptible to the thoroughness of the past we all share in those spacelets, and the many hours at the window of the kitchenette and the many back-bendings over babies in the bathroom can (just) still bring a nostalgic glazing of the eye . . . But I ramble.

[. . .]

I've done a couple of Glanmore sonnets also, but will hold them until they are sure of their shape. They are dear to me, because, among other things, they broke a block, a silence, whatever it was. Meanwhile, love from the place of writing.

Seamus

To John McGahern

MS Galway

12 September 1988

Glanmore Cottage, Ashford,
Co. Wicklow

Dear John,

Two days in the silence of the country is all it takes for the best part of the being to be activated and the right letters to get started. We got a chance to buy this gate-lodge that we lodged in 1972–76. Ann Saddlemyer wisely decided not to retire into our native sireland, so gave us the chance at it. Were you ever here? I most remember you being present at the first-footing of the other teepee . . . It's stone, slate, dormers, shutters, tiles, mustiness, tongue-and-groove, latches, bars and bolts, cold water, open hearths . . . you expect to hear somebody rattling a bucket and coming in with a hurricane lamp.

Sligo was messed up for me by over-enrolment of postulants in the poetry workshops, but more so by the placing of a Field Day meeting on the Friday of the week. That was my one free day, when I hoped I might slip out to see you both, and escape from my status as Mascot. I did national service at Galway, Sligo and Glenties. Made a cod of myself by the day. Moved from Fascism by the Garavogue to (strained) Socialism in the Rosses. Anyway, I was very sorry to miss Foxfield.

I'm writing to ask if you might take part next February (on Saturday 25 or Sunday 26) in a David Thomson commemoration of some sort. (His first anniversary is that Sunday.) Martina would come over, I would do something – ten minutes about him as a writer – maybe a folklorist another 10 minutes, maybe you to speak of him in relation to Leitrim/Roscommon, or to read a bit of his that you like; then probably a bit of music; and a piece from a historian. Brisk, competent, dignified etc., an acknowledgement of how much Ireland meant to him, he to Ireland. It's all true enough, even if it sounds blathery. I'm going over on 22nd, will see Martina then. If you feel like calling in the meantime, do. Love to Madeline. See you,

Seamus

The Garavogue is a river in Sligo, Yeats country; the annual MacGill Summer School, at which SH had newly been appointed Poet in Residence, is held in Glenties, near the Rosses, in Donegal; Foxfield in Leitrim is where McGahern lived.

To John Wilson Foster

MS Emory

12 September 1988

Glanmore Cottage, Ashford,
Co. Wicklow

Dear Jackie,

Years ago at school at this time of the year, we did *Portrait of the Artist*-type retreats. Self-abasement, silence, purposes of amendment. And it seems I am beginning to revert . . . I've come out to this gate-lodge on my own, into an old stillness of stone walls and stealthy fields, and am on my own for the first time in months. You had been much on my mind and your courtesy and patience in letters must be the obverse of a bewilderment and rage elsewhere in your breast. The book and my not having written about it to you became a neurotic locus in my life. I kept saying I would take a weekend to it – I'm such a slow bugger at the joined-up letters that it does take me a long time to get through a volume – but naturally, since it wasn't a deadline, the deadline-induced tasks took precedence. Then your grace in the follow-up note paradoxically paralysed me, and when Hammond told me you were wondering about my playing possum – no, not the way he put it – I simply played possum. My apologies. I guess it's like the Dublin bus-driver: when asked what he most disliked about his job, he replied, stopping for passengers. So opening new books begins to build up a resistance factor, especially when they represent all the procrastination and self-sourness that afflicts one . . .

But what a madness not to have gone at the thing long ago. The broadening of the Revival canvas beyond the usual crowd is, for a start, a great animation. Your discussion of Dunsany, for example, is wonderfully just and critically spot-on. I respect you very highly for the pressure of attention and pitch of critical endeavour you maintain over such a long stretch and broad spectrum. I read some Dunsany years ago and could not quite have expressed my dissatisfaction as exactly as 'indulgent conventionalism', 'pure story devoid of the mystery of tradition as well as of the relevance to life'. 'Well-staged entertainment', with 'very little presentation of the self'.

But the introduction first: it moves me as a thoroughly argued statement – and as a testimony. It is full of things that come home closely to me and meshes with the web of my own selvings and relapsings. When I read about the drama of the self versus the imposed selflessness of church and nation, I know I am at home with a salutary intelligence. The pith and gist of your perceptions are under what I was at in *Station Island*: the 'Sweeney Redivivus' things were meant to be – or at least to sponsor – free self-impulse, and were meant to be seen to issue out of the Joyce *envoi*. But why don't I keep off the 'me' for a moment – except that I want also to praise the riff on 'The Dead'. Gabriel's needing to escape *through* rather than from the surrounding cast, his crucialness as you define it, that seems to me excellent. (And incidentally, that bit about Lady Gregory resenting Synge and Synge resenting the scholars and clergy is pure gold. Indeed your incidental anecdotal information, your tossed-in quotations and throwaway remarks – Stygian fate! – are vital to the book, give it a panache and a Fosterness that seals the deep intimate scholarship.)

It's a sense of you both talking animatedly about the plight we are in on the island now – the veiled entanglements of the ideological and the literary never get cleared – and talking with bracing professionalism about texts – this double attentiveness is what makes the book your book. You are right to draw attention to the way you have taken literary care of Colum, Pearse, Corkery, *etc.* And your judgement of Colum, for me, was also fair and fortifying, in spite of its limiting character. As you know, it is very hard to hold the whole jing-bang of material in the head, after the big read-through. What I come away with is a sense of a necessary book, an act of clarification for the writer and a contribution to the culture. The actual intent body of close reading is locally, serially full of rewards, and the book will be consulted for its discussions of individual authors. What I like best finally is the oath-bound, helpless engagement at the ford, the facing into the backward and abysm of the cultural composts you/we grow out of, and either enrich or complicate. It is truly serious Irish criticism, not in a 'revival' sense of the Irish, but, if you will, in a 'Renaissance' sense.

Blessings and apologies
Seamus

John Wilson Foster (b.1942), Belfast-born literary critic and cultural historian, had first met SH through Benedict Kiely and his wife Frances, and SH's habit of addressing him as 'Jackie' – not how he is generally known – was picked up from theirs.

The book SH had finally got around to reading and appreciating was Foster's *Fictions of the Irish Literary Revival: A Changeling Art* (1987).

To Michael di Capua — MS NYPL

12 September 1988 — 191 Strand Road, Dublin 4

[. . .]

By this letter I have to raise another permissions matter. My friend John Montague is doing a revision of his Irish poetry anthology and faces the old problem of purse-strings . . . My relations with John involve the *comitatus* of poets and the *pietas* of a shared background in the North, as well as a twenty-five-year friendship. I would like him to be able to use the longer poems – I enclose a copy of his letter – and while I hesitate to interfere in your good action on my behalf, I consider it worth doing in this case. Penalize my share of the proposed $700? I know you'll not want to give it to *Scribner's* for nothing but my *geasa* are with J.M.

[. . .]

Michael di Capua was an editor at Farrar, Straus and Giroux, under whose imprint John Montague's *Bitter Harvest: An Anthology of Contemporary Irish Verse* was to have its US publication the following year.

For a sense of *geasa*, see footnote to SH's letter to Thomas Flanagan of 25 October 1974.

To Michael Parker

MS Parker

22 September 1988 London Tara Hotel

Dear Michael,

The postal strike is a cast iron excuse; anyhow, I am very grateful to you for sending me these chapters and more than gratified by what they contain. I do recognize and appreciate the commitment and sensitivity at work in your writing and hope that any yelps and outbursts that came from my pen have not hurt either attribute . . . It's just that – as you know – I'm jumpy as hell about all this. It is certainly a record of what happened but in the midst of my gratitude there is always a voice ready to start up and to say, 'All this is fine, but you're not so far away from it yet – it's like a biography too soon.' This voice is not meant to accuse you but it comes along now and again to discombobulate me.

In spite of it, having just finished the read through – and I have marked what needs revising, correcting or checking – I salute your generous and detailed account, and must say that I got much pleasure being awakened to many of the memories again.

On the Montague section, you should check out the first edition of *Poisoned Lands* against the revised and updated one. It's not for me to say, but the later one contains Heaneyish poems that were not in the original volume. The ones added in would have been even more useful to me at the start – but this is definitely non-quotable, off the record information.

Our love to Aleksandra and the girls.

Marie and I are over for a couple of days. Aer Lingus and *Irish Times* are announcing a literary prize – hefty, £20,000 (punts) – and I function as a mascot on their party. Still, two nights in the *Tara* and executive class seats! Patrick Kavanagh scowls under the Monaghan clay. But Joyce, the sponger, applauds from Zurich? Blessings.

Seamus

SH was in London, enjoying 'executive class' treatment as guest speaker at a celebration of the centenary of T. S. Eliot's birth.

'On the Montague section': the first edition of John Montague's *Poisoned Lands*, which included the poem 'The Water Carrier', arguably, if anachronistically, describable as 'Heaneyish', appeared in September 1961; the second edition, of 1971, is strikingly different and makes more room for poems on rural themes.

To Brian and Anne Friel

MS NLI

28 September 1988 191 Strand Road, Dublin 4

Dear Brian and Anne,

Back from the land of the Britons and the *pléaráca* of TSE. The chairman of Lloyds bank said that another famous poet had worked for them – Vernon Watkins, for 30 years, at Swansea. He continued: 'Watkins, of course, was a branch man but Eliot was always Head Office.' New game: divide the penpeople into said categories.

[. . .]

'*pléaráca*': revelry. The early books of the Welsh poet Vernon Watkins (1906–67) were published by Faber under Eliot's editorship.

To Valerie Eliot

MS Eliot

29 September 1988 191 Strand Road, Dublin 4

Dear Valerie,

A week ago we were at the happy and excellent reception at Lloyds bank; back here, I think of myself as branch office, once again . . . We had an unforgettable time and cannot thank you adequately for the honour you did us by inviting us, in particular to the dinner last Monday. Finding myself at your table, in such company, I could hardly believe I contained somewhere inside me the bewildered boy who sat in the benches at St Columb's College and tried to put his reactions to 'The Hollow Men' into words. Marie and I were both proud and delighted by the whole event. You gave everybody such an historical occasion, yet you also gave us a truly personal, pleasurable time. All of a sudden, we all felt friends.

One of my favourite Eliot quotations is the one about the 'use of memory', from 'Little Gidding'. I felt everything, over the centenary, was renewed, 'in another pattern'.

Marie joins me in sending our most affectionate wishes.

Sincerely,
Seamus Heaney

'Pattern' is a significantly recurring word in Eliot's *Four Quartets*; SH is here alluding to 'Little Gidding', III, ll. 14–16.

To Mel McMahon

MS McMahon

8 October 1988 191 Strand Road, Dublin 4

Dear Mr McMahon,

So many books come hurling through the letterbox that I never have time enough to read them as carefully as they deserve or to write at the length their authors might expect. But I do think there's a genuine personal note in your work and that you have a gift for the good rich phrase. I feel in the presence of a sensibility. I like the directness of lines like 'drowned with small flies in the font'; 'Rain or shine I am there, with / Night-water, small-lighted moonstones.' I liked the runty pears too. It's probably natural for you to strain a bit, overwrite a bit, wobble a bit. But I wonder if you mightn't get pleasure and example from reading, say, Elizabeth Bishop?

I am sorry that at the moment I cannot undertake a reading at St Mary's. My best wishes all the same, to Brian Hanratty – and to you and your work.

Sincerely,
Seamus Heaney

Mel McMahon (b.1968), a student at St Mary's Teacher Training College, on meeting SH in Newcastle, Co. Down, was encouraged by him to send him some poems, and this was the response. Brian Hanratty, once taught by SH, now taught at St Mary's.

To Paul Durcan

MS NLI

9 October 1988 191 Strand Road, Dublin 4

Dear Paul,

The blessing you give with your letter. All year, at times of hurry and at other times of sudden pang and awakening, I say 'Oh Christ, I haven't written to Paul Durcan!' Your letter about *The Haw Lantern* was generous and cleansing as downpour and should have been answered right away. Then, somehow, the departure for America for the year was upon us, what had been neglected fell behind like a broken-off lump of life, and we were on the conveyor belt again. Happily, you give me the chance to retrieve that broken-off chunk . . . *Gratias ago*.

[. . .]

I've not actually got your letters with me but I remember the gist of your recent one from last summer. I shall send you copies of some things I've been doing recently, just to run up a poem-flag in response. They are swift things, in execution and probably in the reading; there's no particular sense to them, but if they could be maintained, I'd think of calling them 'Squarings' – which, in marbles, was a term for the fore-dreamt accuracies of your shot. The shot itself, of course, was most likely inaccurate . . . Anyhow, I'd like them to represent memory-spots or dreamt-up word grids that my soul would be happy to go through when it is on its way, back or away. They are, as they say, in progress, but I feel that letting you see some of them will advance the progress for me.

[. . .]

To Michael Longley

MS Emory

13 October 1988 [Cheltenham]

Dear Michael,

Ever since your letter in August I've been on the verge of answering – which makes a change, I suppose, from Sir Boyle Roche's 'I'd have answered your letter six weeks ago except it only arrived this morning.' All that you remembered and told in it was good and relevant and I appreciated the mixture of formality and generosity. I am sending you here the full text of the lecture from which I excerpted the bit for the Dún Laoghaire *fest*. It was given as one of three lectures in memory of Richard Ellmann at Emory University, last April, and will appear in a bookeen (of the three, plus introduction) at the end of the year. In the States only, entitled *The Place of Writing*. Everybody will say that I copied your introduction.

Of course, the Elizabeth Bowen position about finding everything in a single face is perfectly right – one thinks of Dante, so to speak. But it is possible to apply this truth too inexpansively or too self-deludingly. Obviously when you embrace/promulgate a position like that, you do so after going through a thick wall of complications, all your valiantly endured and principled work at the Arts Council, all that we all know about the back-doors and false bottoms of the liberal as well as of the bigoted psyches of beloved Ulster. Your palpable knowledge of it, your care for it as well as hurt and rage at it, give you the right to proclaim the visionary obliteration of it. Yet everything is indeed one thing, and what I wanted to do, I suppose, was to suggest that the tolerances and transcendences that we win are necessarily linked to the aboriginal set of conditions which they go beyond. It's not that one poet is more 'political' than another; it's that some make the (perhaps, though not necessarily always) artistic mistake of espousing 'politics' in the verse. I hear you groan. I enjoyed that.

I also enclose that odd little riff of twelve lines that rose unbidden one morning recently. The bestirring of the Newry memory in your letter is no doubt behind it. It's not altogether a poem but I've been fiddling around with forays like it, piling – no, scraping – up glimpses and flitters, looking forward to a coalescing of them, maybe, one day . . .

Actually, I'm not in Dublin as I write but in Cheltenham, *chez* Alan Hancox, where I have an hour on my own, mid-morning, in a booklined room. The peace and mellowness of the place make me wish I could have a fortnight's silence, or a year's. At the moment, I have a sabbatical from Harvard (quarter salary for a year, since my year's salary is, as it were, a half-year salary, and the sabbatical allowance is half of your usual . . . Christ, what a sentence) – and I won't be going back until the spring of 1990. After that, I'll have to think again. Age of fifty, and all that. Do I want to keep stepping on planes? Living among the acquisitive brilliant young of Bush-ville. The querulous self-salving rhetorics of the million books of useless poetry. The requests for blurbs . . . The urge towards an elemental purifying move is mighty. But the anxiety about dropping the safety-net of a salary – Marie not working, the middle-aged sofa-life and drinks-cupboard standard of living being here to stay – gives me pause. Eight months off work for four months on is a terrific arrangement, but it may have to go, for the sake of new life. This is not an announcement, if you know what I mean, just a kind of rambling towards what could happen . . .

Your MacNeice book is first-rate and along with Edna's constitutes a real contribution. Already the right noises are beginning to sound out. I haven't seen many of the reviews, one in – I think – *The Independent* gave the right cheers. Do you remember the MacNeice reading we did in The Chimney Corner road-house out beyond Glengormley, when my colleague at St Joseph's, John Sherlock, had gone into the hotel trade and sought respectability? Big square-chinned Sean Fulton bringing all the staunchness of Larne to the appreciation of 'Carrickfergus'.

When I was at St Thomas's, McLaverty gave me the afternoon off one day to take 4B out to Carrickfergus, and we did the walkabout – listing Christ, Chichester ruffs, the Irish quarter, the castle. A number of the kids were subsequently killed, no doubt on 'active service'. Ballymurphy rule not OK and yet not bad. Jack Holland was also in the class. I'm reminiscent too soon. But I expect Hancox soon and want to finish and get this off, unfinished as it is. Just to salute and put on hold. Blessings on Longleyville.

Seamus

Sir Boyle Roche (1736–1807) was an Irish parliamentarian, notorious for his self-contradicting pronouncements: e.g., allegedly, 'We should silence anyone who opposes the right to freedom of speech.'

The Place of Writing actually appeared in 1989.

Alan Hancox (1932–2013) was the bookseller and book collector who founded and ran the Cheltenham Festival of Literature.

'elemental purifying move': see Larkin's 'Poetry of Departures'.

Michael Longley's 'MacNeice book' was *Selected Poems* (1988), published by Faber; Edna Longley's was *Louis MacNeice: A Study* (1988), also from Faber, in the firm's 'Student Guide' series.

'Christ, Chichester ruffs, the Irish quarter, the castle': see Louis MacNeice's poem 'Carrickfergus'.

To Seamus Deane

MS Emory

Thursday 17 [November 1988] 191 Strand Road, Dublin 4

An odd thing happened at that point on Tuesday evening. Peter Fallon came to the door with various bits of business which stalled me at the letter; and as he left he presented me with a forward copy of your *Selected Poems*. A lovely book, in print and look. The new poems at the back gave me the *frisson*. 'Homer Nods', 'Tongues', 'Aisling', 'The Churchyard at Creggan' – these ones manage to be in the high registers and high risk areas and hold the note beautifully. The 'Úrchill an Chreagáin' is doomed to be a classic. The yellow bittern of its time – MacDonagh's, that is, not Mackers. Hope you'll do that at London on December 10 when you get back – back, as Friel once greeted me, to the mouse race!

(Here I move from slouching in armchair to tensing at desk – hence better handwriting.) Frielo I have not seen since Derry and opening of *Making History*, but I've seen the play again twice. I have a real unease about Hugh O'Donnell in the thing – he has a strong element of the buffoon, indeed of Kennelly *bufún*, not only in the way he's played but in the lines he's given. And the overall feel of the thing is not as true and springy as you'd want it to be. It's as if a Platonic dialogue on the writing of history got conflated with a sketch for a realistic period piece . . . I voice these uneases to you, while keeping the world at bay with level meditative venturings like, 'Well, of course, it's not *meant* to be realistic, . . . one thinks of Shaw . . .' But not even Shaw do I mention to Brian.

Walk again among us, o fair youth. Teach the bondsmen how to blaze. Forgive the brevity and spottiness of this. I just wanted to greet you once, if late in the day. I have not ventured into the news of Stewart Parker's suddenish death by cancer or news of my trip to London for Eliot's centenary. These matters can be plied in some snug before long, I hope; when I shall have written the lecture I am to deliver on Edwin Muir – next week, in Glasgow, under the bottle-bottom glare of Hobsbaum and the tremulous courtesy of Peter Butter. What fun, as Brigid, I hope, will cry.

Marion is joining the cast of *Making History* and a few other rakish Paddies – Frank McGuinness, Michael Farrell – at a wee party here to-morrow night, after the thee-ater. Danger is that Hammond may come from Belfast. And me needing a clear stretch of weekend to do Muir . . . Lucky you, in the cold of mid-west; We're looking forward to seeing you.

Love,
Seamus

The second part of an interrupted letter.

Deane, whose *Selected Poems* were published this very month, was about to return from the USA to Ireland.

In 'The Yellow Bittern', Thomas MacDonagh (1878–1916) made the classic translation of the poem 'An Bonnán Buí', by the Irish writer Cathal Buí Mac Giolla Ghunna (?1680–1756); SH was to do his own version later. Deane had included his translation of Art Mac Cumhaigh's (1738–73) aisling 'Úr-Chill an Chreagáin' among his *Selected Poems*.

Red Hugh O'Donnell, the character in Brian Friel's play *Making History*, was played by Peter Gowen.

Buffún is a character in Brendan Kennelly's (1936–2021) epic poem *Cromwell*.

The Northern Irish playwright Stewart Parker (1941–88) had, like SH and Deane, been a member of Philip Hobsbaum's Group.

'Marion' was Deane's first wife, Marion Treacy.

To Rosemary Goad

MS Faber

29 November 1988

Extempore Effusion on Missing Rosemary's Party

Dearest Rose, this is in lieu
Of drinking loving cups with you
Chez Groucho le jeudi prochain –
Which means we're on French leave again.
We're sorry that we have to miss
Another chance to reminisce
About those first shy Faber lunches
Where at first we pulled the punches
But quickly grew relaxed and dafter
As large ones doubled up the laughter.
If you were there, with Charles between us,
We'd tell you what you mean to us,
Why you are highest on the list,
The Goad we never kick against,
How your good will and loyalties
Were icing on the royalties.
We love the way you know the score,
And at a glance can spot the bore,
The way you keep your counsel, yet
Know in a flash who's dry, who's wet.
We add these verses to the pile
To celebrate your unfooled smile,
To hope the party's wild and starry –
And bring you love from me and Marie.
Seamus

The party was in honour of Rosemary Goad on the occasion of her retirement from Faber and Faber. This message, signed and dated, was probably delivered by hand as no address is given.

1989

A landmark year, as momentous for SH as either 1970 or 1972. Freed from his teaching and lecturing duties at Harvard, approaching his fiftieth birthday, he had leisure to scan the horizon and contemplate in a broader way what his next steps might be.

The Chair of Poetry at Oxford had fallen vacant: when first asked if he might consider standing for election to succeed Peter Levi (1931–2000), poet, Hellenist and ex-priest, whose five-year term was now up, he appears to have been cautious, only growing more committed as the campaign organised by his allies within the university gathered momentum. Many of these allies were Irish.

Ted Hughes made clear his interpretation of the nature of this academic coup when, after the election, he wrote to congratulate SH: 'I'm looking forward to seeing how you seize the Oxford opportunity . . . Any operation you can perform there will be like an operation on the pituitary gland – of England. It will soon affect the whole country . . . Has there ever been a successful advocate, in England, for Ireland's side of all the cases? As an opportunity, given your standing with Oxford students, it's maybe unique. Inject a whole new understanding, to the right audience at the right age.' SH's own ambitions may have fallen short of this, but he could intuit the possibilities that such an eminent post might open up.

The appointment, however, was also a factor in exposing him to ever greater intrusions on his privacy; two letters that follow, the first to a person identified simply as 'Liam' (31 August), the second to Francis Murphy of the Arts Council of Northern Ireland (16 December), show him defending what he could of his private space.

To Bernard McCabe — MS J. McCabe

1 February 1989 — 191 Strand Road, Dublin 4

Dear Bernard,

St Brigid's Day. First Day of spring, and truly vernal it was. I walked free on the Strand for half an hour, around two o'clock. I almost said aloud, my father and mother are dead, I am fifty and my son is leaving home. It's all old hat to a Methuselah like yourself, but Michael departs for Paris to-morrow morning at eight o'clock. We feel atremble on his behalf and indeed he must be atremble himself, what with the standard (epsilon) of his French and the fact he has no job lined up and the generally tender inside of his nature. But it is all a good thing for him to do, a bit of the simple venturing forth and riting the passage . . .

At any rate, it left me feeling on a cusp. That may have been helped by the immense relief I felt at being shed of public lecture tensions, after my foray to Derry on Saturday. Guildhall. Five hundred and thirty people in the audience. Derry people. Hundreds of the usuals showing the flag for Yeats, for me, for Derry, for a sort of 'we'll show them – ourselves even – that we're up to a certain level'. I was proud and glad: it was a public occasion, well conceived, well supported, tacitly inflationary for all concerned, and no bad thing. Flaming-faced Friel introduced, *poitín*-head Hammond attended, wonderful wife persons disposed well and dispensed, and the text is still in its first pen-labour state . . . I keep promising Yeats bits and will bring some on *17th*. We arrive London 16th, for *Shaughraun* – wifey and Cappy and me. Will call in the meantime.

However. No mercy. 4 groups of twelve poems envisaged (each poem 12 lines long). Whole thing to be called 'SQUARINGS' (tee hee). First section – 'Lightenings' – provisionally complete. 2nd: 'Holdings' – not really conceived right yet, a couple of possibles included. 3rd: 'CROSSINGS' – or 'FARINGS'? – almost there. 4th: 'Offings' – two bits. All enclosed for carding and palping and snuffling and pissing on and scratching and sloughing.

Much love to you both. Will telephonee soonee.

Seamus

On 29 January, at the celebrations in Derry marking the fiftieth anniversary of Yeats's death, SH gave a talk that was then printed, under the title 'In the Midst of the Force Field', in the *Irish Times*.

The Shaughraun, by the Irish actor and playwright Dion Boucicault (1820–90), was enjoying a rare, brief run in London, with Stephen Rea in the leading role.

'Cappy': i.e. Captain Ann; i.e. daughter Catherine Ann.

To Tom Paulin

MS Emory

6 February 1989 — 191 Strand Road, Dublin 4

Dear Tom,

Many thanks for your kind note about not being able to make the Yeats lecture. It did go well, good sense of occasion, the middle-classes at full tide, and me shamelessly riding same. When I get the thing typed, I'll send you some of it, anyhow. *Fortnight* want to do bits of it and I thought, why not. But won't give Edna the satisfaction of putting in my little retort to her.

Meanwhile, in the week since it, I've been writing at last. I got started on these twelve-line things, and – they're operating like tin-openers, except the tins are all about the size of a wee John West salmon tin. But a way of swooping in on impulse and getting out. Only way I could address the Yeats numen in verse. (enclosed)

Love to Giti and the littl'uns. Best! Seamus

Fortnight, a cultural magazine that ran from September 1970 to January 2012, based in Belfast and hosting a broad range of contributors, published excerpts from the Yeats lecture in its March 1989 number.

Giti is Paulin's wife.

To Stanisław Barańczak

MS Barańczak

6 February 1989 — 191 Strand Road, Dublin 4

Dear Stanisław,

This morning *Zeszyty Literackie* came thumping into the letter-box and I was more pleased and proud than I usually am. Because you did the work. Because of the poems you chose. And because of the manifest care you took – even I can see the attention to chimes and rhymes in the sonnets. Naturally, I am also always honoured to be translated into Polish, and on this occasion the company in the magazine is heady indeed. Anyhow, I felt the need to greet you and thank you.

These feelings of being blessed by the powers – and the people – lie behind the poems I enclose. I send them <u>not</u> for your translation, or comment, just as a semaphore from the western island, with much affection to Anna and yourself.

Sincerely,
Seamus Heaney

Barańczak was co-founder of the Paris-based, internationally hospitable magazine *Zeszyty Literackie*.

To Bernard O'Donoghue

MS O'Donoghue

4 April 1989 — 191 Strand Road, Dublin 4

Dear Bernard,

Some reluctant power in my subconscious keeps tugging me away from sending on the enclosed. But the die is cast . . . My apologies for the sluggishness.

If you get any official blurb about the tasks and remuneration associated with the thing, I'll be glad to see a copy of it some time. Would the 'inaugural' – whoever gives it – be in the autumn of this year?

Why did I ever get into it!!

Best wishes to Heather.

S.

In February 1989, Bernard O'Donoghue (b.1945), Irish poet and lecturer at Magdalen College, Oxford, had written to SH suggesting that he might allow himself to be put forward as a candidate for the Oxford Professorship of Poetry; the 'enclosed' was a signed declaration of willingness. Heather O'Donoghue, Bernard's wife, was at this time Fellow in Medieval English at Somerville College.

To Medbh McGuckian

MS Emory

5 April 1989 — 191 Strand Road, Dublin 4

Dear Medbh,

Your letter after the Yeats lecture should have been answered long ago, and now your card with its inscribed verse and free lucent poem, initialled and all, have me tempted to preen in the thought of your good estimate. What you and John conveyed, that night in Derry and then in John's review, made me feel happy and of some use. I often feel that the pomp and sonority of such occasions as the Derry lecture, and the high rhetoric that they tend to bring out in me, the po-faced and solemn-eyed altar boy aspect of my make-up, are a kind of error. I mean, the low-key, throwaway, ironical touch of a Mahon or a Muldoon, that dodge away from the Bishop's-Pastoral-note, often seems more durable or serviceable as a way of handling the public tasks. So. Anyhow. A thousand thanks.

I'm heading off with Marie this Friday, and we'll be on the train for

Rome, from Calais, on Saturday. We had promised ourselves this holiday for a long while. I've never been to Holy City-ville before, and I'm looking forward to it very much. We'll have the anniversary spaghetti on April 13. (Same as Beckett, you know, very posh dating.)

'The Child of Loyalty' is wonderfully fleet and opulent in its moves and associations; it brings me through an expansive and renovating element. It was a fine thing to receive and I appreciate it greatly. Love,

Seamus

The Northern Irish poet Medbh McGuckian (b.1950) is married to John McGuckian, also a poet; 'The Child of Loyalty' is an uncollected poem by her.

To Joseph Brodsky

PC Beinecke

[April 1989] [Postmarked 'Rome']

'Astraddle on the dolphin's mire and blood' . . . Why did I wait so long to see this city? In danger of believing in civilization as a credible project! Wish you were here.

Love, Seamus and Marie

The postmark bears an illegible date, but the card must have been sent at the time of the Heaneys' birthday jaunt. The image on the card that calls up the line from Yeats's 'Byzantium' is from a mosaic in the Basilica di S. Clemente and shows a winged sea-god on the back of a dolphin.

To Paul Durcan

MS NLI

28 April 1989 191 Strand Road, Dublin 4

Dear Paul,

Last Saturday I got back after a two-week dodge in Rome. I had never been to Popesville before but realized what I had been missing . . . the old heart sang and the webbed head cleared. It was like walking into the unconscious of the first Latin class and the choral transports of the first communion. But anyhow . . .

Your poem in the post when I landed here was another great lift. Fluent and generous and oven-good . . . redeeming even the birthday poem genre. Your impatience with the cant and the mascot stuff entirely spot-on. I am blessed by it, 'steeped in luck'. Enclosed magazine, not for the blather but for the Ellmann / Pasternak / lucky poem, and the 'Lightenings' which I was wobbling into months ago when I wrote to you.

All this poetry on my head is like a christening for the second childhood.

Sláinte!
Seamus

Durcan's 'poem in the post' was 'Seamus Heaney's Fiftieth Birthday', included the following year in his collection *Daddy, Daddy*.

To Margot and Donald Fanger — MS Fanger

18 May 1989 — 191 Strand Road, Dublin 4

Dear Fangers – or is it Margot and Fanger –

The warm embracements are just the thing. And I hope you will not feel they are answered with the could – cold, sorry – shoulders if I suggest a slight deflection of the Dublin visit, away from the cheery season. Last Christmas, the young – now not so young, 22, 21, 16 – put in a request that we might have Christmas on our own. Perfectly fair, since in fact when they were younger, they always had company (and our invitation was based on that habitual open house attitude), and now they just wanted a bit of quieter, family indolence. So in keeping with this newly developed philosophy of Yule, we would like to revise the proposal and suggest you find a weekend on the calendar, preferably before the turkey-kill – ours, that is, not your late November one – though, come to think of it, that might be a good date? What about Thanksgiving in Dublin?

Anyhow, *chers amis*, I know you will not misunderstand our reshuffle of the Christmas date. It's simply to make sure that optimum conditions prevail, pertain, when you're here.

We'll be in Ireland from mid-October. So. Find the weekend. *Arrivez.* Our phone here is 011.353.1.697569.

Now I am a candidate for the Oxford Professorship of Poetry. £3,000 p.a., at least 3 lectures. An election on June 2. Fifty-year-old, smiling, self-doubting man. Love, Seamus

SH had been introduced to Margot and Donald Fanger by Robert Tracy. Donald (b.1929), who is a Russianist and taught at Harvard, began to be addressed by his wife and others as 'Fanger' to avoid confusion when he shared an apartment with another Donald, and the usage continued and spread. The Fangers did celebrate Thanksgiving in Dublin.

'turkey-kill': one of the Heaney family's Christmas rituals, of great importance to SH, was the drive north to collect a turkey from his brother Hugh, who bred them.

To Michael McLaverty

MS Linen Hall

21 June 1989 — 191 Strand Road, Dublin 4

Dear Michael,

Unfortunately, I cannot be with you this afternoon for the launch of *In Quiet Places*. I've got a mid-summer flu and feel like Daniel McNeill felt in *Call My Brother Back* when he lay cooped up under 'blue skies . . . grained with twirls of cloud', when 'the heat of the room was as thick as the bed-clothes'. That was always one of my favourite passages in the book, by the way, but now I know it on the pulses, as Keats would say.

I'm very sorry not to be there to tell you in person how delighted I am that Sophia got this book together. I love it because it is so truly yourself. As I read it I kept thinking of the conversations we used to have in the early sixties, sometimes when you were giving me a lift home from St Thomas's, sometimes, later on, down at Killard. (And I remember in particular one trip to the big estate outside Dromore in Co. Down, where Hopkins had resided for a short while.) All the sureness and earned conviction in you about Hopkins and Chekhov and Mansfield and – equally – McGahern and Friel – all that passion about the pure literary thing, or rather the pure thing that subsumed the literary into the spiritual, or vice versa – all that was immensely educative. It gave me a glimpse of the meaning of terms like 'discipline' or 'commitment to writing'. What I find in the book is that same pure, selfless, attentive love of the thing that is done perfectly; a year by year printout of the sensibility of a writer pressing on past 'the middle of the journey'. It is full of 'the fine delight'. It is, to quote Keats again, the work of an intelligence being schooled into a soul.

But you'll be resisting that praise so let me tell you also how proud I was to find myself overpraised in the last pages. It all reminded me again of the unco-ordinated kind of life writers had in Belfast in the early sixties. I'll always be grateful to you for introducing me to John

McGahern and Roy McFadden, and for sending me out to meet Padraic Fiacc in Glengormley. So I am sorry not to be with you all to-day. I had hoped to go with John Boyd and whip you out for lunch – but maybe we'll manage that some day later this summer. In the meantime, Marie brings you all our love and we salute the marvellous things that are always there, under our readers' noses, *In Quiet Places*.

Le grá,

Seamus

In Quiet Places, subtitled *Uncollected Stories, Letters and Critical Prose*, was edited by Sophia Hillan (b.1950), academic and writer of fiction, who had been a student and, later, colleague of SH's at Carysfort College. Michael McLaverty's novel *Call My Brother Back* was published in 1939.

'. . . and Mansfield': McLaverty was an enthusiast for the stories of Katherine Mansfield.

Roy McFadden (1921–99), Northern Irish poet, was the editor of two historically significant anthologies, *Ulster Voices* and *Irish Voices* (both 1943), as well as of the poetry magazine *Rann*; Padraic Fiacc was the pen-name of Patrick Joseph O'Connor (1924–2019), Northern Irish poet and anthologist; John Boyd, playwright and producer at BBC Northern Ireland, was also an editor: first, of the wartime magazine *Lagan*, and later, of *Threshold*, to which SH had contributed.

To Michael Hartnett

MS NLI

2 July 1989

Magdalen College, Oxford OX1

Dear Michael,

Over for a weekend, to meet 'the electorate'. Through the good offices of Bernard O'Donoghue, I'm attached to this college where they have a deerpark, one of Oscar Wilde's rings and two of Joseph Addison's shoe buckles. Other surprises are in store, no doubt. But in the meantime I thank you for your generous greeting when the thing was announced. *Beannacht*!

Seamus

Elected Professor of Poetry by a large majority, SH could now enjoy the hospitality of Magdalen College, where Oscar Wilde had been a student from 1874 to 1878, and the poet and essayist Joseph Addison (1672–1719), a Fellow.

'*Beannacht*!': a blessing.

To Thomas McCarthy

MS Princeton

3 July 1989 Magdalen College, Oxford OX1

Dear Tom,

Your letter and your gift of the Graves book meant much to me on the occasion of the professorship. To have the channels of good will opened so readily and intelligently was very reassuring. I have always valued the candour and generosity of your impulses and commitments and this latest gesture was another good confirmation.

They've made me a 'supernumerary non-stipendiary fellow' here, and I'm over for the weekend, feeling it out.

What the lectures are to be about I am not yet sure of, but I look forward to some weeks of quiet in Glanmore during the summer, and the emergence of some glimmer of themes and inspirations. Meanwhile, all good wishes to you for your own work, and blessings on you and your family. Seamus

Thomas McCarthy (b.1954), poet, librarian and, at this time, editor of *Poetry Ireland*, had sent SH the gift of Robert Graves's *The Crowning Privilege* (1955), which includes Graves's Clark Lectures 1954–5. Graves had also been Oxford Professor of Poetry, from 1961 to 1966.

To Helen Vendler

MS Harvard

11 July 1989 Dooey, Lettermacaward, Co. Donegal

Dear Helen,

I'm still on my travels, but on a different leg. Last weekend I wrote that mad quick ice-breaker – or ice-cracker, at least – and have been skimming around since. Trinity gave D. Walcott a degree – Terence is starting an MA course that includes Anglo-Irish and 'related' literatures, and wanted to broaden the sweep of the honorary doctorates – so I was over at Ballylee and Coole Park for a couple of days (with D.W. and girlfriend). Then came here to Donegal to be painted by a blasé, high-class (socially) portrait painter called Derek Hill, this as a result of Fabers commissioning him. I stayed *chez lui* two nights and have spent the past two nights with the Hammonds, in whose kitchen I write this on the morning of the last sitting, looking at the glittering sound and the seals' heads (still here) scanning everything. It's all very fine, but it's not my own time, in the Wicklow silence.

I hope to get to Wicklow on Thursday and to be there, with forays away, on and off, until the end of September. Glanmore is only 45 minutes from Strand Road, so whether one resides in Dublin or the cottage doesn't matter . . . The place is workable as study visited daily or as holiday home.

What I want very much is to have you spend a night or two there. For a thousand reasons, I want you to have the place as a memory and hope that you'll go there on 26 and/or 27 August. Let's meet, however, on the evening of the 7th, after your sleep. I'll be coming back on 6th from the tedious Longley-infested John Hewitt Summer School. (The man was not cold in his grave before they were nailing their Ulster colours – or banners – to his mast. Mixed metaphor, but what the hell.) Nancy will be with us from August 4, so that's why I'd prefer to leave our chance for a couple of days of talk-through, between ourselves, to the latter end of your stay. It will be madness and I shall feel badly deprived and askew if we do not make the time for at least a couple of days' *causerie* and refurbishing of all sorts. Please, unless you have other plans made, plan to be indolent and vagrant on that 26/27 occasion. And to break bread with us all on the evening of the 7th – or 8th, if you'd prefer to rest through. I'll telephone nearer your departure.

I feel so at a loss in face of both your unstinted blessings upon *Government of the Tongue* and my long spells of un-letter-writing. The rewards I am given are immense and I feel like a thin leaf on a mill-race, sustained and pitched ahead on a hurl of energy that is beyond me, and for me. Your absolutely tuned sympathy and vertical take-off intelligence have greatly helped me to proceed with whatever I have and am, as creature and writer, so at a moment like this, when I settle and convene myself, I am unnerved at the way I have *not* been in touch. Anyway, self-flagellation is its own reward too, so I'll shut up and hope to get back into the talk that buffs and braces when we meet next month.

[. . .]

Derek Hill (1916–2000) was an English artist living and working in Donegal.

To Katrina Porteous

TS Porteous

14 July 1989 191 Strand Road, Dublin 4

Dear Katrina,

Thank you very much for your letter and forgive the brevity of this reply.

I prefer the lines as they appear in the poem now. In other words, I'd be inclined to make no change at all.

I feel that all your instincts are for keeping the lines – for musical, prereflective reasons almost – and all the reasons you give for changing them are rational, almost moral. I believe that the instinctive sixth sense preferences that are there in you for the original lines are the things to obey in this case. At least, that's the lines upon which I myself usually work.

I am glad to think that you may be in Cambridge next year. Please be sure to get in touch when you are there. And many thanks for your good wishes on the Oxford Professorship. Keep writing.

Yours sincerely

Seamus

PS Sorry to be dictating. I'm in a rush!

As a Harkness Fellow at Harvard, in her early twenties, Scottish poet Katrina Porteous (b.1960) had attended one-to-one seminars with SH in the autumn and winter of 1983–4. Since then, she had occasionally sent him her poems for comment, as was the case here. The point under discussion was Porteous's use of an archaism about which she had vacillating thoughts.

The postscript is in SH's hand. He actually writes 'doctating'.

To Robert and Rebecca Tracy

MS Tracy

31 July 1989 Glanmore Cottage, Ashford, Co. Wicklow

Dear Bob and Becky,

It's not the Stone House but it *is* the bastion of silence and at last we have been able to stow away here together. Ann Saddlemyer gave us the chance to buy it – she had intended to keep it until her retirement and then work on it, but all that began to seem too improbable so, bless her generous heart, she let it go. We have done some work – insulating and painting it white inside to lighten and freshen it – and thrown out or transported some of the old furniture and all of the old carpets . . . It is a Godsend; and absolutely necessary the way things are going. The phone never stops in Dublin and I get about 15 pieces of mail, on average, every day (post only comes 5 days a week, I admit). Somehow the clamour and attrition are like tides, rising and eroding. But here the world turns on the hub of quiet and the spirit begins to align itself and be concentric with that still, turning point.

And then through that clarified and soundless lens arrives the tall shade of self-rebuke; and I want to avoid his gaze the way I have for too too long avoided the blank paper meant for your letter. Always deflecting the thought with the second thought that there's not enough time to write the *real* letter, the big one that will take us through all the hoops of old news and big crises. The news of your cancer diagnosis was a shock, Bob, but happily less unnerving than it could have been. Still, the brush of the wing that brings that word anywhere near is always an ominous one, and I hope your spirit and body have come through the treatment; it is shameful that we have not been in touch with you until now. Maybe I'll feel freer to telephone you in a couple of weeks.

Meanwhile, the exactness and good disposition of your *Haw Lantern* review should have been acknowledged and praised long ago. What I took pleasure – and, well, yes, pride – in was the way you caught the stricter note inside the 'slight lyric grace' of the poems. I very much appreciated the power you had over the whole *oeuvre* (whoever thought that the lad would end up with an *oeuvre*, for Christ's sake? But let that pass . . .) the way you could make the connections from beginning to end. It all made wonderful sense and amplified the notes. The commitment that yields a piece as attentive and complementary and shapely in itself is a blessing to me. To end with such grace in the silence of the sonnets, after the exemplary reading of the 'Haw Lantern' poem, to allow me the latitude of movement from 'moral' to whatever the other dimension is – poetic? – that was the kind of perception the book was in need of.

Syracuse University Press is a place worth thinking about for the Tracy book. They did a Yeats book by a man I like called Douglas Archibald, whom I'll be seeing next week in Dublin; and they also did another Irish book, about what I cannot now recall. Maud Wilcox I have not been in touch with, as I have not been in touch with anyone in the great school. Apart from occasional postcards to and from Helen V., who also arrives next week, kind and devastating all at once, torrent of energy and insight and adept in the higher echelons of the academic command. She always brings me to the realization that a frantic action is proceeding in the word-processors of America, one that I forget about easily and happily once I cross the Atlantic. But she is also a source of good thoughts about who might be the right person to read what manuscript. Paul Zimmer at Iowa UP struck me as an excellent man, by the way, serious and humorous and devoted. He's a poetry editor – I think – but well worth a try. Please say I suggested it, for we spent a merry couple of days a couple of years ago in Kansas.

Catherine has been in France for a month on a class of an Irish-girls-in-the-Loire-Valley-instead-of-the-Gaeltacht camp. College in the morning, *la piscine* in the afternoon, *la vie de famille* in the evenings, and whatever else *eros* and resource can manage. She had a great old time and is still the darling. Christopher sets out on a 10-day Soviet Union In-Tourist type excursion on Friday (Estonia included!). He has completed his three years of Russian at Trinity and proceeds to the final year of Spanish in October. Dear old Michael concluded his MA – successfully, 2/1 – last autumn, went to Paris for two months (with pals) in the spring, found no job, moved to London *chez* Marie's sister Helen and is now treading water and oppressing the delinquent orders by writing summonses in a court in Brentford. Ideological unease and less than desirable salary may have him at new tasks soon, but he intends to hold out in the land of the Britons until Christmas. Then, he will ponder anew what he *really* wants to do . . .

Pondering is what the Professor of Poetry at Oxford is at also. I have to give three lectures each year for the next five . . . and an inaugural in October. Heavy, man. Much focus and scrutiny. Irish/English match, basically. So I have put up a real cheeky title: 'Doing English: Poetry and Redressal'. It's a bit of coat-trailing, for I don't intend to do much of the British/Irish stuff they're all half-wanting and half-bored with. It's just a gleam of possibility, a stimulant that might lead towards the more general idea, uttered by Ellmann, that the poet never accepts the common sense solution, and is drawn to redress the balance of circumstance by the weight of imagining – latter conclusion mine, not Ellmann's. We'll see.

The Long Island ambassador will be here in late August. He's a judge with the *Irish Times* literary award and will be flown in for consultations about whom to award £25,000 to for a novel. Americans, British and Irish all eligible. Much agitation and twinkling in store.

Much love to you both. As I say, when I feel physically fit for the phone, I'll lift it. Marie sends, as I do, what Don Fanger assures me are the conventional thing at the end of all letters in Polish: warm embracements.

Seamus

Robert Tracy and his wife Rebecca had been members of the gregarious circle of Irish scholars who welcomed SH to Berkeley in 1970; their friendship had deepened during the months of 1972 that the Tracys spent in Dublin. The 'Stone House' was a summer rental they had taken for several weeks, in Brandon, Co. Kerry; from there, Rebecca Tracy had written a letter describing the place and its inhabitants.

Robert Tracy had written about *The Haw Lantern* in *Berkeley Fiction Review 8* (Fall 1988). The 'Tracy book' was eventually published in 1998 as *The Unappeasable Host: Studies in Irish Identities* (University College Dublin Press).

Douglas Archibald (1933–2020), Yeats scholar, taught at Colby College, in Waterville, Maine; Maud Wilcox (1923–2009) was an editor at Harvard University Press; Paul Zimmer (b.1934) is a poet as well as having been a publisher.

The 'Long Island ambassador' was Thomas Flanagan.

To Ted Hughes

MS Emory

31 August 1989

Glanmore Cottage, Ashford,
Co. Wicklow

Dear Ted,

Glad to have your letter and your heart-ploughing book. The poems of first place, first consciousness, first fear/pain I find deeply moving. I am at home in them and they in me and all-in-language. 'Dust As We Are', 'Source' (especially), 'For the Duration', 'Leaf Mould', 'Walt' – these are the ones that touch bottom immediately, they are both plasm-tender and rock-sure. Content and grace at once. And they are bonded and hefted up out of pre-reflective time into time-and-place by 'Slump Sundays', 'Climbing into Heptonstall' (wonderful ending), 'Slump Sundays' and 'Anthem'. Once again, as the man says somewhere in *Gilgamesh*, you have established your name stamped on brick. The 'Conundrums' are powerful and along with 'Take What You Want' they amplify the birth-of-soul, schooling-of-an-intelligence, exit-from-the-chamber-of-maiden-thought motif that keeps weaving in and out.

Reading it excited me. And as you well know, that kind of excitement is rarer and rarer. Part of my delight was that something of my original joy in your work as I first encountered it in the early sixties woke again. Maybe because conditions have been generally good this summer – more silence down in the house, writing channels of my own re-opened to child-sources, permission granted from somewhere below to relish the language all over again. At any rate, the good whole thing happened in the listening circle down near the centre. *Gaudeamus.*

[. . .]

Nothing has been more public or marked or remarked upon – in this country at any rate – than the Oxford business. A case of Irish dog wins English race, all right. But beyond expectation. The only thing that has really sunk in. Poetry be damned, the boy has got a big job in England. Odd, if understandable. And a bit of a distraction.

I'm going to call the inaugural 'The Redress of Poetry'. But I want to think of that redress more in metaphysical, poetic terms than politically. In fact, politics out for a year or two. I'd love to get a good grip on and good truth out of George Herbert. Dodge the expectation of being a propagandist for the marginalized. So straight in and annex the centre.

The thing will be on October 24, and I'll be in Oxford from 18th → 27th. Some time before (perhaps) or after (better) we should really try to meet and rough out a *School Bag* plan.

If I get my photo-copying machine into action, I'll also afflict you with the bits I've been doing in the last year. They are not quite 'a sequence', more a kind of waftage, bits sustained on the same lift of excitement, like the webs on the back of a wave. If you do get them, don't feel you have to say a thing. It's just that their oddity will have been lessened for me if I get them into the hands/eyes/ears of other people ready to permit them their oddity/bittiness.

Anyhow. If you have any suggestions for a late September or mid-November overnight summit – here, *chez-vous* or in a breakaway weekend place (four of us in a thatched, pewter-glittering inn, oh no), drop a card. Love to Carol, and big salutes to the book. Blessings.

Seamus

The 'heart-ploughing book' was Hughes's newly published *Wolfwatching*.

To Liam [Surname not provided] MS Emory

31 August [1989]

Dear Liam,

Thank you for the letter outlining the plans for your video and audio pack aimed at the US market. Seamus had indeed mentioned this to me, and it is the presence of so much relationship and friendship in the personal mix that confuses the issue for me somewhat. My unconfused response over the last fifteen years or so has been a simple no to all proposals of videos and tapes. The only time I wavered was about 8 years ago, for a Faber and Faber speech cassette. But Fabers were my own publisher for almost twenty years at that stage, and I was reading my own verse. Otherwise, as you can imagine, I would have high-tailed it from them also.

Several distinguished American firms have made similar proposals. I continue to decline because of an innate resistance bred of my experience of seeing, now twenty years after the event, images of myself <in an old UTV film, shifted to Time-Life films in US> rambling and yapping, for ever the same, on celluloid. The rip-off involved in the contract and subsequent marketing is one thing (and I appreciate greatly the contractual proposals you outline) but the clincher is the fact that there is no stopping the thing once it is released. No recall or revision.

The Yeats video I cannot undertake. The dimensions of the thing are too big and my shyness of uttering on film too ingrained. I declined to do Yeats things last year for this year's 50th anniversary, and my one collapse here involves a reading of his poems for a Field Day film to be shot in Thoor Ballylee. I feel up to that – just about – because it is reading alone, and because after years of declining similar projects with my friend David Hammond, we have hit upon one that is possible. So, in addition to all the above, I would not want to be doubling up on Yeats 'appearances' since I'm sure the Hammond job will be for US distribution too. Sorry about all this.

Sincerely, Seamus

Neither the source of the proposal to which this is SH's response nor the identity of 'Liam' has been traced.

To Bernard McCabe

MS J. McCabe

1 September 1989

Glanmore Cottage, Ashford,
Co. Wicklow

Cher Ami,

Here I am, fairly tipsy, in the *dún* of silence, at one a.m. Marie came down this evening to join me – I slipped away on Wednesday, exhausted by Flanagans and Vendlers and Marie's sister Helen-plus-familyette, etc. etc., all beloved but draining – anyhow, the *cara vidua* arrives, rotten with a cold and eager to bed herself by herself. So fine. Exit, at 10:50 p.m., the greybard, down to the pinthouse. Suddenly it's all like 14 years ago: I remember coming back here around midnight, excited and inebriate, convinced that I should commit myself to a throwaway (but writing) life, sitting in the sleeping house, elate, then waking hung-over and diminished . . . Anyhow, that inebriate, animated mood is upon me. And I simply fill this page in salute, in pleasure and celebration of our luck between all four of ourselves; doing a zany semaphore; blathering for pleasure . . .

I'll heap a certain amount of verse in with this. Maybe also the contents (proposed) of a new *Selected.*

Whatever arrives will be what I pack in with this, in sobriety, in Dublin, in a couple of days (and depending upon how much photocopying I get done).

Much love to Jane and you. May all your haunts be murmurous.

Love,
Seamus

'*dún* of silence': 'fort of silence', i.e. Glanmore Cottage; '*cara vidua*': 'dear widow', i.e. Marie Heaney.

To Peter Balakian

MS Balakian

14 September 1989

191 Strand Road, Dublin 4

Dear Peter,

Your Roethke book arrived from Louisiana, for which many thanks. Your introduction makes a wonderful case for him, and the historic moment, the forerunner aspect of *The Lost Son* was something I would never have paid attention to. I guess up until now I have been too ungrateful for the opulence, the listing, the catalogue of it all. He has genuine marine underlife to him, and he sways and gleams beautifully. Of course I love the first greenhouse poems, always did, always will. But you argue a wonderful case in relation to the deep image boys and the confessional boys and girls. Walk tall. (And what terrible things you suffered through Lockerbie: forgive me for not being in touch since all that distress.) Love to all. Seamus

'Your Roethke book': *Theodore Roethke's Far Fields: The Evolution of his Poetry* is the title of Balakian's study. Yeats was a large influence on the US poet Theodore Roethke (1908–63); and it may be that SH had his erotic, Yeatsian poem 'Light Listened', with its line 'She'd more sides than a seal', somewhere on his mind when alluding to the poet's 'genuine marine underlife'.

'terrible things': one of Balakian's students had been on the transatlantic flight Pan Am 103 on 21 December 1988 when a bomb caused it to crash near the Scottish town of Lockerbie, killing all on board.

To Karl Miller

MS Emory

4 October 1989 191 Strand Road, Dublin 4

Dear Karl,

Here's the proof. No doubt you caught the corrections already, but still . . .

Again, I am sorry to miss your party – my formal regrets to Jean McNicol – but as I said, I am bound as the newest fellow (even as a 'supernumerary non-stipendiary' one) at Magdalen to speak at their Restoration dinner. An ironical duty: the dinner commemorates the college's resistance to the imposition of a Papist president by James II, and the glorious relief brought by William . . . I shall have to speak a word for the Jacobites. Have a good time on the night. Seamus

Bernard O'Donoghue, who heard SH deliver his 'Restoration' speech, recalls only that he addressed the ticklish situation humorously.

To Helen Vendler

MS Harvard

15 November 1989 [Glanmore Cottage, Ashford, Co. Wicklow]

Dear Helen,

Excuse the stationery, but I'm in the armchair where I had you imprisoned on that Sunday – memorable for me because of the joy of having your response to 'Lightenings' but unforgettable to you for the mounting illness in you and the unremitting demands being made upon you. (And after that, to hurl you into Heaney-home-turmoils and Soviet circus-life!) Anyhow, I just mean to say that this jotter is to hand at a propitious moment and rather than forage upstairs for pure white bond, I babble on.

The Oxford stint has come and gone. On October 18 I went over, with the lectures written for once, and spent ten days in England, all of them busy. Much college dining, much sociable action *chez* John Kelly, Tom Paulin, Craig Raine. A reading. A family dinner sponsored by Matthew Evans of Faber at Les Quat' Saisons, a restaurant supposed to be the best in England. £50 *table d'hôte*: for Michael, Christopher, Catherine and parents. (Michael came up for the week, Chris came over for the inaugural, Catherine flitted between Oxford and her London cousins.) The high points of that visit were – the lectures themselves, the reading and my inauguration as supernumerary, non-stipendiary fellow of Magdalen. The latter occasion involved kneeling to the president, giving faith – *do fidem* – promising, I should say. Then being welcomed by the begowned, encircling ring of fellows, all of whom say 'I wish you joy' as they shake hands. Then, as you emerge from this little ceremony into the cloisters, the bell of the great tower is ringing – for you. It rings on for 45 minutes, during which time you are dining at high table, and the next time it rings for you, you will *not* hear it. It rings twice only . . . and I've heard all I'm going to by now.

Sombre thought, which recalls all the weary weight that you had upon you in this chair in August, and all the extreme sorrow you have gone through since. I feel like some preserved species, trundling along in the charabanc of domestic life, and spared the cruelties of chance. There was something unremitting and unfair about the way Meg's disease felled her and bound you, and then something bewildering and unmoored in the absence – release – of her. How you have come through I do not know. But I am sure that even after giving yourself so utterly, you dipped deeper, in both senses, sinking down and scooping up the ultimate resource. I felt a wild Hopkinsian distress in your note and also an inadequacy in face of your high engagement, before and after the loss. Maybe the mania of Harvard work has quelled the other turbulences somewhat. I hope at any rate that you have not surrendered the indomitable part of yourself and that Thanksgiving will find you if not in a mood to give thanks (thanks a lot) then in a position to rest for a weekend.

But, of course, you probably will be going as fast as ever, holiday or no holiday. The Oxford business has robbed me of weeks when I'd thought I might be down here. But it has also given something. I *do* respond to the megaphone aspect of the position, the *cathedra* and the succession of it. The inaugural – which I'll send you soon – was sort of low key in the end. High sense of occasion on the day, all the same: six hundred and fifty persons, a beadle with a Mace, the vice-Chancellor in cap and gown, me in gown, all that processing and galumphing in the Examination Schools. Biggest crowd since Graves/Auden. Etc. Etc. But the truth of what I had to say, about a notion of poetry and about the virtues of George Herbert – this was not of the newsmaking, demagogic sort. Sans protest. I felt that was the right pitch, especially after our conversations in the summer. Any political stir-up would have constituted 'obedience to the force of gravity' which, Simone Weil says, is 'the greatest sin'. But I have this feeling that people – whoever they are – wanted something 'sexier'. Of course they did.

Anyway. Then on the Tuesday after the inaugural I did one on Robert Frost, much more relaxed and springy, in that the tension of the beginning was over, and a freer personal address to the audience became possible. (By the way, how do you feel about 'Two Look at Two'? Seems to me to get away with it beautifully: the reward of my re-reading.)

We went for a couple of relaxing days then to the McCabes in Shropshire, and on the Sunday visited Herbert's birthplace in Wales. (Me going on about his Englishness!!) Montgomery is really a delightful village, which you may have visited already. But it is worth a diversion some day.

We got home on Monday 30 October. On the Thursday I went to Belfast – for three days in a radio studio – BBC are doing a dramatized reading of *Sweeney*; then I went to Oxford, saw students (office hours for the poet-eens and poet-ettes); attended John Carey's Eliot Lecture in Canterbury (driven down in Bentley hired by Valerie Eliot, accompanied by herself, John Bodley from Fabers and some American pal of V.'s called Bob. Gin and whiskey out of a picnic basket en route!); came back to London on Tuesday, did a famous BBC programme called *Desert Island Discs* – almost the equivalent of taking a knighthood. Then to Oxford for more student poets on the Wednesday. Then to Belfast Festival on the Thursday, reading and attendance at a Youth Theatre version of *Station Island* – enough.

What it all amounts to is a sense of busyness and institutionalization. But I thank God for this bunker (in Wicklow). Here I am with the grim settle-bed and the still dripping mistlands and familiar down-to-earthness of cold water and latch noise. I love it and get refreshed from it every time. Indeed one of the things that I am going to miss most when I get back to Harvard is the chance to come here for quick or slow injections of my quieter self.

[. . .]

'Excuse the stationery': written on sheets of lined and punch-holed paper.

To Craig Raine

MS Faber

26 November 1989 — 191 Strand Road, Dublin 4

Dear Craig,

Your letter arrived last Friday, when the house was full of American Thanksgivers . . . they stayed until yesterday and I am entering the dry land of this week like a gasping fish. (Something wrong there, but that's only to be expected.) Anyway, this is to say how much I appreciate both your praise and vigilance. Delighted that you can find exactly what I'd like to be present in the twelve-liners and that the airiness and supply (my reason for keeping going) are available in the written thing itself. All your wonderful detailed attentions are a joy to me, and in a few days I'll know better about whether or not to go ahead with the thing as it stands. What do you think, for example, about the translation section? Not the poems in themselves, but the structural feel of it?

It's not that I don't think the thing would not work as it stands. And it's not that I am exuberant with new work – I'm not. But I have this vague intimation of a book more generously loosened out, with a few more draperies of meditative, discursive things and a more spacious patch-work of the bits – pieces-of-twelve.

Meanwhile, again, your perfect pitch as a listener and your committed attention to the plus and minus life of phrase and echo is cherished.

The people who were here at the weekend were called Fanger and Donald (a Slavicist at Harvard) assures me that it is good to end a Polish letter as I shall end here,

With warm embracements.

Seamus

Raine had written to SH on 20 November after reading an early draft of the collection that was to be called *Seeing Things*. He spoke of having had to adjust to the new, relaxed style of the sequence 'Lightenings', before seeing how 'each poem grows out of the one before – like *matrioski*, those Russian dolls within a doll within a doll'.

To Tim O'Neill

MS O'Neill

3 December 1989 191 Strand Road, Dublin 4

Dear Tim,

Did I ever even acknowledge receipt of the lovely piece on the scribe O'Duigenan – so full of immediately interesting bits – and your own richly packed article (for *Archaeology Ireland*) on the early Christian book? There's something salubrious and restorative about reading about vellum and ink and book satchels, a kind of natural good is associated with the whole process, and the whole paraphernalia. It is very good to have you practising the art among us; but even better to have you as custodian of the memory of the great practitioners. *Beannacht!*

Seamus Heaney

Tim O'Neill has a particular interest in Irish manuscripts. He and SH first met in 1983 during Kilkenny Arts Week, when SH came to an exhibition of O'Neill's calligraphy.

David O'Duigenan (or Dáibhídh Ó Duibhgeannáin) was a seventeenth-century Irish scribe, whose manuscripts included unique copies of ancient texts including *Buile Shuibhne*.

To Francis Murphy MS NLI

16 December 1989 191 Strand Road, Dublin 4

Dear Francis,

Ever since Thursday week I have been uneasy about the scale of the enterprise at the Sperrin Heritage Centre, and I want to outline formally my feelings about the whole thing here. As you know, I have always had misgivings and hesitations, but the sight of all that personal matter leaving the house brought the thing to a head.

First, as it were, the conclusion: I cannot face the prospect of 12/16 sides of exhibition boards devoted to me being on display in Plumbridge. It is a 'commodification' of me, and a displacement, which is both exaggerated and premature. As I have already made clear, the Plumbridge/Strabane area is altogether outside my world. Beyond the mountains. In emotional and familiar terms, I am in fact more an Antrim man than a Sperrin man. Ballymena and Slemish were points of imaginative as well as physical geography to me. (The chance of my having the Glenelly valley poem signifies, in a way, that I felt strange there and saw it as a strange, other place.) So, to have myself in the Sperrin Heritage Centre is already a misrepresentation. And, if I am worth representing in a 'heritage' context, I am doing an injustice to my own South Derry area in allowing the business to proceed in the Strabane area. This kind of display, after all, cannot be done twice, so it should be in every way right from the start.

Leaving aside the location and the propriety of that, there is the whole other question, personal and cultural, about my being the one up for this kind of treatment. Of course, I am aware of the good impulses behind it; but already I have been made too much the mascot. The Irish dog who won the Oxford race, and all that. It is imperative for me not to connive in the overstatement of my own meaning, and the erection of this display, which ignores, for example, Flann O'Brien, Brian Friel, Benedict Kiely and – say – Charles Donnelly, all of whom belong properly in the area, the erection of this display is certainly an occasion of inflation (and self-squandering, in so far as those more private photographs and manuscripts would be subtly rendered personally meaningless).

I got involved with this project because I misunderstood the scale of it. I thought, one glass case with a couple of items, among an array of others – OK. I continued in the arrangements because of friendship with you and John, and because of a desire not to upset unnecessarily the work of the Arts Council with the Strabane District Council. That seems to me an excellent co-operation. But I now *necessarily* have to disrupt the plans.

I suggest that the whole thing be re-thought to include at least the people I've mentioned. That my part in the thing be confined to the old 'In Glenelly Valley' poem, plus other agreed items. That it truly therefore be a Sperrin Heritage Display. As the plans stand, I only end up part of the tourist industry, overexposed and subtly undermined, since I am out of place and invaded. I'll talk on the phone after Christmas. Sorry for all this. Affectionately, Seamus

The Arts Council of Northern Ireland, of which Francis Murphy was an officer, no longer has this letter, either verbatim or revised, in its files. The text here is taken from a photocopy shown by SH to Brian Friel, with a note in red ink: 'This is self-explanatory, perhaps a bit self-important; but as you see, it *might* concern you'; and with the marginal explanation that the rejected proposal had been for an 'exhibition based on life and works of S.H.'

To Desmond Kavanagh and family — GC Kavanagh

Before Christmas [1989]

All good wishes for a very happy Christmas; and a plenary indulgence to each member of the Kavanagh family who actually reads it.

Love,

Seamus, Marie and family

In the Catholic Church, a plenary indulgence frees the individual from temporal punishment for his or her sins. The Heaney Christmas card for 1989 carried SH's poem 'The Settle Bed' inside the fold, and Catherine Heaney's drawing of the eponymous item of furniture on the front.

To Michael Parker — MS Parker

28 December 1989

Michael,

I have just written the enclosed, which is highly illegible, but I did it in the drowse of a seat by a turf-fire, and in middling light, and I am not up to rewriting it. I guess you'll get the gist of it anyhow.

Feeling very exposed and overwritten, or rather written over, at the end of this year. So much publicity in Ireland. So many photographs of me, so often, in the newspapers. Shortlisted for GPA literary award, a member of committee for the Irish Times/Aer Lingus awards, Oxford Professor, Person of the Year, photos, photos, photos. The fucking Taoiseach even made a *faux-pas* and spoke as if I had won the Nobel Prize – on the day of the announcement. So I am very raw at the thought of a book that takes the first intimacies even of Co. Derry into the realm of public possessions. Every time I think of it I wince. If you have a copy of the early chapters, as you envisage them, handy, can you send them? I'll send them back pronto.

Much love to Aleksandra and the girls. Blessings.

Seamus

See immediately below for 'the enclosed'.

The Taoiseach was Charles Haughey (1925–2006); the actual winner of the 1989 Nobel Prize in Literature was the Spanish novelist Camilo José Cela (1916–2002).

To Michael Parker

MS Parker

28 December 1989

Glanmore Cottage, Ashford,
Co. Wicklow

Dear Michael,

In the summer I read your 'Exposure' chapter down here but did not act on it – I had the excuse of your holidaying then. Now I have read it again, prompted by your letter and card, for which much thanks.

It's all very supportive and inward with what I was after in the poems, and I appreciate the way you feel out things, and research the backgrounds. There is, of course, a swirl of differing reasons about the move to Wicklow; they appear in interviews, at different times and with different interviewers. There is no reason, duty or sense in baring one's soul to a journalist asking why. The tax stuff was a simple, truthful but completely inadequate reason: but it was not a wounding thing to say at the time. Hammond and various people all know that there was a submerged, disaffected element at work, but they would have been badly hurt if I had said what I said to Deane at the time. (I say all this not in order to have it incorporated, but to emphasize the various plyings of motive, then and in retrospect.)

Anyway. You are very sympathetic to the work and empathetic with me and I appreciate it.

A couple of things worth attending to: your 'perhaps' allows you to opine about those May '69 poems being a response to politics. All I can say is that I did not think so at the time – although, on second thoughts, many of the unpublished ones did have political content! Stet.

At footnote 15 (just to locate us in your text). Are the metaphors really 'from' marriage? I'd say 'consonant with' rather than 'from'.

Between footnotes 29/30. 'Celtic' is a bit too picturesque. I mean my old 'Ulster' antecedents, admittedly Catholic/Irish.

In discussion of 'Other Side', in paragraph between quotations ('I lay . . .' and 'For days . . .') – the neighbour in the poem is not dismissive about 'The Heaneys' land', the pollen does not drift over 'Heaney' and the young are not 'young Heaneys'. This equivalence is one I'd like to have you avoid, even though I entirely understand the reasons for it. Similarly, after note 88, *Marie* must go (the wife, the woman?) and 'the elder Mrs Heaney' must be 'the mother'. And after note 94, not '*his* wife and *his* readers' but, say, 'to a wife and to readers'. Incidentally, going back to 'Other Side' – at the end, the boy is not thinking about slipping away from prayers. He is at prayer. Still, or rather, the poet is imagining a different scenario: the praying child is now the grown poet, standing ghostly in the yard, listening with the neighbour. Should he slip *away from the neighbour* or etc.

Going back to 'Summer Home' – the discussion of 'Seamus' as the 'name', and the direct movement between Heaney, in and out of the poem ('his wife's tears', 'the naming of him', 'relationship between Marie and the water') – can we do something to depersonalize that, dis-establish the equation of Heaney (me) with 'the speaker in the poem'? And the speaker's wife.

After note 146: These Irish texts were (a lot of them) part of a suggested CSE curriculum.

In 'A New Life' it should be 'a fit' that comes on, not 'a fir'. (Nothing botanical!) (Between notes 203/204.) On next page, title is 'A New *Life*' (not *Song*).

And, of course, I *love* 'verecund'!

Sorry to be nit-picking in such a healthy and luxurious pile! The riches are there and I salute them.

S.

N.B. Rand McNally: a well known US brand name. Manufacturers of maps. Like Phillips Atlas people here.

Please forgive the scrawl. I have written this, slumped in an armchair, forgetting that it will have to be decoded!

SH had asked Parker, who had completed his MPhil, to send instalments of the book he was now working on, *Seamus Heaney: The Making of the Poet*, specifically so that he could correct errors and misidentifications and prevent it from taking too biographical a turn. Here, he responds to a draft of what would become Chapter 4 of the book.

To Tim O'Neill

MS O'Neill

29 December 1989 191 Strand Road, Dublin 4

Dear Tim –

On Saturday 20th January I head back to Harvard. Spalpeen of the seminars. *Ochone agus ochone.*

On 23rd I have to go to a 60th birthday in New York. Derek Walcott, poet and dramatist from the Caribbean, and a man who is just about to bring out a long poem called *Omeros*. Over the years, I have joked a lot with him in the Homeric vein, quoting mostly Joyce's Buck Mulligan: 'One thinks of Homer.' . . . So, suddenly, I thought that if I could have the enclosed passage done out by you, it would make a unique gift for him.

However, if this is going to strain you too much, please do not hesitate to decline. I, of all people, know how the demands come in upon the desk and rob you of the time you had saved.

On the other hand, if you can do it, I'll leave it to you to decide on format and treatment. I'll probably get it framed for him; and it should probably carry some legend. What that should contain, I'm not quite sure.

We'd need the information that it's from James Joyce's *Ulysses*; that you are the scribe, and that it is done for Derek Walcott on 23 January 1990. I don't think that I need to come into it. I'll bring it to him.

If you like, give me a call at 607569. One way or another. And again, I emphasize: don't hesitate to decline if it's too late for me to be asking. And also understand that this is a professional request: whatever the rate is, charge it.

Blessings.

Seamus

‘Spalpeen’: from the Irish *spailpín*, meaning a seasonal hired labourer; ‘*Ochone agus ochone*’: more strictly *ochón agus ochón*, translatable as ‘alas and alack’.

The passage that O’Neill copied was from the ‘Scylla and Charybdis’ section of *Ulysses*: ‘Halted before me . . . One thinks of Homer.’

1990

A Lannan Award, an honorary degree at Stirling University and the invitation to lecture in Japan were among the public recognitions that were more and more coming SH's way and keeping him internationally on the move. 'EI 117', the Aer Lingus flight out of Dublin, appears so often at the head of his letters that he might reasonably have considered having special notepaper printed.

On 1 October, *The Cure at Troy*, SH's one dramatic contribution to the Field Day repertoire, opened at the Guildhall, Derry, but a mention of 'agitations' and 'distractions' in his letter to fellow director Brian Friel, of 9 November, may hint at the differences that would bring the Field Day venture to crisis point.

To John McGahern

MS Galway

22 January 1990 191 Strand Road, Dublin 4

Dear John,

EI 117 moves out from Dublin in twenty minutes and I'm doing the last things that I should have done long ago. I have intended to write to you over the last couple of weeks – since reading the proof copy of the new book. Joanna sent it to me from Fabers. It is a work of heart-breaking purity and surety. Cello and honey, as Mandelstam said of bits of Dante. It wakened me and read me inside out. I am happy and proud for you. The *bail ó Dhia* was on the *obair*. Love to you both. I wish I was going to Aughaboniel this morning instead of Boston. But then, it could be worse. See you. Seamus

McGahern's new book was *Amongst Women* (1990); Joanna Mackle was Publicity Director at Faber.

For an explanation of 'cello and honey' and its relation to the Ugolino episode of Dante's *Inferno*, see SH's letter to Czesław Miłosz of 17 October 1987. SH's translation of the episode, 'Ugolino', is the final item in *Field Work*.

'The *bail ó Dhia* was on the *obair*': scrambling Irish and English, SH plays on the phrase *bail ó Dhia ar an obair* ('God bless the work').

To Bernard O'Donoghue

MS O'Donoghue

25 January 1990

English Department, Warren House,
Harvard University, Cambridge,
MA 02138

Dear Bernard,

The *Poetry Review*, with all your generous and supportive commentary, arrived just as I set out. It was a wonderful booster, and gave me good motives to get my thinking cap on for No. 3.

Meanwhile, I was in New York for D. Walcott's 60th birthday party and met the book designer at Farrar, Straus and Giroux who is doing the cover of the American *Selected*. She would like to do a kind of panelled job, full of little active or ordinary images, like the little seasonal marginal illustrations in Flemish calendars and books of hours. Boys playing marbles. Wood-chopping. Digging. *Etc.*

All of a sudden, I was sorry I hadn't my selection of Bodleian cards – I remember Heather and I shared our pleasure in various odd little images – cats and hares and kissers and diggers and all that. I wonder could I trouble you to send me a selection of those cards; and if you or Heather had any suggestions for sources or images that might either be reproducible or form the basis of a design, I'd be glad to know.

Sorry to bother you again, but you both sprang into my mind as the ones who would have a feel. (Is there a set of 'Flemish Calendar' cards in the BM? I remember seeing them years ago, before I wrote 'The Seed Cutters.') (She has in mind something like the grid here – I think.)

Anyway: if you could send a few of the cards, I'll be for ever grateful. And shall find ways of *redressing* the balance with ye when I get back over. Best! Seamus

O'Donoghue had written an account of SH's first two Oxford lectures for the British magazine *Poetry Review*.

The O'Donoghues might have had a 'feel' for what was wanted on the cover of the FSG *Selected Poems*, as both were medievalists, but in the event it bore an entirely different design (see letter to Bernard O'Donoghue of 10 February 1990).

'like the grid here': a rough sketch is in the margin.

To Joseph Brodsky

PC Beinecke

[Late January?] 1990 [Postmarked 'Boston']

Well met at the feast of Farrar and the wassails of Walcott. This is just to put in your mind again the name of the poet Mahon, to whom a chance to teach for a one to three year period in the New York area would be immensely beneficial. Blessings

Seamus

Writing on an Irish postcard showing a framed copy of 'The Liberator' Daniel O'Connell's (1775–1847) defiant address from Richmond Prison, SH may have had in mind Brodsky's own experience of prison in the USSR. Although the year on the Boston postmark is clear, the month is faint and the day indecipherable. It was presumably written after Derek Walcott's birthday, though, which was 23 January.

Derek Mahon's situation at this time was dire: alcoholically disabled and creatively barren. Perhaps SH knew that he was planning to move to the USA, initially to take up a residency at Yaddo, the writers' and artists' retreat in Saratoga Springs, New York. It is not known if Brodsky assisted in finding him any of the university appointments that followed, all of which turned out unhappily.

To Bernard O'Donoghue

MS O'Donoghue

10 February 1990 En route by train between Boston and NY

Dear Bernard,

The shaky nature of the calligraphy is truly due to the moving train (great symbol of the continent and all that) and not to the can of Budweiser that shimmers to my left . . . Many thanks for the 'care-package'. I had a notion of putting sowing, green-branching, mowing and threshing all together – leaving off the Zodiacal signs – but then the 'great ebullient' Vendler said to me, you've 'done' the past, why not think of an abstract painting? She meant that I should not connive in the comfort, nay the kitsch of pastoral imagery, and she is/was right. So, suggestible creature that I am, I am unlikely to be using the Heather and Bernard Bequest in the jacket design. I thank you for sending it, however, and hope that in the arms of the bricklayer we shall all be gathered in reparation, in gratitude and – well – in redress for your kind and prompt help.

Did I ever tell young Master Reegan that I would not be averse to a May Day Ruskin College reading? In the evening, of course.

Love to Heather and the young. And to all the Oxonian faithful. Seamus

'in the arms of the bricklayer': the Bricklayers Arms, a pub in Old Marston, near Oxford.

'Young Master Reegan': Stephen Regan, then English tutor at Ruskin College, Oxford, where SH did in fact give a May Day reading.

To Katrina Porteous

PC Porteous

4 March 1990 [Postmarked 'Flushing NY']

Dear Katrina,

Very sorry to have been so pressed these past 3 weeks. I'd have liked to have had more time to spend on the poems – but it was one thing after another, until this ultimate outing to Memphis, to read. Had not even the time here to visit Graceland! 'Dunston Staiths' made me think you have a northern 'Under Milk Wood' in you. No? A free-wheeling radio poem? 'Ragwort's' lovely. 'Sluggard'? 'Convulse'? in 'Coke Works'? Seamus

The card shows a photograph of the front gates of Graceland, Elvis Presley's home.

Porteous did indeed go on to write long poems for radio broadcast. Here, SH questions her use of the words 'sluggard' and 'convulse' in a poem that remains unpublished, 'Norwood Coke Works'.

To Ted Hughes

MS Emory

April Fool's Day 1990 EI 117, Between Dublin and Shannon

Dear Ted,

My excuse is that I'm doing a version of *Philoctetes* – S. Deane says I'm to call it *Pus in Boots*, but I favour *My Right Foot*, though it may end up as *The Cure at Troy*. Or *Marching Orders*. Which brings us to *The Kit Bag*. I hope to make a more considered, or at least more annotated response, before the end of April. I really am like a man on a ship when I'm at Harvard, all watch-duty and bunk-zonk. I have to apologize for not writing to you after those quickening letters of yours, and had intended to do so during the past week, when I was on a mid-term break. But honestly, it was all go, between family in Dublin and Derry, then mail that was not as important but that was 'waiting', then (new for me) talk about actors and directors and even visits to the theatre to see some of the former in action . . . Anyhow. The plan is that I'll have the version finished by June, and then, on with the anthologies.

I do like the idea of the *essential*, quickie, nutrient item. The twenty-second-century survival-kit. And I also agree that in *The School Bag*, there should be more, but the three-volume job might not turn out to be effective. Worth putting down, like the wine, but unlikely to be taken up in its entirety.

Also, I think that one more book is what we are allowed on that market – I'd prefer not to load, or rather overload, with three separate publications. *The Kit-bag* seems the way to go, and it would be at once a School-bag and a viaticum.

My one unease – and this is to blurt out something too quickly, perhaps – is *The Kit Bag* as a title. Nothing fundamentally out of the question, but a hovering reluctance about it. It has a shade too much cork-helmet certitude about it for me. The big sorrow-sac of Flanders is weighty at the centre of it but there's a prim, swagger-stick, knock-them-into-shape selvedge to it also. At my present altitude over the Bog of Allen, I wonder if we might not call it *The Black Box* – the container of the essential records – or *The Flight Path* – where we've been, how far, how high, how free, how pitched. But the main thing would be to assemble the contents and that *can* be done with expedition. I feel something of a cod, all the same, having urged it all forward and now putting it all back. My excuse remains this sudden play-version: in January I said to a Field Day meeting that they'd have it by June 1. Deep down, I knew that unless I did something reckless like that, I'd never break the caution. B. Friel quite rightly insists that it is almost my duty as a poet to fail in the attempt to write a play.

The turbulence of descent is under us or upon us. And I want to post this at Shannon. Marie and Catherine are on the flight, coming out for two weeks. I'll be over to do an Oxford lecture at the end of the month – 30th – but that will be all hurly-burly also. The true promise has to be for contents and ponderings in the early summer. Much love to Carol. I'm very glad that the Arvon dinner was such a high-octane affair. But it still would not have been up to sausages and hash and ye fish-cakes of St James's.

Now to join the earthlings. Blessings.

Seamus

The film adaptation of the memoir by Christy Brown (1932–81), *My Left Foot* (1954), typed out by the author, who had cerebral palsy, with the toes of one foot, was released in 1989.

The Kit Bag was one of a number of titles at different times toyed with for the anthology that Hughes and SH had been commissioned to edit after the success of *The Rattle Bag*. Not only the title, but the very purpose of the anthology, was undecided until *The School Bag* was finally settled on. For a glimpse of Hughes's side of the discussion, see *Letters of Ted Hughes* (2007).

To Brian Friel

MS NLI

17 April 1990

Adams House #F.21, Harvard University, Cambridge, MA 02138

Dear Brian,

It's half-seven in the morning and I'm up at the desk, so it must be America. But I wish it was Abbeyland and I could be at the *Dancing* next Tuesday. I've just finished reading the script – couldn't really get at it until my house cleared here and Marie and Catherine went back.

From the minute I started I felt myself at the centre of the right place. The kites and the radio, the sycamore branch – they were only outward and visible signs (very privately potent, nevertheless) of a cleared psychic/dramatic space where – if I may quote myself – 'the extravagant once passed under full sail / into the longed for'. The double-life of the thing is richly in sync: mythic underlife and realistic presentation move very happily and at the right distance. What is naturally, domestically, realistically flowing between the women is inescapable, credible and yet mysterious, and it is also symbolically rampant in the beyondness of Uganda and the back hills. I can see why you might have wanted 'Ceremony' in the title, but *dancing* is better, because it does not instruct or direct the response but simply reports on the action.

All this sounds too abstract. The riches of the moments are what make it alive and heart-breaking. I feel the whole web of sister-life very buoyantly, and, of course, the invisible boy and the magnificent Jack and the beautifully problematic (for the characters) Gerry are woven seamlessly into the web. The work, and workings, of the piece are masterly. If I were Denis Donoghue, I'd say *plenitude*. But the denial of plenitude is so helplessly a part of its invocation too . . . Cornucopia and empty shell.

I wish I could be there for the triumph. It feels like a masterpiece, from inside out. It's whole and it's big and it rises and sets. Salute yourself. Kill a goat. A rooster. Dance. And if you happen to get this on Shakespeare's birthday, consider you have met a one-horned cow. *Beannacht!*

Seamus

Friel's *Dancing at Lughnasa* opened at the Abbey Theatre, Dublin, on 24 April.

To Thomas Kilroy — MS Galway

2 June 1990 [In transit]

Dear Tom,

The defamiliarized conditions of travel at 1290 mph, with caviar and crayfish – not to mention the gilded and the occluded, young and old – have me in an airy mood after an anxious day. I'm en route for a doctoring at Wesleyan. I did a reading at the National Portrait Gallery at 3 p.m. (they've bought a portrait, there's a postcard even), I got on this grey, fleet bird at 7, and I'm to land at Kennedy at 6. Then by bus to New Haven. Then by car to Middletown. A party. Flanagan (Tom) and wife. Bishop Tutu (fellow graduand). Etc. . . . etc. . . . What's happened?

Anyway, *cher ami*: You are the person I think of and feel to be the right one to consult/inform just now. I met Stephen, Bob Crowley and Gary McK. at lunch. They are this minute meeting with Judy Friel, on a pre-arranged casting session. To think how we can combine cast of B.F.'s Macklin with S.H.'s Sophocles. *BUT*: it came out when we met that Stephen and Bob are definitely against doing the Macklin. Artistic grounds, length of Sophocles, general feeling that farce will subvert the heavy stuff, blah, blah . . . Well. Of course, all very well. Except that the double bill was set up, and B.F. has (I think) pulled the Macklin out from Blinkie. And he will feel hugely betrayed by S.R. again, and enraged against B.C. – whom he likes in person, I think, but distrusts in profession (well, he just don't rate designers, that's all I mean). I myself feel a bit paralysed, a bit compromised and a bit of sympathy for Stephen and Bob. I'll be away until next Friday – June 8. You may not get this before then, but if/when you do, you might try to suss out with Stephen or Gary what's going on. You are much more experienced in all these shiftings and feints of the pre-production process, and might have views, advice or orders to give.

Meanwhile, I am only up to line 850, and there's 1460 lines. But I'll be free to go at it *sans* interruption (nearly) when I get back. I'm relying on you for true response, severe truths, practical suggestions, instinctive prediction, emotional protection and a yea or nay to the title: *The Cure at Troy*.

Love to Julie and the dewdrop. From a half-cut jet-sitter, at 52,500 feet at 1310 mph, –53° outside. And whatever you're having yourselves.

Blessings,

Seamus

PS What do you think of substituting a volcanic eruption ('the Lemnian fire' of ye older texts) for the appearance of the god Hercules out of the machine? Soliloquy/Chorus to internalize/transmit change of heart (cure beginning on Lemnos). Looney notion. But maybe? *Hein*? S.

Bob Crowley (b.1952) is an Irish but internationally employed theatre director and designer; 'B.F.'s Macklin' is Brian Friel's *The London Vertigo*, adapted from a play by the Irish actor and dramatist Charles Macklin (1699–1797), which premiered at the Gate Theatre in 1992, neither as a Field Day production nor in combination with *The Cure at Troy*.

The Irish theatre producer Noel Pearson was known locally as 'Blinkie', in allusion to the famous West End producer Hugh 'Binkie' Beaumont (1908–73).

'out of the machine': i.e. the decisive or revelatory dramatic moment commonly termed *deus ex machina*; the script of *The Cure at Troy* includes, in its final pages, stage directions calling for '*mountain-rumble far off*' and '*eruption-effects*'.

'Julie and the dewdrop': Kilroy's wife and daughter, Hannah May.

To Tom Paulin

MS Emory

17 June 1990 — 191 Strand Road, Dublin 4

Dear Tom,

Back into the deep litter of the attic, and into the self-recriminations of the procrastinator also. I should have dropped a card to you the week I was at home in late May. I read *To the Empire Room* then with a happy sense that zesty, zappy work was under way. I admire the way it pelted through the record, the pace and despatch of it. The way the characters were Rolf Harrised in, in a flash; and the almost cartoon-flash edge of the whole story. Let it be done, I've said. And if I can, I'll read it again before we meet. I'm up to the oxters in Philoctetes' fluxes, of course. Love to you all.

Seamus

On Field Day notepaper, with home address in SH's hand.

Paulin's *All the Way to the Empire Room* was, in spite of SH's 'Let it be done', never given a Field Day production, but it was eventually broadcast on BBC Radio in 1994.

'before we meet': for a Field Day board meeting.

'Rolf Harrised': as one of his turns, the Australian TV entertainer Rolf Harris (b.1930) – later disgraced and imprisoned – painted portraits rapidly, while chattering, in front of the cameras.

To Alasdair and Elise Macrae

MS Macrae

2 July 1990 [In transit]

Dear Macraes,

The Broomielaw was a snip . . . It's seven o'clock and we're jammed among supporters. The airport was a stadium full of rejoicers. What it would have been like if they/we had won, I can't imagine. We couldn't get a taxi, and just as well . . . the meter would be up around £90 by now. We're on the bus, but we're not moving. Should be home by midnight. But we're not complaining. We've been filled above the brim with good spirits. Never had as restorative a time since the fiftieth birthday in Rome. The music of what happened was of the sweetest and most heartlifting kind – including the ululations of Raasay and the jocund whinnyings of Taynuilt. (Not to speak of the consoling drones and chanters of the internal combustion engine, by inver and strath and airport.) We cannot thank you enough and I won't go on. *Nevertheless*, as Norman said, you must know what an extension of the good life it was to meet the poets at your house, to hear you praise this one so generously and affectionately on the platform of the Albert Hall, to dine with you on your anniversary, and to be in the loveboat of Fernbank for four days . . . (Tricolours wave at the windows, thumps are given by exclamatory punks.)

Monday

I thought, all the same, that it was ridiculous to continue writing in the middle of such scenes. We did get home in two hours after all, and all I did was doze and watch the England/Cameroon match.

Anyhow. It was a great, great time, and the spaciousness and confirmation of it have entered the memory, and entered also the scale by which we measure joys past and to come.

We'll see you here, there or beyond in Vinland. Yiz are great.

Love,
Seamus

On Harvard notepaper, but, as SH writes below the university address: 'In the middle of a traffic jam, July 1, among half a million Irish supporters lining the road into Dublin . . .' – the Irish football team having reached the quarter-finals of the World Cup.

Alasdair and Elise Macrae had held a party to celebrate the award to SH of an honorary doctorate at Stirling University. The poets alluded to here – Sorley MacLean, who was born on Raasay, Iain Crichton Smith, who lived in the village of Taynuilt, Argyllshire, and Norman MacCaig – were at both the award ceremony and the party.

The Broomielaw is a road in Glasgow.

'the meter': SH has 'the metre'.

The following verses were included with this letter:

THE STIRLING STANZAS

At times in Dublin life is tame
So when a certain letter came
And said in June if I was game
And came to Stirling
They'd put new letters to my name –
My heart went birling.

For Stirling was a place I'd been:
I'd read my poems there and seen
The ancient castle and the green
And famous campus
That had transformed grey academe
Into a pampas.

But how could any place be grey
That had been lucky in its day
To rank a prince of poetry
Among its members:
MacCaig (or Norman, as we say,
Who lisp his numbers)?

And other friends and potentates –
Like that biographer of Yeats,
The Norman who abbreviates
          His name to Derry,
Who edits poems and annotates
          Things literary –

I mean, of course, A. Norman Jeffares,
Though there's a score of his successors,
Scholars, critics and professors
          I could praise too;
But just one more name – Alasdair's –
          Will have to do.

I'm being personal, of course,
But I could speak until I'm hoarse
Impersonally and perforce
          On your behalf
To name and flatter and endorse
          The entire staff.

Instead, I hasten to conclude,
To thank you for my gown and hood,
To say what pride and gratitude
          I feel to be
A graduate of this great and good
          Academy.

We 1990 graduates,
We bless our lucky stars and fates,
Our *alma mater*, parents, mates:
          We're on our knees
To offer thanks and celebrate
          Our new degrees.

To William Corbett

MS Corbett

9 August 1990

Glanmore Cottage, Ashford,
Co. Wicklow

Dear Bill,

Your letter saddened us a bit – not that it was a sad letter, but the pile-up of tests that you underwent this summer must be hard. The suddenness of your mother's death, and the far-awayness of it, and the ash-scattering – all that has the feel of something strange and homesicky. And I am sorry about the fierce actuality of the hand. Literary precedent in the Beckett extremity is little consolation there. Your own stamina and level verified spirit are under pressure again, I suppose, to bear the brunt. It's hard and unfair that it comes to you, without reason or reward. GRRRR, as they used to say in the *Beano*. Beat upon the earth with your cast. Practise sound effects for 'An Old Man's Winter Night' – one [of] the best ones, that, by the way. And I hope you got that thick blue putty, and that it warmed up in your palm . . .

Anyway. We're down in the cottage. I'm upstairs here in a room with a trunk-lid fit and shape to the ceiling. Dry as snuff. Looking out at ivy on the hawthorn, and ferns and still ash trees. Yellow ragwort. Stone walls. Barley. Tree hush on the skyline of the near hill. It's all very good for us. And unfortunately, we cannot enjoy it enough: back to Dublin to-morrow to see the orbiting Mark Strand, then into the summer school circuit next week – duty-dancing at Sligo and at Glenties in Donegal, birthplace of 'The Navvy Poet', socialist and spade-wielder Patrick MacGill. Who wrote 'The Navvy's Address to his Shovel'. Better than the theory dreck that some young Turks and Turkettes will be broadcasting at the Yeats event. But enough.

Michael toils valiantly 9–5, 5 days a week in the Fred Hanna book emporium on Nassau Street. Christopher got a 2.1 and is giving Spanish lessons on and off to private pupils. What next, I'm not sure. The Captain, as we call her, is aswim in the summer of herself and admirers. Out disco-ing – too much, I feel, but then how can I Victorian-father her to stay at home when I am away with the old lady here, in the Sabine twilights of Glanmore? When I go up to-morrow, I'll put a few new poemies in with this. My dead daddy is beaming himself up in gratifying ways again. (And you should have a copy of the *New Selected* soon.) Love to Bev and you from us. Seamus

The poet, editor, and founder and proprietor of Pressed Wafer, which published mainly poetry, William Corbett (1942–2018) was resident, with his wife Beverly, in South Boston; they were famously hospitable to visiting poets and others.

The affliction that Corbett suffered from in common with Samuel Beckett was Dupuytren's contracture, which painfully draws the sufferer's fingers towards the palm of the hand.

The *Beano* is a weekly comic magazine for children, published in Scotland.

Patrick MacGill (1889–1963) had worked as a navvy before turning to writing novels and journalism.

The 'new poemies' enclosed with this letter were 'Seeing Things', 'A Retrospect' and 'Wheels within Wheels', all addressing childhood and family memories.

'my dead daddy . . .': Corbett was later to publish *Furthering My Education* (1997), a prose account of his father's disappearance and his own attempt to discover the truth of what had happened. The different importance of fathers to the two men may have been a topic of conversation between Corbett and SH.

To Helen Vendler

MS Harvard

10 August 1990

Glanmore Cottage, Ashford,
Co. Wicklow

[. . .]

The Japan outing was quite wonderful. We stayed in Tokyo with the Irish ambassador for the first three and a half days. That de-jet-lagged us and worked us into familiarity with the unfamiliar. And it also culminated in a visit to the Imperial presence. We went on Monday 9th July, with Jim Sharkey, the ambassador, first to be at a concert – private – given by a young Irish harper for twenty minutes in the presence of the Emperor and Empress (herself a harpist), and then for a private visit with the Empress, which lasted for almost an hour and a half. Our other member in the party was Masako Saito, an ex-nun who was with the Sacred Heart order, and whose sister is a lady-in-waiting at the court. Masako also attended the workshop I conducted in California in 1984, and has been a member of a poetry-reading group which the princess/empress/poet/translator has occasionally attended. Anyhow – I begin to sound like a court gossip – the whole visit was very easy once the emperor moved off after the harp bit. Herself has excellent English, is alive – she did wonderful, spontaneous imitations of different bird-calls – is highly susceptible to poetry and in general is a pleasure to be with. It was, of course, strange. I kept saying – this is the Empress of Japan, even as I chirruped on about George Herbert (she was able to quote bits of 'The Pulley' from memory, and I was prevailed upon to read it for her from the text of *The Redress of Poetry*, which I'd brought, and also to read 'Love'; and I quoted the Sweeney trees, since her own special emblem/totem/love is the birch tree, and she has a birch grove at the window, in her own garden). It was a genuinely friendly, trustworthy, enlivening time. I felt there was a friend there, and a real sensibility.

Then to the conference at Kyoto, where first I was met by Akiko and introduced to her Dean and chairman, and colleagues, including young Constable and Peter Robinson. After that, I was with the

Anglo-Irish literature side a bit more, and attended all the feastings and some of the papers. Gave a lecture myself on the old theme of social responsibilities outstripped by/subsumed into the free artistic act (title: 'Keeping Time') and serviced the conference topic of 'Literature and Contemporary Society in Ireland' by glancing at poems by the young 'uns – well, not so young nowadays – Ciaran Carson, Nuala Ní Dhomhnaill and Paul Durcan.

But this is becoming a schedule in itself. The main thing to recall is the sheer richness of our lives during the two weeks there. The dense reality of gathered pastness in the gardens and shrines and tea-houses. The extreme, directed and animated hospitality, the sprightliness and humour shimmering around all that, the food and drink. Some quite wonderful moments: going on the river on the last evening in Kyoto to watch cormorant fishing; walking the streets – to visit the floats that would represent each district in the big festival procession – on the eve of Gion Matsuri; meeting a Noh master; going to a Kabuki play that we found for ourselves in Tokyo; and, of course, the raked gardens and the bamboo groves.

[. . .]

James A. Sharkey (b.1945) was Irish Ambassador to Japan; though not yet enthroned, Akihito (b.1933) had become Emperor the year before; SH and Marie Heaney had been befriended by his wife Michiko (b.1934) on their previous visit in 1987; Masako Saito (1931–2004) was a novelist. *The Poetry of George Herbert* (1975) is one of Vendler's earliest books.

Akiko Murakata (1941–2017) taught in the English Department of Kyoto University and was personally known to Vendler, who had been there herself as a Visiting Fellow; John Constable (b.1963), editor of the letters of I. A. Richards, and the British poet Peter Robinson (b.1953) were also teaching there.

The poet Nuala Ní Dhomhnaill (b.1952) writes exclusively in Irish; SH translated two of her poems, under the titles 'Miracle Grass' and '*Mo Mhíle Stor*', for her 1990 English-language volume *Pharaoh's Daughter*.

Gion Matsuri is Japan's great national festival, extending over the whole of July.

To Ted Hughes

MS Emory

12 August 1990

Glanmore Cottage, Ashford,
Co. Wicklow

Dear Ted,

This is unseemly paper for a birthday greeting: but it's to hand. Marie and I have had five days in the house of stillness, and feel the better for it. Must away to-morrow back to Dublin, however, where I hope to post this.

I've always wanted to dedicate a poem to you, because of a thousand reasons, but most especially because of the verifying and releasing power *Lupercal* et al. had for me in 1962. So when this floated up, and the birthday was in sight, I thought it might be a possible one.

I'm not sure that 'gathering' is the technically correct word, so that, and maybe another word or two, will have to be changed.

Meanwhile, blessings on you and the work, and love to Carol. *Sláinte!*

(Anthology business later.)

Seamus

The 'unseemly paper' was a plain A4 sheet with punched holes for filing. Hughes's sixtieth birthday fell on 17 August. The enclosed typescript of the poem dedicated to him, 'Casting and Gathering', ends with a handwritten message: 'For Ted, with love and gratitude for helping me to hear myself. Happy birthday. / Seamus / August 1990.'

To James Crowden

MS Crowden

26 August 1990 — 191 Strand Road, Dublin 4

Dear James Crowden,

You will have to forgive the speed and impressionish aspect of this letter in response to your MS. I'm overloaded with correspondence, but I did skim the verse and admired the sure true feel of what's there. I mean, the sense of a committed lived life behind the verse is very strong and appealing, and as a whole work, I think the thing would probably work well with photographs or drawings or some record of the year or the place that supplements and grounds the verse itself. It's not that the writing does not conjure and fix a world. It does. But it seems to put itself (most attractively) in the service of true record rather than lyric flight/transformation, and a publisher would be more likely to think of it (I suspect) as a 'country' book than as a poem-book. (If it *were* a Zen scroll, you'd have *all* kinds of brushwork going on, images, drawings, as well as characters.)

My favourite riffs, for what it's worth, were on the following pages. At these points, a vitality and refreshment and brisk, thorough quality appealed to me in the writing. Pp. 6/7, 10/11, 14, 17 ('out of the one'), 26, 28, 31 and 33/34 (the apple sequence).

I respect the thing you are doing. I feel great integrity in it, but I have to say that as a poem, it might benefit greatly from pruning. Yet 'poem', in the self-contained 'verbal icon' sense, is not quite the word, maybe. Call it by David Jones's word: 'a writing'?

(You're up against *Moortown* too, alas.)

Forgive the scrawl and flight of all this. Sincerely,

Seamus Heaney

James Crowden (b.1954), a former army officer living in Somerset as a jobbing farm labourer, had shown SH a draft of *Blood, Earth and Medicine*, his account of a year in farming. Crowden reports that SH's comments, particularly the reference to Zen scrolls, helped him to organise the book, which he published himself the following year.

'up against *Moortown*': *Moortown Diary* (1979), Ted Hughes's book of poems about farming.

To Michael Parker

MS Parker

10 September 1990 — 191 Strand Road, Dublin 4

Dear Michael,

Thank you for the letter and the bit of text. Acknowledging drag does equal – well, not equal, but gives access to – permission to fly, as you say. And I think 'SI' *is* about the legitimacy of lyric action, or at least a defensive push towards belief in the legitimacy. (Here I am agreeing with your formulations, rather than formulating 'statements', so let's not regard this card as quotable.)

I'd be grateful if you would modify the line about 'a fourteen line "speech" by F.H.' to read ' . . . "speech" by a hunger-striker who could easily be based on F.H.' There's enough problems without getting the Hughes family and the Sinn Feiners on my back. And I think I'd prefer the phrase 'financial security' to 'financial success'. The latter sounds as if I made a kind of kill and came into a fortune. *FD Anthol.?* Next year! Love to all. Seamus

'F.H.': the hunger striker Francis Hughes.

To Thomas Flanagan

MS Amherst

25 October 1990 Les Martins, *par* Gordes, Vaucluse

Dear Tom,

After hectic days and weeks I am in some silence and relatively unimposed upon. I was very sorry not to have seen more of you and Jean when you were in Dublin. The shock of the *global* stuff must have been severely unnerving, and I'd have liked to have been less anxiously fretted about my own various businesses. But what with Marie's father's death and the bloody play and the Oxford lectures, I was simply a bundle of selfish needs. Anyhow, I hope you've got into your stride – if that hearty figure is admissible in the context of more teaching – and that the body is conducting itself satisfactorily.

Marie and I will be here for another four days. We're in a bijou residence – a bijou barn, to be exact, spacious designer tile-and-beam-and-flag-and-fireplace stuff – across the yard from Bernard and Jane McCabe, who rented the whole complex. Deep down, I'd rather be in Wicklow, but we had the plans and the promises made, and after all, the wines and cheeses and *daubes* of beef and prospects of *châteaux-forts* are better than watching Gay Byrne . . . Beckett was here, at Roussillon, during the emergency. In the Resistance. *On dit*. It's all acceptance with me, I fear.

Our love and best wishes to you and Jean and all the family.

Seamus

Marie Heaney's father had died on 30 September.

To Tom Paulin

PC Emory

29 October 1990 [Postmarked 'Paris Sorbonne']

The Sweeney of the warm south! We've had much needed days of quietness among the olive trees and autumn vineyards. Had *Vernacular Verse* with me and got an enormous charge from it. Wonderful upfront energy all through it. New and lovely things – the Welsh boys in Gurney, the 'burnie' in Clough; and old and lovely things renewed – Burns, Jonson, blues, Lawrence *etc. etc.* Great. Love to you both.

Seamus

Paulin's *Faber Book of Vernacular Verse* was just out: among its contents are 'First Time In', Ivor Gurney's (1890–1937) poem about encountering Welsh troops in a trench, and passages from *The Bothie of Tober-na-Vuolich* by A. H. Clough (1819–61), which is set in Scotland.

SH's postcard shows the mural *Dénicheurs d'oiseaux* from the Chambre du Cerf at the Palais des Papes in Avignon.

To Brian Friel

MS NLI

9 November 1990

Glanmore Cottage, Ashford,
Co. Wicklow

Dear Brian,

Was able to get away down here yesterday afternoon, and after 24 hours of padding about, all I can do is contemplate the agitations up ahead. Well, not agitations maybe, but distractions, certainly.

It was very good of you to haul yourself to Dublin last Tuesday. It meant much to me to have you there, and to have your care in the foyer. It was a big proud moment, whatever about the quality and impact of the play. As I said to the family, if it had been the Moscow Arts Theatre, the sense of history would have been sharper all round. Just because it's the Abbey, and the theatre of Yeats, Synge, O'Casey, Gregory, Friel . . .

The Mary Robinson thing is a bit of a lift. I know she's earnest and gruff, but the woman presence and the sense of a historical eddy that might be a bend is full of potential. It will die down, of course; but wasn't it breath-taking to hear B. Lenihan assume the moral high-ground at the announcement of the result, and insinuate that the offence was with the other parties?

Who cares? Do you(s) want to come down to the party I'm having for the cast on Saturday night, after the last Dublin performance? Matthew is coming over with Caroline. I've asked McGahern and Madeline, by this post, but it's hard to know with them. Deane-o too. But mostly just the company. Think about it.

I'll be in Scotland from Wednesday morning until Friday afternoon. Sorry if that does not mesh with your rehearsal visit. Stay, sure, until Saturday?

Love to you both.
Seamus

Friel had come to Dublin for the premiere of *The Cure at Troy*.

Mary Robinson (b.1944) had just been elected President of Ireland; the Fianna Fáil politician Brian Lenihan (1930–95) had stood against her.

'Matthew' and 'Caroline' were Matthew Evans, of Faber, and his partner, the literary agent Caroline Michel (b.1959).

1991

Busy as he was, much of the correspondence of this year, and of the years that followed, shows how obliged SH felt to keep up with the productions of his fellow poets, both of his own generation and younger, and to send back appreciative or helpful comment on books and manuscripts sent to him unsolicited. The circle of those who received his attention, advice and encouragement, and sometimes benefitted without knowing it from his putting in a good word for them where it counted, extended internationally.

Public eminence brought not just additional duties but vulnerability to attack as well, and at the beginning of the year he was the target of a full-on attempt to demolish his reputation when the Irish cultural commentator Desmond Fennell (1929–2021) issued a pamphlet under the title *Whatever You Say, Say Nothing: Why Seamus Heaney Is No. 1*. In private and confiding to friends, he was rattled by it more than he need have been (see letter to Paul Durcan of 20 June 1991).

To Stanisław Barańczak

MS Barańczak

7 January 1991 191 Strand Road, Dublin 4

Dear Stanisław,

I think it was Bellow's Herzog who described himself as an industry that produced personal history, but whoever it was, it gives me a way of thinking about Barańczak as an industry that produces musework. Magnificent things you are doing. Thank you for the animal confessors and the dismayed cannibals. I'm proud to be in the former and immensely enlivened by the latter. What energy and hack-saw edge and intelligence. The variety is wonderful, but what makes it extraordinary is the intensity of each excellence. I've quoted already – in an introduction I've had to do for Robert Fitzgerald's *Odyssey*, for the new Everyman – those simple, stunning lines of Kamieńska's: 'I believe in a brightness / miraculously increased / to shine on all things.' *You* are an industry that produces that brightness in English for Polish poetry, and vice-versa. Kamieńska and Hartwig ('A Need'!) go straight in. And Krynicki. A great service to Polish poetry and English-speakers. It's one of the books that will stay within arm's reach of the bed: laying hand on it will be a form of hand brake setting, an entry into the place where the books will still be. *Gaudens gaudeo*.

To think you are also using your time and talents on this scribbler too! I look forward to seeing you when I get back there, in a couple of weeks. Of course, the permission is given, with éclat! That it's for love poems is a special pleasure. More power to your elbow, and love from Marie and myself to you and Anna.

Sincerely,
Seamus

'animal confessors': Barańczak's book of light verse, *Zwierzęca zajadłość: z zapisków zniechęconego zoologa* ('Animal Ferocity: From the Notes of a Discouraged Zoologist') is dated 1991, as is *Spoiling Cannibals' Fun: Polish Poetry of the Last Two Decades of Communist Rule*, edited by Barańczak and Clare Cavanagh. Anna Kamieńska (1920–86), Julia Hartwig (1921–2017) and Ryszard Krynicki (b.1943) are among the poets represented there.

'*Gaudens gaudeo*': SH puts in the present tense a phrase from the start of a Gregorian chant, '*Gaudens gaudebo in Domino*' – literally, 'Rejoicing, I will rejoice in the Lord.'

To Medbh McGuckian

MS Emory

15 January 1991 191 Strand Road, Dublin 4

Dear Medbh,

Your book, which I have read through twice, is rich and strange and utterly poetry. I'm writing on this makeshift notepaper so that you can read my too brief comments on you and others in the course of a lecture I gave at Oxford last April – subtitled 'Old Ireland and the Young Poets'. Totally inadequate space, but an earnest of my belief in the newness, rareness, realness and opulence of your work. It is so inventive, so fluid, so different, so resistant to the clomp-clomp of linear narrative, the one-two-three addy-uppy and draw-a-line kind of writing, that it is, of course, very hard to write about. But as I open the book again, I recognise and relish the inner logic and lateral vision of 'View without a Room'. The language has been pulled outside in, as it were. I feel this poem shows the lining of its poem-life, as it were. There's intimacy and rawly exposed structure to it, the way you see the seams at the oxters and the conjunctions of the stuffs in an inside-out jacket. There's a feeling of the whole book being fluid, coming from a source that is cloudy with mist all round it, but is pebbly-hard and watery-clear behind that gratifying aura. Immensely inventive in its changes, very sound-of-sensey in its movements and – admittedly – hard to work out. Nevertheless, immediately believable in. Completely original. True to you. True to the process that is yours. Your faith has made it whole. 'Many congratulations, abs'lute triumph!' as Charles Monteith used to say to me after a reading. Love to you and yours. You have done precious and valiant work. Seamus

McGuckian had sent SH her 1991 collection *Marconi's Cottage*. The 'makeshift notepaper' on which SH's letter is written consists of typescript pages from a lecture on younger Irish poets that was not included in *The Redress of Poetry* when he came to choose from his Oxford lectures. In this one, he speaks of McGuckian's 'finding access to a vestibule of consciousness where an entirely new "hosting of the sidhe" became possible. Not *sidhe* in the Yeatsian sense, not the Gaelic *sidhe* of the land of fairy, but the (s)he of the land of feminism, a manifestation of womanly impulse and resistance.' *Sidhe* – pronounced 'she' – means 'fairies'.

To Adrian Munnelly

TS

15 January 1991 — 191 Strand Road, Dublin 4

Dear Adrian,

Proposal of Michael Longley for membership of Aosdána

It seems to me a matter of regret that the poet Michael Longley has not yet been enrolled as a member of Aosdána. Longley has been a foremost practitioner of the art of poetry for a quarter of a century, and has established a distinguished place for himself, artistically and historically. Any anthology of modern poetry in the English language is likely to carry his work, and in particular he is, as you know, copiously represented in all the standard collections of Irish poetry.

He is a lyric poet of acknowledged mastery and his absence from our ranks is something that we must immediately redress. I therefore propose him as a member of Aosdána, in the knowledge that he will bring as much honour to that body as membership of it will confer upon him.

Yours sincerely,
Seamus Heaney

SH himself had been a member of Aosdána, Ireland's limited-membership association of writers and artists, since its foundation in 1981; whether or not because of this prompt, Michael Longley was elected later in the year.

To Roger Straus

MS NYPL

3 February 1991

English Department, Warren House,
Harvard University, Cambridge,
MA 02138

Dear Roger,

Forgive me for not being in touch to thank you for your warm and confirming words about the poems and the play. Perversely and unfailingly, I neglect to write the pleasurable and happy friend letters while going tense and hunched towards the duty-pile. At any rate, I am high as a kite at the prospect of *Seeing Things* coming out here, and feel the spirits coursing like a line through the rod's eye. (Glad the fisherman in you wakened to the spinning reel stuff . . .) And, of course, I'll be down in New York before that.

To have Jonathan as my new Farrar, Straus and Giroux editor is, as Lady Macbeth said of the man,* to have it all. It's a wonderful prospect and I am gratified to think that Jonathan was in favour of it too. He has written to me, so I'll be in touch with him immediately about *The Cure at Troy*. I hope I might be able to see him on the morning of February 22. I'm doing a lecture – one of the higher babble sort – at Fordham on the previous evening.

Maybe I'll catch a glimpse of you that day – 22nd, I mean. Just now I'm off to Boston UFA to attend to the bard of St Lucia. And to think it's only four weeks since the master of Morton Street and myself were reading Mandelstam in London! What a list, you cry! Us too. More power to you, and all who sail with you.

Sláinte.

Seamus

* her man, not Jonathan.

Roger W. Straus, Jr (1917–2008) was one of the founders of the firm over which he now presided.

By 'spinning reel stuff', SH presumably means the poem 'Casting and Gathering' in *Seeing Things*.

Jonathan Galassi (b.1949) edited the poetry list at Farrar, Straus and Giroux.

Derek Walcott had a home on the Caribbean island of St Lucia; Joseph Brodsky, a flat on Morton Street in the West Village, New York City.

To Fred Marchant

MS Marchant

26 May 1991 191 Strand Road, Dublin 4

Dear Fred,

Forgive the bad management of my time and the panic stations it caused in the last few days of my stay in Cambridge – I seemed to be always rushing and dodging . . . Now here I am on a flight between Toronto and Boston (and due to take off for Dublin later to-night) trying to put some final order on my life next spring. Obviously I would very much like to oblige and to be part of your program at Suffolk. But I have been very ravelled this year through these kinds of engagements and am doing my best to steel myself against even friends, and to keep a few weeks clear. It's not just the time and energy of the engagement itself, it's the tension before and the subtle wastage-by-exposure of one's meaning and specific literary gravity – or rather, literary specific gravity. But, having made moan like that, I'm going to suggest that we try to work out something on March 18 or 19th, 1992. If you can leave the actual detailed arrangement until next February, well and good. But I'll consider one of those afternoons committed.

Don't worry about the fee. I appreciate the high range of the $1500 figure, but you should probably spread your budget around. Half of that will do fine. I'm doing this, as you will appreciate, not for the dough but for the friendship's sake. For which sake I am also sorry not to have been able to go with you to Iruña. To say, among other things, how I admired the discreet opulence – linguistically and spiritually, as it were – of 'Directions Down'. Sincerely, Seamus

Fred Marchant (b.1946), whose friendship with SH began at Harvard, had returned to teach English at Suffolk University, in Boston, where he planned to establish a course in creative writing. SH knew of Marchant's intention and his acceptance of the engagement discussed here was calculated to help it come about.

Iruña was a Spanish restaurant in Boston, where SH particularly enjoyed the *angulas* – fried baby eels. 'Directions Down' is the introductory poem to what would become Marchant's first collection, *Tipping Point* (1993).

To Paul Durcan

MS Durcan

20 June 1991 Magdalen College, Oxford OX1

Dear Paul,

A letter like the one you sent me deserves more than a letter in return: some kind of jubilant dance, a day of kites and banners, dappled sea-borne clouds . . . To have your answering calls in response to those poems and lines, and to have them registered in the element of your true and far hearing is immensely reassuring to me. There was a certain amount of letting go and unclenching and flying back in the book, and to find those little flutters setting up answering flutters in a reader was great reinforcement.

I saw you at the Aosdána but didn't have the right words and the right place to tell you my pride and gratitude. And to thank you for the passion and immediacy of your response to the Fennell thing. I'm afraid that I kept my head down in Harvard for the duration, and had a sort of mini-withdrawal. I was greatly embarrassed by the terms of the assault, especially the jibes about adapting to market forces. Of course, there is indeed a case to be put for the poets who have felt themselves unfairly put out by my having been so much put in to the story. Of course, too, I know – nobody better – about the inflated reputation, and about the unfair share of critical attention my work has received. But I'm damned if I'm going to go cap in hand to tell this to D.F. I had a sort of a row with him at a do in TCD when I got back here three weeks ago. He circled and came up and said, 'I've been having some fun at your expense,' all bland smiles. Too easy an approach altogether. I lost my cool, told him he had no authority to patronize me and that his tone was that of a schoolboy debater's.

But enough. The care and love of poetry you set free around me are worth the badmouthing to the power of *n*. See you soon,

Seamus

'dappled sea-borne clouds': see Chapter 4 of Joyce's *Portrait of the Artist as a Young Man*.

D.F.: Desmond Fennell (see 1991 headnote).

To Monica and Tomas Tranströmer

TS Tranströmer

16 July 1991

Glanmore Cottage, Ashford,
Co. Wicklow

Dear Monica and Tomas,

Lines in rhyme
Must mitigate my fault and soften blame.

For months I've said, 'Tomorrow I shall write,'
And every morning put it off till night,

And every night again, *etcetera* . . .
But you don't want to know. Far better a

Culprit who dispenses with excuses,
Says *sorry*, and gets on with it: no ruses

Rhetorical, poetical or flirty
Can wipe a slate clean that has gotten dirty!

So after all, dear friends, what can I say?
It seemed that night had capsized into day

The day we heard about Tomas's stroke.
Fear reared and bolted. The reins of danger broke.

It was a scaresome, intimate sensation,
A kind of family (almost) visitation

I experienced at the time. I felt close –
Which makes the lateness of this letter worse;

Yet though I'm late, remorseful, truly sorry,
This still brings sympathy from me and Marie,

And brings news of a strange thing that befell us,
A thing unique and slightly marvellous

Which was like a grace bestowed. Last night we stood
Watching the sea from a high place in a wood

Not far from here (we're in the country now,
Down in our silence-den in County Wicklow).

At any rate, what happens? A young fox
Is suddenly beside us on the rocks!

His fine, long, white-and-ginger nose, his brush,
His slender, feral vigilance in the hush

Of trees and twilight, his just being there
Beside us, and not showing any fear

Of us or of the world felt heaven-sent.
It verified a word like *innocent*.

It made me trust the commonwealth of love
And half-persuaded me I'd be let off

For being too long silent. *Mes amis*,
Love overflows to you from her and me,

Abiding like the air above that wood
Where a fox appeared to mean the true and good,

And made its lovely, frail, symbolic stand
Against those bolts of fear that rule the land.
Seamus

The Swedish poet Tomas Tranströmer and his wife Monica had met SH at the Morelia International Poetry Festival that they had all attended in 1981. Later, after a visit to Ireland in 1985, Tomas wrote to his friend, the US poet Robert Bly (1926–2021): 'We met Seamus and Marie Heaney, our old friends from Mexico, and the talk continued effortlessly at the point it was interrupted then.'

In November 1990, Tranströmer had suffered a stroke that for the rest of his life deprived him of speech and the use of his right hand.

To Jane McCabe

MS J. McCabe

17 July 1991

Glanmore Cottage, Ashford,
Co. Wicklow

Dear Jane,

Forgive my tardy response. We've been down here, on and off, for the last two weeks, and it has done us a world of good. You had to join the letter queue, alas, because I am relatively well paid up in your area – my big anxiety was to get off a screed to the Wallace-Crabbes, which was owed to them since July 1988 – so there! And then, things like a late letter to Tomas Tranströmer, who has had a stroke; and various responses to people who sent their books. I'm *not* moaning, for I sort of enjoyed doing those things at a certain unhurried pace: I suppose I'm really boasting. So what else, you cry? An entry on Lowell for the *Oxford Companion to Twentieth Century Poetry*, a preface to a book on Ulster townlands and (now the pigeon-breast swells and the fantail fantails) a new car. A Nissan Bluebird, so there! I remembered a guy I knew and liked since the old days here – a motorman, risen in the world of car-packed forecourts to be a kind of Wicklow Nissan-shōgun. So there I was, familiar with the boss, being given the rundown on the stock. 'One owner, an auctioneer, serviced every 3,000 miles, worth the price, Seamus, o worth it. We'll not see you stuck. Does Marie drive too?' Anyway, the relaxation and long sleeps have soothed us greatly, and I'm only sorry I have to break cover to-morrow morning in order to head north to a poetry workshop (one-off 'appearance') that Jimmy Simmons is running.

Next June or July in Ludlow. It would be bold not to; in fact it seems to be the kind of tie-up that will ensure we chomp and lap soon after my return from Beanburg. So let's say yes, and work out dates by the speak-wires. Also, I greatly appreciate the great fee mentioned, but must say to you: big fee no needee. Him outloud scribble-stuff for coloured beads, OK? In other words, if there's strain (the slightest), scandal (the slightest), or surliness (hmm, maybe we up the ante there) SH ready to drop by three-quarters. All we need is Bluebird-seed and ticket for her ship-roost. Plus widowticket and bard*billet*.

I'm sober, I think, so don't know to what to attribute the wordbleeps above, if not to the sheer joy of being in communication with you both. We must murmur together soon. [. . .]

The McCabes now lived near Ludlow, in Shropshire, where Jane had invited SH to give a public reading.

'Wallace-Crabbes': Chris Wallace-Crabbe (b.1934) Australian poet teaching at the University of Melbourne, and his partner, the painter Kristin Headlam (b.1953).

'Beanburg': i.e. Boston, 'home of the bean and the cod', according to John Collins Bossidy (1860–1928) in his four-line squib, 'A Boston Toast'.

To Alasdair and Elise Macrae

MS Macrae

17 July 1991

Glanmore Cottage, Ashford,
Co. Wicklow

Dear Alasdair and Elise,

Aye boy! That Shelley fellow didn't idle many days! I did 'Julian' and re-did *The Triumph of Life*, and had a go at the 'Defence' for the first time since my Senior Certificate. I'm the better for it, of course, but I've got the wind up me from the coherence and condensed learning of your introduction, and the spot-on helpfulness of your commentary and notes at the back. Flags up and out. Hats off. Thumbs up . . . But I'm not sure that I can face doing an Oxford lecture on the bard just yet. I think I told you I had a notion of doing C. Marlowe, D. Thomas and A. N. Other in between. P.B.S. would be a possibility – I want a writer of verse who has something of the high drone, axle-hum verse of the other two – Hart Crane, say, though he's a bit too close to the Welsh boy. Anyway, I burble.

[. . .]

Macrae had just published his edition of Shelley's *Selected Poetry and Prose*, in which 'Julian and Maddalo', *The Triumph of Life* and 'A Defence of Poetry' are included. He had sent SH a copy, with the suggestion that Shelley might provide the subject for an Oxford lecture, but that never happened.

To Sorley MacLean

TS Macrae

3 September 1991

Dear Sorley, English may be wrong,
Not quite the setting for your song –
Like having just a single tong
        To build the fire
Or being served short drinks when long
        's what you require.

Yet this Burns stanza was the first
Art speech I heard. His lines conversed
In local accents and rehearsed
        A local rhythm.

The whole of Ulster was well versed
            In the lilt o' them.

His shrewd art pleased them in that land
Where life was fought for hand-to-hand
And elders had you understand
            Each inch was won;
The soul lay wee as riddled sand
            When they had done.

So that was that, Burns Rule OK.
For who'd begrudge him or gainsay
Such gumption, solidarity
            And hardy feeling?
And yet, the *ceol mór*'s majesty
            Sent all that reeling.

The sunsets of the psyche's west,
The sense that doomed ways might be best,
That heartbreak has the right to crest
            And amplify,
That what has been may be suppressed
            But will not die –

I heard you, Sorley, and expanded.
My ear and being were commanded.
It was as if the Prince had landed
            And won the day.
I did and did not understand it:
            Poetry!

Poetry by its pitch and tone,
Its crises suffered in the bone,
Its tragic magma and ozone,
            Survived translation.
The spirit's cover had been blown
            By inspiration.

Which is how poems help us live.
They stretch the meshes in the sieve
We put ourselves through and so give
            Potential speech.

In order to be transitive
    Poems need not preach.

Sorley, all I say is this:
Your work and you have grown priceless.
There Gaelic finds its fort, its *lios*,
    Its empowered will.
Hallaig survives the clearances.
    The wheel turns still.

The Cuillins' visionary blue,
Conscience, world and self askew,
Love hurt and justice overdue –
    Your transformed days
Will live for ever, big and true
    As the men of Braes.

Written for inclusion in *Somhairle: Dáin Is Deilbh*, a book of tributes to MacLean on his eightieth birthday. In a note added to the typescript copy sent to Alasdair and Elise Macrae, SH writes: 'It's not good enough, but I *had* to get something in for the Skye book, so it was a birthday card verse in the end.' For all that, the poem's argument shares themes developed at greater length in the Oxford lectures.

'*ceol mór*': the 'great music', i.e. a more stately and complex music than that of common airs and dances, and associated particularly with the Scottish Highlands – MacLean territory.

'*lios*': ring-fort.

The Cuillins and Braes are on the Isle of Skye, where MacLean lived.

To Michael Parker

MS Parker

27 September 1991 — 191 Strand Road, Dublin 4

Dear Michael,

Spot on. A very handsome harmonizing of your intelligence to the book. Merciful and perceptive. And truly into the underlife of the thing. I myself had forgotten how afflicted we all were by the torn skies of troubles. I wrote the Chekhov, by the way, when I was in* France in the summer of 1981 – same time as I wrote the review of Mandelstamiana – and it *was* during the hunger strikes, and I'm afraid my ignorance of a map-image of Sakhalin did help me to promote it to Northward. You're quite right about its equivalence to Long Kesh.

(But note (?) revision in *New Selected Poems*, where, as you know, I also drop the April 13 stuff from the Joyce section of *SI*.)
[. . .]

I am very gratified that you respond so freshly to the 'Sweeney Redivivus' stuff. I think it's the best bit of the book. I'm hurtling now.
[. . .]

* Also, that was when I visited the caves. Took a lot of notes at the time. Also visited Rocamadour, bird swept over me on the road there; had intended to put a sermon at centre of *SI* where priest would talk about his visit to Rocamadour. Funked it. Found Miłosz's *Bells in Winter* – end of Section II, 'Diary of a Naturalist' – it blew me away. I see my copy is the 1981 third printing, so the sermon was knocked to hell. But I felt closer still to C. Miłosz!

In response to the discussion of *Station Island* in Parker's book-in-progress.

To Colette Nelis and Gary McKeone MS NLI

27 September 1991 191 Strand Road, Dublin 4

Dear Colette/Gary,

Sorry for the hold up on my part re – the playscripts. I read them both a while ago, and did write a note to T. Eagleton in May. But, as director . . .
[. . .]

The mooted possibility of a reading of the Eagleton play is certainly something I'd want to support. The play itself may well be workable. I found it, for my own taste, a bit too set in its rhetorical and political ways. Subversive and paradoxical and wonderfully gifted speech by speech, but overall, a feeling of predictability – the correct subversion, the well-placed aggravation. But then, I suppose, that's the point of it, to flush out the old irked reactionary in one. I'd not be against doing it, by any means, but not very strongly for.
[. . .]

Colette Nelis was Field Day's Administrator, Gary McKeone its Company Manager.

Terry Eagleton (b.1943), literary theorist and critic, had had his play *Saint Oscar* produced by Field Day in 1989, and a pamphlet, titled *Nationalism: Irony and Commitment*, published by the same company in 1988. The play SH comments on here was not taken up.

To Bernard O'Donoghue

MS O'Donoghue

1 October 1991 [Venice]

Dear Bernard,

Last year we rewarded ourselves with a jaunt to France after the Oxford outing. This year the timing isn't so good, although the place is beautiful. Thanks to the blandishments of Bernard and Jane McC., we signed up for six days in Venice. I approached it all with a certain surliness – I really should be hard at it in Wicklow – but now that we're here, the great sweetness flows into the breast, and laps there like the canal under the window.

Anyhow, it was thoughtful and very helpful of you to write about* Bertie – 'it had to be Bertie', I see, in the *TLS* – and Louis. I remember Dan Davin's *Closing Times* with great affection, and hope we can put a spin on all that before the end of the stint. But for better or worse I think I'm going to have a shot at Marlowe and D. Thomas – and, *maybe*, 'Rime of Ancient Mariner'.

But while that's in balance, I've been reading *The Weakness* – and I thank you for sending it to Marie and me, with its much appreciated inscription. The fullness of the book, its complete trustworthiness, its path at the boundary between life-love and language-care really hold up and hold a strong, sweet line. To begin at the beginning, the tenderness and factiness of the first two poems get the mixture exactly right, and act like a tuning fork for the whole collection. The eroticism of that shock contact with what Montague would call 'the hen weemin'! And then to end at the end with 'Lastworda Betst', so intricately and un-insistently implicated with the shape and hurt of other poems like the title poem and the one for Josie – it's a real guarantee of the authenticity of the underlife of the writing, already so joyfully supplied for me with other guarantees on the surface, like those bigboys I told you about before who stole the stick or those heartbreakingly right 'lunar blue' oats on the grain loft. And you making your visits, on the opposite page.

[. . .]

Anyhow, be proud of it. We're proud of you. I keep reading bits out to Marie and she keeps saying, 'Aw – yes.' There y'are! Love to Heather and the 'chisellers'. Forgive us our disgraceful freedom here.
Seamus

to me to be a poem of great joy, judgement and panache, full of wise and quotable truths. First stanza on p. 20, for example; second last one on p. 21. The cheerful, daring, morally bold rhyme of 'awe' and 'claw' on p. 18! It seems to me that all through the 'Letter' you have the proper reckless drive, on the crest of intuition and the roll of a metre simultaneously; impatient with the sanctimoniousness that surrounds your subject. True, ready to be true, like a very good old friend. The short first Plath poem is more of a gloss – in spite of its intensities and felicities, or maybe because of them; and in the quick, end-stopped lines of the penultimate stanza, it seems more stylistically indebted.

But your original, big, open-weave musical and imaginative slides in 'Journal Entry' are all your own. The weather of the poem and its transitions. The spacey free life it lives in its stanzas and its historical/meditative reach. I greatly admire it; and the grave inward melodies of 'Elegy' – the 'finish' of this latter being particularly satisfying. 'The Other House' poem sings itself into wonderful freedom and insight: I feel the last five stanzas are really out on their own, in poetry-country: the first five are steps on the stair. My paper is done. And I am late for lunch. Forgive me. Love,

Seamus

* Two months later, they were in your book when I opened it in the hotel here.

Anne Stevenson's *Bitter Fame: A Life of Sylvia Plath* was published in 1989, and her own collection of poems, *The Other House*, which includes 'Letter to Sylvia Plath', a year later. The poem is, naturally, freer to voice the author's personal feelings than the more objective biography was able to.

'SPORTY, I mean': large capitals to correct a possible misreading.

To Seamus Deane

MS Emory

19 October 1991 [New York]

Dear Seamus,

Saturday afternoon in New York. Just lunched with B.F. and stole this notepaper. Am seated outside the New York Public Library drinking coffee before heading for Kennedy.

Historic sighting earlier today: first glimpse of the boxed-in anthology in B.F.'s hotel room. A square tabernacle, as awesome and potent.

I got an enormous shock of pleasure and pride. You have done a prodigious work and done Field Day and the country a service that could not have been anticipated. Forgive the orotundity, but I feel as if some immense transmission of power has taken place. A genius-transfusion. Call when you get back. Love,

Seamus

Later the same day, on the flight home, SH was to pen a more circumspect four-page 'Memo . . . to Brian Friel and Seamus Deane', expressing his 'apprehensions' about the launching, in different places, of the *Field Day Anthology* and what he perceived to be the 'absence of co-ordination, consultation and general preparation' for them.

To Rand Brandes — MS Emory

19 December 1991 — 191 Strand Road, Dublin 4

Dear Randy,

My apologies for not replying earlier to your letter, and thanking you for sending the review of *Seeing Things*. The review was full of fresh responses to the new book and I liked it well in that section. I was less happy with the Concorde scenario and all that lingo about literary stardom, stellar life, diplomatic hobnobbing (hobnobbing?), globe-trotting, and so on. Surely you, of all people, know from the inside that what appears as 'stardom' and 'globetrotting' is often simply the result of a decent sense of obligation to a person running a conference, arranging a lecture, whatever. Even honorary degrees come as pious duties to old friends or *alma maters*. I did not enjoy those warm-up paragraphs, but I did respect the care and good disposition of the whole thing. But that's enough, and there's no fall-out – in either sense.

There's no chance of my going to North Carolina on the Wednesday before the conference. (Marie will be with me, incidentally, at that time.) I'm teaching a lecture course and am involved on Wednesdays all through the semester. When I get to the States and get into harness, I'll give you an exact arrival time. Obviously, you'd want to know a month or more ahead, and that can be fixed, OK.

Please let me have a copy of the conference program as soon as you can, so that I can have a sense of what to expect. I know that the hospitality will be high and the company heartsome, but I'm so used to getting feminist uppercuts or Marxist fleshwounds nowadays at these events that I like to (Tiresias-wise) foresuffer all, and so be freer to enjoy myself when the time comes.

This term has been distressingly busy. No doubt *ILS* will cover our Field Day promotion last month. But there have been the Oxford lectures and a thousand recommendations (it seems) as well. I wish I had more time in Glanmore before heading for MA 02138.

Happy Christmas and blessings on you and yours.

Sincerely,

Seamus

Brandes had reviewed both *Seeing Things* and *Selected Poems 1966–1987* in the Fall 1991 issue of the *Irish Literary Supplement*; on reflection, he himself regards the language and tone of the piece as 'too cute'.

To Ted Hughes

PC Emory

20 December 1991

Dear Ted, In lieu of the letter I hope to write soon, to say *your* letter came like a sign from Zeus who views the wide world. I felt the power of it and the good, great force of it and the incontrovertible wisdom of it immediately. It was as if I put my back to the oak and my ear to the ground all at once. I had the administrative equivalent of the warp-spasm and went through the letter pile with the no's flashing and the heart – so to speak – rising. Still beset by the bits and pieces of pre-Christmas domesticity and society. But look forward to the dip before the new year. Love to you both from a man who has been houseled, appointed and annealed. Seamus

The postcard, from the Bodleian Library, shows 'The Whale' from the Ashmole Bestiary (*c.*1210), and was sent in response to a long, confiding letter from Hughes dated 28 November 1991. SH had told Hughes of his worries about heart fibrillations that he had been experiencing, and Hughes had written to advise him over several pages characteristically combining medical wisdom with more speculative or magical propositions.

1992

For all the fine, scholarly work that it had performed in rescuing many centuries of Irish writing from neglect, the three-volume *Field Day Anthology* was immediately and justly criticised, the 'ire of feminist Ireland', as SH calls it in his letter to John Wilson Foster of 8 January, being directed at its failure to give adequate representation to writing by women. One of the quickest to bring this to public attention was Nuala O'Faolain (1940–2008), journalist and television presenter, who in an article in the *Irish Times* wrote, 'While this book was demolishing the patriarchy of Britain on a grand front, its own, native, patriarchy was sitting there. Smug as ever.' SH was not alone among the editors and contributors to the anthology in feeling the sting of such reproaches and he adverts to this in a number of the letters below.

To John Wilson Foster — MS Emory

8 January 1992 [m.d. 1991] 191 Strand Road, Dublin 4

Dear Jackie,

As usual, the delay in writing has been disgraceful, in perverse proportion to the honour and pride I felt when I read your essays in *Colonial Consequences*. For the past week I have been hurtling through work that was due on 31 December – a long introduction for the new Everyman Library of *The Odyssey* in Robert Fitzgerald's translation (Robert was Boylston Professor before me at Harvard, and a person of Homeric courtesy). Anyway, one of the recurrent features of the work which is still potent is the idea that grey-eyed Athene can put a god's brightness round her chosen lad at any moment. And I've felt myself girdled with that kind of light since I read your wonderfully well-disposed and well-grasped essay on 'the redress' business. Not only that, but the whole thorough, focused, upfront, intellectually heartsome venture of redefinition through inquisition, self-inquisition and creative riffs deserves big saluting: I mean the total gift and effort of the book itself. 'Who are the Irish', for example, is a tonic, an example and a challenge, and should attain great currency. These days, with the (entirely justifiable) ire of feminist Ireland gathering round one's *Field Day* head, and with an enforced sense of one's 'old fashionedness' for being unable to go with the swish revisionist (entirely justifiable, or maybe *not entirely*) tide, for still remaining dully conscious of the petrified rings in the Ulster tree, and the plastic wood-filler in the southern one, I found it wakened me and buffed me into a sense of possible meaning to be reading you. Indeed, it all constituted an invitation to be 'more serious', as P. Larkin had it; or at least, to enter into the cultural critical world that you have made less cant-ridden, more generous, more helpful. It's odd – why should it be? because of the 'academic' or 'professional' or 'factional' nature of so much of the 'cultural debate'? – to open a book and feel enlivened and implicated rather than accused or dematerialized.

But of course, the stamina, accuracy, long-haul intelligence and beautifully cheering swiftness of the new essay on my work is the jewel-brain of the thing for me. When I got the book first I skimmed it, and should have written immediately. But of course I procrastinated, waiting for that more prepared moment when I would have a surer, deeper sense of what you had said – and had attained a more purposeful and clarified idea of what I wanted to say in response. The fact is, I have this deplorable shyness or self-deflecting habit when it comes to reading things that are in praise. I suppose it is a caution, but it ends up as a boorishness. At any rate, that you, with your complete intimacy with all that we 'grew out of', and with your veteran care for true accounting in/at the dangerous intersection, that you could give such assent and take such meanings from the *oeuvre* is one of the most courage-founding and love-inducing things that have happened. When I took the silence and time to read in earnest, I was moved in a way that I have not been heretofore by an 'assessment'. Of course, it was because of the high terms and bold commitments of the literary estimate; but it was also because of the witness of it all, and the positive trust, and the feeling I got of a representative act of grave import being deliberately, publicly and valiantly performed. You made me believe in what I've been inclining to declare, by your wonderful formulation of the 'constitutional' trope. And the kneeling priest metaphor, while it sets off the watch-it-for-self-regard alarms, also touches me profoundly. I suppose I've always tried, or if not tried, adhered to a notion that I ought to be honest, especially in relation to the kind of creature I am, and true to the usual dirt in the sump of the Ulster psyche. But I also hope I did so in a spirit of sharing the blame, of invitation to all hands to come away from defensive, pre-emptive strikes into something more reflective. Not, of course, that one should avoid putting in the boot when the occasion warrants (see the enclosed self-injunctions). (Those vials of hormone from the male side of the ledger are beginning to take, I hope.) But my hope was that a northern Protestant could read the work and not feel 'erased' or excluded, at least certainly not unfairly assailed. But your whole reading – both in the sense of giving an account of what's going on in a book like *Preoccupations* or *North*, and in the sense that you divine drifts and motions (as in the discussion of 'Frontier of Writing') – makes me want to shout 'hats off'. The margin – how self-congratulatory can one get – is full of wee ticks and side-linings. And not only between pp. 168–202. Great stuff there on post-war Ulster poetry, and a reminder that that 'Open Letter' probably needs some kind of follow-up, sooner or later. Clarification, more 'archipelago' acknowledged, admission that it was a 'jag' at Ultonians rather than at the Saxon oppressor, so to speak. But that's for another day. The main thing to say now is that *Colonial Consequences* is full of inner freedom, mind-virtue and invigorating gumption. Like the work of a man who's thrown off the coat and squared up, throwing a few punches in the air and giving off the message of being in good form, unhostile but up for it! Blessings on the work. *Gaudens gaudeo*. And I thank Lesley for the cheer and kindness of her Christmas note. I'm off to Harvard in a week's time – on January 18th. I've been very busy, so again, please forgive the discourtesy of this late dip of the flag.

Sincerely,

Seamus

Foster's *Colonial Consequences: Essays in Irish Literature and Culture* includes a chapter on SH that lays particular emphasis on the political, questioning nature of his writing.

To Gibbons Ruark

MS Ruark

16 January 1992 [m.d. 1991] Glanmore Cottage, Ashford, Co. Wicklow

Dear Gib,

Excuse the notepaper. I'm down in the silence-fort, with the briquettes burning down to the last flutter and dust, and I've been reading

Rescue the Perishing. It's very odd and even mysterious, how a book of poems will find its moment to enter. There it was, for the best part of a year, in and around my desk and shelves. Shocking to think that the peace and marksman's focus so necessary to receiving and endowing poems comes so rarely. Anyhow, I'm babbling and free associating because I'm still aswim in the gentleness and precision of the book, and am feeling an old pride in being part of the furniture here and there, in Glasnevin and around the Joyce tower. Of course, I have read the book long ago, and know the poems from away back – well, a goodly number of them anyway. But this evening was the Ruark moment. They were coming carefully upon their hour. I went through from beginning to end, dreamily but vigilantly too. I was so delighted that the Enniskillen diptych was up to it, and that the wild flower poems – the bloody cranesbill especially, but the Edward Thomas one as well – did more than hitch a beautiful ride with the flowers' names, and came through, moved, carried their imagining over and further. The outer and inner delicacies and distances so finely matched – especially in 'Dawn Address' and 'A Small Rain'; and the one place and the other so rarely woven in 'At the Graves in Memory' and 'Transatlantic Summer Elegy'. And then too I liked the contrary, downgrading impulses of 'St Stephen's Green'.

All in all, I just want to say that it has been one of those too rare moments when reading really did occur. I'm so much on the move, and so overloaded with tasks (not unique in this, I know) that I seem less and less to have the right conditions for receptivity. And you have been on my mind, especially since you took the time to write your heartening and encouraging words about *Seeing Things*.

My best to Kay and the girls. I'll be on my way to Harvard in a couple of days. I'll be teaching and busy. Strange to know ahead of time that there won't be any silence or location there with the purchase and pleasurable drag of this in the stone house in Wicklow. Why do we ever leave the engendering places anyway?

Blessings on the work.

Seamus

US poet and teacher at the University of Delaware, Gibbons Ruark (b.1941) initiated his friendship with SH when he wrote him a fan letter; an exchange of letters followed and eventually the two men met in Dublin. Ruark's 1991 collection *Rescue the Perishing* contains a poem dedicated to SH, 'With Thanks for a

Shard from Sandycove', as well as one titled 'Glasnevin', about a joint visit to the cemetery there, and another, 'The Enniskillen Bombing', about the notorious massacre in 1987.

To Thomas Flanagan

PC Amherst

16 January 1992

Portrait of a Michael Longley on reading his headnote in the Kiberd section of volume three . . . Ululation, as Sweeney has it *chez* Flann! Why did we ever start . . . I hear you did us proud in *Washington Post*, brave man. Meanwhile, the general editor is rather like Macbeth on the battlements, fully expecting woods to move at any minute. Faithlessly, I go to New England soon. But have just taken delivery of *Tar Beach* and thank you and Dick. See you soon.

Seamus

The photograph on the other side shows the isolated figure of a fierce, bearded hammer-thrower at the Highland Games, Edwardian period. In his introduction to the *Field Day Anthology*'s selection of Michael Longley's poems, the literary critic Declan Kiberd (b.1951) had remarked on the narrowness of their concerns, arguing that they had 'more in common with the semi-detached muse of Philip Larkin and post-war England than with Heaney or Montague'.

'*chez* Flann': i.e. in *At Swim-Two-Birds*, the novel by Flann O'Brien (1911–66), in which Sweeney appears incongruously and is portrayed as a figure of absurdity.

Tar Beach is Richard Elman's (1937–97) novel of 1991.

To Rand Brandes

MS Emory

15 March [1992]

English Department, Warren House,
Harvard University, Cambridge,
MA 02138

Dear Randy,

Please excuse the pencil. I'm on the plane and cannot face disentangling my jacket in the overhead bin from the jackets and effects of other jocks all around me. And besides, my rain stick would have them all wetting themselves . . .

Before the memory slip, as MacNeice says, I dwell upon the Hickory trip. You made it a first rate occasion at the College, but you and Beth added real grace and memorable meaning to the interlude by the quality of your welcome and the good life of your home. There was something vernal and good about our Sunday morning, just as there was something both merry and ceremonial about the Thursday of the triumphal entry into Taylorsville.

Love to you both, and to Blake. I shall listen to the rain in the stick for and with and by you – another 'river in the trees'. *Sí?*

Yours pencilly,

Seamus

SH was returning from the Irish Studies Southern Region Convention that Brandes had organised at Lenoir-Rhyne College, Hickory, North Carolina, where he taught. The rain stick, subject of the poem that stands on the first page of *The Spirit Level*, was a parting gift to SH, who had refused to accept an honorarium for his attendance at the conference; the 'triumphal entry' refers to the welcome into their home that Rand and his wife Beth, to whom 'The Rain Stick' is dedicated, had offered him.

To Czesław Miłosz

MS Beinecke

24 April 1992

Dear Czesław,

That was an epiphany at the podium – great reading, sure-footed, magnanimous, beguiling.

Any poem, but one that won't tax you. I'd thought of 'What was great . . .', simply because I'd loved it in translation . . . On the right hand side of the page, *s'il vous plaît*.

And I wish I had a copy of Yeats's poem, 'The Man and the Echo', for you. It, and 'Cuchulain Comforted', are wonderful late poems of *his*.

I hope we can meet in Ireland. My home address is: 191 Strand Road, Dublin 4. My home telephone, *unlisted*, is 2694221. If you – or you and Stanisław and Anna – would like to have a day or two or an hour or two in a car round the literary sites or the non-literary sights, please do get in touch. Marie and I are going to be in Ireland for the summer.

Gaudens gaudeo. It was a great honour to be allowed to introduce you, and a confirmation to talk.

Sincerely,

Seamus

In *Stepping Stones*, SH says, 'I couldn't say that I ever knew Miłosz well. I was always a bit in awe of him.' Even so, his affection for the man was plainly equal to the awe, almost filial.

'Any poem . . . *s'il vous plaît*': at home in Dublin, SH kept a sort of autograph book in which he asked visiting poets to write one of their poems; the first to do so had been Robert Graves. SH must have taken this book with him to Harvard in the expectation of adding to his collection there, for it includes Miłosz's handwritten poem of 1963, 'Rivers Grow Small', signed and dated 24 April.

To Paul Muldoon

MS Emory

28 May 1992

Adams House #I.12, Harvard University, Cambridge, MA 02138

Dear Paul,

Thomas Moore's birthday, I think – at least, on 28 May 1979, when we were here, we had a bicentennial party for him. But no matter . . . I appreciated your call a couple of weeks ago, and should have been in touch with you myself, especially after that sorrowful and unnerving evening with Walt when you received the news about Mary's death. It was shockingly disturbing, for you it must have been devastating, to be between the absolute cruelty of the news and the genial hosting of Walt. The easy path into slightly too much drink was not one that you could take, but it seems to have been the way I and a few of the company went. In the meantime, there is little chance that you have gained equanimity and freedom from the odd fierce blow of her end, but at least the immediate shock will have dispersed. I wrote to J.F. at the time; very strange to be talking to a father about the death by cancer of a daughter younger than oneself.

[. . .]

Seamus

Mary Farl Powers (1948–92), US artist living in Ireland, had been Muldoon's partner; she is the one addressed in his extraordinary elegy 'Incantata' (*The Annals of Chile,* 1994); the novelist J. F. Powers (1917–99), who treated mainly Catholic ecclesiastical themes, was her father.

'Walt' was the literary critic A. Walton Litz (1929–2014), a colleague of Muldoon's in the English Faculty at Princeton.

To Thomas Kilroy MS Galway

17 June 1992 [191 Strand Road, Dublin 4]

Dear Tom,

Clutching at straws, I suppose, using the stationery of a professor of poetry as I sit in the attic scratching out a few remarks to be made at the Caen symposium. I write during one of my frequent dull pauses in that activity to apologize for not having been in touch before now to acknowledge your letter of resignation from Field Day. You will understand it was not any resentment at your decision which caused my silence. Far, far from it. The thought of such a withdrawal must have occurred to all of us on several different occasions. It's just that I suffer first of all from a constitutional slowness to write to friends on personal and central and fragile matters, and that this sluggishness is intensified when I am at work in the States. Somehow, a pane of separation becomes operative the minute I give myself over to the Harvard function, partly because of busyness, partly because of the by now fairly coherent, slightly occluding and provisionally satisfactory nature of my life over there among other friends, preoccupations and pressures. So, before we meet in Normandy, I want to say how I sympathized with the crisis of decision which you had to undergo and how I admire the clarity and grace with which you came to your conclusions. Something unnerving has happened to Field Day in the last year, to some extent because of the Brian/Stephen wobble, and obviously, more immediately, because of the publication and reception of the anthology. Speechlessness seems to be the only negotiable means of proceeding from the latter, but it is a deplorable and inadequate means. Not that one did not foresuffer the consequences of no women directors and no women editors: but given that, *some* attendant boldness should have been prepared *corporately*. But then, the *corpus* was more mystical than operational at all stages of its history, and your bracing need for clarity and declarativeness – not to mention your justifiable sense of being excluded even when you had made the bold gesture of including yourself – carried you where you had to go. There's more enterprise in walking naked . . .

Anyhow, I look forward to seeing you in Genet-ville. It will no doubt be jumpy enough in my case, with the volatile and always potentially rancorous Montague on parade, and the prevailing open-season-for-the-phenomenon still running. Banville is not coming until the Saturday – confessed he could not face being challenged in the late-night drinking flytings! But who knows? People may behave.

How little things improve with the years. Nothing in the conduct of one's peers to lift the heart – apart from the occasional salubrious laugh from Drumaweir House. I'll be on the carpet there for being snapped with Durcan at the Fallon-fest. But at least it will be enjoyable.

Love to you all. I'm back to the discourse.

Seamus

The first page is written on Magdalen College headed paper.

SH and Kilroy were getting ready to attend a conference of Irish writers on the theme of creativity, in Caen, Normandy, organised by Professor Jacqueline Genet; John Montague, John McGahern and John Banville were among those also invited.

Yeats's poem 'The Coat' ends with the lines, 'Song, let them take it, / For there's more enterprise / In walking naked.'

Brian Friel lived at Drumaweir House.

To Paul Muldoon and Jean Hanff Korelitz — MS Emory

24 July 1992 — 191 Strand Road, Dublin 4

Dear Paul and Jean,

Great news. I'd heard about her arrival before I got the poem – thumbs updown, the judgement passed. I'm writing this just to keep in touch and enclosing an odd little amulet which I've had about me for years. I got it at the church in Shropshire where there's a monument to George Herbert's mother – it (the amulet) commemorates some cult to the BVM on the spot there. There was something so humble and brown about it I couldn't resist it. I hope it will be a token of love and welcome to Dorothy Aoife until I find something else for her. Jean, I hope these papist fetishes don't disturb you, and that you grow back to oneness and threeness and happiness together.

Much love and delight from Marie and me.

Seamus

The poem sent by Muldoon was 'Birth', which exuberantly celebrates the birth of his daughter Dorothy Aoife on 7 July.

'papist fetishes': Muldoon's wife, Jean Hanff Korelitz, is Jewish.

To Alasdair Macrae

MS Macrae

9 September 1992

English Department, Warren House,
Harvard University, Cambridge,
MA 02138

Alasdair,

Forgive the fancy notepaper. It's to keep the limit short . . . But no matter . . . In haste.

Peden's mask would be useful enough to a Field Day director nowadays, by the way. I thank you for it. And I am sorry to say that with characteristic patriarchal regressiveness, I have to be in Derry on October 13 to introduce Ted Hughes at a Field Day reading. The office arranged this, as part of FD's contribution to a Derry City civic festival, and I am naturally lassoed in. I'm very sorry – I *would* have done the Stirling swerve with pleasure. (Wrote to the organizers a long time ago regretting the February date not possible next year.)

Very much enjoyed your letter. Our ones all in good shape – Catherine in Paris for summer. The ould doll hard at the legends. Love to you both

Seamus

'fancy notepaper': i.e. Harvard stationery.

The Rev. Alexander Peden (1626–86) was a prominent Covenanter; the fearsome, bearded mask he wore as a disguise is now in the National Museum of Scotland.

'patriarchal regressiveness': see headnote to 1992.

The 'ould doll' Marie Heaney's first book, her telling of Irish legends, would be published in 1994 under the title *Over Nine Waves*.

To Brian and Anne Friel

MS NLI

16 September [1992]

Glanmore Cottage, Ashford,
Co. Wicklow

My Dears,

That was a great spin. Regenerative. I even wrote a few verses about the swans along the Flaggy Shore, but there may be too much Coole in the air – and not just because of Mount Vernon – for them ever to see the light of print. But I'll probably not be able to control myself in the end.

Thank you for the treats at dinnertime. A joy to be out for the day and taken care of like that, socks and all.

Much love,
Seamus

The 'few verses' must be 'Postscript', which inevitably saw 'the light of print'.

To Tom Paulin

MS Emory

22 September 1992

Glanmore Cottage, Ashford,
Co. Wicklow

Dear Tom,

This letter should have been written long ago, but on the evening of the last Field Day meeting I had to flail back to Dublin and go to the Netherlands the next day. And between one thing and another, the usual slippage took over. But I did read, swiftly, two weeks ago, on the morning of the meeting – in bed in the old Co. Derry haunts – your version of the Strindberg. I know it's not finished, but I have to say that I loved the jing-bang energy of the thing. As you know, that early scene with the stuff being hurled in on stage is irresistible; but the theme and the language and the cartoon force/pace of the thing are infectious all along. If it could be done *à la High Time*, at an intelligent lick, at a certain angle to text and audience which would grant the danger quotient in the subject and yet keep the faint alienation effect of the treatment (both the writing and the acting) you'd be in business. I regret that I don't have the text of it here. But it stays with me as a pace and an edge. Wonderful combination, in your work and in the play and characters, of putting the boot in politically and figure-skating freely in and round and through the political on the sheer fluency of artistic/linguistic invention. (Also, by the way, I take my hat off to Sunday's *Independent* poem: that one sticks. Mixture of boot and beauty. Hair-raising, in the good Housman sense.)

Anyhow. The Field Day is shaken and sorry. The acknowledgement at meeting level of the theatrical 'split' and the wobbly nature of our approach – if that's not too strong a word – to volume 4; not to mention Seamus's fall-back in the face of the hostile reception – it has all been dispiriting. I sense a kind of den-hugging, boundary-spraying mood growing in everyone. You, at least, went into the fray and bore the fight into the camp, which was a valiant act on behalf of the group and a spiritually verifying and renovating thing for yourself.

I look forward to having a word with you next month in Oxford. My first stint is brief – Oct. 20–Oct. 22. But I hope to get back for 10 days. Love to Giti and the boys.

Seamus

Paulin's *The People's King*, unpublished and unperformed, is a version of Strindberg's *Erik XIV*.

'volume 4': the addition of a fourth volume to the *Field Day Anthology*, that would make good the failings of the first three, was under discussion; in the event, two additional volumes were published in 2005.

Giti is Paulin's wife and mother to Michael and Niall.

To Ted Hughes

MS Hughes

24 September 1992

Glanmore Cottage, Ashford,
Co. Wicklow

Dear Ted,

It would be a great thing if you could get a couple of free hours during your Ireland visit to come down to see this place. That's by the by, but it's what struck me when I lifted the pen. All you commended to me a year ago about gathering towards the focal point of self and surety and fate comes through as a breathing truth when I'm down here on my own. I'm by now like one of those hens that 'laid away' – the nest is out under the nettles, not in the orange-box compartments in the henhouse. But I digress.

The mythic poet supplement is utterly convincing. I've been reading MacDiarmid and been distressed, really, by the disparity between effort and effectiveness in that life. And it seems suddenly clear that your chemical separation of realist and mythic endeavours/susceptibilities makes a diagnosis possible there: the early lyrics are the real mythic thing and then the Leninist materialist hijacks that 'reactionary' visionary. Hundreds and hundreds of pages of quite extraordinarily disabled writing by somebody with a proven gift for transformations. He almost gets into the true element – in fact he often does – as in the main body of 'A Raised Beach' and the opening of 'Island Funeral'

Seamus Heaney, reading from *North*, 1970s.

Charles Monteith and Rosemary Goad at Faber, 1975.

Michael Longley, SH and Derek Mahon, outside Marie Heaney's family home at Ardboe, 1970s.

John Hume, Seamus Deane, Brian Friel and SH, St Columb's College, Derry, 1987.
John Montague, SH and Liam O'Flynn, Gate Theatre, 1989.

SH, Helen Vendler and Czesław Miłosz, 1990s.
Derek Walcott, Ted Hughes and SH, Stratford, 1992.

Michael, Catherine, SH, Marie and Christopher, at the Nobel Prize ceremony, 1995.
Tom Sleigh, SH and Sven Birkerts.

(*above*) Barrie Cooke.

(*left*) Paul Muldoon, 1986.

(*below*) SH and Carol Hughes, at the memorial service for Ted Hughes, 1999.

Dennis O'Driscoll and SH, Lannan Foundation in Santa Fe, New Mexico, 2003.
SH and Karl Miller, National Library of Ireland, Dublin, 2010.

(flattish but floating, all the same) and 'In a Cornish Garden' – but the looney embrace of the Tolstoyan do-goodery combined with the McGonagallish tendency in the natural run of his speech proves fatal. But I digress again – it's just that I've finished a lecture on him for Oxford where I don't say this as clearly as you do, without even mentioning MacDiarmid. I love the deep clarity and sure purchase of your argument and your metaphors, and was greatly moved as well as brought cheering to my critical feet by your account of the Sylvia poems. It's shocking that you had to be as explicit as that about the rules of the game; obtuseness and hostility and galvanized vindictiveness combined helplessly at first and then proceeded wilfully against you. I've had a faint taste of it this year myself through association with *The Field Day Anthology*. It's Deane's baby, of course, but cabinet responsibility dictates solidarity, and the book sins indefensibly in many areas: no women editors, no 'feminist discourse' section (all true, all hubristically foreknown by S.D., but he has collapsed under the vehemence of the reception); too much 'non-revisionist' historical perspective. Vah! But I am more alive than before to the immense rage which man-speak, or even men speaking, now produces. The historical tide is running against almost every anchor I can throw towards what I took to be the holding places.

[. . .]

I enclose something I like of things I've done during the summer. I'll probably take the dedication to the brother off it. Love to Carol. I greatly look forward to seeing you, even tho' the Hancox thing will be wonky. Michael Foot! We could do a salmon-leap, or let fly a *gáe-bolga*. More power to you.

Seamus

'mythic poet supplement': presumably 'Appendix II', at the end of Hughes's monumental study, *Shakespeare and the Goddess of Complete Being* (1992).

The enclosure – 'something I like' – was a typescript of the poem 'Keeping Going', dedicated to SH's brother Hugh.

The 'Hancox thing' was *Poems for Alan Hancox*, an anthology honouring the director of the Cheltenham Literature Festival, which included not just poems by SH and Hughes but one by the Labour Party politician Michael Foot (1913–2010).

'*gáe-bolga*': Gáe Bolga was the name of Cúchulainn's spear.

To Derek Mahon

MS Emory

9 October 1992 — 191 Strand Road, Dublin 4

Dear Derek,

Great news about the *Irish Times*/Aer Lingus bounty. Would have been a disgrace it if had gone any other way but, as they say at Harvard, shit happens. Not that Medbh or Paula are . . . Christ, now that Larkin's letters are out and Longley's are in archives, I'm beginning to panic about putting down a line! (I did a postcard to a Cork poet last year and now he asks can he use it as a blurb. Jaysus.)

I haven't been in touch, partly because I felt that if you'd been in the mood for visitors, you'd have rung, partly because I've been, as usual, boke-anxious about getting my Oggsford lectures done. All go . . . But have done out sixty pages of the joined-up writing on MacDiarmid and Clare, so some respite in that quarter.

Big Ted Hughes en route for the town – and then to read in Derry. I'm going up to introduce him – then on to Dunn-sville, in St Andrews. Then back for a couple of days and on to Oggs. and – Spain. Hollyer there for a week, with widda.

The bad news is that I shall be burbling about you on the RTÉ book programme, with Nuala O'F. next Thursday. They wanted to have it *before* the result, and I did it a while ago, but then, of course, they put the Yank proseman on first. However, I hope you'll put up with it – I cannot recollect what I actually said, but Nuala asked for starters what would have happened if you'd gone to Queen's. Lovely, fuckin' lovely.

I hope the heart keeps up and that the spirits are good. Call us when you're in the mood. Wish the *IT* bounty was up to the Walcott handout! Love,

Seamus

The *Irish Times*–Aer Lingus Award went to Mahon for his 1991 *Selected Poems*; books by Medbh McGuckian and Paula Meehan (b.1955) had been on the shortlist. Mahon himself was at a low point, being looked after in St Patrick's Hospital, Dublin, when the award was announced.

'Dunn-sville': i.e. St Andrews, where the Scottish poet Douglas Dunn (b.1942) was Professor of English at the University.

Derek Walcott had been awarded the 1992 Nobel Prize in Literature.

To Rand Brandes

TS Emory

13 October 1992 — 191 Strand Road, Dublin 4

Dear Rand,

A brief response to your questions about poetry and violence.

Denis Donoghue remarked on the number of violent images in *Death of a Naturalist*. He reviewed it for, I think, *Encounter*. That would have been in 1966 probably after July or August. At any rate, that would be a bit of a scholarly reference for you.

As I recollect, he said this book was simply the outpourings of a country boy who had seen too many war movies. So there you are.

Seriously though, I did not watch TV, simply because there was no TV in those days. And when I began to have a television set of my own, I think I was beyond influence in any subliminal way. At any rate, I don't think that the media images of violence have affected me in more mature years.

As to the earlier imprinting, there may be something in it. Six-shooters, cowboys and injuns, the radio programme *Riders of the Range*, Audie Murphy and all that – it probably did have an effect. For the record, I have found TV and films neither distracting nor (I hope) detrimental to my work or imagination in general. But then, who is to say what's what to the imagination?

This is all pretty hasty, I regret to say. I'm en route for St Andrews, and then to Oxford, and then to Spain. You'll not be hearing from me for a while. Hang in there.

Yours sincerely,
Seamus Heaney

Working on conference papers on SH's poetry, Brandes had asked about extra-literary influences on his imagination and their bearing on some of the violent imagery in his first few books. The copy of the letter, presumably dictated, from which the text above is taken is unsigned.

To Alasdair and Elise Macrae

PC Macrae

October 1992 [Spain]

Irish poets, learn your trade? The old lady and myself have been on the road via Barcelona and Madrid – the former a first visit. Great. Nearest thing to Casa Fernbank down on the Mediterranean. Yiz should go some weekend. Seamus

The Yeats quotation adverts to the image on the face of the card: painting by Francisco Goya (in the Prado, Madrid) of two men sunk up to their knees, in a barren landscape, fighting with cudgels.

To Thomas Flanagan

MS Amherst

13 November 1992

English Department, Warren House,
Harvard University, Cambridge,
MA 02138

Dear Tom,

Adams House has replaced its ancient mailboxes with new ones, and I am so inept at operating the combination lock that I prefer to use the English Department address. What's more, the new box is at floor level, so the embarrassment of failure in the area of manipulation is equalled only by the Falstaffian scrambles and flushes and maladjustments of the body as it attempts to get down that low.

I've been in harness now for a couple of weeks, and in residence for three. Have got over the first few days of withdrawal and self-bewilderment – the why-am-I-here-and-not-back-in-the-Lawrentian-blood-intimacy-of-hand-to-hand-home-life kind of thing; am back to being a happy functionary. Cheerful with colleagues, almost. Glad to see the ironic points of light (Pinsky, say) and the warm glows (Shaun O'Connell) and the hot stoves (Helen V.?). Anyway, as Beckett might say, accuse even, I'm going on.

This year I've very deliberately cut back on the readings, lectures, travels, social services . . . Kevin Cahill sent me to see Eoin O'Brien at the time when my fibrillation was becoming part of the agenda (I went for shock treatment after the November Field Day trip but it didn't jump me back to the regular beat, so now I'm meekly at the aspirins) and Eoin suggested that I take the opportunity to change the rhythm as far as possible in my own favour. This doesn't mean that I'm absolutely homebound, but it does mean that when I go next week to Gainesville, FL, on a long-arranged reading, I'm going to spend the weekend after it at Charleston, SC (Marie arrives on Sunday, so it's a class of a mini-holiday.)

Daithí Ó Ceallaigh tells me you have been most kind to D. Mahon. I have not seen him since the summertime. What I'd prefer to do would be to meet him rather than begin the phone-call life. It's all very heartsome when he's in shape, but as you know, the inchoate and sorrowful creature-in-cups is as harrowing as it's heartbreaking. I do sense, all the same, that matters have been most serious there and hope that some contact will be resumed in the course of the semester.

We're bound to be towards NY before May. Certainly, I'm to be at Wesleyan on April 11, so perhaps the night before that an expedition might take me islandwards, Manhattan or Long . . . The main thing is that I just wanted to greet you both and to say that we'll call before long. Love,

Seamus

The poet Robert Pinsky (b.1940) was a Cambridge neighbour of SH's; Shaun O'Connell taught Irish and American Literature at the Harvard Extension School.

Eoin O'Brien (b.1939) is an eminent Irish cardiologist who has also written on literary topics.

Daithí Ó Ceallaigh (b.1945) was an Irish diplomat.

To Helen Vendler — MS Harvard

11 December 1992 [Dublin]

Dear Helen,

All these addresses . . . The stationery available to me is a cautionary tale in itself . . . And so is the fact that I use this in Dublin. Where am I? Well, more at home than usual, in that I did my third Oxford lecture last week (on E. Bishop – OK, readings, close, and generalizations, unexceptional, one or two moments worth it) and have no deadlines ahead of me for a good long time. Much socio-literary activity, all the same – lunch with Mahon coming up; reception for GPA Literary Award this evening (Updike overall judge,

McGahern probable winner, me – thanks be to Jaysus – not on the shortlist, Mahon instead); Field Day is more or less collapsed, with debts and meetings (not a heartbreak, this, but a problem); deferred schools visits <to read poems!>; then, before Christmas, the tithe-gathering and bounty-spreading trip to Co. Derry. Ever since we went to Wicklow twenty years ago, I've gone up to collect a turkey. First my mother reared them, now Hugh: about a dozen, for friends and relations. The brothers assemble to pluck them, then they <(the turkeys, that is)> hang in the engine house – the place where our yard pump used to be housed. This year I am very delighted that Michael and Christopher expressed a desire to go on the jaunt also: they always did as children, and now are beginning to indulge me as I head towards second c.h., I suppose. Michael has moved into a house in Inchicore with three friends and has a perilously established but creatively satisfying job these last couple of months with the *Dublin Event Guide*, a handout newspaper subsisting on ads, where he does a centrefold of notes on gigs and bands and releases of new pop/rock music. He does it very well. Works at it and at last gets something out of what he's working at. I'm glad to see his face clearer and know that he's generally in better nick. Chris continues with the English teaching and is now drumming with a band called the Revenants. OK name, anyhow.

[. . .]

At least I *see* them. I know what you mean about David and Xianchin: phones all very well, but the savour of the den life is reassuring. I hope your journey to the western reaches was not a strain and that the whole merciless pile-up of recommendations at this time of year does not entirely overpower you. I can't imagine the volume of that kind of thing that must break over you. My own desk gets loaded, and my feelings all twisted: filling in those ratings. Above Average, Average, First 5%, First 33% . . . If you could be sure that honest brokers were at work all along the line . . . But slack-mouthed, dud-promoting gnomes are surely at work all over, so do you join the inflation game? I suppose the answer is one of those back-of-the-bus reluctant long-drawn-out *yeses*. But not quite. I hate it when one can't say totally positive things, but I enjoy it also when I can characterize my reservations. I suppose thinking about it worse than doing it.

Heigho! Ledwidge enclosed. A pious duty. He's nearly no good, but he moves me – at least, the idea of him. And a few of the things get there. (I shudder to think of you coming on a certain misquotation, but I still want you to have the book.)

Suddenly I couldn't bear the thought of coming back in the Fall. Phil was wonderful. More on that later – I just want to take a breather after Oxford and all clears up next year.

I am so proud of my figure of the universe. Thank you for everything, all your acute kindnesses to all of us. Catherine and I (another Christmas 'tradition') will buy the tree to-morrow. We'll be thinking of you as we deck it – and not only then. Love, Seamus

Congratulations on the Trinity Degree. Absolutely right. Many people here will be proud for you and TCD. I arrive Jan. 24, probably. Enjoy France.

'All these addresses . . .': the letter is on Magdalen College headed paper.

'E. Bishop': Elizabeth Bishop, on whose work Vendler is an authority, and to whose poem, 'The Moose', 'one of those back-of-the-bus reluctant long-drawn-out *yeses*' alludes.

'pile-up of recommendations': on behalf of graduating students.

'Ledwidge enclosed': SH's introduction to *Francis Ledwidge: Selected Poems* (1992), edited by Dermot Bolger.

Vendler was due to receive an honorary DLitt from Trinity College Dublin in July 1993.

1993

SH's publication of greatest significance this year, and his first piece of work done since the fall-out from the *Field Day Anthology*, was the Gallery Press volume *The Midnight Verdict*. Coming at his implicit subject by way of translation, he added two passages about Orpheus from Ovid's *Metamorphoses* – the second describing his death at the hands of 'a band of crazed Ciconian women' – to an episode from Brian Merriman's dream-vision of being charged in a punitive female court. Furthermore, one of the last lectures he gave as his Oxford Poetry Professorship came to an end, delivered on 21 October, was 'Orpheus in Ireland: On Brian Merriman's *The Midnight Court*.'

To Michael Longley

MS Emory

12 January 1993 191 Strand Road, Dublin 4

Dear Michael,

Forgive me for not writing earlier in response to your card. I was troubled when D. Hammond told me that you had remarked that you'd not got a Christmas card this year (from me, I mean) – and thank you for yours . . . For once, the poem-at-yule habit was broken. And my approach to the whole thing was both desultory and surly, a fuck-it-anyhow, why-should-I-always-anyhow mood. Nothing intended or personal, sheer neglect in general.

I'll do a seconding for R.P., with great pleasure. And I read your letter with admiration for the emotional and imaginative boldness of it. And the poem too – envying a prod's freedom to invoke Our Lady. If Big Shay opened his cheeper to herself, think of the heaped scorn against Marianism, the boos at the boyish piety. It would be good to see you for a minute before I head away: I'm for the States on Saturday 23rd – and all mucked up with trips to Wales and other jobs in between. But give us a call at 2694221 if you think we could have a drink – maybe Thursday 14th, early evening, or the following Wednesday. It's all go.

I hope my information is right that you're in TCD now.

Obeisances to Ovid job too. The heart o' corn, thon ould pair.

love,

Seamus

The sending of cards constituted a significant part of the Heaney family's Christmas ritual. Catherine Heaney recalls that every December her father 'approached the task with the rigour and planning of a small military operation'. The cards themselves carried poems, often newly written, or lines from his poems, and might be illustrated by a member of the family.

The 'seconding' was on behalf of the artist – also expert on and illustrator of Ireland's wild orchids – Raymond Piper (1923–2007), whom Longley wished to propose for membership of Aosdána.

The poem envied for its 'prod's freedom' was Longley's 'Burren Prayer', included in *The Weather in Japan* (2000); the 'Ovid job' was 'Baucis and Philemon' ('thon ould pair'), one of his several contributions to the anthology *After Ovid: New Metamorphoses* (see footnote to SH's letter to Bernard McCabe of 8 July 1993).

To Bernard O'Donoghue

MS O'Donoghue

29 January 1993

English Department, Warren House,
Harvard University, Cambridge,
MA 02138

[. . .]

Please forgive me for not answering your note to me before Christmas, enclosing the lucid and bracing (to me) chapter on *Government of the Tongue*. You rendered the whole effort of that book very clearly and helpfully. I do wish, however, that I had done or could do something on Shakespeare, say, and dramatic poetry – for you are quite right to discern that which I too now see all the more clearly because of your acts of attention – I've been focused needily on lyric. Nothing wrong with that at all, of course. But still, it would be nice to face into your man from Stratford. (Too much, too big for me, I'm afraid.)

[. . .]

O'Donoghue's essay on *The Government of the Tongue* was added to *The Art of Seamus Heaney*, edited by Tony Curtis, when a new, expanded edition was issued in 1994.

To Bernard O'Donoghue

MS O'Donoghue

4 April 1993 Aer Lingus flight EI 135

Dear Bernard,

Between Dublin and Shannon, after a hurried few days at home for Spring Break – and I rejoice to think of y'all heading for Duhallow. Annie Murphy will preoccupy you now, no doubt . . .

Once again you'll have to forgive this too fleeting salute to the new chapter you sent. As an introduction, it seems to me wonderfully brisk and pointed, defining exactly what your purpose is, giving lucid and lively examples of how your readings will be conducted. (I love the 'Broagh'/'Anahorish' stuff – and I don't know if you could take notice, or have taken notice, of the Ireland/England vowel/consonant analogy in that early *Preoccupations/Guardian* piece in relation to penultimate stanza of 'A New Song'?) I am of course very proud and moved by your strong and kind approbation, and worry in case personal friendship inhibits your critical freedom – please revise and come down on me/the stuff as you honestly feel you want to. It *will not interfere* with the nurture and pleasure of our company. I am so elated by the terms of your understanding and approach that I truly am at ease with whatever negative things you might need to say. (I relish the middle voice riff!)

[. . .]

Duhallow is the name of the barony in north-west Cork where O'Donoghue's home places are located. Annie Murphy was the American woman, the discovery of whose relationship with Bishop Eamon Casey (1927–2017) precipitated his resignation.

O'Donoghue had sent SH the first chapter of his 1994 book, *Seamus Heaney and the Language of Poetry*.

The 'early *Preoccupations/Guardian* piece' is 'Christmas, 1971', part two of the essay 'Belfast'.

To David Constantine

MS Constantine

5 June 1993 [In transit]

Dear David,

The Aer Lingus stewardess at Dublin (I'm en route to Boston, *again*, having been at home and at Oxford and at boiling point for two weeks) was somebody I knew, so she put me into the executives' lounge and I purloined the fancy notepaper . . .

When I got back to Strand Road, your post-Greece letter was waiting for me. Please excuse me for not replying sooner to a wonderfully spontaneous and trust-inducing note. I am sorry that after following your good impulse and writing like that, you've had to wait so long for an acknowledgement.

Anyhow, I could feel the magic carpet of pleasure had lofted you both on your travels and was delighted that the 'lightening' and the steeped-in-luckness of it all implicated me. I've never – shameful – actually been in Greece, although Marie and I hope to go next May, in the company of a Greek-American sculptor and his English wife. (Dimitri Hadzi, who taught for years at Harvard, and Cynthia, who is still attached to the Carpenter Center for the Visual Arts.) Dimitri speaks the language and knows the stones so we hope to make up for lost time.

But I rejoice in your own *peregrinatio* or *immram* or *turas* (TURAS – the Irish word for a journey, also applied to a pilgrimage, a ritual visitation of the fixed Stations). And I envy you the boost of the long poem. Always, your combination of focus and supply both reassures and rebukes me: I feel rebuked simply because I've let myself get into a life of hurry and podiums and senatorial pomps, not sufficiently attuned to the silences and oldness at the centre, but feel reassured by the measure and access and active passage of energy which your work represents. The way it combines two kinds of knowledge – cultural, acquired knowledge and fore- or pre-knowledge . . . But I babble.

Perhaps I'll get a glimpse of you and Helen when I'm over for Encaenia. Before then, I've got to proceed (now) to Harvard and Dartmouth, then get back to Dublin, then go to the Poetry International at Rotterdam. July, August, September for recuperation. Love to Helen.

Seamus

The 'fancy notepaper' is headed with the emblem of the Aer Lingus Gold Circle Club.

The poet David Constantine (b.1944), who at this time was Fellow in German at The Queen's College, Oxford, and his wife Helen had got to know SH, first by attending his lectures, then, more intimately, through social gatherings with their friends and neighbours Bernard and Heather O'Donoghue.

'Encaenia': Oxford pomp at which honorary degrees are awarded.

To Joseph Brodsky

MS Beinecke

19 June 1993 Hotel Central, Rotterdam

Cher Poète,

Why is there no time?

Skimmed them again. 'Cappadocia' is the full orchestra, magnificently managed. Some notes in need of tuning here and there, I think. I've annotated where I think the sound wobbles. But I admire the big slam.

'Lullaby' the surest note, I think.

I can see the swashbuckling intent and can appreciate the rattle and flourish of 'Anti-Shenandoah' – but I don't love it as much. It's brilliant but I feel the speed of the lines – no, not the speed – the inevitability of the fit between cadence and intelligence is not *always* there. I babble. But throw the hat in the air too –

In haste.

S.

Brodsky in his later years wrote poems in English, although his command of the language, its structures and idioms, wobbled as much as the sounds did; here it appears that SH had been shown poems that would appear in Brodsky's final collection, *So Forth* (1996).

'In haste': the sprawling handwriting, covering two sheets of Hotel Central fax paper, says as much.

To Bernard McCabe

MS J. McCabe

8 July 1993 191 Strand Road, Dublin 4

Dear B.,

Restore 'doomed and bridal' – but make it 'Bridal and doomed', for the metre's sake.

Herewith, for *strictest* invigilation, is my shot at the opening of *The Midnight Court*. You know the poem? A court of love, war-of-the-sexes work, over a thousand lines. I'm thinking of doing the end as well (where poet is assailed by vengeful Connemara – or rather Clare – maenads) and putting it with this opening and calling it 'Orpheus in Munster . . .' But I feel uneasy about metrical wobbliness (though I simper to myself about some things here, quite faithfully rendered as well as OK to my ear) and would welcome any comment – whenever.

Vol. 3 *juste le billet*. More scope than ever. Great prospect . . . Also, forgive my sending me first sestina, etc. Love, S.

'Bridal and doomed' is from SH's 'Orpheus and Eurydice', his contribution to the anthology *After Ovid: New Metamorphoses* (1994) edited by the poets Michael Hofmann and James Lasdun. A fortnight earlier, SH had sent work-in-progress on this to McCabe, with a note saying, 'You'd better get your strength up now, if you are to detect the many revisions – for the sake of metre, tone and diction – in the enclosed.'

Brian Merriman (*c.*1747–1805) was the author of *Cúirt an Mheán Oíche* (*The Midnight Court*). Later in 1993, Gallery Books issued *The Midnight Verdict*, in which SH's Ovid was sandwiched between the two passages from Merriman mentioned here.

'me first sestina': presumably 'Two Lorries' (*The Spirit Level*).

To John Wilson Foster

MS Emory

20 July 1993

Glanmore Cottage, Ashford,
Co. Wicklow

Dear Jack,

It did my heart good to read 'A Runagate Tongue' – bright shoots of everlastingness started through me – although I also realized how transient the words are too. Heartbreaking, in a way, that the jubilation of recollection which 'crigs' and 'hoachin' and 'heck' and 'gulpin' provoke in me is so short-circuited, generation-bound, culture-bound, ezettera, ezettera, as my father-in-law said. I loved the finer points, words which I would hardly have considered un-standard – shade in the hair, dinge in the hub-cap, whinge, tartles. (By the way, I was faintly disappointed lately to see that *jap* is standard – I'll send you a few lines of *The Midnight Court* I did in the last couple of weeks just for the sake of hallion and clabber and japs.) *Boor* was my wishful-thinkin' etymology – the poem began as a dedication to John Hewitt and then, *in situ*, in the Glanmore sequence, I felt it would be overdedication, so to speak, since Ann S. was the head-bummadeer (bombardier?) in that context.

S. Deane (Indiana Deane now, according to T. Browne!) wrote a poem when he was at Queen's addressed to Wallace Stevens which began 'Of the svelte diction, master!' So there's echo for ya.

[. . .]

'A Runagate Tongue, or, English as We Speak It in Ulster' was an article by Foster that appeared in the *Irish Literary Supplement* on 1 September 1993. Foster had shown SH a copy in advance.

'bright shoots of everlastingness': see 'The Retreat' by the seventeenth-century Welsh poet Henry Vaughan.

'*jap* is standard': in his poem 'Underground', SH conceives of 'some new white flower japped with crimson'; '*Boor*': 'Soft corrugations in the boortree's trunk' is the first line of 'Glanmore Sonnets V', from the sequence dedicated to Ann Saddlemyer.

To Audrey C. Davies

TS HomePlace

19 August 1993 191 Strand Road, Dublin 4

Dear Dr Davies,

Many thanks for your letter. I am both proud and daunted at the thought of you all working away at those *Selected Poems*. And I sympathise with your problems over 'King of the Ditchbacks'. You are right in thinking that the Sweeney figure is at the centre of it. As a matter of fact, it was written at three different moments – the three parts gathered themselves together only gradually. The first one was done in the early 1970s. It's born out of memories of walking along the road as a youngster, at night, and being haunted by sounds on the other side of the hedge. And, of course, you are right: it is an 'other self' whom I imagine there beyond the bushes. Then, I think the second one in order of composition was actually Part Three of the poem. That is based on a pigeon-shooting event in County Kilkenny when my friend dressed me up in the manner described and we went out into the fields. Once again, the Sweeney presence is there in the figure covered in twigs, dressed like 'King of the Ditchbacks'.

The oddest bit, of course, is the central prose section. That is a memory of translating *Sweeney Astray* in Wicklow in the early 1970s. The governing notion in it is that the Sweeney figure equals somehow my little self, the little self that was at home in the hedges and ditches of County Derry. And in the various nightmares, dreams, etc. that little self is crying out for preservation. But all of that is, of course, slightly looney . . . I just mean the second section to be a kind of suggestive phantasmagoria.

John Montague is the dedicatee of the poem because he too was interested in Mad Sweeney. What bother it has given you! I hope the above is some clarification – although, God knows, the reader could never be expected to know the half of that. What a strange business it all is.

Yours sincerely,
Seamus Heaney

PS Forgive the speed of this dictation, and its near incoherence, but I wanted to answer you right away. And thanks for the stamps!
S.H.

Dr Davies has not been traced. This letter to her was found inserted into a second-hand copy of *The Spirit Level* in an Orkney bookshop, passed by the finder to the Heaney HomePlace in Bellaghy, then passed again to the editor of this book.

The postscript is handwritten.

To Niall MacMonagle

TS MacMonagle

27 September 1993 — 191 Strand Road, Dublin 4

Dear Niall,

Many thanks for your note of a while back requesting permission to turn the photograph into a postcard. I have, I'm afraid, a real hesitation about this. And it is aided or strengthened or whatever you do to increase a hesitation by Marie's unease. So, nothing personal, but can we let that one rest? Among other things, Marie's gardener's pride has always been wounded by the broken aspect of the garden seat. There y'are. See you soon.

Seamus

PS I like the idea, of course, even tho' I'm writing this card!

Niall MacMonagle (b.1954) has worked as a teacher, literary critic, promoter of poetry-speaking, and anthologist, among other things. The photograph he hoped might become a postcard, by Arnold Edge, shows SH seated in the garden of the Heaneys' Dublin home; the family dog, Carlo, sits at his feet in stately profile.

The postscript is handwritten.

To Bernard and Jane McCabe

ms J. McCabe

9 October 1993 — 191 Strand Road, Dublin 4

Dear Bernard and Jane,

Just a quick note to apologize for not having written you a long letter. For no particular reason except friendship and pleasure. As usual, too much running around and doings. Just back, a bit crocked, from Belfast and D. Hammond's 65th birthday party. The usual gulping and plucking of instruments and rhythmical utterance. Late night and boozy morning. Now we're in an interim between our train journey from the north and our car trip in half-an-hour's time to the American Ambassador's residence for a reading by E. L. Doctorow. My God, I have fizzled out my life with finger food.

Big literary do here three weeks ago: International Writers Festival. Had squiring rights and duties to Edna O'Brien, Nadine Gordimer, R. Wilbur, Judith Herzberg (Dutch sibyl), P. Muldoon and Big Toni M. – before she got the bounty of S. Many excellent readings and larks and scrapes – remind me to tell you about my *two* flat wheels in Wicklow with N. Gord., then having to find a driver to take us on a veldt-trek across the Calary bog, to Bray, where we put her on the DART and then went on the tyre-trek. And a dinner with E. O'B., so fevered and frantic and pitched that I couldn't sleep after it.

Meanwhile, my Fulbright funded bibliographer, Rand Brandes, is in the attic every other day, and I'm with him, excavating the layers. We're simply boxing the detritus in heaps – letters, MSS, publications, keepsakes – and making some initial progress. I want the attic to turn out like a den where chaps can go and play darts and drink beer at the top of the house.

[. . .]

Merriman lecture limply readyish. O. Wilde's *Ballad of R. G.* subject for second one. Wish I could deliver something worthy of the great fruit (who said the C in balcony should receive more emphasis than it customarily does) but 'twill be drab. Last yelp of amazing news: she and I head for Palermo in Sicily on Wed. – an Italian prize was awarded to me for *Station Island* in Italian! Millions of lire. TV and seminars in Sicily. Back late on 17th! Love to you both. Seamus. PS Cyril Cusack gone to the great upstager in the sky.

Among the International Writers, South African novelist Nadine Gordimer (1923–2014) was recipient of the 1991 Nobel Prize in Literature, US novelist Toni Morrison (1931–2019), of the same prize in 1993; US poet Richard Wilbur (1921–2017) and US novelist E. L. Doctorow (1931–2015) were not so favoured.

The 'flat wheels' story concerned a puncture that had humiliatingly cut short SH's attempt to drive Gordimer around some of the local sites.

The lectures on Merriman and Wilde are both included in *The Redress of Poetry*.

To James Simmons and Janice Fitzpatrick TS Emory

20 October 1993 191 Strand Road, Dublin 4

Dear James and Janice,

Many thanks for your letter. I am answering briefly because I am off to Oxford this afternoon. And, indeed, Oxford and all that has a bearing on my response to your invitation. I am, of course, flattered to be asked to be external examiner – especially when I know that my rating as a verse writer could be higher in your own eyes. But at the moment, I am more involved in shedding responsibilities than taking them on. The Professorship of Poetry ends for me next June, and I am determined not to get into that kind of duty-dancing again. Moreover, when I come back from Harvard, the last thing I want to do is to get stuck into other people's manuscripts. I am hoping to have a sabbatical next year also, and want to keep the desk clear.

I would feel worse about declining did I not also feel that my hat and face had already made some contribution to forwarding the cause of Poet's House. Sooner or later, a return visit, perhaps. But I regret that I won't be examining.

Sincerely,
Seamus

Simmons and his American wife, the poet Janice Fitzpatrick (b.1954), had founded the Poets' House, in Portmuck, Co. Antrim, in 1990. An educational establishment, it was the first in Ireland to offer an MA course in creative writing.

To Bernard O'Donoghue

MS O'Donoghue

27 October 1993 Magdalen College, Oxford OX1

Dear Bernard,

You and Heather have done so much to make me completely at home, I don't know how to thank you. I'm sorry I didn't write before now to say again how memorable and mellow and lustrous the Adlestrop/Stones/Tew afternoon was, and then how thoroughly happy and free the feasting and hosting was on Hilltop Road. And I deeply appreciated your care in signing in for the high table.

Rand had a full Oxford experience, and we all felt safe in your good company. The Irish joke perfectly timed and placed, too.

Will deliver the Reading message. See you Thursday evening? Looking forward to Friday. Love to y'all.

Seamus

O'Donoghue had driven SH around the Cotswolds, on a trip that took in Adlestrop, scene of Edward Thomas's poem, the ancient Rollright Stones near Chipping Norton, and the Falkland Arms at Great Tew.

The 'Irish joke' and 'Reading message' have been forgotten.

1994

Foreign travel this year included a return to Tollund, in Denmark – the territory that in his poem 'The Tollund Man' (*Wintering Out*) SH had called 'the old man-killing parishes' – just at the time when the IRA announced the 'cessation of military operations' that would help make the Northern Ireland peace process possible.

Other trips were to Mexico, Australia and Poland. Connection with the last-named, already sentimentally lodged in SH's mind, was reinforced when he and his Harvard colleague Stanisław Barańczak began to collaborate on their translation of Jan Kochanowski's great book of elegies, *Treny* (see letter to Barańczak of 23 June 1994 for something of the care and labour that this involved).

To Ted Hughes

MS Emory

25 March 1994 [In transit]

Dear Ted,

By a mad coincidence this is the only stationery I have in the bag. An anglophile professor-nut from Ann Arbor gave it to me a while ago and it has survived at the back of the briefcase until this needy moment. By another coincidence, this also happens to be the Feast of the Annunciation and I've just heard the angel of poetry make her re-entry into English discourse – discourse in English, that is – in 'Myths, Metres, Rhythms'. I've been away for two days in Montana, at Missoula, a town with a river and fishermen almost at the centre of it, and a real sense of audience around the university. But the chief virtue of the trip was to have four hours' sustained silence on the way back to-day, when I rode the thermals of your pages. *Winter Pollen* is a great book and I was elated to find myself testifying in Bill Scammell's introduction. I have rarely felt as transported and nailed down into grain of poetry. The last time I was lifted and laid with anything like the same force or faith was when I encountered Mandelstam's 'Conversation about Dante' and 'Fourth Prose' and *Journey to Armenia*. Completely different genres – at least the Armenian book – but the same sense of all of a culture's and a language's and a person's ultimate genius being rolled up into one ball and hurled. Partly a marvel, like Cúchulainn's ball hurled and caught, partly a world-scare, like the Gáe-Bolga being given a test run . . . The sense of deep learning, deep, long, detailed, loving possession of the detail of poems as well as their DNA; the sense of a defence of poetry being written single-handed, in desperate love and anger. I read it and felt like a child on the edge of one of those old excavations/road works, feeling the intentness and focus and big strength of men at work close to the mains and the powerlines. In awe. Reminded of the absolute seriousness of the venture. I have yet to read the Coleridge essay, but I will do in the next few days. I'm actually on my way home for mid-term break – one week, returning to Harvard on Easter Sunday – and am at present ensconced in a lounge at Kennedy Airport waiting for an Aer Lingus flight in a couple of hours.

Of course, I am distressed at not having written to you in response to your January letter. Marie forwarded it, but because of the odd dislocation and hurry of Harvard, and because I could not find Sylvia's journals, to take another look at your introduction, and because somehow I felt inadequate to the job of saying anything commensurate with your own great 'durance', as G.M.H. might call it, the whole thing went into abeyance. There I was, walking around with a jewel of pain in my pocket, as it were, strenuously forgetting it in the trivial pursuits of the busy life. And then, casually, I heard a few days ago about Aurelia Plath's death, and thought what new shock-waves and rebounds this would bring for you. Maybe you were over in the States at the time even. Anyhow, I wish I could have absorbed some of the shock that you are applying to yourself a bit better. And I hope your self-flagellation has eased. Which is easy to say: the fate that you have lived out and lived in for thirty years has only gradually dawned upon me: something to do with getting older, something to do with the – mild enough – experience of enmity and false-image making that inevitably has gathered up around me. At any rate, more and more when I think of you, I think of the immense complexity of your sorrows and constraints, of the stove-hot labyrinth you've been caught in; what one took for granted – the abundance and ecology of your whole work – seemed a marvellous feat of total integration, intelligence, total vocation, sacrifice of the social self to the imagined dimensions of the calling. But now even that profile of self-yielding and making seems a pale ghost of the 'war within' you have undergone. You should not be bothering yourself about the small hurts delivered incidentally in the *Journals*, although it is a token of the self-laceration that you have lived with. And you shouldn't be so hard on the Introduction you wrote – if it is the one reprinted from *Grand Street* in *Winter Pollen*. In fact, it seems to me that with the Shakespeare book and this one, you too have done what you say there that she/Sylvia did – you have overcome, by a stunning display of power, the bogies of your life. There is a magnificent sense of combat and exultant resource, as if a Proteus grappled with a Proteus, and the world began to experience a beauty of transformation through the brilliance and desperation of their mutual feats of metamorphosis and resilience. I can only say how I experience the great invention and intensity of your prose as a kind of Amergin-like summoning of power to overwhelm the Fomorian spells and mists and menaces walling and welling up against you – in you, of course, too, as well as around you. There was irrigation for me in the beginning in reading those early 'listening and writing' pieces; there was a jump-lead joy about the Shakespearean afterword – and introduction – when they appeared. There were the parables of poetic life that lay at the centre of the Sylvia annotations. All that has reanimated itself in me as I sped through the book; but the transposition of the scrutiny and analysis – the passionate, simple coherence and preternatural lucid sensitive readings – in the 'Myth, Metre and Rhythm' chapter is an extraordinary boon. The piece on Wyatt is breathtaking, and incidentally is a reminder of how utterly the academy has abandoned its responsibility to the culture. And the marriage history of the anima/genius of the language is one of the headiest – and funniest – riffs I've read.

I've not seen any reviews. My nose has been to the grindstone, I've been to and fro to New York – Marie has been here launching her book in Boston, undergoing parties, enjoying the hullabulloo. My dreamtime has been obliterated, my browse-life has been nil. But I hope there was a salute (for *Winter P.*) that rose to the occasion. (When I get home, I'll have a pile of literary gossip-sheets in the form of *TLS* and *LRB* which may have some reports/responses.) Meanwhile, the next leg of the journey is on. I'll call you next week to finalize things for Oxford. And by the end of June I hope to be off the treadmill for a year and a half. No return to US until January '96. I hope I can break the concrete that has hardened over the well. I need to lap and lick. But there's always the dread that the font is dust.

My love to Carol – what a shitty way they put her dedication over the publication data! Heigho. And love to you.

Seamus

On the letterhead, SH has crossed out an Ann Arbor address, leaving the bold typeface of 'On Her Britannic Majesty's Service', but not giving an address of his own.

William Scammell (1939–2000), poet and teacher, had chosen the material for *Winter Pollen* from Ted Hughes's prose writings, old and more recent, 'Myths, Metres, Rhythms', 'The Snake in the Oak' (on Coleridge) and a number of pieces about Sylvia Plath standing out among the latter. By 'those early "listening and writing" pieces', SH means the broadcasts to schools that were gathered in Hughes's *Poetry in the Making* (1967), extracts from which are included in *Winter Pollen*.

Aurelia Plath, Sylvia's mother, had died on 11 March.

'G.M.H.': Gerard Manley Hopkins.

In Irish mythology, Amergin is bard of the Gaelic Milesians, while the Fomorians are a race of malevolent supernatural beings.

To Heather and Bernard O'Donoghue — MS O'Donoghue

8 May 1994 — In the air, with British Air

Dear Heather and Bernard,

Everything not only flows, it turns into bloody white water. It's rapids nowadays . . . Somehow, I feel the days skimmed past and I never did solemnize, as it were, sufficiently, to your faces, how much your great true kindness (and kind trueness) has meant to me (and Marie, but I'm thinking of the way you made a home context for me on Hilltop Road when she *wasn't* there). I felt I was your young brother, the way you both took care of me. I am very aware how much sacrifice of time and convenience and emotional energy your 'good attendance' involved. Knowing from experience how family life goes into a 'holding pattern' when visitors are around, I appreciated all the more acutely the practical adjustments you always made to make my life a convenience to *me*. And I know that I took Bernard out on expeditions that the *whole* family might have enjoyed, had I been more devoted [to] *your* pleasures. I'm thinking of the trip to Stratford, in particular – tho' there was great compensation at Babcote Hythe. And Boar's Hill. And Garsington. Adlestrop and Rollright were for the boys, admittedly, but 'this is what you're up against . . .'

The last few days in particular were sweet and thorough. The reading was a huge lift for me, and I'll never forget that you, Bernard, and Christine took it all on and underwent the stress. But it *was* one of the great memorable events of my life (and, I suspect, of Ted's), and as such was a perfect cresting of all good currents that have flowed for the past five years.

Please know you and yours will always be welcome with us, and get in touch with us whenever there's a chance we can meet again, in Dublin or in what I shall henceforth call Ballybullán . . . Love to you all.

Seamus

SH's thanks are for hospitality received from the O'Donoghues over the five years of his professorship.

'Babcote Hythe': SH refers to a jaunt in 1991 when Bernard O'Donoghue conducted him on a tour of sites associated with Matthew Arnold's 'The Scholar Gypsy', including Bablock Hythe.

The reading referred to took place at Oxford's Sheldonian Theatre, when SH shared the platform with Ted Hughes; Christine Kelly was the principal organiser.

Ballybullán: an Anglo-Irish play on 'Oxford'.

To James Fenton

MS Emory

10 June 1994 — 191 Strand Road, Dublin 4

Dear James,

When this letter failed to get written straight away, it kept being put off until the moment when 'the real letter' could get done. As Tomas Tranströmer says of deferred correspondence, 'it puts on weight'.

It was great – if well expected – news that the vote went so decisively in your favour. No messing. The only way to take the trick. I was delighted and am proud to have been the prelude to your theme, or the tug to your liner or the chaser to your pint – not that anybody wants to be a pint, and can a chaser come before? So, me pint, *you* chaser. Enough.

At least, as I said to P. Levi five years ago, it's not the Grove at Nemi. Magdalen will let me go and take you back as supernumerary and non-stipendiary, no doubt. And I hope I can take shelter with T. Smith in the autumn when you do your inaugural. I'm going to be in Melbourne, at the Writers' Festival, until some time around October 24. So I'll miss you if you are earlier than that, but will catch another lecture before the end of your first year.

I greatly appreciated your coming to the Sheldonian in May. It was a wonderful bonus to what was a wonderfully rewarding reading. Sorry not to have exchanged a word then, and sorry that it has taken me so long to congratulate you. You will have a great time doing the lectures and I am sure you will kick your critical heels more jubilantly than I did, and probably range more widely. I'm afraid I was very canonical;

I think you should be more scampish altogether.

I did not see enough of Darryl this semester. But his presence brought Harvard to life in a new way. As will the new professor at Oxford. Until we get down to the chasers, then, blessings [. . .]

Seamus

SH's tenure of the Oxford Chair of Poetry concluded in the summer term of 1994 and James Fenton was elected to succeed him; Peter Levi had been SH's predecessor. The succession of the priesthood of Diana at Nemi involved mortal combat.

The playwright and novelist Darryl Pinckney (b.1953) is Fenton's partner.

To Brian Friel

MS NLI

15 June 1994 c/o McCabes, Ludlow

Dear Brian,

We came over here yesterday to see Bernard McCabe. He had a bad turn of angina in April and had angioplastic surgery – the balloon in the artery treatment – so we promised ourselves when we were in the States that we'd make the journey to see him pronto. He's as right as rain, although naturally cautious for himself and inducing caution in us. But he has long ago mastered the art of quiet living: a beautiful hilltop brick house, an English garden, a stereo, a view of Ludlow and Housman's 'blue remembered hills'. It has been a great twenty-four hours of quietude, and while I regret that I did not read *Molly Sweeney* before now, I am glad to have read it in the end in such good conditions . . . It's electrifying from the first word to the last.

[. . .]

Anyways, it breaks the heart and lifts it at the same time. Seems to be full of those things which Eliot called 'some deep personal reminiscence never to be explained, of course, but to give power from well below the surface'. I wish I had written it. I envy you the possibilities and highs of the weeks ahead in rehearsals. And I'll talk to you when I get back. I have a notion of bluntly cutting out of Field Day myself, sans consultation with anyone. Rea and Deane have behaved scandalously there. But what is that to you, old cock? *Gaudens gaudeo*. Love,

Seamus

PS Last August I did my own blind woman poem which you may have seen in the *New Yorker*. Our previous talk had brought her sweetly back to me, and I realized she belonged in a poem I'd always wanted to write – about Marie's habit of closing her eyes when she sings. But I hope the world will link her to *Seeing Things* rather than to *Molly S.*, even though *Molly* brought her forth.

The heroine of Friel's play *Molly Sweeney*, which premiered at the Gate Theatre in August 1994, undergoes surgery to regain her sight. 'At the Wellhead' is SH's poem evoking 'sweet-voiced, withdrawn' Rosie Keenan, who was blind, 'knew us by our voices' but would 'say she "saw" / Whoever or whatever.'

Omitted: almost two pages of SH's enthusiastic remarks on the play: 'A musical inevitability about it, a true ring to the whole cadencing and movement that is of a piece with the human truths being represented or rehearsed' – and so on.

In an undated letter of 1944 to his friend John Hayward (1905–65), T. S. Eliot wrote, of 'Little Gidding': 'The defect of the whole poem, I feel, is the lack of some acute personal reminiscence (never to be explicated, of course, but to give power from well below the surface).'

To Breon O'Casey

MS O'Casey

15 June 1994 — 191 Strand Road, Dublin 4

Dear Breon,

If I wait another day, it will be Bloomsday and the literary stakes will have been raised too high altogether.

I envy you your anvil and I am proud that you feel enough for 'The Forge' to use it as a starting point for a work of your own. I'm more elated by this than agreeable to it. And don't worry about the sales aspect. Give me a few copies of the edition, then sell what you can through your own channels. The accounting is too fussy. My reward is your regard for the poem.

Now, off to buy those kidneys . . .

Love to you both.

Seamus

PS On second thoughts, of course: Faber Copyright would need to be contacted some time, if the poem is being reprinted.

S.

Breon O'Casey (1928–2011), painter, sculptor, jeweller and, incidentally, son of the playwright Sean O'Casey (1880–1964), had made an etching inspired by SH's 'The Forge' (*Door into the Dark*): in it, the poem is printed above O'Casey's near-abstract image of an anvil.

To Stanisław Barańczak

MS Barańczak

23 June 1994 191 Strand Road, Dublin 4

Stanisław –

Better get this off before Mexico can change the mood . . . Here's hoping.

Great work on my attempt – *all* works together towards good!

l. 86: 'Blind' is spot on.

l. 104: maybe previous version is better – just a bit Lowellesque in its triadic adjectival form?

l. 113–114: *Gaudens gaudeo.*

l. 135: 'New peace' is a spondee to my Ulster ear. But even before I heard from you, I had in mind another shot at 133, 134:

'You must accept, although your wound's still raw,
The rule and sway of universal law
And fill your heart with new peace, banish pain.'
Maybe, maybe not.

l. 143: What about 'self-mastery' and then in l. 144: 'You've helped them over it, etc.'

l. 156: 'Never forget –' for 'Keep that in mind'??

Enclosed – or rather, to follow – a version of No. 17.

Meanwhile, here is a list of things that niggle at me as I re-read our versions so far:

Lament 2, line 20. The 'but' seems to me just too archaic. Can we add a 'for'? 'Applies to all, for man is fortune's fool.'

Lament 4: Delete comma after 'for' in penultimate line.

Lament 7: Every time I read it, I have a temptation to change that 'you' in line 3 and line 5 to 'they'. I know it would be a real interference with the original. I only mention it to allow you to be aghast at me. Line 12 – substitute 'last' for 'hard'?

Lament 9, line 3: 'purge' for 'cleanse'? Line 4, delete 'the'. Line 12: substitute 'what's' for 'just'? End line 14 with a period?

Lament 11: I know I'm going to come back to 'but not by us' – the line seems ever so slightly forced, off-centre, not quite right. Later, later . . .

<Lament 11, also – The most tentative of thoughts for line 2: Substitute 'it is' for 'in truth'?>

Lament 13, line 4: Go back to your 'What else, what else . . .'?
line 7/8: 'but, when we wake at dawn,
Our hands are empty and the gleam is gone'
line 18: 'Her father's joy that slipped his loving hands.'?
line 19: her grave/this grave? No? 'The' grave generalizes early death as the rule? Too much?

Lament 15, line 8: substitute 'sorrows match' for 'beings know'?
line 33: 'This tomb keeps no corpse; this corpse keeps no tomb:'?

Lament 18: I know, I said it was untouchable – but 'ere' in line 9 bothers me a wee bit.

Lament 19: Bernard McCabe, my merry friend in Ludlow, pointed out that Cockney rhyming slang for 'wife' is 'trouble and strife' – so merrily suggested a revision at lines 59/60:
made her years
One long declension into strife and tears.'
Maybe it *is* better. 'Tis all one to me!
line 88 – a comma before ', safe,'?
line 104:
'Interlude, short-lived but innocent.'
(As it stands, it limps a bit).
line 115:
. . . *That* burden's placed upon (?)
<PS line 10: Substitute 'rise' for 'come'>
line 136: Delete comma?
line 138 – delete second 'that'?

FINALLY
LAMENT I, l. 8: On and off it has struck me that 'remorse' is not exactly what K. is feeling. Death might be remorseful for having snatched Ursula away, but not her father . . . I wonder. It's a lovely

forceful word, a clinching rhyme, but I have to question it at this crucial moment, in order to calm my fears. Alternatives:

. . . I am left without recourse.

. . . it left me no recourse.

Not as absolutely rammed home as the remorse line, but is it truer to the sense? Maybe not. But making better sense in English. *Ochone, ochone*, he keened . . .

Love to you all. Come on, Jack's army!   S.

PS Good to have 'The Spanish Doctor' – he would have been an equal curiosity in our own fair land.   S.

The collaboration between SH and Stanisław Barańczak that eventually produced their translation of *Treny* (*Laments*, in English) by the Polish poet Jan Kochanowski (1530–84) sprang from a discussion between the two men one Saturday afternoon in April 1993. Barańczak then excitedly began the process by sending SH four of his own English versions – 'rather insolently in verse', as he himself put it – of these classics of Polish literature, poems of grief over the death of Kochanowski's infant daughter Ursula. The letter above gives some insight into the to-and-fro of drafts that then followed.

SH's first comments concern the last and longest of the laments, subtitled 'A Dream'. 'Blind' (line 86), for instance, which seems to have been Barańczak's suggestion and which occurs in a passage about those who 'Are wrecked on blind reefs when the gales start blowing / And drowned and lost', survives in the published text; readers can ascertain for themselves what was finally decided in other cases.

SH's valediction actually appears on page 3 of this four-page fax – in haste, presumably.

To Gibbons Ruark

GC Ruark

19 July 1994

[. . .]

Well, of course, it's vulgar but that's what I liked about it. And the fact that it seems to be quite in earnest. Or is it . . .?

Well, and of course, put the name down and we'll put the boosters in again. It used to be I had successes on my Guggenheim hands, but nowadays some of the starriest kites I've been tail to have failed to fly. I begin to wonder if I'm a dead weight . . . But I know Joel Conarroe, so no, I don't think so. Anyhow, we'll shoot in a letter when the time comes.

I'm in a good – and yet panicky – situation. Oxford Professorship over, a year off from Harvard, no alibis and no poems. Translations, hopes, revisions of Oxford lectures for publication, etc., etc., but not even 'a few weeds and stubble'.

Unfortunately, too, I had to pull out of the Morans trip. Bad aches and pains in the back: decrepitude but no wisdom. Arrival of Canadian – well, Canada-dwelling – brother. Several factors. A bit of a let-down. *Mea culpa*.

Love to Kay and yourself. Seamus

'Well, of course, it's vulgar': the letter is on a folded picture card which reproduces *A Beauty* by Monte Dolack: painting of an enormous gasping trout filling an entire sofa, with two paintings and a Japanese print of nude or partially clothed women on the wall behind it.

Joel Conarroe (b.1934) was and remains president of the John Simon Guggenheim Memorial Foundation, which awards fellowships to writers; applying for one, Ruark had asked SH to write a reference, but the application was unsuccessful.

'a few weeds and stubble': see Robert Frost's 'Desert Places'.

To Paul Muldoon and Jean Hanff Korelitz PC Emory

4 September 1994 [Postmarked 'Copenhagen']

We went to moss this morning: brought out to Tollund, where they found your man. A familiar ground, of course: rushes and bushes and mossholes and a picnic site in off the side-road. But, happily, no mention of himself or his discovery. The usual old silence. Perfectly satisfactory . . . Love to you all. Seamus

The Silkeborg Museum postcard shows the 'Tollund man'.

'We went to moss': 4 September was a Sunday.

To Rebecca and Robert Tracy MS Tracy

10 September 1994 191 Strand Road, Dublin 4

Dear Becky and Bob,

Well, the ceasefire has held for a week and a staunch – and heretofore unfavourite – Unionist, John Taylor, has pronounced himself inclined to trust the Provos' good faith, so we may be moving from the atrocious to the merely desolate . . . Anyhow, *chers amis*, this is just to ask a favour. I enclose a cheque which I hope might go towards the framing of a hand-printed poem I am sending by DHL to Bob's Wheeler Hall address (thought it would be safer – people on the spot to sign, *etc.*, *etc.*). The poem is to celebrate the Dominic and Lisa nuptials, a wedding present, I suppose.

[. . .]

PS Submerged Mandelstam in fourth last line.

John Taylor (b.1937), at this time the Ulster Unionist MP for Strangford and a member of the hard-line Conservative Monday Club, was among the first in his party to support the peace efforts of its leader David Trimble (1944–2022) when he made public his 'gut feeling' that they would succeed.

'Dominic' is in fact Dominick, the Tracys' son, and the gift to him and his wife Lisa, an autographed broadside print of 'The Poet's Chair', of which the fourth last line goes, 'Of the poem as a ploughshare that turns time / Up and over'. As a translator of Mandelstam, Robert Tracy may have been quick to spot the reference – possibly to Mandelstam's poem 'Black Earth'?

To Tom Paulin

MS Emory

9 October 1994 Novotel, Launceston, Tasmania

Dear Tom,

You're probably in Princeton, I'm in Van Diemen's Land, in the town of Launceston – a kind of Coleraine of the South, except there isn't as much bad poetry (yet) in Coleraine. The Tasmania Poetry Festival is on here and at the event where I read last night there was one of those open-reading sessions – a 'slam' – where the winner was decided by an applause meter. Wyndham Lewis would have been useful – apparently when Eliot was doing his porno rhymes, Lewis said it was the policy of his magazine not to publish anything that rhymed in -unt, -uck or -ugger. No such ban operates in Launceston. Incredible stuff.

But Australia has been a great experience. We came via Bangkok where I dealt in silks (two shirts) and loved the river ferries and the temples. Then we landed in Melbourne and stayed with the Wallace-Crabbes to get our bearings. Thence to Brisbane, where there was the first and most relaxed of the festivals so far. I was interviewed in public by a fair dinkum Ocker populist poet Bruce Dawe – perfectly amiable event – and did a reading at the Irish Club of Queensland. Strictly non-sectarian, of course. But the best thing in Queensland was a drive up through the country – red earth and white-barked gum trees – to the town of Nambour, near where my Uncle Charlie, my father's twin, ended up in the late 1920s, on a sugar cane farm. After Queensland, four great days in Sydney, courtesy of the Celtic Studies Department of the university. One day of tasks, and three days to ourselves, but with the direction and company (if we wanted it) of an entirely pleasant young couple, an Anglo-Australian woman and a Welshman called Geraint Evans, for Christ's sake. Then to Hobart for a couple of days where I repeated a new and improved lecture on *The Ballad of Reading Gaol* – saying it was as much part of the protest literature of the Irish diaspora as 'The Wild Colonial Boy' or the ballad of 'Van Diemen's Land'. (Added piquant circumstance – sodomy still a crime in these quarters.) My one regret is that I did not get to see the penal settlement at Port Arthur – about which Robert Hughes has much to tell in *The Fatal Shore* – a book I read with great pleasure and profit before heading off.

[. . .]

The Field Day thing is a shambles. What the hell is the money situation, the staffing situation, etc.? I swerve away from thinking about it every time, yet I know I am conniving in something less than useless – deplorable, nearly. I don't really believe that *Uncle Vanya* will come off, and yet I understand that thousands and thousands of pounds are voted towards it by the Arts Councils. But I swerve again – I'm in the foyer of the hotel here listening to a jazz band made up of men fatter and older than myself.

Raine's book, apparently, got a lot of attention. But I missed it – and also M. McG.'s remarks about yours. What's she on about anyway? I remember she was bad-mannered in the *IT* about a previous collection. Did Muldoon get any showing for *his* new stuff? Love to Giti and the boys. I'll see you. Seamus

The poet Bruce Dawe (1930–2020) had parents who were farmers, but probably would not have cared to be described as 'Ocker'.

Charlie Heaney (b.1910) emigrated to Australia before the Second World War; while it is known that he worked on a farm in Queensland, when and how he died are a mystery.

The Fatal Shore (1986) by Robert Hughes (1938–2012) is a history of the early colonisation of Australia, including the penal settlements.

Frank McGuinness's version of Chekhov's *Uncle Vanya* was never produced by Field Day.

'Raine's book': Craig Raine's verse novel, *History: The Home Movie*; Muldoon's 'new stuff' was *The Annals of Chile*.

To David Constantine

MS Constantine

27 October 1994 191 Strand Road, Dublin 4

Dear David,

You should have heard from me before this, but unfortunately I had just departed for Australia when you sent *Caspar* and I did not get back until a week ago. Last night, however, I read the first three cantos and this morning – from dawn, down in Wicklow, alone in the cottage here – I read the rest. From the moment I heard the confidence and good cheer of the opening tercet (the cheer is in the rhyme, both shouldered off and shouldering through) I knew the whole work was on course, aligned with something deep and capable of great out-ripple and cross-current. It is very strong and very lovely, breaks the heart and lifts it all at once. The agony and purity of Caspar's being and doings are opened up by the narrative, and the tone, and the wonderful epic imagery. The Homeric simile rides again – those chestnut trees at Whitsun, those 'winds of the stratosphere / In the hurtling planet's bright delighted hair', the whole orchestration of the pit/cellar life and of the angel brow* <*and the time-heap, in all its dispersals>, all that you planned and then discovered in a dimension of invention you could not have planned for – I loved it. The tenderness and usefulness of it all is implicit in that image of Caspar/any child being walked on its father's feet: extraordinary care and love finding a way to broadcast itself in the 1990s. The eighth canto is a risk which you had to take and which you get away with – not least because of that early daring lyric entry made by the poet *in propria persona* at the end of the second part of Canto 1 – the fresh water on the salt ocean. There's no risk in the truth and ache of what you have to tell, it's more that the insistence on the contemporaneity of the fable is a defiance – thrilling – of all the old show-rather-than-tell orthodoxies. But you know all that already.

The characters are totally convincing. Clara, with the diaphanous yet substantial garmenting and the credible heats, is a wonderful Tír na nÓg at the centre, but I must confess to loving the trusty Daumer above all. Through them, you found a way of speaking directly and, as it were, heftily. The poetry came crowding in like a white flock of gulls after the black effort of the narrative plough.

If all this sounds a bit eager, it sounds right. I just want to let you know, a few hours after I finished it, how thrilling it was to encounter work that did not disappoint, did not flaunt itself, was at full stretch and focused upon its own errand of sympathy and transformation. To end with a rhyme on make/broke! Or whom/name! Hosannah! It's history, the big movie – although, to be fair, I haven't read the home movie yet. But I thought that the short line, so to speak, was not going to be up to the long haul.

Your good presence and your constant hospitality at Hilltop Road will always be part of the good memories of Oxford: but *Caspar* is beyond us both now. A work. Love to Helen and y'all, as they say down south of the Mason-Dixon line.   Seamus

Constantine's *Caspar Hauser*, subtitled *A Poem in Nine Cantos*, was published in 1994.

'diaphanous yet substantial': SH writes 'diaphonous' and 'substantantial'.

'home movie': see footnote to letter to Tom Paulin of 9 October 1994.

To Seamus Deane

MS Emory

22 November 1994   191 Strand Road, Dublin 4

Dear Seamus,

This won't be the letter that's waiting to be written, the poem of the changes, the arc of the attrition. I feel so inchoately the shifts and disjunctions of the past few years, not only in the context of Field Day, but in some mid-life crisisy way inside myself; and I feel them as an effect of and affecting relations between us all personally – to the point that an autobiography rather than a letter is what is needed. I'm beached on the soft sands – or mud, is it – of this sabbatical leave and feel only waste and inertia within me. Fat grief, I admit. But disappointing.

Very glad to get your letter. I'll send a couple of things for the literary magazine, but won't be surprised if Valerie doesn't want any of them. The 'Mycenae' piece was really scringed out. I've always had this great affection for the Watchman at the beginning of the *Oresteia* – setting the whole fuck-up in motion by having to announce the victory fires and the return of big Aggie – and I felt I could merge with him somehow. But it all feels so dutifully clinker-built, coopered and hooped, no madness or getaway. Ah well.

Field Day has gone dead for me. I cannot believe in the reality of the theatre work that is going afoot and don't feel related to it. I don't mean this to be a challenge or a declaration of intent to withdraw, just a statement of the emotional case. Of course, the ashy element is in all of my life, and has to do with the stalled 'creativity' – which has to do in its turn with too much that should be – should have been – ploughed up and grubbed down in other areas of my life and work. All the same, almost a year after that holding action of that meeting in January in the Wellington Park, I am even less devoted to the idea of carrying the FD banner. I'm trudging with the good remnant of Rea and Deane, but don't have the spring in the step. The lodge is dispersed, really. There was a sense of breach after the resolutions of January failed to become resolutions of spirit. Colette – what does she do, what is her future to be? I panic and resent all at once when I think how the deck-clearing and dis-engagement that went on with Gary was all gone back on, somehow. We are going to be in huge debt, I feel, before long, on fronts other than the anthology. I got a letter from Orla K. telling me she had been appointed by FD (before I got the recent bulletin) and it made me both bewildered and angry. Angry because, again, I cannot credit that we are really an organization capable of employing anybody. I'm rattling on here and won't re-read what I've written because I know it [is] incoherent and I'd want to throw it away. I suppose the coherent thing *would* be to get out. But I'll talk to you after December 22 [. . .]

Seamus

The '"Mycenae" piece' was 'Mycenae Lookout' (*The Spirit Level*): each of its five sections is voiced by a different character from Aeschylus's *Agamemnon* ('big Aggie'), the first play in the *Oresteia* cycle; the first voice heard is that of the Watchman.

To Stanisław Barańczak

TS Barańczak

23 November 1994 — 191 Strand Road, Dublin 4

Dear Stanisław,

This Friday evening, in Dublin, I am doing a reading with an Irish piper, Liam Og O'Flynn, who plays those deep-toned, deep-droned, elbow-bellowed jobs – the uilleann pipes, from the word *uile*, meaning elbow in Irish. It sent me back to the *Laments*, because Liam has many slow airs and laments from the traditional repertoire and I wanted to choose a selection from Kochanowski to match the music. But, of course, I got stuck into revisions – initially because I wanted to give the diction of the first lament a Hiberno-English feel for the occasion – using 'lament' and 'slow air' in the poem itself. But then I thought, why not *retain* the change? It sounds wonderfully but not picturesquely Irish. And so, of course, I was off . . . I enclose the results and hope you won't go apoplectic. This time I was going through the lines with Jonathan Galassi's demurral in mind – his feeling that in places the clinching, confident quality of the rhyming worked against the authenticity of the grief. And I did feel, for example, that the eyes/sighs pairing so soon in 'Lament 1' was not what we wanted – especially when we fly the banner of threnodies/Simonides so magnificently at the very start. At any rate, *cher ami*, I'm hoping you'll agree to some of the proposals. I am especially attracted to my worst transgression/liberty at lines 17/18 of the first poem. But I'll let you suffer the rest without forward warning, and hope that this will have reached you before I reach Kraków on Friday week. I greatly look forward to the whole visit. To seeing you both and to seeing the country. To swanking in Polish translation and mooning around in your light. Love to all Barańczaks.

Seamus

Liam O'Flynn (1945–2018) performed on the uilleann pipes both as soloist and with other musicians; he and SH would go on to collaborate in concert programmes of poetry and music that took them not just around Ireland but abroad as well, and a studio recording of the two of them was released by Claddagh Records in 2003 under the title *The Poet and the Piper*.

To John Kelly

TS Kelly

30 November 1994 191 Strand Road, Dublin 4

Dear John,

Full marks and grace notes. Boke of the Month Club stuff. I read most of it in the real presence as he and I jigged south to Cork for a gig last Saturday. Unfortunately, I didn't get to the bit where our hero becomes Liam Og, but there were multiple yelps and tremors and abacks of laughter, so much so that L.O. was showing signs of becoming as irked as the spouse in the bed when too much of the yelp and tremor and aback is going on (from one's reading in a book, you fool) while she is trying to get to sleep.

You got a great race at it and you got a great go at it – like your man the sergeant who does the long jump in *At Swim-Two*. And you took off. There's a marvellous freewheeling vivacity and a spot-on ear. Wonderful fly insinuating cadences. Brilliant swerves and dashes and solo runs. I loved the way the cornerboy chic and the high-class Hibernoid and parodic allusive are kept going at full tilt neck and neck to the end. The mode you establish lets you get away with nearly anything. What matters is the ould plausible rascality of tone. It lifted the heart. And it covered a lot of ground, literally and memorably. That big man with the boots on the back of the lorry in Dungloe. Och aye. And the unanswerable. Much preening as well as much admiration. Don't do it down, even though you may have written it quickly. Solemn oafs are going about the world with unapologetic self-regard, so if only to twart them (as the Covey – is it – says) walk tall. The writing has got a touch of lightning in it, so just let the rumblers go to hell. Tell Hammond to tell you my story about McLaverty's story about Somerset Maugham and the reporter . . .

Meanwhile, I'm away to the land of the zloty. But should be back home for midnight mass.

Seamus

The Northern Irish broadcaster and writer John Kelly (b.1965) had recently published his first novel, *Grace Notes and Bad Thoughts*, which he now describes as 'basically sub-Flann O'Brien eejitry for the amusement of friends'.

The 'real presence' was David Hammond, who had first introduced Kelly to SH; 'L.O.' was Liam O'Flynn.

There is a character in Sean O'Casey's *The Plough and the Stars* (1926) called the Young Covey.

To Adrian Rice

PC Rice

7 December 1994

Dear Adrian, I'm sorry to have been so dilatory in getting in touch. I am headed at this minute to Munich: I was in Kraków and Warsaw for the last 5 days. I feel like an old wireless dial.

[. . .]

To Jerzy Illg

MS PNL

12 December 1994 — 191 Strand Road, Dublin 4

Dear Jerzy,

You will excuse – I hope – this brief note: you deserve an epic symphony of gratitude and celebration because of the immense kindness – and efficiency – you displayed during my visit to Kraków. I shall never forget it. From the first moment of welcome at the airport (when I knew immediately that I was in good hands) to the way you arranged – at great expense – to have the trumpeter play, I knew this was going to be one of the special moments in my life. To meet dear friends like the Barańczaks, to have a book of poems published in Polish, to receive a phone-call from Czesław, to meet the extraordinary Szymborska, to feast and drink with poets in your home, to meet your wife, your children, your excellent staff in the bookshop – my cup flowed over, as they say in Scripture.

Thank you also for arranging the flight. I look forward to meeting you again, in Kraków perhaps.

With great respect and affection.

Seamus

The literary critic, journalist and teacher Jerzy Illg (b.1950), as head of the publishing house Znak, based in Kraków, had welcomed SH to the city for the launch of Stanisław Barańczak's translations of his poems under the title *44 wiersze*. SH had remarked to Illg on the trumpet call that sounds every hour from the tallest tower of Kraków's St Mary's Basilica, and was told that it had been arranged as a fanfare for him.

The poet Wisława Szymborska (1923–2012) would go on to receive the Nobel Prize in Literature the year after SH himself.

1995

This was the year of the award to SH of the Nobel Prize in Literature, the public announcement of which reached him while he and Marie Heaney were holidaying with friends in Greece.

Letters to Henri Cole and Tom Sleigh, written prior to that, are printed here to show something of the society that SH found congenial during his periods of teaching at Harvard; letters to other friends and feasting companions are included in later sections.

This was also the year when SH, after long hesitation, accepted a commission from the US publishers W. W. Norton and Co. to translate the Old English heroic poem *Beowulf*, then immediately set to work on it.

To Patrick Crotty

TS Crotty

8 March 1995 — 191 Strand Road, Dublin 4

Dear Patrick,

Your sending the autobiographical/critical sketches was much appreciated. As I may have said to you, one of my favourite anthologies ever was Miłosz and Peter Dale Scott's *Postwar Polish Poetry*, done in Penguin some time in the late sixties; and what made it so alive and convincing was the sense of the editors' personal engagement and deep reading and seriousness of purpose – all communicated without strain in the statement that preceded each poet's entry. Your book will have a unique claim because of your hard work and readiness to make judgements – the *tone* of your headnotes distinguishes them every bit as much as the content. It will also be an enormous help in undergraduate courses, and will probably give the Blackstaff anthology a commercial edge over competitors in the end. Which is why you should be sure to look to the contract and try to see ahead and take care of reprints and American rights and so on. You could have a steady seller on your hands.

Any praise I want to give you will be suspect, of course, as some form of payback for the high and gratifying terms in which you talk about this particular scribe. I am very proud and touched that you can shoot the rapids of the Yeats and Lowell rivers, and carry yourself and your cargo so confidently through. Usually I wince and wobble, even when such invocations are well-intended; but somehow you manage to up the ante and at the same time to sound persuasive. Because, probably, you *write* rather than just annotate. And this assured phrasing and phasing of your critical judgements all through give me immense pleasure. I'll just go through some of my favourite formulations, if only to assure you that your efforts and felicities have one deeply receptive reader. (This is by no means a total list of the exhilaration points – just a brief list where the applause meter needed a few extra gradations at the top.) Kavanagh being read 'a shade too comfortably'; and the 'ostentatiously ramshackle' aspect of things in 'The Hospital'. Hats off for the curry-combing of *Autumn Journal* in regard to De Valera's Ireland; and to Rodgers turning to sexual love 'with the zeal of a convert'. Geniality and social justice is such a fine pairing for Hutchinson, and agility and grandiloquence (plus their sources) for Kinsella. Longley's 'bulwark' and Derek's 'whimsy into vision' are fine perceptions. And then there's nice stricture too, in relation to Paulin's 'ultimately equivocal critique'; and nice puzzlement over Medbh's seesaw between 'post-modernist relativism and radical feminism'. Your note on Matthew Sweeney is a masterpiece of the genre, not only because of the clinch and elegance of 'miniaturist of estrangement' but the (to me) soaring bonus in the use of the word 'discommoding'. I wish I had done that first . . . Anyhow, the whole thing is carried through with great integrity and care and I salute it. I just wondered about one sentence, in the Richard Murphy piece. I am being over-scrupulous, I know, and over-protective of a master of self-distancing, but I felt when I read that sentence about his being excluded from the world of unselfconscious intensity of seals and girls that there could be a little indication that it is 'the speaker in the poem' rather than 'the poet in real life' who is being characterized: could you substitute 'presents himself as' for 'is finally'? Excuse the fuss . . .

I'm delighted too that we'll be seeing each other at and maybe before and after the Synge school. We'll be in touch nearer the time, I'm sure. In fact, I'll be in touch with you again – or maybe my Harvard printing person will – to let you have a look at a few poems. Not altogether a settled book but a thrown shape. Some time, if you have boos or boasts or suggestions or censures, I'll be glad to hear from you. But in the meantime, this is just to acknowledge with gratitude and admiration your own 'keeping going'. Delighted to hear that the *bean a' tighe* is taking to the teaching again. All our love to all of you. And never ate black puddins on a Friday.

Drown the shamrock!
Seamus

Patrick Crotty (b.1952), himself a poet, then lecturer in English and Welsh Studies at Trinity College Carmarthen, was the editor of *Modern Irish Poetry: An Anthology* (1995), published by Blackstaff Press.

Czesław Miłosz was in fact sole editor of the Penguin *Post-War Polish Poetry* (1965); the Canadian poet Peter Dale Scott (b.1929) occasionally worked with him on translating his poems into English.

Among the poets and poems in Crotty's anthology picked out for comment by SH: Patrick Kavanagh's 'The Hospital' opens with 'A year ago I fell in love with the functional ward / Of a chest hospital', and concludes by asserting, 'we must record love's mystery without claptrap, / Snatch out of time the passionate transitory'; the Scottish-born, Irish-raised Pearse Hutchinson (1927–2012) travelled widely before settling back in Ireland where he was supported by a pension from Aosdána; the Northern Irish W. R. Rodgers, after serving as a Presbyterian minister, spent most of his working life in London, where Matthew Sweeney (1952–2018) was currently living.

'Drown the shamrock': a St Patrick's Day (17 March) ceremony involving the dipping of a shamrock into the glass before a toast to the saint is drunk.

To Ted Hughes

MS BL

14 March 1995

Glanmore Cottage, Ashford,
Co. Wicklow

Dear Ted,

Matthew's letter jolted me. And not because of its frank address to money matters and its real interest in moving things along on the *Schoolbag* front. It made me wince that I had not long ago written to you, to thank you for – among other things – the new *Selected* and the paperback *Pollen*. When I saw 'Chaucer' in the *New Yorker* a few weeks ago I reeled for joy. The emerald and the laundry. They were like the streamers of spring, of the Shelleyan spark scattered, new life from huge sorrow. The poem began and ended with immense promise. And in between all was exalted. And then I opened the 'uncollected' section of the new book and found myself like canvas in a big wind. Which I could not rebuff. The poem about the vision of your mother and her sister and you mistaken for her brother – well, I suppose that [is] what the poem is about all right, but what it is is sheer poetry. And it is wonderfully placed as a prelude to what follows. I was deeply moved to find 'The Earthenware Head' again, a poem which had stayed in me from the moment I read it years ago. But I was quite unprepared for the agon(y) of 'Black Coat' and 'The God' – like a 'Prelude' turned inside out. The total engagement of those poems is exhausting and beautiful because of the total candour and the unleashed, justified anger. Intelligence rampant, as it were. So head on, and not just with the 'you' of the poems; as much, more, with the ring of 'them' at bay around the poem-hearth. It is all really quite heart-breaking to contemplate. The positive truth in it all is that your book is as lightning-packed for me in the final pages, in the 1990s, as it is/was for the me who read the early poems in the 1960s. Those Sylvia poems and 'Opus 131' and 'Lines about Elias' set the guy-ropes thrumming. Groundswell and emptiness. Your courage and endurance and fecundity and brave solitude count for everything. When I read the poems, I just want to dwell in the daunting feel of them, but even if blurting out impressions is a kind of misrepresentation of the reality of the experience of reading them, I still want to let you know how gratefully shaken I was when I went through them. And there's all the rest of the book as well. *Gaudens gaudeo.* (And I was proud of T. Paulin the other night on the *Late Show*. I'm sure somebody must have told you that he said – rightly but so strangely in the context of that rabid gossip arena – that you were to be revered. As poet and as example of good behaviour. The verb was both unexpected and elevating.)

The month of April is more or less clear for me, and much of May, and I could do something purposeful then for the anthology. But I feel we should realign, take squarings again, pow-wow for an hour, sit and look at the same horizon, just to get in tune. Would April Fool's Day be a possible date for a visit? I am to do the recording for the new Faber cassette series on Friday 31, in London, and I could make another day of it, if it suited you. Or perhaps you might like to come to London, either for dinner on the Friday night or for lunch on the Saturday? See what you feel like, and don't feel you have to do anything. For God's sake, don't change any arrangements you might already have.

[. . .]

I've been flirting with the anima and have written a very few poems. But there are weeds in the cracks at last. Love to you both.

Seamus

Matthew Evans at Faber and Faber had reminded SH and Hughes of their long-unfulfilled contract to produce an anthology of poems for use in schools.

Hughes's *New Selected Poems 1957–1994*, recently published by Faber, included poems which later formed part of his *Birthday Letters* (1998) but which, presented in this context, received scant attention from reviewers of the book; SH, however, evidently saw them for the bold, intimate revelations that they were. 'Chaucer' was another poem destined for *Birthday Letters*.

Tom Paulin, a frequent guest on the BBC arts programme *The Late Show*, had fiercely and eloquently defended Hughes's *New Selected*, and Hughes's reputation in general, against the disdain and carping of fellow guests.

To Henri Cole

MS H. Cole

14 March 1995 — 191 Strand Road, Dublin 4

Dear Henri,

The time, the speed, the distance . . . All of a sudden it's almost a year since we did the interview and still no conclusion . . . Australia, Christmas, some poems, much distraction intervened, but this weekend I got involved again with the big draft and will be sending Roxann a revised version of most of it in a few days. Then, if you don't mind, I'd like to look at it all again. I'll have Roxann send you a copy of the preliminary revised text: the revisions I'm making are mostly in the cause of legibility, sense, grammar – trimming the style, making the statements more compact and pointed, and so on. I am not altering the substance of what was said.

What may require some thought is the blocking of it, the shaping or I should say re-shaping. Of course, there is much to be said for a certain randomness but I'd like it to be the best randomness we can arrange, so to speak.

Anyhow, I am confident that I shall be putting in another spurt after I get the clean copy out of the computer, and at that point we can talk again. Perhaps after reading period, in May? I know you'll be going fifty to the dozen between now and then . . . And am very conscious that I am adding to your woes with the Boylston Prize. I thank you for taking it on and was gratified to learn that we have a rabbi to represent 'the pulpit' this year.

Meanwhile, I have been reading *The Look of Things*. I hope you did not take it amiss that I did not supply a quote for the jacket. Apart from the hurry in my life when the request arrived, there is a whole history of my *not* having done this kind of thing for many friends and acquaintances – a circumstance which makes it easier to repeat the refusal and harder to contemplate acceptance (what would X and Y say now that he's doing it for Z?) But enough. Thank you for the gift of the beautifully produced book and buoyantly composed poems. The combination of susceptibility to colour and sensuousness and awareness of desolation and pain makes for a kind of sorrowful richness. The blackcurrant liqueur and octopus ink of the opening poem run together in an emblematic kind of way in my mind, bitter knowledge and relished sensation. Of the latter, what beats 'The Bird Show at Aubagne'? For the former, what excels 'Aix'? And the combination is there, subtly and sadly, in 'Supper with Roy', 'Sacrament', 'Harvard Classics', 'The Christological Year' . . . I could go on. But, of course, I rejoice greatly in 'Une Lettre à New York' as well, where the rapturous tendency is given its head and earns its keep entirely. 'Tarantula'! 'And He Kissed Me . . .', 'Christmas in Carthage'. The book has a real force because the seriousness and pain behind the poems get transformed into their doings as 'verbal contraptions' selving, going themselves, transforming. And so too, of course, the pleasure behind them also becomes a pleasuring, of language, through language. The blessing of that cabbage-butterfly is all the more because of its placing! I was glad to hear you say that the Harvard reading gave you a lift, because so it should. There is a trueness that touches, a far thing in the work that brings it close. Close, that is, not dose . . .

Time I stopped, obviously. My love to all the Kirklanders. Drown the shamrock, if you have not already done so . . .

Affectionately,
Seamus

The US poet Henri Cole (b.1956) was at this time Brigg-Copeland Lecturer in Poetry at Harvard; his interview with SH, commissioned by the *Paris Review*, eventually appeared, much revised, in issue 144, Fall 1997, of the magazine; Roxann Brown was an administrative assistant in the English Language and Literature Department at Harvard, assisting SH.

Cole's fourth book of poems, *The Look of Things*, was published in January 1995.

'selving, going themselves': see Hopkins's 'Each mortal thing does one thing and the same . . . Selves – goes itself . . .' ('As Kingfishers Catch Fire').

Harvard's creative writers had offices in a house on Kirkland Street, Cambridge: hence 'Kirklanders'.

To Tom Sleigh

MS Sleigh

13 April 1995

Glanmore Cottage, Ashford,
Co. Wicklow

Dear Tom,

It's not that I have not been thinking about you. I have, quite a bit. And the thoughts have as ever been tinged with second thoughts: for example, I was sorry after you rang that time in the summer that I had not urged you to come over. The usual hunched, wild-eyed panic about how I could do this and that and still have time for the spacious pleasures of Sleigh-rides in Wicklow intervened too automatically. Somehow, the chance had come and gone in a moment. And then too I've been bugged by the idea that I saw a letter from you in a big mail-pile – perhaps when I came back from Australia or Poland last autumn – and that I put it aside to read properly, after the rush-through for crisis-stuff, and then never found it. At any rate, I am haunted by this notion and only hope I am mistaken.

It's my birthday and it is a day of utterly vernal Easter. Holy Thursday indeed. Fifty-sixth birthday. The fact that I'm actually sitting out in the open air (cf. Mark Twain on the English countryside) will give you some idea of the extraordinary pause and poise of the weather. Loveliest-of-trees time. In fact, the Housman cherry is blooming its snowflakes over my head – and there aren't no fifty springs left no more 'to look on things in bloom'. *The Work*. The work. Chimes at midnight. La la. Awful but – well, not cheerful either.

Since early December – no, January – I've managed to get down here to the cottage every week, sometimes for three nights, more usually for two. I do my 'correspondence' with my helper-woman on Monday, and phonecalls and fuckabouts, and try to get away 8/9-ish in the evening. Going back then Thursday lunchtime. It has been extremely good for me, and even though I have been back and forward to England and the north at weekends, for various readings and meetings, I have managed to pivot myself on silence and work time. Wrote six or seven poems in late January, early February, had a rush of conviction and threw the shape of a book together. But it is not yet 'there', although my anxiety is somewhat allayed. Meanwhile – hush, hush, I guess – I've started on *Beowulf*. You remember I turned down the commission in the early '80s, and have kept backing away ever since? Well, finally (clearly no rush on *Beowulf* – this correspondence has been in suspension for 14 years!) the editor wrote and said, OK, we know you're not going to do it, so just recommend somebody else. I replied by return (on March 21) that I'd do it myself, and have knocked off 400 lines since. Voices singing in the ear that this is all folly. Other insurance-policy voice saying, well, at the end of the year, at least you'll have *something* to show for the Sabbatical. Some of it – anywhere that a boat floats – very bewitching. Most of it pretty hall-troop and Weland's work kind of stuff. The formal speeches especially. Ah well, Fitzgerald gets Homer, Pinsky gets Dante, Walcott gets both and Seamus gets *Beo*. Serves him right for doing Anglo-Saxon in the first place. (Made up my own kenning – when the *Beowulf* boys come off the boat and stand their spears up I call it the 'seafarers' stook' – but is it worth doing three thousand lines to get one touch of originality?)

Had a lovely weekend in Cracow with S. Barańczak before Christmas. His translations of my verses came out and we did readings there and in Warsaw. But the feel of Cracow – great square, market place, cafés, baroque churches, closeness of quarters of old town, kitchen-life of the poet-persons (practically *Sol Poste* in its credibility) – was something unique. It had duration-life, as the Gutenberg elegist might say. I came away from it as if I had been for an indeterminate but salubrious time immersed in Miłosz. (Who called the kitchen where we were after the book-launch and told me I was there 'in very good hands' – but with wonderful Slavic slouch and trail to the words, as you can imagine.)

I love being off teaching and as the spring weather opens up and the whins go gold and the sycamore fantails for us, I ask myself how I am going to face Warren House and a lecture course and a workshop. Not much, in a way; but a whole absconding from this open-souled time.

Will *The Work* be out soon? It stays with me as a pressure and bulwark of a book. A line drawn, a ground stood and a pain constellated. Also a book that makes me want to write myself, because of the way it has found a ground for its sounding, a first stratum which is the string, the strum, that the whole thing is tuned to. I've not read it recently, but it has found its place in me as a certain register.

My love to Ellen. The one thing I truly miss this year is the rejuvenation of Stinson courting and Dothan-doting and Washington wonking (I *said* wonking). My love to them all, and to any ambient Ukrainian you may encounter. Four years, and I'll be visiting schoolchildren – again.

Love,
Seamus

Poet, essayist and academic Tom Sleigh (b.1953) had been Professor of English at Dartmouth College, in New Hampshire, since 1986. He and SH met in 1984, after a reading at the Fine Arts Work Center in Provincetown. When Sleigh sent him his first book of poems, *After One* (1983), SH invited him to lunch in Cambridge and friendship developed from there.

Mark Twain had called the English countryside 'too absolutely beautiful to be left out doors'; allusions to Housman, Shakespeare and Elizabeth Bishop (her poem 'The Bight') follow thick and fast in one of SH's more than usually packed paragraphs.

'*The Work*': a sequence of poems Sleigh was writing after his father's death, its title altered to *The Chain* when it was published the following year.

SH's 'helper-woman' was Susie Tyrrell.

Sol Poste was a Portuguese restaurant where SH, Sleigh, Sven Birkerts (b.1951), essayist and author of *The Gutenberg Elegies*, and Askold Melnyczuk (b.1954), writer, translator and the 'ambient Ukrainian' of the final paragraph, were wont to gather. Ellen Driscoll was Sleigh's wife and they lived at Stinson Court, while Birkerts and his wife lived on Dothan Street, in the Boston suburb of Arlington.

To Stanisław Barańczak

TS Barańczak

28 April 1995 [Glanmore Cottage, Ashford, Co. Wicklow]

<I wrote this down in Wicklow earlier to-day, on my increasingly beloved laptop . . . >

[. . .] I have been bogged deep in another translation. Although you don't get bogged in ironworks, come to think of it: *Beowulf* (for that's what I'm at) is composed of ingots of Anglo-Saxon, peremptorily dumped clang-lumps of language, brutal bard-ballast that modern English cannot budge or break open. Like trying to assault that castle in Cracow with knitting needles. I see and hear my lines like clotheslines pegged out with little tinkling trinkets and tin-bits and keepsakes, while the original is something brutal and Soviet steelman-stalinesque, more tanklike than trinketty. But after all, as you can see, I do enjoy the impossibility of it, which means that with combine-like tedium, I keep facing it down in Wicklow, a bit entranced, a bit reluctant to leave the labour of it. Anything more different from *Treny* is hard to imagine. No anima in the poetry, it seems – except when the sea enters. Bóats bring óut the beáuty in the médium. (Christ! an Anglo-Saxon line, unpremeditated, I swear, noticed afterwards as I read through this.)

[. . .]

To David Batterham MS Batterham

23 May 1995 [Arklow, Co. Wicklow]

Dear David,

Funny the places I end up writing letters in . . . Usually I find myself pacing the pages against the pilot as he takes us in to Heathrow or Shannon – a definite perversity, that, doing it airborne and against the clock. But to-day I'm in the foreman's office in a garage in Arklow, Co. Wicklow. Marie left the keys of the house and the keys of the car in the door of 191 the other night and they were gone in the morning (the milkman?) so much re-boring and rebuffing and all that, including this visit to Behan's, the Nissan people of Wicklow. (As a matter of fact, it gives me more of a high to have access to a Behan office than, say, a Blackwells one – I feel grown up at last when the garage man treats me as a friend and not a fool. This particular contender I got to know in the 1970s in Ashford – went boozing with him on the night when his first – and only – child was born. The bondings!)

[. . .]

The London-based antiquarian bookseller David Batterham was married to Marie Heaney's sister Val (1943–2023). He is also the author of a book of highly amusing letters to the painter Howard Hodgkin (1932–2017), *Dear Howard: Tales Told in Letters* (2018), largely about encounters with eccentric book dealers in France and elsewhere.

To Bernard and Jane McCabe TS J. McCabe

28 May 1995 191 Strand Road, Dublin 4

Dear Bernard and Jane,

Apple PowerBook. Collapse of archaic man. Farewell to the quill, the vellum, the scratch of the *pen* – of course! that's where the word came from! – the ink-spurter, as Flann O'Brien called it . . .

Enclosed are slightly disturbing evidences of new poetic activity. I deeply enjoyed writing the 'Dialect Versions' but would not be surprised if you enjoined me to cut it out . . . there is an element of schoolboy humour, I agree, sixth form snigger. Does one get away with it? I ask because I so much valued, Bernard, your response to the whole manuscript and the beautiful alertness and care with which you picked up on those tics and habits. *I* should have been more alert and careful and answered promptly – in case you thought I was huff-huffing, than which nothing could have been further from the case. I burbled something into your answering machine too late, I think, since you had already pleasured away to gooseland. Anyhow, I did act on the recommendations, brought 'The Rain Stick' up to be the first poem in the book, put the MacDiarmid poem in the penult. posit., dropped 'Damson' (there goes an 'I love'), changed 'I love' in 'At Banagher' to 'And more power to him . . .' and did a job on one or two of those 'alls'. Cadenced closure injunctions to be treated soon . . . (I'll be interested, of course, to see if you think I get away with the new Mycenae things.)

Gooseland. Roman remains in museum at Périgueux. *Les grottes.* I personally am very regretful that I could not be there for a while, because I have this 'epiphany' poignancy in remembering a late arrival in the Périgueux museum one afternoon in July 1981, while we were at Domme, near Sarlat, in a gîte, the kids all 14 years younger . . . Anyhow, I didn't have enough time in the place and promised myself to come back. I also remember sitting later on with small sharp wife (Herbert, the dog!) in [a] sunsetty, mellow tile 'n bricky *place* or *parc* as the boules clocked and borped and we considered where to go for some good old *ancienne cuisine*. End of flashback. No doubt you had mellow soirées and poignancies and rich munchings, riparian sloths and fluvial reveries. Reverruns. Gras-sy banks. Meanwhile, s.s.w. has been constantly and anxiously bowed to the books, the fine swimmer's back and shoulders humbly hunched, the sauce-sniffing, herb-scenting nose to the grindstone, the whole energy concentrated on getting through to noon on Tuesday 30 May when it all stops. She has been greatly focused and truly tense about it all – nobody should be doing exams in their fifties! – and I am glad to have been around, even if it was only to keep out of the way. I believe she will, of course, pass the whole thing with *les couleurs* flying, but she has not had much joy these past few weeks. Reward in our case is a trip to Spain, to Anne and Ignacio in Asturias for three weeks in July. Hoorray.

[. . .] Did I tell you I have finally agreed to translate *Beowulf* for Nortons? Anyhow, Grendel's mum and all that looms. I have just got to line 845 where the *mod-werig* Grendel goes to the *nicor-mere* and the melody of mourning becomes irresistible. I suppose one does it for those keens and slow airs that swim up out of the fenmists (fenmist criticism, *ja*?) and for the bewitching interludes – so few, so short – of sea-travel, the floater on the waves, in close under cliffs, the foamy-necked, most like a fowl. No anima, it would seem, elsewhere in the poetry. [. . .]

The 'Dialect Versions' are not readily identified.

'Herbert, the dog!': Bernard's brother, the Dominican priest and theologian, Herbert McCabe (1926–2001).

'nose to the grindstone': Marie Heaney was completing her MPhil in Irish Studies under the aegis of University College Dublin.

To Donagh Cronin

TS Cronin

9 June 1995 191 Strand Road, Dublin 4

Dear Donagh Cronin,

The harvest bow you sent is a lovely specimen, and I hope you don't mind if I keep it. The ones my father made were from new wheat straw and consequently were a bit larger and shinier.

Unfortunately, I don't feel I can go along with the project you suggest. It is an original idea, of course, and I am flattered that the poem should have inspired you to think of it. But there would be far too many crossed lines in it for me. The poem would be, as you suggest, a sort of up-market tag to ratify the product, and my instinct is that such a use of it goes against the ethics of the art.

There's no reason why you shouldn't go ahead with the sale of the harvest bow on its own. It's a beautiful thing and you clearly have a good supplier to hand – and people would be glad to wear them.

I appreciate the notice you gave me, the preparations you made and the proposal all round. I am sorry not to be saying yes.

Sincerely,
Seamus Heaney

Donagh Cronin explains: 'A local man, by the name of Jimmy Howard, made harvest bows. My proposal to Seamus Heaney was that we sell the harvest bows attached to a card with the poem printed on it. The card could also include a little history of the bows and the poem.'

SH's poem 'The Harvest Bow' is in *Field Work*.

To Dennis O'Driscoll

TS Emory

7 September 1995 191 Strand Road, Dublin 4

Dear Dennis,

By a happy coincidence, your letter arrived on a day when I was at last getting some dream-time: I was headed for Glanmore to have a final think about the poem MS and to clear my head about – among other things – the title, when lo and behold, your wonderful, exhaustive, attentive, and (for you) all too time-consuming pages came to hand. Like you, I too have had a summer of toings and froings. Luckily, the time in Spain was utterly rewarding, utterly quiet, but too short. I had two weeks in the same place, the same house, no phone calls, no duties other than self-imposed ones like taking my in-laws to eat out or applying sun-tan oil to Mrs H.'s fine swimmer's back and shoulders . . . And at the beginning of the trip, en route to Pescara to pick up the Premio Flaiano bounty, I lost my address book. Left it on a phone shelf in the International Arrivals lounge at Milano. *Sì. Sì.* What would Freud have said anyway? It upset me for a day and then I took it as an absolution from and by the world. (B. Friel wrote me a card later to say that it was on display in Kenny's where they were turning a page a day.) Anyhow, I came back in early August and got on the school bus. To Oxford for Robert Graves, to Sligo for Willie, to Derry for Sean O'Casey – or rather for Shivaun. Then a bit later, Swansea. And then Finland, for the best part of a week. A book of selected poems (called, in Finnish, *The King of the Ditchbacks*) out there and an appearance at the Helsinki Festival. The reward was a chance to talk to Brodsky for a couple of hours. Like yourself, he brings me to life with a combination of care for poetry and good judgement, not to say horse sense, about it and about life in general. Then the usual pile-ups of mail and entries of visitors, familial and professional.

[. . .]

Your worries about the title focused a vague unease in myself and I immediately telephoned Fabers, only to find that they have printed next Spring's catalogue with *The Spirit Level* irretrievably advertised therein. You will see from the attached queries – which I put together last night and am sending to Chris Reid – how I propose to do some damage limitation in this situation, but I want to thank you for being so clear and honest about your reactions in the first place. You will also see that I have taken cognizance of many of your suggestions and probings and can be sure that I'll pay attention to others at the proof stage, such as, for example, your vigilance about the discrepancies of spelling and phrasing in 'The Swing'. I had dropped 'A Transgression' in the meantime, and in 'Tollund' I may well go back to grags and quags. I just suddenly took a notion that I was too like myself altogether in that bit of burring and agging, but of course I have a soft spot for the hard a's.

Needless to say, I am moved and helped by the generous things you say about the poems and personally very delighted that 'The Gravel Walks' comes home to you so sweetly. And that 'Postscript' and 'Keeping Going' ring the bell or at least roll the drum. I know what you mean about 'An Architect' but somehow I have manoeuvred myself into a position where if I take it out it will look to Robin W.'s family that I am slighting the memory of the dead. *Ochone*, *ochone*. 'The Thimble' is a *jeu*, partly a criticism of the whole whimsical/inventive genre, partly an indulgence in it. I have a soft spot for it too because I wrote it in ten minutes in bed one morning and didn't know where the hell it came from.

[. . .]

Simon Armitage's new book is terrific. I skimmed through it on my way to Oxford, after he had interviewed me for *Stanza*. The big long poem at the end about the bonfire is hugely on to something, wonderfully ram-stamming into the actual conditions and at the same time up and away in the language, unfettered, the new recklessness with an old caring deep at the heart of it. Hats off. I agree, he's the goods. (I did not see Hofmann's review, but Armitage will come through all that – and, alas, is probably due some more, just because he's bound to race the envy pulse. Not that I'd expect it to throb in Hofmann . . .)

You are too scrupulous about the shredding of correspondence to me. Please do not worry about that. I greatly and for ever value our friendship and your verity and it would be a source of pride to me to think that it might be preserved in some shape or form.

My love to Julie and my good hopes for your life in the new/old house. 'Ketu' will always be associated in my mind with your help and guidance at that crucial moment of my life.

Love to you both
Seamus

PS News just in of the death of a dear old aunt in Co. Derry. My mother's sister, one of the 'don't point, don't stir' school of sisters . . . We'll see you sooner rather than later, I hope.

S.

'your wonderful . . . pages came to hand': O'Driscoll was a valued – perhaps increasingly the most valued – and very diligent reader of SH's work in progress, commenting, in this instance, on what was to be *The Spirit Level*.

'Premio Flaiano': in a letter of Thomas Flanagan on 5 June, SH had written: 'Meanwhile, the good news is that some Italian outfit – Premio Internazionale Flaiano, situated in Pescara on the Adriatic – are going to hand over a wad of *lire* in mid-July.' He was the first non-Italian winner in the poetry category of this prize.

Kenny's is a bookshop in Galway.

'Chris[topher] Reid' had succeeded Craig Raine as Poetry Editor at Faber in 1991.

'An Architect' is about the Irish modernist Robin Walker (1924–91).

The new book by Yorkshire poet Simon Armitage (b.1963) was *The Dead Sea Poems*, which Michael Hofmann (b.1957) had reviewed cuttingly. *Stanza* was the name of a radio show that Simon Armitage presented at this time.

The 'dear old aunt' who had died was Annie McCann, who worked in nursing and care in the Belfast area throughout her career, and lived in Castledawson.

To Ted Hughes

PC BL

7 October 1995 [Postmarked 'Baile Átha Cliath' (Dublin) '17 October']

Was telephoning on Friday evening, immediately after I heard the news. Wanted to say how much you were on my mind and how deep the sense of gratitude takes hold – for all that you have done to help me and the effort. Seamus

PS En route from Athens.
PPS Forgot to post this. Your letter a fort for the soul. S.

The 'news', received while the Heaneys were on holiday in Greece, was that SH had been awarded the 1995 Nobel Prize in Literature. The card, written in Greece but mailed from Dublin, shows a view from inside the entrance to the Treasury of Atreus, Mycenae.

Back home, SH must have found waiting for his return the letter of congratulations of 8 October in which Hughes wrote: 'Like a sea-god on a great wave you emerged and inevitably took it [the Prize], by sovereignty of nature' (*Letters of Ted Hughes*, 2007).

To Sorley and Renee MacLean — PC NLS

7 October 1995 [Postmarked 'Baile Átha Cliath' (Dublin) '17 October']

It could be Skye . . . Thinking of you at this moment, en route back into the fray. Seamus

Sorley MacLean and his wife Renee lived on Skye. The postcard shows an image of the Acropolis at Mycenae: mainly low stone walls, rubble, grass and trees, under a cloudy sky.

Like the card to Hughes, this one was written in Greece and mailed from home. It seems likely, from these two examples, that SH was eager to communicate at once with poets of a stature that might equally have been recognised by the award of the Nobel Prize.

To Mary and Desmond Kavanagh — PC Kavanagh

12 October 1995

'Our shells clacked on the plates . . .' No more perfect celebration of our happiness could be devised. We ate them deliberately. Pure verb we were. Poetry and freedom. A thousand thanks.

Seamus

The postcard shows Barrie Cooke's painting *Megaceros Hibernicus*; SH's message alludes to his *Field Work* poem 'Oysters', the Kavanaghs having sent a gift of oysters to congratulate him on the Nobel award.

To Bernard and Jane McCabe — MS NLI

31 December 1995

Dear Bernard and Jane,

More than usual, I don't want this old year to end. Feel that the day must be marked with recollection, of all our joys with you both since the Nobel news. I'll never forget the happiness of driving with you from Cheltenham that Saturday morning. Our magical pub stop. The sense of extraness in nipping in to the house in Snitton! The utter rightness of the restaurant. The hare. The *vins*. The pleasure of collision and come-uppance with the next door/next table swank-fart. *Et alors*, Stockholm. All the hooray-ore that underlay us there. And to have the children on the spot with both of you: such circle-closing and heart-stirrings and laugh-launches and love-lifts. Down to the *scriptorium* tale on radio! I wanted to embrace ye every time I saw ye. Will see ye again as soon as poss. in the year ahead. NO Horncastling either: it's our turn. Eeek, as Catherine used to eke in anticipation. The cup flows over. Love,

Seamus

The McCabes had attended a reading given by SH at the Cheltenham Literary Festival; Snitton, in Shropshire, was where they lived; and they had been part of the intimate group of family and friends invited by SH to the Nobel award ceremony in Stockholm.

'NO Horncastling': referring to an occasion when the Heaneys and McCabes had competed to pay the bill in a restaurant in Horncastle, Lincolnshire.

1996

'There's no such thing as a free Nobel Prize,' Marie Heaney is reported to have said, and SH himself had to come to terms with its consequences for him, both in the wider world and closer to home.

His friend and fellow Nobel laureate Joseph Brodsky died on 28 January.

To Tom Sleigh

MS Sleigh

5 January 1996

Fitzpatrick Manhattan Hotel,
687 Lexington Avenue, NY 10022

Amigo,

A cold coming . . . well, it *is* nearly that time o' year, and in fact herself and I are swanning it a bit, using frequent flier points to sneak in and out of NY for the weekend. Brother Friel has a play opening on Sunday evening (*Molly Sweeney*, about a blind woman cured – and uncured by the cure) so that's the excuse. He was directing in NY and couldn't come to Stockholm, he who might have been expecting the call himself . . . All very delicate, and very free too, of course, nothing fraught, just fluid and animating underground activity. The usual . . . But I felt that a brow on the floor, or at least a grave and formal inclination from the waist, to acknowledge seniority, majesty, friendship, love even, was called for. There I go, making excuses for the affront of transatlantic travel with no *work* or duty involved . . .

Your letter did me good and more than that, it gave me the rarely experienced feeling of delight in my own work – specifically, your praise of the 'Cassandra' piece restored me. Naturally, I am conscious of all that it is due to call down upon its slender form, but in the end I decided to abide by the words and weaves that came so quickly and definitely as I wrote it. It sped out of its own little coil, reminded me of the verity of lyric, of the thick-wittedness of certitudes which precondition the delicacies of *ars*. The ars and the elbow hand in glove – but enough, enough, enough.

I seem to spend my time in the executive part of my being, or in the domestic, escaping too rarely into the opener, scarier emptinesses of the writing part. Hence the good of your letter, with its account of your solitary reading of the *Redress* and its lovely account of how conditions on the train journey to and from Kansas constituted a kind of weather in which the book was taken in – it reminded me of the mysterious reliability of those moods in which 'the affections gently lead us on . . .' Made me envious of your Iowa far-awayness and the bounty of the new poems that came to you there.

Anyway, this is just to greet you and thank you. You probably have heard by now that I am not going to be at Harvard this semester. I had a sudden realization in mid-November that I would annihilate myself as a sentient creature if I had to turn around about now, abandon the confusion and cram of mail and obligation, pageantry and business that the prize has brought in its wake, and head into the tensions and givings-out of a big lecture course in a cold temperature. I just wrote to President, Dean and Chairman saying, 'No can do. Sorry. See you in the Fall,' and they gallantly responded, 'Understood, fine, but no money in the meantime.' Fair enough.

I go back home on Monday. We really did come here as a kind of *hommage* to Brian. And as a chance to see Tom and Jean Flanagan and sit with them in gratitude and sage memory, friendship and wonder at what can happen to a youth from the fields . . . Also as a chance to pow-wow with Joseph B. – lunch and laughter and more nose-rubbing. What creaturely creatures we are, after all.

You will have remarked the pace of this hotting up and the coherence slipping away. Marie is ready to go out and I am to attend. She sends her love and I do too and hope you and Ellen have good life and work in 1996. *Urbi et orbi* to all the tribe – or are we conscripts? Conscribed, somehow, certainly, Love, Seamus

'that time o' year': i.e. Epiphany, the subject of T. S. Eliot's 'Journey of the Magi'.

'Your letter did me good': Sleigh had written to thank SH for showing him the poem 'Mycenae Lookout', and to express his appreciation of both the skill and the courage with which it addressed difficult moral and political questions.

'the affections gently lead us on': see Wordsworth's 'Lines Composed a Few Miles above Tintern Abbey'.

'all the tribe': see letter to Tom Sleigh of 13 April 1995, where SH names several members of the extra-academic gang in whose company he relaxed while teaching at Harvard.

To Charles Simic MS New Hampshire

12 January 1996 191 Strand Road, Dublin 4

Dear Charlie,

The weeks after Christmas – well, the week – are/is the best time of the year for me. A dip into hibernation stillness. Quiet and far in. I spent hours with the different books you sent, which had been adjacent to the bed and dipped into on and off over the last few months. Intention was to write immediately. Intention is a word that should be banned from my vocabulary.

Anyway, the coherence and lambency, the mixture of pebbly truth-to-things and jubilant truth-to-impulse, the invention and laconic clued-inness of the work you've been doing is really heart-lifting. Everything seems all of a piece and your very own – the service you do others and the Serbian language and poetry in general could only succeed as it does with your own particular gifts. There's a lovely buoyancy and plenitude about having all the books together – and the *Hotel Insomnia* gets an annex. Your Cornell book is particularly moving. Wonderful mixture of intellectual stamina, sheer relished and stored, unpredictable association. I was doing a lecture on Elizabeth Bishop at Oxford in November and used 'The Gaze We Knew as a Child' as a path into her work. Your whole good will towards sensation and your readiness to go with the breeze of association gives a wonderful salubriousness to all the writing. The black marks against life are all registered in the black box at the back of the mind, but the coloured-crayon imp of perverse creative joy keeps drawing the graffiti that we love. With your work, there's no need to keep adding makeweights of reassurance to oneself – 'oh, other people must get something that I'm missing,' all that compensatory carry-on that usually accompanies the reading of verses – the thing brims above its level, the more-than-enoughness of the spot-on job prevails. *Gaudens gaudeo.* See you in the springtime, some time. Love to Helen. Congratulations.

Seamus

Charles Simic (1938–2023), born in Belgrade (then capital of Yugoslavia), now American poet and translator from the Serbian, had got to know SH personally on his regular visits to their mutual friends in Boston, William and Beverly Corbett.

‘pebbly truth-to-things’: alluding primarily to ‘Truth? A pebble of quartz?’ from the last line of Frost’s poem ‘For Once, Then, Something’; perhaps also hinting at the poem ‘Pebble’ by the Polish poet Zbigniew Herbert, whom both Simic and SH admired. The ‘Cornell book’ is *Dime-Store Alchemy* (1992), Simic’s prose meditation on the US artist Joseph Cornell (1903–72).

To Marion Meek

TS Emory

January 1996

Dear Marion,

I am sorry to say that I cannot attend on Friday in Bellaghy. In fact, I would have liked to have been able to show up at the Bellaghy Development Association on Thursday night also since they very generously wanted to talk to me about some kind of post-Stockholm reception but none of that is now possible. On Friday, I am going to Asturias, and won’t be back until next week.

Thank you very much for your congratulations on the Nobel Prize. It was a great honour but it has also entailed great pressures on my time and energy and I am therefore anxious to get some matters cleared up as quickly as I can – and these obviously include commitments already made in relation to the Bawn.

1. First of all, I must reiterate clearly the message which I think I communicated in a blurred kind of way to Francis Murphy some months ago: I am not thinking of housing the archive of my manuscripts at the Bawn. Last April as I walked over to lunch in the company of the librarians, there was indeed a kind of heady speedy conversation about the prospect of lottery money, purchase of my papers, and so on; and I know some follow-up did occur via Emory University. But I wish to put on record here and now that I have no plans to go ahead with any such disposition of my papers. In fact, I am incapable of making a decision on this matter so it is unlikely to come to any resolution for years.
2. It was with mixed emotions that I read of your acceptance of bookings for ‘a literary tour’ next October. Obviously, this kind of thing may be exactly the kind of spin-off many will want from the restoration of the Bawn, but I am enclosing

my memorandum for the meeting of February 24 last year which outlines my uneases about turning a home ground into a stamping ground. All I can do is urge you and the members of the Steering Committee to read it and think about it and continue to take cognizance of it as the project develops. (Barney Devlin's forge at Hillhead is a possible stop on such a tour; the site of the old clayworks at Toome – see 'Bann Clay' in *Door into the Dark*; the eel fishery at Toome – 'A Lough Neagh Sequence'; Lagans Road; and so on. But again, I am ambivalent about mentioning them.)

3. My feeling is that I should talk in detail with the designer before too long. Obviously, the function of the room will dictate to a large extent the nature of the materials and the method of display. Once again, I refer you and the committee to the memorandum and to the copy of my September 1992 letter (also enclosed). As I envisage it, the room would not be a scholarly archive but a well-stocked educational resource. Much look and learn, 'See this!' kind of things. Also things that can be taken to the adjacent room for consultation – tapes, videos, poetry books by myself and others, books of criticism, etc.
4. I enclose a copy of a letter I drafted last year. I meant to send it out to a number of the poets but never got round to it. Would the best thing be for you or Clodagh to send it out with some kind of covering note? Or would you prefer me to proceed on my own?
5. Having had some slight brush with the idea of setting up a trust recently, I know how complicated it can be. I also know that this has to be the next stage of development in the structure of the administration. So, before the final decisions are taken on that, I wonder if a document can be prepared and circulated to all of us – some lucid explanation of what exactly a trust means, what its responsibilities and powers will be and so on. Just so that we can see what we are working towards. Something in lay people's language. I know it's a tall order, but worth a try, I think.
6. Even though I am not altogether sure what a trust is or does, I feel it should contain at least one person with a sense of the pre-Bawn language and culture of the district. In my letter of

6 March 1995 I suggested to Clodagh that we might involve Dr Dermot Devlin of the Irish Department of the University of Ulster in our activities. But for a trustee, I would also want to put forward the name of Dr Brendan Devlin (no relation) of St Patrick's College, Maynooth. He is a senior figure, a tower of common sense and a cultivated scholar. He is from Gortin originally and has written a play in Irish about St Patrick's bell and its curatorship by the Mulhollands.

[. . .]

The project to convert Bellaghy Bawn, a seventeenth-century fortified farmhouse in SH's home town, had been mooted in 1992; Marion Meek was Senior Inspector of Historic Monuments at the Department of the Environment for Northern Ireland, the body concerned with it; Clodagh Harvey was Project Manager; Francis Murphy was an officer of the Arts Council.

While lending the project his support in principle, SH had also expressed misgivings, which mainly concerned what he feared might be the impact on members of his family. In a memorandum sent to a meeting of the steering committee in February 1995, he wrote: 'I want to emphasize again that several members of my family live in the immediate vicinity of Bellaghy. Already they find their privacy is vulnerable because of the way that some people interested in the poems feel free to arrive on their doorstep. One of my brothers, a busy man, has on occasion found himself with a Japanese professor in Toner's Moss when he should have been with his cows in the milking parlour. My sister finds herself under siege by sixth formers eager for a glimpse of my mother's scrapbook in order to give that extra piquancy to their term essay. (High marks to the sixth formers, I agree, but still symptomatic of the kind of visitation that could be on the rise.)'

To Charles McGrath

MS

6 February [1996]

Dear Charles McGrath,

I had two-thirds of this written before I knew you might like to see it. So it may not be your thing. Also, I feel that it would be better to appear sooner rather than later, given its tone, so unless you can run it (assuming you like it enough) before long, it might be better to leave it. Anyhow, see what you think.

Seamus H.

This faxed communication and the following one, both to members of the *New York Times Book Review* staff, concern the eulogy for Joseph Brodsky that SH had written immediately after Brodsky's death on 26 January. In it, SH praises the 'intensity and boldness of [Brodsky's] genius, plus the sheer exhilaration of being in his company', as well as his 'valour and style'. In a fax to Jonathan Galassi, his editor, and Brodsky's, at Farrar, Straus and Giroux, showing him the poem 'Audenesque', written 'in memory of Joseph Brodsky', SH said, simply and eloquently: 'Big black hole punched in our days.'

To Katherine Bouton MS

14 February 1996

Dear Katherine Bouton,

Thanks for the copy.

Line 17: I agree: what about 'his death last January *was* . . .'

line 21: Joseph Brodsky? I want the name Joseph to appear on its own once or twice. The whole point of this piece is that he is and was 'Joseph' to me. I understand about the decorum of a public tribute and about demands of house style, but it would make a deep and disabling difference to the piece if the personal connection represented by the first name disappeared . . .

So restore 'Joseph' here to make the point straight away? ~~Maybe it's a bit soon. Make it 'Joseph Brodsky'. Agreed.~~ On second thoughts, this seems the place to make the point . . .

[. . .]

To Jean Kennedy Smith TS

5 March 1996 191 Strand Road, Dublin 4

Dear Jean,

Unfortunately, I cannot be at the great event in New York next Monday. I was honoured to be listed among those 100 names and would have liked to have been free to attend the banquet, especially since President Clinton is going to be guest of honour, but I have to be back here in Dublin all next week.

If you get an opportunity, please tell the President how much Marie and I enjoyed meeting him and his wife. It was a heady moment and I'll always be grateful to you for the privilege of a private audience with them on that historic day. Grateful too to have been able to tell him, without flattery or exaggeration, that his visit to Belfast and Derry had made a difference for the better. It was impossible not to sense the shift of mood and the fortification of good purposes that he caused at levels that were both personal and public. And, of course, I was proud not only to have been quoted in the President's speeches but also to be able to tell him about my long-standing affection for Arkansas – especially a certain hardware store in the town of Conway! More power to him and to you and to all around you who are working for that 'great sea-change / On the far side of revenge'.

Sincerely,
Seamus

Jean Kennedy Smith (1928–2020) was United States Ambassador to Ireland at this time; the 'great event in New York' was the presentation on 11 March of the Irish American of the Year Award, by the magazine *Irish American*, to President Bill Clinton (b.1946).

In his final sentence, SH quotes words from *The Cure at Troy* that Clinton had quoted the previous year, in a speech delivered in Derry as the peace process was being brought to a resolution.

To Gary Snyder

MS Davis

9 March 1996 191 Strand Road, Dublin 4

Dear Gary,

Now I own the Greenland of Trinity. I am monarch of all you surveyed. I am elevated by that and by your including me in your circle of sensibility and practice. Your own work and doings have brought verity and dignity to what the word poet means in our time and I have always honoured you for that as well and taken sustenance from the poems; so it was a great reward to have your dedication – and your letter. My love to Carole and you. Bug chirps across the whale-road!

Seamus

SH had been introduced to the US West Coast poet Gary Snyder (b.1930) in the course of one of his periods of employment at Berkeley in the 1970s, and lately Snyder had offered to dedicate his poem 'Icy Mountains Constantly Walking' to him. The poem, which came out of a visit to Ireland, mentions both Trinity College and Greenland in a single stanza and describes Snyder's reading of his own poems in Galway as 'just the chirp of a bug'.

To Robert Crawford

TS Crawford

[March 1996]

EPISTLE TO ROBERT CRAWFORD

Lord, Crawford, but I cursed you often!
My heart was hard and wouldn't soften,
My smile like varnish on a coffin,
    My study brown,
All winter as I starved far off in
    Dublin Town.

What I was up against was this:
My Bicentenary Lecture promise
To speak on Burns and Ulsterness –
    It had me spancelled.
I'd have dealt with Ould Nick or Ould Dis
    To've had it cancelled.

For a title, you'd suggested
'Burns's Art Speech': why resist it?
I thought, yes, go ahead and list it,
    Ideas will come.
But then my brain got blurred and misted,
    The mind went numb.

Yet something in me always knew
I'd winter out and see it through.
One morning, words would fall like dew
    On my writer's block.
I'd wake and start to stretch and crow
    Like a ballad cock.

After all, Burns' words and rhythm,
The Scots the Ulster Scots brought with them
Got birled across from Down and Antrim
    West o' the Bann
And had to be deep laid within
    My inner man.

So part of me did feel connected
Although a sixth sense half-detected
Some hint of something disaffected
            Just out of reach
Like royalties that Burns suspected
            Were owed by Creech.

I mean to say, the 'Rhyming Weavers'
Don't thread my looms and throw my levers
Or link me to the Border reavers
            As they did Hewitt:
'His own' he called those old believers –
            Which I could not.

And yet, my neighbours *bummed* and *blowed*
And *happed* themselves up till it *thowed*.
By *slaps and stiles* they *thrawed* and *tholed*
            And *snedded thrissles*
And when the rigs were *braked* and hoed
            They'd wet their whistles.

Old men and women getting crabbèd
Would hark like dogs who'd seen a rabbit,
Then straighten, stare and have a stab at
            Standard habbie:
Custom never staled their habit
            O' quotin' Rabbie.

And who could blame them, or resist
Those rhymes like bowls that rolled and kissed,
Those line-endings that crossed and crissed
            En suite, *en face*,
Their overrun and final twist
            And *coup de grâce*.

And surely there's a lesson still
In Burns's vauntie voice and skill
That set the pace, provide the thrill
            And have the answers.
If anything can foot the bill,
            It's those trig stanzas.

Surprising by their fine excesses,
Like bottled stuff that effervesces,
The lines fly past like fast expresses
        Or ton-up bikers
Or surge like crowds who seek redress as
        General strikers.

Such confidence outstrips perhapses,
It compensates us for our lapses,
It forks like lightning through synapses
        From head to foot:
The wired-up bardie freaks and taps his
        Finger to't.

But heartsome as it is, and frisky,
Excessive rhyming can be risky
Though (this I learned from Kochanowski)
        Still well worth trying:
There's no such thing as a large whiskey,
        Said Flann O'Brien.

Enough is not enough in art.
We overplay to play the part
(The rules of play being from the start
        Well understood).
We need the horse before the cart,
        The open road.

And that's what's marvellous in Burns.
He overflows the well-wrought urns –
Like buttermilk in slurping churns,
        Rich and unruly
Or dancers flying, doing turns
        At some wild hooley.

But far down underneath all that,
Behind the banter and ould chat,
I sometimes wonder if there's not
        Something foreclosed,
A no inside the habbie note,
        A breadth refused.

What we all love in it's the tone
Of knowing who and what's your own,
Of being fit to stand alone
            And independent:
The bondedness within the bone,
            How Hewitt kenned it!

Agrarians who 'took their stand',
The Fugitives, the Lallans band,
The colonists who worked the land
            Till it was theirs,
This tone suits them down to the ground
            Of all their fears.

Which brings us to the great debate:
Authority and holding out
By holding on to pride and root,
            That's where we're landed,
And, Crawford, I both credit it
            And *cannae stand it*.

I want to shout a *Yeah, yeah, yeah*,
Or cisatlantic *Blah, blah, blah*
When another drone lays down the law
            And blows his horn
And quotes "A man's a man for a" . . .'
            Need I go on?

An independence harped upon
Is herd emotion before long.
A value turns into a slogan,
            The bloom goes off
And then the causes you believe in
            Can bore you stiff.

Lallans, even, Faroese,
The Blasket *blas*, Kiltartanese,
Boeotians, Inuits, Basques, the wees
            Versus the bigs –
Sure aren't they long since off their knees
            Like Orwell's pigs?

Devolved, evolved, in touch, empowered,
Tingling fit as if they'd showered,
Small languages that one time cowered
    Beneath the great
Are rising like a flooded ford
    In spate, in spate.

'Nostalgia,' said Mandelstam,
'For world culture.' To be at home
But homesick still for Greece and Rome,
    To plough and plod
The ground of Bunyah and Mossbawn
    In step with Hesiod!

Burns was a freeman of this world.
Before its banners were unfurled,
Before its rescue bagpipe skirled
    His voice was steadfast,
His accent thick, his Scots *r's* birled,
    His talent vast.

And though his first tongue's *going, gone*,
And word-lists now get added on
And even words like *thole* and *thrawn*
    Have to be glossed,
The poet's element is gain,
    He 'lides what's lost.

Ultimately, Burns is big.
His stanza may sound cramped and trig
But once he sets the sail and rig,
    Away he goes
Like Tam-o-Shanter o'er the brig
    Where no-one follows.

The poet in him overcomes
The *ayes* and *noes* of fifes and drums,
The kirk, the lodge, the drawing rooms,
    The party whips.
His poems buck and follow whims
    Like mountain *tips*.

Eros runs with *Libertas*.
No one lives or loves *en masse*.
The risen people aren't a class
          Or devolution.
The motto could be *Kiss me, lass,*
          For revolution!

At this point, then, I heard *blah, blahs*
Which I took, Crawford, for applause
So I quit the rhyme and made a pause
          And wrote some prose
Which, finally, with all its flaws,
          I now enclose.

The Scottish poet and academic Robert Crawford (b.1959) was organising a series of lectures to celebrate Robert Burns's bicentenary, under the aegis of the University of St Andrews and the British Library Centre. SH delivered his, which, following Crawford's suggestion, was titled 'Burns's Art Speech', in front of a live audience at BBC Scotland, Queen Street, Edinburgh, on 26 March, and it was broadcast in full on the radio later that evening. It was collected, with other lectures, in the book edited by Crawford, *Robert Burns and Cultural Authority* (1997).

To Derek Mahon

TS AND MS Emory

6 April 1996

191 Strand Road, Dublin 4

Dear Derek –

You may have heard by now that the Department of the Environment is going ahead with a plan to make Bellaghy Bawn a class of Heritage Centre. They also have plans to devote one of the rooms to poets and poetry. In the beginning the plan was to concentrate on this particular bard, but for all sorts of reasons I thought that the focus should be widened. So, while I am going to give them a lump of material – manuscripts, books, poster poems and that sort of thing – I am also anxious that the rest of us/you should be represented also. To begin with, it would make sense to gather materials that would be of interest to visiting students. Schoolchildren, sixth formers, undergraduates, maybe even professors. So I am writing to ask if you could donate (or lend for a protracted period) worksheets of a poem, for example. One or two or three pages showing some kind of development (of the poem, that is . . .).

I know this is an intrusive request. But I still think you should know that these plans are going ahead and should have an opportunity to contribute, in case you might want to. Poster poems, pamphlets, books – anything like that would be very welcome. Something that can be laid in a portfolio and taken out and studied – or something that can be put on a wall or otherwise displayed.

I am not very clear about what kind of guarantees/ownership/guardianship arrangements will be entailed here. An outright gift to the Department of the Environment is one way of thinking of it (they'll have good security). Or it might be some kind of loan. Or the material held in trust for you. In fact, the people in charge have not yet clarified their own minds about how exactly it will be done. At this stage, the main thing would be to know whether you might be interested in making a contribution.

The building is still being got ready, but the hope is that the first exhibition would be available for display in mid-June 1996. In the meantime, Marion Meek (Environment Service, Historical Monuments and Buildings, 5/33 Hill Street, Belfast BT1 2LA) is the person to contact. [. . .]

I apologise for adding to the volume of begging letters. I do so only because of the Bellaghy connection. And again, please understand that what is being requested is not a large amount of material – just something that would show your good will towards the scheme and would be of interest to young writers (the project includes the dream of weekend creative writing courses).

All good wishes.

Seamus

More bother . . . Meanwhile, I enclose a ram-stam made at the ould bittern. Was doing a lecture on R. Burns and wanted to draw a comparison between 'Bittern' and 'To a Mouse'. Just lunged happily in to do a one-off version. Now I like it. Aaagh!

Derek Mahon is the addressee here, but this was a standard letter that went out to other Northern Irish poets as well. The postscript, though, is personal and handwritten.

'the ould bittern': SH's translation of 'An Bunnán Buí' ('The Yellow Bittern') by Cathal Buí Mac Giolla Ghunna.

To Jerzy Illg — TS PNL

9 April 1996

[. . .]

The New York commemoration of Joseph was wonderful. Almost two hours of poetry, music, choirs and prayer. All in an immense cathedral. Cold as the Baltic. A kind of hangar emptied of God. It was marvellous to meet Czesław – and Tomas Venclova whom I had not met. Plus a host of other Russians and émigrés of all sorts. I think Joseph would have enjoyed it himself. Certainly, the fact that only his own poems were read would have made it palatable to him . . . Not to mention the vodka afterwards. We had a real banger of a party in Greenwich Village. Pity you were not there.

[. . .]

The memorial service for Joseph Brodsky had been held at the Cathedral of St John the Divine on 8 March. Illg was the Polish publisher of both Brodsky and Czesław Miłosz; the Lithuanian poet Tomas Venclova (b.1937) was, like Miłosz, a political dissident and émigré.

To David Hammond — MS Emory

6 June 1996 Air Canada

Dear David,

The thing is out of control: I've just flown over 'the cold coast of Greenland', en route from London to Edmonton. Yesterday (hush hush) as part of Ted Hughes's confidential advisory committee on the Queen's Gold Medal for Poetry, I had lunch in Buckingham Palace <not with herself, no>. Last Tuesday, as part of the family, I had to go to see Aunt Jane in a convent in Drogheda. Last weekend, as a consequence of the life we've all lived, I had Bert Hornback and Rand Brandes on my social hands. Since I landed back from the US ten days ago, I was on the go moment by moment, and away again yesterday morning at half past seven. As I said to somebody lately, all I do nowadays is 'turn up' – I'm a function of timetables, not an agent of my own being. And it's going to be like this for weeks and months still.

[. . .]

'The Cold Coast of Greenland' is the title and refrain of an old whaling song.
Bert G. Hornback (b.1935) taught at the University of Michigan, Ann Arbor, where he also ran a series of Tuesday readings.

To Desmond Kavanagh

PC Kavanagh

[? June 1996]

I was always haunted by the feeling that I might have had a vocation, and when I saw your man front left I realized how it could all have turned out . . . Greetings from Auntie Bridie in Montreal. Seamus

The postcard, sent from Canada, shows *La Noce*, the painting of a wedding group, by Henri (Le Douanier) Rousseau (Montreal Museum of Fine Arts); the figure SH draws attention to, identifiable as the priest officiating, bears a faint facial resemblance to him. For 'Auntie Bridie', see postcard to Kavanagh of 18 May 1982.

To Ted Hughes

MS BL

8 July 1996 Galan 1, Salinas, Asturias

Dear Ted,

At the weekend I got to Santiago de Compostela: Raleigh and his scallop shell much on my mind, of course, but I was soon inundated with memories and sensations below and beyond schools and schoolbags. We happened to be in the Cathedral on Saturday night at a Mass where an ordination was taking place. Two priests taking final vows, three deacons being consecrated, bishops in mitres, litanies in Latin, Gregorian chant, murmurous responses – the whole underlife of my childhood and teens rallied and wept for itself. The stone and the squares, at once 'southern' and Atlantic, lashed with rain and holding out for something more; it was potent because there is just enough 'living faith' around the place to make you feel the huge collapse that has taken place at the centre of the Christian thing . . . At any rate, when I got back I wrote a couple of pages that could serve as an afterword or a foreword to the anthology and I have just realized that the eschatological mood of the weekend must have been at work in the last paragraph. I'll copy it out here (imagine, I've actually composed it on a lap-top computer, for which I have no printer to hand . . .) because I think it may provide you with a prompt or an opportunity to do a piece about memorizing poems. I'll send you my complete note at the end of the month, once I get through the mail-ramparts and fax-middens. It is a minimal statement about our title and its implications, our inclusion of Irish, Scottish and Welsh material in translation, our one-poem-per-poet decision and its implications, plus peroration, thus:

'We think of our readers as people in search of the ancient salt which Yeats declared to be the best salt for the survival of poetry. To some extent we even think of them as poets in the making, beginners who want to know what is needed before and after the achievements of the recent past. People, at any rate, who want to remember poetry, know it by heart and make sense of it in their lives.'

The past few days have been deeply restorative. I suppose it is too much to expect to be able – at this stage – to change the mode and pace of life, but in 1997 an effort will be made. I go – for the last time, I think – to Harvard in September. I hate the thought of teaching students (*School-bag* editor or not). Whatever the Stockholm effect will be finally, its immediate result is a desire to quit the job and try to get started again *in propria persona*. Imagine being able to come to Asturias three or four times a year; or to Donegal; or, indeed, to Devon. To the sources again, at any rate.

I'll (soon) send a heap of not very well translated Celt-verse. And hope that we can do the most of the final ordering and inning and outing in early August. Much love to Carol and you from both of us.

Seamus

Sent from Salinas, in Asturias, where the Heaneys had retreated to the home of Marie's sister Anne.

Sir Walter Ralegh's poem 'The Passionate Man's Pilgrimage' begins with words that must have had an extra resonance for SH at this hectic time: 'Give me my scallop shell of quiet.'

'I wrote a couple of pages': the foreword to *The School Bag* is by SH and concludes with a modified version of the lines he puts in quote-marks here; Hughes wrote an essay propounding his method for memorising poems, which appears as afterword.

'for the last time, I think': it wasn't.

'Celt-verse': among the poems that were to be included in *The School Bag*, as correctives to the Anglocentric canon prevailing in places of education, were 'The Reverie' by Egan O'Rahilly (aka Aodhagán Ó Rathaille) (*c*.1670–1726), translated by Frank O'Connor, and 'The Shadow' by the fourteenth-century Welsh poet Dafydd ap Gwilym, translated by Joseph P. Clancy.

To Roberto Mussapi

TS Emory

12 and 26 July 1996 191 Strand Road, Dublin 4

Dear Robert Mussapi,

Here are some (very swift) responses to your questions.

1. 'Grass dust' is the old dried-up matter on the bit of the horse's bridle. The vestiges of grass which would have been wet and chewed while the horse was harnessed.
2. 'To beat real iron out, to work the bellows': these words are to be taken literally, translated for what they are. What they imply is that the blacksmith turns away from the hurry and distraction of the road outside in order to return to more permanent and durable concerns. Bellows has a remote, submerged association with inspiration. The smith is, of course, a potent symbol of creative endeavour.

   [. . .]
4. What is being described is a process of thawing a water pump which has frozen. The kind of pump involved is a vertical, standing pump. During hard winter weather, the plunger/sucker used to get frozen within the iron cylinder. This involved a process of thawing. One way to thaw out the pump was to light a fire around it, hence, straw was brought and set alight in order to free up the motion and workings of the pump. By the way, I was thinking of calling this particular poem 'Persephone'.
5. 'Reflection': some sense of the mutuality that comes from sexual love, some sense also of a face reflected in water. The 'undine' is at once a woman presence and a water presence. A spirit of the water.
6. In 'Cana Revisited': the analogy – a bit heavy, perhaps – is with pregnancy. 'Virtue' is used in its more or less Latin sense, meaning power or efficacy. It is meant to be about the wonder of conception.

[. . .]
Here are a few swift reactions to your new questions:

Pharaoh's 'visitations' were the plagues of locusts etc. The magnified flies remind the speaker of these locusts.

I used the phrase 'fly *an* umbrella' in the original. Meaning that they form an umbrella of wings etc. over the boat. But a misprint turned 'an' into '*and*'! So in the misprinted version 'umbrella' has to be a verb of sorts . . .

'Vision': The child was told that unless he allowed his hair to be fine-combed, i.e. combed with a specially fine-toothed comb which would comb out the lice, the lice would gang up and drag him to the river. Gruesome fantasy to promote hygiene in the young! But then, as an adult, when he sees the eels crossing land, moving in the grass, it's as if the gruesome louse-procession has come true. The 'he' is, I suppose, the poet.
[. . .]
The speaker in 'The Plantation' is getting lost among the trees, or remembering getting lost. He keeps passing mushrooms and stumps and assumes that he is passing them for the first time. But then he is not sure. Is he passing them a second time? Going round in circles? The 'you' is like the French *on* here.
[. . .]

The Italian poet and translator Roberto Mussapi (b.1952) had written to ask SH to explain details of poems from *Door into the Dark* that he was translating, the poems elucidated here being 'Gone', 'The Forge', 'Rite of Spring', 'Undine', 'Cana Revisited', 'Ardboe Point', 'A Lough Neagh Sequence', 'Vision' and 'The Plantation'. A tiny drawing in the right-hand margin at the foot of paragraph 4 completes SH's description of the thawing process.

To Clare Reihill

MS Clare Reihill

4 September 1996 191 Strand Road, Dublin 4

Dear Clare,

I'm on the aeroplane for Boston. Last night, I opened a Faber package that came weeks ago – I'd just ripped it open when it arrived and presumed it was all tapes of *The Spirit Level*. But in the frantic run-up to departure I was putting things away, into some kind of storage, and in the process discovered your beautiful, original gift of the little level. I have it in my luggage now, and will have it on my mantelpiece in Adams House for the next four months. I love it and love you for getting it and am very sorry not to have seen it earlier. You must have wondered what kind of a shit I was . . . And the odd coincidence was I had met Robin only a couple of hours earlier, at the Deane-fest. Anyhow, a thousand thanks. We must go out on the batter and off the level and celebrate it one day. Love, Seamus

Clare Reihill was working at Faber as Matthew Evans's assistant; she was married at the time to Robin Robertson (b.1966), poet and publisher.

'Deane-fest': the launch of Seamus Deane's *Reading in the Dark*.

To Ted Hughes

TS BL

7 October 1996

English Department, Warren House,
Harvard University, Cambridge,
MA 02138

Dear Ted,

Just a sudden, late-night thought or two about the *Bag*. We forgot to put in a McGonagall. I think he earns his keep, so to speak, so let us press for the Tay Bridge when the proofs arrive. [. . .]

Cambridge in the autumn is a great deal kinder than Cambridge in January: I should have been coming at this time of the year all along. When I began the connection, September was the month when the young were switching to new schools, so Daddy's defection would have been out of the question – there was a lot less resentment factor inherent in a January departure; besides which, Harvard always likes to have you on hand in the spring, for thesis marking and prize adjudication and general end-of-year duties. I suppose it's just that at the age of 57 I'm beginning to realize that it's time to focus on my own convenience since for sure nobody else is going to focus on it. And the young are now in their mid-twenties . . .

By a strange coincidence, I was in Cracow last week on the day the Szymborska announcement was made. Znak, a small publishing house there, had done Marie's book of legends and a selection of my essays into the Polish tongue, so we were there for a couple of days post-Frankfurt. Szymborska is a marvellous *cailleach*, a chainsmoking sibyl, as wily as MacCaig and Stevie Smith put together, but less defensive somehow, a touch of Elizabeth Bishop kneaded in, a bit of Beckett bottom-linery too. But it was a surprise, nevertheless.

I hope you are getting work done. I feel like I'm on the edge of

Sandymount Strand and the tide of writing is away out there on the horizon. I'm even getting to like the absence and desire and lostness of being at the barren edge. *Ochone agus ochone*. Much love to you both.

Seamus

[On envelope:] Maybe start the whole thing with 'Long-Legged Fly'?

'The Tay Bridge Disaster' by William McGonagall (1825–1902) was duly included in *The School Bag*, and the book opens with Yeats's 'Long-legged Fly'.

'*cailleach*': Irish term for either an wise woman or an old crone.

'Szymborska announcement': of the award to the Polish poet Wisława Szymborska of the 1996 Nobel Prize in Literature.

To Desmond Kavanagh and family

GC Kavanagh

Before Christmas [1996]

To all at Roslyn, with love at this season of sweetest and surest memories.

Seamus and Marie

With apologies for a poem that's more like an A-Level test than a Christmas card verse . . . My three old Scottish bard-friends all went away out of the light in 1996.

The Heaney Christmas card for 1996 carried the elegiac poem '"Would They Had Stayed"'. The three Scottish poets who had died in the course of 1996 were Norman MacCaig (on 23 January), George Mackay Brown (13 April) and Sorley MacLean (24 November). Oddly, the poem's title is taken from Macbeth's exclamation after the disappearance of the Witches in Act 1, Scene iii of his play.

'out of the light': as against those lamented by Henry Vaughan in his poem 'They Are All Gone into the World of Light'.

1997

SH's two most significant publications of this year were, first, *The School Bag*, the second of the two anthologies he co-edited with Ted Hughes, and secondly, *The Spirit Level*, which went on to win the Whitbread Book of the Year Award.

To Brian Friel

MS NLI

18 January 1997

Glanmore Cottage, Ashford,
Co. Wicklow

Dear Brian,

Got back from the final Harvard lap on Thursday, and went to ground here for purposes of 'recollection'. And to read – having found the manuscript of *Give Me Your Answer Do* secluded in the Adams House mail room. It was stowed as a 'parcel' and had been on what Tommy Devlin used to call 'the high shelf'. I was doing a last check before heading away.

Anyway, what a geometry of desolation. The geometry of it exhilarating, the 'content' inescapable. Naturally, I went through it more or less ravenously and ended up both exhausted and satiated. The sense of an unfolding action, of each character's simultaneous freedom and corneredness, of inevitability without interference – that's what really exhilarates. Merciless but not punitive. Mirrorings but no manipulation. A wonderful total sense of the characters' givenness and authenticity. As fierce as *Faith Healer* in its way, and yet more buoyant. Another quotation springs to mind – 'The shortest way through is out' – I beg your pardon, magnificent Freudian slip in the circumstances – the other way round. 'The shortest way out is through.'

Well, there it is, an instinctive attempt to dodge the inescapable truth of it. But the audience will get a great lift as well as a great confrontation.

[. . .]

Friel's new play, *Give Me Your Answer, Do!*, in which a novelist's anxiety about the sale of his papers to an American college library supplies the premise, opened at the Abbey Theatre two months later.

To Hughie O'Donoghue

MS H. O'Donoghue

5 February 1997 — 191 Strand Road, Dublin 4

Dear Hughie,

Nowadays I find it harder and harder to get away to work, so when the opportunity came to spend this week in Wicklow, I grabbed it – hope the Gallery gave you my apologies for not making it on Tuesday. But then, for God's sake, I got a flu that has kept me in bed here for the last couple of days. And then, I got your gift of the Catalogues.

I got a real sense of large emergence in the work represented in those publications, for which I thank you, not only because of 'the thought' which does indeed count, but also because of the quality of the volumes themselves. I share Christoph Vitali's sense of occasion about *Via Crucis* and find myself imagining the copiousness of the paintings from the reproductions – something at once chthonic and deeply meditated, the reward of long, complete attention. The prose poems to the colours (from your notebooks) are like sounding lines, guarantees of the depth of the commitment, proof that you have been out there, logging the voyage and keeping on solitary course. 'Like a long-legged fly on a stream,' as Yeats said. (Who also said that that poem, 'Long-Legged Fly', was 'about the importance of silence in the lives of creative people', something your own work proclaims too, in spite of the resonances of the art *as* art.) *Via Crucis* is a title that raises expectations and the paintings are more than equal to them, something I'd have thought well nigh impossible. They manage to know, and to be burdened by knowledge, yet at the same time to begin afresh, neither abashed nor ironical – atremble, rather. And up to the task. *Lines of Retreat* seems like a gift-richness, a paean as well as a prize, a bounty after the line of advance by the way of the cross. I look forward to seeing the exhibition. Sorry to miss you. And thanks again for the catalogues.

Love to Clare. Seamus

Hughie O'Donoghue (b.1953) is a British artist of Irish extraction who spent periods of his childhood in Ireland; he had first met SH in 1995 when they shared a stage at the Whitworth Art Gallery in Manchester, in front of one of the large canvases that O'Donoghue had been inspired to paint by photographs of the Tollund Man. At the time of this letter, two of O'Donoghue's exhibitions were running simultaneously: *Via Crucis* at the Haus der Kunst, Munich, and *A Line of Retreat* at the Purdy Hicks Gallery in London.

To Bernard and Jane McCabe

MS J. McCabe

8 March 1997 — 191 Strand Road, Dublin 4

My Dears,

Saturday afternoon here, just back from Glanmore – I posted that poemie to you on the way down yesterday.

Anyway, this morning Marie came down – in *her* vehicle – with the news that my sister Ann was going to have to go into hospital for a mastectomy next week. I'm sorry and very worried for her – she's the one who lives on her own and is celiac, or however you spell that gluten-problem condition. We're going up to see her to-morrow, before the surgery, but I feel that I should go and stay with her next week. She gets out on Patrick's Day and to be honest, if I went ahead with our plans, I'd have a sense of reneging not so much on a duty as upon a chance to give her something back for all the years she gave our parents . . . So I am sorry to say that I don't think I'll be in Wales or Ludlow. It just suddenly seems not the thing to be doing in the circumstances. At least that's how it feels at this moment, and I thought I'd better write about it rather than telephone. I'll speak to you in a couple of days' time. Forgive me for this change of plan. Much love,

Seamus

To Louis de Paor

PC de Paor

18 March 1997

Mac Gearailt got the trade beyond in Nzakara? The 'bill's' not a bird's after all? Anyhow, I hope you like the enclosed. I've always wanted to have a go at doing it, ever since I read Joan Keefe's version in the early '70s. I enclose the original I worked from, in case you want to parallel the texts. But that's probably over-doing it. Anyhow, I hope *Sean* likes it. Seamus

PS 'Runkly' is in the 13 vol. OED – wrinkled.

Louis de Paor (b.1961), poet and editor of the Irish-language journal *Innti*, was putting together a collection of poems and translations in honour of Seán Ó Tuama. In response to de Paor's invitation to contribute, SH had offered his version of Eoghan Rua Ó Súilleabháin's (1748–84) '*A Shéamais, Déan Dam*', which was later to be included, as 'Poet to Blacksmith', in *District and Circle*. Séamus Mac Gearailt was the blacksmith to whom the original poem was addressed. The postcard image is of copper tribute blades from Nzakara in the Central African Republic.

Joan Keefe was the compiler and translator of *Irish Poems from Cromwell to the Famine* (1977).

SH later dropped 'runkly' in favour of 'wrinkly'.

To Ted Hughes

PC BL

1 April 1997

Ted – After we spoke this morning, the postman brought in *Tales from Ovid*. I've read 'Pyramus and Thisbe' and (again) the opening chapter; 'Phaeton'; 'Bacchus and Pentheus' – they really take the gate off the hinges. Great work. The mighty wind, the word-hoard going like a foamy-throated longship into the Mediterranean. Total excitement. 'Bow down, archangels, in your dim abode – ' and read this. And I love the jacket art. S.

Stimulated by the commission he had received from the editors of *After Ovid* (see letter to Michael Longley of 12 January 1993), Hughes had set out to translate many more episodes from *Metamorphoses*; *Tales from Ovid* was the result. Like *The Spirit Level*, it would go on, the following January, to be voted Whitbread Book of the Year.

'Bow down, Archangels . . .': from Yeats's 'The Rose of the World', a poem celebrating solitary endeavour.

The jacket art was from a fourteenth-century illuminated manuscript of the *Roman de la Rose* illustrating the story of Narcissus. The image on SH's postcard was *A Lion Attacking a Horse* by George Stubbs (Paul Mellon Collection, Yale Center for British Art).

To Tomas Tranströmer — PC Tranströmer

1 April 1997

Dear Tomas, Our ghosts watched it from a Swedish clifftop. A Scottish monk made the sign of the Kipper from the prow of a currach. A Viking hurled a herring-javelin that turned into a flying net. Then *The Sorrow Gondola* sailed out of the Baltic and everybody wept for joy. My ghost wanted to be re-incarnated as a Tranströmer. Yours had been a T. already and just wanted to write more poems . . .

Love and more love to you and Monika from Marie and me. Seamus

Tranströmer had sent SH his new bilingual volume, *The Sorrow Gondola*, English translations by Robin Fulton, published by Gallery Press that year. It was the first book of his published after the stroke that incapacitated him in 1990. SH's whimsical vision of northern seafaring takes its cue more from the title of the image on the postcard – 'Battle of the Herrings 1429' by Jean Chartier (1500–80) – than what is actually depicted there.

To Thomas Flanagan — MS Amherst

20 May 1997 Poros

Dear Tom,

Now there's a writer's address. For 'the shit in the chateau' as Larkin called him. The Larry Durrells of the world . . . But I could get used to it, all the same. We're here among orange groves and olive groves, on a site overlooking a fishing village, with a view of the roan hills of the Peloponnese. We have been on a self-improving tour of sites and sanctuaries left unvisited after the Swedish interruption of 1995, and are taking a couple of days of a pause in a house owned by a chap called Manolis Savidis. His father taught at Harvard, and was the editor and friend of Seferis; also head of Cavafy studies and chief Ellmann type authority on the Greek modernists. I met him a couple of times there and between one thing and another have ended up here, and now . . .

I am not altogether made for the grand tour, however; keep thinking of the mail piling up at home and the faxes gulping and slithering into one's life and the requests for recommendations and introductions lurking . . . A feeling that sunlight and silence and free time on a Tuesday morning on a Greek island is an affront to the workers of the world. On the other hand, it's the kind of time that gives the mood and the freedom to write to one's friends, something I've been remiss about.

I suppose you are back in Long Island by now. Your February letter was certainly proof that the Californian migration works perfectly and I sense that the three-nest life is the right one for you both from now on. I myself am pondering – but the word is too founded and saturnine for the flittery fluttery thoughts I have on the subject, the subject being the purchase of the house next door to us on Strand Road, our other half, under the roof with us, our possible two-nest future. The owners are a young couple who may move inside the next 3/4 months, and they let us know about the possibility ahead of time, in case we were interested. And after much banishing of the thought, I am beginning to imagine a more spacious and ordered existence – an office where things could be stored and Susie could be in charge of her secretarial life and part of my life as well; book space; possible roosting space for the fledged family; a house each, Beckett style, for the moulting mates. I'll let you know what happens.

What happens, of course, will depend on the money situation. It is conceivable that the bloody place could be bid up to around the £200,000 mark, and even though I may now have a certain camel-proportion in the eye of the needle, the hump is still a relatively small one. Indeed, I have failed to maximize my financial chances by letting the Nobel doubloons lie inertly in the hold of the Bank of Ireland. A mixture of country stealth, timorousness and inertia. A dislike of the youth sent by the bank to smooth-talk investment talk with me. Obstinacy. A helpless secretive inclination, not wanting others in my accounts, as private as my sheets . . . But I've got over it, or almost. So. A school friend, same class as Deane and myself, called (deceptively) Mullarkey, is now chief of the Department of Finance, adviser to the minister and friend to (among others) Lew Glucksman. And Mullarkey I trust and will be led by, and he has led me towards a money honcho with whom I am to dine when I get back to Dublin next week. What I would like to arrange is some way of being sure of a decent yearly income; and at the same time, to be able to assist the fledged ones to nests of their own. But all this is so usual and generational, I wonder why I am writing about it . . . To convince myself about the rightness, if not the justice, of purchasing 189.

I'm not working at poems and am worried about it. Hope to heave through the last 1000 lines of *Beowulf* before the end of September, which gives me an alibi of sorts – even though there is something dead-weightish by now about the hardy-under-helmet warrior and the foamy-throated wave-floater under his resolute tread. Before I set out on this *immram*, I did a piece on Roy Foster's mage book and found myself unnervingly out of touch with whatever once upon a time wrote reviews for me. I had read about half the book when I was in bed with flu in February, and found it simply hard to *keep* reading. The cargo of data was awesome, and the revelation of the Yeatsian bundle as an intended if not a complete thing at all stages of his life was exhilarating. But I was not at that stage getting much joy from the page-turning. And when I came back to it, it was not joy, but there was an immense gratitude for the sweep and garnering aspect of Foster's work. And I did begin to feel this was a book that matched its subject and was not a let-down. W.B. gets bigger and firmer and more 'opinion' prone than he would have cared to admit.

Anyhow, I sensed from your piece in the *NYT Book Review* that you probably weren't altogether in love with the style of it but that you did rate the book as being up to the task. Certainly, Roy has had the accolades, without which it would have been very hard for him to forge ahead. I don't know how these cargoes can be assembled and annotated by somebody who is doing all the other professional and domestic thing as well. Twenty lines under the alliterative hammer and I'm beaten for the rest of the day.

We're travelling with the Hadzis, again a couple I met at Harvard. I was never close friends with either of them, but was always very relaxed in their company, and gradually the idea of a Greek trip got firmed up. And was very successful for the five days it lasted in 1995. Naturally, we felt that there had been an element of let-down involved for them when bounty of S. called us back home, so this second round was planned. It has gone well, partly because of the potency of the sites – Olympia, Delphi and (a second visit) Mycenae; and partly because everybody is on their best behaviour. But in all honesty, one week should be the limit for two-couple travel.

[. . .] I enjoyed a sup from the Kastalian spring and the site of the (current) omphalos, 'a dismal object' as Peter Levi accurately terms it. Levi was my predecessor as Prof. of P. at Oxford, and his translation of Pausanias was something I picked up casually but have enjoyed immensely – especially the footnotes.

I also enjoyed the coincidence of parking the car on Antigone Street in Thebes; of staying in Hotel Hermes in Delphi, since I'd begun to think of my father, hatted and ashplanted and booted, as an aspect of the pathbreaker; and hearing the cuckoo at the temple of Apollo in Bassae.

Enough. I look forward to seeing you when you land among us – and send our love to you and Jean in vine leaves and libations.

Seamus

Manolis's father, George Savidis (1929–95), was a Visiting Professor at Harvard and eminent editor of the texts of modern Greek poets. By 'chief Ellmann type authority', SH is referring to Richard Ellmann (see headnote to 1988).

'purchase of the house next door': this never happened.

Paddy Mullarkey, contemporary of SH at St Columb's, was now in command at Ireland's Department of Finance; Lewis Glucksman (1925–2006) was a financial trader and chairman of Lehman Brothers, Kuhn, Loeb Inc.

R. F. (Roy) Foster (b.1949) is an Irish historian and author of, among other books, a biography of Yeats, the first volume of which, subtitled *The Apprentice Mage*, had just been published. In spite of his difficulties, SH completed a review of it, which *Atlantic Monthly* printed in November. 'Yeatsian bundle' alludes to Yeats's own dictum that a poet, though writing from his personal life, is 'never the bundle of accident and incoherence that sits down to breakfast'.

To Desmond and Mary Kavanagh PC Kavanagh

24 May 1997 Rome

The soul drinking at the healing waters . . . Thinking of you as we go shamefully free day by day in sunlight and leisure. After a self-improving trip around the pagan sites of Greece, we're back among the familiar images of Rome. *Benedicat vos, omnipotens deus* . . . Love, Seamus and Marie

The card which SH dates as above but which is postmarked 22 June shows a stag drinking from a stream: a detail from a mosaic in the Basilica di San Clemente in Rome. The Latin means, 'May almighty God bless you'.

To Tom Sleigh TS Sleigh

31 July and 8 November 1997 191 Strand Road, Dublin 4

Dear Tom,

You have been on my mind, and indeed all my Cambridge friends have been on my mind. Missed poignantly at moments, then unthought of, then flitting in in the small hours like shades or consciences. I owe letters to everybody and when you see them you can tell them that I know I owe them . . .

You're probably migrant in Europe at this time of the year, but sooner or later this should reach you. I've had a disconsolate sort of a summer. Or if not quite disconsolate, then disordered, torpid, blocked, in disarray. Just now convalescent, getting some writing done, and hoping to re-establish a grip on things. In July I had three free weeks, more or less, and had anticipated doing three hundred lines of the dread hand-locked, stress-linked lines of *Beowulf*, but it was not to be. I went down to Wicklow and gazed and gazed. When I went to open the word-hoard, the key just wouldn't turn. I was like a sullen old truck up to the hubs in mud slick, spinning, spinning, spinning. (*To Glanmore then I came . . .*) Me that in my time was a great caterpillared vehicle, crunching the text gravel with all those Co. Derry gears so blithely grinding. Still, as I say, the chain is beginning to tighten again and a certain haul and purchase being felt.

I think it was partly because of the illness of many friends. My sister Ann had a mastectomy in April and has had chemo-therapy and is now in hospital for radiation treatment. Another woman we know is in the last if undetermined stages of cervical cancer. Hammond's fluctuating Ménière's disease has taken a bad turn and he is from hour to hour, day by day, afflicted with tinnitus and terrified of total deafness. Off his head, in a newly exorbitant way. In general, there has been a failure of the genial spirits, as Wordsworth termed them. They have been suffered to decay.

But I am also anxious on another front: you gave me a manuscript of your new work and I took a race through it at the time, with admiration and a certain awe for the density and sustained explorative drive in it. I am ashamed to say, however, that since I got back here I have managed to mislay the manuscript. I don't want you to send another, because I know exactly the cost (not only financial, but the time and the hassle) but I want you to know that the poems as a body of work stayed with me.

The mislaid text reminds me of another reason for my torpor, which is a feeling of being overwhelmed by mail, old and new, by paper, by books, by unfiled archival material, letters, manuscripts, shit of all kinds, some of which should be treated as bullion. The letters I've had over decades from friends are not filed, I dwell in what was once a pleasing shabbiness but has now become a disgraceful mess. A feeling of stasis and crisis, if such a co-existence is possible. Boredom and unglory.

What a drear note. [. . .]

The mislaid manuscript was of Sleigh's 1999 collection *The Dreamhouse*.
For 'Ménière's', SH writes 'Meuniers'; for 'tinnitus', 'tintinnus'.

To Louis de Paor

MS de Paor

1 August 1997 191 Strand Road, Dublin 4

Dear Louis,

The poem looks fine, except that I think I should add a colon at line 9.

Meanwhile, I did a version of '*Gile na Gile*' – impossible, of course, a clank and clump where there should be *seinm* and sidereal melody . . . But I thought I'd let you see it in case you had any preference. I think the Ó Súilleabháin works better because the task is easier; but Seán is an Ó Rathaille man and it seemed right to have a go at an Ó Rathaille. But I honestly am not pressing this on you. It just happens to be to hand.

Send me a couple of M.D.'s, with Béarla help, and we'll see how it goes.

Seamus

SH's translation of the aisling '*Gile na Gile*' (literally 'Brightness of Brightness') by Aodhagán Ó Rathaille would eventually be published in a political context, by *Index on Censorship*, in 1998.

'*seinm*': verbal noun of *seinn*, 'to play music'. Ó Rathaille's poem is an outstanding example of the musical deployment of metre. The Seán referred to is Seán Ó Tuama, of whom SH says, in *Stepping Stones*: 'Seán was somebody whom I could talk to honestly and merrily and get honest and merry truths from in return. Sharp as a tack and full of knowledge.'

M.D. was Michael Davitt (1950–2005), poet and founder of the magazine *Innti*; de Paor was at this time editing a bilingual edition of his work.

'Béarla': the English language.

To Helen Vendler

TS Harvard

15 August 1997 191 Strand Road, Dublin 4

Dear Helen,

The Feast of the Assumption. On this morning the Ancient Order of Hibernians used to march out from the 'tin hut' – a corrugated iron barn that was their hall – with pipes skirling and banners flying to the tune of 'I'll Sing a Hymn to Mary'. To-day there should be banners hefted and astream and massed pipes and drums for the hymn to Helen. I am sorry not to have written before now in response to such wonderful letters from you, after Cambridge and after completion of the book. And I am further cast down by my inability to lay my hands on the latter just at this moment, more evidence of the moult-down in self and study. There is such jubilation in all that you do, such volts of your own spirit. It is as if Hopkins were to turn the bunsen of his younger, exhilarated being upon one – I feel not only blessed that you have written the book, indeed could bear to write it; but magnified by your constant huge kindness and care. At dinner here last night, for example, I was waving your gift of the Oxford University crest aloft over John and Christine Kelly (and Lester Conner et al., it being late Yeats School time), conducting the chorus of praise that arose. Genuine need for people to testify – in your absence – to the intensity of their gratitude, because of good deeds you've done for them, but really to their delight in your being who you are and giving yourself to all of us – all the powers and dazzles you embody and manifest. I cannot imagine how you live at such a pitch of devotion to the work you do and the people you know. If I think of the achieve of it, I'll sink under my sheer plod, go cindery rather than gold vermilliony.

The spirits have lifted a bit. I was deeply reassured to have your account of the drug list that could be checked with the GP, but I never did get round to going back to see him. I somehow even enjoyed the slough. The fact that I had weeks free was a bad thing maybe, I simply wasted time. I meant to have six hundred more lines of *Beowulf* completed by the end of August – counting out from early June – but have let all that slip. Kept up with the business mail but did not write a human letter. Have not had Tom and Jean Flanagan to the house – lunches out and all that, but no zest.

[. . .]

Membership of the Ancient Order of Hibernians, founded in New York in 1836 and predominantly American, is restricted to Catholic men who are Irish or of Irish descent.

The 'hymn to Helen' was owed in gratitude both for the letters mentioned here and for *Seamus Heaney*, Vendler's study of SH's work, published by Harvard University Press the following year.

The Oxford crest had been a birthday gift; John Kelly (b.1942) was (is now Emeritus) Research Fellow in English at St John's College, Oxford and a specialist in Yeats and Eliot; his wife is Christine.

'If I think of the achieve of it . . . gold vermilliony': see Hopkins's 'The Windhover'.

To Helen Vendler

TS Harvard

21 October 1997

Glanmore Cottage, Ashford,
Co. Wicklow

Dear Helen,

You should have heard from me long before this: I had rain sent to my roots by your wonderful big long letter of so many weeks ago and should have at least acknowledged it, if not answered it on the spot. But I wanted to have read your book about the poems, and while I have occasionally swooped and stolen into it for short spaces of time, it was only this morning that I gave myself over to silence, Glanmore and autumn and read the whole manuscript at a sitting. Madness not to have done so before, but you will know my hamperedness when it comes to reading about myself. It always tends to be the same rhythm, even with you – swift glancings and gleanings to begin with, then a later, more deliberate attentiveness. In this case, it was such a honeycombing and harvesting, such a granary of rewards, that I am more than usually angry at myself for not having read the thing earlier and sung out my hallelujah. I am all atingle with the seraphic – your own word of approbation that slew me altogether – quality of your writing. I remember from my first literature lecture in Queen's a definition of style (quoted, the man said, from Conrad) as 'nervous energy translated into phrases'. The phrases you found to commend or describe different poems from different phases revivified me entirely – the 'flirtatious revenge' of 'The Thimble', the movement from 'fact to consequence' in 'The Old Icons', the perception of 'the perceptual as a never-to-be-forgotten standard of veracity and plain speech' – language-joys and brilliant illuminations flashing and fleshing on very page. I cannot possibly tell you of my every elation, but among the ones that had me most trampolining off my own delight were your many 'Second thought' adducings ('Peninsula'/'Postscript', 'Damson'/'Mossbawn', 'Oracle'/'In the Beech'); your inexhaustible capacity to take pleasure in and see the point of poems which I had forgotten – ones I had loved at the time of writing but which had become part of the strata, down there in the shell midden, such as the whole 'Sweeney Redivivus' riff – your etymological forage and fillip at the end of 'The Scribes' was baton and wand, Mozart and Merlin altogether – and how delighted I am to have 'The Old Icons' and 'The Stone Verdict' and 'The Riddle' so jubilantly celebrated and rated. But delicious as each local praising is, what lifts the whole thing beyond anything that has been written on me ever before is the conceptual plane you establish, your organizing ideas of anonymities, archaeologies, anthropologies and so on – The Seven A's, The Seven Arguments as opposed to sacraments – the way they are at once true to the questing, what-nextness of the life and the need behind the poems and also revelatory of qualities actually inherent in the writing. It is utterly heart-lifting and mind-sifting. It overjoys me that you should be able to say what you say about the work because a) it is *you* who are saying it and b) what I am hearing is a preternaturally sensitive articulation of that which resides in the language of the poems as a matter of premonition and intuition. 'Deserted harbour stillness', for example, is even more credible to me after your reading. But all of them are. I hope you won't mind my noting too some mini-slips (mini-slip = a fact in a mini-skirt?) which you might want to attend to in proof. (Will put them on separate page.)

Matters you mentioned: Derry? Londonderry? I think your notion of indicating that you are falling in with my habitual usage rather than imposing your own nomenclature is a good one.

Louis O'Neill went, as far as I know, to a 'Catholic' pub. Devlin's, his usual haunt, was shut. The bomb was delivered presumably because the pub was disobeying the IRA's call for a curfew: pulling down the blinds but continuing to trade. I better double check that and let you know by fax if there is a problem.

[. . .]

Helen – just a few pernickety points, to head off the nit-pickers. If 'head-off' can go with 'nit-pickers'. Also some points of information that might be helpful.

1.5 In 'Anahorish' it should be 'neighbours', strictly speaking, and not 'family' at line 4. The Gribbin family lived in/on Anahorish and we'd see their hurricane lamps going about the farmyard after dark.

1.8 As a matter of interest, the title 'Requiem for the Croppies' echoes Geoffrey Hill's 'Requiem for the Plantagenet Kings'. Only the title . . .

2.11 In summer 1969, the police do not confront the Civil Rights marchers in Derry; 'the police and residents were involved in what came to be known as the "Battle of Bogside".'

3.2 Ledwidge not a Northern Ireland poet. Born in Slane in Co. Meath and lived there. (I love all the resemblances you help to outline there, the implied self-portraits.)

4.1 My own mistake here, evidence of how other Belfast and all that really was. Dockers, apparently, were Catholic, the labourers who worked at loading and unloading the boats. What I am describing is a shipyard worker, who were typically and notoriously from East Belfast and Protestant. This was later pointed out to me.

4.5 Better say the interlocutor was English rather than Protestant (line 4, para. 2). He was in fact one Mr Paige Smith from Stroud in Gloucestershire whose English purred with the same upholstered calm as his Rolls-Royce.

5.1 Aunt Agnes rather than Grace. Grace survived.

5.11 Again, as a matter of interest, the last earl was Hugh O'Neill, with whom the Earl of Essex parleyed rather than fought in 1599 (I think) and thus earned Elizabeth's final rejection, not to say his execution.

6.6 The woman in the wheelchair was my Aunt Mary but there's no big need to tell them so.

PS As I was skimming through the notes to pick up these references I came across other things that had made me go yippee in the margins, such as the comment that the allegories in *The Haw Lantern* were written 'not to escape the censor but to escape the topicalities of political journalism'. And then, re. the twelve-liners, 'Shaker simplicity'. Shiver me timbers!

PS Also, just remembered that in discussion of weather forecast sonnet (Glanmore Sonnets) you say there is a storm – it's a sort of imagined event, suggested by the gale-warning on the radio. Fuss, fuss . . .

Before sending the final draft of her book on SH to the publishers, Vendler had asked him to check her chronology.

To Derek Mahon

MS Emory

27 October 1997 Magdalen College, Oxford OX1

Amigo,

Here briefly, at the fall of the leaf. The deerpark misty, the choir angelic, the heart aswim . . . Just finished a second read-through of *The Yellow Book* and, as they say, happy for you. 'The hot drink far from home' – the note perfect all the way, the opulence of means and melodies, the *pleure dans le cœur*, the combination of buoyancy in the verse and ballast in the feeling. The poems to Eugene L., the Christmas in Kinsale, the Chelsea Arts Club, the night-thoughts: I couldn't place one over the other in my mind just now, just have this Baudelairean dusk-mood of gratitude. I see Miłosz calls poetry a dividend from ourselves: high yields, *mon vieux*. See you.

Seamus

'opulence . . . buoyancy . . . Baudelairean dusk mood': all true of Mahon's *The Yellow Book*, in which two of the twenty poems it contains are 'after Baudelaire', and a richly allusive, *fin-de-siècle* mood prevails.

In a letter to Dennis O'Driscoll of 27 November, SH thanks him for introducing him to Miłosz's aphorism through *As the Poet Said* (1997), a collection of remarks about poetry selected from a column O'Driscoll had written for *Poetry Ireland Review* and edited in book form by the Irish poet Tony Curtis.

Below the signature, in Mahon's hand, on the actual letter in the Emory archive: 'Pompous ass.'

To Paul Muldoon

MS Emory

13 November 1997 [In transit]

Dear Paul,

After the rickshaw (post-colonial crime but photo-opportunity) and the sushi 'n sake *agus a leithéid*, we're on the plane home. Kenzaburō Ōe did me good, as they say; we were on a forum about 'the peripheral and the universal', but we talked of other things as well, including P.M. He's a great tonic, sharp and sheer. You feel at home with him.

Before I left Dublin, I had lunch with S. Deane. I'd not seen him for a few months, so the 'business lunch' aspect allowed us to get restored to ourselves. However, business was indeed plied, and the Norton/Field Day/Hean-o/Deane-o/Muldoon-o triangle half-squared. As you sensitively realized, there are considerations which weigh, impersonally, on all persons involved.

There was – and still is, as far as S.D. is concerned, an understanding that Nortons might do a paperback, one-volume digest of the three-volume hard-back *FD Anthology*. Now, of course, there is the added complication of Volume 4, the vol. of atonement. So to speak. Seamus is understandably bound to stand by this publication also, but he is willing (and this is the first time we have settled this proposal) to go ahead with a paperback that includes material from this fourth volume also. So, given my prior link to the Field Day, I thought I should begin by standing by this proposal, and should perhaps co-sponsor (not co-edit) the paperback proposal.

This obviously complicates the position vis-à-vis Norton's proposal about the Muldoon/Heaney editorship of a book of Irish literature. Nortons may have decided already upon some course of action in relation to the FD paperback, but for the moment I must not make any move to accept the offer made to you and me.

Other thoughts arise and swim around. It may be that two anthologies with Ted are enough. It's one thing to join up, it's another thing to seem to be sewing up. Not that the *seems* matters a damn. It's just that I have some instinct that enough may have been done, now that *The School Bag* is out.

You yourself would also be freer without me. You will understand that the prospect of the actual work in tandem is/would be pleasant and heartsome – all the toil and trouble of it apart – but a) I wonder if I should not stop taking on big commissions like this anyhow and b) I have had this notion of fiddling towards my own *Kings, Lords, Commons* type of thing, and the Norton book might disturb/overload that circuit.

All this like the nerves without pattern on a screen. I look forward to seeing you next week. Will fax this when I get home. *Le grá*. Seamus

Fax headed 'On way home from Japan', the second and third sheets on Imperial Hotel, Tokyo notepaper.

'After the rickshaw': SH had already sent Muldoon a postcard from Japan, reporting his 'god's eye view of the world – the poor human back hard at it – from the top of a rickshaw'.

'*agus a leithéid*': 'and the like'.

Kenzaburō Ōe (b.1935–2023), Japanese novelist, had won the Nobel Prize in 1994; he and SH were among a group of Nobel laureates being fêted in Japan (for more, see letter to Alasdair Macrae, 23 November 1997).

The idea for an anthology co-edited by SH and Muldoon petered out.

Final paragraph: see 'as if a magic lantern threw the nerves in patterns on a screen' (T. S. Eliot, 'The Love Song of J. Alfred Prufrock').

To Alasdair Macrae

TS Macrae

23 November 1997 191 Strand Road, Dublin 4

Dear Friend,

This day two months ago, we had our autumnal Sunday evening drink in Glasgow, this day two weeks ago I was in Kyoto with a bunch of beet-rua-ing Japanese, at a hooley organized by the Paddy faction in that city (well, there are paddy fields, aren't there?); and this day week I was on my back in St Vincent's Hospital, my left leg in a plaster-cast and my two eyes fixed incredulously on the ceiling – the doctor had just told me I'd be in the cast until after Christmas and that it would then take another couple of months of painful physiotherapy to get the limb into any kind of working order again. This evening I'm on top of the bed at home, still plastered, so to speak, but attached to my laptop. Writing on impulse, briefly, just to thank you for the postcards – I especially appreciated the moustache on the redcoat – and the wedding news and the confirmed invitation to read in Stirling, and to let you know about this fuck-up.

Marie and I had a glorious week in Japan (4–12 November), treated like royalty, flown first class and limousined about, farting through silk, eating through chopsticks, committing crimes against humanity (if only for the photo-opportunity) by riding on a rickshaw, and generally just swanking – which is what our function was. I was part of a Forum which the newspaper group Yomiuri Shimbun has been sponsoring for the past ten years or so, called 'Creativity towards the 21st Century'. Basically, it's a bit of corporate self-promotion and self-congratulation: they put half a dozen N. persons on display at different universities, take photos and write stories about it all in their own columns. I accepted because the other literary customer this year was Kenzaburō Ōe, whom I'd met and liked; and the peace person was big Shimon Peres (whom I only met at the final reception, as it turned out, since we hunted in different packs). Anyhow, the treatment was truly splendid, we were alive and high in a refreshing way, a feeling of Tír na nÓg, and then wham, back home to the Oisín syndrome. Twenty-four hours after we land, I go back to the airport to meet two American friends, fall, tear the muscle, grow to be three hundred years old in a second, get stretchered and ambulanced, anaesthetized and knifed, the knee itself stitched like a laced-up football, the leg like a post attached to the hapless trunk. Dashed inconvenient, what!

I'm in good enough heart, and can footer about on the crutches. Secretly glad to be able to get out of several (not, alas, all) social duties; and feeling that I may be able to get a bit of time to myself as a recompense. Awkward in the bed, all the same, having a terra cotta pipe instead of a bendable limb. And I won't be in my attic study for a long time. Enough. My love to Elise and yourself. And my thanks – along with the scholar's – for your congratulations to her for all her work and pomps. Or should that latter stay in the single for once?

Seamus

'N. persons': Nobel Prize winners.

Tír na nÓg: in Celtic myth, the Otherworld, returning from which the poet and warrior Oisín fell to the ground and immediately became an old man.

To Ted Hughes

MS BL

14 December 1997 191 Strand Road, Dublin 4

Dear Ted,

There's that image early in the first Canto of the *Commedia* where Dante compares himself to a swimmer cast up on the shore, looking back at the immensity of the thing that has delivered him – it came to me when I took out this paper and asked how I could salute you after the immensity I've come through these last few days, reading – and re-reading, once – *Birthday Letters*. I was very gladdened and excited when Joanna told me you said I could see the manuscript, but was overwhelmed when I began to read it. Poetry and wounded power gathering and doing the Cuchulain warp-spasm, the salmon-feat, showing a wild Shakespearean back above their element. What is so magnificent from the very beginning of the sequence – but which gathers to a greatness as it proceeds – is the way the quotidian and the sacrosanct commingle, the simultaneity of astonished 'my-God-this-is-what-actually-happened' and 'o thank God, what actually happened has gone round about the dark of the mind's moon and come back beyond me as poetry'. The impact is head-on and heartbreaking all at once. I feel inadequate to the need to tell you how the poems rocked and sweetened me. I want to list out favourites, but that would run to paragraphs, and equally want to cite passages. What I actually did first was to write the enclosed. Only a poem could relieve what for me was the psychic equivalent of 'the bends'. I had been down so deep, at such levels of pressure, in such submarine contact with the sadness and endurance of the undertruths, I gasped, as it were, when I closed the manuscript and could hardly re-enter the daylight life of the house here. Luckily, I am living in fairly mid-ocean conditions these days, on a raft, a kind of drifting stage, since I wrecked my leg a month ago and had the bed moved downstairs (more of that in a moment). At any rate, I was able to live in the aftershock of the first reading longer than usual, without the dispersals that are usually inflicted by being on the move, and I could let the poem happen. I hope you don't think it is either too close or too oblique. At this moment, I think I would like to publish it round the time when *Birthday Letters* appears, but it was not written with that in mind. 'A timely utterance gave that thought relief' – it was more that kind of thing by 'one not used to make a present joy the matter of my song' – or something like that, I think, is what he says.

You have two powerful lenses turned on the matter of the story – the lens of personal memory and the lens of mythic understanding, and each is potent on its own as a single view-finder, and I think you could find poems where one of the lenses is almost the only thing being trained on the subject. But usually they are being aligned, for magnification of detail or for distancing and contracting, for a longer view. The poem about the flounders, for example, is so up-and-at-them, tell-what-happened that the gift-myth dimension of it is almost going to be unnoticeable to those after only the story, but then the ending – achingly, simply, incontrovertibly – turns narration to illumination. Which reminds me of 'Epiphany' and 'Chaucer' and 'Earthenware Head' (those two I've loved from the moment I saw them) and 'Wuthering Heights' (with its Shakespearey/Milton-y turn at 'the moor wind') and 'Daffodils' and 'The Fifty-Ninth Bear' and 'Grand Canyon'. But I don't, as I say, want this to turn into a list. Of the other comprehended-through-the-theme kind of poem, the one that comes in from the circumference of your understanding towards the meaning of what happened, I most love, perhaps, 'Picture of Otto' – and maybe that is because of the Owen allusion – and the elm table poem and 'Black Coat', and 'Rag Rug'; then there are the poems that work because of the saw-tooth truth – 'A Little Touch of Timon' and 'The Literary Life' – and others because of the total, intimate, irresistible surge of the recognizable, like 'Stubbing Wharfe' and 'The Beach'. And then there's the sheer poetry of 'Freedom of Speech' and the sheer riveting story (poetry too) of 'Fidelity'. I could go on . . .

What is hugely a triumph and a relief is the sense that this book can now be placed like a sandbagged wall against the wash and slush of forty years, that it heaves and creates a backwash that rocks the whole tide backwards; it is very daring and bewildering, for you an unprecedented kind of solitude and exposure all at once, seismic both in terms of your own being and in terms of the literary and cultural history of our times. No doubt you dread the vulgarity and vehemence which publication may unleash, but it is hard to know in advance. I myself cannot imagine it not being greeted with awe and tenderness. Even those who don't know the transfigured nature of the achievement will be helpless before the density and utterly amazing candour of the tale.

What an *annus mirabilis* – with a touch of the *terror, terribilis* too – this has been for you. In the course of writing this note, I got a call from Barrie Cooke who reported that he'd spoken to you and that you sounded good. I greatly appreciated your letter sent during the summer and had been meaning to write, but lay instead with my ear to the pillow or the rail or the trail and hoped that the pulse that was coming in from North Tawton was a jubilant one. I know you've come through having been gone into, as it were, and the arrival of *Oresteia* convinced me that all was well. I read the *Agamemnon* right through on the afternoon of November 19 – I know that because I came out of hospital on Tuesday 18, and began my raft-life on the downstairs bed that night. You may have heard my tale of woe: I fell, inexplicably, drastically, on the level floor of Dublin airport at 8:30 in the morning on Friday 14th. Maybe not so inexplicably after all – I'd been in Japan for a week, had come back, not slept for a couple of nights and had driven myself to rise on the Friday in order to meet a woman from Boston – she has done my taxes in America for the past twelve years, never accepted a halfpenny in payment, was coming to Dublin (first time) for a long weekend and so, of course, I promised I'd be in Arrivals . . . Anyhow, muscle torn off the left knee. Surgery. Cast from arse to ankle, due to stay on until 30 December. Then physiotherapy for weeks, the gleaming smile of the torturers. 'Spring in the step' takes on a whole new meaning. Philoctetes' revenge? Antaeus' revenge for my 'Hercules and Antaeus'? Still, there have been rewards, such as the chance to dwell with reading and – even – writing. And I must say the effect of reading *Birthday Letters* has been to shake me into poetic wakefulness, if not action. The first time you did it to me was in 1962 – I remember the tension and promise as I got the idea for a poem about turkeys, after reading 'View of a Pig' – but this time I feel called upon to do more. To get through to 'freedom of speech'. We'll see. (First fruits, or some of them, I shall also enclose – 'Red, White and Blue'.)

Haven't read the rest of the *Oresteia* yet, but know that the medium, that lean, toledo-bendy, cleavery-come-hithery verse line, is yours to do anything with now. The speed. The jump-cut, dropped-weight thunk of the scenes – more apparitions than scenes, and yet more solid than apparitions – that's what comes through, or what I remember coming through. Above all, the sense of nothing intervening, no translation, as it were, just the flame of telling licking along and firing up. It should go very powerfully on to the stage. Nothing like it – it's a match for reality, the trilogy.

Meanwhile, my neck is as sore as you describe in one of the 'Letters'. It probably has to do with the crutches, the reawakening of an old arthritic mine in the shoulder, the reflex-mysteries of lying with one leg flat in its terra cotta pipe and the other raised at the knee, supporting the shuffle desk as I write . . . For whatever reason, I am spiked and spurred, glowing with bone-burn, and not sure how to proceed. It's been with me for a week. Painkillers have no effect. I take sleeping pills at night. I'm seeing a 'rheumatologist' to-morrow. But I'm going to try to get at it now by taking a glass of whiskey. It *can* help.

My love to Carol. I know she will have close and testing relation to the January book, but also to you in the course of your own health-tests of the past few months. The blessings of the season, as they say, upon you both.

Seamus

PS I haven't shown *B. Letters* to Marie yet. Nor mentioned it to Barrie. It's probably best to keep it like that for a few weeks still? S.

PS 'The Prism'! 'Fever'! Enough!

Joanna Mackle, Publicity Director at Faber, had sent SH a typescript of *Birthday Letters*, Hughes's account in verse of his life with Sylvia Plath and its legacy. Both speed and secrecy were required to prepare the book for publication on 29 January 1998 and very few people outside the firm were allowed to see it before then, SH being a privileged exception. On 1 January 1998, Hughes wrote a letter to SH that began: 'Your letter overwhelmed me. I dearly wanted to know what you would feel about all those pieces and about the niceties and not-so-niceties of publishing them – your opinion above everybody's (as a veteran of ticklish declarations).'

'What I actually did was to write the enclosed': a draft of SH's poem 'On a New Work in the English Tongue', subsequently revised.

'A timely utterance . . .' and 'one not used . . .': in both cases, SH is quoting Wordsworth, first from 'Ode on Intimations of Immortality', then from *The Prelude*.

'from the moment I saw them': 'Earthenware Head' and 'Chaucer' were both in Hughes's *New Selected Poems* of 1995; 'A Little Touch of Timon' was not included in the collection as published.

Hughes's translation of the *Oresteia* was not published until the year after his death, in 1999, when it was first staged at the National Theatre's Cottesloe Theatre.

'your own health-tests': Hughes had been undergoing treatment for cancer.

To Thomas Flanagan TS Amherst

16 December 1997

[. . .]

And so too, as you see, I have become an injury bore. I have a 'stoppeth one of three' need to blurt it all out to everyone, especially since I can add that inside a week of getting out of hospital, I developed gout in the big toe of the injured leg (excruciating, but cleared up quickly with the pills) and then ten days ago was revisited by an old sorrow in the neck, a pinched nerve, unmercifully painful and constant, weakly assailed by pain-killers but inextinguishable as the fires of hell. It was of a similar complaint suffered by Montague that Deane-o remarked, 'Oh, the brass is wearing out?'

[. . .]

'I have become an injury bore': this follows an account by SH of his airport accident.

To Carol and Czesław Miłosz

MS PNL

30 December 1997 191 Strand Road, Dublin 4

Dear Carol and Czesław,

Many thanks for your card at Christmas, and for your sending that agent on my trail . . . True to my sluggishness, I have done nothing about it yet, but I hope to contact him before long.

Seeing you both was one of the high points of recent years, and I am just sorry that I wasn't more available or more alive when you were in Dublin. For about six weeks this summer, I went into a kind of dip. I've never been depressed in any full, desperate sense of that term, but for July and August this year, I felt like perished elastic, incapable of my usual 'go'. If I had been my full self, I'd have been more to the fore, perhaps even have crossed the country to Galway, but the inertia was upon me. And then there was the clash of dates between my Kilkenny duties and your R. S. Thomas evening – but I believe that was a good event, and there were surely enough poets there at the one table.

Meanwhile, Marie and I greatly look forward to seeing you in April in LA. Indeed, we may even give you a call in March, since I am due for 'honour' – I feel like an old bull being stuck with rosettes – by the Ireland Funds of San Francisco early that month. It will be a flying visit and I am not sure how free we will be, but we shall dip the flag, for sure.

Meanwhile, farther up your boulevard, at 1175, my old Berkeley friend Tom Flanagan and his wife Jean have rented for the springtime. Tom was in Berkeley when I was there in 1970/71, but went to SUNY at Stony Brook in the mid-seventies. Now that he is in his own seventies (I think) the sun has called him back west.

I've just read a book (in proof) by another friend of mine Darcy O'Brien, called *The Hidden Pope*, all about Lolek and Jurek, Jerzy Kluger and the great poet of the Vatican . . . I've no doubt Czesław will be sent in and be stirred. It is a very positive account.

Much love to you both.

Seamus

Darcy O'Brien's *The Hidden Pope* is subtitled *The Untold Story of a Lifelong Friendship that Is Changing the Relationship between Catholics and Jews*, the friendship in question being that between Karol Wojtyla (1920–2005), who became Pope John Paul II, and the Polish Jewish businessman Jerzy Kluger (1921–2011).

1998

Early in the year, SH was elected by members of Aosdána to the high office of *Saoi* ('wise person'), after which he was drawn back into the now inescapable round of 'hurtling and being hurtled' – as he puts it to Thomas Flanagan in his letter of 5 May – to various parts of the USA, Britain, Italy, Japan . . .

Opened Ground: Poems 1966–1996, a deliberately more substantial volume than SH's *New Selected Poems, 1966–1987*, appeared with his Nobel Prize lecture, 'Crediting Poetry', as tailpiece.

Appointed Emerson Poet in Residence at Harvard, a position that carried with it lighter duties than the Boylston Professorship, he had hoped that on returning from his first semester in that capacity he might meet up again with Ted Hughes; instead, he found himself attending Hughes's funeral.

To Dennis O'Driscoll

TS Emory

31 January 1998

Dear Dennis,

My apologies for not having written to thank you for your letter of a couple of weeks ago and the enclosed Stuart tape. I had indeed heard it on the radio and got some relief from it. I had been agitated by the *Je ne regrette rien* factor and had spoken to a couple of other people about it – Derek M. and Michael L., both of whom seemed less troubled than I was, but then neither of them had been voted a *saoi* by the outfit. I had deferred arrangements for any formal conclusion to the *saoi*ship because of the Philoctetes leg 'n knee factor and was really giving myself time. Had F.S. not made his murmur of retraction, I would have felt under pressure (from myself, from the shade of Brodsky, from the eyes of many other friends) to decline the honour which he had accepted. I was helped to think about it all more clearly by Wilfred Owen's phrase 'the eternal reciprocity of tears' and had persuaded myself that Stuart's Piafism refused that reciprocity and was therefore not to be excused – although excuses could be fairly mounted – confusion, dotage even, mischievous editing etc. Anyhow, for better or worse, I let myself off the hook after the broadcast, and later in the year will be torc-ed, *saoi*-ed and ordered by Mary McAleese. At which stage, it might be worth making some small allusion to the helpfulness of Big Francie's apology, although the dirt-stirring potential of such a remark is probably worth remembering too.

[. . .]

There are no more than seven *Saoithe* at any one time. Francis Stuart, an unrepentant Nazi sympathiser who had spent much of the Second World War in Berlin, had accepted the honour two years before. Máire Mhac an tSaoi had objected to Stuart's election and, when the matter was taken to a vote and her motion defeated, she resigned from Aosdána. SH's own election went ahead in May.

To Tom Sleigh

MS Sleigh

20 February 1998 [In transit]

My Dear Boy,

No other salutation will do on this stationery . . . After the Sweden-swank I was proposed for this Tory haven by a publisher (not my own) and was 'brought aboard', as they say, by a Rule 2 concession – i.e. they break the rules because they want the N. word. Still, the place was founded by, among other people, Humphry Davy, and they have a splendid portrait of Matthew Arnold in the foyer. (Which reminds me – tell Bro. Pinsky to research the death of Arnold and add him to the D. o. P.s list.)

I am, as ever, writing 'on the road'. In the plane, in fact. Marie came over with me to England last Tuesday, partly because I am still a bit anxious about moving around on the leg – it's weak and soreish at times, but not unworkable. For the past week, I have been able to go upstairs like a normal stepper, left, right, left, but until then it was very much one stump at a time. The ruptured quadriceps is a serious injury. I was made a fellow of the Royal (in Dublin!) College of Surgeons recently and had to meet many of the chief cutters, and they all nodded, and pursed, and looked at their toecaps and told me it would get better, but it would be slow. I was lucky enough to have Ireland's head knee-knacker on duty the day I was brought in: general anaesthetic, fourteen stitches, the knee looking (still) like a laced-up football, etc., etc.

Which etc. etc. reminds me of Brodsky, and one of my readings, with

Irina Ratushinskaya, to the Russian Poets Fund in Keele University. I am a patron of the thing, and this was a long promised trip – to glamorous Stoke-on-Trent – and I had hoped that by the time I set out I'd be clear of *Beowulf*. But alas, no – the 3 months I had kept free of engagements, between November 12 and February 17, when I meant to hammer the last 600 lines into submission, were all taken up with the leg. I was daunted and had the wind taken out of my sails. Five weeks on a bed downstairs in the living room, then gradual re-entry into the walking classes. I have not been in Glanmore once in the meantime, because I cannot drive, the knee being so weak. I actually did almost all the *Beo* in Wicklow, alone, like a boxer in the ring with a sparring partner, and I sort of need to be in prime physical shape to square up to it. Also, I cannot altogether work in Glanmore if M. is on the premises, so I didn't want her to be driving me and hovering. But she has, in fact, been my driver everywhere else for months now.
[. . .]

'Tory haven': the headed paper is that of the Athenaeum, one of the grandest of London's private members' clubs.

'tell Bro. Pinsky to research the death of Arnold': referring to a macabre, charade-like game, played by SH and his non-Harvard Cambridge friends, in which the deaths of poets, mainly those who had met grisly ends, were mimed by a player using only forefinger and middle finger, while those watching had to guess the poet in question. Matthew Arnold died of heart failure in 1888 as he ran to catch a train.

The Ukrainian-born Russian poet Irina Ratushinskaya (1954–2017) was, like Brodsky, a dissident and in exile.

To Tom Sleigh

TS Sleigh

28 February 1998

[. . .]

What I did not know on the plane – or when I wrote the poem – was that you too had written about your visit to Epidaurus, so when I sat down a couple of hours ago and started my rapt and chastening reading of 'The Incurables' I was transported, so to speak. First of all, you have achieved what Lowell yearned to achieve, the effect – not 'an effect' – of being heartbreaking. The pressure and lucidity, the mixture of intellectual agility and cargoed spirit, of unmonotonous sublime and resolute down-to-earthness make this opening movement of the book a noble thing, but also (for your friends especially) a transformative experience, an example of that high state of civilized readiness that I once (rather high-flownly) prescribed as the desirable condition for the poet between poems. The pitch, the 'plane of regard' as Brodsky would have called it, made it for me the equivalent of the 'spiritual reading' which was always being urged upon me by the voices of my early and earnest and admirable Catholic education. And it is also, of course, complementary to and richly consonant with the sorrow and opulence of *The Dreamhouse*. I had read those poems again over the past week and came to an even deeper regard and respect for the coherence – and not just the wonderfully elaborated artistic coherence – of the book and the translations and now, the prose. The interview at the end of *Bodily Transport* is also amplified by the opening, although no amplification was necessary – it is grave and sure in a very personal way, yet it has wonderful general enforcements in it, as have the reviews in between. (I hadn't seen the Tranströmer piece, for example, which is brilliant on the Celan/Ashbery distinction, as well as the trivializing of the former and the dumbing down of the latter.) I am babbling but truly the charge I am getting is powerful and instructive, and I am proud for you as well as delighted. [. . .]

Sleigh had supplied a typescript of his collection of poems *The Dreamhouse*, to be published the following year. *Bodily Transport* was the working title for the book of his essays that would appear in 2006 as *Interview with a Ghost*.

To Michael Longley

MS Emory

13 April 1998

Glanmore Cottage, Ashford,
Co. Wicklow

Dear Michael,

Down here on my own for the day: my birthday present to myself. The house in Dublin is in great disarray; builders in the place since late January, a grey film of dirty dust on everything, squalor and torpor disabling me in equal measure. Wicklow, however, never fails to soothe the breast and give an illusion of continuity, coherence, even the possibility of purposeful work . . . I feel I have pushed myself to the edge of my own life by getting caught up in travel and caught down in doings of all the usual sort – festschrifts and endorsements, receptions and eloquences, committees and patronships. I even wrote paragraphs about C. S. Lewis last week – David Bleakley's campaign to reclaim him for Belfast.

At least, something good happened on Friday. It could be the holy door, but the rush to get through hasn't altogether started, so the caution persists. But still. *Oremus*.

This is just to thank you for the *poème-à-clef*, the who-he-Horace, oy-me-Vergil one, which I enjoyed in equal measure for the stately and scampish elements in it. It, and 'The Literary Life' – in the *New Yorker* a while ago – are whetting the edges. Sato's blade beneath the silk.

Epidaurus – the sanctuary of Asclepius – we revisited last May. Small report enclosed – another duty dance, for the Irish Hospice Calendar, for which no doubt you too are being asked to deliver.

I have not forgotten the Sacks test.

See you in Princeton. Me post-LA, for God's sake – Coleslaw Meatloaf conference there, unrefusable too. Up the Poles, so to speak.

Seamus

The literary scholar, Christian apologist and writer of allegorical novels for children C. S. Lewis (1898–1963) was born in Belfast; David Bleakley (1925–2017), Northern Irish politician and peace campaigner, had known Lewis personally and wrote a book about him under the title *C. S. Lewis at Home in Ireland* (1998).

'something good happened on Friday': on 10 April 1998, the Good Friday Agreement was signed by the British and Irish governments and the four major political parties of Northern Ireland – Sinn Féin, the Ulster Unionists, the Social Democratic and Labour Party, and the Alliance Party – formally bringing the Troubles to an end.

'*Oremus*': let us pray.

Longley's '*poème à clef*' is 'Remembering the Poets', later included in *The Weather in Japan*, described by the poet himself as 'a learned leg-pull'.

'Sato's blade beneath the silk': see the second stanza of Yeats's 'A Dialogue of Self and Soul'.

The poem enclosed by SH was the twelve-liner 'Hygeia', included in *The Whoseday Book*, published in 1999 by the Irish Hospice Foundation, but not in any of SH's own subsequent volumes.

'Coleslaw Meatloaf': or Czesław Miłosz, whose achievement was to be celebrated at a four-day festival at Claremont McKenna College, in Claremont, east of Los Angeles; Helen Vendler, Robert Pinsky – then US Poet Laureate – and W. S. Merwin were among the participants, as were others named in the letter immediately below.

To Thomas Flanagan

MS Amherst

5 May 1998

Glanmore Cottage, Ashford,
Co. Wicklow

Dear Tom,

I am here for a one night sit, so to speak. A desperately needed fix of silence. Since I saw you, I have been hurtling and being hurtled . . . Most recently in LA for the Miłosz *hommage*, which I greatly enjoyed and was sorry to have to leave early. Helen V. and Robt Hass were there, plus the Lithuanian Tomas Venclova and the junior Pole-bard Zagajewski, these latter two being a cross between Gaeltacht paranoiacs and European intellectuals, and hence mightily sympathetic. And of course Miłosz and spouse, hale and 87 . . . It gave me great pleasure to get between the rhetorical shafts and roll out a waggonful of sumptuous praise. There's so much to salute.

Then it was cross-continent to rather thinner air. Muldoon, the Longleys, Princeton. Not that Paul M. was not kind and gallant – he is a true lad and a class of a genius – but the big generous mood of the Lithuanian arch-bard was missing. But young Muldoon's anxiety to get to bed early kept me out of the late-night booze-ups and ritual carve-ups which are the usual requirement on these occasions. A good taste in the mouth, a good reading, worth it all . . .

Then back to Marie's graduation (she's better qualified than me now, MPhil in Irish Studies) and then – well – yes – I did – I went to Windsor Castle, to a 'Celebration of the Arts' arranged by herself and the Dook. More like a Wembley fan stampede. Anyhow, I thought that in post-agreement conditions I should show my fenian face, but who cared. Her Majesty 'mingled', we met, I said, 'You know a friend of mine, Ted Hughes.' She, marbly and not as bad as this sounds, 'Yes, my mother knows him better,' and that was more or less it. [. . .]

Then on Friday I was made a *Saoi* – wise person, me and Francis Stuart and Ben and Louis Le Brocquy and Tony O'Malley are now the 5 elect ones. I have the gold torc which once gathered heat from/upon the neck o' Mary Lavin, handed over by our ring-giver and gold-friend, Mary McAleese. At least I knew not to put the thing round my neck. I had been present when Tony O'Malley had been invested or engorged and had seen how ridiculous a grown male looks in a collar and tie, plus a bronze age neck ornament. So the photographs show the

Uachtarán and the Derryman gazing at the gorget in its presentation box. Nae sae bad . . .
[. . .]

The gathering of Irish poets at Princeton was to mark the donation to the university's Firestone Library of the Milberg Collection of Irish Poetry.

Of SH's fellow *Saoithe*, Ben was Benedict Kiely, while Louis le Brocquy and Tony O'Malley (1913–2003) were painters; the late Mary Lavin (1912–96) was a fiction writer most admired for her short stories. Uachtarán: the Irish President, Mary McAleese (b.1951).

To Diarmaid Ó Doibhlin

MS Cork

28 May 1998 191 Strand Road, Dublin 4

A Diarmaid,

Here's my version of 'Hallaig' – done to be read out at a conference in Strathclyde last September. I sent it to Renee just for courtesy's sake, but I won't be publishing it. Renee has enough anxiety dealing with other requests without complicating things. (I suppose I should spell her Rianai, come to think of it.)

The problem is the place names. I've anglicized them as if I were a character in Friel's *Translations*. I wanted the thing to 'run' in English – but of course I heard the master's voice at the back of my head.

More power to you.
Seamus

Diarmaid Ó Doibhlin: i.e. Dermot Devlin, referred to in SH's letter to James Simmons of 11 January 1980.

In fact, SH's translation of Sorley MacLean's most admired poem was published, a few years later, in a bilingual, limited-edition pamphlet by Urras Shomhairle: The Sorley MacLean Trust; on receiving it as a gift Ó Doibhlin wrote to SH: 'Many thanks for the copy of "Hallaig" which I value very much. I'm sure the Somhairle I knew is delighted.'

To Thomas McCarthy

MS Princeton

17 September 1998 191 Strand Road, Dublin 4

Dear Tom,

I'm in Co. Wicklow for the day, down in Glanmore, and

wondering why I don't spend more time in the place. It's a silence-fort, a fuchsia *dún*, a ráth of rumination altogether . . . So why am I going away to Harvard for six weeks this Monday?

Glad to have your letter about the *Cork Review*. When I get up to Dublin I'll certainly send you something. I have a longish chunk in quatrains called 'The Locking Up' which I am oddly fond of – because *it* is odd – and I might try it out on you for starters. I have other 'safer' things, so let me know (617 496 8737 is the Harvard fax) if you have any hesitations and I'll send you something else.

I was sorry about that Triskel wobble, but I was wobbly myself earlier in the year, and worn, and well booked up forbye.

Blessings on the work –

Seamus

Back in Dublin – I changed the title to 'Screenplay'. What do you think?

As editor of the *Cork Review*, McCarthy had asked SH for poems. He took the one here titled 'The Locking Up', later 'Screenplay', a strikingly uncharacteristic piece in which SH imagines his widowed father leaving The Wood and locking the front door as he had never needed to while his wife was alive. In what it describes rather more than in its language, the poem seems to echo the final stanza of Wordsworth's 'Timothy': 'Perhaps to himself at that moment he said: / "The key I must take, for my Ellen is dead" . . .' SH did not include the poem in any subsequent volume.

dún is the Irish for fort; a *ráth* is a defensive enclosure.

'Triskel wobble': SH had promised McCarthy, on the board of the Triskel Arts Centre in Cork, to read there, but nothing came of it.

To Ted Hughes

MS BL

19 September 1998 Ballynahinch Castle, Co. Galway

Dear Ted,

A morning after a reading the night before – in Clifden. I don't know if you ever were in this hotel, but it is our favourite in Ireland. River and wood. Belonged to an eighteenth-century Irish MP, more recently to a Maharajah. Now to a consortium – but if ever you wanted to come, silently and unapprehended, the man to contact is Des Lally. A book reader and submanager here.

But what I should be saying is how elated Marie and I were to hear about the OM. You should have had a letter from me long before now.

Somehow the Eliot – and Forster? – precedent shines through and the honour not only ratifies you in the order of the present time and our present lives, but it magnifies itself by being continuously present, as it were, in the poetic tradition, subject to what they used to call in our Christian apologetics 'continuous creation'. There's something about the O_2 in OM, whether it is said or seen, that makes for an aura or halo effect. It is qualitatively, imaginatively different from the other distinctions and will always be more so, now that it has been best-o-ed on you.

We went to *Phèdre* – ideal conditions, in that we landed in Hazlitt's around 4 on the Saturday, found that there were seats and were in the theatre by 7:20, out by 9:30, as if we'd gone like Quaker Oats – remember – 'shot from guns'. The pace and drive of the play were terrific. It gathered and forced and broke oceanically in the last twenty minutes. The big horses speech will always be with me. I'd seen a version – couplets, couplets, couplets – by Derek Mahon in the Gate Theatre in Dublin a couple of years ago which carried itself very differently, and in which that speech (naturally) also stood out. But oddly, the verse was like reins on the tumult, whereas the hugeness of the outer and inner story, the god and the plot coming up at the same moment, rose more extraordinarily in the prose. Not that prose is the right name for the medium: it was a match for the alexandrine, it seemed to me, a kind of diction cushion which established a certain level and convention, and then opened and touched deep. The cast was terrific also – I especially admired Hippolytus's confidant – whose name I forget, but it is not fair to single out one of them. And Diana Rigg got more and [more] powerful as the thing proceeded.

What excitement and purchase. And to think that *Alcestis* and *Oresteia* are still to come. Our night in the Piccadilly wakened me to theatre again. I have to say I enter the places without much anticipation or expectation but all that changed on September 5.

I'm off to Harvard for my reduced-duty and shortened-time round of service as Poet in Residence. Back in Ireland on 31 October. Due to be in London in mid-November when – perhaps – we might meet. Meanwhile, after all my arsing about, the *New Yorker* is going to publish that post-*Birthday Letters* poem, in some special edition due in the next month or six weeks. There's an O in the title of it now – they wanted to call it by the title that I had used to explain the kind of poem it was. I'd said it was as if I had written a kind of 'On first looking into

T.H.'s *B.L.*' – and I'm afraid that's what they've persuaded me to call it. To get round their rule of no dedications, and to put their dumbo readers in possession of the facts. Heigho.

Love to you both. Seamus

PS House now looking and feeling good. Books coming back to shelves – hmm [or could it be 'home'?] – but energy returning also. Keep well. S.

'I don't know if you were ever in this hotel': Ballynahinch Castle, in Co. Galway, where Hughes may well have stayed on one of his fishing expeditions, and where Des Lally, whose literary interests include modern Irish theatre, was assistant manager.

SH must have heard in advance that Hughes was to receive the Order of Merit, considered the highest honour the British monarch has to bestow. T. S. Eliot and E. M. Forster both received it.

'There's something about the O_2 in OM': SH actually writes the small '2' beneath the 'O', like a cedilla, perhaps meant to signify 'doubly oxygenated' as a chemist might have expressed it.

Hughes's translation of Racine's *Phèdre* had enjoyed a successful run at the Albery Theatre in London, directed by Jonathan Kent and with Diana Rigg (1938–2020) in the title role; 'Hippolytus's confidant', Théramène, was played by John Shrapnel (1942–2020). In a late burst of translating from classical drama, Hughes also produced versions of Euripides's *Alcestis* and Aeschylus's *Oresteia* that were performed posthumously. He died on 28 October.

To Laurie Anderson

MS Emory

9 October 1998

English Department, Barker Center,
Harvard University, Cambridge,
MA 02138

Dear Laurie Anderson,

Please forgive me for not being in touch. I have been all over the country in the meantime. I apologize for not having been able to give the material you sent a decent span of attention, but I am glad to be associated with your project and to have the poem like a little pennant on the great craft you are launching. Success attend you.

Seamus Heaney

PS Can you add 'big' before 'hull' – and restore original lineation?

The American performance artist and musician Laurie Anderson (b.1947) had requested permission to incorporate the poem 'Lightenings VIII' – about the mysterious boat that appeared to the monks of Clonmacnoise – into the prelude to her multimedia stage show *Songs and Stories for Moby Dick* (1999).

To Donalda Crichton Smith

MS Emory

6 November 1998 191 Strand Road, Dublin 4

Dear Donalda,

You should have heard from me before this: Alasdair Macrae wrote to me when I was in Harvard with the news of Iain's death and the sorrow was both sudden and abiding. His presence on the earth meant there was always that much more trueness and tenderness and merriment: in his case the pureness of the spirit and the pureness of the poetry were continuous with each other. Alasdair used to enjoy imitating Sorley's tremulous exclamations about 'the Bless-ss-ed Iain' and the adjective was the right one. I know he also had his sorrows, and that there were periods when you too must have been distressed for *his* distress; but he *made* something of all that and kept himself a whole and healing person by the huge hurting effort of his art. One of my favourite books of his is one called *In the Middle* – many of the poems in it simply break the heart, and when I got home earlier this week, I couldn't stop reading it. I reviewed it on Irish Radio twenty years ago at least, and read out the one called 'When Day Is Done'; but almost any poem in there finds a path into the centre of the self. 'Around the iron fades the fresh dew.' All his tenderness and stoicism, his challenge and his kindness, are in those poems; so in one sense there is nothing to worry about – he belongs to the future, and as long as the languages keep going, all that he brought to the fore out of himself and his culture will stay working. But your emptied-out house will be a site of hurt for you; none of us will miss him the way you will. Marie and I send all our love; and I apologize for the slowness of this letter. (Iain once said I was a slow poet, but he meant that the rate of the word-music was slowed down . . .) Somehow, when I was 'on the road' in the States I couldn't centre myself in the right kind of silence. And then, suddenly, I was called home because of the death of Ted Hughes. Shocking times. Love from the both of us.

Seamus

'as long as the languages keep going': plural because Crichton Smith wrote in both English and Gaelic.

To Desmond and Mary Kavanagh

MS Kavanagh

28 November 1998 Tamlaghtduff, Bellaghy, Co. Derry

Dear Des and Mary,

Last night I was in Derry and did a reading in the Orchard Gallery (the basement of St Columb's Hall, transformed) and came down here to my sister Ann's. Have the chance now to lie about for a few hours, because I'm due to go to Belfast to-morrow for *pléaráca* to celebrate D. Hammond's 70th birthday. (We were in Asturias last weekend, for Anne Devlin's 60th, so time's going on.)

It's going on for you too. I thought Fr Dick's sermon was perfectly pitched, about memory and the transition from the numbness of grief to the pain of loss. Strictly and theologically speaking, that pain is hell upon earth. Your lives have been irrigated by sorrow and all the plenitude of your love and delight in Rory has been turned into a sorrow river flowing through you. None of us want to think of it. I was gladdened to hear that Colette had read the poem, and by coincidence I had been footering with it again. Somewhere in me was an unease with the thin, shortlined sections. The change of rhythm, the pulse, didn't seem right. I think the version I am sending you now is the final one – and I especially like the word 'plout' at the end – a countering irrigation and plenitude, a pentecost. In classical elegy – as at the end of 'Lycidas' – the dead one is resurrected in a beneficent landscape and I can think of none more nurturing than that river country around Ahascragh.

Also I'll enclose three other poems. I don't know if you ever saw the Shakespeare/St Columb's one. I read it in Derry last night and Colin Fox appeared and told me he had played 'the black' among the three suitors for Portia's hand in Rusty's *ad hoc* classroom reading of *The Merchant of Venice*. Thomas Mullarkey was in the audience and I thought, Christ, he'll be expecting to hear *his* name, but then he was never a thespian . . .

You'll recognize where the other two short ones came from. I told you that I always associated – since your sorrows came upon you both – Hugh Bredin's and your boyhood tests in the piano practice room at St Columb's with a capacity for facing the music in the more familiar sense of facing a test. So that's where 'The Breard' came from, a condensation of things you saw earlier. (Carol Hughes, in a Victorian veil, Jacqueline Kennedy-like, in the village church in North Tawton, must have supplied the unconscious prompt for the image of the bride.)

Ted's death left me feeling bereft. He'd had colon cancer (known in May 1997), had his operation and treatment, lost his hair, got it back again and, alas, contracted it in the liver. But because of the lovely undisfigurable quality about him – a Rory in his 60s – we simply assumed he was not in immediate danger. Stupid, of course, but when he and Carol visited Dublin in June we felt he had climbed the ladder again and was in peak physical form. Now we realize it was a kind of 'last look' trip he had been taking to Ireland. Luckily, I had written to him before setting off to Harvard, about his OM and the translation of Racine's *Phèdre* which M. and I saw in London in September also.

And another wedding. Great news. I don't know whether the home game means that the supporters go wilder than at the away game, but we'll be on the terraces.

Before that, however, we're on the planes again. The Japan Foundation – a kind of national PR outfit that invites guests to their nation – have been putting courteous and unremitting pressure on me to honour a promise made (too casually) to go to Japan under their auspices. Four years ago I had said 'before 1999'. So, take-off, for two weeks, on December 4. Hah! Or perhaps it should be Hahh! How do you represent that pounce of Japanese breath, quick heft of *huh*, like the quick blunt sound [of] a sensible tweed skirt hitting the floor at her ankles . . . but I digress.

Love to you both –

Seamus

The Kavanaghs' son Rory, who had died in his twenties, is the dedicatee of SH's poem 'Clonmany to Ahascragh', which is included in *Electric Light*, as is 'The Real Names' – the 'Shakespeare/St Columb's one'.

To Brian Friel

MS NLI

10 December 1998

Dear Brian,

Odd to be on a holiday that you didn't altogether want to go on. A sign of lost control, probably; but I'm nearly half-way through and all the jokes about getting home early with good behaviour have come home to roost. Also, all the pens I brought with me have run out of ink, so I'm operating with a mini-brush, one of those Japanese calligrapher's jobs. The whole thing is breaking down.

Three years ago this Japan Foundation invited me to be a guest of the nation, so to speak; you could stay for months, if you wanted; a great offer, but not one I had any desire to take up. But the ambassador (Japanese) was courteously unrelenting and the Irishman in Tokyo kept pushing too. Instead of cutting brutally early on, I kept putting off and then decided it had to be done before the end of this year. The one worthwhile activity I arranged was to go to places that Bashō visited and wrote about in his *Narrow Road to the Deep North*. That comes up next week, but we have been on the go now for five days, from Kyoto via Hiroshima, and now en route to Tokyo. My plan was to spend the mornings in the hotel, writing letters – I thought I could repair a lot of collapsed correspondences – but even that isn't quite working out. There is much shrine going and museum haunting and handshaking, shoe-taking-off and slipper-putting-on. Much inculcation of statistics. The population of Kyoto, the proportion of Japan that is mountainous, the number of cars in Tokyo. But still . . . We sat through 2 hours of a Noh play on Sunday. A mixture of sean-nós and high Mass, but actually an experience; coming out of it was a bit like coming out of a bullfight. You definitely had been through something.

12th, in Tokyo

The above was blurted out on the plane on Thursday morning. We've been in Tokyo now for a couple of nights and have this Saturday to ourselves. Mostly what we want to do is lie about and take pleasure in the very spacious hotel quarters. We've been in the company of guides since we landed, and in the meantime have seen a *Kabuki* and a *bunraku* performance, both greatly helped by the supply of those English language headphones you'd be inclined to disdain at [the] time. The *bunraku* is the big puppet event, done with three puppeteers to a puppet, and the most magnificent thing I've seen. Real theatre poetry. There were nine puppets on the stage at one point – 27 handlers – and no sense of the puppeteers' presence being an interference. Narrator/ chanter, the stringed instruments, the clappers – the whole Yeatsian paraphernalia in great shape. Brilliant colours and costumes. I thought that if ever *Beowulf* was to be treated – and murmurs about it are being made – it would have to be bunrakued. (Other worthwhile sighting, of course, on a menu – a section devoted to VEBERAGES.)

[. . .]

I'll give you a call when I get back. Maybe connect up in the dark days after the feast, although my time is messed (by me again) at that season also. Love to Anne, David and all the Yuletide visitors. *Kanpai.*
Seamus

'operating with a mini-brush': it suits SH's hand.
'sean-nós': old customs and traditional unaccompanied singing in Irish.
'*Kanpai*': Japanese for *sláinte*.

To Valerie Eliot

GC Eliot

[Pre-Christmas 1998]

Dear Valerie – Sad 1998, with loss of great loved Ted, 'now the land / will have to manage without him'.

With much love at Christmas – Seamus and Marie

On the Heaney Christmas card: SH slightly misquotes lines from 'The day he died', one of Ted Hughes's *Moortown* poems about his father-in-law: 'From now on the land / Will have to manage without him.'

1999

Busyness as usual: travel for both public reasons (USA, Mexico, Brazil), and private (SH's sixtieth birthday celebration in Rome).

Private and public may be said to have come together in the eulogy SH delivered at the memorial service for Ted Hughes in Westminster Abbey on 13 May; some months later, his translation of *Beowulf* was published with 'in memory of Ted Hughes' on the dedication page.

A wholly new exercise was the provision of words to fit pre-existing music, in this case that of the great Czech composer Leoš Janáček (1854–1928). The song cycle that, in SH's version, came to be called *Diary of One Who Vanished*, received its first performance in Dublin in October, with Ian Bostridge (b.1964) singing the role of the protagonist, and Deborah Warner (b.1959) directing.

To Deborah Warner, Lucasta Miller, Ian Bostridge, Julius Drake, Neil Wallace TS NLI

11 January 1999 191 Strand Road, Dublin 4

Dear All,

Yesterday was a great encouragement. I was elated to find that a fair number of the lines did fit the music and to hear them being lofted past themselves by Ian; and then to discover that we could repair the ropy ones so that they became tight-ropy, so to speak, and held up . . . I look forward greatly to March 8.

Twelve pages follow. I may have taken down a few wrong transcriptions, but I think the gist of the new version is here. I'll be interested to know if Deborah has any views on the tar at line 4. (And yet, if the sloe/briars alternative is singable, we might consider that too. And maybe birch is better than mushroom at l. 3)

Section V: Do you still want it in the past tense, Deborah? I like the turning-and-turning-in-a-narrowing-gyre of the present, so just need to ask one more time before I preterite it. Pretterittit.

The here to-day is the gone to-morrow, no? *Diary of One Here To-Day*? Or just *The Here To-day* – Louis MacNeice has a poem with the same title, but I don't think that would be a big problem. It's probably a bit winsome, but it won me for a while . . .

Seamus

PS On second thoughts, sloes rather than tar – if poss.

Written after an early try-out of SH's words for *Diary of One Who Vanished*. Among the number addressed here, it was Ian Bostridge's wife, Lucasta Miller (b.1966), who had conceived the idea of getting SH to provide a fresh English translation; Julius Drake (b.1959) was the pianist, and Neil Wallace, of Offshore Cultural Projects, producer. SH spent two days with the company as they tested the singability of his text. Bostridge recalls: 'Julius and I would try things out and if they didn't work Seamus would make another suggestion. He also wanted all of us to chip in – we were nervous at first but he was so welcoming that it ended up being an incredibly joyous and open experience.'

The 'second thoughts' are handwritten.

To Dorothy Walker — PC NCAD

24 February 1999 [Postmarked San Diego, CA]

Good ole Daniel made it to Mexico. We had a brilliant and rich time in Oaxaca and Mexico City and now, alas, reside for 2 nights in Las Vegas, the metropolis of the meaningless.

Love to all, Seamus and Marie

'Good ole Daniel': the postcard image, Diego Rivera's *Las Mansiones de Xibalba*, while including what could be lions, illustrates not the Bible story but a Mayan legend.

To Dennis O'Driscoll — MS Emory

26 February 1999 as from: 191 Strand Road, Dublin 4

Dear Dennis,

The real address is somewhere above Kansas City, Missouri: the captain of United Airlines Flight 12 has just announced it. I have been on the road since February 1 and now head back to a busy enough springtime. In my briefcase there was a small fardel of personal letters that I had intended to answer in what I imagined might be leisurely conditions somewhere along the road, but alas, this four-hour trans-continental hoist is the quietest stretch I've had since I touched down in Berkeley.

The whole trip grew from a Berkeley commitment: they have an exhibition of Irish Art at the University Museum and so I agreed a couple of years ago to be the Avenali Professor – for a week. Then one thing led to another – including a week in Mexico, where two books were launched (a limited edition and a translation of *Seeing Things*); plus 3 days in a peacock 'n pool 'n palm tree house in San Diego; ezzettera, ezzettera, as Marie's father used to put it. Marie has been with me since February 9 – just as well, since we also had to survive 2 days in Las Vegas . . . I'm sitting at an angle in this cramped airbus seat, so I apologize for the odd angle of that last page.

But I have more than that to apologize for. I should have replied long ago to your very full and very acute responses to the manuscript I had sent you. Every point you made about those poems gave me pause and I agree with many of the detailed suggestions. I'll hope to see you and let you see the poems (again) some time in the coming months. Now all I can do is plead the madness of my schedule during the months just past as an excuse for not having written.

[. . .]

The fact is, I was slightly astray, in withdrawal, denial, whatever you want to call it, because besides being under starter's orders for the translation to be completed and the lectures to be done, I was behind with my drastically overdue income tax. The entry of the builders into the house and the dispersal of all paper middens and secret base camps of letters and accounts was one thing, but the sheer impossibility of getting a good long clear stretch to hunt and arrange the stuff paralysed me completely. The big push is on now, however, when we get back. I have to prepare accounts back to my pre-Nobel year – bad slippage – and then must seriously think again about what to do about the children, the manuscripts, the possibility of putting money into a house for Michael, think again about trusts ('n tax) . . . Good resolution time all round. My hope is that by June there will be breathing space again. Before that there is much on and off travel (including a trip to an E. Bishop conference at Ouro Preto, in May – after Ted's memorial service in Westminster Abbey on May 13) (and including too a wee breakaway to Rome for the 60th birthday).

It is too long since we have seen you and Julie in our place. We saw the Miłoszs in Berkeley. They are so true and vivid – even though Czesław had a real distress about his hearing on the day we arrived he was full of gallantry and go. (He'd had wax removed which had – paradoxically – made him deafer than ever, but that condition did eventually pass.) Being with them reminded us that the company of the trusted and the beloved should be caught and kept, so let's meet soon. Call any time. In haste, as we pass Cleveland, over Lake Eyrie, and are approached by a stewardess, bearing the snack trays. Heigho.

Seamus

As fifteenth Avenali Professor, SH had lectured on 'Getting It Right: Reflections on Art and Artists in Ireland'. His host in San Diego was Marianne McDonald (b.1937), classics scholar, promoter of early Irish literature and, later, dedicatee of *The Burial at Thebes*. The Mexican translator of *Seeing Things*, and of other collections by SH, is the poet Pura López Colomé (b.1952).

The manuscript that SH had sent O'Driscoll, well ahead of publication, was of *Electric Light* (2001).

To Mo Mowlam

TS Emory

16 March [1999]

Dear Mo,

It was a great pleasure to hear from you about Josefina de Vasconcellos and her generous gift to the Stormont Estate. I am touched that she would like to meet, but embarrassed at not being able to say a simple yes please. I am in and out of Dublin a lot and increasingly at the end of my work-tether. I am desperate to save some days in order to hide away and do what I am meant to do, i.e. stay off the road and write. I'm sure you know the problem.

I should, for example, have written to you, long ago, to say how deeply I have admired your work as Secretary of State, your spirit and stamina and good undeflected force in building a future for Northern Ireland. You increased the possibilities and lifted the heart, all by your indomitable self.

Yours sincerely,
Seamus Heaney

The Labour Party politician Mo Mowlam (1949–2005) served as Secretary of State for Northern Ireland from 1994 to 1997; she is widely credited with a key role in bringing about the 1998 Good Friday Agreement through the qualities SH praises her for here.

To Paul Muldoon

MS Emory

13 April 1999 c/o Russell Hotel, Russell Square

Dear Paul,

According to the original sources, I came in Dr Kerlin's bag this day 60 years ago. It was great to hear from you and to have the good news that the doctor is going to be landing with you and Jean again next month. May 19 was the date of my re-birth as SH – Faber published *D. o. N.* on that day in 1966. So, *musha*, Moishe may coincide. [. . .]

SH's sixtieth birthday. The Russell Hotel, now with a different name, is situated on Russell Square, close to the original Faber offices, scene of SH's 're-birth'.

'*musha*': 'ah, well' (Irish slang); but Asher, not Moishe, was the name given to Muldoon's son.

To Matthew Evans

TS Faber

10 May 1999 191 Strand Road, Dublin 4

Dear Matthew,

It's a bit late to be thanking you again for the bountiful birthday you gave us: every time I enter the closet in this office (which serves as a humidor) I am reminded of the personal largesse behind it all – and of relishing the caviar, so beautifully iced and bound, on the little balcony of our hotel near Campo de' Fiori. Hopkins's Herbert is retained in its book-shrine, removed occasionally for veneration . . .

On that day, we were all a bit high and decided that the thing to do with *Beowulf* was to issue it with a parallel Anglo-Saxon text. Generous and stylish that would be, but in the meantime I wondered if such a publication might not entail a more edited and annotated volume than the one we envisage. If we give the original, does it promise a scholarly engagement with the material? And even if we don't do the Anglo-Saxon, I wonder if some kind of received academic wisdom about the poem is not required in the apparatus, or introduction. I ought to speak to Paul about this, and I hope that I might be able to have a word with him on Wednesday afternoon. (Will call.)

Matthew, please don't think I am against the parallel text. I greatly appreciated the readiness with which you agreed to the proposal, and am merely facing the reality of the thing, wondering a bit . . .

I look forward to seeing you in the course of the week.

Seamus

Evans's sixtieth birthday gifts to SH included the mid-nineteenth-century edition of George Herbert's poems that more than a century before had been a gift to Gerard Manley Hopkins from his Aunt Fanny. Evans and his wife Caroline are the dedicatees of *Electric Light*.

'Paul' was Paul Keegan, who was at this time Poetry Editor at Faber. The idea of presenting SH's *Beowulf* in parallel with the original Old English was dropped.

To Carol Hughes

MS Hughes

19 May 1999 — 191 Strand Road, Dublin 4

Dear Carol,

The unbearable month of May, with all its life: only gradually did I realize what Eliot's line about 'cruel April' could mean. Even without the stroke of personal grief, this time of the year begins to melt the heart.

But last Thursday was a great ceremony and again I was proud and blessed to be admitted to the centre of it. Strange how we were all there, heavy in the big glittering net Ted had woven out of his poetry and personal beauty. I sat there, looking across at you and Nicholas and Frieda, Olwyn and Gerald, thinking how strange and unforeseen it was that Marie and I were attending this historical event in Westminster Abbey, with the Queen Mother ('she looks so like Mammy', Marie kept whispering) and the prince across the aisle. Their presence ritualized and sanctioned the solemnity of the occasion, but the solemnity was in the hearts and minds of the congregation. There was a verity and specific grieving gravity in the air. And the assembly at the Atrium afterwards was good: a gathering of literary sorts and samples, 'all of us there', everybody on their best behaviour and fuelled by their better nature because the main man was presiding *in absentia*.

God, I loved that photograph on front of the *Independent* next day. And in general, the coverage wasn't bad. Plath-plaint totally uncalled for but probably part of the rote responses. But it was recorded seriously and photographed respectfully. The whole three days, in fact, beginning with the rehearsal (which I found important, not simply because we got some notion of the way to sound the readings forth, but more because we had a chance to dwell in the ampleness of the space, be reminded of the dimensions of reverence Ted inspired among us, as his on-living friends); but, as I say, the three days were a proper and lovely pause for Marie and me, a re-minder of Ted in the fullest sense. Sitting at the Ivy, in the natural free trust of the table, and enjoying the absolute rightness of the food and wine, it readied us for the elevation of the Thursday morning.

[. . .]

One of my special personal 'literary' regrets is that Ted is not here to be the dedicatee of the translation of *Beowulf* that I am getting ready – due out in October. For his sixtieth <no, 65th> birthday I gave the Faber people an extract from it for the birthday-book, an oblique *salaam* in that the passage was about Beowulf as 'the biggest presence' in his heroic world. On the dedication page I want to put 'in memory of Ted Hughes', not only because he fostered me as a poet, but because he was like the minstrel who sings in Heorot Hall, 'telling with mastery of man's beginnings, / how the Almighty had made the earth / a gleaming plain, girdled with waters'. And so on. It belongs to him. (Another literary regret is that he didn't have the time to do *Sir Gawain*. I had this notion that the extract he translated for *The School Bag* would have got him galloping off into those green thickets that he felt so at home in.)

We'll see you again, I hope, before too long. The May 13 Pembroke College notion keeps beckoning. But maybe in the meantime also. Much love,

Seamus

PS I'll send this in the mail too.

Carol Hughes is the widow of Ted Hughes, at whose memorial service, held in Westminster Abbey on 13 May, SH gave an address. 'Nicholas and Frieda, Olwyn and Gerald' were Hughes's son, daughter, sister and brother.

The hyphen in 're-minder' has a caret beneath it and is evidently an afterthought.

SH's contribution to the 'birthday-book', *A Parcel of Poems*, privately printed and presented to Hughes on his 65th birthday, is titled 'Sea Interlude, with Hero'.

'I'll send this': a typescript, with handwritten revisions, of SH's memorial address.

To Andrew Motion

MS Motion

7 June 1999 Ballynahinch Castle, Co. Galway

Dear Andrew,

'The shit in the chateau'? Please forgive me for not having written to you earlier to congratulate you on the laureateship. I had said in a letter to one of those advisory quarters (before the appointment) that my only worry about your being named was that you were in a great way of writing at this time and that you might find the office interfering with the creative lift. (I did feel that your last book had a crest and crescence, as it were, that said you were away out there in yourself.) But that's a scruple. You're the right man and fit for the task – since you can make it what you want it to be.

I wouldn't worry too much about the mini-shittinesses that are thrown up by the passage of your car, so to speak. Drive on, as you have done. (I loved your reading of that accident, or near accident poem at Grasmere.) If you can link your own personal matter to an occasion, do it like that: publish a dedicated poem (like the 'Rain-Charm') to mark a moment or an event, without necessarily making the event or the personage the subject.

Enough. No advice. Hats off. Bows from waist. Glasses raised. Up and away.

Marie and I came down here – a fisherman's hotel, really, that you and Jan should think about if you ever go west to Connemara – because we were to meet another couple and have an indolent weekend. Other couple didn't show. Better still. I actually got a couple of human letters written.

Our love to you both

Seamus

On Ballynahinch Castle notepaper.

'The shit in the chateau': slight misquotation from Philip Larkin's poem 'The Life with a Hole in It'. Motion (b.1952), whose appointment as Poet Laureate had been announced on 1 May, was Larkin's first biographer; his own most recent book of new poems was *Salt Water* (1997), while his *Selected Poems 1976–1997* came out in 1998.

To Alasdair and Elise Macrae PC Macrae

8 June 1999 [Postmarked 'Baile Átha Cliath' (Dublin)]

Somehow Hardy reminds me of roosting-nest pockets . . . I'm ashamed not to have written long ago to thank you for the wren-muffler and the robin-roofer – utterly original and desirable things. Where to situate them *still* a matter of contrariness. I put the wren-hole at the head of the bed . . . It was great of you to come down to the gather-up. Unforgettable for M. and me. Will have to see you before *too* long. Seamus

The postcard shows Olive Edis's photograph of Thomas Hardy in beaky profile (1914).

'wren-muffler . . . robin-roofer': SH's kennings for a woven pouch designed to be hung in the garden for birds to roost in.

To Brenda O'Hanlon MS Emory

10 June 1999

Dear Brenda,

At the opening of Tony O'Malley's exhibition at the RHA in 1997, I said that the thought of Tony's work produced a great sense of carnival and delight in those who knew it, because of the way it has developed over the years. It has a mixture of lent and easter in it, but in latter years, the easter element, the revelry in colour, the readiness to celebrate the radiant and the erotic has been predominant. That's why I dedicated the opening lines of my translation of 'The Midnight Court' to him, because there too the deliciousness of the summer world is given the full treatment. I also wanted to salute Tony's rootedness in the *dúchas* of his Clare Island ancestors, the connection between the peacock colours of his palette and the brilliant world of Celtic marvels. He too is the artist as Merri-man . . .

Seamus Heaney

'*dúchas*': heritage, birthright.

The freelance writer and journalist Brenda O'Hanlon does not recall receiving this fax, a copy of which is in the Emory archive, though she knew Tony O'Malley and was at the Royal Hibernian Academy exhibition mentioned by SH.

To Sue Roberts

MS Roberts

[June 1999]

Dear Sue,

Over the weekend I daydreamt and fiddled with *Beowulf*, trying to get it down to ten fifteen-minute sections, and succeeded, I think. Hopefully, each section can be read in 14 minutes. I've timed myself and am satisfied that we are close enough, that we have a 'rough cut' that an editor can get into the slot.

Some afterthoughts then complicated my satisfaction with the timing . . . I thought that you'd perhaps want a voice telling the audience, at the beginning of each reading, 'the story so far', or at least, where we are in the story. And that that would probably require a minute. And then I wondered if you'd want music. I'm not sure what it might be. I'm not sure if it's needed. I feel if it's to be used it should be strong and sparse, a punctuating harp-note, a plucked, a tucked string . . . (There's a recording on the old Claddagh label of Jackie MacGowran speaking Beckett which you should get a listen to for its own sake, but also to hear Beckett's contribution – a few solemn, slight gong-strokes.) I wondered if the 'Finnsburh Lay' (1070–1158) mightn't be topped and tailed with a note from the 'tuned timber'.

Fuss, fuss. Thoughts of a focused author who will be unfocused in the meantime . . . But I did think it better to let you have the text well ahead of the recording date, so that you too can get a think about it. I look forward to seeing you and Simon in Bristol on 22nd July.

Sincerely,

Seamus

PS The manuscript is marked by two different systems of editing, to be ignored. The occasional inter-linear headings in italics are for Norton's student anthology; the ancient mariner glosses are Fabers/FSG's aid to beginners . . .

Enclosed with this letter was a third page showing how SH thought *Beowulf* might be divided into ten sections for the BBC Radio 4 broadcast of the poem scheduled to coincide with its UK publication. Sue Roberts, wife of the poet Simon Armitage, produced the programmes; SH was the reader; a BBC announcer prefaced each broadcast with narrative continuity.

To Carol Hughes

MS Hughes

1 July 1999 — 191 Strand Road, Dublin 4

Dear Carol,

You are often on my mind. I think of you in your cool thick-walled house with the flourish and thick delicious life of summer going on while you are left with your grief. Each time, I would like to transmit a pulse of sympathy, just a waft on the airwave to say we are with you. So this morning, on impulse, here this goes . . .

Love
Seamus

To Carol Hughes

MS Hughes

9 September 1999 — Hotel Teatro di Pompeo, Rome

Carol – Something good about the date, anyhow . . . We were all humiliated and enraged by the vile story in the *Sunday Times*. Matthew rang me on Saturday and you have been in our mind since. To hell with them. The only consolation I had was remembering an old low-class joke made by Oliver St John Gogarty at the turn of the century. 'You don't swim in the Liffey,' he said, 'you just go through the motions . . .' You are the clean strong swimmer, my love. Don't break your stroke . . . Seamus

PS If you ever want to go to Rome for a quiet weekend, this is a lovely place. S.

'Something good about the date': a row of '9's, even if, in SH's writing of it, the month becomes 'ix'.

The 'vile story', which need not be recalled here, was typical of the British press's ceaseless hounding of Ted Hughes even after his death.

To Michael Donaghy

MS Madeleine Paxton

17 September 1999 — Glenlo Abbey, Galway

Michael,

Last night we stayed in this baronial *schloss* on the Corrib shore, courtesy of University College, Galway, where I gave a – disgracefully *organized* – 'millennial lecture'. '*Us* as in *Versus*' I called it. More disgrace.

Anyhow, the morning being sunny, cerulean even, and the summer being late, we decided to sit on Corrib-viewing until check-out and to read what we had not read. And I had your *Wallflowers*. It's a real blinder. The reel thing. Foot and mouth poem. A dazzle adazzle. It brought me to my senses, regulated me by the *dérèglement* method, played the regulators, the hardest art of all, maybe. Congratulations. The book makes a stir. Full of life and mind. Take the floor!

Seamus

Michael Donaghy (1954–2004), Irish-American poet and musician who had settled in London, argued in his *Wallflowers: A Lecture on Poetry* for certain correspondences between poetry and dance. 'Regulators' are the lower chordal notes on a set of uilleann pipes, used to lend colour to a tune at given moments. It was Rimbaud who wrote of '*un long, immense et raisonné dérèglement de tous les sens*' as a function of poetry.

To Michael Alexander

MS Emory

24 September 1999 191 Strand Road, Dublin 4

Dear Michael,

Faber sent me two copies of this book (I'll get more, I assume) and I thought you should have one of them straight away. Your own translation is so buoyant and has such purchase and relish, such at-homeness with the wave-cutters, such kenning-cunning and hoard-hoking, that there is small need for another. But, as the Introduction explains (p. xxii), I got into the job gradually. I feel a bit uneasy, turning up at your hall, putting my tuned timber to work in your rafter-room, so to speak, but the George Jack memorial seemed fair enough. I valued your graceful salute when you sent the Student Edition, and have to admit that it was a great help. Custody of the eyes, however, was practised with regard to the translation – until I got through to line 3182 . . .

I look forward to seeing you, if again too briefly.

Seamus

Michael Alexander (b.1941) was a Professor of English at the University of St Andrews and is a distinguished translator of Old English verse whose own translation of *Beowulf* has been in print since 1973. George Jack, who also taught at

St Andrews and was editor of the student edition of *Beowulf* mentioned here, had died recently.

To Charles Boyle MS Faber

29 September 1999

Charles,

Ropey rhythms that I've lived with for the sake of the singing are humiliating me as I contemplate letting this stuff into the world. At XV: would a break after line 8 (ending on an exclamation!) help, and then, quatrain, slight revision at 9:

Now I dread my summons:

S.

The problem is, this will be a divergence from the sung text, that which is set in the ENO's music. And I have not informed/got permission from Deb. W. for this, or other changes.

The poet – later, fiction writer and proprietor of his own press – Charles Boyle (b.1951), who was then a copy editor in Faber's production department, was overseeing proofs of SH's *Diary of One Who Vanished*, to be published as a booklet in time for the first performance.

This brief note and the excerpt below show SH worrying over tiny details of the text, rescuing it from compromises necessitated by demands of the singing voice.

To Charles Boyle MS Faber

29 September 1999

[. . .]

PS i) Your poet's ear: 7, 8 in VII

Banal, banal, banal, but: if we said 'Fate lands . . .', would that be millimetrically better? Maybe not.

ii) Poet's ear: XI: if it were quatrained, would it be even more tum-tee-tummy? Maybe.

[. . .]

To Philip Reed

MS NLI

4 October 1999

Dear Philip Reed,

Thank you for your fax. Poem XII is a very good addition.

I am hoping you haven't gone to press with the programme note, since revisions are needed on page 1. My son read it and convinced me that I could not use the word 'tinker' so blithely. It's a bit like other abusive race terms at this stage, so I suggest we 1) say 'a crowd of grown-up men' at line 5, deleting 'grown-up' from line 6. 2) at line 11 'gipsies proper were another people.' 3) at 17, 'travellers, still in those days pursuing their traditional ways as tin-smiths, etc.'

Please, if you can, incorporate these changes, which I've also marked on the accompanying page. I'll be at Hazlitt's until Wednesday morning.

Sincerely,
Seamus Heaney

To Valentina Polukhina

MS Polukhina

13 October 1999

191 Strand Road, Dublin 4

Dear Valentina,

Since we met, I have been travelling – to Manchester, St Andrews, London (again) and Italy. I came back here exhausted and afflicted with the thought of further travels. Also, very complicated by the way the whole Brodsky event is becoming a site of tension. I am all the more sensitive about this because I did not attend the actual burial in Venice, and feel that it might add insult to injury if I were to go through with the birthday party next May. My real problem, however, is the developing pressure on my calendar. I am due in Greece for the launch of a book of translations, May 9–14; in Washington DC for a JFK memorial on 17th, an Oxford University event (in DC) on 18th and an honorary degree at Philadelphia on May 20/21. It being the millennial year, Harvard have also requested that I attend their commencement in the first week of June, so I return to the States within ten days of getting back to Dublin.

Sore as it is to you, and reluctant as I am to do it, I nevertheless must renege on the Venice/Brodsky event. What I undertook as an uncomplicated celebration has turned into an occasion of tension and a locus of crossed loyalties, and I am constrained to withdraw. I am very sorry, but sadly resolved.

Sincerely,
Seamus

PS Many thanks for the renewed photo package.
PPS Marie is insistent that I cut down – and out – of my travels.

The Brodsky scholar, then Professor of Russian at Keele University, Valentina Polukhina (1936–2022) was organising an international conference in Venice, timed to coincide with what would have been Joseph Brodsky's sixtieth birthday on 24 May 2000. SH was a patron of Polukhina's charity, the Russian Poets Fund.

The photographs mentioned had been taken by Polukhina's husband, the poet and translator Daniel Weissbort (1935–2013), on a visit to the Heaneys in Dublin.

To Tom Paulin

MS Paulin

16 November 1999

Bell Tower Hotel, Ann Arbor, Michigan

Dear Tom,

Rub-a-dub! Ribby-dib-dibs! Hulla-baloo-bellay! A twenty-one gob – or gub – salute is what's called for for *The Wind Dog*. An absolute utterance. Jubilant and rangy, seven-league-booted sound. Comes in very close, near and wee, and then off on its sweeps and bow-bends . . . I am proud and gleeful to be a dedicatee. Am writing this after the luxury of lying in late and reading through the whole thing again. The book is so much of a piece, and yet in no way does it feel designed to have designs. It's hefted up, a terrific sense of each poem hurdling towards its own ends. Abundance and readiness, a capacity for the sudden, a way of knocking in one sound wedge so that the whole grain of a memory life falls open. The title poem is more than a tour-de-force: for all its exhilarating speed, it's a kind of 'poetics of reverie'; and of course 'Door Poem' is tamped and rung and hammered into me entirely, as I too have come forth into the air. I feel the book heals and anneals, not in any corny thematic peace-processy way, but in puddling and muddling in the phonetic dough, allowing us all to be wean-scops together while keeping us up to scratch intellectually. In other words, it's poetry. The intimacy and tendresse of origins played out into structure – and sport – in the medium. And then you manage to do that lovely Verlaine/Bournemouth into the bargain. And to 'get in' Drumcree in that dragon's tooth-ladder. And to fly with Chagall and fledge with him, nay flare with him. We're proud of you, as they say in Bellaghy. Not musical, my arse!

I'm here for a week's 'residency'. Bleak enough. But quiet in the mornings, at least. Marie will get a read at the book when I get back. But she and I send all our love and gratitude. And to Giti too.

Seamus

Written on hotel notepaper.

The Wind Dog, newly published and with the dedication 'For Seamus and Marie Heaney', was Paulin's sixth collection.

'bow-bends': see Hopkins's 'The Windhover'.

Among the poems SH mentions, 'Door Poem' refers by name to SH's own *Door into the Dark*, while 'Drumcree Three' absorbs news of the 1998 loyalist arson attack in which three Catholic boys, Richard, Mark and Jason Quinn, were murdered.

'wean-scops': i.e. infant bards, SH's neologism.

To Ciaran Carson — PC Emory

17 November 1999

Cranfield is one of my own original places: the poem after the Clonmacnoise one in *Seeing Things* is set there: there was a photo of the aunts and the wean in our house for years. So I had an extra-vivid response to the book, having entered by that portal. It's a marvellous abundant extravagant *turas* or *immram* or cabinet of capaciousness – lovely tribute to your father too, but a revelation and restoration of things to themselves. Hermetically unsealed. Congratulations.

Seamus

In his prose book *Fishing for Amber* (1999), Carson writes learnedly and lyrically about Cranfield in Co. Down.

The 'poem after the Clonmacnoise one' has the first line, 'A boat that did not rock or wobble once'.

The postcard, from the National Museum of Modern Art in Tokyo, is of Henri Rousseau's *Liberty Inviting the Artists*.

2000

At a ceremony in London on 25 January, it was announced that SH's *Beowulf* had been named Whitbread Book of the Year 1999. The subsequent press attention, which included a jarring interview in London's *Sunday Times* and the insinuation of plagiarism in another Sunday newspaper, the *Observer*, may have soured the experience, but boosted by the award *Beowulf* itself went on to be a surprise best-seller.

In February, the Heaneys paid the first of a number of winter visits to the Caribbean island of St Lucia, at the invitation of its most illustrious son, the poet, playwright and painter Derek Walcott, and his partner Sigrid Nama. SH had got to know Walcott through their mutual friend and fellow Nobel Prize winner Joseph Brodsky.

To Liam O'Flynn

TS ITMA

5 January 2000 191 Strand Road, Dublin 4

Dear Liam,

You need to see 'The Uilleann Pipes', not because of any great distinction in the verse, but because the thing draws so much on your words and stories and grows from the power of your playing, and presumes indeed on our friendship. I've been fiddling with this Japanese form called the tanka – two lines longer than the haiku, and a development of it – consisting of five lines of five-seven-five-seven-seven syllables. It's like a wee pastry cutter I nick into the ould dough inside the head, just to give it shape. Verse-nips from Nippon. Ah-so soundbites. You might have seen a set of them in the *Irish Times* last Saturday (following here) – full of quotes from poems about blacksmiths.

I may change these round a bit, but I still think you should see them before anybody else.

And it gives me a chance to give you and Jane a happy new year, and to set the sail towards Manannán's island.

Seamus

PS Marie and I did go to Hardy's grave on New Year's Eve and read his poem 'The Darkling Thrush' – written 31 December 1900.

'Tankas for Liam O'Flynn', the poem offered here, was not included in any subsequent collection by SH, although 'Midnight Anvil', which shares the form, is in *District and Circle*. The poem for O'Flynn begins:

Security men
Puzzled by the long flat case
The piper carried,
Stopped him. 'Is that a gun, sir?'
'O worse,' he declared, 'far worse.'

The Isle of Man is etymologically associated with Manannán mac Lir, mythological guardian of the Otherworld.

The postscript is handwritten.

To Eamon Duffy

MS Duffy

7 January 2000

Glanmore Cottage, Ashford,
Co. Wicklow

Dear Eamon,

There I went, writing '99 . . .

Many thanks for the letter before Christmas, and my apologies for the tardy response. I've got so far behind with letters – I mean letters to friends, not 'correspondence' – that it practically requires a retreat to get me started. Glanmore has become a class of a retreat house . . . Phoneless but not quite heatless (storage heaters), neglected but not yet squalid, just the place for a soul perched in the rafters of a lost discipline. I mean I've lost whatever grip I had on the self-respect-pleasure-reward that comes from keeping alive by friendships. I've not written to Helen in months, but think of her constantly and hope she's all right. But, but, if this *is* a retreat house, you are not my confessor. So, to the business . . .

I enclose, for the Magdalene anthology, 'The Loose Box'. The Hardy appearance in it makes it the obvious choice. I wrote it a couple of years ago and trust it, in spite of the slightly crazy turns in it – well, *because* of them, to be truthful. I'm still not quite sure about the servant girls at the end of the Hardy section, but I feel something of the violence and sexual exploitation of the Tesses of the world is implicit in the rutting thresher. (The third section of it was my Christmas card in 1998.) It will appear in my next collection – *maybe* before the end of this year – but it has not been in any other publication yet.

Edna is a first rate choice for the Parnell fellowship, and I would enjoy turning up for the evening of 6 March. I am reluctant to promise, however, because I have fought for over a year to keep the weeks between January 27, when I have to do a 'Friends of the Library' reading in York, and April 14, when I have to show up for honorary doctoring in Cardiff, free of all commitment. Marie and I intend to behave the way American academics behave – go 'away' for three or four weeks. An enormous luxury. We're not yet sure exactly where or when, but the ultimate *luxe et volupté* is the fact that we can leave it, or go it, whenever, because there are no other marks on the calendar. (Or *weren't* – John Hume has sent a message that we're 'a-lookin' for' in the White House on St Patrick's Day – and when John calls, at least this year, it behoves us to pay attention.) So. On hold for 6th. [. . .]

SH and the Irish historian of Christianity Eamon Duffy (b.1947), who is a Fellow of Magdalene College, Cambridge, had met through the offices of Helen Vendler when she was appointed to a Parnell Fellowship at Magdalene, a one-year post which Edna Longley had recently taken up. The 'Magdalene anthology' to which SH, himself an Honorary Fellow at Magdalene, had contributed, was *Figures of Speech* (2000), edited by M. E. J. Hughes, John Mole and Nick Seddon. The servant girls had gone by the time 'The Loose Box', SH's contribution, appeared in *Electric Light*, published not in 2000 but in 2001.

John Hume (1937–2020) had been one of the recipients of the 1998 Nobel Peace Prize, for his part in securing the Good Friday Agreement, while US President Bill Clinton, who in 2000 was nearing the end of his second term in the White House, is credited with helping to bring the opposing sides together.

To Heather Clark — TS Clark

24 January 2000 — 191 Strand Road, Dublin 4

Dear Heather Clark,

Sorry to be slow in replying to your letter of September 8 last year. In the end I took advantage of it to remind myself of other things besides the Group that were going on in Belfast at the time.

I don't think of Philip Hobsbaum as my teacher. Even though I was still in my early twenties when the Group began to operate, my way of reading and responding was already formed. I had written and published my first poems, such as they were, and whatever 'craft and style' I may have had, they grew from my predilections as a reader and from my temperament and general make-up. On the other hand, Hobsbaum was more than a 'mere organizer'. His sympathy for the kind of writing I did and his positive response to it were important in firming up some kind of confidence in my own style.

But the 'pre-Group' history is important too. For example, while I was completing a postgraduate course at St Joseph's Training College in Belfast in 1961–2, I did an extended essay on literary magazines in Ulster during the twentieth century. This gave me a certain purchase on what had been happening at Queen's and in Belfast during the 40s and 50s, so I ended up with a good sense of the efforts made at that time to get a 'regional literature' going. I knew about the work done by people like Robert Greacen and John Gallen in the *New Northman* at Queen's in the early 40s, by John Boyd and John Hewitt in *Lagan*, and by Roy McFadden (see Hobsbaum's recent obituary in the *Irish Times*) in *Rann*. At this time I also met Michael McLaverty (I did my teaching practice in his school and subsequently taught there in 1962–3) and the painter T. P. Flanagan. Through Terry and Sheila Flanagan I got to know the artist Colin Middleton and eventually became personally friendly with John Hewitt. All this grounding in a pre-Hobsbaum, pre-Group, pre-Longleys and Mahon context was important to me. For example, in the period before I left Belfast in 1972, I suppose I had a stronger sense of John Hewitt's work and a stronger sympathy with it than any of my contemporaries: Louis MacNeice and W. R. Rodgers, whom the Longleys and Derek Mahon had coincided with in Dublin were *their* 'master' poets. I visited John and Ruby more than once in Coventry and they came to see Marie and me in Belfast.

Another helpful local context that pre-dated The Group was the little coterie surrounding Mary and Pearse O'Malley's Lyric Theatre, and their magazine *Threshold*. The Flanagans were active in the Lyric, and Hewitt was a trustee of the magazine. In the O'Malleys' house, for example, I first met John Montague, and I saw my first Yeats plays in their little theatre at the back. When the foundation stone of the new Lyric Theatre building was laid in 1965, I was commissioned by the O'Malleys to write a poem for the occasion, which I did. (Reprinted in *Eleven Poems*.) Austin Clarke and Thomas Kinsella also wrote and read special poems on that occasion.

Another extra-Group context that was important to me then was my friendship with the singer David Hammond, and through him a connection to an older generation of writers, such as Sam Hanna Bell and Joseph

Tomelty. These met in a café in Fountain Street, in the company of Jimmy Vitty, chief librarian of the Linen Hall Library. They were not particularly 'influential' at a stylistic level, but they gave one a strong sense of local context, of creative endeavour having been there from the start, of high (or highish) artistic ambition proceeding in an Ulster accent.

I mention all this in order to remind myself, as well as you, that the Group was only one part of the field of force, even though it was a very important part. It marked a new configuration. It linked, uneasily but energetically, an 'on-the-ground' crowd (Stewart Parker, myself, Joan Watton/Newmann – whom Philip had 'discovered' in a WEA class) to a new group of returned natives (Michael Longley, James Simmons, Derek Mahon – and yes, I know he didn't really attend) and to another crowd of about-to-be-naturalized-in-Belfast people like Harry Chambers and Edna Longley. Then there was the English diaspora of Queen's faculty members like Arthur Terry and W. J. Harvey, and other English people in the Ulster swim such as Norman Dugdale and Norman Buller. At the time, in other words, the actual gatherings in Hobsbaum's flat were crowded affairs, miscellaneous enough, held together by his organizational flair and his pedagogical gifts.

Still, the reading out of poems that followed the discussion of the 'set' author for the week was a wonderful part of the proceedings. Hobsbaum would champion the claims of Peter Redgrove, Robert Lowell, George Crabbe, William Langland, Francis Berry, Martin Bell – people from the London Group, as well as eccentric voices from the canon. Edward Thomas would be an agreed enthusiasm – Edna Longley had done postgraduate work on Thomas and had just arrived as a lecturer in Queen's. Arthur Terry would read the new Larkin and introduce us to Catalan poets such as Salvador Espriu. My enthusiasm would run to Ted Hughes and Patrick Kavanagh. Michael Longley would give us Hart Crane, perhaps, or a new Richard Wilbur.

A crucial service was performed by Philip when he sent round the Group Sheets to his old poet pals in London. Edward Lucie-Smith with whom he edited the *Group Anthology* got these texts, and passed them on to literary editors. It was, at any rate, through the Hobsbaum/Lucie-Smith connection that poems of mine made their way to the *New Statesman* in late 1964. I remember Karl Miller, who was then the literary editor, telephoning me at St Joseph's College, after he had accepted three poems for publication. That appearance – 3 poems was a real showcase event – led to Charles Monteith of Faber and Faber contacting me and asking me to send a manuscript. Imagine the elation.

Marie and I were friendly with Philip and Hannah Hobsbaum. We once drove them down to Dublin for a weekend, during which Philip met (I think) Patrick Kavanagh. I had a closer personal link with Philip, I believe, than Michael or Edna. As much a matter of temperament, perhaps, as anything else. Maybe something political too, although all that was in the pre-1968 world of middle-class, academic Belfast. But Philip did empathize with the minority and I remember he was in favour of my doing a 'big' Irish poem, maybe something on 1798.

As to the *Honest Ulsterman*, I am not the best witness. I was never as closely involved with it as I was with the Group. I suspect I was already being regarded as a kind of established presence, a slightly stick-in-the-mud (or in the frogspawn) figure, rural and un-racy. James Simmons had a much more urban, tin-pan alley sense of what was what. A desire for a 'popular' poetry, a devotion to the common touch, and yet a 'liberationist' agenda. I didn't find it all that convincing, for all the genuine purpose and hope behind it. Too 'fly', as they say in Ulster. Jimmy was slightly paternalistic, for all his pretence of subversion. Impose-a-freedom; stock-broker belt rebellion.

One writer whom the *HU* helped to establish was Michael Foley. Totally vigorous, street-wise but culturally and politically informed, at ease with his resistances, a voice from the chorus, as Sinyavsky calls it. Jimmy, I always felt, was more of a choir-master. Frank Ormsby, who later edited the magazine, would be a better person to ask about all this. And also a poet who steadied his keel in those *HU* pages.

When Philip Hobsbaum left, I ran the Group for a couple of years, but never with force or conviction to equal Philip's. We met at times in my house on Ashley Avenue, at times in a room in the English Department, once at least in the Club Bar. Paul Muldoon read his poems, I think, as did Ormsby and Foley. But you better check all that with them. The Group Sheets are in Emory now.

I'm a bit puzzled that you find a statement which I regarded as simple information as 'mystification'. Hobsbaum sent out poems by the person whose work was to be discussed to all members of the Group.

We came together, discussed them ('sat upon' them as in court) for an hour and a half or more, came to certain judgements and tended to enforce those judgements upon the author. When I say 'the canon was settled' I mean there was more or less common agreement about which poems 'worked', which didn't, which were the best. (By canon, I mean our local, beginners' mini-canon.) In the end I suppose that kind of foreclosure or group orthodoxy seemed more of a constriction than a corroboration.

You probably don't need advice about sources for your research, but if Solly Lipsitz, Joan Newmann, Arthur Terry or Harry Chambers are not on your list, you might think of trying to get in touch. Solly never did attend the Group, but as a jazz-man and friend of Michael Longley, he might have his own perspective on the way we all influenced one another. He was astute, older and an insider of sorts – but without any 'side'.

All good wishes,
Seamus Heaney

Heather Clark was researching for her book *The Ulster Renaissance: Poetry in Belfast 1962–1972*, eventually published in 2006.

Among the host of names mentioned in this letter: Robert Greacen called the *New Northman*, the Queen's University magazine he co-edited with John Gallen (d.1947), 'the literary voice of Ulster'; Roy McFadden was a lawyer and poet; Colin Middleton painted both outdoor and Surrealist scenes; Sam Hanna Bell (1909–90) was a novelist, playwright and broadcaster; Joseph Tomelty (1911–95) was an actor and writer of the radio comedy series *The McCooeys*; Arthur Terry (1927–2004) taught Hispanic languages and literature at Queen's; W. J. Harvey (1925–67) was a literary scholar; Francis Berry (1915–2006) was a British poet; Solly Lipsitz (1920–2013) was an art school lecturer, jazz musician and music critic.

The poem written for the new Lyric Theatre was 'Peter Street at Bankside', which did not graduate from *Eleven Poems* to *Death of a Naturalist*.

To Dennis O'Driscoll

MS Emory

4 February 2000 [m.d. 4 Jan.] Glanmore Cottage, Ashford, Co. Wicklow

Dear Dennis,

Every now and again I need to get down here, to get into the Diogenes tub, as it were, or the Colmcille beehive hut, or the Mossbawn scullery. At any rate, a hedge surrounds me, the blackbird calls, the soul settles for an hour or two. Your letters were too much. You put far too much pressure on yourself with all your attentiveness. Needless to say, the balm and virtue they represent are sweet and strong elements in my life, but I know how hard a hard-pressed man like you has been driving himself every time the welcome inditing shows on the envelope. You must leave the more detailed letter you promised – leave us a chance to meet later in the spring and just have a chat; your initial swift, thorough and thoroughly instructive reaction to the manuscript told me that important thing about *Known World*. I don't know how you do it: day job, steady and intense intellectual duty of reviews and commentary, self-born impetus and supply-line of the poems, chain-gang labour of poetry judging, conjugal proofing (what?), letters to friends, and all done as if you 'had that one trade alone'. I loved that *TLS*, Bartleby-refusing poem, and by God I knew how fervently it had to be meant. Its irony was steely. The hard job of the head-on truth being done with the necessary mixture of barefaced feeling and artful dodge.

Cosmo. Well. I knew it was sullied ground I was entering, but it was a bit dismaying all the same. There's such a headmaster/headboy aspect to me, I just couldn't handle it. Like being treated familiarly by a shit you would normally cross the road to avoid. The rural hauteur got the better of me. But the real sin was in submitting to the rules of the Whitbread Publicity caravan. If you win, these will be the expectations, Radio X, TV Y, Journalist Z etc. As a matter of fact, I suspect that Jerry Hall would have been a hell of a lot more reticent and cultivated company than Mr C., but the speed and vulgarity with which he came out with the questions, and the immediate understanding of the shit he was hoping to stir made me lose all wit and presence of mind. Stolid lumpen respectability came like the ox upon the tongue. Anyway, as the Anglo-Saxon stolid-speaker said, that passed, so will this.

The whole Whitbread hullabulloo was unexpected – i.e. I didn't expect that *Beo* would be chosen (Ted's poems for two years, me in '97, Harry Potter's popularity, the 'good thing' angle to Children's Literature being a contender etc. etc.) so I went to the proceedings with a certain equanimity. I did not make the mistake, however, that I had made in '97, of not having the *cúpla focal* ready just in case. And by Christ I was glad I had taken the precautions. The Gibbons man in the *Guardian* got it right when he said I appeared shocked. Marie thought I was going to faint, I got so white. And the Co. Derry ones knew I was in dire straits as I began to look more and more like my father . . .

Still, the bigger shock was the dimensions of the news coverage. Due, I suppose, to Harry Potter and Jerry Hall, but implicating the sixty-year-old smiler, all the same. Maybe it can be survived, but I'm not sure. The lookalike who goes to the platforms and the camera-calls has been robbed of much of himself these past few weeks, and I just hope the scullion/scullery man can nurse himself to secret strength again.

[. . .]

And then, on Valentine's Day, the bride and I break for St Lucia. 'Island in the sun' said the villainous Friel. For twenty years Derek W. has been 'at us' to come over, so we're off. He has some class of a hen-house or turf-shed on the premises where we can be on our own. Separate quarters. We'll see. Much love to you both. Watch yourselves. And my deepest gratitude. Seamus

SH dates the letter '4 January', which has to be wrong.

'Mossbawn scullery': the child's-eyes experience of which is vividly evoked in *Stepping Stones*, the book of interviews on which SH and O'Driscoll were soon to collaborate.

In addition to the heavy responsibilities of his employment at the Office of the Revenue Commissioners in Dublin, O'Driscoll was a formidably busy and conscientious reviewer, editor and encourager of other poets. His poem in the *Times Literary Supplement* of 7 January was 'No, Thanks' (later in *Exemplary Damages*, 2002).

'Cosmo' was Cosmo Landesman (b.1954), the journalist whose interview with SH was printed in the *Sunday Times* of 30 January.

Other contenders for the Whitbread Book of the Year had been the novelists Rose Tremain (b.1943) and Tim Lott (b.1956), the biographer of Hector Berlioz, David Cairns (b.1926), and J. K. Rowling (b.1965), whose *Harry Potter and the Prisoner of Azkaban* was the first children's book to be considered for the overall award. The model Jerry Hall (b.1956) – 'Gerry' to SH – was one of the judges.

'*cúpla focal*': 'a few words', stock phrase used in self-deprecation.

'scullion/scullery man': the Heaney and Scullion families of Bellaghy were related.

The 1957 film *Island in the Sun* has, among its themes, racism, adultery and murder.

To Matthew Evans

TS Faber

6 February 2000

Dear Matthew,

It could be that you are on your way to China and free of the gossip columns; but in case you're like the rest of us, in the sewage spill, I thought I'd better write about

The Browser/The Observer

In today's *Observer*, there's a nasty little piece in The Browser's column implying that the final lines of my *Beowulf* were lifted from Michael Alexander's translation. It as much as accuses me of plagiarism. I can see how the similarities may have put the thought into somebody's mind, but the fact of the matter is that I did not check Michael Alexander's translation against mine, otherwise I would have noticed the similarity. (I avoided consulting verse translations for help with construing, precisely because I didn't want to be influenced.) However, had I indeed noticed the similarity, it's likely that I might have retained the version as it is now printed.

The Browser's piece casts a slur on the integrity of the work done, and I am anxious first of all that you and the people at Fabers (Paul and Jane especially) have a clear picture of the kind of effort that went into the passage in question.

I am sending with this letter seven pages which are taken from my correspondence with Prof. Al David during the final stages of the translation. I have sidelined the places where the treatment of the final three lines is discussed. Since these lines are among the most famous and most scrutinized, I had an anxiety about how to render them. What I am sending you is simply the documentary proof of that anxiety, first of all, extracts from my letters of May 8 and May 17/19 to Al David. Then you will see how Prof. David (in the last line of first page of his May 21 fax – the top of second page didn't come through very well) recommends that I incline towards 'the kindest of his people' rather than 'most caring' and how on the second page of that same fax from him I have entered the longhand revision of the lines. I also enclose his May 31 query and my June 1 last word.

I think that the Browser should be let go to hell for the moment, but if any more serious questions are raised anywhere, we can have a talk about how to proceed. I don't propose to respond in any way, but if we ever need to, we are in a strong position. When all is said and done, these lines have a kind of simple clear sense, and the more literal you are, the more likely you are [to] coincide with other renderings – especially since the alliteration sends translators towards the same choices – 'keenest', for example, rather than 'most eager', since it alliterates with either 'caring' or 'kind'. But enough. I just thought you should have the evidence.

I'll call you to-morrow.

Seamus

SH was wise to put his trust in Evans, who had shown in the past that he was ready to take up the public scraps and legal causes of his more valued Faber authors in a fighting spirit; in the event, action was unnecessary.

'Paul and Jane' were Paul Keegan and Jane Feaver, Assistant Poetry Editor.

Alfred David (1929–2014) was the academic specialist – among other things, editor of the medieval section of the *Norton Anthology of English Literature* – who was appointed by Norton, the firm that had initiated SH's translation of *Beowulf*, to advise him.

To Basil Blackshaw

MS Emory

14 February 2000 191 Strand Road, Dublin 4

Dear Basil,

Your gift of the picture means more to me than I can say without sounding as if I'm overdoing it. I've always loved that statement that Constable made somewhere about old muddy banks and puddles and sheughs – not his word – having made a painter of him. What moves and steadies me at one and the same time in *A Glimpse of the Bann* is the sense of homecoming I have, first in the pigment and painted-ness of the picture itself, and then through and behind that artistic reality into the verity of the Bannside. And oddly enough, the Bann has begun to figure a bit more in my own writing recently. It's partly the colours, so suggestive of the 'clay-sucked stride' as Hewitt puts it; the glar and glit, the cowdung and the red cow's hide; but it's also the vigour of the painting in catching the sluggish thing in the ground. I cherish it and am proud that you bestowed it.

I'm sending a couple of the 'Bann-related' things I've done. The Moyola and the lint-hole were closer to me as a youngster, but the Bann at Toome was always a radiance. 'The Perch' comes from a memory of standing on the bank at Toomebridge when I can't have been much older than six or seven. And the 'Eclogue' combines Virgil's 4th Eclogue – about the birth of a miraculous child who will herald a world change – with the coincidence that a niece of mine in Bellaghy was going to have a baby coming up to the millennium.

Marie and I are away to St Lucia for 3 weeks. Our love to you and Helen. Blessings on the work. Keep glimpsing. Seamus

The painter Basil Blackshaw (1932–2016) was born in Co. Antrim and lived and worked there; in 1990, he had supplied the cover illustration for the first edition of *The Cure at Troy*, and SH's 1998 Christmas card, produced by Gallery Press, carried a painting by him.

In a letter of 1821, John Constable wrote: 'But the sound of water escaping from mill-dams, willows, old rotten planks, slimy posts, and brickwork, I love such things'; and this is likely to be what SH is recalling here.

'Perch' and 'Bann Valley Eclogue' are both in *Electric Light*.

To Thomas Flanagan

MS Amherst

17 February 2000 c/o Derek Walcott, St Lucia

[. . .]

Marie and I arrived in St Lucia the day before yesterday. For decades, Derek has been urging us to visit, and now that he has a place of his own, with an adjacent, separate cottage for travellers, we thought the time had come. I had fought to keep the month of February free of all commitments, and half-intended to go to Andalucía for a break, but when we encountered Derek and Sigrid in New York last November, we caved in to the notion of the Caribbean. Already I have drunk coconut water from a trepanned coconut, shown my pale belly to the dismayed beach-persons, wobbled in the turquoise waters of the sea, drunk the habit-forming rum punch and generally slackened – as I write this, we are summoned away for the second beach-bask.

*

Well, unless you get the thing done in the morning, that's it. The rhythm involves beach 'n swim 'n doze 11:30–1:00; a cooked lunch at home on the verandah; a drugged siesta; a slow awakening; a rum punch . . . not conducive to sustained effort. I even smoked a cigar on our – separate – cottage verandah last night.

It's the first time I've relaxed in a couple of years. In any sustained way, I mean – is it relaxation if it has to be sustained? The post-Christmas hibernation, that breakdown of self-belief and onset of low-heartbeat, is one thing, but this lotus interlude is indeed a trip. So far, at least. Three nights spent, about sixteen still to go. 'Sustain' may indeed be the word. [. . .]

'Derek and Sigrid': Walcott shared the last years of his life, in both New York City and Gros Islet, St Lucia, with his German companion Sigrid Nama.

To Rachel Buxton

MS Buxton

19 February 2000 Gros Islet, St Lucia

Dear Rachel Buxton,

The address is too good to waste. I am here with my wife, staying for a rare holiday with Derek Walcott. One of the things I'm doing – to earn my inner keep, as it were – is answering letters that are months overdue. Please excuse me for not having replied to your query about Frost long ago.

'Out, Out –' is the poem I remember making the deep impression. First. I believe Laurence Lerner handed it out on one of those practical criticism sheets – cyclostyled/xeroxed jobs – that used to be the staple of the seminar room. It connected with me because of its intrinsic head-on narrative force and its – I now realize – beautiful, delicate pacing. (A friend points out that Frost's 'So.' in this poem predates my translation of *Beowulf*'s '*Hwaet*' – I don't think there is an actual echo, but it's a piquant point.) It also had a powerful impact because that kind of rural tragedy was familiar to me when I was growing up – and I suspect that the death in a road accident of my young brother Christopher predisposed me to the poem also. I certainly recognized the conduct of the people in the last line who, 'because they were not the one dead . . . turned to their affairs': I think Lerner regarded this as a symptom of emotional callousness, but as far as I was concerned, it was a correct rendering of the fatalism and resignation, the slightly punch-drunk resolution, of the too-often assailed.

I do remember the sheer recognition factor – of the people, the situations, the practices – in my first reading of a greyish coloured Penguin *Selected*, done by C. Day Lewis. I think I must have had this as an undergraduate. Certainly I dwelt in it during the sixties, and lectured on/from it. 'Home Burial' hit hard. And I enjoyed 'The Fear' and – because of descriptions of hay-cock building – 'The Code'.

I seem to remember beginning my first arts lectures on Frost with a reading of 'The Gum Gatherer' as a kind of allegory for his practice as a verse-writer – 'overtaking you and taking you in' – a bit like Muldoon, in fact; the Frost and the Muldoon poem falls into step, comes level with your listening pace, so to speak, and engages you – but I digress.

I never did teach a course on Native American Literature, by the way. I took a couple of classes on 'Modern American' once upon a time, standing in for somebody else, probably Michael Allen. My teaching was mainly on 'Modern British' with the honours classes, in seminars and tutorials, and with First Arts, in a big lecture once a week, and in tutorials. Probably Paul Muldoon heard one of these first arts lectures and probably attended a tutorial. Can't be sure. His main Frost teacher was Gerard Quinn, at St Patrick's College in Armagh, and – I suspect – Edna Longley.

I suspect I got my green Cape *Collected* in the mid-sixties – I've mislaid it – when I also got the first volume of the biography (? or was that later) and a volume of *Selected Letters*. My Liverpool lecture was concerned to say that Frost was a 'wizard' – a transmuter of things into language – and that the hillside thaw poem was a paradigm for his fluency and mastery. Pound's review of *North of Boston* in which Frost figures as a realist of sorts is what set me off to say he was a language-conjurer. I believe I gave a little disquisition on the beguiling strengths of 'The Pasture' and demurred at the too neat clinch of 'Design' – a poem much celebrated *in illo tempore* – thanks to (?) Brooks and Warren's *Understanding Poetry*.

Frost helped me to think about poetry, how it linguifies things, if you'll excuse the expression. And this was where 'Directive' came to fit in, years later. If I can locate the pages in my unpublished Oxford lecture called 'The Playthings in the Playhouse', I'll send them to you. In later years too, I came to love 'Two Look at Two', 'To Earthward' etc. – and all those ovenbirds and phoebes.

'The Wife's Tale' – in *Door into the Dark* (1969) – is bred out of Frost, and knows it, but I don't think his trace is audible in any obvious way in my work. He's there more as an insistence on the rightness of making your own sounds in your own way. His notions of 'tones' and 'the sound of sense' – as well as his essay 'The Figure a Poem Makes' – are all part of my first base. All good wishes,

Seamus Heaney

– I sent the original of this for typing to my secretary in Ireland, but now that I look again at the copy, it seems legible enough. My best to Tom – S.H.

A DPhil student at Hertford College, Oxford, where Tom Paulin taught, Rachel Buxton had met SH at the Yeats Summer School, where he encouraged her to send him questions arising from her research into the possible influence on his poetry of Robert Frost.

To Sven Birkerts

MS Birkerts

26 February 2000 Gros Islet, St Lucia

Dear Sven,

If the pen cannot be put to the paper here, when will it ever be? Last night as I reminded Sigrid how to decode FUNEM/SIFM, I knew it could be put off no longer. Indeed, one of the reasons I gave myself for coming to this lotus land was that it would give me time to write letters – although I am surrounded by scoffers. Derek simply does not write them and others seem to possess no emotional answerability to their correspondents.

Still, the sun and sea do such a dumbing down on all faculties that even the act of hefting a *Uni-ball fine* becomes something of an effort. As I write, Dame Heaney otters her way through a pool on the very margin of the Carib sea and I sit bare-backed under one of those broad-sweeping, Graham-Greeneish fans, at a window that looks out on our little verandah that looks down a lawn where iridescent doves iridesce and the occasional old coconut cocos in the hedge. We have been in St Lucia for the best part of two weeks and are immensely the better for it. I found myself jogging – involuntarily, bubbily, and not too breathily – on the sand yesterday and realized that such an exertion would have been impossible at the start of our stay.

Derek has an inflexible law about swimming and lunching. We all go [to] the beach every day at around 11:30 a.m. and stay until around one o'clock. Then it is back to a lunch cooked by a cook and – for me, usually – a siesta. Marie goes off on the occasional local shop tour, market-researching *mit* Sigrid, and we all usually assemble again for rum-punches at sunset. Even tho' big D. doesn't actually drink them, the years of rampage have not been in vain: his recipe is splendid. Somehow, a few scraps are thrown together for a supper and we often find ourselves on our backs around 8:30, and with lights out at 9:00 p.m. What has come over us?

Naturally, we were worried about whether the togetherness would work out. Our own, God knows, as well as the foursome – we are in a one-roomed cottage – open-plan-kitchen-sitting-room-bedroom, with separate bathroom, a kind of bothy adjacent to the main bungalow; so far, however, herself and myself have been as softly inclined to each other as sunflowers, indolent as algae, honeysunning, in a manner of speaking; and the separate quarters, combined with the time-tabled aspect of the day, make the foursome meetings both easy and energetic.

Derek has a separate studio as well, and spends a good bit of time painting. There's a caretaker lad on the premises as well – all the year round, a necessity given that their grounds are in an isolated enough situation, on the shore, well out of town. And a cook, as I say, and a lady who cleans. So the *calme, luxe et volupté* aspect of things is sustained constantly and unobtrusively. But the real bonus is the access to the life of the place – we attended the independence day celebration concert and met the people who run the joint – judges, lawyers, merchants – and heard the *à bas gorge* (fiddle) music, the calypso, the gospel, the jazz and so on; attended also the launch of a book of plays by Derek's twin, Rodney, who is at present seriously ill in Toronto; went to a big open air 'food fair' – something like those Cambridge/Harvard Square *fests*, with music and booths and booze – but this one distinguished by the presence of a fourteen-piece steel band.

As to the actual island, it's like living in a Walcott poem. We drove in along the country roads, up the mountainsides, green tree ferns, casuarinas, mango trees, banana plants; and little houses, stuck there on stilts, built out on the slopes, lots of the people on the road, a woman with a gas cylinder on her head, a multitude with ghetto-blasting equipment at every rum shop, the ribs of beasts and giblets of fowls cooking on small barbecue pits at every crossroads. Need I go on? I shan't go on.

We think of you and Lin and Liam and Mara and know that you'll be in Ireland one day. But don't leave it too long. Meanwhile, I'll be in Cambridge for the Stratis reading – hastily, en route – and back for a couple of days in June. Maybe during the latter swoop we can assemble the Sunsetters. Love from us both –

Seamus

PS The plan was to do a lot of work – a review of the Russian/Soviet poet Nikolay Zabolotsky, for example – but truly the heat puts a halt to much head-work. (*Beowulf* responsible for alliteration evils . . .)

'FUNEM/SIFM': 'Have you any ham?'/'Yes, I have ham' – in mock German accent.

The playwright Roderick Walcott (1930–2000) died just over a week after this letter was written.

'Stratis' was the Greek novelist and poet Stratis Haviaras (1935–2020), curator of the Woodberry Poetry Room at Harvard and co-founder of the *Harvard Review*. 2000 was the year of his retirement from the university and return to Greece.

To Matthew Evans and Caroline Michel   MS Emory

20 April 2000   191 Strand Road, Dublin 4

Dear Matthew and Caroline,

Easter in Gloucester. The peaceable kingdom greening and golding, the lads and the lambs, the Aprilling Mabel . . .

Delightful to think of you all there at this time of the year. I always loved Holy Week when I was an adolescent at boarding school, coming home religiously – in all senses – ascetic and rhapsodic, all bulb and bloom . . . And now this year we can rejoice a little blasphemously in *our* risen lord.

Enclosed is a manuscript which I'll submit before long to Paul, and I hope you will accept the dedication on the dedication page – best thing in the book – as a celebration of the peerage and of our dear-age, if you'll excuse the expression. I've had it in mind for years to do this, and nearly went for it with *Opened Ground*, but at that retrospective moment, Marie seemed to be the right one, once again. And I'm glad now, because so much comes together at this season.

As the fellows say when they welcome a fellow to Magdalen, 'I wish you joy' – both, for this time the 'you' is plural – and beloved. By both of *us*.

Seamus

Matthew Evans and Caroline Michel had a house at Temple Guiting in Gloucestershire; Mabel is their daughter; he had just been raised to the peerage as Baron Evans of Temple Guiting. *Electric Light* is the book SH dedicated to them.

To Alice Doherty, Melissa Hanson, Niamh Boorman and Joanne Doyle   TS Emory

26 April [2000]   191 Strand Road, Dublin 4

Dear Alice, Melissa, Niamh and Joanne,

Thanks for your recent letter. I can see that you've been busy hunting up information about me. Congratulations on all that net-surfing.

I hope you don't mind if I answer your questions in a letter rather than fill in the nice big form you prepared for me.

I suppose what I enjoyed most about my childhood was the safe and secure atmosphere of the countryside in those days. Everything was much quieter. Very little traffic on the roads, mostly just horses and carts, people walking, people on bikes. Everybody seemed to know everybody else.

When I was very young, I used to get up early and go with my Aunt Mary to the byre where she would milk the cows. I remember once on a winter morning watching the sparks going up from a neighbour's chimney. It was still dark and they were lighting the fire. On mornings like that I liked to be in [the] heat of the byre, in the hay, in the light of the hurricane lamp.

I often helped to bring in the cows and to herd cattle when we were moving them field to field. I also often went with cattle from the Broagh down [to] the Wood farm in Tamlaghtduff, to stand in gaps along the road and 'cap' them. When I was older, I used to work in the hay during the summer holidays.

I didn't particularly like school when I started, but I liked the teachers all right. Miss Walls is mentioned in 'Death of a Naturalist' and Master Murphy in 'Station Island'. I didn't get slapped much at all, and in general nobody did. I used to like going into the school garden, for 'gardening classes' – mostly just digging.

My best friends in Anahorish School were the Gribbins, Henry and his cousin Eamon; Philomena MacNicholl took me to school on the first day, and of course Tommy Evans lived over the road from us and was part of the crowd on the Lagan's Road every morning and evening.

When I went to St Columb's I knew Gerald McCann from Ballynease, who was there ahead of me. My favourite teachers at St Columb's were the Latin teacher, Fr McGlinchey, and the English teacher, Mr O'Kelly. When I was at primary school I was good at 'sums', but by the end of my time at St Columb's I didn't like maths very much. I ended up preferring English, although Latin gave it a close run as my favourite subject.

I didn't really write poems at St Columb's. In my fifth and sixth years I used to 'act the cod' a bit, with mock poetry, some of it even in Latin.

I hope this will be of some use to you in your project and that you have good luck in the All Ireland Community Games final.

Yours sincerely,
Seamus Heaney

Written to pupils of St Mary's Primary School, Bellaghy.

To Harry Chambers

MS Hull

28 April 2000

[Glanmore Cottage, Ashford,
Co. Wicklow]

Dear Harry,

I'm actually down in the cottage in Glanmore – probably my equivalent of your chapel. Our own house has turned into a kind of office, a site of fax and phone, of administration and importunity. I had to build on an extra room to make a work-space where letters would be answered and stored . . .

It is a great sadness to hear from you about Lynn. And I sense a bereftness in your letter. How else could it be. I only hope the spirit holds up and that the old Harryesque stamina keeps bogging in and bogging on. But there's no getting away from the sorrow of it, and the loss that is implicit in the sturdy words you wrote for the Reverend Wilton. But Hannah and the grandchild must lighten the heart for you. Marie sends her deepest sympathy too.

I wish I had more heart for poetry readings. The way things are this year, I am in a kind of suppressed rage at myself for having taken on so much. I'm writing to you by return, for example, because I know that I won't have a quiet, personal moment for the next couple of months, no silence-time, only travel and executive-self stuff. I go to Greece (not the end of the world, I know) because of a book of translations being launched, then the States for the ever-present, national-service-type Irish arts fest, then Harvard for graduation duties, then Beowulfian, archaeological travels in Denmark . . . And so on. Harvard again in the autumn. Plans for a trip to St Lucia next February. The family have shown me the yellow card. I appreciate the care and financial support you offer, but have to ask to be excused, for the moment. I feel like Gulliver, pinned down by single liens of obligation. No one of them is a big thing, each has singular meaning, but taken all in all, they panic me. Seamus

Having moved with his second wife, Lynn, to Cornwall, Chambers ran his poetry press, Peterloo Poets, from a converted chapel overlooking the River Tamar. Lynn died in 2000.

To Robert Woof

MS Wordsworth Trust

3 May 2000 — The Athenaeum, Pall Mall, SW1Y

[. . .]
I think the 'uplifting poetry' could be rephrased in Nobel-speak – the prize was left for works that had an idealizing tendency or some such term. 'Ideal' goes towards uplift, but is minimally less pious-sounding. A prize for works 'fostered alike by beauty and by fear'. A prize for a work that reveals, illuminates, celebrates 'the growth of a poet's mind?' Now maybe that would be an interesting thing to reward – and adjudicate. Publishers to submit the volumes? In haste – I head for Athens – where else from here. Love to P. – Seamus

Robert Woof (1931–2005) was Director of the Wordsworth Trust, in Grasmere, Cumbria. In this final paragraph from a dashed-off letter to him, SH appears to be musing *ad lib* on the possibility of a poetry prize awarded according to specifically Wordsworthian criteria. No such prize was established, but something of the same spirit may have contributed to the decision of the Wordsworth Trust in 2009 to take on administration of the Michael Marks Awards for poetry pamphlets, a scheme that SH publicly and heartily endorsed.

To Heather O'Donoghue

MS O'Donoghue

3 May 2000 — The Athenaeum, Pall Mall, SW1Y

Dear Heather:

'Solemn approbatory truth': that phrase, as praise, lifted the heart greatly when I read it in your review of *Beowulf* – Bernard sent me a manuscript of it. And now I am doubly elevated by the s.a.t. of the review itself. Obviously, the wording of every line of my translation could be challenged and bettered or battered, so I was touched that you left that side of things to others in the field. But the big points of carry-over, from the *Beowulf* poet's world to the *North* world made strong sense, especially since you understand and state so clearly that there is no allegory involved. And I so love the proclamation of the poem's 'centrality, authority, a profoundly wide-ranging and reliable humanity'. Almost everything to do with the appearance of the translation has been a pleasure, but the sense that you and Bernard could associate yourselves so positively with it was a great steadying and sweetening factor.

Odd to be writing about our northern epic in this vestibule to the warm South: they invited me to join after my visit to the Swedes. And, by another happy coincidence, Marie and I are now heading for Athens, to the launch of a book of translations. Only for four days, but still, better than Philadelphia. Love to you all.

Seamus

Heather O'Donoghue had reviewed *Beowulf* for *Poetry in Translation*.

To Thomas Flanagan

TS Amherst

6 July 2000

Dear Tom,

This time a couple of years ago I published 'The Marching Season', but maybe I should have held it . . . Timing, timing, as Deane would say.

'What bloody man is that?' 'A drum! A drum!'
Prepossessed by what I know by heart
I wait for Banquo and Macbeth to come,
Unbowed, on cue, and scripted from the start.

The Drumcree Brethren are beating about the hill, the drum is sounding in the townlands, the roadblocks are being set up all over, the mood is eerily like the mood before the workers' strike fucked up Sunningdale *in illo tempore*. Croppy stands up and Billyboy rampages. Dangerous moment.

I have been doing the usual marching myself. After the slow heartbeat and amniotics of the Carib sea in February, I entered the Phlebas lands of profit and loss, and podia and commencements. All very elevated and busy, but not conducive to prolonging the moment of contemplation. We were at Finisterre in Galicia this day week, on a sort of Amergin *immram*. Sent Kinsella a postcard, quoting one of his most haunting lines – from an Amergin poem called 'Finisterre': 'I smelt the weird Atlantic.' We were twenty miles from Santiago de Compostela, but didn't get to it this time, being in the care of the University of A Coruña. They have (and they have good right to) an interest in Irish Studies, so I was doctored in that cause, during a four-day stay at Coruña – Sir John Moore's tomb still there on the ramparts, the 'Tower of Hercules', their Roman lighthouse, still on the headland. Late one night we took part in an anti-witch ceremony – fire-water being set alight and the glimmering drams being ladled into individual glasses, blown out and emptied down. Warm glows and *aroint thees* all round . . .

The week before that, four days in Denmark. Old Globby connections there, of course, now much revived by Heorot and Hrothgar, not to mention Jim Sharkey, a veteran of the St Columb's gulag who is the current Irish ambassador. One morning at eleven o'clock sixty consenting adults congregated in a field to hear *Beowulf* read in translation. The thinking is that Heorot Hall – if not *the* Heorot, then certainly *a* Heorot – stood on the site at Lejre, which is not far from Roskilde, not far from Copenhagen. I went with anxiety, but the thing worked fine. Sunshine and scholars, then a few Tuborgs. A Merriman-type lark in the skaldic air. I could go on enumerating these landfalls . . .
[. . .]

'The Marching Season' was first published in the *Irish Times* of 10 July 1998, two days before 'the Twelfth' (see letter to John Montague of 12 July 1976). The annual dispute over the assumed rights of the Orange Order to take their traditional parade, to and from Drumcree Church and through largely Catholic neighbourhoods in the town of Portadown, Co. Armagh, in 2000 threatened to erupt in outright violence and destroy the recently established Belfast Agreement. The quatrain SH includes here is the first of his 'Ten Glosses' (*Electric Light*).

To David Ferry

TS Emory

26 September 2000

English Department, Barker Center,
Harvard University, Cambridge,
MA 02138

Dear David,

Why has it taken so long to get these to you? Anxiety, perhaps, at having had a go at Eclogue IX. You'll remember I had 'Bann Valley

Eclogue' done a while ago. It appeared in *TLS* some time last autumn – October, I believe – in a slightly longer form. What prompted it was, of course, your own translations: they opened a sweet sure path back into my memory of reading the eclogues at school – in translation then also, in prose, in one of those old Pelican purple-rimmed editions. *Murex* even . . . Two of my nieces were expecting babies at the time, and to one of them in particular I am very attached, so I experienced an almost fatherly *tendresse* at the news of her pregnancy, not unwanted but not, as they used to say, within wedlock. Anyhow, the child on the way, in the aftermath of the eclipse in August, and the promise of the Belfast Agreement and the setting up of the new assembly – it all came together thanks to re-reading Eclogue IV. And I also went to Wendell Clausen's commentary and found it wonderfully enriching. Then I had to do something to contribute to a volume of essays and poems on J. M. Synge, and since our cottage in Glanmore was once a gate-lodge on the old Synge estate (ancestral – J.M. was born in suburban Dublin, although he did haunt the Wicklow place as a young man) and since Ann Saddlemyer had made us tenants there for next to nothing in the early seventies, and since I was still susceptible to the pastoral weather, I got started on 'Glanmore Eclogue'. And then, when it came to placing them in the manuscript of a new book due out next year, it seemed that an actual translation was needed to put keel or anchor under them, so I launched into IX and did it all of a sudden a few weeks ago. I used your version and Paul Alpers' as my cribs and got great pleasure out of the whole thing. What a beautifully tilted angle those poems are set at. I keep thinking of Miłosz's 'The World' – radiance at the centre, danger at the horizon, delicious language under and over all.

We'll see you before long.

The US poet and translator, largely from classical poetry, David Ferry (b.1924) does not recall receiving this letter, the text of which is taken from an unsigned, possibly unsent, copy held in the Heaney archive at Emory University; but Virgil is prominent among the Latin poets he has translated – his bilingual edition of *The Georgics of Virgil* would be published in 2006 – and I am prepared to risk the attribution.

To Williams Cole

TS W. Cole

29 September 2000

Dear Bill,

I am very, very sorry not to be able to go to New York to-morrow. Your father's memorial service was something I wanted to attend and looked forward to attending. I loved him and had some of my sweetest moments in his company. On my first visit to New York in 1969 when Galen and he welcomed me to that book-grotto on West Fifty Fourth, it was like entering a good dream that turned out to be no dream at all but the real thing – there was always an open channel between us, an affection and trust and merriment that never failed. Marie and I came to cherish those rides up in the elevator with the Carnegie Deli's corned beef sandwiches in one hand and the vodka in the other. Next thing it would be Delia Murphy on the record player and a discussion of who was good and who was godawful among the old and young bards of Ireland. We seemed to come more and more to our senses, even though there were occasions when we managed to lose them. In memory of it all, I woke this morning and had a vision of him by the banks of the River Moyola, and slipped into terza rima as easily as I slipped into a reverie many an afternoon in the armchair under the bookshelves. I send the lines with love from Marie and myself to you and Rossa and Galen and all the rest of the family and friends; with the deepest regrets at not being able to attend. Long-standing locked-in Harvard engagements for to-day and to-morrow keep me here. I'll try to telephone you at the weekend. And I'll be humming Thomas Moore's 'Oft in the stilly night' around four o'clock to-morrow: 'When I remember all / The friends so linked together / I've seen around me fall / Like leaves in wintry weather, / I feel like one who treads alone / Some banquet hall deserted, / Whose lights are shed, whose garlands dead, / And all but he departed . . .'

Williams Cole's father was the publisher, anthologist and writer of light verse William Rossa Cole (1919–2000); the poem SH sends with his letter is the uncollected 'In Memory of Bill Cole', which imagines a meeting similar to that of Dante and Casella early in the *Purgatorio*, only with the setting transposed to the 'earthly paradise' of the banks of the Moyola.

Delia Murphy (1902–71) was an Irish singer and collector of ballads whose husband, Thomas Kiernan (1897–1967), held many diplomatic posts, including Irish Ambassador to the USA; her LP, *The Queen of Connemara*, was issued in 1967.

To Sarah Broom

TS Emory

19 November 2000 — 191 Strand Road, Dublin 4

Dear Sarah Broom,

Thanks for your recent letter and apologies for the brevity of this one. Anyone who has committed so much time and attention to my work could well expect more of a response, but I have been in Harvard for a couple of months and just returned to a Himalaya of mail. You were lucky – your note was near the top.

I did the translation of *Philoctetes* almost entirely in Harvard. Between January and June 1991. I have no Greek, but even so, I looked at the Loeb Classical Library edition, which gives you a sense of the metrical shapes, of the strophe and anti-strophe in the choruses – even though it is all couched in deadly Victorian/Edwardian-Shakespearean verse. I also kept to hand David Grene's translation (or at any rate the one that is in the Chicago University Press series that Grene's involved with), and the one in Penguin Classics. What was most useful to me, however, was a book, or rather pamphlet, that I found on the shelves of the Widener Library, a schoolboy's crib, really, a word-for-word translation done sometime in the late nineteenth century, I think by somebody called Mongan, and published in Edinburgh(?). This had no elegances of style and was designed, I suspect, to help with homework, in the construing of the Greek directly. As such, it was the one that interfered least with what one might do with the text.

Needless to say, I added those extra bits of chorus without reference to anyone.

I wish you all the best with your work. And again am sorry not to have more to tell you.

Sincerely,
Seamus Heaney

After studying at Oxford for a PhD on myth in contemporary Irish poetry, Sarah Broom (1972–2013), a New Zealander, was now back home and writing a book that was to include a discussion of *The Cure at Troy*. She was also a poet. Misreading her name, SH begins his letter, 'Dear Sarah Brown.'

The Antigone / Sophocles – 'literally translated by Roscoe Mongan, BA' and published by James Brodie Ltd – does not bear a publication date.

2001

Some time in the autumn, SH and his trusted younger friend Dennis O'Driscoll drew up the agreement that was to lead to the publication, in 2008, of *Stepping Stones*. The interviews that form the book were to involve considerable labour for both men; even so, the immersion in the past that they entailed for SH – and from which a text of Proustian richness was to be the reward, particularly when the sensations of his childhood are evoked – looks like a salutary holding action, a touching of base or recourse to first things, in the midst of a life ever more taken up with international travel and public appearances.

To Angela Bourke

MS Bourke

7 January 2001 [m.d. 2000] Glanmore Cottage, Ashford, Co. Wicklow

Dear Angela,

This is about the only place where I ever write a personal letter nowadays, and indeed about the only place where I can get any sustained reading done. So I regret to say that it took me until now to read *The Burning of Bridget Cleary*. The only bonus, I suppose, is the fact that I have had the silence and the time to read it all, and intently, which means that it has been an experience rather than a skim, and an experience that vindicates entirely your claim in the final page that story has the power to convey ideas. The book has the feeling of completeness that comes from its scrupulous working through of all the evidence and the implications of the evidence; but there is the aesthetic/emotional satisfaction that comes from that shaped artistic projection, that touch of the artist (which you credit and show to be at work in the system of fairy lore itself). Something in me rejoiced at the completeness of your response, the breadth of your sympathy, the care you took with your words. Of course, the theoretical comprehension of the case, your placing of it in the dark liminal zone between fairy and official Ireland, between *lios* and ledger, and your demonstration of how it figured in the politics of the newspapers – all that is admirable and illuminating and vividly relevant to 'the way we live now', a hundred years on. The vilification of Irish nationalism in a country which owes its independence and 'modernity' to the nationalist effort is somehow reminiscent of the spurned and simplified (and anxious) repudiation of 'superstition' at the time of the trials. But what makes the whole book so trustworthy to me is your scruple of language, never going down the motorway of theoretical jargon or into the side-roads of local in-talk. A matter of tone – a firmness and an open-ness. We're proud of you. See you. *Le grá* – Seamus

Some years before, in 1991, SH had written to the Irish historian and academic Angela Bourke (b.1952), congratulating her warmly on her story 'Deep Down', which she had sent him because it shared a source with his own poem 'Lightenings viii', about the ship that appeared to the monks of Clonmacnoise while they were at prayer. In *The Burning of Bridget Cleary* (1999) – SH spells the name 'Brigid' – Bourke recounts the true story of a notorious murder in Tipperary at the turn of the previous century, and unfolds its cultural and political implications.

'*lios*': a fairy fort.

To Bernard and Jane McCabe MS NLI

7 January 2001 191 Strand Road, Dublin 4

Dear Friends,

As I told Bernard, I had this transcribed and photocopied for my brothers and sisters, and my cousins, the Joyces (children of Susan Heaney) – it was my Christmas present to them. But since ye are siblings and part of the inner trustworthies, I thought you should have it. Nobody else outside the family has a copy. Quite right.

Love,
S.

Accompanying *Heaneys and Scullions in Broagh, Mossbawn and The Wood: A Personal Account* by Sarah Heaney. SH introduces the work as follows: 'Some time in the nineteen eighties – I'm sorry not to be able to remember the date more precisely – I asked Aunt Sally to write down memories of her early life, so that the rest of us would have some record of who was who and what was what in those hard times. The following pages contain a transcript of her handwritten account.'

To Carol Hughes

TS Hughes

8 January 2001

The crucial letters I write are written in guilt and confusion, usually because they have been unconscionably deferred. You did me the honour of writing with great generosity about my memorial address for Ted and I should have answered immediately. So I'll not be surprised if you just stop reading here. But if you don't, please accept my apologies and be assured that my silence has been a greatly embarrassed one. A hangdog and head-hung interlude.

Our mutual friend and soul-guide – *lo mio maestro e 'l mio autore* – would not thank me for evading reality at this stage, so I must confess that my natural impulse to meet and salute your kindness was complicated by all kinds of remote control systems deeply lodged in my own personal and public life. Derek Hill used to scold me and push me about not going to Sandringham, saying it had to be 'political', and I would tell him no, it was not. Which was true, insofar as the reason I declined any invitation always had to do with calendar clashes and a reluctance – even given a prince's favour and fond invitation – to enter the formal pomps and flourishes of a grand weekend.

But above and beneath those immediate social facts was a shadowy web of complication which I trust we'll be able to bring to light and acknowledge together some day. History – as Stephen Dedalus said – it seems, is to blame. For the moment, I only hope you will accept my apologies for the long delay in thanking you for your letter and accept the enclosed proof of my new book as a belated token of gratitude. But I also send it because it contains a poem in memory of Ted (pp. 59–61).

Marie and I first visited Court Green maybe as long ago as 1970. Ted took us for a walk that night on Dartmoor where we heard the power station in operation underfoot, so that memory brought about the allusion to the ghost dead of the First World War in Wilfred Owen's 'Strange Meeting' ('Sullen halls where encumbered sleepers groaned'). And the reference to 'fretting no more' goes back to a phrase in Joyce where Stephen Dedalus – that man again – hears an English Jesuit speaking (English) and thinks, 'My soul frets in the shadow of his language.' But this is getting too much like a seminar.

I also enclose a copy of *Beowulf*. In its way, it's something of a millennial poem. Certainly there are moments when the sense of refreshment and renewal and escape from the shackles of the past comes across with delicious power. One of my favourite bits comes at line 1605:

> Meanwhile, the sword
> began to wilt into gory icicles,
> to slather and thaw. It was a wonderful thing
> the way it all melted as ice melts
> when the Father eases the fetters off the frost
> and unravels the water-ropes, He who wields power
> over time and tide . . .

Best wishes to you and yours in the new year and new century.

The text here, lacking both salutation and signing-off, is taken from SH's own typed and faxed transcription of an original letter which has not been traced.

'*Io mio maestro e 'l mio autore*': see Dante's address to Virgil at line 85 of Canto I of the *Inferno*.

The 'enclosed proof' was of *Electric Light*, soon to be published, and the 'poem in memory of Ted' is 'On His Work in the English Tongue' (pp. 61–3).

To Thierry Gillyboeuf

TS Emory

30 January 2001 191 Strand Road, Dublin 4

Dear Thierry,

Many thanks for your recent letter with the good news about the publication of *North*. Congratulations first of all on the translation itself – a valiant achievement since parts of that book are more like fossil English than a fluent, transparent idiom, so you had your work cut out for you, as they say. (That expression must go back to seamstresses/sempstresses?) I've just read again one of my own favourites in the book in your version – 'Lumière de Soleil' – and find the cadencing and management of line breaks, etc., just as I'd like them to be.

Please accept my apologies for not having written before in response to your letter of last November. The truth is, I am a bit overwhelmed by mail nowadays, and put many things on the long finger. I should have at least answered your queries about 'mother-wet' – by which I meant wet as a creature that has just emerged from the mother's womb, alluding to the exposure of the archaeological finds just at that moment when they are still glistening with the damp of underearth.

'Betrothal of Cavehill' – mad, submerged, mythological coding, incomprehensible to most people . . . Basically, the diagram of the thought behind the poem is this: shooting in Belfast results from male Protestant Ulster saying no to Union with female Catholic south/republic. Even so, speaker of poem remembers that on the morning of his wedding, neighbours practised the old country custom of shooting over the bridegroom's car as he set out for church. Hence speaker, implicitly, finds a possibility of union, shifting forward of political process from 'Ulster says no'. North 'betrothed' to south an emblem of move towards new relations between both places. (All of this, sorry to say, is extremely programmatic when spelled out. I do so only to try to clarify things for you. Poem was actually cut from four to two stanzas, so that didn't help the clarity . . .)

Conor Cruise O'Brien, writer and commentator on Irish affairs, Minister of Posts and Telegraphs in the Republic during the seventies. A controversial figure then and since. He has written on Burke. Billy Hunter a name of a schoolboy friend. His name appears also in a little rhyme in the 'Reading' section of Mossbawn chapter in *Preoccupations*.

Meanwhile, I confess that I cannot lay my hands on the copy of *Crediting Poetry* that you sent long ago, so if it's easy to have the publisher send another copy, I'd appreciate it. But I don't want to be making more work for you. You have enough on your hands with the foreword to *North* to be written, *Death of a Naturalist* and *Door into the Dark* to be construed and domesticated to your language and voice. I simply want to thank you again for the commitment and the effort and the thoroughness of your attention.

Sláinte!
Seamus

Thierry Gillyboeuf (b.1967) is a French translator from both English and Italian of a wide range of prose writers and poets; his translations of SH's early work were published by Gallimard as *Poèmes (1966–1984)*.

To Thomas Flanagan

MS Amherst

17 February 2001

Durrants Hotel, George St, London W1

Dear Tom,

Here to pause for a day and two nights, before proceeding to St Lucia. The time in Berkeley was rightifying. It was a resettlement of lives and loves and it did me good to be in the house and take part in the Sunday memorial. You spoke beautifully and proudly about that early life Jean and you lived in New York, and as you did, the feeling of the purposeful light shining on certain people at certain phases was shared by us all. Heart-mysteries and broken hearts.

The Eoghans have done a wonderful thing in offering the house, and there will be the extra sweetness of old summers flitting and fleeting through the place. The right way to come back this time.

Meanwhile, I was going like a sprinter since I left your door. Home on the Monday, in Scotland until the Friday, Saturday to Wednesday two income tax returns for US and Ireland, tons of old mail, late Guggenheim recommendations (they haunt me still). Then to Cambridge on Wednesday for Helen Vendler's Clark Lectures. Stayed in Trinity College: splendour falls on college walls – in the chapel, sculptures of – among others – Newton, Bacon, Tennyson, Macaulay, plaques to Housman and the lesser *lares*, portraits of monarchs and murdered wives – enough.

Keep your heart up. Will send you a card from under the bam . . .

Seamus

After retiring from his job at Stony Brook, Flanagan had returned to live in Berkeley, where his wife Jean died in January 2001.

'under the bam . . .': SH alludes to the song in T. S. Eliot's *Sweeney Agonistes*: 'Under the bam / Under the boo / Under the bamboo tree.' This became his reliably recurring joke about holidaying on St Lucia.

To Karl Miller

MS Emory

29 March 2001

Enclosed – in haste as I head from Faber for Oxford reading – are the Henryson versions I was blabbing on about. And you were right – after the *Beowulf*, I felt the need of a 'day job' – but I also loved the iambic pace and the rhyme.

Anyhow. They're not finished, but they'll give you an idea of what I'm at.

[. . .]

'Henryson versions': early mention of a project that was not to take book form until 2009, SH's translations of *The Testament of Cresseid* and *Seven Fables* by the fifteenth-century Scottish poet Robert Henryson. As a literary critic, Miller, born in Loanhead, Midlothian, wrote mainly on Scottish subjects.

To Thomas Flanagan

MS Amherst

10 April 2001 — 191 Strand Road, Dublin 4

Dear Tom,

Last before America. Sorry indeed not to have been in touch before this last minute. I go to New York to-morrow morning and come by indirection to Marin on 19th.

The Tracy man spoke to me and told me about your angiogram and possible -plasty to-morrow. I'll be thinking of you . . . Bernard McCabe astonished himself a few years ago by watching the whole show they made of him on closed circuit TV, so you may develop an interest in that too . . . Not anybody's favourite viewing. I'm glad Kate is going to be with you.

Don't bother yourself by trailing out to Marin. It's 45 minutes of reading to an auditorium that's meant to hold 2000, for Christ's sake. And then there's a repeat of the Seamus and Bob Hass show – 'in conversation'. We'll converse in Berkeley. Marie and I will come over on Monday. I'm going to be indolent on Saturday in the hotel the agent has put us in, and see Maryon D.L. on the Sunday. Will call you on the Saturday anyhow. Won't get into SF until Friday P.M.

I hear you're in full tilt on J. Ford. I hope he's keeping you if not up, from going down . . . The house on your own must be hard. See you soon – S.

PS Am sending you a copy of *Electric Light*. I've been all over the place 'launching' it.

'Kate' is Flanagan's daughter Caitlin.

Robert Hass (b.1941), US poet, taught at Berkeley.

'full tilt on J. Ford': Flanagan was reviewing a biography of the film director John Ford for the *New York Review of Books*.

To Dennis O'Driscoll MS Emory

16 April 2001 Dam's Mark Hotel, Colorado Springs

Dear Dennis,

Well, my excuse is that it's not all that far from Santa Fe . . . About a year and a half ago I agreed to go to Houston (Adam Zagajewski's American station) and then one thing led to another and I ended up taking in a reading in New York on Good Friday (was to do it on 12th/ Thursday, until I found out that John Montague was also due to read in Manhattan that evening and postponed mine rather than have to put up with all that) and coming here on Holy Saturday, just to catch my breath (it's high) and get ready for a week of girded going: to-day Colorado College, to-morrow Houston, Thursday UCLA, Friday Marin County. Czesław was due to be co-reader in Marin, but sadly he's still in Cracow. His ninetieth year . . . His ABC so abundant. His new book of poems with one called 'Against Philip Larkin' or something similar. What a great one.

Anyhow. Your letter deserved an earlier response and I apologize to have been so long. The simple answer is that I believe the proposal is a good one and mightily honorific and there's nobody I'd rather do the work with, and nobody with a better right or capacity to do such a book. Your own honesty would keep me honest and the prospect of spending time together is an extra invigoration. So, in principle, I'm all for it and proud that you would take it on.

In practice, things are complicated by the fact that I agreed a couple or three months ago to do a book-length set of interviews with Jerzy (from Łódź) and Jerzy (from Znak) Illg. A Polish book to come out of that, to be published by Znak. It so happens I am to write to J. Illg about this, but now that your proposal has materialized, I think I'd better wait until we have had a chance to talk. But that won't be very soon, I'm afraid.

[. . .]

The title of the poem in which Miłosz states the case against Larkin's nihilism more bluntly than SH ever did, even in his Oxford lecture 'Joy or Night: Last Things in the Poetry of W. B. Yeats and Philip Larkin', is 'Against the Poetry of Philip Larkin'.

'I believe the proposal is a good one': O'Driscoll's first move towards the intensive collaboration that was to bring *Stepping Stones* to fruition.

'Jerzy (from Łódź)' is the poet and academic Jerzy Jarniewicz (b.1958); writer, poet and critic Jerzy Illg is an editor at the publishing house Znak, based in Kraków. For more on SH's diplomatic negotiation to avoid possible conflict of interest, see his letter to Illg of 30 October 2001.

To Carol Hughes

MS Hughes

18 May 2001 [Oporto airport]

[. . .] it will be a huge task – I feel that it should be a bit like Wade's *Letters of W. B. Yeats* – which was the standard edition for years. A hefty volume done with ambition and thoroughness, not a stop-gap. I mean the editors shouldn't think of their task as being to hold the line until the 'real' Collected comes along. The book will be a revelation of Ted's huge range of interests, his holistic meaning for his correspondents, the passion and focus of vocation. I remember suggesting to him one time that he should undertake a mighty prose book – almost autobiographical, but more like 'the growth of the poet's mind', a cross between Wordsworth's *Prelude* and Nadezhda Mandelstam's *Hope against Hope*, something that would allow the coherence of his inner life to be manifested. Of course, when you combine the *Winter Pollen* book with the Goddess/Shakespeare book, plus *Birthday Letters*, you do have the aurora of his intelligence and imagining revealed, but a big well-contoured and seriously chosen book of letters would be an easter occasion, I'm sure [. . .]

Written on Aer Lingus Gold Circle Club notepaper, in answer to Carol Hughes's request for advice on how to proceed with the publication of her late husband's uncollected writings. Here, he is thinking of Hughes's letters.

To Daniel Weissbort

TS Emory

30 June 2001 191 Strand Road, Dublin 4

Dear Danny,

Late though it is, and ashamed as I am to have been so long in getting round to finishing your Joseph diary, I am still writing even though I know I will be too brief. Marie and I are going out to a seventieth birthday party in a couple of hours' time. But if I don't write at this moment, I fear I'll not get round to it to-morrow and then the whole thing will slip again.

[. . .]

At any rate, I've had all day to-day, and hours on and off earlier in the week with your manuscript, and apart from anything else, I've had my writerly conscience pricked by the example of your own great tenacity of purpose, the way you made time and made effort and composed a meaning and exhibited a love: the way you were true, recording the (yes) nitty gritty of the daily doings, but also staying true to the spirit, dealing fairly with the 'shadow', not simply out to please him: honouring the intimacy, facing up to the figure you may have cut in his eyes, but not shirking your own hurt at hurts done.

The thickness, as they say, of the treatment is what is powerful. That, and the complete care you take of everybody mentioned. Recently I was watching those Picasso programmes on TV, presented by John Richardson, and what I loved was the fact that Richardson was not 'presenting' at all: he was a man with a life of his own and wherever he went to report on Picasso, he was re-entering that life and meeting friends who also happened to be friends or relations of Picasso. What flowed from all this was a complete sureness of tone, an attentiveness to the subject in hand and a self-forgetfulness on Richardson's own part – no anxiety for himself as a performer, just an effort at getting it right, at telling what happened. And the same kind of thing happens in your diary/journal. Each new entry or essay has a note of 'let's see now, let's try to get this straight, or straighter' about it. Always the focus is upon Joseph, or if upon yourself, then upon what your dealing with him and your sticking with him entailed. As in the poems to Ted, you give unique expression to what a friendship means over a lifetime. Both sequences are 'In Memoriams' for our own day. Of course, the technical question that's being pursued, about what Joseph's English amounts to, how 'admissible' it is, gives you a course to hold to that's not the usual memorialist's course, but even so, the book ends up being as much about the toils of friendship as the toils of translation.

It's an anthology of good things said – by you and by others – about the problems and is an education in itself. A translator's Prelude, the growth of a poet-translator's mind. The unremittingness of the questions about Joseph's English and the repeated testing of the 'May 24' poem are guarantees of the passion that sustains it. Over and over again you reveal how much is at stake for you, how much you have been prepared to give of yourself in order to get a rightness in *it*. I myself suffered a kind of shock when you report how Joseph took the Zabolotsky you had laboured over and treated it so offhandedly, as a sort of first draft. But the largeness of spirit is in the quietness of the treatment.

I cannot begin to enumerate all the places where I underlined and rejoiced in what you attend to and how you express it. Just leafing through, in no particular order, I see phrases like 'his scrupulous informality' and sentences like 'it was something of a mystery to me that I could not love the poems as I did the man'. 'He was fond of the word "job".' 'Joseph's reading exalted language as such.' 'In the dock Joseph was a kind of Candide.' And then, your conclusion: the Dido line and the Akhmatova quotation and Joseph's comment on the empress theme – it took my breath away. You have raised the monument, you have kept beauty (Hopkins, by the way, always makes his entry most appositely) and you have nearly persuaded me that Joseph was going about a work that could be made to work – Russianizing English. But the wonderful thing is your *lutte* with the languages, your need to be true to the poet-daimon in yourself who cannot leave Joseph's figurings and disfigurings alone. The drama of concession and refusal is wonderful, the destabilizing (in the realm of translation) of orthodoxies, the attempt to find the way out by going through.

If I were a publisher's editor, I might suggest some cuts – only for the convenience of 'the general reader', but, come to think of it, no such creature will be reading the book. The long lists of specific rhymes and the inexorable record of the versions of the 'May 24' are both crucial and testing.

And of course, I was gladdened to find 'Audenesque' getting in and getting through, as it were.

Forgive me also for not writing sooner to congratulate you and Valentina. It was a great delight for Marie and me to hear about your decision to marry and we are moved to be included among your guests on September 15. Kisses kisses . . .

Seamus

Daniel Weissbort, poet, translator from Russian and teacher, had been a friend of Ted Hughes's at Cambridge, and with him founded the influential magazine *Modern Poetry in Translation*. A year or two before this, SH had read and offered comments on Weissbort's collection of poems about Hughes, *Letters to Ted* (2002). Here, SH addresses his prose account, *From Russian with Love: Joseph Brodsky in English* (2004). Weissbort's wife-to-be was the Russian literary scholar Valentina Polukhina, herself an authority on Brodsky.

'(yes) nitty gritty': SH alludes to Brodsky's recklessly unidiomatic use of the phrase 'nitty gritty' in his poem 'May 24, 1980'.

To Karl Miller

MS Emory

2 August 2001 191 Strand Road, Dublin 4

Dear Karl,

The son of a landscape painter probably doesn't need another landscape, but even so . . . This birthday card was done by one whom Yeats thought of as 'a great painter born / To cold Clare rock and Galway rock and thorn'. It's one of a group of watercolour sketches I got at an auction last December, offered for sale by a Ms Cathleen Kennedy, grand-daughter of Lady Gregory. They were done by the Irish airman himself, Robert Gregory, and the tower surely has to be the one at Ballylee. I didn't frame it, in case you want to do a special job to show up the dame on the back of the 'scene'. It comes with love and best wishes for 'the day that's in it'.

Seamus

PS The auctioneers were Mealy's of Castlecomer, the auction was in Tara Towers Hotel, Dublin, on 5 December 2000. You have part of lot 594 . . .

Miller's father, William, had earned his living working for the Post Office, but as a graduate of the Glasgow School of Art was a talented and dedicated painter as well.

Robert Gregory (1881–1918), Irish artist, sportsman and member of the Royal Flying Corps, who died in a flying accident, inspired a number of Yeats's major poems, including 'In Memory of Major Robert Gregory', from which SH quotes here.

To Adrian Rice

TS Rice

8 August 2001 191 Strand Road, Dublin 4

Dear Adrian,

Kieran Furey sent me this collection of poems. It landed in the post this morning and I am sending it on to you with a copy of the letter that accompanied it. (I hope the Abbey Press is still in production.) I don't know Kieran Furey but I sympathize with his situation. My own situation is to be in this position constantly, being sought to give opinions on manuscripts or to promote them. I've made it a rule now to stay out of the blurb game, since the requests are unending and even if I had time to read and decide, I couldn't for my own credibility do more than one or two a year. Still, I read these poems and feel there is something in them worth attending to. Not every poem earns its keep, but there's a sturdiness about the imagining, a sense that something has been carried-through and connected-up, and I'd be grateful if you could give them a reading and consider whether they might not make a small book in your list. I'd begin with the sonnet sequence 'Water' because it seems to me firmly written, with good thematic and historical thews running through it, and even if there are places where you'd want to make changes, such as the very last couplet of poem 2 and poem 6, it has imaginative grip.

There are many places, of course, where the poems could be improved in detail. The first couplet of the first poem, for example, could go, and there's a problem of decorum in a phrase like 'peeled-spud moon' – the visual image is fine, but 'spud' is a hard word to handle – maybe he gets away with it in the last line of *The History House*, because of the satirical jag?

Anyhow, I in turn apologize for landing you with more obligation. See what you think. I'll let Mr Furey know you have the poems.

And more power to your own work.

Seamus

Adrian – In fairness, as they say in Cork, I thought you should see my note to K. Furey. I just want you to see that I didn't build him up.

The Northern Irish poet Adrian Rice (b.1958) was also the proprietor of a small publishing outfit, Abbey Press; he did not take on Kieran Furey's poems.

In his 'note to K. Furey', SH had written, 'You have a claim on a reader's attention, I think, because the poems communicate a strong sense of an apprehended world: they sound as if they know what they're talking about' – before specifying his dissatisfactions with other features of the collection.

To Eamon Duffy

MS Duffy

21 August 2001 191 Strand Road, Dublin 4

Dear Eamon,

Sir Christopher has conquered. The book is a heartbreak. The love and insight you have lodged in it come through constantly and powerfully. And it's so beautifully shaped and paced. Please excuse this unregulated babble, but I just want to tell you how entranced and delighted and instructed I was, even if I have not enough time to do so properly (I am away to Macedonia this morning, for six days – getting in won't be a problem, but getting out? Anyhow . . .)

The completeness of your understanding, the terms of your conception, the delicacy of your deductions, the alertness and sympathy in every act of interpretation – it's all *dulce et utile*. And the big overall elegy for the death of the old sacralized community, that comes through – to me at least – as a not so objective correlative for the world of loss we ourselves have known. From the morning offering to breakfast TV, the May altar to the camcorder. The chapter on the 'dismantling' of the Parish, where you read the mood of old loyalty under the cowed conformity, and make that wonderful new reading of the ms. To link it to the camp men – it's like cello music. Drawn out and climactic. But so intimatily prepared for. My toes curled when I read the burr-words and then I warmed to them as to old friends all through the text – the vawnte, the awter, the wolde, the vyre bykin . . . Yet it is the wholeness of your own response and the mixture of springiness and focus in the writing that keeps the whole book alive. The amount of knowledge/felt truth you evince from the 'accounts' is extra-ordinary. The significance of the change from 1st person recording, for example. The fleshing out of the 'chrismers' story. The ongoing drama of the black vestments. I just wanted to let you know before the excitement cooled. I have a chapter to go, but must, alas, go myself. Poetry-fest in Struga. But *gaudens gaudeo*. Beavers aloft! Seamus

'away to Macedonia': recently the scene of an armed insurrection. SH had been invited to the international poetry festival held annually in Struga, to receive its most prestigious award, the Golden Wreath.

Duffy had sent SH his newly published book *The Voices of Morebath: Reformation and Rebellion in an English Village*, in which the manuscript records of Sir Christopher Trychay, vicar of Morebath for much of the 1500s, supply evidence. The 'camp men' were five men from Morebath who had joined the camp around the besieged city of Exeter; the '"chrismers" story' concerned children who had died soon after baptism and were referred to as 'Chrysom children', or 'chrismers'.

'intimatily': unambiguously what SH wrote – not, I think, mistakenly, but as a neologism meant to imply a process of intimation.

To Paul Muldoon and Jean Hanff Korelitz — MS Emory

7 September 2001 — 191 Strand Road, Dublin 4

Dear Paul and Jean,

This seemed like a good idea at the time – i.e. a couple of weeks ago when I phoned Willie Devlin in Ardboe and asked him to get me an eelskin. What he sent me was one he had just unpeeled – or peeled – with instructions to me to 'put a wee lick of salt on it and lave it for a while'. As the reek of the thing will tell you, it seems not to have been left long enough. If there had been more sun on the garden table where I spread it, it might have been less rank. But still, my loves, it's meant to wish you both your happiness – Seamus

With this unusual gift came the typescript of an uncollected poem, '"A Present from Old Ardboe"', with the dedication 'for Paul and Jean'. In it, SH slyly alludes to Muldoon's own poem – 'for Seamus Heaney' – 'The Briefcase'. Neil Corcoran's essay '"A Languorous Cutting Edge": Muldoon versus Heaney?' throws light on the sometimes coded and loaded exchanges between the two poets.

To Dennis O'Driscoll — MS Emory

17 September 2001 — 191 Strand Road, Dublin 4

Dear Dennis,

Devastating week . . . My freedom to arrange my own time meant that I spent hours in front of the television and hours in a kind of torpor, feeling inadequate yet uneasy about marching into public grief. Feeling wrong in not making some kind of declaration, feeling there was nothing adequate for the declaring.

Meanwhile, your excellent 'business' letter has been in front of me, to remind me that one helpful response is to attend to the work in hand. All that you outline is appreciated as a good record of our conversation and agreed as a basis to proceed on – except that the question of your remuneration must be attended to with special care and in consultation with Patrick Lannan. In fact, you pay too much attention to my money matters and too little to your own. All to be discussed.
[. . .]

'Devastating week . . .': SH must be referring to the events of 11 September, when four American airliners were hijacked: two were flown deliberately into the towers of the World Trade Center in New York, the third into the Pentagon in Virginia; the fourth crashed in a field in Pennsylvania after passengers fought back. Although he felt unable to make 'some kind of declaration' just then, his poem 'Horace and the Thunder', later to be titled 'Anything Can Happen' and subtitled 'after Horace, *Odes*, 1, 34' was written quickly enough to be printed in the *Irish Times* on 17 November, then included in the Urbino lecture that he reports on in his letter to O'Driscoll of 25 November.

O'Driscoll's 'business' letter followed a discussion initiating the collaboration between him and SH that was to result in *Stepping Stones*. In the eventually published book, Patrick Lannan, son of the J. Patrick Lannan who had established the Lannan Foundation as a cultural charity, is thanked for the 'very generous support and encouragement' received from that quarter.

To Jerzy Illg — TS PNL

30 October 2001 — 191 Strand Road, Dublin 4

Dear Jerzy,

You know the old song – 'You always hurt the one you love, / the one you shouldn't hurt at all . . .' I am very sorry to have been slow in replying to you, and sorry that this reply, being written late at night, more in order to break silence than to settle the many matters pending, will not be as full as it should be.

First of all, I'm truly delighted that Stanisław is doing *Electric Light*. I've come to regard the Polish translations and the Polish audience as a kind of extension of the home enterprise and feel it a real honour that Staszek has stuck by my work. I only wish that I could say an uncomplicated yes to your tour of Poland proposed for next May, but already last May I had committed myself to several other events around then. A visit to the Muldoon campus and others in USA in late April <2002, i.e.>, honorary degree trip to Prague, much else. I am slightly distressed at the way the calendar is ruined for months ahead. Reluctant even to think about planning. In denial. Hence slow reply. And inconclusive response even now.

The Dennis book. About to begin. Conceived of as a big enterprise. Ideally, I'd *write* the answers to the questions. It would be an ongoing 'ambitious' attempt, not a 'second string' job but a fully engaged bit of work, building up to a substantial, 'authored' book, albeit one prompted by the O'Driscoll questions. But we'll have to see how it goes, whether we can get any 'rate of production' established. My whole life and time are tied up for months. A week in Italy later this month, ten days in Stockholm next month (will you be there with Wisława? probably not Czesław). A series of formal lectures to be written for a residence in Cambridge in February. Jesus, Mary and Joseph! as my mother would have exclaimed.

So can we put the Znak interview on hold, and see what has accumulated by springtime? As for the book tour, you know I would love to be with Jane and Danny in May, but I simply cannot say yes at the moment. I am frazzled. I feel a total mascot. I spent two days at the University [of] Ulster yesterday and to-day, launching a new academy, a 'smiling public man'. Next week I go to decorate a pomp and circumstance fund-raising event in my old alma mater at Queen's in Belfast, then show myself to the corporate world again at a fund-raising dinner for them in London. At this moment, I just cannot contemplate taking on more exposure of myself. It would be irresponsible, a mortal sin because it would be a 'grave matter' of neglect of other (inner) responsibilities, done in 'full knowledge' and with 'full consent of the will'.

Dear Jerzy, you know I am well disposed to the Polish connection and cherish my Polish friends. You have been a great host and a great publisher, a most patient correspondent. Put up with this procrastination for a while. Give my love to Czesław. I was so bloody well put upon by other, outer things that I didn't write the poem I'd hoped to write for his birthday. I feel a little panicked. In fact, pushed to the side of my first self. And even if that's the late-night inner man speaking, isn't he the very one we should all attend to?

Fondest wishes to you and yours.

Seamus

Światło elektryczne (2003) was Stanisław Barańczak's third volume of Heaney translations to be published in Poland.

The question of possible conflict between the Znak book of interviews that Jerzy Jarniewicz would have conducted, and the one planned with Dennis O'Driscoll, had already been raised awkwardly in correspondence between SH and Illg earlier in the year.

To Brigid Murtagh-Sheridan TS Emory

30 October 2001 191 Strand Road, Dublin 4

Dear Brigid Murtagh-Sheridan,

Your letter arrived here a week or so ago. I was upset to hear about the hurt your daughter felt and could sympathize immediately with the hurt and disappointment you felt on her behalf. I apologize to her. Clearly she sensed that she had been singled out for unmannerly treatment, but the last thing I'd want to do would be to slight anyone vulnerable.

The last thing I wanted to do on the evening of the Hartnett launch, however, was to remain in front of that crowd signing my books. Michael Hartnett's partner was in the front row and it was a Hartnett memorial. There were certain courtesies called for. I realized that I would be approached to sign and had decided from the beginning to depart promptly, without putting pen to any paper, because if you sign one book in a crowded situation like that, it's unfair not to sign them all. So, before the reading began I had gone to excuse myself with Nuala Ní Dhomhnaill and Dermot Bolger, telling them that I'd be fleeing afterwards. And indeed fleeing was what it felt like – as I pushed out people were even holding up Hartnett books for signing. Which would have been, in my view, a trespass of sorts.

David Hanly I have known for thirty years. He came in late to the reading and would have expected some greeting – but I had to pass him also without speaking to him. Whatever 'embrace' he got had little to do with his 'fame'.

I wasn't sure whether to reply to your letter, since you called it 'a sad day for poetry' and had decided to your own satisfaction that I had been 'lauded by many famous people and perhaps . . . forgotten the ordinary ones who read [my] poetry'. As far as I am concerned, it was a good evening for Michael Hartnett's poetry. I was there, as many were, to honour him and his work. It's just a pity that your daughter was bruised in the crush. She was not singled out. I certainly did not, in any demeaning sense of the term, 'turn my back on her'. I hurried out of a crowd.

Yours sincerely,
Seamus Heaney

To Dennis O'Driscoll

MS Emory

25 November 2001 BA 2561, Above Cisalpine Gaul

Dear Dennis,

Well, that's done, but for once, I'm not all that glad it's over. M. and I set out last Tuesday for Bologna – and ever since have been on the go in Italy, but rewardingly so. Coming home enriched rather than exhausted. Perhaps there's a lesson here – if you're going away, build in a couple of extra gazing-and-drifting days. Although, as we both know only too well, calendar will usually say no.

Gabriella Morisco translated – along with Anthony Oldcorn, professor of Italian at Brown University – *Station Island* into Italian. Years ago. She then taught at Bologna but is now appointed at the university in her home town of Urbino. Anyhow, she had wanted me to accept an hon. doc. at Urbino just after the Stockholm avalanche, but I had to dodge it then. Yet in the end, of course, had to atone. So this outing was a kind of climax, and turned into a series of pomps. The Poetry Centre at Bologna University seems to have some good young poets and critics attached to it – the reading they arranged, at any rate, was a first class affair, very good audience and good literary company at the various lunches and dinners. Bologna itself a beautiful, venerable town, where we have been already, recently; then, reward day, by car to Ravenna. The mosaics in the different churches and mausolea are entirely available and un-arcane. Virgins and martyrs, emperors and empresses, Roman-style naturalism and Byzantine-style stylization, the colours hard and clear, the greens and whites and golds beyond the usual. Anthony Oldcorn was in the company all week and drove Marie and me (from Bologna to Ravenna to Urbino) – introduced us also to a couple of retired schoolteacher-sisters who knew every tessera in the town and guided and gossiped us through the place in a completely familiar Irish way – the *béarla* was at one of them, fluently – like my Aunt Sally-sur-Adriatic. I babble, I know,

but I'm reminding myself as much as telling you why the whole thing holds up so well. Urbino, for example, is a mighty walled town, dominated by Federico da Montefeltro's palace. W.B. and Augusta G. were there in 1907, and no doubt we stood where they stood, in the palace room where Castiglione read out *The Book of the Courtier* and in the Duke's study – marquetry-panelled, unchanged, small and workable-in. 'Urbino's windy hill', Yeats refers to, and what I've brought back is a poem by Pascoli – a class of a contemporary of W.B.'s – native also of Urbino – a poem about flying a kite in Urbino *ventoso* when he was a lad. So that should keep me happy in the chair by the Yule log.
[. . .]

Gabriella Morisco, who had invited SH to Urbino and escorted him around the city, has remarked on the resonance of the lecture SH delivered there, two months after the atrocity of 11 September, under the title 'Towers, Trees and Terror'. It was she who, incidentally, introduced SH to the work of Giovanni Pascoli (1855–1912): 'A Kite for Aibhín', the concluding poem in SH's final collection, *Human Chain*, is 'after' Pascoli's 'L'Aquilone', in which the poet recalls flying his kite as a child in Urbino. The seven translations, some substantial, from Pascoli that are to be found in Marco Sonzogni's 2023 edition of *The Translations of Seamus Heaney* suggest the strength and depth of the Urbino poet's appeal to him.

To Cathal McCabe

MS C. McCabe

25 November 2001 Bologna Airport

Dear Cathal,

A week has passed and I've seen and done much in between – uttered poems in Bologna, gazed agog in Ravenna, been doctored (academically) in Urbino. A rich and busy week – but, happily, I've had an hour in the quiet of the lounge here, and have been able to read through – too speedily, I know – *Poems & Letters*. There's real go and real finish in the manuscript – my favourites among the poems seem (as Lowell once said to me about some of my own) 'to have come through a sadness', even if the occasion and the art itself are happy. I suppose I'm only saying that there's a real sensibility behind the work. My favourites – just leafing through again, and leaving aside the big set-piece letters – are 'The Harbour', 'Epithalamium', 'Philoctetes', 'Three Poems' – well, the first two* <*No 3 OK in itself, just a bit muldoony for comfort> – 'In Memory of My Mother', 'A Postcard from London', 'From the River

L.', 'Summer in K.', 'My Childhood', 'In Donegal', 'The Stone', 'The End of the Journey'. I have left out some beautifully done work, such as 'Kerkenna', 'The Marten' and 'Light and Love', because the actual forms and postures of the writing were too Mahonesque for me (or better say, for *you*) – although sections II and III of the former hold their own, by dint of subject matter and self-sitedness, so to speak, against the influence. What I like about all of the above is the sureness of touch, the way your own note and the chosen shape are in harmony, and the trustworthiness of the feeling – to use an old-fashioned term. The light touch, in other words, is not a sign of light weight.

The big 'Letter from Łódz' : I frankly think it is *too* big, but I hate saying so, because there's so much packed or loaded into it. The historical moment, the historical transition in Poland, the freshness of your own response to the data and drunken-ness of things being various, the sheer heft and haulage work being done by the stanzas – I take the hat off to all that. But here and there I think the metre wobbles under the weight, and in other places – I can't say where since I'm hurrying to finish this before flight is called – the data clogs a bit. My hunch is that Paul Keegan might feel much the same: which is to say he will recognize a poet at work, bringing it off in his own way, hitting the spot definitely and sweetly – but he may hesitate a bit when faced with the big one. The last thing you'll want to hear is a suggestion that it might be shortened – or maybe sectioned – but you might think about it. Which thing having been said, it should be ignored by you if your hunch is different. The main thing is this: the manuscript should be sent to Paul K.

I'll let him know that he'll be hearing from you sooner or later and that I think the manuscript deserves careful attention. (I'll copy this when I get home and quote some of my favourite poems – and comments – to him: will probably write in a couple of days, since I head for more hullabulloo in Stockholm in a week's time. No peace till Christmas.)

It was great to see you in Dublin – Flight awaits –
Seamus

SH's friendship with Cathal McCabe (b.1963) had begun the year before when SH accepted McCabe's invitation to read for the British Council in Warsaw; later they established the Ireland–Poland Cultural Foundation, for which they received the Gloria Artis medal from the Polish government. Most of the poems SH singles out for commendation here went into McCabe's *Outer Space: Selected Poems* (2016).

2002

'I desperately need rehabilitation with the muse,' SH confides to Sonja Landweer in a letter of 26 January 2002, but the usual whirl of distractions and travel, which this year included trips, some more restful than others, to St Lucia, Canada and South Africa, as well as appearances at a large number of US venues, conspired to make that difficult.

A major personal loss was the death on 21 March of SH's friend from his first days at Berkeley, Thomas Flanagan.

To Sonja Landweer

MS Emory

26 January 2002 191 Strand Road, Dublin 4

Dear Sonja,

Forty-eight hours ago I breasted a tape of sorts . . . finished the last of four lectures I am to deliver in the course of the next two weeks – one at Oxford on Tuesday and three in Cambridge the following week. A tension in me for the past four months, really. Literary criticism, a need to speak for an hour . . . It's what I've done on and off since my late twenties, since I got a job in the university system. I was never 'qualified', only had a BA, never did a 'higher degree', and hence always felt I would prove myself by doing what the academics were supposed to do – lecture and write criticism – but in a way that was still my own. I didn't want the mystique of 'the poet' to be a union ticket. I wanted, in a proud, puritanical sort of way, to 'pay my way', not to be beholden, to be as good or better at the job than my 'non-creative' colleagues. I think the impulse was right. The *hauteur* was right. And much of what I did was truly helpful to me: a clearing of the head, a declaration of loyalties to certain masters, a paying of creative debts, a standing up for the art, a teacherly duty, a service of sorts . . . But now I fear it may have become an alibi. I desperately need rehabilitation with the muse. Need to graze, to go 'on an overgrown path' – this is the title of exquisite small-high-cloud-drift piano music by Janáček that I've been listening to recently – and I am writing to you like this, suddenly, because, I suppose, you'll know what I mean, but also because time and retrieval are opening up ahead. The builders are in Glanmore. The spring is ahead. My year is by no means free, but next year is and will remain so. It's Saturday night and I feel fit to climb the rigging and tackle the jobs, with the good prospect of coming into some kind of harbour in mid-February. Marie and I keep promising to visit you and hope to do so later in the spring. Forgive me for this surge of talk about myself.

Love, Seamus

PS Sonja – all prompted by the fact that your letters are here and there on my desk and remind me of personal truths as I hurry through the business and efficiency side of things. Too much of that . . . S.

To John Breslin

MS Emory

1 February 2002 191 Strand Road, Dublin 4

Dear John,

You could have done with a reply to your November 21 fax – and follow-up – before now. I've carried the review in my little travelling fardel of 'personal letters to be written soonest' – first to Stockholm and other Swedish destinations during 10 days of revels and tasks to celebrate the Nobel Prize Centenary, and most recently, this week to Oxford, Leeds and *TLS* Centenary reading in London. All to no avail . . . until I get to Heathrow, and here we pause. High winds in Dublin hold us up, or rather down, and it's an ill wind that etc. . . .

There's such fullness in the experience of reading Miłosz and you testify richly to that in your piece. I'm on record as saying that when you read him, you want – and have him – as your boon companion and confessor. The weight and the sprightliness of his mind are the marvel: gravity and grace indeed, great readiness to grieve or to rejoice. The bits you quote, of course, go straight to the centre of the want in me. I suppose I read him as a kind of spiritual director, really. Life, religion, and then, as you say, in its place, literature . . .

When I get home, I'll fax this and send also a copy of a Horace Ode I adapted – took off the first stanza and – how dare he – put on an extra one. It was breathtakingly close to the September 11 situation, which we all feel in so many confusing ways.

Bail ó Dhia ar an obair.
Seamus

PS 'Ode' to follow –

Fr John Breslin (1943–2016) taught English at the Jesuit Le Moyne College in Syracuse, New York. His review of Czesław Miłosz's selected essays, *To Begin Where I Am*, was written for the 21 January edition of *America*.

'*Bail ó Dhia ar an obair*': God bless the work.

To Carol Hughes

TS Hughes

11 February 2002 191 Strand Road, Dublin 4

Dear Carol,

You deserved to hear from me before this, and by the pen and ink method, but it's Monday morning and there's a certain brightness in the air and I'm up in the skylit skull of the house and the blank gaze of the computer is saying, come on, so even though the shade of Ted is shaking his head at this desertion of the scribal tool, I'm off . . .

[. . .]

I've been careering around like hell, doing a lot – both in terms of written and spoken work, and in terms of student societies, college dinner tables and all that. One good result of it was a word with the Master(?)/President(?) of Pembroke at a reception last week after the Tanner Lectures. He reminded me about the Ted window and urged me to call. Which I did – a porter, former sergeant major, big moustache, big heart, guided me to the top of the stairs and into the room. The window was more than I expected, a wonderful bold open energetic honest-to-god and honest-to-ground rendering of the words and the images. What I liked was the value given to the texts, and the choice of poems – some of my own favourites, like 'Fern', 'Thought Fox', 'The Horses'. The quality of pale, from-over-the-horizon light was also right, I thought, and when you see the big horizon-light/skylight of the glass-work outside over the stairs, it all connects in a heartlifting way. I think Ted would have liked it. At any rate, I felt the better for having seen it, and for having been in the college again. [. . .]

Faxed from Strand Road. When SH, in his attic study, confesses to 'desertion of the scribal tool', he alludes to Ted Hughes's stated belief that any intervention of the mechanical is bound to have a deleterious effect on writing.

The windows by the German artist Hans Gottfried von Stockhausen (1920–2010), with their imagery derived from poems by Ted Hughes, are in the Yamada Room at Pembroke College, Cambridge.

To Ian Kilroy

MS Emory

20 February 2002 191 Strand Road, Dublin 4

Dear Ian,

Forgive me if I don't present myself for interview. I feel I've talked myself out on this art and politics topic. It's forever new and forever old and there are only individual solutions to it. There's Brecht and there's Beckett: one telegram – 'uptherepublic' or whatever it was – versus a whole *oeuvre*. Beckett declared his political opinions as a citizen, Brecht expressed them as a writer. But a passion for justice can come out in black humour as well as in didactic epic. A writer/artist is involved in some kind of wager that calls for him or her to lay an important part of himself or herself on the line. The written line, that is, which can be in its own way a kind of front line. It's the truth – artistic as well as moral truth – that counts, that's what people want, and they recognize it not in the volume or the message, but in the pitch of the tuning, the emotional urgency of what's at stake. There are times, of course, when the hugeness of some public wrong will make writers feel small if they don't come up with a big headliney response, but they will feel even smaller if they make the headlines but don't make the grade artistically. I've said before that I'm susceptible to both of these contradictory statements: first, a quotation from Miłosz, familiar by now – 'What is poetry that does not save / Nations or people?' and Joseph Brodsky's equally persuasive, 'If art teaches us anything, it is that the human condition is private.' Miłosz's question, however, comes in a poem of what we might call 'survivor guilt' – addressed to the dead of his own generation just after the war in Poland. And it might be said that the saving that Miłosz actually achieved during the Nazi occupation was to write a poem not about the world as it then was – he said it was a mistake to try to compete with the Nazi hell-force – but the world as it is wished for. An idyll, an act of defiance, not an innocent poem but a poem that risked visionary good in face of the drastic evidence. But then he also wrote *The Captive Mind*, a kind of Orwellian *j'accuse*, a polemic, if a highly intellectual one, against Marxism. There are different ways of doing things, at different times. The worst thing is to fake it, good or bad . . .

Seamus

PS 'The World' – written in Warsaw in 1943 – is the poem in question.

The journalist and playwright Ian Kilroy (b.1969) was writing a piece on the artist and political commitment for the Irish current affairs magazine *Magill*.

Beckett's '¡UPTHEREPUBLIC!' was his laconic response to the questionnaire that Nancy Cunard sent out asking writers to state their positions in regard to the Spanish Civil War.

To Czesław and Carol Miłosz ms PNL

21 February 2002 191 Strand Road, Dublin 4

Dear Czesław, Dear Carol,

What a joy to receive the books with their ever-to-be-cherished inscriptions. I felt like Yeats in his state of bliss: 'I was blessèd and could bless.' I felt it all the more because I was mad at myself for not having written personal greetings at the time of the big birthday last June. What I'd have liked to do was to write a poem, of course, but somehow that wasn't possible – I was too busy, too far away from myself, hurtling through prose and fulfilling engagements. I managed to write a piece – a far off birthday card, really – for the *Irish Times* – but the world was full of gratitude for Czesław's life and work at that time and I was just another – glad, glad – voice in the chorus.

We think of you and rejoice that you're there in Cracow: not that Grizzly Peak was not a *locus amoenus*, but the good old reliable streets and squares and speech must be a sustenance. Like sitting in the wishing chair of the whole world.

I'm making bold to send a short poem that I feel belongs to Czesław and that I may dedicate to him, hanging it up thereby on a sky-hook . . . The 'we' are a family of neighbours who had a slaughterhouse near to us – but *I* am one of them, insofar as I remember the troops arriving. But they were neither damaged nor did damage in our place. Much love – and from Marie too – Seamus '*locus amoenus*': congenial place.

'Testimony', the poem SH sends and inscribes 'for Czeslaw / with love and honour', is a version of 'Anahorish 1944', which was included without personal dedication in *District and Circle*. That collection, however, also contained the set of three poems, 'Out of This World', which bears the epigraph 'in memory of Czeslaw Milosz'.

To Ian Parker

MS Emory

1 March 2002 — 191 Strand Road, Dublin 4

Dear Ian Parker,

Thanks for the reminder about the Roger Straus profile. This in haste: I'm off from here later this morning.

Joseph Brodsky used to call Roger 'Boss' – to his face, that is, banteringly, very affectionately, but meaning it, even so – and that covers something of what I myself feel about the man. My first book with FSG was in 1979 and I didn't meet Roger until a bit later. What's great about him is the head-on strength of body and personality, the forthrightness, the swiftness of his judgements, the immense largesse.

You know how they call publishing firms 'houses': often the term doesn't match the reality, but 19 Union Square West is Roger's house in a domestic as well as a commercial way. He's the head of it and the heart of it. He's proud of it and the writers on his list are proud of him. You could even say it's the literary equivalent of a 'safe house'. You're going to be looked after. You come in as his guest and lo and behold he seats [you] at his right hand in the Union Square Café. He and Dorothea turn up at your reading, the current quickens and strengthens. And the great thing about it, it's all so uncorny. There's nothing 'luvvie' about the love he inspires.

Sincerely,
Seamus Heaney

To Dennis O'Driscoll

TS Emory

26 March 2002 — 191 Strand Road, Dublin 4

[. . .]
When the poetry clog cleared, on Sunday, Marie and I went to Glanmore where she bogged into kitchen clearing and [?]xing and I stuck into

book shifting and we generally left the world of contemplation for action. But this week I got back to the interview and hope to keep at it now for a while to come. Earlier in the month, and during the working hours in St Lucia, I stuck with the *Antigone* job. I wanted to get deep into the text and ended up with half of it done, so I'm pausing there for the moment. Don't want to get behind with our three month to a book programme, but on the other hand don't want you to be overloading yourself with that formidable task. The amount of thought and note-taking and ordering and re-ordering that went into the questions so far has been immense – when I think of the work you've done for *Door into the Dark* alone, I'm overwhelmed. I feel you mustn't go at the other books so exhaustively – both for the sake of your own time and your other work, and for the sake of the interview book. I'm worried about a self-indulgence, perhaps, creeping in if I keep on in too much detail about too many things – even though I relish and respect every turn and twist of your questioning. Nothing is in fact otiose, but now that I'm getting into it again, I worry that a disproportion may establish itself. I've got up to fourteen pages of text for the new chapter (your questions included) but I've only dealt with six of your pages and there are 25 more to go.

Having said all that, I realize it may sound unconscionably ungrateful for the job you've done. You know that's not the case. I'm just anxious about overload for you and overlength for the chapters to come – just blurting out what swam wraith-like through the head as I got re-started.
[. . .]

'poetry clog': in the preceding paragraphs, omitted here, SH comments frankly on an international gathering of poets that had just taken place in Dublin, for which O'Driscoll had delivered the keynote address.

'[?]xing': possibly 'axing', only the squarish mark on the page, the size of a single letter, oddly indecipherable in a piece of typing, does not particularly suggest an 'a'.

O'Driscoll's introduction to *Stepping Stones* explains fully the modus operandi, not yet established, by which his almost 500-page interview with SH was put together over a number of years.

To Carol Hughes

MS Hughes

15 April 2002 Nassau Inn, Princeton

[. . .] The trouble with the Devon date is, finally, my body. More and more, I am unable to place myself in a metal cylinder and have me hurled at great speeds in different directions for great distances round the curve of the globe. [. . .]

To Caitlin Flanagan

MS

16 April 2002 Nassau Inn, Princeton

Dear Kate,

Marie and I are very sorry not to be with you on Saturday, but in an odd sort of way the couple of days I spent in the house with Tom at the time of Jean's memorial stand now in good stead. There was something strange and solemn about Jean's absence, Tom's loneliness and my own sense of being welcomed – as it were – home. We were both getting a lesson in mortality and in the preciousness of the life we are given. In the value of silence, at homeness and loving.

He has only himself to blame for a lousy line like that. He was a walking quotation bank and his habit of crazy-paving the conversation with lines from Yeats and Joyce had a powerful, happy effect on me. It was all part of a re-orientation that happened during that magical year we spent in Berkeley from September 1970 to August 1971. We were mothered and fathered by Tom and Jean, feted and treated as equals by people senior to us and superior to us in standing and achievement. We basked and flourished in their kindness, and all the while, from Tom's deep familiarity and sense of personal relationship with Irish writers and the figures of Irish history, I was learning to take new stock of myself, intellectually and imaginatively.

I'd had an undergraduate education in English Language and Literature within what was essentially a British university, and what I got from Tom, in the nick of time, was a re-education, ongoing until last month. That year, parties in the house on Bret Harte Road were a cross between a singing session and a seminar: stylish and testing company, Irish and American, everybody being their astonishing selves at full and fuller tilt – Schorers, Bridgmans, Barishes, Tracys, Raders,

Michaels, Alpers and then, from the home ground, the Cruise O'Briens, the Keefes, the Dillons. We went back to Belfast exhilarated and liberated, and a year later I resigned from my lectureship in Queen's to re-settle and re-dedicate in Glanmore. Meanwhile, Tom and Jean and you girls had spent the intervening year in Dublin, *The Year of the French* was begun and we all shared a fullness of experience that marked us and made me for life. From my friendship with Tom came stronger bonds with those whom we knew as mutual friends, both in Ireland and America: Ben Kiely and Frances, Kevin Sullivan and Fran, Bill Chace and JoAnn, Darcy and Suzanne. So Tom, I can say without exaggeration, meant the world to me.

Over the years, the Flanagans would arrive among us like the summer itself. The bright smile, the bright shirts and ties, the whole Brighton Road experience meant scenes well set and excellent company. But it also meant occasional breakaways, drives in the car when Tom was as brotherly as he was fatherly, when the exchanges between the driver and the passenger had the eyes-ahead, tell-all, go-in-peace quality of the confessional. Although needless to say, there was a touch of the snug about it too, not to mention the ongoing tutorial. Which is why I was able to quote – as a valediction to Tom with love – the lines I wrote about my own father after his death: 'there was nothing between us there / That might not still be, happily, ever after.'

Love to you all next Saturday –

Seamus

Caitlin is the daughter of Thomas Flanagan, who had died on 21 March.

To Marco Sonzogni TS Sonzogni

3 July 2002 191 Strand Road, Dublin 4

Dear Marco,

The usual apologies for the lateness of this reply. I took your letter of May 14 with me to Canada last month but was too busy all the time to get round to any mail-work – in May, would you believe it I was absent from home from 15th to 23rd and in June from 8th to 18th. Pressure, pressure, pressure.

I received with admiration the *Translation Ireland* that includes 'Reality and Justice' plus the other translations. I agree that the Arabic and Hebrew versions are a great thing to have – and they *look* formidable too. And that terrific blast by Ezra Pound. Who is there to do that kind of unfussy, knowledgeable, committed sort of commentary now, off the cuff but worth listening to, opinionated and show-offy but in earnest and entitled to sound off . . . The journal is to be congratulated. You are all doing admirable work, which makes me wonder if the *Honest Ulsterman* might not overload you. Your work in the translation area integrates you, in some way at least, makes sense and use of your bilingual, transnational/cultural situation – doing what you do now, your autobiography and your *oeuvre* cohere and at the end of the year something has accrued from your efforts that situates you better in your world. I feel that there would be a hell of a lot of distracting work in the editorship of *HU*, that a lot of it would be give, without much return. Which is not to say that I don't think the *HU* is not worth saving or that the work is not worth doing; it's just that I'd be afraid it would put too much strain on you. (I only go on about this since you do me the favour of asking my advice.)
[. . .]

The Italian academic and translator Marco Sonzogni (b.1971) had been a teaching assistant at Trinity College, Dublin, and studying for a Master's degree there, when he first met SH at the Yeats Summer School in 1995. In this letter, SH acknowledges receipt of the issue of *Translation Ireland* in which, as editor, Sonzogni had included his essay 'Reality and Justice: On Translating Horace', and the translation in question, under the title 'Horace and the Thunder' ('Anything Can Happen' in *District and Circle*). As well as the Arabic and Hebrew, there were translations into Irish and Italian of the same ode.

In the end, Sonzogni did not apply for the editorship of the *Honest Ulsterman*.

To Thomas Lynch

TS Lynch

23 July 2002

Noble Person,

Which is to say, in Synge-speak, *a dhuine uasail.*

Apologies for slow response to the very attractive proposal of reading with Ó Coileáin and Ó Loinsigh. In principle it has to be done, in practice it's a bit tricky.

Two considerations: I read – agent-sponsored and hence overpaid – in Chicago Art Institute last April. Not averse in any way to returning, but would need to extricate myself from agent for our occasion. (As far as I'm concerned, whatever fee is going will go.) Also: finding the moment is a problem. I've been refusing everything for 2003, and so far have not caved in – except to one Notre Dame date in late September. (Deane put me on the friendship rack and I cracked.) How soon do you need to fix definite date for the unlocking of the Hibernian word-hoard? Could we hold for a month or six weeks? I'm up to my oxters in anxiety-work and run-arounds and need to get the head cleared before any final calendar marking can be contemplated.

Very good to hear from you –
Seamus

A cutting from the *Irish Times* headed 'Intoxicated undertaker drove hearse dangerously' is at the head of this fax: the US poet and essayist Thomas Lynch (b.1948) is also by profession an undertaker.

'*a dhuine uasail*': formal greeting.

'Ó Coileáin and Ó Loinsigh': alias Billy Collins (b.1941), at this time US Poet Laureate, and Lynch himself.

To Elizabeth Lunday

TS Lunday

1 August 2002 — 191 Strand Road, Dublin 4

Dear Ms Lunday,

Forgive my long delay in replying to your letter. [. . .]

You've read, I think, the remarks I made about the poem in the *Paris Review* interview. That says most of what I can confidently or usefully say about the thing. I had been in Australia in October 1994, at the Melbourne Festival, and came back in a kind of rage at myself for not having got enough writing done. So I sat down and gritted my teeth and very deliberately started in with the couplet as a kind of crow-bar to open a way into the Watchman's speech. And then the other pieces came – when they came – quickly, especially 'Cassandra' and 'The Nights'. My own favourite piece may be 'Cities of Grass'. I suppose what I want to emphasize is that there was no real communiqué factor at work in the poems, there was the excitement of utterance, the writing was after and into something other than commentary. It was a surge-up through language. I was buoyed by the doing rather than relaying any message.

I never have studied Greek, but I've read the *Oresteia* in a couple of versions. Lots of *Agamemnons* – MacNeice, Lowell, Grene (is it?). I even looked at the Loeb when I was considering a full translation.

I read about the well/stairway on the acropolis in early, pre-Hellenic Athens in a Penguin history of Greece. A very brief reference, but it was most suggestive. I didn't know about the one at Mycenae until we visited the site in October 1995, but naturally that was a great thrill. As was the act of reading 'His Dawn Vision' to my wife and the Hadzis up in the megaron of Agamemnon's palace.

As to the vehement language, especially in 'The Watchman's War', I think it results partly from the wilfulness of the couplet: at that early stage in the writing I was driving hard, forcing it, as if the rhyme were a bit and the two pentameters were directed to it and through it like the handle/shafts of a pneumatic drill. Then too there's a bloodbath element in the Aeschylus play – the butcher-shop aspect of Clytemnestra's welcome probably induced a more brutal approach to the northern Irish killings. So you're on to something true when you suggest there's a sense of 'weighing in'/'no more mr niceguy' in the poems. I can see the rightness of adducing that 'prophesy, give scandal' line.

Another thing that produced a fierce readiness to go physical was a story I heard on a TV documentary about a notorious bombing incident in Birmingham in the seventies, where twenty people or more were killed in a pub. A fireman or ambulance man was recalling what it was like and came out with the shocking information that when he got home and went to bath, he took off the clothes he had worn in the haulage and carnage and found his whole body was red with blood. It struck me that that's how the killer-heroes would have come in off the battlefield, if they had come in. And that's where that odd beginning of the water section came from.

The 'space for hope' quotation is now available at the end of a chapter called 'Cessation' in *Finders Keepers*. Which is a reprint of an article done immediately after the IRA announced their ceasefire. (The following Sunday, by the way, I was in Jutland, in the bog at Tollund, and wrote 'Tollund' almost immediately afterwards, in a shorter form that it would eventually attain in *The Spirit Level.*)

I hope this is of some help.

With warmest wishes to you – and George –
Sincerely
Seamus Heaney

PS Reply coupon appreciated.

Elizabeth Lunday, a graduate student, had written to SH at the suggestion of George Lensing, of the University of North Carolina at Chapel Hill; her 'Violence and Silence in Seamus Heaney's "Mycenae Lookout"' was eventually published in the Spring 2008 number of *New Hibernia Review.*

The 'incident in Birmingham' was the 1974 bombing of two public houses in the city, of which the six men subsequently accused and found guilty, were later – having spent sixteen years in prison – shown to be innocent.

To Carol Hughes

PC Hughes

4 September 2002 [Postmarked Cape Town]

After all the worry and hurry, we have had ten terrific days. Busy at first, but very good people in charge, and then four days to ourselves in lovely Cape Town. But it is the most distressful country: desolation and delights cheek by jowl. Hard to forget the wretched as we revel. Much love – Seamus

To Bernard and Jane McCabe

PC J. McCabe

5 September 2002 [Postmarked Cape Town]

A lion lay twenty yards away and roared – whether at us or for us, I'm not sure. We saw maidenly giraffes and mud-forged rhinoceros. We saw the overfilled cemeteries and henhousey dwellings of the tragic townships. I lectured and lectured and interviewed and interviewed. To-day we whale watch, to-morrow we Cape Town. It's hearse country, in its way – sumptuous and sorrowful. Love, Seamus and Marie

To Massimo Bacigalupo

MS Bacigalupo

25 September 2002 191 Strand Road, Dublin 4

Massimo – Were it not for the mini-crises of departures for long trips, I'd maybe never get round to answering the letters put aside for 'personal' answers . . . Even at 63, I've not learned that what's put aside stays aside. Anyhow, as I rise to fly to Harvard for 6 weeks, I'm very conscious that I've not written to congratulate you on the *Beowulf* and thank you for the Italian boost. The word-hoard of the Anglo-Saxons will now be a lovely Tuscan terra-cotta instead of a glum wet Wessex wattle. The book is beautifully turned out and the apparatus wonderfully brisk and to the point. I just wish I knew your language, but I rejoice in the clear song of the skilled poet, the head-clearing register of the Rapallo minstrel.

So. Sorry to have delayed but exultant to have your ratification –

Seamus

SH is writing in appreciation of the trilingual edition of *Beowulf* edited by Massimo Bacigalupo (b.1947) and published in Rome. Bacigalupo was and still is Professor of American Literature at the University of Genoa, much concerned with the theory and practice of translation and himself a prolific translator of poetry from English into Italian; he was born and brought up in Rapallo, where Ezra Pound, one of the poets in whom he has specialised, lived in the 1930s.

To Carol Hughes

MS Hughes

8 October 2002 Four Seasons Olympic Hotel, Seattle

Dear Carol,

This corporate pomp is simply too good to waste . . . Seattle Arts and Lectures keep their contributors in this ziggurat and the sponsors bear the brunt, even seem to want it . . .

Marie and I crossed the ocean a couple of weeks ago and on Sunday I flew from Cambridge, MA to this destination. [. . .] A huge audience here – they turn up for the series – of about 2½ thousand. A rally rather than a reading.

The other rally is the one being mustered by Bush. He spoke on the television for twenty minutes last night, statistics and accusations and insinuations all telling us about what weapons Iraq had and might have, but not proving the need for aggression. The Democrats are sheepish and the UN probably resigned to being a stalking horse, and there seems to be no realization or care that an American attack in Iraq will send recruitment for Al Qaeda sky high and create general Arab disaffection. Oil, oil, oil. Bush prefers to go to war than to raise the price of petrol.

I'm writing this on impulse, before check-out – going to Portland to-day, then San Francisco . . . M. still in Cambridge. She'll be home next week, I'll be in Harvard until Hallowe'en. Will keep in touch –

Love,
Seamus

'corporate pomp': the letter is written on notepaper headed 'Mr Seamus Heaney / In Residence at the Four Seasons Olympic Hotel'.

To Tom Paulin

MS Paulin

31 October 2002

Dear Tom,

You should have heard from me long ago – but I wanted to get a look at the Tintern Abbey programme first, and only managed to do so a couple of days ago – and, yes, passed it on to Helen.

The Milton/*Paradise Lost*/solitary way ending(s) worked beautifully and completely persuasively, and the proposal that the secret life of the poem had to do with post-revolutionary survivor guilt and post-Annette worries had a big suggestive power. What was brilliant was the contextualizing by date/flashback of the compositions – 14 July 1789/13 July 1793 – it jumped the poem into a new context, as did the Bristol/ Birmingham co-ordinates and the mightily inventive co-ordination of the Priestley soda water. I loved the spark and prompt of all that, the sheer alertness and knowledgeableness. I woke up. But I still wasn't sure how far we/I could go to feeling that Wordsworth was as alert to it all as you were. The high jinx and high perceptiveness of copse/corpse and *sick*-amore, not to mention gunfiring cataracts had me cheering – and wondering. Gleeful and pondering. The whole programme was an aerated version of the waters and their inland murmurs . . . Just sorry

I won't be here to raise a fizzy or a wee still glass in a couple of weeks' time.

Hope you had a good time back at home. I'm off on Saturday.

It was, as ever, a great sweetness for Marie and me to see you in New York. And I loved the masquerade with Edna. What larks – love –
Seamus

Paulin, who was teaching at Columbia University for the fall semester, had sent SH his essay 'A Republican Cento: Tintern Abbey' (included in *Crusoe's Secret*, 2005); shortly afterwards, he presented a documentary film on the subject for the BBC.

The 'masquerade with Edna' was a lively dinner, in the company of Edna O'Brien, after a reading given by SH in New York.

To Tom Paulin

MS Paulin

3 December 2002 191 Strand Road, Dublin 4

Dear Tom,

You'll be back soon, and I hope to speak to you on the phone soon – I missed you a couple of times last week and then was away from Thursday to Sunday in England – but still, your letter meant so much to me that I just want to let you know in the joined-up writing.

David and Brian F. had both told me how down you sounded on Sunday week, and so the news about Jorie and Peter and the threats to you, to them – was kind of supplementary to that. You have indeed seen that republic at its best and its worst. The first thing I ever saw in the States, the first impression, was in February 1969, when I went to do a poetry reading in Richmond, Virginia. I landed in Kennedy and was met by Polly Devlin's husband, the Old Etonian Andy Garnett. Anyway, we go out through the door of the arrivals hall and there's a big accoutred cop with a hard – hickory? – night stick beating the erect fin of one of those long-loined American cars. Ding, ding, ding. Hammer and anger. Casual as fuck. And then, of course, Andy guided me to a wee MG sports car that hardly reached up to the mudguards of all the other motors on the motor-way. And took me to an apartment on E 89, under the roof with the Guggenheim, where I slept for the first time ever in a four-poster bed. So much for the New World.

We were with Bernard and Jane in Ludlow, where we also had arranged to see Carol Hughes. All spoke with admiration – nay, love – and sympathy for what you've had to go through. And Bernard was sorry not to have written to you about *The Invasion Handbook* – which has not been properly saluted yet by any of us; so far-ranging, trampolining, both heavy duty and pleasure-principled. The year has been shockingly darkened for you and the shadow line drawn through your days. The one unshakeable thing has been your dignity and courage: it's not much consolation, but you can sing the song of the man who has come through. [. . .]

'how down you sounded': in an article published in an Egyptian newspaper in April 2002, remarks made by Paulin, critical of the occupation of Palestine by Israeli settlers, were distorted, then quoted widely in the British press, in the US and elsewhere. The controversy that followed involved protests against Paulin, including death threats, so that, when invited to give the Morris Gray poetry reading at Harvard in November 2002, he decided not to go ahead with it despite support from members of the university's English Department, including Helen Vendler and the poet Jorie Graham, as well as Graham's husband, the painter Peter Sacks (b.1950).

'Song of a Man who Has Come Through' is the title of an emphatically exultant poem by D. H. Lawrence.

To Dennis O'Driscoll MS Emory

4 December 2002 191 Strand Road, Dublin 4

Dear Dennis,

A month since your reading. I can hardly believe it.

Meanwhile, I've been living with *Exemplary Damages* and meaning to write and meaning to write . . . It delights me for its own sake and for your sake. The amount of world that is between its pages is more than you get in half a dozen average novels. The abundance, the variety of good and ill, the big grief-factory and the thousand home-industries of joy. The Wordsworthian imperative – to throw over the scenes and incidents of common life a certain colouring of imagination – so unsentimentally fulfilled, the clear eye aiding the sympathetic mind. And Keats's soul – to whom the miseries of the world *are* miseries – shining through also, his schooled intelligence that becomes a soul . . . But I wax a bit solemn. It's just that the sense of *lacrimae rerum* gives the book a terrific wise steadiness, while the populousness of it and the non-exclusiveness in terms of subject and language and feeling make it as heartsome as those plovers rising like doves from a conjuror's hat. You're in full flight, the sense of supply is unmistakable and gives the whole thing a unity that supplements the thematic patternings and so on.

[. . .]

Your September letter and supplementary questions were here when I got back from Harvard and I apologize for not getting to them yet. The amount of work you've done there deserves a better response, and will receive it before long. All being well, the days will be workable, rhythmical, lookable forward to again before long. Not that there's any great problem here and now, just circumambient botheration and the sorrows of friends – Dorothy Walker seems very far gone and a couple of others are newly in thrall to the dread stalker. We count our blessings, which include so richly Julie and yourself – Love –

Seamus

O'Driscoll's 2002 collection *Exemplary Damages* carries this as a dedication: 'FRANK, SEAMUS, MARIE, DECLAN, EITHNE / as it was in the beginning.' In addition to the qualities SH praises, it includes among its poems a satirically accurate and gleefully thorough demolition job with the title 'England'.

To Joseph Woods

TS Woods

18 December 2002 191 Strand Road, Dublin 4

Dear Joe,

That's a good Simmons idea, but I won't be able to show up. Nothing to do with readiness to join the roster – just that Marie and I have made plans to set off that week for a bit of silence, exile and sunning. I'll be working like hell, lecturing and 'appearing', for a month before that, and we decided to take off after the opening of renovated church in Bellaghy on February 10. The gigs we get to do! Thanks for the Poetry Ireland card – and the blessings of the season on you and your other PIrelanders.

Sincerely
Seamus

Joseph Woods (b.1966), poet and, at this time, director of the promotional organisation Poetry Ireland, had invited SH to take part in an event commemorating James Simmons, who had died in June 2001.

To Paul Muldoon

TS Emory

22 December 2002 191 Strand Road, Dublin 4

Dear Paul,

Sunday morning, no complacencies of peignoir, more regrets of the correspondent . . . I should have written long ago to say how much your nomination of *Finders Keepers* in the *Irish Times* and *TLS* meant to me. More than you might realize. As a volume, it's a bit *emmenthally* so it needed that little touch of *caprice des dieux* to bring out the best in it. At any rate, as the man said, 'I go about the house/Like a man who's published a new book.'

I wish I'd published one as Telling and tolling and tintinnabulating as *Moy Sand and Gravel*. Another book I read with great elation this year is *Veil of Order*, conversations with Alfred Brendel – full of great quotations. Apparently Schoenberg said that art springs 'not from ability but necessity', so it's a marvellous moment when the ability and the necessity make a grand conversation and mutually give way. The book maxes out like those solvent hawthorns and gimlets piercingly in through that eyelet of bone. As ever the truth to the domestic down-to-earth carried away in the arms of the extravagant up-and-away. Rich and strange. A canal-change. An ever further range.

One surprise this Christmas: my brother Hugh will be sixty on the day. The two sisters who follow me I've always regarded as the same issue, so to speak, with the three boys that followed on a lower Frys-ad level. Definitely 'younger'. So when the young brother is sixty, you know it's in earnest. But here's hoping we can hold out against 'paltry thing' status for a while longer.

Much love to Jean and yourself and Dorothy and the well cradled Asher. We'll pull a wishbone for yiz.

Love
Seamus

'complacencies of peignoir': see Wallace Stevens's poem 'Sunday Morning'.

In a poem in the *Times Literary Supplement*, under the title 'Caprice des Dieux', Muldoon had likened various Irish poets to different cheeses; SH was an Emmenthal.

'Telling': upper case, because the Swiss rebel William Tell features, amongst a multifarious cast of characters, in *Moy Sand and Gravel*, Muldoon's new book; 'canal-change': because Muldoon lived on Canal Road, Princeton.

In *The Veil of Order: Conversations with Martin Meyer* (2002), the great Austrian concert pianist Alfred Brendel (b.1931) shows himself to be a compelling verbal communicator as well.

'a lower Frys-ad level': SH seems to have in mind the brand of Fry's milk chocolate that showed five expressive faces of a little boy, all in a row, on its packaging.

2003

Work proceeded in earnest on the chapters concerning SH's early volumes in *Stepping Stones*, while professional demands took him to Russia, England, Scotland, Poland, the USA and Spain.

To Dennis O'Driscoll

TS Emory

9 January 2003 [m.d. 2002]   191 Strand Road, Dublin 4

Dear Dennis,

This won't be a very systematic note – more a snatched jotting before I go out to lunch with Christopher and Michael – but I just want to spell out in no particular order things that come up.

[. . .]

Cannot just now be very clear about the shape of the rest of the interview, but feel that for both our sakes we should aim at having it conquered, or a good bit of it, by September, so that you can come back with the thing off your hands if not out of your mind. The only worry about that is the pressure it puts on you. I realize that it's easier to respond to questions than to frame them; you have the fore-stress and envisaging to do, all I need to do is run at the mouth. So I am conscious that this suggestion may overload and overstress the already supercharged O'Driscoll machinery.

[. . .]

The above is nothing but my entirely first-time sketch, not previously pondered. But even if each chapter went to 40 pages, we would still have a book of about 300 pages, which is workable.

One thing I do notice, though, is that my focus is autobiographical rather than explicatory. When I get the *Death of a Naturalist* chapter finished – soon – we'll have some notion of how the balance between specifics and general story might be balanced out and fitted in. In the meanwhile, I'm off . . . M. and C. usually take me out before Christmas, but last year was too gouty and they are now *hommes* of their own affairs.

Much love to you both – Seamus

To Dennis O'Driscoll

TS Emory

20 January 2003 191 Strand Road, Dublin 4

Dear Dennis,

Last Thursday I sent the drafts of the first three interview chapters to Jonathan Galassi and Paul Keegan as well, with injunctions to keep them – and the news that we are at work – confidential.

[. . .]

Meanwhile, other confidential news. Ben Barnes at the Abbey approached me before Christmas to do a translation – well, it would have to be a new version of versions – of *Antigone*, for the Abbey's centenary, coming up next year. Something in me yawned a little. I thought of Paulin and Aidan C. M. and B. K., not to mention Anouilh and Fugard and Brecht, I thought of human rights and women's rights and Hegel and Steiner, and thought, as Empson didn't quite say, we don't want ideology and the whole thing there. And then I thought again, of the moment in the world, and of the Abbey moment, which I'd like to be part of, and plunged suddenly in. I'm established in labour – hundred lines or so to hand at this stage, including a shot at the famous chorus, to follow. I just went at it with the Anglo-Saxon line in my hand like a bill-hook, my main thrust to get through, and enjoyed it immensely. Translation as hedge-facing.

Anyhow, the main point is this: there's no pressure to get *Door into the Dark* questions into shape: I have plenty to keep me busy. An introduction to Gabriel Ferriter, translated by Arthur Terry, long, long overdue. The *Antigone*. A Robert Henryson project. A host of readings and commentaries on piled-up manuscripts. You know the drill [. . .]

'Jonathan Galassi and Paul Keegan': Farrar, Straus and Giroux and Faber were publishing US and UK editions of *Stepping Stones*.

Ben Barnes was Artistic Director at the Abbey Theatre, where *The Burial at Thebes* was to receive its first production in April 2004, the Abbey's centenary year. Tom Paulin's *The Riot Act*, which Field Day had produced, *The Antigone* by Aidan Carl Mathews (b.1956) and Brendan Kennelly's *Antigone*, each derived from Sophocles' play, had all been performed in some part of Ireland in 1984. The French playwright Jean Anouilh (1910–87) and Bertolt Brecht (1898–1956) had written their now classic, modernising versions, while the South Africans Athol Fugard, John Kani and Winston Ntshona incorporated a performance of *Antigone* into their 1973 prison drama *The Island*.

'You don't want madhouse and the whole thing there,' is what William Empson (1906–84) actually wrote in his poem 'Let It Go'.

To Czesław Miłosz

MS PNL

23 January 2003 191 Strand Road, Dublin 4

Dear Czesław,

A month since you sent *Orpheus and Eurydice*. And longer since I left a message on your California phone. Forgive me for not writing to you then, at the moment of your loss. But now that the big rite of lamentation has been conducted in this poem, it is easier to speak. It's heartbreaking work. I too 'wept at the loss / Of the human hope for the resurrection of the dead', and yet the poem is as delicious as it is desolate. A marvellous span, from the cybernetic phantasmagoria at the start – those electronic dogs! – to the pastoral symphonics at the end. It's as if you are wading helplessly in the river of the intimate and the contemporary, and the myth is a shadow looming on the water. And the strong, sweet, resolute lost one is there like 'an armful of lilacs' in the vale of tears. *Gaudens gaudeo.*

We think of you often and often, with love. Robert Hass told us that you said to him that you were 'surviving by incantation' – and we others survive more abundantly because of that. I pray that I may be able to see you later in the year in Kraków: I had made a resolution not to travel *anywhere* in 2003, but Adam Z. and Jerzy I. are strong persuaders, so my resolution may falter.

Meanwhile, because of the coincidence, I'm sending a translation I did of the Ovid Orpheus passages. I juxtaposed them with bits of an eighteenth-century Irish language poem – a kind of burlesque dream vision, where the poet is *nearly* killed by a troop of Hibernian maenads, but escapes in the last line . . .

Keep singing the canticles. Much love –
Seamus

Carol Thigpen Miłosz (1944–2002) died, of cancer, in August 2002. Robert Hass helped Miłosz translate his poem of mourning, 'Orpheus and Eurydice', into English.

To Paul Muldoon

TS Emory

6 February 2003 — 191 Strand Road, Dublin 4

Brilliant things. Wheekers, as my father would have said. Real wheekers. Clinkers. 'Tithonus' a featherlite and a left hook all at once, 'The Procedure' a procedure indeed . . . Hats off again.

And hats off for P. Fallon: he's one of the Mannix Flynn Seven. 'Well, now that's done . . .' – and done the only way we'd want it – one-off, clean procedure.

Many thanks indeed for thinking of March 23. I'd love to assemble that morning. And will, in spite of 'shock and awe' ahead of us, I fear. A couple of things follow: no good poems go unpunished — S.

SH here praises poems that Muldoon had sent in MS and that would duly appear in his 2006 volume, *Horse Latitudes*.

Gerard Mannix Flynn (b.1957) is a Dublin politician and writer; he and Peter Fallon, occasional publisher of both SH and Muldoon, were among seven individuals recently elected to Aosdána, which appears to have made them members of a gang sounding a little like the Magnificent Seven.

To Carol Hughes

MS Hughes

23 April [2003] — Glanmore Cottage, Ashford, Co. Wicklow

Dear Carol –

Shakespeare's birthday. Chaucer's sweet showered month. It was lovely to hear from you on [the] 13th, and I'm impelled to give a chirrup from whinny, hawthorny Wicklow, since last night was the first night I spent here on my own in the renovated cottage. First footing new floors, regaining old silences. The ghostly silt of the old untouched place has been dispersed, but the new space and freshened airs are a fair compensation. For months I felt the good had been irreparably taken out of the house. The first set of builders were tramps, really. The actual structural job they did in the beginning is/was OK – stone walls, dormers, slates, all that OK. But then they subcontracted to fly-by-nights in the electricity, plumbing, tiling, all that . . . The taste went sour. I felt sullied and angry at myself for not following my original instinct to have nothing to do with them. But then, after the necessary fall-out, our good man who had worked on 191, our house-healer, stepped in. And eventually, after him, a health-bringing landscaper, a countryman from around here . . . so I rejoice . . . Also rejoicing to see the *Collected Poems* announced – and to see that terrific photo. We'll talk soon. I just want to flap the leaves of the hedge-school – Love – Seamus

Ted Hughes's *Collected Poems*, edited by Paul Keegan, with on its cover a handsome photograph by Noel Chanan (b.1939) of Hughes seated and in profile, was launched later in the year.

To Dennis O'Driscoll

TS Emory

9 May 2003 — 191 Strand Road, Dublin 4

[. . .]
The *Door into the Dark* unanswereds can creep in somewhere else, I'm sure. If you have the *Wintering Out* stuff gathered, just send it. I agree with your notion that the book should be in earnest, but I'd like [to] keep shooting for the pace we aimed for in the beginning, if not even faster. I'm now up to the end of the Tiresias scene in *Antigone*, but slowing down instead of speeding up, probably because the excitement has dwindled – although I've still enjoyed doing it. Slog-work from now to the end, but not a huge distance to be covered. Given the right mood and the free time, I could probably do it in three days. But of glum, grim days, probably six or seven are necessary. I was thinking, by the way, of calling it something like *The Burial at Thebes*. Seriously. It's all about burying. And the *Antigone* title could do with refreshment; when you hear that word, a slight air of exhaustion overcomes you, it's been done so often.

One of your favourite tasks is completing your tax form: I've always loved – too mild a word – the moment in the New Testament when we're told that 'a great gulf' separates Dives in hell and Lazarus in bliss. Equivalent of said gulf suddenly opens between here and The Gallops when you tell me something as astonishing as that. In fact, it makes me more frustrated than ever not to have been able to get a satisfactory way of saying or re-saying, 'Wonders are many and none is more wonderful than man . . .'

Much love to Julie too. I'll be back next Thursday. Happy computing.
Seamus

O'Driscoll not only 'toiled in Revenue' (his phrase), but was also editor of the magazine *Tax Briefing*. The Gallops was the estate in Naas, Co. Kildare, where he lived.

To Robert Tracy

MS Tracy

10 May 2003 Delta 128

Bob,

You should have heard from me long ago, and so should the proud parents of DDT. It seems that the long flights are useful as reverie time – I do more personal letters when I'm miles above the earth than at any other time. Am beginning to realize that 191 is as much office as domicile . . . but now at least Glanmore is coming into use again, after a year and a half of being builder-bollocksed-up. We've even got the place landscaped – gravelled paths, whins in the ditch and, most delicious of all to me, great railway sleepers from Poland, hard as iron and black as the black earth, as kerbs.

We rejoice for you as grandparents and for dear Dominic and Lisa. Michael and Christopher may learn something there, but then neither of them had the stamina to follow through a purpose like Dominic's doctorate. All that is as wonderful for you and Becky, I know, as for the lad himself. A big case of the *gaudeamuses*.

Gaudies coming up for us too in the next couple of days. We're en route to Atlanta – to Bill Chace's school. I'm afraid I caved in to his invitation to do the Commencement address this year – after more or less vowing (that's an Irish form of resolution) never again. But Bill is about to retire and big Ron Schuchard added his voice, so here I am, grave and orotund, trying to say something that won't be spoilsport on a celebratory occasion, but that won't ignore the dark times. Will read 'Horace and the Thunder' and refer to Wilfred Owen's feeling more repelled by 'insensibility' at home than German fire-power a hundred yards away in the next trench.
[...]

'DDT': Robert and Rebecca Tracy's grandson, Declan Diego.

'Bill Chace's school': Emory University, Atlanta, Georgia, where William Chace (b.1938) was President and Ronald Schuchard Professor of English, and which houses one of the world's great collections of Irish literary documents of the twentieth century. SH was not only to deliver the commencement address, but he was also to be made an honorary Doctor of Letters there.

To Adolphe Haberer

MS Haberer

10 May 2003 Delta 128

Ado –

Why does it require a journey of six to eight hours, at a height of three to four miles above the earth, to get me writing letters to friends? I spend days in 'correspondence', jumping to it as the cutter of the fax machine rolls out another request like a head from the guillotine (well, no, but it's the French connection) but weeks pass and the letters from the true ones sit there waiting, like parents or relations we are due to visit . . .

Marie and I are en route for Atlanta, where I have to do the Commencement Address at Emory University and attend the pomps and be conferred (two old friends in high places there could not be dissuaded). It will be busy and genial, plus we'll have the company of Carol Hughes, who is going over to see Ted's papers in their magnificent literary archive at the Woodruff Library. But the big bonus is the time for reverie on the plane.

I've been gazing at Janine's delicious icon, so firm and so light, as dreamt as it is delineated. I love the lad who is 'casting his garment' on the ground, and the airborne branch-breakers . . . I was once in a Zen monastery in Japan, a sunlit morning, silence, gravel, gardens, trees, and then I heard this constant, delicate, grasshopper gleeful snip-snip, snip-snip, and couldn't see what it was – until I look away and up, just a little, to see two lightweight monks, trimming the treetops in the garden, swaying on the boughs like scissor-wielding blackbirds . . . Their buoyancy is in that icon.

This is just an affectionate casting down of the Heaney garment and a down-flutter of leaf from a deciduous Delta flight to say this sixty-four-year-old was glad to see that card and letter –

Fondest wishes –
Seamus

The friendship between the French academic and specialist in Irish literature, Adolphe Haberer, and SH had grown from their first meeting at the 1992 conference in Caen to which a number of Irish writers had been invited (see letter to Thomas Kilroy of 17 June 1992); a regular exchange of letters had followed. 'Janine' was Haberer's mother-in-law, who had taken up icon-painting on her retirement; her 'delicious icon' shows the entry of Christ into Jerusalem, with figures perched in trees – like Zacchaeus, in Luke's Gospel – to get a better look.

To Gibbons Ruark

MS Ruark

10 May 2003 Delta 128

Gib –

A one-room schoolhouse in Montana – it trumps everything. The name of that State meant romance and freedom ever since I was a youngster: a man who worked for us was nicknamed 'Montana' and I felt the big sky, the far wind, the rocky skyline – although there may be no such skyline there . . .

I was glad to hear from you and am as ever regretful not to have been more in touch. But honest to Jesus, I seem to do little else these days than respond to the ruthless cut of the paper-cutter in the fax machine. I've stayed away from e-mail because I feel I'd be inundated entirely with queries from grad students and indeed grade schoolers doing their essays, but the relatively backward means of fax and postman keeps me busy. It can be managed, but at a moment, high above the Atlantic, with all the reverie-time that a Dublin–Atlanta flight affords, I'm suddenly conscious of how administrative my days have become. I rarely write letters – merely respond to correspondence . . .

Anyhow, it was great to hear from you in April. Marie and I took off for two days to Kerry. Stayed overnight on a Thursday at one of those Blue Book country-house places (The Mustard Seed, outside Adare, great food and a habitable four-poster), then spent all day Friday in 'the Kingdom' – returning to Dingle Peninsula, Gallarus Oratory, the view of the Blaskets and the visionary Skelligs. It was quick, but it did us good. Apart from anything else, I drove my scandal – a second-hand, but relatively sumptuous Mercedes, automatic, lumbar-hugging, deep-surging vehicle. First time in my life I had any conscious sense of the auto I was in . . .

Good for Kay. Pillow talk rather than briefings. (My father once cried out in exasperation to my brother Colm, who was lying in when he should have been milking cows in the yard, 'Do you think you're living private?') Let the dame live private and the poet do his circuits.

I'd love to see you in Clarinbridge. Remind us when you land. Our hush-hush number is 01-269 1594. Love to you both – Seamus

PS Going for 4 days to Emory: Commencement Speaker. You'd think I'd have learned by now – S.

The 'schoolhouse in Montana' was a property owned by friend of Ruark's, where he had been invited to give a poetry reading. See SH's poem 'Montana' (*Electric Light*) for a fuller portrait of 'the best milker ever // to come about the place'.

Co. Kerry has for many centuries been known as 'the Kingdom'.

'Good for Kay': SH congratulates Ruark's wife on leaving a long-time job.

To Jerzy Illg

MS PNL

[23 May 2003?]

'To kill the bottle' means to finish off all the drink. So it's late in the evening and the Bushmills bottle is empty . . . You know how it is –

Best – Seamus

Written at the foot of the fax on which Illg had asked for the phrase 'the Bushmills killed', in SH's poem 'The Bookcase', to be explained: the fax is dated 23 May and this has all the appearance of an immediately faxed response.

To Thomas Lynch

TS Lynch

11 June 2003 191 Strand Road, Dublin 4

[. . .]

What I remember is the problem of cracking the backs of the lobsters . . . The Reids were in residence in the cottage and had acquired the creatures wherever: mighty movers, a match for Dürer's rhino any day. Did we splatter the shells with a hammer on that flaggy floor? I think we may have. There was, at any rate, a sense of a feast that had been fought for. Great debris and great delight.

[. . .]

This paragraph responds to a request from Lynch for verification of the story of the hammer, which was true; it is referred to in Lynch's poem 'Heaneyesque', written in Yeatsian quatrains to celebrate SH's sixty-fifth birthday in 2004. SH used the same verse form in the stanzas that accompanied his letter of 5 April 2004, thanking Lynch.

Lynch has a cottage in Moveen, West Clare, and had allowed my wife and me to stay there for a week, free of charge; SH and Marie Heaney drove over for dinner one evening; the lobsters were local and magnificent.

To Ben Barnes

MS NLI

25 June 2003 191 Strand Road, Dublin 4

Dear Ben,

Here's a draft of *Antigone* to be going on with. No doubt there'll be revisions, but this is the version that will be the foundation.

One main thing: it's done in verse, and the metres mean something, I hope, so when it comes to casting, the capacity to speak verse, or at least to have clear and firm utterance, should be a big consideration. I have a few voices in mind, but that can wait, maybe. Gerry McSorley, e.g., as Tiresias? Anyhow, all in good time.

Another consideration. I hesitate to interfere in a director's freedom, but I must declare a definite prejudice against imposed 'relevance' – videos of trouble spots, black berets; all that . . . The power of the thing is in the thing itself, as it were, and the bolder and more declarative the presentation of the words and characters, the truer we'll be. But, as I say, I'm now entering the artistic realm of another –

In haste, as usual –
Seamus

In a letter to SH of 10 July 2003, Ben Barnes, Artistic Director of the Abbey Theatre, had announced the Canadian actor and director Lorraine Pintal as director of *The Burial at Thebes*, and Andrea Ainsworth as voice coach. In the event, Stephen Brennan, not Gerard McSorley, took the role of Tiresias.

To Dennis O'Driscoll

TS Emory

27 June 2003 Glanmore Cottage, Ashford, Co. Wicklow

[. . .]

Tremendous time in Russia. Was there from 12th to 20th of the month. Beginning in Petersburg, going by overnight train to Moscow, ending up at a lunch in the writers' house in Moscow – now a fancy private club of some sort, of course. Intense and often heartbreaking moments. A visit to Joseph B.'s room and a half especially so. But also I did a hommage to Joseph in Akhmatova's Fountain House, opened an exhibition *teach* Nabokov, Bloomsday lectured in St Petersburg University, dined on an Irish navy ship (the *Eithne*) that was on a goodwill visit, tied up in the Neva – and accompanied our commodore and ambassador to lay a wreath in memory of the dead of the Leningrad siege. Goose-step and guards of honour. Not to mention Guinness in the Shamrock pub. We were treated like heads of state but had a similar schedule. Book launch of translations in Moscow, lecture, press conference lunch, visit to Yevtushenko, likewise to grave of Pasternak and his house/museum (still a strong sense of the ghostly silt about the place, silent, simple, a site of work and spirit, trees, a piano, a gathered meaning in the air). Edzeddera, edzettera, as Marie's father used to say. [. . .]

'*teach*': Irish for 'house'; so '*teach* Nabokov' (the word is not italicised in the actual letter) is the St Petersburg house in which the novelist and poet Vladimir Nabokov was born in 1899.

To Tim O'Neill

MS O'Neill

29 June 2003

Jurys Great Russell Street Hotel,
London WC1

Tim, *a chara* –

More bother: every time a letter comes in, it's somebody looking for something . . . At least that's how it is on Strand Road.

I'm on the go quite a bit these weeks and days, but on August 7 I set out for Ludlow, for an eightieth birthday. Bernard McCabe, the man you met, by happy coincidence, when you delivered the papyri, he to whom I dedicated *The Haw Lantern* (with wife Jane), Bernard is the birthday boy.

I'd love to give him another Tim-text. I leave it to you . . . It can be one word 'Scriptorium' or one poem 'The Scribes' or a word-devising of your own . . . Here's the background that prompts me to bother you . . .

In 1982 (I think, maybe '83) Marie, Michael, Christopher, Catherine and I spent a fortnight with Bernard and Jane in Provence. They had rented one part of a small 'big house', we were in the ample stone barn (converted) at the other side of the courtyard. I was writing some of the 'Sweeney Redivivus' poems, including 'The Scribes'. I sent Catherine (8 or 9 at the time) across the yard to Bernard to ask if it was 'scriptorium' or 'scriptarium' . . . imagine the ignorance . . . and she came back with the message.

So a fitting salute would be 'The Scribes' with 'with love from Seamus, Marie, Michael, Christopher and Catherine-Ann'; or simply the word 'scriptorium' decorated with 'To Bernard on his eightieth Birthday' and a showing of our names . . .

I'm sorry to be coming late with a request. Sorry to be so suggestive. It's just that I've bethought me, here, late at night, aled by the Newcastle Brown, and decided to go ahead and overload you.

I'll be home later in the week and give you a call. Love to Christine and the littl'un forbye – Seamus

'*A chara*': 'My friend'; 'Strand Road': where both SH and O'Neill lived.

The 'papyri' were several versions, on papyrus, of the two-line poem with which SH had dedicated *The Haw Lantern* to Bernard and Jane McCabe. For Bernard's birthday, O'Neill inscribed the whole of the poem 'The Scribes' on vellum.

To Jerzy Jarniewicz

MS Jarniewicz

2 July 2003 [In transit]

Dear Jerzy,

This is typical: I am writing on an aeroplane, and also writing late: you should have heard from me sooner with gratitude for *The Bottomless Centre*. It is a book of many strengths – a steady gaze at the whole *oeuvre*, a wonderful alertness to what is happening in particular lines of particular poems, real sensitivity to the historical context (and literary-historical, not to say literary-local-cliquish), but what most moves and gratifies me is that somebody of your critical and poetic stature is an advocate for the poems. And the advocacy is distinguished by an admirable combination of learning and lucidity: you are rightly sensitive and revealing when you refer to the 'centering' (O American spelling!) that rural background and Catholic upbringing have had – and then to give the insight such specific application when you see the bricklayer's trowel as equally and naturally at home (or transported) in the world as Odysseus' sword; but then I love especially the 'History in Everyday Objects' chapter – and also appreciate, for different kinds of reason, the 'discontinuities' chapter. The old schoolteacher in one kept putting ticks of approval in the margin and (more school*boy* than teacher) bits of underlining in the text. The whole book is not only a pleasure to me, but often a refreshment and enforcement of the poems. I hope you'll excuse this too brief salute – I've just been for three days at a conference for teachers (sponsored by the Prince of Wales, for God's sake, and meant to affirm the value of the canon, the traditional syllabus etc.) and am on the way home, after a rather unexpected outburst of press attention. I actually prepared and delivered two papers on the topic of the conference, but was wheeled out – naked PR, the N-word and all that – to 'speak to reporters'. Of course, the whole jabber was about 'how relevant is poetry to the young in the age of pop, electronic media, *blah, blah*' and after being harried and bored I ventured to say that 'this guy Em & Em' – the deplorable rapper – 'has a kind of verbal energy and has sent a voltage through a generation'. Well, one sentence out of thousands gets the attention and I'm reported as 'hailing' the genius of a homophobic corrupter of the young . . . The British papers were full of it – jokingly and vulgarly – and subtly demeaning. Anyhow, am glad to be going home.

And glad also to be heading soon for Cracow. I'm not sure if you'll be there this time, but I look forward to seeing you some time before long so that we can set a little vodka crown upon your much cherished effort. With good wishes, from high above the Irish Sea –

Seamus

Written in the sky, but faxed from Dublin.

The full title of Jarniewicz's book about SH, published in 2002, is *The Bottomless Centre: The Uses of History in the Poetry of Seamus Heaney*.

The 'N-word' here is Nobel, as SH explains in a later letter. Numerous newspapers had taken up the story of SH's 'praise', while answering questions from journalists, for the controversial US rap performer Eminem (b.1972), whom, as 'Em & Em', SH seems to associate loosely with a US brand of chocolates.

To Brendan O'Neill

MS O'Neill

17 July 2003 191 Strand Road, Dublin 4

Dear Brendan,

Your collection of skulls is a real treasure and I was delighted to see and hear about each one of them. It made me think of a poem by the Scottish poet Hugh MacDiarmid, called 'Perfect':

I found a pigeon's skull on the machair,
All the bones pure white and dry, and chalky,
But perfect,
Without a crack or a flaw anywhere.

At the back, rising out of the beak,
Were domes like bubbles of thin bone,
Almost transparent, where the brain had been
That fixed the tilt of the wings.

The skull of the gannet you showed me was one of my favourites, but I also liked greatly the rabbit's wee front teeth.

If you keep collecting, you'll have things that will be of value to you for ever. All good wishes –

Seamus Heaney

Brendan O'Neill, Tim's son, still has his skull collection.

MacDiarmid's poem, beautiful as it is, was actually lifted, with minor alterations, from a passage in a short story by the Welsh writer Glyn Jones (1905–95).

To Bernard McCabe

MS J. McCabe

20 July 2003 — 191 Strand Road, Dublin 4

Dear Bernard,

Looking forward greatly to seeing you next month. Meanwhile, your homework is enclosed. I finished this a couple of months ago and haven't read it since. I got started with the metre of a poem in Irish 'Caoineadh Airt Uí Laoghaire' – 'The Lament for Art O'Leary' – a three-beat line – dee dáh dee dádda dóo / dee dá dee dádda dóo – and then the Old English gnomic swam in for the first chorus. So off we went . . .

Busy days but worth the busyness – Preston, Dundee, Kraków, falling towers, fading Heaneys then at a wedding in the north this Friday. Much society to be handled between now and Ludlow, but Ludlow is the shining horizon light.

Love to you both in the meantime –

Seamus

Of the poems in SH's next collection, *District and Circle*, the two that most closely conform to the metre described here are 'To Mick Joyce in Heaven' and 'The Blackbird of Glanmore'; if the stanzaically detached lines that come at every sixth line in the latter count as choruses – the first, 'It's you, blackbird, I love', having what might just be called a 'gnomic' quality – then that's the one he is presenting to McCabe.

To Stephen Stuart-Smith and Hughie O'Donoghue

TS H. O'Donoghue

21 August 2003 191 Strand Road, Dublin 4

Dear Stephen, Dear Hughie,

Thank you both for the timely, tender reassurances. I was suffering some kind of panic attack. I was awake all Tuesday night, bunsen-eyed and full of bracing self-doubt, and passed the time with the manuscript. But the fit has passed, even though a crack in the foundations remains – or perhaps better say a floodmark on the wall that shows how high the doubt-waters can rise. What is needed, I more than ever realize, is a cogent introduction and that I hope to provide soon.

However, a definite contributory factor in my panic was a feeling that I might do better with other work on the Henryson front. Three years ago I saw a manuscript of his 'moral fable' 'The Cock and the Jasp' in an exhibition called 'Chapter and Verse' in the British Museum. I had forgotten about Henryson for years until that moment, and circumstances now made me look him up again. I had recently given a reading of the *Beowulf* translation in the Lincoln Center and afterwards the director said to me, why don't you do something dramatic, something that could be performed. So there and then in the BM I thought, ha, versions of Henryson's fables – very wily work, vernacular, merry, dark, full of gumption and insinuation. And in fact I did 'The Cock and the Jasp' quite soon after that. Then I got a notion of preparing a wee volume in the Faber 'poet to poet' series, a 'choice of Henryson's verse' kind of thing, and calling it – for the echo – 'Four Fables and a Testament'. The big problem, however, was the challenge of the *Testament* itself, so acting on the principle that you bog into the hard bit first, I did just that, and ended up flattened, with the big fish landed, but a feeling that I had worn out my enthusiasm. Still

I managed, out of sheer pleasure, 'The Two Mice' (town and country) and have still a notion that I might do more – especially if I can track down a performer. All of this to explain my sudden turn: the note of the fables is flyer, lighter, more beguiling than the note of *Cresseid*. But for our purposes, the two wouldn't work together. The Aesopic stuff almost asks for woodcuts, or some kind of antic illustration, something so stylistically far from Hughie's work that it's just not on. But still, I want you both to know that the fables could turn up some time in the future. But there's a lot of rhyme royalling to be done before then.

Again, I thank you for your gallant, kind responses.
Seamus

Stephen Stuart-Smith is the Director of Enitharmon Press, in London, which publishes occasional collaborations between poets and visual artists: in this instance, although SH and O'Donoghue were eager to join forces, SH himself was not yet convinced that his translation of Henryson's *The Testament of Cresseid* would be the right text. A *de luxe* edition did, however, appear from Enitharmon the following year.

To Dennis O'Driscoll

TS Emory

25 August 2003

Glanmore Cottage, Ashford,
Co. Wicklow

[. . .]
Many thanks for the big welcome to the *WO* chapter. I realize I have 'passed' on several childhood questions, and that something must be done about that. I think my inhibition comes from a feeling that the rhetorical mode of Q & A requires a certain reticence or at least a sparingness with regard to the inward note. Or maybe a fear that I have overdone the childhood landscape. Your remarking on my refusal of the lures, however, makes me realize that I should try to work in some more of that particular material.
[. . .]

'*WO*': *Wintering Out*, which contains a number of poems of a more than usually intimate nature.

To Dennis O'Driscoll and Julie O'Callaghan TS Emory

3 October 2003 Adobe Heaven, Hill Country, NM

Dear Dennis and Julie,

The music of the Indian flute floats beneath our raftered roof, the whitewashed walls say 'Quiet' – and stay quiet, the oxblooded floor takes what comes. Meanwhile, as you drove away to Albuquerque this morning we dozed away until nine o'clock and then lay gazing out at the brush, listening to the chickadees. (Were they chickadees? I like the sound of the word anyhow.)

It has been a blessed time. From the moment Julie took to the wheel to the moment we osculated outside Andiamo!, there was sweetness in the breast. And the work that got done was well done and worth doing – there never was a reading that meant more to me. The introduction wasn't just a boost but a bond. And then the interviews – so assiduously prepared, so lightly conducted, so gravely in earnest, and just at the right moment, I feel, to perk the written papers.

To-day is not so sunny but nevertheless the naturist impulse persists: I have been in the hot tub one more time and am beginning to feel the entitlement of the rich: my gate locked, my driver on call, my whim of iron. We may even do the plutocratic thing and take a car to Taos this afternoon. But first, silence, i-Book and sunning.

[. . .]

The Lannan Foundation (see letter to Dennis O'Driscoll of 17 September 2001) had invited SH to give a reading at their headquarters in Santa Fe, New Mexico, and O'Driscoll to conduct a public interview with him there on 1 October. Andiamo! is a trattoria in Santa Fe.

To Carol Hughes MS Hughes

29 October 2003 Glanmore Cottage, Ashford,
Co. Wicklow

Dear Carol,

Ted's *Collected* arrived: so much a reminder of the dimensions of the achievement, the inner radiance and call. And the physical book does honour to the integrity of the vocation. Paul Keegan's work has been unstinting and will stand the test. Amazing to have done so much in the time available. Passion and precision, as Yeats said, are made one. The introduction and the apparatus a guarantee of the selfless devoted quality of the service.

But then: the poetry in between. Daunting and beautiful, brave and far out; you feel he was an organism with toes in the ground and fingertips on the horizon – as much integrated and interred in the whole earth of the English language as he was alive to the physical world. The genius running like lightning everywhere, and the old genetic thunder, the old wisdom of the species, always growling away as well. It made me angry to read a shitty little piece by one Robt Potts in the *Sunday Times* – but then, again thinking of Yeats, these are the eunuchs gazing on Don Juan's 'sinewy thigh'.

I thought you might like to see a far more perceptive and just piece by Harry Clifton, that appeared in the *Irish Times*. Apart from anything else, the photo is terrific. And I also want to send the article that appeared in the same issue – about the transfer of the papers to Emory . . . I knew that it would all be cause for comment eventually, but if this is all that's made of it, I'll feel bloody lucky.

Excuse the haste of this – I'm in Wicklow trying to get some work done, and loving the quiet. But looking forward also to seeing you next week.

Paul says there's no need to speak very long at the reception. I was wondering if I mightn't use the enclosed 'Stern'? Did I send you a copy of it before? Maybe not.

Much love –

Seamus

Robert Potts's review of Ted Hughes's *Collected Poems*, edited by Paul Keegan, had appeared in the *Sunday Times* on 19 October; Harry Clifton's, under the Yeatsian title 'For the song's sake, a fool', was in the *Irish Times* of 25 October, and celebrated the balance achieved by Hughes 'between his sacral leanings and his genius for physical evocation'.

The poem 'Stern', subtitled '*in memory of Ted Hughes*', is in *District and Circle*.

To Simon Armitage

TS Armitage

2 November 2003 191 Strand Road, Dublin 4

Dear Simon,

Thanks for sending those first fitts of *Gawain* . . . Or should I say fits, since there had to be fits of pleasure when you got started. You've hit the note and you're definitely on your way. The rhythm and run of the verse are wonderfully caught, so your alliteration isn't like a duty being performed but just part of the stride of the tale – and it's a triumph to get those other wee quatrain-tails so neatly trimmed and tacked and rhymed into the bargain. The whole thing passes the jealousy test . . . It's compelling as narration in a living voice but it's also audibly and materially a transfusion – Dryden used the word about what happened between himself and Chaucer – of the Middle English. I don't think medievalists are going to worry about what you call your occasional indiscretion. In the reviews of *Beowulf*, for instance, the specialists seemed to take more pleasure in the riff of minstrel's song, where I paid less attention to the literal content and went for the 'feel' of the poetry. And the editor of the Norton Anthology who rode shotgun on me when I was a word-hoard haulier, Al David, isn't just a supervisor of word-for-wordness but somebody of a real literary sensibility. I'm sure Norton's would want to send it to him, since he's in charge of that section of the anthology.

Anyhow, this is just to throw the hat in the air and rejoice in what you've done. All you need to do now is keep going. The work promises to drive the green force of the old poem through the Armitage fuse and set it a-buddin' and a-bloomin' for the new millennium.

Love to your ladies. See you at the British Library before long.

Seamus

Simon Armitage had sent SH early stanzas of his translation of the late fourteenth-century poem *Sir Gawain and the Green Knight*. 'Seamus was an encouraging voice in my decision to translate *Gawain*,' Armitage recalls, 'and it was Seamus who put me in touch with the US academics who had worked with him on *Beowulf*, as well as his editor at Norton.' The translation was eventually published in 2007.

To Karl Miller

TS Emory

17 November 2003

Glanmore Cottage, Ashford,
Co. Wicklow

Dear Karl,

Herself and myself are down here in the bothy, nowadays the only place where I seem to get reading done or letters – as opposed to correspondence – written. The gate-lodge is so nestled in its bosky corner that the mobile phone rarely works. We have no 'land line', no television and can get no real BBC radio reception – hence I missed the dramatization of the *Justified Sinner* last night. But missing that reminded me I'd been remiss in not saluting *Electric Hogg*, which page by page made me gleeful and grateful. It's a wonderful book, in close to its man, in close to its own sentences, full of the joy of writing. All your other books pave the way for it, with the result that it has big emotional and scholarly weight. It packs, if you'll excuse the expression, a double punch. The subject calls forth your subjectivity, you just can't help writing vividly about him. He has been shepherded all over again, brought properly into the fold at last. There's an equal feel for Ettrick and Edinburgh, for the country codes and the city styles, all the different clandestine modes. Every character seems like somebody you have known for a lifetime. And your sentences at once sentence and reprieve them. Even Maginn. Rammed with life, the whole book, rife with utterly interesting report (one bit that I particularly loved was the 'species of Scottish praise' you quote, meted out by that William Dunlop) and in the end just heartbreaking. Never has the Wordsworth effusion felt more true to life than when you quote it at the close – the old cut atoned for, the sweetness of the poem guaranteed now more than ever by the (new to me) account of the earlier put-down. I don't want to babble on about it: what I'd like to do is to quote you back at yourself, 'in terms of praise'. You do more to reinstate Scots as a language than many a Lallans bard. As well as delivering the usual Millerfest of intelligence, irony, sympathy, love even, you give a social history of the times, a history of the magazines, a biographical dictionary, a dictionary of quotations, a more than enoughness that deserves the *momentum exegit* of approval. Apart from anything else, we all know so much more now – like the full meaning of personality. And

somebody will have to incorporate your paragraphs on parody in a dictionary of literary terms.
[. . .]

James Hogg (1770–1835), the subject of Karl Miller's book *Electric Shepherd*, and author of, among other things, *The Private Memoirs and Confessions of a Justified Sinner*, acquired his nickname, 'the Ettrick Shepherd', from the parish of Ettrick, in the Scottish Borders, where he was born and in early youth worked as a shepherd's assistant. Wordsworth, author of the 'Extempore Effusion upon the Death of James Hogg', also wrote of him, 'He was undoubtedly a man of original genius, but of coarse manners and low and offensive opinions.'

'*monumentum exegit*': see Horace's boast 'Exegi monumentum aere perennius' ('I have raised a monument more lasting than bronze') in his *Odes*, Book 3, no 30.

To Ben Barnes TS NLI

19 November 2003 191 Strand Road, Dublin 4

Dear Ben,

Yesterday was very well done: a great start to the centenary, and a genuine lift to the Abbey enterprise. I thought the presentations were substantial and impressive. The promise well set up by Eithne, thoroughly urged by John and convincingly settled by you. The publication a very handsome earnest of things to come. Great attendance too. And completely successful 'cradle of genius' digest by the actors.

Meanwhile, for *The Burial*, two additions, revisions, alternatives:

i) at page 39, I had dropped a short passage (some scholarly murmurs have declared it 'an interpolation') which I have now restored at the urging of my editor, Paul Keegan. It may be worth restoring to the acting script also, since it reinforces/explains the logic of Antigone's action.

ii) an alternative version of 'the wonders chorus'. I did this as a self-contained speakable poem, leaving out some of the original text and breaking the symmetry of the stanzas, but I believe it may be a more cogent speech on stage also. See what you think. Substitute it if you wish.

Congratulations again on *Aristocrats*. As I told Brother Friel, it held, and held, and held the note.

See you.
Seamus

To Lorraine Pintal

TS NLI

21 December 2003 — 191 Strand Road, Dublin 4

Dear Lorraine Pintal,

Many thanks indeed for your letter. I was very glad to know that the translation has your approval and that there will be something more in it for the actors than the mere semantic content. I look forward to meeting you when you get here for the rehearsals and am sure the production will gain in energy and excellence from your involvement.

There was obviously some misunderstanding about the business of the Chorus. I always assumed that there would be at least two voices, so the casting of two actors came as no surprise. Be sure that I don't have the slightest problem with that decision. I was a bit on edge, however, when I heard incidentally that the Chorus's lines had already been divided up and assigned. Having dwelt closely with the script for four months, I had (and retain) a protectiveness about the lines and felt that I should have had some say in their redistribution. That is why I asked to see the manuscript with the reassigned Chorus parts.

As it turned out, I agreed with almost every one of your decisions. I hope you have received the letter I sent to the Abbey some time ago, outlining my responses to that version (and including several revisions). Before the actors' scripts are finally given to them, I'd like to have a last check, just to make sure there has been no slippage.

The real problem – in so far as there has been one – has been lack of communication, or perhaps better say lack of understanding about the parameters of responsibility and consultation. For example, my immediate response to the casting of a woman in the part of Tiresias was dismay. I have the highest regard for Olwyn Fouéré and not the slightest doubt about her ability to make the role haunting and powerful, but I felt that I might have been let in on such a radical casting decision. (Of course, there is mythological justification for a trans-sexual Tiresias, but I'd argue that that is a separate matter from [the] play and the cadencing of the character's lines was established with a grave, senior male voice in my ear.)

Please understand that I am very happy with Olwyn in the part. It was just that it was unexpected first time round and, as I say, my proprietorial attitude to the manuscript I'd submitted received a shock.

I'm writing all this down in order that we begin with a clean emotional slate, as it were. Just to let you know the story so far. I am glad that we are in contact and that you wrote a fax. I myself prefer to write things down: even for an English-speaking Irishman, the phone can be an obstacle to clear expression.

With all good wishes for Christmas and the New Year,

Sincerely,
Seamus Heaney

The cast on the first night, 5 April 2004, included Ruth Negga as Antigone, Lorcan Cranitch as Creon, Barry McGovern as Chorus and Stephen Brennan as Tiresias – a serious road accident having prevented Olwyn Fouéré from taking that role.

2004

The Seamus Heaney Centre for Poetry at Queen's University Belfast opened on 17 February with an official ceremony and SH in attendance; the premiere of his second work for the stage, *The Burial at Thebes*, took place at the Abbey Theatre on 5 April; the death of Czesław Miłosz had him travelling to Poland in August for the funeral of his revered friend; other foreign countries he visited in the course of the year included the USA, Greece and Sweden.

To Matthew Hollis

PC Hollis

8 February 2004

Matthew – your book arrived as I set out for an event in Delphi so I took it on the plane and have had a chance to dip into it, on and off, over the past few days – and as I read I felt 'found, happy and at home'. Wonderful relish of words and reliability of *Ground* – literal and emotional, all that mor and mull. In many places, 'the take was deep and real . . . the change was made'. I like the reach out – 'The Orchard Underwater', 'The River Drivers', 'One Man Went to Mow' – and the reach in – 'The Wash', 'In you more than you'. (And 'The Fielder' had such an uncanny parallel feel to a poem I wrote recently that I'll send it with this when I get home.) Congratulations. Take pleasure in the book. In 'whiffletrees' and 'harwonder' and that 'busying' rain. Seamus

Matthew Hollis (b.1971), Editorial Assistant at Faber since January 2002, had brought out *Ground Water*, his first collection of poems, the previous month. The words 'mor and mull', 'whiffletrees' and 'harwonder' occur in the book.

The postcard, a Greek one, shows a photograph of the young Cavafy; the poem accompanying it was 'Quitting Time' (*District and Circle*).

To Dennis O'Driscoll

TS Emory

21 February 2004

Glanmore Cottage, Ashford,
Co. Wicklow

[. . .]
I was sorry to hear about Eugenia Murray. I recently wrote to John Montague about a poem, 'big' yet in ways problematic, in which he confronts his dead brother, but there was nothing problematic about his calling the cause of death 'the glutton cancer'. It's ravening everywhere.

The opening of the Centre was a good event. A great turnout, of people from all walks. [. . .] The Longleys ran a pleasant party afterwards, which was their blessing on the affair, and which it was good for Marie and me to attend. Not quite a reconciliation since there was never a fall-out there, but certainly it represented the closing of a distance that had grown over the years and might just as easily have widened, because of simple lack of contact. It would be unfair to say you missed nothing, but it is fair to say you did not need to be there or to apologize for it. I thought C. Carson did very well. My mother used to talk of young men 'filling out' – attaining some kind of physical stature and substantial presence – and the phrase now applies to the professor. No charmer, God knows, but committed to doing the work at the centre, whatever it is, and making a go of it. What I like is the fact that he is gifted as a poet, has made a name for Belfast as well as himself, speaks Irish and is in nobody's pocket.
[. . .]
I didn't get back to the interview until to-day. Did another few pages on the Nobel subject and hope to-morrow to dip into the 'politics' section. But what kept me away from the job was a sudden dive into a Cavafy manuscript that Stratis passed on to me. He has retired from Harvard, spends most of the time now in Athens, and has done a new translation of the 153 (157?) poems in the canon, with an introduction by Manolis, who is now Mr Cavafy-studies and is going to do a biography. Stratis wanted me to write a prefatory note of some kind (the thing will come out first in Greece, in some series sponsored by Manolis) but as I nosed into his texts, I found myself itching to change some of the lines and then beginning to scratch and in the end to scrawl

whole new versions of several poems. The result is that I now have rewritten versions of a number of the early poems and am both hooked on the idea of bogging into the whole manuscript and at the same time terrified to show Stratis what I've been up to. I did tell him in a preliminary note that I'd have suggestions for him, but that warning shot would not prepare him for what I've done to the stuff (and therefore his self-esteem) already, which is the equivalent of a pummelling by artillery. But by God, Cavafy is wonderful and tempting. It strikes me that a collaboration with Stratis would be as rewarding as that with Barańczak on Kochanowski, but we'll have to wait and see. The job would be big, but I feel I could do it fast. Certainly, I was obsessed for the whole week after I came back from Greece. But what, I hear you cry, about the interview? I seriously don't believe it would interfere. I can only do so much at a time with it – or with any focused writing. Intense bouts. Exhausted fall-backs. This is all you know on earth and all you need to know.

[. . .]

Eugenia Murray was a solicitor in Naas, Co. Kildare, where O'Driscoll lived; she died on 14 February. The Montague poem that refers to 'that glutton, cancer' is 'Last Court', in *The Drunken Sailor*.

The Seamus Heaney Centre for Poetry was incorporated into the School of English at Queen's University Belfast; Ciaran Carson was its first director.

Stratis Haviaras had been at Harvard for forty years, both working and studying there. During SH's time at the university, as Curator of the Woodberry Poetry Room, he was responsible for the acquisition of poetry books and recordings of poets. The translations SH speaks of here were published as *C. P. Cavafy: The Canon* by the Harvard Center for Hellenic Studies in 2007. If SH offered his improvements to Haviaras, he is not credited in the book, and it is likely that, for reasons of tact, he simply took his own versions elsewhere, contributing, for instance, six poems to the Trinity College Dublin classics journal *Hermathena*, no. 179 (Winter 2005). 'Cavafy: "The rest I'll speak of to the ones below in Hades"' is included in *District and Circle*.

To Bernard McCabe

TS J. McCabe

4 March 2004 191 Strand Road, Dublin 4

Amigo, caro, cher ami, a chara,

Jane rang this morning, Matthew rang last night with news of your nuisance pneumonia. *Grr*, as Lord Snooty's Gang would have said. No toothbrush chorus for that. Which translates into Bernardese as *Bugger!*

You are ever on my mind. I, alas, am ever on the move. Going to Belfast in the morning to read verses with the gorbellied Longley. Due to meet the deregulated Hammond. Accompanied by the one whom Herbert denominated 'small sharp wife'. Wish you were there. With the bun-sated ones.

Matthew told me that Alex and various McCabe-lings are due in the next few weeks. If you are allowed visitors beyond those familial degrees of consanguinity, please let us know. We miss the chance to have seen you and Jane and Al and his bride in March, in Mulligan's back snug and Heaney's big front room, but what the hell? We will rise again, as Con Howard used to cry in his drunkenness. (Con is the man who christened the ambassadorial service to which he belonged as 'The Irish Dipsomatic Corps'.)

I am inebriated and the pretence of sobriety is hard to maintain any longer. Thank God for word-processors – you should have seen the number (I first wrote 'the umber') of mistakes I've been making as I struggled to get this far . . .

Much love to you. Rise again soon. Love to Jane too.
Seamus

PS I am much entangled just now in rehearsals of the *Antigone*, in the Abbey. 'Theatre business, management of men?' No way, buddy. It's press interviews and gossip column photographers.

PPS What you really need to get you on your feet is a visit from O'Malley. 'AAH! The Great McCabba!' You'd be out of the bed in a shot!
Love – S.

'Lord Snooty and His Pals' was a long-running comic strip about a boy toff and his unruly gang, in the British comic weekly *Dandy*; the 'toothbrush chorus' is less easily identified.

Matthew and Alexander are two of McCabe's eight children.

'Theatre business . . .': see Yeats's 'The Fascination of What's Difficult'.

Con Howard (1925–2009) was a legendary Irish diplomat, whose most significant posting was to the USA; Peter O'Malley, of *Ploughshares* and the Plough and the Stars in Cambridge, was a mutual friend, whose 'valiant' style SH salutes in a letter to the McCabes dated 22 October 2004.

To Askold Melnyczuk

MS Melnyczuk

17 March 2004

Glanmore Cottage, Ashford,
Co. Wicklow

A Dhuine Uasail –

Literally, o noble person! Hiberno-anglicized in Synge-song: Mr Honey! And how well these salutations suit . . . On St Patrick's Day, especially. Not that our patron would have been entirely at home in the native Erse, him being a *civis romanus* before he became an Irish slave. But I digress. And for a purpose. The wily secret sharer in oneself trying to put his interlocutor off the trail . . . Deflect him from his memory that a letter was owed him since the new year, since the Brodsky/Darwish/Bundle communication (B. McCabe called me 'The Bundle', intertexting with Yeats's observation in 'A General Introduction' that the poet is never 'the bundle of accident and incoherence that sits down to breakfast'.)

That was a swift incision, a proper cut, a risky right writing. I was proud to be part of your thought. Reminded how much is called for. There was an element of foundation-rocking in those few pages. Semtex material of a sort. (No, censor, please, I speak in metaphor.)

Wish you were here. Love to you both. Perhaps I'll send a couple of verses when I get back into town. Seamus

PS Thanks too for your Dalai Lama photo: my sister recently sent me a cutting from the British *Independent*: a gossip column reported that I was named – along with Dalai L., Germaine Greer and others – by a survey in *Erotic Review* – as among the top 50 sex gods in the world.

Askold Melnyczuk, founder of the literary magazine *AGNI* and writer in a broad range of genres, was one of the convivial group of non-Harvard friends whose company SH enjoyed while staying in Cambridge, Massachusetts. The 'Semtex material' was Melnyczuk's essay, in *AGNI*, 'Gentlemen's Disagreements: Brodsky, Darwish, Heaney, Translation, and the Purposes of Poetry'.

To Thomas Lynch

TS Lynch

5 April 2004 191 Strand Road, Dublin 4

What an undertaking, Tom:
Tum-ti, *tum*-ti, *tum*-ti, *tum*,
Beating with the metre stick,
Keeping time by talk and tick.

Talk that isn't cheap, I know –
Gaudens, wherefore, *gaudeo* –
Talk that's light but carries weight,
Ballasted but still *en fête*.

Talk from one who's learnt the trade,
Nailing down all things well made,
Lines and lids, the varnished boards,
Brass plates, the bone-house box of words.

(Burials are on my mind,
Theban ones, the holy ground
Antigone threw upon a corpse
Honouring gods, facing the worst

Creon could devise for her:
Ireland's Abbey Theatre
Premieres *Antigone* to-night
In this old stager's new rewrite

So this reply, dear Tom, is brief,
Straws where what you need's a sheaf.)
Heartened, honoured, more alive
Thanks to you, at sixty-five,

Keeping going's still the thing.
As you well know, whose trochees ring
The changes true! *Heaneyesque*
Makes it worthwhile at the desk.

Supplementing a handwritten and faxed letter in which SH declares himself 'elated and moved' by Lynch's 'buoyant, unstinted birthday card' (see letter to Thomas Lynch of 11 June 2003), these lines addressed to one professionally concerned with attending to the dead cannot by coincidence alone have been written on the day *The Burial at Thebes* was to open.

To Rand Brandes

MS Emory

22 April 2004 Madison Hotel, Morristown, NJ

Dear Rand,

Sorry for the delay on this – I'm en route from Columbus, Ohio to Newark, NJ – three readings done, one to go, plus one lecture . . .

Titles: What usually happens is that I start to look for one or hope for one once a 'critical mass' of poems gets written. I find that if I have a working title at that stage – say when half a volume is in existence – the title itself can help in shaping, or at least inclining and suggesting, the poems to come. Hence, most recently, *The Real Names* was a useful working title for *Electric Light* and – as far as I remember – the winter theme was a governing one in the bleakish mood of the late 60s, early 70s poems in what eventually became *WO* – *Winter Seeds* having been a previous notion.

I can't remember when I fixed on *D. of N.*, but I suspect it was quite suddenly, when the bulk of the MS was finished. *Advancements of Learning* was the title of an earlier MS submitted to Dolmen Press at the end of 1964, and that title may have been my 'working title' until *D. o. N.* came up – itself a revision of the earlier 'End of a N.' poem title.

Door into the Dark was there very early: 'The Forge' was one of the first poems I wrote, post *D. o. N*, and the minute the first line came, I knew I had a title.

Can't remember when I fixed on *North* – but there was never any doubt. (As I said, the poem itself had earlier titles, like 'North Atlantic' and 'Northerners' – or was it 'Northmen'?)

Field Work came after other working titles had been floating around – all of them suggestive of a more temperate mood than the *North* mood.

SI – settled from the start.

The Haw Lantern – a late enough arrival, as far as I remember. You know the consideration that made me drop *The Stone Verdict* . . .

Seeing Things: I believe 'Squarings' and 'Lightenings' *might* have been floating in my head, but when I wrote the 'Seeing Things' poem – I think in the summer of 1990, after I came home from Harvard, early summer – I suddenly knew that I had the name of the volume.

Spirit Level you know about; but frankly, I'm not sure that I shouldn't have stuck with *The Flaggy Shore*. It's windier and stranger – nobody quite liked it, but I always felt it had a contrary rightness about it. A lesson there – go with your own contrariness . . .

Duncan's Horses would have been my preferred title – if D.W. hadn't come up with *Tiepolo's Hound*: again, an odd, off-centre title, but with a certain phonetic unshakeability to it . . . We're in Newark. S.

The essay that resulted from Brandes's enquiries was 'Seamus Heaney's Working Titles: from "Advancements of Learning" to "Midnight Anvil"', which is included in the *Cambridge Companion to Seamus Heaney*, edited by Bernard O'Donoghue (2009).

The Stone Verdict was dropped as a title because Richard Murphy's *The Price of Stone* was to be published in the same year, 1985.

'Duncan's horses' appear in 'The Real Names' (*Electric Light*).

To Thomas Kilroy MS Galway

24 April 2004 Aer Lingus flight EI 104

Dear Tom,

Two weeks ago is when I should have written, the day your review came out – but I was on the road with Catherine (home for Easter and eager to go 'away' for the weekend) and Marie. And then when we got back, I was pelting towards departure for USA, where I've just spent nine busy days, ending up with a lecture to the American Philosophical Society in Philadelphia – on translating *Antigone*.

You gave me a good generous booster and I deeply appreciated the well-disposed tone; but equally I appreciated the attention drawn to the crux wonder/terror word. The first two lines of that chorus had me chopping and changing uselessly and inconclusively all along. I didn't want to use 'awesome' since it has been so done down and dumbed down; and I was haunted all along by the dematerializing irony of Mahon's 'Glengormley' – 'There are many wonders in this world / And' – no – 'Wonders are many, and none is more wonderful than man / Who has tamed the terrier, trimmed the garden hedge, / And grasped the principle of the watering can . . .' But the bigger neglect, I agree, was the dropping of the death line. I had it in an earlier version published last year in the *New Yorker*, but I was so intent on making the end of the thing applicable to Bush that I elided the big D.

What bothers me more is the thought that you may not have received an invitation to the opening. I assumed that all Abbey writers would be on their list, but this time, because of the Post Office dispute, many of those on that list didn't get their invitation until too late – Felim Egan, for example, down the road from us on Strand Road. (And Lucy McKeever, who deals with tickets etc., apparently broke her arm just before the run started – a follow-up on the accident that happened to Olwyn Fouéré – the thing could have been re-titled *The Emergency Room at Thebes*.)

You can probably get a ticket or tickets any time you choose, from Lucy. I hope you'll get a chance to see it – not that I quite know what to think about the production. I like a lot of the work that's done by the cast, and of course I schooled myself into some kind of solidarity with the team effort, but *in principio* I wasn't too hot on the director's conception. For a start, she said she was going to set it at the time of 'the Colonels' war' in Greece. 'What war?' I asked, but then, just left it . . .

I saw *The Shape of Metal* on the last day and came away both settled and enlivened. Lovely armature and illumination in the writing, and terrific service from your cast, especially your lead. I felt that you had been renewed greatly in the process of the writing – that an idea, or rather what Philip Sidney called a 'fore-conceit' – had opened and complicated and generated. There was real intellectual and moral purpose. Work done – a certain force moved through a certain distance.

If you come to Dublin, maybe we can meet, if it suits you. I'm up to my oxters in society this next week, but let me know if there's a pint moment. Much love to your ladies – Seamus

Kilroy's positive review of *The Burial at Thebes* had appeared a fortnight earlier; in it, though, he had taken SH to task for avoiding the Greek concept of *deina* – the 'crux wonder/terror word' – which Kilroy regards as central to Sophoclean tragedy in that it combines the ideas of beauty and horror.

'The first two lines of that chorus': the published text of *The Burial at Thebes* has: 'Among the many wonders of the world / Where is the equal of this creature, man?' The version in loose quatrains that had appeared in the *New Yorker* under the title 'Sophoclean' omits all mention of 'wonders', and the 'death line' which

SH regrets having chopped goes: 'He survives every danger except death.'
'Colonels' war': presumably the junta of 1967 that was led by army officers and brought about seven years of dictatorship in Greece.
Sara Kestelman (b.1944) played the lead character, Nell, in the Abbey Theatre's 2003 production of Kilroy's *The Shape of Metal*.

To Rand Brandes

TS Emory

3 June 2004 191 Strand Road, Dublin 4

Rand –

Just back from six days in Portugal, before that a walkabout with Liam O'Flynn in Iceland, but so far, no Morocco.

When you say 'heart issues', I hope you don't mean serious physical problems. God forbid. Have taken note of your concerns and hopes.

'Tête Coupée': probably the term came into my vocabulary from archaeological material I was reading in the seventies, although it may have come from accounts of Louis le Brocquy's head images: Louis talked often about the cult of the severed head, the heads in the Celtic sanctuary at Roquepertuse, for example. And there was all that stuff in Anne Ross (quoted in 'Feeling into Words') about the head cult in Celtic religion.

'Strange Fruit' was once one part of a poem triptych, which was meant to be analogous to the tricephalic stone carving known as the Corleck Head (100 BC–100 AD) in the National Museum of Ireland. The sections I dropped were about Oliver Plunkett's head in the cathedral at Drogheda and the head of the turnip-man (our equivalent of your pumpkin head).

By the way, I just remembered a couple of days ago that one of the very serious contenders for a title to what eventually became *Electric Light* was *Known World*. Still attractive, no?

Looking forward to seeing you in Sligo. I'll be in Hardy country late July, hoping to get to Sligo on 4th. Not sure of movements after Sligo – a desperate need for seclusion being felt, after a year of overexposure. But if you're in Dublin, we'll see you surely. Lie the night in 191, at any rate . . .

Seamus

Written in answer to Brandes's continuing questions about titles (see letter to Rand Brandes of 22 April 2004).

In the Rainbow Press limited edition of *Bog Poems* (1975), with illustrations by Barrie Cooke, 'Tête Coupée' was the title of the poem that later became 'Strange Fruit'.

To Henri Cole

MS H. Cole

25 June 2004 Flight BA 632 London–Athens

Dear Henri,

Sophocles was born in 496 BC, so the Greeks are holding his 2,500th birthday party in Delphi, and have invited all kinds of old journeymen to do their party pieces. Mine, since I've just provided a version of *Antigone* for the Abbey, is a twenty-minute piece about the trouble maker from Thebes. So off I go again.

But these outings have their advantages – dream time of sorts in lounges and on planes, reading time, drift and slack time – so I grabbed an *APR* as I left the house this morning and as I killed a couple of hours in Heathrow I came upon your poems and interview. And your words – in poems and in interview – woke the sleeping poet in me, touched the core, sounded deep. Those sonnets – 'The Lost Bee' and 'Mirror' are what's needed. You talk brilliantly and honestly about the male/female poetry thing – the absence of 'explosion of consciousness' in those competent, confident male poems – but it seems to me that our changed and daunted world – changed from the old beautiful and repressive Catholicism we knew and from the pre-callous imperium of Bushland – the changed world finds its way into the filmic, fretful, phantasmagorical scenarios you manage to slip into.

And 'Pearl' is rare, 'far and free', to misquote e.e.

(The height is wreaking havoc on this Pilot-pen, and the meal arrives, but we'll see how things proceed – pen now improving.)

My lashes were wet when I read what you had to say about Helen and me, and I was proud and helped to be named among the poets you admire, because I trust your words and know you don't go in for the sucky-uppy stuff.

But I also found the courage and the first-place, last-ditch quality of your statements about love and poetry rare and renovating. Hence this sudden paean. You are in great creative and spiritual shape, I feel, doing necessary and durable work – a compensator for all the fakery and disappointment that attends our mystery.

When I get back, I'll send you a couple of things I've written recently – small enough jobs – that chime with things in *APR* – on 'listening', for example.

Anyhow, *cher poète*, here's to you –
Seamus

Henri Cole's poems and the interview with him appeared in the May/June 2004 issue of *American Poetry Review*. In the interview, Cole said that he admired SH for 'remaining socially responsible and creatively free', and that he regarded SH and Helen Vendler, Harvard colleagues, as 'liberators' who had taught him 'as much about life as they did about art'. He added: 'I love them both.'

'far and free' alludes distantly to E. E. Cummings's poem 'in Just-'.

To Lorraine Pintal

TS NLI

9 July 2004 — 191 Strand Road, Dublin 4

Dear Lorraine,

My apologies for the delay in answering your recent letter. I have been in Delphi, for a week-long conference on Sophocles, and have fallen behind in my correspondence.

When I think seriously about a translation by Marie-Claire Blais of a translation by me of an original by Sophocles, I have very strong doubts about the enterprise. It would surely be better for Marie-Claire to do her own version directly. If she were to put mine into French, there would be problems of attribution: would she be translating me or Sophocles? And think of the difficulty of the 'billing'. I believe the whole enterprise is problematical.

On the other hand, I don't want to veto the proposal. It's just that I'd be less than honest if I didn't voice my doubts.

Anyhow, I've had my chance for second thoughts and just want to give you a chance to have yours.

Sincerely,
Seamus

Pintal, as Artistic Director of the Théâtre du Nouveau Monde, Montréal, had written on 15 June to promote this translation by French-Canadian Marie-Claire Blais (1939–2021), which despite SH's misgivings went into production in 2005 under the title *Antigone, de Sophocle, texte français . . . d'après la traduction de Seamus Heaney*. Other translations of *The Burial at Thebes* have followed, including one into Italian, as *La Sepoltura a Tebes*, by Angela Teatino.

To Askold Melnyczuk

PC Melnyczuk

[Autumn 2004] [Postmarked 'Baile Átha Cliath' (Dublin)]

'Girls'!
'Shakespearean thunderstorm – a tempest!' That Oksana can conjure the winds and you can catch them in an English sail. Between you, you have upped the language ante. The whole thing charges and discharges. This, as the Lord Geoffrey hath it, is plenty, this is more than enough. Meanwhile, have been to Kraków, have seen Czesław's mighty marble tomb and found myself in tears. Met the Zag. and other scribes. Drank the vod. Wished you were there. Much love to Alex and you from herself and me – Seamus

PS This quill overdid itself – hope you can read the stuff written with the front of the nib – S.

Girls is the title of a novella by Oksana Zabuzhko (b.1960), which Melnyczuk, who describes her as 'Ukraine's most celebrated writer' and 'a very "public intellectual"', translated and published.

'Lord Geoffrey': the English poet Geoffrey Hill, in residence at Boston University at the time; 'more than enough' alludes flippantly to Hill's sombre poem 'September Song' (*For the Unfallen*, 1959).

Czesław Miłosz had died on 14 August, and SH attended the memorial service for him, in Kraków, on the 27th; 'the Zag' was Adam Zagajewski. The postcard is a Polish one, the stamp and postmark Irish.

To Adrian Rice

MS Rice

23 September 2004 191 Strand Road, Dublin 4

Good ould Samuel Taylor . . . And then there is Sir Philip Sidney, whom I quoted lately at our own Christopher's wedding:

My true love hath my heart and I have his,
By just exchange one for the other given:

He holds mine dear and his I cannot miss –
There never was a better bargain driven:
My true love hath my heart and I have his.

It's a bit posh, I know, but it has to be said – Marie and I are going to be in Sweden next Saturday and so will miss the Baronscourt revels.

But we rejoice at the news of the hoe-down and knot-tying in the North Carolina mountains and send our love –
Seamus

Rice had invited the Heaneys to his and his American fiancée Molly's pre-wedding party, held at Baronscourt, home of the Duke and Duchess of Abercorn. Their invitation had quoted all ten lines of Coleridge's 'Answer to a Child's Question'.

To Tom Paulin

MS Paulin

29 September 2004

Glanmore Cottage, Ashford,
Co. Wicklow

Dear Tom,

Just when I was getting ready to thank you for your gutsy, generous remarks in the Elizabeth Bishop article – so spot on, un-pussy-footing, whistle-clean, hear-ye, hear-ye – along comes *The Road to Inver*. Bloody marvellous. Hopkins had this brilliant image of Browning like a man jumping up with his mouth full – or something on those lines: well, page after page I wanted to jump up, wave the book, point at the poem, show it to the imagined world out there. You have managed to open the channels, utterly, between what's in you and what's in the original poems. And the staring angels go through, as the man said. Language and perception startled into terrific alert action. The full resources of the orchestra mastered: from the stanzaic tread of the Horace (1.4) and the take it or leave it panache of the French Sonnets (I love the Baudelairean Briar) through the up-and-away tour-de-force of the title poem and 'The Caravans' to those ur-Paulin, far-out, up-north scrimshaws on 'Voronezh' and 'Landsflykt' – and I haven't even mentioned the Greeks or the Italians. The book really lifted my heart and you should rejoice in it without doubt or stint.

Meanwhile, you may have seen J. Fenton having his sport in his recent Clare pieces in *NYRB*. I had been in touch with Barbara Epstein (I'm doing a brief preface for Tom Flanagan's essays, to be published by them, and I also had a bit of Sophocles in this new issue, in memory of Miłosz) and she half-urged me to write a response. I enclose* <*I don't: it needs revision. And polishing. S> something I wrote to-day, but I'm not entirely sure if it's worth sending in. On the other hand, the harp-smiting and the flax-dam/father/sex-pool stuff is just that wee bit too snottery . . .

I'm away to Harvard on Tuesday, for six weeks. Maybe see you when I'm over in England, lateish November. Much love to dear Giti and the boys. (Christopher's reminded me lately that when he and Michael were kids, M. McLaverty used to refer to 'Little Marie and the terrorists'. Sounds like a band.) Seamus

Of the several articles that Paulin had written on Bishop, the one most likely referred to here was printed in the *Irish Times*: in it, he noted Bishop's influence on such Irish poets as SH and Paul Muldoon. *The Road to Inver* is Paulin's collection of verse translations from a wide variety of languages.

Hopkins had described Browning's 'way of talking (and making his people talk) with the air and spirit of a man bouncing up from table with his mouth full of bread and cheese'.

The piece by James Fenton in the *New York Review of Books* that SH had taken objection to was titled 'John Clare's Genius' (23 September 2004); in it, Fenton had written, 'Of the Irish, Patrick Kavanagh and Michael Longley wrote poems about [Clare], while Tom Paulin and Seamus Heaney (as we shall see) turned him into a quasi-political figurehead'; Fenton had then gone on to poke fun at SH's reading of Clare's 'The Mouse's Nest' in SH's Oxford lecture 'John Clare's Prog'. Barbara Epstein (1928–2006) was then Editor of the *New York Review of Books*.

To Andrew McNeillie

MS Bodleian

2 October 2004 [In transit]

Dear Andrew –

Excuse this tired old stationery – I'm on an aeroplane with my old briefcase and pulling out whatever I can. Marie and I have just been in Stockholm for another spot of Swedish bounty-hunting, as it were: there has been a joint issue of stamps by Sweden Post and An Post in Ireland – featuring W.B.Y., G.B.S., S.B. and guess who – and why. Anyhow, mine will act like one of those old white bread poultices used to work – it'll draw out all the venom in the literary system of the island. 'Let them not forget this contribution / to their jealous art.'

Anyhow, talking of poultices – that bisected cat that cured the horse . . . Marvellous stuff. Your father's book is a kind of Caledonian *Georgics* – and not just because of the bees. You're quite right to link Clutag to Mossbawn – we even had a Hillhead a mile up the concrete road – where Barney Devlin had his forge. And the world of that first place kept coming back in the 'bright shoots' of single words and images. The word 'planting' – I loved ours and hadn't heard the place called that in years. That hinge that 'wailed'. The rats in the corn. The sheer sexual thick-wittedness in the term 'buck rabbit'. (Nearly always kitted with his epithet 'big' in Co. Derry.) The grunt before the grace. The wire-meshed turnip baskets for the turf. And so many wonderfully rendered moments – the pony's fall and the grandfather's accident; the visit of the horsedealers; the saga of Steel Arm – and that beautiful last paragraph of the whole childhood account. It's marvellously written and a marvel that you found it and were able to publish it. And what a beautiful jacket – Gail's painting is spot-on.

You mention the poetry pamphlet and I'm wondering if it's not too late to present you with an alternative set of contents, here enclosed. These would be the opening poems of a new collection – by no means ready, not promised or to be rumoured even – and I suddenly thought that they might be better, more up to the moment, less odd, than the Henryson. I'd suggest *A Shiver* as the overall title, if we went ahead. See what you think.

I agree that P. Fallon has done great work on *The Georgics*. I've reviewed it for the *Irish Times*. And I said a word, not in disparagement, about C. Day Lewis. I'm very glad that you think so highly of it because I was very enthusiastic in private and have given the quotable quotes in public, and I'd not want it to end up looking like a case of log-rolling. Anyhow, it would be great for PF if he ended up in World's Classics.

Now I'm buckling the safety belt [. . .]
Best wishes – Seamus

PS I go to Harvard for 6 weeks on Tuesday morning.

Ireland and Sweden had jointly issued a set of postage stamps honouring Irish winners of the Nobel Prize in Literature (see postcard to Desmond and Mary Kavanagh of 5 October 2004).

In the lines about 'their jealous art', SH misquotes his own poem 'The Scribes', from 'Sweeney Redivivus' in *Station Island.*

Andrew McNeillie (b.1946), poet and editor at Oxford University Press, had found and published, under his own imprint, Clutag Press, a manuscript by his father John McNeillie (aka Ian Niall, 1916–2002). Its title was *My Childhood* and it is recognisable as an earlier, more candid version of the book by John McNeillie that had been published in 1967 as *A Galloway Childhood.* Andrew McNeillie sent it to SH on the hunch that the world it described would have had many features in common with Mossbawn. The 'Steel Arm' refers to an artificial arm that McNeillie's great-grandfather, a blacksmith, had devised for a farm labourer who had lost his real one. Gail McNeillie is Andrew McNeillie's daughter and an artist.

A Shiver, containing poems that would later appear in *District and Circle*, was brought out by Clutag in 2005.

Virgil's *Georgics*, translated by Peter Fallon (b.1951), publisher – occasionally SH's – and poet, was duly incorporated into the series Oxford World Classics.

To Desmond and Mary Kavanagh

PC Kavanagh

5 October 2004

[Postmarked 'Baile Átha Cliath' (Dublin)]

Ah, well . . .

Love –
Seamus

The Swedish card shows a view of Stockholm; the Irish stamp shows the head of SH, more heroically square-jawed than in real life, against a stretch of Irish coast.

To Maura Cregan

MS Cregan

15 October 2004

191 Strand Road, Dublin 4

Dear Maura,

The dedication of *Lost Fields* sends me out confirmed – a second time – and sweetened. I feel blessed and honoured and am deeply grateful.

It so happens the book arrived at more or less the same time as I did this morning. I've been in Harvard for the past two weeks, and have to go back (for a month) on Sunday. So your timing was perfect.

And thank you for your earlier note: I thought the whole event was completely right. As a civic gesture, an artistic tribute and a dear reminder. And the moment of the unveiling of the plaque was wonderful – it went to my heart, as they say.

When I get back to my wee computer in Massachusetts, I'll send you a copy of my words on the Saturday morning.

Fondest wishes
Seamus

Maura Cregan is the daughter of Michael McLaverty, under whose headmastership SH had his first taste of schoolteaching; his novel, *Lost Fields*, just reissued, was originally published in 1941. The plaque is outside McLaverty's home in Killard, Co. Down.

To Jane and Bernard McCabe   TS J. McCabe

22 October 2004   English Department, Barker Center, Harvard University, Cambridge, MA 02138

Dear Jane, Dear Bernard,

Up early, for some reason, with an hour to spare before I meet a reporter from the *Crimson* for breakfast (and, yes, of course, an interview) in Adams House. But in the matutinal silence wistful rememberings of *les très riches heures de* Berkeley Street are upon me. Chimes at dawnlight. New realizations of how kind you were to me in those days when I would haunt porch and kitchen, Heineken Heaney, the six-pack scavenger, the lonely began, the Sheraton demander . . . Lovely times. You are among the *diversi sancti* . . .

Meanwhile, I have been among the ones you know so well: have given a couple of lectures already and there they were on the benches, kindly attenders, living in a sort of eternal Cambridge present, Alfie and Sally, Softpad and B., Jack and Ann C., Frank B. and Robert P., Helen V., Dimitri and Cynthia, Heather Cole, Robert Gardner, Rose Styron, and many younger scribes and older crazies. *Le tout* 02138.

Not in attendance but beating the bounds like a maneater, the O'Malley: valiant and tweeded, toothless because of the effect of radiation treatment being undergone for some damned cancer of the oesophagus, undaunted in his great boasts (billions, he said, he and his company had just offered in a takeover bid in Australia), set up (he says) in apartments both here and in New York, living on expenses, banking his salary/earnings for security in age – he is a great creature, really. But after an hour and a half of his genial broadcasts across the lunch table (we had lunch yesterday with his delightful, now 31-year-old son, Gabriel) I was glad to reel away, my head athrob like one long pent in ear-splitting disco now set loose . . . He loves you both. And yes, we love him. Courageous, lonely man. Blowhard veteran of the hard blows.

And speaking of the hard blows, how are you both? In my Yeatsian way, I delight to imagine you, if not exactly under the plum blossom with an ancient glitter in your sleek and seeing balls, still adjacent to the girlish birches and the garrulous Teme, the air recommending itself unto your gentle senses. But it's a sore situation, I know, with mother Johnston in her sad state and Ms McNab not able to see her – even though Mr McNab sounded in great shape when we spoke on the phone last Sunday.

Much love. Wish you were here.
Seamus

PS Sleek and seeing etc.: what Hopkins called the eyeball. Just in case you thought I was, er,

On Harvard notepaper. *Crimson* is the university's student newspaper. The McCabes' old Cambridge home was on Berkeley Street.

'lonely began': see Hopkins's sonnet 'To seem the stranger lies my lot, my life', which concludes with the lines, 'This to hoard unheard, / Heard unheeded, leaves me a lonely began.'

'one long pent': spinning off Keats's sonnet 'To One who Has Been Long in City Pent'.

'mother Johnston': Jane McCabe's mother.

To Andrew McNeillie

TS Bodleian

9 December 2004

Dear Andrew,

Sorry for the hold-up. To-ings and fro-ings continue, but there was also the uneasy feeling that certain revisions needed to be made. In 'Ajax', for example, the phrase 'gathers head' appears, having already shown up in the Horace, so that has been changed. And I cannot get the middle of 'Helmet' right – go with what's there, for what it's worth.

There are a couple of other wee corrections, plus another revision – 'conqueror' for 'conquering drover' in Ajax, but the main change I'm proposing is in the placing of 'The Tollund Man in Springtime'. He has grown a couple more sonnets into himself, and with his general revivification, I think he'd better go at the end of the pamphlet. And if we put him there it's goodbye, I think, to the Cavafy. I like it for what it is in itself, but it starts off in a new direction rather than rounds off, so I think it should go.

See what you think. I'm sorry not to have e-mail. This goes into the post, with hopes that it will get to you before Yule.

All good wishes,

Seamus

PS As well, Andrew, we already have two translations. Enough?

Here SH communicates his corrections to the text of *A Shiver*. The postscript is handwritten.

2005

By this time, Dennis O'Driscoll had become SH's principal correspondent, with even more letters passing between them than are shown, or partially shown, below, as work on the *Stepping Stones* project intensified. In addition, SH continued to depend on O'Driscoll as trusted reader of, and frank commentator on, his poetry in progress.

To Dennis O'Driscoll

TS Emory

13 January 2005 191 Strand Road, Dublin 4

Dear Dennis,

Every now and again I am suddenly overwhelmingly conscious of how much our interview is costing you in terms of your own writing, your time and energy and head-room. And when I got those exhaustive, exhilarating questions about *Station Island* I did tremble again with anxiety for you, but with an immense, exhilarated gratitude as well. I feel we're into the home stretch and I hope to have this chapter finished in a month, or maybe even sooner. I got a terrific renewed energy just reading through the pages, but I was also conscious of the extent of my debt to you. Awesome, as they say. The depth and detail of your knowledge of the stuff I've written over the years and the stuff that has been written about it were not gained without steady gleaning and concentration, and all that before we even consider the expense of spirit and time required to generate and order the questions . . . As I turn up the old soil and get a new sense of myself from doing so, I constantly think that this 'sensation sweet' is owed to you, and more and more I'm conscious of the immense service you have done me in taking on this task. The routine way we talk about it should not obscure the sense of privilege and promise that underlies the whole job.

I'm also conscious of a stylistic limitation that comes, I believe, with the genre. What I like about the interview format is the scope it gives for setting down a record and keeping the pitch of the exchange relatively sharp, or at least springy. So there are times when the questions would seem to require more inwardness in the answer than I am prepared to give. Although I am writing the responses, I'd prefer them not to sound 'written', and for that reason a fully realized account of the inner man just doesn't always emerge. I'm not saying there's evasion or deception, just that the stylistic means aren't quite fitted to some subjective ends. I occasionally stay at a certain safe level when I could possibly go down into the shadier levels. It may be that a shorter autobiographical reverie could eventually supplement our big survey, but that is not in any way a plan, just a wispy notion.

[. . .]

O Lairdy! I didn't see the *Sunday Times* piece, but I felt for Montague when I read the hammering he took in the *Guardian*. From a critical point of view, there was a lot to agree with, but it was unnerving to watch a 75-year-old being used for target practice. But I shouldn't get myself into too much of a lather since I got a very nice letter from the Cookstown man recently, expressing gratitude for books of my own . . . 'She would plunge all poets in the ninth circle . . .'

Much love to the poets of Gallops –

Seamus

'O Lairdy!': the poet Nick Laird (b.1975, in Cookstown, Northern Ireland) had taken a stern line when reviewing John Montague's 2004 collection *Drunken Sailor* in the *Guardian*.

The penultimate sentence is a self-quote, from 'An Afterwards' (*Field Work*).

To Dennis O'Driscoll — TS Emory

28 January 2005 — Becune Point, St Lucia

Dear Dennis,

A swimming pool, the foaming Carib Sea, big leafed growths of every kind – palms, rubber trees, banana plants – outside the window, but inside the breast the slight tension of a man who has just packed and has half an hour before he's due to be picked up for the airport . . .

At least I covered thirteen more pages in the course of the week – your questions included, of course; and there were other rewards. On Sunday night last, a reading and a performance of a couple of extracts from Derek's *Odyssey*, but then as a surprise there was also a cut-down version of *The Burial*, done by actors from St Lucia and Trinidad, some of them terrific speakers. Poets who came from Trinidad were Ralph Thompson and Eddie Baugh, who also did the Derek Walcott Lecture on Derek Walcott last Wednesday. And what a happy surprise to find that Ralph knew you and had been in correspondence with you. When he bought a copy of *Finders Keepers* at the bookstall that evening, he could hardly believe the dedication page. All in all, the week was well worth it, and the heliotropic spouse returns tawny and teed up for all the functions and receptions that await: Friel first night, Queen's pomp re handing over of *Beowulf* papers, the PEN do in Dún Laoghaire. I wish they were all over. A reading in city of culture Cork with the assiduous Delanty will be a snip compared with walking across a fully assembled Gate Theatre foyer. Gird the loin and prepare the face . . .

I apologize for not getting back to you concerning Joseph Parisi's enquiry about the St Xavier honorary degree. I hope it's not too late to ask him to restrain the good sisters. Once again I find myself in a familiar bind, caught between gratitude for the honour proposed and an increasing sense of honour-overload or degree-fatigue. Crossing the ocean has become increasingly hard and I honestly could not face the trip to Chicago with the proper degree, if you'll excuse the expression, of wholeheartedness. I do appreciate that this is a highly honorific thought on the part of Sr Sue Sanders and don't like declining, but much better to do so ahead of time than at a later date, when all the committee work and faculty ratification has already been gone through with.

Other matters later. I'll fax this when I get home and get it printed. Then will crash into bed and the mailpile, hoping to have surfaced by Monday. Meanwhile, surf faces me still, but not for long. Love to you and Julie – also beloved of the poet Thompson.

Seamus

PS In Glanmore, Sunday morning: we were so zonked when we got to Dublin yesterday afternoon, we parked the cases in the hall, unparked the car and came down here directly, for the big sleep. In the meantime, not at all gruntled (I've been reading Wodehouse again) to miss your name on that *Irish Times* shortlist published yesterday.

The entertainments SH describes here were for Walcott's seventy-fifth birthday, which fell on 23 January.

Ralph Thompson (1928–2022) was a Jamaican businessman, educationalist, painter, and the author of books of poems and a verse novel; Edward Baugh (b.1936), a Jamaican poet and academic authority on the work of Derek Walcott.

Joseph Parisi (b.1944), whose twenty-year editorship at the Chicago magazine *Poetry* had recently ended, was now Director of Publications at the Poetry Foundation. Susan Sanders, a Sister of Mercy, was then Vice President for Mission at St Xavier University, Chicago.

To Hughie O'Donoghue

MS H. O'Donoghue

15 February 2005

Glanmore Cottage, Ashford,
Co. Wicklow

Dear Hughie,

The depth of imagining in *The Prodigal Son* series is rich and strange. The Flanders mud and the mangel-wurzels, the Arras woundie (like an escapee from Bosch) and the boy in the yard – beside what we used to call 'a turnip snedder'. To have elevated the pathos and sensory purchase of those secret, sorrowful images into the structure and size of the whole work is a marvellous achievement – a man at the peak of his powers, following the hint to the hilt, if you'll excuse the mixed metaphor.

I'm very sorry not to be able to attend the opening in the Fenton.

Love to Clare and yourself –
Seamus

O'Donoghue, who is dedicatee of 'The Turnip-Snedder', the first poem in *District and Circle*, has written his own account of how the chance discovery of a collection of glass plate negatives, including a poignant image of a stolid young man standing beside such a machine, gave rise to one of the paintings in his series *The Prodigal Son* – the painting in question being titled *The Dutiful Son.*

The Fenton Gallery is in Cork.

To Dennis O'Driscoll

MS Emory

23 March 2005

Glanmore Cottage, Ashford,
Co. Wicklow

[. . .]

So much has flowed in from your teeming brain and busy printer – the letters, the copies of the reviews, the Muldoon mullarkey, the

Beo-blather – I feel deeper in your debt than heretofore – if that be possible. I'm especially thankful for the very true account of 'Artemis'. 'Mick Joyce' I knew for what it was, a hurdling over the half-line alliterative course, fourteen more or less Anglo-Saxon verses – or rather seven halved ones – legging and footing towards sonnetdom, stanza by stanza. All done before, in 'The Sandpit' and 'Damson'. But I just got carried away. However, I'm more doggedly interested in my Aunt Sally and have dug in and around the William Street garden and turned up the ground in different shapes which I'll let you see eventually. Also, over the weekend, been happily at work on three translations from Rilke's *New Poems* – don't worry, though – no archaic torsos or panthers.

[. . .]

'Artemis' may be among the 'heavy' Greek poems ultimately dropped from *District and Circle* (see letter to Paul Keegan of 19 May 2005); SH's Aunt Sally is pictured, gardening, in the first section of 'Home Help', in that book, where two poems 'after' Rilke are also to be found; 'The Sandpit' was in *Station Island*, 'Damson' in *The Spirit Level*.

To Dennis O'Driscoll

MS Emory

29 March 2005 191 Strand Road, Dublin 4

Dear Friend,

Which is how they used to begin their 'Christian' leaflets in the north . . . But you are a friend indeed. Wonderful to have your focused, unfaltering responses, if hard, hard work for you to assemble them. You bring to the fore, into articulation, every hovering uncertainty that can manage to hide at the back of the mind – even from itself. Which is to say that your response to the additional poems of the Tollund sequence struck me as a remembrance. They do end up swerving away from the springtime element . . . And yes, too, in some deep inner Rilkean dark I also knew that the roaring and spattering at the end of the 'cattle in the rain' sonnet was far too violent. Yet the wrongness of its placing was offset by the pleasure of just imagining it. The proof of your rightness, however, was the speed and ease with which I was able to alter things. I changed the final couplet in the queues and cow poem (that bulrush has been waiting to get into the right place for decades) and resituated the straphanger and the tunnel busker in land of Sweeney Redivivus – a country I'd always hoped I might re-enter.

Many, many thanks also for your attentiveness to the Rilkes. 'Heath-house' I did indeed take from Leishman – aware of its oddity, but thinking that the lindens gave a clue that we were abroad in Germania and so could expect/sustain a bit of 'difference'. But my problem is a simple and profound one – sheer lack of knowledge of the language. Earlier to-day I was writing to somebody in the University of Kent who's doing a PhD on Nuala Ní Dhomhnaill and her translations/translators. I headed off an interview by scribbling a page of observations, including the following which suddenly seems *à propos*:

> The ideal situation would be to come at the poems without mediation, but that's an ideal that's rarely lived up to. I know Latin and French, for example, well enough to think for myself about what might be equivalents, but I'd still go hunting for other people's translations, not to rip them off, just for some kind of reassurance that I'd got the sense right. And then, of course, once you see that other version, your instinct is to make your own translation more your own, as it were, make it diverge so that it doesn't look like a copy. (Same thing happens with a good crib . . .)
>
> Come to think of it, that is the problem with cribwork – you're dropping your bucket into the well of meaning all right, but it doesn't go down all the way to the bottom. The haulage work, which is part of the joy of poetry, is lighter than it should be. You may get beneath the surface, but not very far.

With apologies for the self-quotation, but it actually covers my problems with the Rilke. What I appreciated greatly were your absolutely pertinent remarks about 'unreliable' in 'Burnt-Out House' – the thing suddenly made sense when you introduced the word 'importunate' – and your suggestion about the repunctuation of 'Roman Campagna'. The Cohn version of 'The Apple Orchard' reads limpidly and fluently, but I believe (notwithstanding my ignorance of the German) that a certain counter-current, a slow backwashy flow, is called for.

[. . .]

J. B. Leishman (1902–63) was a pioneer in the translation of Rilke's poems into English, his *Duino Elegies*, done in collaboration with Stephen Spender, being pre-eminent; Stephen Cohn (1931–2012), artist and teacher, translated a number of the major volumes from Rilke's *oeuvre*.

To Massimo Bacigalupo

MS Bacigalupo

6 April 2005   191 Strand Road, Dublin 4

Dear Massimo,

Thanks for your recent letter. Yes, Tate's Avenue is where Madame H. had a flat, early on. I suppose it was (at that stage) more a case of 'petting' than 'making love'. The F-word was still 'flirt' in 'Locked Park' Belfast – which was, yes, a town where the parks were locked on Sunday. You could call the poem in Italian 'The Rug', if you liked. I called it that at first.

'Streel-head' is straggly-haired. I supposed 'streel' to be dialect ('Her hair was in streels') but I see it given in the Collins dictionary as a loose woman . . .

'Fiddleheads' is a problem, I can see. Helen Vendler wasn't sure what was going on in it and I have revised it in the meantime to indicate 1) that I see a slightly pubic aspect to the ferns and 2) that Toraiwa was expecting to find more erotic content in my work. The last paragraph simply presents them as a 'delicacy', cooked as in Japan, in a little basket. BUT – if you like, substitute 'To Pablo Neruda in Tamlaghtduff', deleting 'Fiddleheads' and placing Pablo after 'Planting the Alder' and before 'The Birch Grove'.

I agree about using 'My Education'.

I shall endeavour to have a couple of pages on me and 'the state of the art' ready for you before you head for the States. Certainly by the time you get back.

All good wishes –

Seamus

Bacigalupo's booklet of translations from SH's recent work was published under the title *Fuori Campo* (2005).

SH had met the scholar Masazumi Toraiwa, to whom the poem 'Fiddleheads' is dedicated, in Japan.

To Paul Keegan

TS Faber

19 May 2005 191 Strand Road, Dublin 4

Dear Paul,

To-day, or yesterday or to-morrow, some day around now at any rate, is the 40th anniversary of publication of *Death of a Naturalist* so I've made a drive to get the new manuscript into shape.

[. . .]

Anyhow, here's a revamped version of the thing I gave you last month. Fewer translations – the Greek stuff was heavy, the Ajax in fact lumpy, and the Sorley maybe too exotic. The contents are re-ordered, there are one or two new things, and two or three old ones have been dropped. (Was I right to keep the Rilke?)

The main change is the title. *District and Circle.* I came to think of *Planting the Alder* a bit too beautiful. And I have my own district which I've been circling for a while now. Not 100% sure of it, even so.

[. . .]

To the Registrar, Aosdána

TS

14 June 2005 191 Strand Road, Dublin 4

Proposal of Brian Friel as *Saoi*

I wish to propose Brian Friel as a candidate worthy to fill the position of *Saoi* which is currently available.

If anybody deserves this honour, it is Friel. He is the author of classic works that already have lodged themselves in the repertoire of world theatre. For more than forty years his plays have, in Yeats's words, 'engrossed the present and dominated memory'. Just to name them is to be reminded not only of one dramatist's epoch-making achievements, but to remember also the excitement that greeted each work as it appeared and the purchase it has maintained on audiences ever since: *Philadelphia Here I Come*; *The Freedom of the City*; *Faith Healer*; *Aristocrats*; *Translations*; *Dancing at Lughnasa*; *Molly Sweeney*; *The Home Place.*

[. . .]

His work in general manifests a passionate engagement with the political and historical condition of Irish society but eschews didactic or prescriptive responses. He has been exemplary in the purity of his dramatic intent, managing always to grant his characters an inner freedom and linguistic energy that allow them to pit their individuality against their social and ideological circumstances. Nevertheless, they still exhibit the stresses and strains of the times, and, to quote Yeats again, we can 'Ireland's history in their lineaments trace'.
[. . .]

Yours sincerely
Seamus Heaney

Friel was formally elected a *Saoi* the following year.

To Tom Paulin

MS Paulin

23 July 2005

Durrants Hotel, George Street,
London W1

[. . .]
I've been uneasy about not having spoken to you or Giti this long time. You've had it very hard, and there's a mercilessness about the way the slings and arrows have kept coming. It's been a grief for both of you, and it's no wonder that even a spirit as regenerate as yours has quailed. But for sure you're going to bud again and write, and feel the sun and rain and relish versing. You have so much to your credit – not only the exultant poems of decades, but the purely motivated, critically exhilarating books of prose – tonic on every page, heroic in their endeavour to transmute the subjective 'joy or night' into a volt of conscience or jolt to the culture. All that 'sedentary trade' would be enough to wear you down – given the passionate teaching you also do – but when you add to it the expense of spirit in your public witness – in newspaper reviews, on the TV, in readings and lectures – and in the ordeal by calumny that you've had to undergo – it's no wonder, as I say, that you feel, for a while, 'the fell of dark, not day.' But as the old English line has it, *þæt ofereode, swa will þis* – or something like that – 'that passed over, so will this'.

Paulin had been invited to Columbia University to give a lecture on Edmund Burke in February 2005; again, as had happened in 2002 when he was invited to Harvard (see SH's letter to Tom Paulin of 3 December 2002), there were objections and protests, but Professor Akeel Bilgrami (b.1950), who had issued the invitation, was adamant that the lecture should go ahead. Although ill with flu at the time, Paulin carried on with teaching and other commitments, before falling into the deep, long-lasting depression to which SH refers here.

The line SH is trying to recall, which serves as refrain in the Old English poem 'Deor', actually goes, *Þæs ofereode, þisses swa mæg* – 'That passed over, this may too.'

To Tom Sleigh

TS Sleigh

22 August 2005 191 Strand Road, Dublin 4

[. . .]

I only wish I could pant out a Molly Blooming yes to your invitation to read at Hunter with that hosting of the scribes, but this autumn and next spring the calendar says no. I've been on the go a hell of a lot since April this year and need to pull back. Since returning from Sligo, for example, I was three days in London (uxorious, paternal, laved in an unpermitted ooze of sentiment, celebrating the 40th wedding anniversary with herself, the boys and their partners, and Catherine – marvellous, really); then to the Faroe Islands with the piper O'Flynn (hallucinatory sheer green hills upstanding in the Atlantic, dried whale meat, smoked puffin breast, Viking lookalikes and luckily also the analeptic schnapps); then off to Athenry in Galway for centenary celebrations of the birth of the poet Padraic Fallon (Kavanagh and MacNeice last year, Beckett next, so it goes). But I digress. I need to stay put for a few months. Apart from anything else, I'm heading for Hong Kong next month – literary festival, but really because of Susie Kennelly, who used to work as my part-time secretary and became my guardian angel before betraying me and going east with her husband; then when I get back I'm into a mini-tour on this side of the ocean to mark the publication of a new book. I think I'm going to call it *District and Circle*. I had decided on that title before the London bombs, then hesitated, thought of other titles, then wrote a couple of extra sonnets into the little sequence (enclosed) and decided, to hell with it, this stuff is haunted enough to bear scrutiny.

Sleigh is Distinguished Professor and Director of the MFA Program at Hunter College, New York City.

By 'London bombs', SH refers to events on the morning of 7 July 2005, when bombs were set off in a co-ordinated act of terror that targeted different parts of the city's transport system, including the underground Circle Line.

To Paul Keegan

TS Faber

25 August 2005 — 191 Strand Road, Dublin 4

Dear Paul,

Many thanks for the catalogue copy, so closely considered and beautifully written. You have a gift for discovering the uniquely applicable words. It's a prose poem, really, pondering the assay and timbre of the book with safe hands and a marvellously true ear, and I am sensible of my transgression as I send back a revised version. Your estimate of the manuscript does me honour and I apologize for rearranging its many felicities. It all comes, I'm afraid, from having had the weekend in Glanmore, with too much time, for once, on my busybody hands.

I wanted to reduce somewhat the number of references to spades and harrow pins and trowels and the like (God knows, they're there a-plenty in the text), to draw some more attention to the element of the contemporary (automatic lock, melting glacier), and to try to make the thing sound a bit less of a miscellany. Also, since I have added the supplementary phrase 'doing / the rounds of the district' in 'To Pablo Neruda' (revised text following) I thought it would be no harm to use it in the copy in order to flag the title that extra little bit. And might it also be better to have lines from an original poem as a coda, even though the translated stanza you choose is one of my own favourites?

My apologies also for reneging on the *Henry IV* tickets. A stupid move, but I've again stupidly landed myself with too much travel.

I look forward to seeing you on Monday week.

Seamus

To Dennis O'Driscoll

TS Emory

25 August 2005 191 Strand Road, Dublin 4

[. . .]

The Tomlinson is unexpected and very good in the end. Every time I read the like I regret that I kept so few notebooks, but then I compensate myself with the thought that record is not the same as retrieval, that the whole thing for me was the hole itself, the mud mouth, the god-puddle, the plaster-seed element (as we called plasticine in Anahorish School). I'm closer to Julie's quick eye for miracle and mammon in the muck than to Charlie's inventory. But I'm very grateful to have it – unexpected, as I say, in the 'human' outreach it reaches.

[. . .]

Cracks in the Universe by British modernist poet Charles Tomlinson (1927–2015) contains a significant number of poems evoking childhood scenes and events.

To Jane McCabe

MS J. McCabe

1 September 2005 191 Strand Road, Dublin 4

Dear Jane,

I don't sit in one of the dives, although it's the day for it, and I wouldn't mind . . . Just to hope that Bernard is doing better than the guy once treated by all the King's horses and all the King's men, and is all together again. Also to say that Section 2 of 'Dist. and Circ.' has been revised. For the better, I have to presume . . . Coming soon.

Love – S.

To Barrie Cooke

TS Pembroke

4 September 2005 Glanmore Cottage, Ashford,
Co. Wicklow

Cher Ami, Cher Maître,

Excuse this printout, but I'm down in the dacha, using the word processor in a fit of correspondence efficiency.

To-morrow Marie and I head away for ten days. First to London where I'm to talk to the Faber sales reps at their sales conference – I'm having a new book of verses out next April (called *District and Circle*) and the reps want me to think of something they can say about it to the bookshops. Then after London to Rome and on to Lerici, for poetry-pomps and decorations.

I thought I'd let you know what I'm going to do with the art paper that Poetry Ireland has just forwarded to me: remember you and I are to 'collaborate' on something for their fundraising auction . . . My plan is to write out the enclosed poem on the sheet and leave it to you afterwards to do to it (or on it) whatever you feel like doing. I know you'll want me to contribute something spontaneous but stolidly I decline. What I intend is to write out the four sections of 'Moyulla' – the sullied name of the River Moyola, memories of seeing the first milky pollution of its stream when Nestlé's started a milk-powdering factory in our district in the 1950s. I'll write the verses in some sort of pattern on the sheet provided and then hope that you can perform on the inscribed surface. One question I have, though, is what should be used for the inscription: Pencil? Pen? Calligraphic ink?

I hope you can bear this. I know I'm landing you again (if you'll excuse the expression) with water – and river and pollution and refreshment – but it could be worse. You could be working with – oh well, just complete that sentence yourself.

Fondest wishes –
Seamus

The arts organisation Poetry Ireland had devised a scheme to raise funds, whereby poets and painters were to collaborate on pieces combining words and images that would then be sold at auction. The buyer of the item produced by SH and Cooke is unknown.

To Tom Paulin

MS Paulin

5 October 2005 191 Strand Road, Dublin 4

Dear Tom,

Crusoe's Secret arrived this morning and your letter was here when I landed back from England yesterday – I had to go to Magdalene in Cambridge to do a reading – Eamon Duffy is President (not Master) and I couldn't really refuse him. Also did a recording for that 'Poetry Archive' project . . . Came home, as ever, a bit ravelled, but that means that I lay leafing and loafing for a couple of hours – 'spread out', as my brother Charlie once said about Jim Griffin, a drunk neighbour who fell off the bike loosely and lay where he fell in the grass of the ditch – 'spread out like an accordion'.

As the song 'The Blue Hills of Antrim' says, 'My lashes were wet' when I finished reading or, to be truthful, skimming the 'Political Anxiety and Allusion' chapter. Such fullness overflowed, such gratitude for the utter receptiveness and extreme reach in your ear and understanding, such rejoicing in the electric flight of language, such sweetness (for me) in the generosity of your disposition, I felt I must write, even though briefly. The whole book is clearly deserving of the deserving praise you give Ted's writing; it's 'an invocation and a celebration which exalts a whole community of writers and readers . . .' and it also exultantly fulfils your own wish for literary criticism, that it 'find a way of communicating with a general audience'. (That Marvell essay, by the way, is transformative: as I read it, I was laid 'sheer and clear'. But then there's Hopkinsian whoosh and juice and jostle everywhere, and the essays are poetry in themselves, in their more than enoughness, all source and savour, not an ordinary utterance from start to finish.)

Another world-righting quality, unique and galvanic, is the 'intransigent honour' which underlies and overbrims in the writing. The insights that both open and steady one's own sense of what literature/poetry can mean in a life (the observation about an individual word or phrase carrying with it the charge of the whole poem) are one thing, but the sense of your endeavour and vocation as a proffer, a principle, a gift is, as they say, something else.

I want to get this into the post before 5:30, in the hope it might get to Donegal for Monday. Blessings on Giti and you, who are so good to yourselves – I mean to each other, not in that rebuking Ulster sense, 'They're brave and good to themselves,' God no – and so good for us to have you among us. I'll call before we set out for McCabe land. I hope you steady as water in a well – Love from us both – Seamus

Paulin's 2005 book of essays *Crusoe's Secret* is subtitled *The Aesthetics of Dissent*.

To Christopher Reid

MS Reid

7 October 2005 191 Strand Road, Dublin 4

Dear Christopher,

Scribendum est – something must be written, and it struck me that Lucinda's name had something of that imperative force to it – she was to shine, to keep the light from going, as perhaps Christopher was to bear a certain weight of grief. Your long truthful valiant life together had the required *consonantia* and *claritas* and *integritas*; now she, like the utterly tested water, lies utterly worn out, and you who have been utterly tested also, must go to again.

Marie and I were distressed to hear the sad news. On Tuesday morning I had flown over to London and actually spoke to Clare Reihill who told me how extremely imperilled Lucinda was that day – I was en route to that studio on Askew Road where you once accompanied me. Then, when I got back here last night, Catherine had phoned – and the whole edifice staggered badly.

You, like Mary in the scriptures, will have kept many things in your heart. You gave and were fit for many things, and the life you lived together manifested the shine and strength of love, all the more so because of a beautiful demure demeanour. Your goodness was undemonstrative and your durable art unpathetic; plus, as they say, your anger was frolicsome and efficacious.

I don't know what to say, I'm simply babbling, so *scribendum est* no more, or not now. All of our love to you, all honour and love to memory of brave, lovely Lucinda –

Seamus

My wife, the actress Lucinda Gane, had died from cancer on 6 October. As she had willed her body to medical research, there was no funeral service, but on the Saturday of the following week SH and Marie Heaney were among the friends who gathered at a party held to remember and celebrate her.

'utterly tested water . . . utterly worn out': see the final lines of 'How Water Began to Play', second of the 'Two Eskimo Songs' in Ted Hughes's *Crow*.

To Jane McCabe

MS NLI

15 October 2005

Dear Jane –

From Berkeley Street
          to Tanza Road,
From Knowbury
          to Lower Broad,

Dear daughter of
          the far Dakotas,
Dear Princess of
          the prize potatoes

Dear birch grove dryad
          at three score
We value, love you
          even more
     Seamus

SH's birthday greeting lists addresses where Jane McCabe had lived, her US origins – her mother had been Potato Queen of North Dakota – and her talent as a gardener, to which the *District and Circle* poem 'The Birch Grove' also pays tribute.

To Iggy McGovern

MS McGovern

4 December 2005

Dear Iggy,

You should have heard from me long before this, but I've been on the go unmercifully. Missed last week's Poetry Ireland Art Auction because I was attending Poetry Archive launch in London. So it goes.

I was very moved by your 'landing in' with the book that night – just I had been a bit hangdog about having scooted out so promptly after the launch – both of us (Marie and me, I mean) being worn down to a frazzle that particular evening. Now, however, I've had a chance to dwell with his suburban majesty and have to say it was a terrific audience altogether. The true voice of feeling and the free play of wit, as rueful as it is resourceful. I really like the combination of verbal roguery and real concern – and of course any friend of the Danish G-Man is a friend of mine. Poems to the dad and to the dame – 'Knight Errant' and 'Seasons' – I am a sucker for, and they're really good forbye. Which doesn't mean I'm not giving thumbs up to ones like 'The View from Dundrum' or 'Errata' or those 'spud-hard muscling legs' on 'Sportsday' – or the marvellous 'zephyr of mayhem, / the whirlwind of peace' in 'Vertigo'. The book has a fine style and despatch about [it] – it renders an account and at the same time has a bit of a romp and altogether passes the 'good crack' test, a seal of approval that Mahon used to require of all slim volumes.

Meanwhile, your 'Errata' prompts me to send a few lines I read out at Ben Kiely's 80th birthday. Muldoon will be after us next for royalties.

All good wishes –
Seamus

Above the letter, where the address might have appeared, there is instead a cartoon of SH standing in front of a pair of what must be students, looking at a sheet of paper and saying, 'You call this literature?'

Iggy McGovern (b.1948), who taught physics at Trinity College Dublin, had been encouraged by SH in the past and was now able to present him with his first book of poems, *The King of Suburbia*: 'Smoking on the Bog', one of the poems in it, alludes sceptically to the work of P. V. Glob ('the Danish G-man').

SH's 'Errata for BK' – 'For BK read OK. / For Tyrone read own turf. / For *amor* read Omagh', and so on – comes '*with apologies to Paul Muldoon*' and imitates Muldoon's own poem 'Errata' in *Hay* (1998).

To Annie Wedekind TS NYPL

5 December 2005 191 Strand Road, Dublin 4

[. . .]

Excisions first, since there's potential editorial challenge/conflict lurking here. On the acknowledgements page I have cut the glossary bit, where Hiberno-English and Ulster-Scots words like *súgán* and braird are explained. I think this explanation takes away from the recalcitrance such vocabulary intends to signify. These words are meant to go against the standard grain so there's a real inconsistency in glossing them for readers before they are actually encountered as a strangeness in the text. On the other hand, 'B-men' probably deserve their citation as 'B-special force of the former Royal Ulster Constabulary'.

Annie Wedekind was an assistant editor at Farrar, Straus and Giroux preparing *District and Circle* for US publication. The pre-emptive glossary was dropped.

To Andrzej Szczeklik   TS PNL

8 December 2005

Dear Andrzej,

In *Catharsis* you have found your Archimedean point. The book is a lever strong enough to move mountains. The faith and force and thought-throughness of it moves and strengthens me – and everyone who reads it will be affected in the same way. It is certainly a reinforcement of our common immunity system, at a time when such reinforcement is desperately necessary. It is no exaggeration to say that I loved every page, and obviously I also learned from it: 'the intellectual sweetness of those lines,' as Yeats says. My copy is covered with underlinings and gleeful margin ticks – what I keep wanting to do is to copy out all the wise and unexpected and holy (I don't think I exaggerate) things that you say – and quote. I was happily enmeshed in the webs of the net you wove, drawn in by the many threads of association that you drew out, delighted by the resource and rightness of your use of myth. I shall return to the book because it is a help. I think of Czesław's remark, made I'm not sure where: 'The child who dwells inside us trusts that there are wise men somewhere who know the truth.' The trusting child in me is full of *Gloria in excelsis* because of the good of your work, on the page and with the patients – and full of gratitude also to Antonia, who has done such a perfectly pitched job of translation. Not a jarring note in the whole text. And what a beautiful jacket.

Please excuse the brevity of this note – it's just a quick yelp of joy. Blessings of the season to Maria and you. With love from Marie and me –

The Polish immunologist Andrzej Szczeklik (1938–2012), whom SH had met in Kraków, was the author of *Catharsis: On the Art of Medicine*, translated into English by Antonia Lloyd-Jones and published by the University of Chicago

Press. Breaking his own rule in what was an exceptional case, SH supplied a paragraph of blurb for the book: '*Catharsis* is a masterful restoration of the old etymological links that exist between what is hale and healthy and holy. Andrzej Szczeklik is professor of medicine, but he is also expert in "the science of the feelings", which was how William Wordsworth defined poetry. His book is erudite, imaginative, intimate, authoritative; at once a reverie about the roots and responsibilities of doctoring, and a timely reminder that health care involves *Caritas* before it involves the economy.'

The fax is unsigned because it is the copy of one sent earlier and presumed by SH not to have been received.

To Paul Durcan — MS NLI

16 December 2005 — 191 Strand Road, Dublin 4

Jesus, Paul! Isn't life gas?
I felt an indescribable surge of surprise and good fortune
When I read your poem.
It was so big it made me feel small.
The only thing I can do is write this out now
Super spotum, as we used to say in St Columb's College.
A kind of grief came over me, as well as immense gratitude.
It had to do with a memory of being with John McG.
In the Rosses in Donegal years ago –
North of our spin country, closer to the *dacha* of Friel –
Anyhow, John was in the car with Marie and me
And we headed for Dungloe or Kincasslagh or wherever,
The lonely road, the turf on the verges, the heather and all,
When into view comes the lone cyclist (no sheepfarmer he)
(But girt like a sheepfarmer, or better say an Aran Islander,
In his *báinín* waistcoat and *crios* and baggy and homespun britches)
Bearded yet trim-bearded, bare-headed, freewheeling and blithe.
And then he was past and we were ongoing at speed,
In post-observational silence. Which McGahern then broke.
'A brush with arts there, I'd say,' says John, full of glee,
A phrase that has come in handy over the years.
But the years, the years-o! That's what I felt, years
Like the big, far, furrowing silence over mountain and moor
We drove through that day – that's what I felt
When I read your 'View of the Bridge'.

But also a great benediction, and desire to bless,
To say of your heart what the song says of those Donegal ones –
'Sure your hearts are like your mountains in
The homes of Donegal'.

Dear Mighty Ireland

Professor of Poetry, dear *file*, dear friend,
If an angel of the Lord had appeared
The tidings of joy could not have been better
Than the tide that came in off and under that bridge.

Le grá
Seamus

Durcan had sent SH a typescript of his poem 'A View of the Bridge', in which a provincial shopkeeper tells of catching sight of SH and John McGahern, 'our two world-famous authors, strolling slowly, / Strolling very slowly, fresh as daisies, arm in arm at eleven o'clock in the morning . . .' The more touchy response of McGahern, to whom Durcan had also sent a copy, can be found in *The Letters of John McGahern*, edited by Frank Shovlin (2021). SH's style of versification here takes its cue from Durcan's poem, which concludes with the phrase, 'Isn't life gas?'

'*báinín*': jacket of white homespun woollen cloth; '*crios*': a belt.

2006

District and Circle was published in April in the UK, in May in the USA.

Some months later, the habitual hurtle and bustle of SH's public life was interrupted by a stroke that laid him low after a celebration with friends in Donegal; but instead of forcing him to reduce the volume of his correspondence, the illness brought him so many messages of sympathy – what he himself was to describe with rueful wit as a 'tsunami of love and kindness' – that as soon as it was possible for him to do so he was writing back to well-wishers and others from his hospital bed.

To Henri Cole

MS H. Cole

6 January 2006 [Co. Derry]

Cher Henri –

Old Christmas Day, as they used to call it here, and I'm actually in Co. Derry, at my brother's house, or perhaps I should say one of my brothers' houses, since there are four of them living within six miles of each other . . . Our sister is in hospital for a mastectomy, so I came up yesterday and will visit her later on to-day.

But just as I was setting out, the mail arrived, and your letter and lovely account of our Dolphin evening were slipped into my briefcase, unread. Just now I have read both and am a bit lightheaded with gratitude and joy. Surprised by the latter, indeed, but not by your wonderful way of inducing it – strictness of report, pinpoint reliability of detail, supply of rich information – about the pronunciation of 'quahog', about the lateral line on a haddock – and general truthfulness. The recall is total and makes me sorrier than ever that I didn't keep a diary all the days of my life. But to be remembered so kindly and so thoroughly by you is more than adequate recompense.

I also greatly appreciate your delicacy and discretion in asking about the non-communion taking and so on. I've no problem at all about the 'tea-pot' being reported, but am shy of making the funeral story more public than it is. Later, yes, when you like, if you wish, but at the moment it just feels too intimate for inclusion.

The direct, inclusive telling is a natural bonus of your forthright, clear-eyed, moral gaze at the world and those of us in it with you. I am honoured and sweetened by writing that has a light touch and enough weight to mark the soul.

I thank you also for the Paris address – but it's unlikely I'll get there. On the other hand, there's a fish restaurant or two in Dublin –
Seamus

'Our sister': Sheena, the senior of SH's two sisters, married to Tony McCormick.
Cole had written an account of a meal with SH at Dolphin Seafood, a restaurant – now closed – on Cambridge's Massachusetts Avenue. A version of it was eventually published as 'Dinner with Seamus Heaney: A Remembrance', in the *New Republic* of 30 August 2013. The incident SH wanted to be suppressed concerned his refusal to take communion at his mother's funeral mass, in 1984; SH and Cole had also confided to each other their mothers' euphemisms for the male genitals, Margaret Heaney favouring 'little teapot' when talking to her oldest child.

To Paul Muldoon

TS Emory

15 February 2005

Glanmore Cottage, Ashford,
Co. Wicklow

Dear Paul,

Horse Latitudes is a great book. Hurt longitudes. Mortal bearings. Or barings. The preternatural rage of reference (I meant range but let that stand) and reach of associations are all aswim with the pain that gives power from below. I had been dipping, as they say, into it, but last night I sat here and read it through, and now that I've been there I won't forget the experience. The opening and closing sequences are far out achievements, the way they combine so utterly *cri* and *crise* and *croidhe*, the crescent high of composition and the cruelties of cancer. The Donne allusions are brilliantly to the point. One little room, one stanza here is up to everywhere. Language jubilates, intelligence investigates. Procedures proceed while the poetry makes its passes. And I rejoice in the way the ancestral Armagh still makes its presence felt and metamorphoses as marvellously and even more marvellously than before. Tremendous writerly joy in the work as well as furious stand-off. Old country and new world mulbooned *abú*. We should be rushing the pitch and carrying you shoulder high.

Love –
Seamus

Horse Latitudes, Muldoon's tenth collection, perhaps his most grieving, is dedicated to the memory of his sister, Maureen, who had died of ovarian cancer in 2005.

Croidhe (the Irish for 'heart') and *cri* are pronounced identically; 'mulbooned *abú*' alludes to Michael Joseph McCann's rousing song of the 1840s, 'O'Donnell Abú' ('O'Donnell For Ever').

To George O'Brien

TS O'Brien

15 February 2005

Glanmore Cottage, Ashford,
Co. Wicklow

Dear George,

You should have heard from me after the good letter you sent before Christmas. But after your petrine poem, there's no excuse. The rhymes and the rock of it I loved. Croagh Patrick/elastic. Tuam and uaim. The boy from the Moy (altered boy?) better look to his aurals. The parochial will report you to the Provincial. You'll be moved to Malin. So just as well you're headed for Lisbon.

Marie and I have been to that town twice and loved it. I envy you Brasilia Café, Casa Pessoa, the fish restaurants, the architecture, the general buzz of the place. I went first as the guest of the Portuguese/Irish society and was kept at Lawrence's hotel in Sintra (see under Byron, in any sense you like). Did a reading for them in aforesaid Casa. And did another in the same place a couple of years ago, en route to University of Coimbra – where once again I bowed my head to the swinging hood. Coimbra also worth a visit, as is Porto, where my very anglified, slightly aristocratic Portuguese translator, Rui Carvalho Homem, hangs out in the English Department of the University. If ever you think of going up there, you should contact him. And at Coimbra, a very decent big quiet man – who perfectly fits Lowell's description of Larkin as 'a large undangerous drinker' – Stephen Wilson, also in Roinn na Béarla. Or an Bhéarla? *Tá mo chuid Ghaeilge caillte agam.*

I regret to say I've not read the whole of the McGahern memoir. Before it was published I listened to the cello as he wrote about the lanes and loanings of Leitrim/Cavan, and attended to different bits digested here and there. And I've taken a big chunk out of the middle of the book where the death gets ready to happen and the move is made to the barracks. John can do the thing truly and heartbreakingly, but B. Friel would more than share your unease. He thinks the mother hagiography is a derogation, almost a scandal. The writery/priesty fragrance is too much for him. And I know what he means, and why you had to take, as you say, 'an obscure line' with the book. I feel – what shits we have to be – he's got too good at what he does.

Not something that will be said of Seamus, mind you – *District and Circle* being due out in April, an amalgam as much as a collection, but for a while I had the George Herbert syndrome, felt the sun and rain and relished versing. I think my own favourite is 'The Tollund Man in Springtime', but there are one or two others. If you send me your Lisbon address I'll get a copy to you. If it says it's for review, it's not – merely a ploy to have Faber's charge it to their list. What shits etc.

It would be great if you were about TCD over the summer. Or if we could get to Lisbon for a weekend before the end of June. But that's not likely to happen. Because of the book, I've written myself into far too many fests and to-ings and fro-ings: a weekend each for the Abbey, Cúirt, Queen Elizabeth Hall, Hay-on-Wye, I could go on . . .

(I'm also doing my best to keep quiet the fact that I share a birthday with centenarian Sam.)

You'll enjoy Lisbon. And deserve to.
Seamus

16.ii.'06 – a day later, since I have no printer down in Glanmore. By a wonderful coincidence I met Stephen Wilson in TCD last night, at a lecture by Durcan (now Ireland Prof. of P.) on Hartnett. He knew the O'Brien writings and promises to send me on addresses etc.

And when I met him, I realized he wasn't large at all – a kindly Englishman who had supplied this large undangerous unsupplied guest (of hon., at reception, where nobody asks you would you like another) with the needful.

Heigho.

O'Brien's 'petrine poem' was, according to his own description, a 'piece of satirical doggerel abjuring the Church ("on this rock") re clerical abuse'. About to spend the spring semester at the Universidade de Lisboa, he never received addresses for either of the recommended contacts.

O'Brien's Moy is the Co. Mayo river, not Paul Muldoon's Co. Armagh birthplace as SH appears to have assumed.

'Roinn an Bhéarla': Department of English; the following sentence can be translated as 'I have lost my Irish'.

O'Brien had written about John McGahern's *Memoir* in *Dublin Review* 22 (Spring 2006).

'centenarian Sam': Samuel Beckett, born 13 April 1906.

To Noel Russell

TS Russell

18 April 2006 191 Strand Road, Dublin 4

Dear Noel,

What to say? So much generous forethought, so much effort of organization of people and time, such a wide spectrum of interests covered, such deeply affecting contributions from everybody who spoke. Yesterday's features moved me far more than I could have anticipated. I suppose I was in some sort of denial about the actual extent of the tribute you were planning, but now I am lapped in a backwash of gratitude.

Great formal thanks therefore to BBC Northern Ireland for the unstinted nature of the celebration. Deepest personal thanks to you for the sustained and almost familial care you took of the preparation and execution of the recordings. And fondest wishes from Marie and all the family in Bellaghy and environs.

My one regret is that I missed a good few of the 'one off' contributions – over the weekend we were in Wicklow with Marie's sister Anne (who sends her warmest greetings to you) so I started in with the marvellous 10 o'clock programme that included sister Sheena, cousin Biddy Joyce and brother ('one poet in the family is enough') Dan. Then there was Robbie Meredith's excellent take on The Group and Marie-Louise and Stan's finely edited job on the book itself. There was something at once relaxed and thorough about it, which was the reward of good preparation. I thought Marie-Louise's questions came across very naturally, and the eventual placing of the formal readings was very artfully timed and, as it were, toned.

Over the years I've been blessed with much welcome for my work, but nothing sweeter or truer ever happened than what happened on Monday. I hope that after all the work you put into it, you will feel with Robert Frost that 'strongly spent is kept'.

With renewed gratitude and regard,
Seamus

On 13 April, SH's birthday, BBC Radio Ulster had celebrated the 40th anniversary of the publication of *Death of a Naturalist* with a number of programmes broadcast throughout the day. Noel Russell produced the programme described in the third paragraph, recording the voices of people in and around Bellaghy who had memories of SH and who read poems they were fond of; Robbie Meredith produced a programme about The Group; Marie-Louise Muir, then presenter of *Arts Extra*, interviewed SH; Stan Ferguson arranged readings of individual poems.

To Jane McCabe

MS J. McCabe

9 May 2006 [Four Seasons Philadelphia, PA]

Dear Jane,

This is crazy – not to have spoken to you before I took off on this 2½ week fly-about. Please excuse me for all those promises, promises on the message machine, message machine, and for being in a Four Seasons Hotel . . . *They* put me here, the sponsors, the trustees of the Philadelphia Free Library – where I am due to read in a few hours' time.

Often you have been in my thoughts – as I hurtle around with too much company, your own left-aloneness comes to mind and I am suddenly aware of the loss we have all suffered, but you in particular, who lived closest to the great solar spirit and felt most his central power and sustaining warmth. Wilfred Owen speaks somewhere of 'a cold star' and that stellar cold must be blowing round you now and again these days – but I hope the vernal airs that blow on the burial ground nearby work their kindlier effects also.

I get back from this jaunt on May 22, and on the following Sunday 28, I am being shipped to Hay-on-Wye for a 'gala opening'. I'm afraid I'll just have to go with the crazy festival flow for 36 hours, and then get away, since M. and I take off for a second American / hon. degree trip on Saturday 3 June. Crazy, crazy, crazy, I know . . .

Let's talk about your coming over to Dublin when things quieten. I mentioned June 14/15 – which would involve my reading at the Dublin Writers' Festival. Maybe, on mature reflection, it might be better to wait for a quieter time, since I'll have a bunch of Poles on my hands that weekend (17–19/20) – people who hosted M. and me in Kraków and who will need our time and attention in Dublin. So it goes.

Isn't this fancy notepaper?

Here's hoping your valiant spirit holds up and holds out and that you keep going.

Listen to that river in the birch trees. Love – Seamus

Bernard McCabe had died at the end of March 2006.

SH's final line picks up on the two-line poem accompanying his dedication 'For Bernard and Jane McCabe' of *The Haw Lantern*: 'The river-bed, dried-up, half-full of leaves. // Us, listening to a river in the trees.'

To Vona Groarke

PC Groarke

2 June 2006

This (overleaf) is why they were called 'dippers' in Co. Derry.

Meanwhile, I've been born again thanks to your letter about *District and Circle*. Flicker-lit, in fact. It does me good to know you like the title poem, which I trust but cannot quite justify other than to say, it's the ordinary thing disordinaried. And 'The Aerodrome': again, it was/ is on the knife-edge between the 'so what' and the 'that's it' – so your notice of it saves it for me. An American edition of the thing should arrive with ye sooner or later. Meanwhile, love to you and Conor and the young. Keep going. Seamus

Vona Groarke (b.1964), Irish poet, was at this time married to the Irish poet, later novelist, Conor O'Callaghan (b.1968). SH's postcard shows John Steuart Curry's painting, *Baptism in Kansas* (from the Whitney Museum of American Art).

To Karl Kirchwey

MS Kirchwey

2 June 2006

Glanmore Cottage, Ashford,
Co. Wicklow

Karl – How delightful and perdurable the Plantin poem and the Kirchwey translation. George Herbert would be proud of you both, as would John Crowe Ransom. Tough reasonableness and much lyric grace. I'm delighted to know it and to have it in its one out of a hundred impression.

And, yes, by God, the other Karl's your man for the anapestic pentameter. Not to mention the feminine rhymes: I thought aura /Gomorrah deserved an ovation – or maybe that should go – a close-run thing in the same stanza – to lattice/gratis.

Gracias, anyhow, my friend. It was a pleasure to see you again, and I walk a little taller because Ma Kirchwey gave the thumbs-up.

Meanwhile, I stagger (or, to be truthful, wing it) back to USA: Princeton honours on Monday and a lecture in the Pierpont Morgan Library on Thursday. No rest for the wicked.

Blessings on you and yours – Seamus

The US poet Karl Kirchwey (b.1956) had sent SH both 'The Happiness of This World', his translation of a sonnet by Christophe Plantin (1520–89), and the poem 'Fireworks' by Karl Shapiro (1913–2000).

'Ma Kirchwey' was, in fact, Kirchwey's mother-in-law, who had voiced hearty approval of SH after a reading at the Y in New York.

To Alasdair Macrae

PC Macrae

21 June 2006

[Hawthornden Castle, near Edinburgh]

Good to hear from La Rochelle. A few days after that K. Miller and I – driven by A. O'Hagan – did our Alloway to Auld Reekie tour, a night in Ayrshire, a night in Tibbie Shiel's inn, a night in Edinburgh. Kirk Alloway, Brig o' Doon, a visit to Eddie Morgan, an ascent of Cairnpapple Hill, a visit to Hogg in Ettrick Kirkyard, a feed in Leith (The Vintners) with J. McMillan, D. Paterson and M. Linklater – all arranged by the vigorous O'Hagan. We must talk about Edinburgh

Fest. nearer the date. Drue Heinz has us kidnapped – at last – and I'm dodging press and radio already. (Had a happy morning to myself – when the southron folk were already on their way – in the Portrait Gallery. Marvellous place.) Love – Seamus

Postcard image is of Sir William Allan's painting, *The Celebration of the Birthday of James Hogg*, in the collection of the Scottish National Portrait Gallery.

The Scottish novelist Andrew O'Hagan (b.1968) describes the jaunt he undertook in the company of Karl Miller and SH in his introduction to Miller's book of essays *Tretower to Clyro* (2011); the poet Edwin Morgan (1920–2010), the first to be appointed Scots Makar (or national poet) lived in Glasgow; the company in Leith included composer James MacMillan (b.1959), poet Don Paterson (b.1963) and journalist Magnus Linklater (b.1942); the cultural philanthropist Drue Heinz (1915–2018) offered hospitality at her writers' retreat, Hawthornden Castle, south-east of Edinburgh.

To Karl Miller

TS Emory

20 July 2006 191 Strand Road, Dublin 4

Dear Karl,

A week ago at this time we were getting ready to leave Tibbie and advance on Eddie: we were in Scotland all right, but even then I felt we were in Tír na nÓg, and in the meantime the feeling has, if anything, increased. Several times since I came home I had an impulse to telephone you, but hesitated because so much had been experienced and enjoyed and satisfied there was not much left to say. Those days were some of the best of my life. *Laus deo*, as Hopkins might have cried, for all the language and laughter. And for Tinker Belle. But *laus tibi* also, for being with us. I came home renovated, knowing it couldn't have been better, knowing all over again that Thomas Moore was right when he said, 'the best charms of nature improve / When we see them reflected in looks that we love.' There's no need for photographs to keep Kirk Alloway, Brig o' Doon, the Hogg headstone, the Ettrick water and the Braes of Yarrow in mind. Or the Duke of B.'s pies for that matter, or the Paterson versus Linklater bout in Leith. Both of them gey sensible men, for all that.

My one worry, and I know it was yours far more, was that you had to leave Jane at a moment when she was still in pain and doldrums. Marie and I hope that some improvement has come and some relief will be felt. I'll ring next week – after I get back from celebrating the Feast of Mary Magdalene at Magdalene College.

No doubt Andrew will be in touch when he gets back from his other holiday this week.

Have you thought of introducing a swear box in no. 26?

Love to you both –
Seamus

For 'gey', Scots for 'very', SH writes, phonetically, 'guy'.

To Dennis O'Driscoll and Julie O'Callaghan MS Emory

31 August 2006

St Catherine's Ward,
St Vincent's Hospital, Dublin 4

Dear Dennis, Dear Julie,

You may have heard that the physios here told Marie to bring in 'one of my tracksuits': I must be the only man who got his first track-suit thanks to a stroke.

It all happened luckily, if it had to happen, in Donegal, surrounded by friends, with my speech and my wits unimpaired. We'd been to B. Friel's housewarming the night before – B. still recovering from his more severe incident in 2004 – and T. Kilroy was there: my reading of the whole thing was 'the curse of Field Day'. (Also present was the greatly depressed T. Paulin.)

I was looking forward to making a big push on the interview this week and next, but now I console myself with the thought that I've gained October (no Harvard this time) . . . M. is keeping me away from the iBook at the moment.

I spent Saturday afternoon on my back on the bed in Viking guest house reading through the Bloodaxe book. Very proud to be cited so often by you in such company. Making a lot of notes in the back for future reference. I thought that Glyn Maxwell's remark about (was it) form – at the start of one of the chapters – was first rate . . . and that the organization of the book was magnificent. It must have taken a hell of a lot of time and work to get the different things into chapters, and the titling of the chapters in itself is a bit of a triumph. Here's hoping it will be greeted with the gratitude it deserves – certainly all poets and readers of poetry will be in your debt. This fellow especially.

Many thanks for contacting Gerry Smyth. He sent a copy of the *Green Knight*, but I'm afraid it may be some time (if that is the right expression) before I'll be delivering my piece. M. (as I said) forbids the iBook in here.

If all goes well, I'll be in rehabilitation to-morrow in Donnybrook. I've no mobile phone in here, but am feeling good. My spirits are greatly strengthened by the fact that movement and some strength have come back into my left leg. On Sunday morning it was as dead as a post, no messages travelling in the timber, no twinkle toe, all log-dull.

So, for the moment, gratitude . . . To you dear ones especially, for all that you have given of your time and yourselves. See you soon. With love –

Seamus

PS I'm telling everybody that the relevant text is Mark 2:1–12.

St Vincent's University Hospital is Dublin's principal general hospital and regional centre for emergency care. SH had been taken there, via Letterkenny Hospital, following his stroke on 27 August. He had woken, the morning after a party at the house of Brian and Anne Friel, to find he could not move his leg, whereupon he and Marie Heaney immediately realised he had suffered a stroke and their response to the situation was swift and effective.

The book of Dennis O'Driscoll's that SH had been enjoying was *The Bloodaxe Book of Poetry Quotations*.

The passage from St Mark concerns the miraculous cure of the man 'sick of the palsy', which became the source of SH's poem 'Miracle', in *Human Chain*.

To Rand and Beth Brandes — MS Emory

6 September 2006 — Royal Hospital, Dublin 4

Dear Rand and Beth,

Even though I began to write October as the month above, I assure you the faculties are all working. By now Marie or the grapevine will have got news to you about my stroke, mild at the time and by now well recovered from. We were up at a party in Donegal to celebrate the housewarming of Brian Friel's new holiday home, and the morning after, in the guest house, I found myself immobilized. Power gone from my left leg and left arm, but speech and mind unaffected. Luckily, M. was in the twin bed, and friends in the neighbour rooms – Des Kavanagh and Mary, Peter Fallon and Jean, Tom Kilroy and Julie, so when the ambulance came there were stout arms and kind faces close by to get the bulk down the stairs. Thence to Letterkenny hospital, where I was scanned and tested and lodged for the next day and a half. Christopher and Michael drove up from Dublin, Marie and the Kavanaghs stayed close, Dan and Mary came over from Co. Derry, Sheena and Tony called on the way from *their* Donegal place – a caravan, not a house – and Brian and Anne Friel came in also – 'Different strokes for different folks,' says Friel, who had his own in November 2004. Anyhow, the good news was that my big toe on the left foot moved on Monday evening, just before I was put into an ambulance that boneshook me all the way to St Vincent's hospital, which, as you may remember, is only a few hundred yards from 191 Strand Road. I was in there from Monday night until Friday afternoon, when I was transferred to this more spacious and generally pleasanter environment – a place for physio and rehab. – now feeling good as the strength and balance comes back and Marie and Michael and Chris and Catherine even (home last weekend) continue their loving rota. Love being one of the reliable cures in this condition.

I hope this hasn't sounded too much like a policeman's evidence, but I wanted to give you some sense of how it all went and to reassure you that I'm in good order, glad of the excuse to lie low for a few months and get some reading done.

Hope all goes well for the pair of you and that Blake continues to tread the path of glory. As to the bibliography, it is now being taken better care of, I hope, if not taking care of itself.

All love and good wishes to the house of Brandes –
Seamus

SH had written a recommendation for Blake Brandes, son of Rand and Beth, who had duly been awarded a Marshall Fellowship; and Faber had recently agreed to take on Rand Brandes's Heaney bibliography, originally to be published by Gallery Press as *A Poet's Album*.

To Grigory Kruzhkov

MS Kruzhkov

9 September 2006 Royal Hospital, Dublin 4

Dear Grigory,

Sincere apologies for the late reply to your letter of July 12. In early August I was 'on the road' in England and Scotland, at Stratford-upon-Avon, Grasmere (Wordsworth's Dove Cottage) and the Edinburgh Festival. Then, two weeks ago, I had a stroke – fortunately a relatively mild one – and am now recuperating satisfactorily. My speech was unaffected, my mind stayed clear and only my left leg and left arm suffered immobilization. Both are happily returned to movement, feeling and strength and my balance steadies day by day. The prognosis is good, as are my spirits.

So. Please feel free to make whatever interventions you deem necessary in the translation of the essays. You are the master and the tuner and the conductor of the Russian score. Your ear for English and your literary alertness to echo and allusion are nonpareil and I trust your judgement completely. So, *cher ami*, proceed. I'm only sorry you have so much work on your hands. But then your hands can be miraculously refreshed by laying them on the beauteous Dasha. Much love to you both, from Marie and me –

Seamus

PS I don't expect to be at the above address for more than a couple of weeks more. S. xxx

The Russian poet and writer of books for children Grigory Kruzhkov (b.1945) has translated numerous English and American poets, from Wyatt and Donne to Frost and Stevens, into his own tongue. In 1985, he happened to be preparing an anthology of Irish poets for publication, when he and SH were brought together by chance and on the spot settled down to a long, detailed discussion of it, poet by poet. The book of SH's own writings mentioned here included not just essays but poems as well, and was published in Moscow as *Chur, moio!* (2007). Dasha was Kruzhkov's wife.

To Willem Groenewegen

MS Groenewegen

12 September 2006 [Royal Hospital, Dublin 4]

Dear Willem,

Please excuse the brevity of this note. Your delightful, most attentive letter deserves better, but at the moment I am in hospital. On August 27 I had a stroke, mercifully a mild one, from which I am now recovering. Speech never affected, feeling and movement restored to left leg and arm, balance steadying.

What I'm not recovering from, however, is the mighty influx of mail that comes in, day by day. All welcome, but not all as rich with recollection and renewed pleasure as your letter with its news of Rutger's enjoyment of our Dublin ramble and reading – and the wonderful photographs. I thought the event in the Project theatre was one of the best of its kind, in that we both suited each other – and the audience.

My fondest wishes, therefore, to Rutger and his wife and to you and your girlfriend – and congratulations to all on the review in the current *PN Review* (no. 171). Seamus

The poetry translator Willem Groenewegen (b.1971) had accompanied the eminent Dutch poet Rutger Kopland (1934–2012) when the latter, before a joint reading with SH, had been invited to lunch in Strand Road. Groenewegen treasures a memory of their host washing cherries at the kitchen sink.

'suited each other': because of similar build, each with shaggy white hair and spectacles?

To Adam Kirsch

MS Emory

16 September 2006 Royal Hospital, Dublin 4

Dear Adam,

Too bad about the hold-up in answering those questions. But to quote the Dublin triad, 'This is it, this is the thing, this is what you're up against.'

The handwriting slopes, by the way, not because of any after-effect of the stroke, but because of the angle I'm tilted at in the bed: the light is directly overhead and if I sit straight, I overshadow the page.

Anyhow, it's 7:00 a.m., and when I woke I thought I'd have a go at written answers – Dennis, I realize, may have made arrangements for a phone link in the meantime. But even so . . .

1. Teaching and writing have tended to proceed on parallel lines, but there have been times when there was indeed carry-over from the classroom to the 'creative' work. In the 1970s, for example, I found myself learning to relish the poetry of Andrew Marvell and Sir Thomas Wyatt, and getting a handle on poetry of plainer speech than I had dwelt with heretofore. Which led me on to a new appreciation of middle Yeats, of the short three-beat line and forward-driving syntax, and that paid in, in turn, to a poem like 'Casualty' in *Field Work*.

   The traffic, however, was usually the other way. My teaching was animated by what I was reading and being excited by as a poet. Early on, Ted Hughes. Very early on, Hopkins. I taught/used Hughes's poems in the school in Belfast where I started as a teacher. I don't miss teaching. I'm learning to take my time for myself. When I was teaching, I gave a lot of my mind and anxiety to it. There was always something clenched and anxious in me until the classes were over.

   Once I was 'on the job', once I had got started, I felt safe enough, but the anticipation made me tense.
2. Harvard created wonderful conditions for me as a writer – but the writing was done, almost entirely, when I got home. The appointment gave me economic safety, writerly support and intellectual self-respect. <Plus 8 months to myself every year.> From the beginning, and before the beginning, as it were, I felt welcome. Even though Helen Vendler wasn't on the Harvard faculty when I came first in 1979, she was a guardian spirit; Robert Fitzgerald gave me the use of his study in Pusey Library. Monroe and Brenda Engel kept open house, Bob and Jana Kiely made me at home in Adams House.

   Then, too, in 1979, Frank Bidart, whom I'd met in Dublin after the death of Robert Lowell – he was over seeing Caroline Blackwood – Frank brought me into his circle of friends, including Robert Pinsky and Jean Williamson. And most amazingly of all, through Frank and Helen, Marie and

I were often in the company of Elizabeth Bishop and Alice Methfessel.

So Harvard meant a lot in my writing life from the beginning, even though I didn't actually do much composition on the spot.

The poems I did write there include 'Alphabets' – the 1984 Phi Beta Kappa poem – and 'A Sofa in the Forties'. And, of course, the John Harvard poem for the 350th anniversary – 'Villanelle for an Anniversary'.

3. Irish readers, British readers, American readers: is it odd that I haven't a clue about how differently they react. Or better say, I cannot find the words to describe my hunch about them.

   Best to say that once a poem is finished I trust it to make its way, and I trust readers will find their way to it, if the thing has got itself rightly expressed.

4. I felt implicated in American affairs in a new way over the past five years. Outraged at the blatant lies about Iraq's involvement in al-Qaeda, at the regime's arrogance and stupidity, Guantanamo Bay and all the rest of it. But the poems at the start of *D. and C.* – 'Anahorish 1994', 'The Aerodrome' – aren't particularly aimed as criticism. On the contrary, there's a recognition of the big contribution to world order made in Europe during WWII. 'Anything Can Happen', on the other hand, is not only about the atrociousness of the September 11 attack, it's also a premonition of the deadly retaliation that was bound to come.

   And also, incidentally, 'Anything Can Happen' is a poem that arose from teaching. I'd talked about the Horace Ode (I, 35) in a lecture I gave at Harvard in the fall of 2000 – entitled 'Bright Bolts' – and remembered it after the Twin Towers attack (see Amnesty Pamphlet: 'Anything Can Happen', Townhouse Publishing, Dublin 2009).

5. 'The feeling I attribute to Miłosz in Part 1 of 'Out of this World' is actually and intimately my own, and is indeed 'the legacy of a devout upbringing'. It more or less sums up the story.

6. 'The Birch Grove' is actually set in one planted by my friends Bernard and Jane McCabe, at the back of their garden in Ludlow in Shropshire.

But yes, I suppose I did feel a certain 'public' pressure always. One of the very first poems I wrote was 'Docker' – 'That fist would drop a hammer on a Catholic' – and one of the sturdiest was 'Requiem for the Croppies', written 50 years after 1916. 'Being responsible' and what it means, what it demands, has indeed preoccupied me – maybe too much. But this is it, this is the thing, this is what you're up against.

It's now 8:05. Hope this will be legible and tolerable, maybe helpful also.

Fondest wishes. I really admire what you've been doing.

Hope we can meet again at some stage.

Sincerely
Seamus

The US poet and literary critic Adam Kirsch (b.1976) had attended SH's poetry workshop as a Harvard undergraduate. His profile of SH appeared in the November–December issue of the *Harvard Magazine*, of which he was a contributing editor.

To George O'Brien

MS O'Brien

20 September 2006 [St Vincent's Hospital, Dublin 4]

Dear George,

Here I am in a corridor of St Vincent's, in a queue for the cardiac boys and girls. The palsy has improved but it turns out that the ticker is sluggish. *So.* A pacemaker has been recommended. But before they can go ahead with that, I have to swallow a camera which will inspect the inner chambers for clots, cloteens or clotlets. And then, if all is safe, they'll make a breast pocket above the left nipple and stitch in our friend. It all goes to prove the truth of Harold Nicolson's remark – printed on my Get Well Card from the poet Mahon – that 'one of the minor pleasures of life is to be slightly ill'.

One of the major pleasures was to have that while/those whiles with you in the summertime, and to get your card and gift of the Machado. I'm very glad to have the latter – and in that particular translation/edition. Machado is a lacuna in my literary awareness, and I'm grateful for the chance to remedy that.

I'm also grateful, to tell the truth, for doctors' orders telling me to take things a lot easier. It may be that I'll be signing off from the big Ulster/April push on DC. All to be checked on later, but I've sent preliminary dousings of the promises to C. Carson. I don't think P.M. was going to bother, one way or another. So.

Bless you, *a chara* – and see you as soon as I can – *O'Neilli an chéad* [. . .]

Seamus

The book O'Brien had given SH was *Antonio Machado: Selected Poems* (Harvard University Press, 1982), translated by Alan S. Trueblood.

In the event, SH was unable to appear in person at the symposium, *Befitting Emblems of Adversity: Lyric and Crisis*, that O'Brien was organising on behalf of the Lannan Foundation, but he sent a recording to be played at the final session instead.

O'Brien says the last few words of Irish, which tail off into illegibility, make little or no sense.

To Donald Fanger

MS Fanger

27 September 2006

Not that there's much froth on what they dole out here . . . I think instead of the Fleurie we shared in The Harvest with Master Fuentes . . . but even there, because of the warfarin, it's one 'unit' a day for many a day to come. Partly because of the obedience to orders and the invigilation of Mrs Heaney, partly because of proper caution. But spontinuity could change all that.

Very glad to have your letter with its cheering news. You're a kind of pacemaker for the rest of us – the thing is on my mind since I'm having one implanted, embedded, insinuated next week. What it does is give me (at last) rhythm. An added preventative measure, anyhow.

The other citizens in this ward – 4 of them – gaze in wonderment at me every morning as I get out the pen and paper, the stamps and the envelopes, and demurely lower the eyes, shutting myself off.

Here's to the success of the Gorky book, which I greatly look forward to. (To which I greatly etc., given that I've been to Harvard, if only as a professor.)

Sorry to miss our biennial colloguings. But, thankfully, there will be another time. Love to Leonie. Keep cooking –

Seamus

'Not that there's much froth': accompanying the two sheets of this letter is a third showing, in photocopy, a cartoon mole reaching for a freshly pulled pint, with the caption underneath: '"His condition is improving rapidly – he is sitting up in bed blowing the froth off his medicine." Flann O'Brien'.

Fanger recalls: 'I introduced Seamus and my friend Carlos Fuentes to each other at a lunch at the Harvest restaurant in Cambridge. Seamus broke the ice by telling about the Mexican who asked an Irishman whether his people had a word in their language like the Spanish *mañana*. "Yes," the Irishman answered, "but with us it doesn't carry the same sense of urgency."'

'spontinuity': an 'inadvertent contribution to English' by Fanger's friend, Polish actor and writer Andrzej Wirth (1927–2019), that delighted SH.

The 'Gorky book' was Fanger's *Gorky's Tolstoy and Other Reminiscences*.

To Anne Stevenson

MS Cambridge

28 September 2006 Royal Hospital, Dublin 4

Dearest Anne,

Many thanks for sending *A Lament*: I'm still in hospital, strength and feeling and balance all restored, but what's missing is a bit of silence. I look forward to getting out of this ward – five men, Bardolphs and Petoes, Malvolios and Horatios, mind-numbers and ear-polluters, but, as Falstaff says, mortal men, mortal men.

I've not read a poem since I came in. Thrillers, yes: Robert Harris, James Lee Burke, Ian Rankin, Henning Mankell – but ne'ery a serious page of literature. My window-sill is heaped with the higher class of volume – the new Donne biography (a thriller too, I believe), Coetzee's *Elizabeth Costello*, a Nadine Gordimer, but there they lie . . .

I yearn to get back to Glanmore, which should be inside the next couple of weeks. In the meantime, this is a laggard note of thanks – and anticipation.

Love –

Seamus

Jesus, Anne! It *reads* like a thriller. When did I last start a book of poems that was – from the start – a page turner?

After I wrote to you this morning, I got permission to go into the 'Family Interview Room' which was free for a few hours and stepped into the flow . . . I know why you might think of the first part as 'better', but there's no telling or deciding. Different buoyancies, velleities, vigours, freshets, risks, frisks . . . There is an utter given, there-you-are-and-where-are-you about the opening strophes, but there is delicious utterance from those shades in the second part. Such lyric joy and literary sport. Real Dantesque truth-telling about the soul/sole poetry of all concerned, stern and accurate, but also the real quiver and swim of excited language; grief and reason, as Brodsky might have said. Glee and gumption. How we'd love Ted and Frances and Peter and Philip (both Philips) to be able to read it. The three-line stanza is a wonderful skimmer along – keeps you limber and trig, trims off the sentiment, tones the muscles all the way down the page.

As M. Longley used to say of the real thing: it passes the jealousy test. Do more.

Much love –
Seamus

Stevenson's 2006 book, *Lament for the Makers*, was described by the poet herself as a 'dream poem' on the medieval model, and among the deceased poets, loved by her, who feature in it are Peter Redgrove, Ted Hughes, Frances Horovitz and Philip Larkin.

To Carol Hughes

MS Hughes

17 October 2006 — 191 Strand Road, Dublin 4

Dear Carol,

What a beautiful, bountiful book. The delights are dolphin-like, the mighty talent rising again and showing his back above the element. I came off my sleeping tablets on Sunday night, but slept only till 4:00 a.m. – then stayed in bed all yesterday morning. In that indolent, slightly bleary condition I got *Selected Translations* and swam in and out of the different coves and caves, safe havens (few) and strange strands. A strong sense of being lifted on the tide of it all, a quickening anticipation of the pleasures of dwelling with it, page by page, and gratitude for Danny's utter gratitude. Marvellous to feel the indomitable quality of the work becoming more and more palpable and obvious. And the volume itself is beautifully jacketed and bound. It looks very good and handles pleasingly. Just the right size/length too, I think.

I got out of hospital last Wednesday – come to think of it, you called Marie just about the time I was due to shift. In the meantime, my pacemaker incision has healed, the thing is in there doing *its* thing (no sense of it, now that most of the tenderness has gone – but lying on the left side at night isn't as easy as it was); generally, I'm steady enough on my feet and confident enough in the world. Just that slight, unpeeled feeling when I walk out – as to the doctor's yesterday, half a mile or a mile to Sandymount. But all that is a matter of (re)building and settling. And the carer is in good order too. Glad to have another phone answerer on hand at home, and to have less driving and visiting.

All well. And, yes, better, now that the warning has been comprehended. Everything cancelled – except our special rendez-vous next July.

I loved the account of the Eliot revels – oh no – it was Ron Schuchard's letter that went into some detail about that – he named Valerie a 'champagne blonde' – but still it seems to have been a jubilant do.

Much love from the carer too.

Seamus

Selected Translations of Ted Hughes was edited by Daniel Weissbort.

To David Batterham

MS Batterham

18 October 2006

[Glanmore Cottage, Ashford,
Co. Wicklow]

Dear David,

A month ago you were in York and I was in the Royal Hospital, Donnybrook – founded 1743, name changed recently from the R. H. for Incurables to something more p.c. – although one wing houses those who won't be going home again. More de-hab than re-hab, but it's all done with great kindness and gumption. The stroke unit has two wards, one for good ole boys, one for tremulous gals, six beds in each, plenty of space between them – since there has to be room for duelling wheelchairs and a table at the centre where they can dock. Luckily, I was the sprightliest among them, with co-ordination, articulation, mastication and my own two feet. My co-mates ranged from one so stricken there was no speech except a desperate trumpeting to a denizen of Dún Laoghaire, a stand-in for O'Casey's Joxer Daly or any of the low life in those Shakespearean history play tavern scenes. He, alas, was articulate, vehement, and wakened early. 'Nurse, nurse, I need the bottle.' 'Nurse, nurse . . .' and then a simple cogent vocative, exclamatory, 'Nurse, fuck it, nurse!' And so it went from 7:00 a.m. until 9:30 breakfast/docking time. Then, 'Nurse, nurse, I need down for a smoke.' At first I couldn't bear him, in the end I enjoyed the performance immensely. He had worked as a joiner in London for 20 years, roamed Kilburn, smoked more than Woodbine and spoke longingly of the Flamingo in Soho. His fantasies were understandable, modest enough, and constantly proclaimed: a six pack or a dozen Guinness, a half bottle of Powers Gold Label, and an afternoon with his fishing rod on Dún Laoghaire Pier. It's only as I write this I realize how much I liked the old bugger in the end.

Anyhow. At this moment Marie and I are down in Glanmore Cottage – I got out of Donnybrook last Wednesday and this is our first night in the dacha. And since Glanmore is a class of a silence-bunker, I incline to write the occasional letter . . . I got great joy from your account of the Wharton victim/victor, your host/harrower in York. Maybe it was as well Val stayed at home. And Joe McCann . . . good at the job, I think, and hence a certain authorial ambivalence in the admiration. I like him, as I do all capable dealers and dodgers – like Bill Clinton, for example, who actually visited me in the Royal. M. and I had been invited to a corporate lunch – we were free, but the corporates were paying €750 apiece, €1000 if you wanted to be in handshake line. Happily, I had my alibi, but I wrote a note to the old rogue, apologizing for having to miss the do. We'd met him in Princeton in June, I'd read in the *New Yorker* how he'd recently quoted a stanza of mine from memory at a celebration of Nelson Mandela in SA, and I'd contributed a verse to his sixtieth birthday greetings album – 'Irish poets, raise your pen, / Bill at three score scores again.' ('Dip' would have been better, but I had second thoughts.) At any rate, it all added up to a certain ease and next thing he landed in the ward, the big arm on the Heaney shoulder, the other hand shaking those of the Dún Laoghaire complainer, the ward sister, the Filipino orderlies, the physios, the tea girls – and Marie's. She had been apprised of his arrival by 'his people' and got in ahead of the outriders. We all repaired to 'the family interview room' and Bill monologued for half an hour. But he's a bright boyo, so the whole thing went off with great brio. And the timing was perfect – that afternoon I went from Donnybrook to another hospital where I would get my pacemaker . . .

Yes, I have one now, in my very own breast pocket. The surgeon was in his togs when I was wheeled into the theatre, everybody masked up, me on my back on the gurney, so he asks, as he strops the knife – 'Have you any questions?' Me: 'Do you come here often?' He: 'Only when I've a couple of drinks on me.' I knew he was the man for the job.

So, now I tick silently. Feel no different. Feel safer, I suppose. Walk again on an equal footing with myself, and plan a regime that derives/deviates from the Joycean triad – for me it's 'indolence, silence and sunning' – for months.

In the words of Flann O'Brien – 'His recovery has been remarkable: he is sitting up in bed blowing the froth off his medicine.'

Much love from us to yous –
Seamus

PS I've been writing this on my knee, in an armchair, and I fear it shows. I got carried away into illegibility. Sorry about that. S.

The letter is headed with a black-and-white photo of armed and uniformed officers standing in front of Crossmaglen RUC Station.

To Jane Miller

TS Emory

22 October 2006

Glanmore Cottage, Ashford,
Co. Wicklow

Dear Jane,

Here we are, the dame and myself, down in the dacha for the weekend. I got out of hospital a week and a half ago, my pace made, my balance steadied, my warning heeded. In the meantime, some old patterns have been cautiously re-established – a couple of glasses of red wine a day are allowed with the warfarin; and some new practices have been tentatively initiated – a walk, for example, to ensure that I now stay on an equal footing with myself.

Sometimes I carry a stick – down here in the country it looks as if I'm out after the cattle – but back on Strand Road the sight of me poking along a footpath would make it look as if I were out swanking in the light of the newspaper reports: last week, for example, the *Sunday Independent* ran a story 'Heaney Recovering from Stroke', and my brother tells me that it appeared also in the *News of the World* (probably the Irish edition).

So, having been issued with the stick, all I need now is the tattered coat . . . I received the current *Raritan*, for which much thanks, and was greatly delighted and instructed by your essay. It is beautifully shaped, Aristotelian even, with that tonic personal beginning, the variegated animated middle and the ineluctable Russian end. Nothing senescent to be found, in the tone or the material, nothing but brio and embroilment with the subject – 'a credible intelligence showing no signs of collapse', to alter one of my favourite (and your attractively fierce) phrases in the conclusion. Not being much of a novel reader, I got a necessary introduction to Rabbit, although all those quotations from Barnes and Atwood and co. had a nice self-sufficiency about them and I didn't feel at the slightest disadvantage. And then the *coup(s) de grâce* in your citation of and commentary upon the Tolstoy and the Chekhov. *Sacré bleu!*

Catherine had told me you wanted to talk a bit about old age/my illness etc., and now I see why. But it might be easier if I scribble something since I tend to clam and flip when a discussion gets personal – and I can see that personal is what's required here.

When I thought about it last night, I remembered a Beckett sentence which typically chases its own tail, but it still fairly well expresses my take on the subject: 'I have been waiting all my life to be old.' Although that in fact is only half of the sentence as it was reported to me, by Derek Mahon. Derek went to see the reticent Sam in Paris, late in his life, and given Derek's own shortness of small talk and Beckett's gift for silence, what happened was less a conversation than a series of quick forays into speech and quick collapsings out of it – as follows:

D.M.: And what do you think of your new fellow laureate?
S.B.: Who's that?
D.M.: William Golding.
S.B. (not quite catching the name, remembering an old Dublin crony): Don't tell me Louis Golding won the Nobel Prize!
D.M.: No, no, William Golding, the English novelist.
S.B.: Oh? I'm afraid I don't keep up enough with these things. Did he write one called *King of the Rings*?

But the relevant foray was this, coming out unilaterally: 'I have been waiting all my life to be old, and you know, it's marvellous. The memory goes, and the vocabulary goes.'

It's not that I have been waiting for to be old, more that from early on I was (in Yeats's phrase) 'beginning the preparation for my death'. When I was young, from first awareness until at least the early teens, I dwelt in the womb of religion. My consciousness was formed, maybe better say dominated, by Catholic conceptions, formulations, pedagogies, prayers and practices. All kinds of simplifications of these matters coexisted with the canonical expression of all kinds of orthodox doctrine. As in: The soul at birth is like a clean white handkerchief and when we die there will be a particular judgement and if the soul is still clean we will go to heaven. Which was another way of saying you would go to heaven provided you died in a state of sanctifying grace. Or alternatively, you would be sent to eternal damnation in hell if you died in a state of mortal sin. So the drama of last things, nay the melodrama and terror of them were there from the start. You'd hardly got out of the cot, yet already you were envisaging the death bed. Along the way then you would learn about the sacrament of extreme unction, learn to talk knowledgeably about holy viaticum and the final anointing of the organs of sense with chrism and so on; you had your being within the great echoing acoustic of a universe of light and dark, death and everlasting life, divine praises and prayers for the dead: as in 'Grant them eternal rest, O Lord, and let perpetual light shine upon them. May their souls and the souls of all the faithful departed rest in peace. Amen.'

All this (which I don't think a great exaggeration [of] what was going on) seems to me to have provided a primal ordering, a structured reading [of] the mortal condition that I've never quite deconstructed. No doubt I might have talked differently, certainly more diffidently, if you'd asked me about these matters thirty years ago. Naturally I went on to school myself as best I could from catechised youth into secular adult. The study of literature, the discovery of wine, women and song, the arrival of poetry, then marriage and family, plus a general, generational assent to the proposition that God is dead, all that cloaked and draped out the first visionary world. And yet in maturity, my growing familiarity with the myths of the classical world (and Dante's *Commedia* – Irish Catholic subculture with high cultural ratification) provided an imaginary cosmology that corresponded well enough to the original: poetic imagination proffering a world of light and a world of dark, a shadow world, not so much an afterlife as an after-image of life.

So, I think in my case getting older has been a matter of fitting in with those archetypal patterns. For years I've been writing poems where I meet ghosts/shades, and among those are some of the ones I cherish and value the most: 'Casualty', 'Station Island', 'The Tollund Man in Springtime', 'District and Circle' (where I more or less ghostify myself). Then, too, one of the things I've done with most relish recently is a version of the Messenger's speech in *Oedipus at Colonus*, where [he] tells of the old king simply disappearing, being assumed into earth rather than into heaven. But then I've always had a weakness for the elegiac.

Your trope of 'inhabiting old age' is wonderfully suggestive. It makes old age, as it were, the right country for old men: souls clapping hands and singing, a surge of bodies hurling sticks and crutches into the air, like some miraculous exodus from Lourdes.

It strikes me, of course, that the airy mood of all of the above comes from my own recent 'turn'. That's what they used to call a stroke in Co. Derry, and what they may still call it elsewhere: the word, at any rate, does convey both the physical wobble involved in being struck down and (if you're as lucky as I am) the psychic reorientation involved in getting going again. At the moment, because of a gratifying sense of having made a recovery and feeling capable of proceeding healthfully into the next however many years, also because of doctor's orders which have entailed my opting out of many engagements, I am like somebody on the threshold of a newness. My old triad – that success in life and art involves getting started, keeping going, and getting started again – seems to be holding good. I do have the feeling of starting again. And can credit it somewhat because I am 'only' 67. At the same time I am more aware of mortal dangers, being careful for the first time about diet, needing to watch myself on stairs and uneven ground, worried about lying on my left pace-made side, and so on. But for the moment I'm in a mood of gratitude and confidence. Much to do with having had all these weeks restored to me, readings and lectures and all the rest scrubbed to hell off the calendar. Which is why, of course, I have this unaccustomed leisure, and have given myself up to all this lucubration. But once a word like that occurs between friends it is definitely time to stop. My love and Marie's to you and Karl. I do realize that for all your undaunted style on the page, your pain in the bone has not ceased so I can only hope it has eased or will ease.

Love –
Seamus

PS I hope to copy one of my favourite old age poems by Miłosz <'Late Ripeness' – but I cannot find the book right now> when I get back to 191 Strand Road, from his last volume, *Second Space*. It's a kind of Catholic comeback in face of Larkin's 'Aubade'.

PPS I remember the first appearance of Philip Hullman's 'The Old Fools' in the *Listener*. I think Karl headlined it as a 'Marvell-ous New Poem'.

Jane – This all swam up because I had time to myself, got reading your essay with such pleasure and gave myself 'permission' to ramble. Unfortunately, I couldn't find *brakes* on my iBook . . . S. xxx

The essay by Jane Miller that prompted this meditation was 'Reading in Old Age', published in the Summer 2006 number of the US magazine *Raritan*; Miller in turn took up issues raised here by SH in the final chapter of her book *Crazy Age: Thoughts on Being Old* (2010).

Louis Golding (1895–1958), English Jewish writer in a variety of genres and hugely popular in his day, is unlikely to have been an 'old Dublin crony' of Samuel Beckett's.

For Yeats's exhortation to 'Begin the preparation for your death', see his poem 'Vacillation'.

The final note beginning 'Jane –' was added by hand at the top of the letter.

To Sven Birkerts

TS Birkerts

1 November 2006 — 191 Strand Road, Dublin 4

Dear Friend,

You're a busy man, but there you go with your *obligatio* as well, having to keep Heaney amused. (I'm sure I told you before that I regard myself as a member of the Mr Sleary school of poetry readings – In Dickens's *Hard Times*, the circus owner Sleary, or Thleary, sinth he hath a lithp, pleads with the utilitarian Gradgrind who summonses him for rebuke after the two Gradgrind children have been detected in the big top – 'Thquire,' Sleary pleads, 'people muth be amuthed.' And he never said a truer word.)

Anyhow. I was delighted to get your fax which arrived on the same morning as forward copies of *Harvard Magazine*, or not so forward, since you had seen the thing before me. Although I have yet to see the Saul-snap – perhaps it was taken on that uneasy occasion with J.B. and co. at BU? Er and um to that one. But I was glad to hear about the gallowglass development of your son and heir, and the freshmanning of Mara, not to mention the colonization of her quarters by the manifestly destined *maman*. (I myself am involved in slum clearance in Michael Heaney's former room – abandoned by him for years now, but still deserving of Brodsky's verdict: the first time he was in Dublin, when I brought him in to see a big communist poster on the teenage wall, the nose went into the air and the response was immediate and fond: 'Smells like barracks.')

Months ago I agreed to introduce your Dublin talk, some time around Nobel Day in December, if I'm not mistaken. In the meantime, I've put a ban on all public smiling man jobs, up to and as they say including a lecture to the Yeats School next August. (This Saturday, for example, I'm betraying the coterie in Belfast by not turning up for the launch of a book by Queen's University,* celebrating itself as a nest of and perch for singing birds – Hewitt, Muldoon, Carson, McGuckian, Deane, Heane and so on.) It therefore seems proper, part of the *obligatio* on this side, to show as a friend in the audience and let somebody else do the honours as introducer. Dennis O'Driscoll would be good, except I don't like asking him because his goodness at the jobs means everybody asks him. But *shantih, shantih, shantih* to all that.

We must, however, see as much as possible of the Birkerts party (or as much as they can bear) and you are to consider my brazen car and the feasting hall at 191 at yours and the family's disposal when you're on the island. Time flies, so we should discourse on the far-speaking device well before you set out.

Here's hoping the wholly ghost consubstantial with the father and the son can be made wordflesh. And here's congratulations on reissues and fresh assays. People do read essays. Didn't Mandelstam mean to write the word when he slipped instead through habit into the same old thing: 'The people need poetry . . .' Bah! Bring on the Birk.

Much love –
Seamus

PS I need to tell you about Bill Clinton's swoop into the hospital to see the palsied bard. But as Charles Monteith used to say, 'Keep for dinnah!'

* And now they have an S.H. Library and an S.H. Centre for Poetry. SHit, they now believe . . .

The issue of *Harvard Magazine* just received was the one that included Adam Kirsch's profile of SH (see letter to Adam Kirsch of 16 September 2006).

'Saul-snap': on 11 April 1994 SH had taken part in a symposium of literary heavyweights at Boston University, at which the novelist Saul Bellow (1915–2005), Joseph Brodsky, Derek Walcott and Robert Pinsky also spoke.

'son and heir . . . Mara': Birkerts's son is Liam, Mara is his daughter.

'the coterie in Belfast': see letter to Ciaran Carson of 23 November 2006.

'Deane, Heane and so on': *sic*.

It was indeed Dennis O'Driscoll who introduced Birkerts at his Dublin reading; and Birkerts and his family were given a memorable dinner by the Heaneys.

To Ciaran Carson

MS Emory

23 November 2006

Glanmore Cottage, Ashford,
Co. Wicklow

Ciaran –

No sign of the blackbird to-day, what with rain-scourge and wind-raze. November in Wicklow. But I just want to let go a note of thanks for your note after the gala night. I managed to hear the *Arts*

Extra recording and caught something of the 'huge resettling' of the poets and poetry into that audience – and the culture in general. A proud and credible moment, and for me a very moving one what with Brother Longley's reading and the wafted good wishes from Frank via the full house.

Naturally I had my pangs and uncertainties about missing the whole thing, but I'm still feeling a bit unpeeled and unready for stand-up action, in public places or on podia. Enjoying it so much, in fact, that I'm inclined to do a Mahon now and in time to be . . . Fondest wishes and thanks for holding the hillfort –

Seamus

PS *Yellow Nib* 2 a cracker. Inaugural lecture for a start, then a lot of poetry earning its keep – Foley, McGrath, Lysaght, Allen . . . Full steam ahead.

To Simon Armitage

MS Armitage

22 December 2006 191 Strand Road, Dublin 4

Dear Simon.

Your inscription on *Sir Gawain* had Gawain-like grace and force, and I've just tried to find your address, but Faber is closed up and Sue's not at the BBC – which is reassuring, at this stage of the Yule. (Dennis O'Driscoll tells me that Ian McKellen did the job on BBC4 yesterday, but I missed that too.)

Anyhow, I just wanted to wheel and bob and fitt a bit to salute the work – marvellous oomph and onwardness from start to finish, a feeling of man at work with the belt tightened and the hand sure. It is a big work to have taken on and a beauty to have in your own words. The only problem I have about praising it is that I did a job on B. O'D.'s for the *Irish Times*, having been hangdoggy in myself since I did my Norton stealth-speak. I was due to have it in in September, but with the stroke and all it was late, and they're holding it for Christmas. So there I am, like *The Playboy of the Western World*, 'between two fine' – well, not women, but you know what I mean. Still, by Jesus and St Julian, I offer thanks for Simon –

Seamus

Faber had recently published Armitage's translation of *Sir Gawain and the Green Knight*. The inscription in the copy he gave SH quotes words of Gawain's from close to the end of the poem:

> There are folk in this castle who keep courtesy to the forefront;
> Let the man who hosts them find endless happiness.
> And let his lady be loved for the rest of her life.
> That he chose, out of charity, to cherish a guest,
> showing kindness and care, then may heaven's King
> reward him handsomely, and his household also.
> For as long as I live in the lands of this world
> I shall practise every means in my power to repay him.

Bernard O'Donoghue's translation of *Sir Gawain and the Green Knight* was published at almost the same time by Penguin Classics.

To Patrick Crotty

TS Crotty

31 December 2006

Dear Patrick,

You'll have more than enough on your hands and desk and mind as you hurtle towards the TCD lecture, but even so, no mercy. These for your perusal, as threatened.

I'm both glad of them and not sure. Obviously, anyone who concurs with the unsureness will only confirm me in the antithetical gladness, so you don't have to worry about telling me they're a shaky venture. Peter Fallon has a notion of doing a set of limited editions next year (Mahon, Edna O'Brien, Roddy(!) Doyle, Heaney have been mentioned) and I'm inclined to see this baker's dozen as my bijou contribution to the series.

You'll not want notes to 'Book Six', but if the episodes were to be given titles (which they won't be), iii would be Charon, iv would be Italia (this out of sequence, obviously, since Aeneas gets to Italy before he gets to Cumae), v the golden bough, vi Palinurus, vii the sibyl shows the bough and gains admission, viii Dido, ix the shades of the war heroes, x the elysian fields, xi the banks of Lethe and xii the vision of the descendants.

So, and as you say yourself, so so. It's the last day of 2006 and we're going out as granny and granda to Christopher and Jenny and Anna Rose this evening. And this morning, by coincidence, I began reading Bryon whatever his name's biography of R. S. Thomas, which had me wondering all over again about perf. of the l. or of the w. – Ers was up at 8 every day of his adult vicar life, in his own room doing his own scribbles until 11, then bread and cheese and more 'study' all day, then parishioners from 5–8, then bed at 10. Nice work if you can get it and are fit for it. But you need to be cut out for it, which I most certainly was not. Only nowadays, post-job, post-stroke, post-cancellations of everything, am I glimpsing the possibility of a writing 'routine'. And I'm still superstitiously suspicious of it and therefore incapable of establishing it. So. Carpet slippers and pantaloon and the Bovril for this one.

I look forward to seeing you the week after next. Give us a call before you set out or when you land so that we can ha-plan the next move.

Seamus

PS I hope they'll allow this through – have just discovered a hoard of penny blacks.

The possibly 'shaky venture' was the poem 'Route 110', in which moments from Virgil's *Aeneid* are embedded in a series of childhood recollections: it was included the following year in a limited edition published by Gallery Press and titled *The Riverbank Field*, then a few years later in *Human Chain*. SH's granddaughter Anna Rose is the dedicatee of 'Route 110'.

Byron Rogers's biography of R. S. ('Ers') Thomas, *The Man who Came Out of the West*, was published in 2006.

2007

The year began with yet another public accolade, when SH was announced, at a ceremony in London that he was not well enough to attend, as winner of the 2007 T. S. Eliot Prize for *District and Circle*.

The illness of the year before continued to demand, and for many months was accorded, a more sedate pace of life from the recovering author (see his letter to Liam O'Flynn of 11 June 2007).

To Valerie Eliot

MS Eliot

17 January 2007 Ballynahinch Castle, Co. Galway

Dear Valerie,

Even before the great news of the prize, Marie and I had planned to come to this lap of Irish luxury, but the fact that we set off the day after the marvellous win enhances things for us even further.

It was a great pity I couldn't be present either at the readings last Sunday or at the revels on Monday. Our daughter Catherine was elated to receive the cheque (which she promises to hand over) and to be photographed in your company. As ever, you were most kind and she came away both honoured and grateful.

Meanwhile, as you know, I've been in withdrawal from readings, lectures, receptions, and – alas – revelry. I had the stroke at the very end of August but after six weeks in hospital was out in good shape, unimpaired in body and spirit, but resolved to follow doctors' (and family's) orders to slow down and make the next year or so a 'no go' time. Hence our absence from the weekend's celebrations, which I hope you'll understand and excuse.

I intend to share a good proportion of the prize money between two good causes, one of which you are likely to know about. It's a memorial fund set up by the people at Dove Cottage to honour the name and work of the late Robert Woof. The other is a fund to establish a drama centre at Queen's University (Belfast), in the name of my friend, the playwright

Brian Friel. But I'll still let fly a few score in sheer celebration – here and elsewhere – my new alcohol consumption limit notwithstanding.

Love and gratitude, as ever, from Marie and myself –
Seamus

Valerie Eliot had inaugurated, and established the funding for, the annual T. S. Eliot Prize in 1993; it is customarily awarded at a ceremony on the evening after a public reading by all shortlisted poets.

The Friel Theatre and Centre for Theatre opened at Queen's in 2009.

To Paul Keegan

MS Faber

21 January [2007]

Dear Paul,

Many thanks for taking care of things (and Catherine) last Monday. It was a great delight to be the chosen one and I appreciated the grace with which people accepted my absence from the events – not to mention the follow-up endorsement by Boyd Tonkin on Saturday which (of course) Dennis sent on to me.

Meanwhile I've read with great delight *The Holy Land* and written to Mossy about the book. And Daljit Nagra's new Synge-songs fairly brought me to my senses – style, as J.M. said, born from the shock of new subject matter. With those books and Simon's 'airing of the green' (Dennis again) the old firm has its foot firmly in the door of the new year.

One of the things I had to do with Mossy was to head off charges of trespass on his fields and fences – especially the electric one. Many of the images and moves in *The Holy Land* occur in the poems I've written since October, so I sent him a few to fence myself, as it were. And now I'm sending you a sheaf that I'd like your advice about. I told you I would enjoy overdoing things and bringing out – Ashbery-like, McGuckian-paced – another quick volume in 2007. I know the title I want, have a notion for the jacket art, and would welcome your honest answer to the question: Is the enclosed a manuscript that would be worth my while and your while publishing? Voices sing in the air that this is all folly, but I'll be doing 'The Riverbank Field' and 'Route 110' (once called 'Book Six') as a limited edition with Gallery and I'd regret not at least raising the possibility of a further publication later on.

So. That's done and I'm not sure I'm glad or mad. Stooped to folly or rose on the afflatus.

So. No hurry – or worry, whatever you feel –

Seamus

PS I also wrote a note to Valerie.

'Mossy' is the Irish poet Maurice Riordan (b.1953), whose 2007 collection *The Holy Land* recalls and meditates on scenes from a rural Co. Cork childhood; the British poet Daljit Nagra (b.1966) had just published his first collection, *Look We Have Coming to Dover!*, which in rhetoric and subject matter is markedly the product of his Punjabi Sikh inheritance and which includes a poem with the title 'Singh Song!'; 'Simon's airing of the green' was Armitage's *Sir Gawain and the Green Knight*. All three were published by Faber, whose poetry list SH turns, by alluding to J. M. Synge and the rebel song 'The Wearing of the Green', into an all-Irish affair. Keegan himself is Irish.

No new book from SH was to appear as speedily as he evidently hoped, though 'The Riverbank Field' and 'Route 110' are both included in his 2010 *Human Chain*.

To Maurice Riordan

TS Riordan

21 January 2007 — 191 Strand Road, Dublin 4

Dear Mossy,

Many thanks for your note about the T. S. Eliot Prize – the bounty of St Louis – which I think I'm going to mete out to a couple of good literary causes (after I take enough for a bit of a holiday and a few celebration feeds; and after I get the cheque from Catherine, who's still in possession).

It gives me an extra push to write the letter I was going to write anyway, to tell you how greatly I relish and esteem *The Holy Land*. I've read it in its entirety twice and dibbled and dallied in it often. I'm a slave to the material, of course, but am therefore all the more aware of what you've made of it. The book isn't just beautifully voiced and cadenced, poem by poem, but richly yet perfectly reticently orchestrated. So many echoes (ole-in-ger-err-er), so many fields full of folk, so many potholes in the lanes, so many takes and ticks in the electric fencing. Credible for its inwardness, admirable for an artfulness that isn't flaunted into cleverness. I could go on. I'm a sucker for it.

If I have a worry it's because I've been doing a bit of electric fencing and understoreying myself. After the palsy, I had a fit of the old twelve-liners, a kind of 'Squarings' relapse – up writing in the middle of the night like Omar Sharif in *Doctor Zhivago*. In the circumstances, I thought the best thing would be to afflict you with some of the pieces where we sail close to the same wind, the one that shakes the fence and blows from Bottom Glen into Back Park. 'The Riverbank Field' and 'Route 110' will be done some time later this year in a limited edition by Gallery Press, and 'Had I not been awake' is one of several where (like you) I use the first line as the 'title'. Plus, as they say, I've a few more prose bits on hand. So all in all I'm going to look like the culprit in the old story about the Cork kids found copying ('The cuckoo is a migratory bird: he have a roundy head') . . .

I even had a half notion of going reckless and swanking it in Ashbery/McGuckian fashion, publishing another one the year after. It might be folly, but why should not a palsied man be mad? The main thing, though, is to rejoice in *The Holy Land* and to hope to have the trespass charges dropped. Fondest wishes –

Seamus

'bounty of St Louis': because T. S. Eliot was born in St Louis, Missouri.

For 'ole-in-ger-err-er', see Riordan's 'The Idylls', number 16, in *The Holy Land*; 'Bottom Glen' occurs in 'Understorey', in the same book; while in 'The Riverbank Field' (*Human Chain*), SH captures a memory of 'coming through Back Park down from Grove Hill / Across Long Rigs on to the riverbank – / Which way, by happy chance, will take me past // The *domos placidas*, "those peaceful homes" / of Upper Broagh.'

To Paul Durcan — TS NLI

7 February 2007 — 191 Strand Road, Dublin 4

Dear Paul,

This is an awkward letter, but it comes from an awkward man – thrown off his step by the gout. It has given me grief for the best part of ten days, and I'm still yielding to it – to the point where I must cancel my attendance at your lecture to-morrow evening. I wouldn't do this were the case not a hard one: for your sake, for Harry's, for the sake of the Professorship, for Hugh Brady's sake, I would wish to be present, but in order to see this pain in the foot doused, I regret I'll be absent.

The right big toe kindled on Sunday week, then the foot itself blazed and shone in earnest last Friday, and only to-day, after a course of pills, has it begun to die down. Now its hue is that of the topmost rondure of a swede turnip, whereas over the weekend it was more like a varnished beetroot. Heretofore when this affliction arrived I could assail it immediately with anti-inflammatory pills but now that I'm on warfarin, in the post-palsy condition, these are not permitted. Result: after a weekend on top of the bed in Wicklow and feeding on the ineffectual Paracetamol (other pain-killers likewise incompatible with the rat-poison) the doctor prescribed a course of tablets based on ye ancient remedie of colchicine which worketh slowly but [at] least it doth work. To-day the throb is, comparatively speaking, a thrib, and the foot is capable of being grounded on its side – from throbble to hobble, as it were – but I still want to give myself three or four days' grace before I venture forth.

My apologies for such a long paean to my pain, but my one defence these past few days has been to give in to self-pity and grim seclusion. I even enjoyed describing it.
[. . .]

Durcan was just coming to the end of his three-year tenure of the Ireland Chair of Poetry and was to give his farewell lecture at University College Dublin, of which the medical scientist Hugh Brady (b.1959) was President, and where the poet Harry Clifton (b.1952) taught.

To Andrew McNeillie — TS Bodleian

11 February 2007 — Glanmore Cottage, Ashford, Co. Wicklow

Dear Andrew,

Glanmore is not Aran or Clutag, but it's a class of an *annwn* all the same, even when I have the gout. I've been afflicted now for the past two weeks, severely after the first few days, not so bad in the past 48 hours. Previously when it struck I could strike back with anti-inflammatories, but after the palsy I was put on warfarin which won't combine with them, and since the sawbones in his caring way regards prevention of stroke the prior necessity, he put me on an older remedy – colchicine, root Colchis, where the sorceress Medea came from. So there's a whiff of the magical about the stuff. But it's a slow magic.

Enough. If this were a poem I'd cut that opening riff. I used to tell the students at Harvard that the first stanza you put down was a bit like the starting handle of yore – you swung it to get the engine started and then you withdrew it so the real work could begin. Which satisfied me but left them a bit mystified, since they'd never 'swung' a motor in their preppy lives.

You certainly got the engine running recently. I apologize for not having got round to dwelling with the recent work until now. Your *Slower* arrived in the middle of a busy summer that climaxed with the stroke, after busy readings and rambles in Ireland, England and Scotland – but not in the land of Platonic trout and prince-poets. Those poems about your father, and the ones about character/poetry/ the character of poet/poetry, and the Glendower sequence – not to mention the 'Arkwork' – plus several others, they 'have it' and do it. My favourites – well, this is risky, but I'll just take the veriest favourites: 'Stones', 'Death', 'Gone for Good' (beautifully placed in *Part of His Life*), 'Natural History', 'Fisher Widow', 'Glendower' v, vi, viii, xv, xxi, xxviii (but this is ridiculous – for different reasons, for different kinds of salute, I should also have ix, x, xi and others, but as Magnus used to say, I've started . . .), 'Meditation . . .' (lovely), 'Slower' – and that's leaving out much and many, the first poem in the book, for example, which is a pure beauty, and the specially privileged, in this quarter, Clutag glosses.

After the Ian Niall book, the latter were like fuses that led back to muffled depths and charges. The whole of that book is not only a duty discharged, it's a body glorified, as it were (not that his Presbyterian spirit would want any of that Romanist idiom wielded over him – you know the glorified body, as Christ's after the resurrection, can pass through walls and have immediate access anywhere) . . . I thought of Hardy's 'After the Journey' as I read 'Natural History', and there's something of the retrieval and gleam that animates 'Poems 1912–13' in *Part of His Life* – happily without the remorse factor. The quick account of John's old age is strong as a tourniquet. And the dues paid to the years of writing, to the unremittingness of the work done by John the Penman, has an effulgent, not just a filial rightness and sweetness to it. And needless to say, it moved me to find those piecemeal references to myself in there.

Elegy in the air here this morning also: Benedict Kiely, novelist, short story man, broadcaster, booze master, scribe, *seanchaí*, *shuler*, lord of revels and misrule, an heir of Carleton and contemporary of Myles/Flann/Brian has been silenced. And three weeks ago Sean MacRéamoinn – he who averred that outside every thin girl there was a fat man (often himself) trying to get in. *Unto the deid gois all estatis* . . .

Meanwhile, when I get back to Dublin, I'll print this out and enclose with it an offprint of a lecture done a couple of years ago – because in it I quote a definition of *dúchas*.* I had decided to do this before I came across your own glossing of *cynefin* late in the prose book, but, since I've started . . .

With thanks for all your care –
Seamus

PS Glad to see Mick Imlah's book too – was he reading Glendower, do you think, when he started that *sequentia Scotiana*?

* p. 413.

Annwn, in Welsh mythology, is the domain of otherworldly delight and eternal youth. McNeillie lived on the Aran Isles in 1968 and published his account of that time in *An Aran Keening* (2001). As in SH's letter of 2 October 2004 to McNeillie, 'Clutag' is a reference to Clutag Farm, Wigtownshire, the subject of John McNeillie's *My Childhood* (2004).

To celebrate the publication of SH's Clutag Press pamphlet, *A Shiver*, in 2005, McNeillie had taken him to lunch at Chez Gerard on Charlotte Street, London W1. Departing for the lavatory, he handed his poem 'Slower' to SH and was delighted by the response it was accorded on his return: '"Slower," he smiled when slowly he'd finished. / "A slow air."' (McNeillie: 'Lunch with Seamus Heaney'). McNeillie recalls, too, that it was on his way to this lunch that SH had the encounter with the Irish busker that is related in the first section of 'District and Circle'.

'Magnus' is Magnus Magnusson (1929–2007), presenter of the TV quiz show *Mastermind*.

The 'Ian Niall book' was Andrew McNeillie's biography of his father, *Ian Niall: Part of His Life*.

Benedict Kiely had, like SH, moved from his Northern Irish home ground to live in the Republic; a *seanchaí* is a traditional Irish storyteller; a *shuler*, a student training for the priesthood; for William Carleton, see letter to Thomas Flanagan of 25 October 1974.

SH raises the Irish word *dúchas* and its resistance to translation – it means something like 'birthright' or 'entitlement' – in his 'Title Deeds: Translating a Classic', given as the Jayne Lecture at Harvard in 2004; McNeillie's 'glossing of *cynefin*' – Welsh for habitat – is in the fifth of his 'Glyn Dwr Sonnets', in *Slower*.

McNeillie's Clutag Press had published *Diehard*, a booklet by the Scottish poet Mick Imlah (1956–2009), the year before.

To Grigory Kruzhkov

TS Kruzhkov

17 February 2007

Glanmore Cottage, Ashford,
Co. Wicklow – Land of the Settle Bed

[...]
I can't 'explain' the import of the busker episode, except to say that this kind of encounter happens to me often as I descend into the London Underground: an Irish musician is there playing an Irish tune, eyeing me just as he eyes everybody else, except that sometimes I have a feeling he recognizes me. But whether he does or not, my inclination is to recognize *him*, for what he is – an artist. And this recognition, I tend to believe, is more real and more respectful if given as a face-to-face, eye-to-eye nod; but at the same time I realize that the money thrown down in the cap would be gratefully accepted also. So every time I am uneasy and uncertain what I'll do until I come down to where he is sitting on the tiles. Hence rolling a coin in my pocket, triggering and untriggering, as it were. Will I give it out, will I 're-pocket' it? This is the 'real life' occasion of the poem, the starting point, but of course as the journey down continues the busker takes on aspects of Charon, which is another importance . . .

I think you definitely should translate the blacksmith translation. I'd just love to hear it sing and swing and ring in Russian.

The Tollund Man is, of course, the Tollund Man, but he is also a second self of sorts for SH. Like me, he is at once capable of going through the motions of life in the virtual city, being scanned by the security cameras and standing in the queues at cash-points, but he also belongs equally and imaginatively in another time and place, among the bogs and bulrushes. As the sequence begins he is something of a 'green' – environmentally speaking – man, but as things proceed he becomes more reminder of the poet's need to keep in touch with the old, damp, Derry sources of his inspiration, to beware of becoming a showpiece, an exhibit, a mascot, for the culture – see 'display case' stuff at the end of poem 3. Poem 4 is about regaining trust in the vital joyful action of poetry itself, its sensuous and spiritual refreshment, its readiness to 'survive in the valley of its saying', to be a surge of the soul rather than a servant of the 'history' or 'society'. Poem 5 is in a way me repossessing the original ground of my inspiration, re-entering my creatureliness – as exposed to the elements as cattle in the rained-on fields and bogs of Co. Derry, obstinately 'out of it', full of 'newfound contrariness' in the age of Walkmen and Broadband . . . And the final poem comes from an actual bunch of rushes I pulled in Tollund Bog and kept for years under the stairs in 191 Strand Road. The dust they have gathered I treat as Christ treated the dust of the road: he cured the blind man, you remember, by mixing it with his own spittle. In other words, the rushes retain a certain miraculous, restorative, life-giving, poetry-inspiring power. At the end I go back to poetry-work like any spadesman spitting on his hands and getting on with the job. Pollen = fertility etc. 'Name' – as if one is a healer healing. 'In the name of the Father' etc.

Does that make sense? The whole sequence could have as its epigraph George Herbert's lines (from 'The Flower') 'And now in age I bud again / After so many deaths I live and write / I once more feel the dew and rain / And relish versing . . .' (quoted from memory and probably somewhat inaccurate verbally, but right imaginatively).

Here's hoping this is of some interest, even if too late to help. I hope too that it gets through the Dashafax . . .

Love to you both –
Seamus

As Russian translator of *District and Circle*, Kruzhkov had sent SH queries about some of the poems in it; the 'busker episode' occurs in the poem 'District and Circle' (see letter to Andrew McNeillie of 11 February 2007); the 'blacksmith translation' is 'Poet to Blacksmith' (see letter to Louis de Paor of 18 March 1997); the rest of SH's elucidations concern 'The Tollund Man in Springtime'.

Punctuation aside, SH's recall of lines from 'The Flower' is perfect.

To David Batterham

TS Batterham

17 February 2007

Glanmore Cottage, Ashford,
Co. Wicklow

Dear David,

Many thanks for your note about the gout. At this stage, the lava has stopped flowing at the joint, but the cone on the side of the big toe is not quite extinct. A little gristly Vesuvio. I hadn't touched a drop for three weeks, but on Thursday night I risked it at a dinner in the Spanish Embassy in Dublin. High society, and me having to rise and utter at the tinkle of spoon on glass. So I risked a couple of glasses of their excellent Rioja, to no deleterious effect. And was all the more voluble when colloguing with Laura Garcia Lorca (Federico's niece) and Sean Scully (himself in all his power and majesty) and others less famous if a helluva lot more familiar . . . What to say about Inigo's poems that you haven't said yourself? Like Marilyn, I'm something of the old fogey in the school of art and craftwork, but not to the extent of denying virtue to other aesthetics/poetics, the William Carlos Williams notational as well as the Wallace Stevens orchestral. The pieces you sent have the feel of sketchbook work, drawings rather than oils, lines that take the line for a walk, as it were. 'Scare Crow', the first of the batch, also seems to me the best realized. It has the vitality and spot-on detail that occur all through the writing, but it has a consistency and finishedness that distinguish it. It has intimacy but is not exclusive, is quick but also shaped. This all sounds so schoolmastery I'll shut up. But the things are born from real impulse and transmit the feel of what Lawrence might have called 'the living present'.

Heigho! Seamus

Laura García Lorca (b.1953) is an actress; the painter Sean Scully (b.1945) frequently works on a large scale.

Batterham had typed out poems recently written by his son Inigo, then shown them to SH. Inigo himself has explained: 'For some unknown reason during a few weeks in 2007 I woke every morning around 6 a.m. with a compulsion to write. I certainly didn't think I was writing poems . . .'; and so he was 'horrified' when his father told him he'd sent 'the stuff' to SH.

To Carol Hughes

MS Hughes

24 February 2007

Glanmore Cottage, Ashford,
Co. Wicklow

Dear Carol,

Just now on the radio I heard 'God Save the Queen' played in Croke Park, and since I wrote the address England have scored their first three points – from a penalty. A historic day this – the tears were in my eyes when the bands struck up. There was huge anticipation and anxiety in case there would be disfiguring protests from thick wits in the GAA or diehards in Provisional Sinn Féin, but going by the radio, people have conducted themselves and history has been made in good and proper order. All we need now is an Irish win.

It was lovely to get your letter and to think of those forty trees in the ring-fort fringe and to see in the mind's eye the daffodils and narcissi and crocuses and snowdrops – which we can happily match on the ditch backs of Glanmore. But this other match on the radio has me distracted – sides now even – so I'll pause here . . .

Half-time, and a big change. I'm not usually caught up in sport, but with this opening up of Croke Park – the centre of resistance for more than a century to 'foreign games' – to rugby, and with the playing of the English anthem on the site of the Bloody Sunday shootings, the whole thing has been overcharged, and now, happily normalized (with Ireland in the lead 23–3).

But enough. Great to know that Christopher has breasted the tape with the letters and that you have some sense of having seen a big wheel turned. And as the big one turns so many cogs and ratchets move elsewhere: it's going to be a great book, a reminder of the spiritual height and depth as well as the artistic, creative power of our lamented *makar*. November 1, All Saints on the eve of All Souls, will be the winter of our new content.

I was sorry to miss you and many other friends at the TSE event, but glad too to have an out from the hype and hullabulloo. Not to say glad to have won the prize. I'm not sure how to handle things at this stage – say, don't enter me (which looks as if you're not ready to defend your title, as it were) or let things go (which looks like greed). Not the toughest situation to be in, but you know what I mean.

I hadn't known about Terence's new trouble: I saw him a month ago at a funeral, frail enough but valiant and to the fore . . . I've been in the pulpit twice, enouncing praise for legendary elders – the wit Mac Réamoinn ('outside every thin girl there's a fat man trying to get in') and the writer Ben Kiely (barman to Ben, mid-afternoon, in Dublin pub: 'Ah, please now, Mr Kiely, no singing. You're here to drink, not to enjoy yourself.') Both in their late eighties. And before them, Michael Yeats. My photo each time in the papers. All confusing the signals – since the message is otherwise – no readings, cancelled engagements etc. But I couldn't refuse to pay the tributes.

To think it's almost ten years since Ted's loss. Those trees must be rooted in your Moortown heart.

Anyhow: I'm actually in great shape – apart from glowing, aggressive gout for the best part of a fortnight lately. No anti-inflammatories allowed because of the warfarin. No wine. No joke. But now the varnished beetroot look has given way to a mildly blushing, faintly bunioned parsnip. So out to-night with the dame to Roundwood Inn, and perhaps a cut of venison and a flowing cup.

Wish you were here. Soon I'll make a crossing of the Irish Sea. Will keep you posted. And am still on for Devon in July – my first stand-up act.

Will see Christopher, who comes here to read at the Dún Laoghaire Poetry festival late March/April Fool's Day. They took my suggestion and invited him. We'll connect with him then.

So. Hurriedly, with love –
Seamus

PS M. cries from the nether room to add her warm embracements – which is, I'm told, the Polish salutation.

xxx

Fourteen people were shot dead by officers of the Royal Irish Constabulary during a match at the Gaelic games stadium Croke Park, Dublin, on 21 November 1920, an atrocity which, in combination with others, led to the day being ever after referred to as 'Bloody Sunday'. The game in progress as SH writes was the first at which an English rugby team, as part of the Six Nations tournament, had been welcomed, the taboo against rugby being played there at all having been broken the week before, when Ireland Rugby hosted the French team.

'Christopher has breasted the tape': I had recently shown Carol Hughes the manuscript of what was to be published as *Letters of Ted Hughes* later in the year.

'Terence's new trouble': the Presbyterian minister and activist for social justice Terence McCaughey (1932–2016) had been a friend of Ted Hughes since they were at Cambridge together, and he had officiated at Hughes's funeral.

Michael Yeats (1921–2007), lawyer and politician, was the son of W. B. and Georgie Yeats.

SH was to deliver the annual Hughes Memorial Lecture to an audience at the Ways with Words festival, Dartington Hall, Devon, in July. The title of the lecture was 'Suffering and Decision'.

The final result of the match at Croke Park was Ireland 43, England 13.

To Liam O'Flynn — TS ITMA

11 June 2007 — 191 Strand Road, Dublin 4

Dear Liam,

Two things prompt me to write: I saw a clip of your upcoming RTÉ programme with Paddy Glackin last night, and on Saturday morning, on a plane from Amsterdam, I briefly met Conor Linehan who was coming home from Sydney for Rosaleen's 70th birthday.

Seeing Conor, I was surprised at how unnerved I felt at being reminded about the plan to go to Australia in January. It has been bothering me all weekend with the result I'm up writing this at 7.00 on Monday morning. I now realize it was over-confident of me to take on the compensatory journey to Sydney; at the time I felt uneasy about having had to cancel last year and wanted to redress the situation. All of a sudden, however, it's clear to me that I spoke rashly. After my meeting with Conor, instead of having the little jag of excitement at the prospect of our *turas*, it was as if some heavy weight had plunged down into the soul. That's putting it over-dramatically, but it describes a radical mood change. I'm afraid, in other words, that I have to renege again. I cannot face the journey in January. The change of pace forced upon me by the stroke has obviously effected changes of attitude at a deep level – attitudes to appearances, to performance as opposed to writing, to travel, to how to use my own time. I have, for example, asked my American agent to decline all requests for readings, and will be holding to that position – to the extent of cancelling a trip to Harvard in October where I was to attend the 75th anniversary celebrations of Adams House (the place where I resided during my stints there).

I haven't yet spoken to Conor or Tom, and indeed could not or should not until you have the news. You'll understand, as friend as much as programme-fellow, that I don't enjoy what I'm telling you, but I prefer the unsettling of things to happen now and the situation to be honestly addressed because, among other things, it may be a prelude to even rarer Poet and Piper performances in the future. But if that were to be so, I trust it would not infringe our own trust.

Once again, I must have recourse to Sean Mac Réamoinn philosophy: 'This is it, this is the thing, this is what you're up against.'

Le meas –

Seamus

To Matthew Sweeney

TS Sweeney

17 June 2007

191 Strand Road, Dublin 4

Dear Matthew,

Near time, Heaney, says you. I should have written weeks ago to thank you for your phone call from Donegal and to hope that your death-duty journey home wasn't too grievous. You've had a troubling time these past few years and I admire your gift for keeping going and keeping at it. I'm not sure whether you're still in Austria, so I'll send this to your Berlin address as well – one of the virtues of the iBook being the copy button.

I've been thinking of you too because I'm heading back to Munster again for the first time since we met there two (Jesus) years ago, in Bantry. Going to see the bould Delanty, as a matter of fact, after many a promise to visit him in his Derrynane hill fort. I have to turn up at a formal hullabullo in Killarney, arranged by the Ireland Funds in honour of one A. W. B. Vincent – a grand old millionaire whose people gave Muckross House to the nation years ago and who himself pours out the thousands into the annual gullet of the Ireland Funds Literary Award. Happily I've nothing to do with that any more, but I did receive it and have known old Billy since the night I was awarded it and Marie fought with him about the North at the dinner afterwards. Call it bonding . . .

Greg, as a matter of fact, has just called me: he's back for the summer and at present en route to Dublin to attend a reading Poetry Ireland has arranged in honour of Kinsella this evening in the Gate. Various bards and priestesses on stage, the great owl (eighty now) installed in the stalls . . . A right and proper *hommage*, but the *dommage* is I won't be in attendance. I decided it would be easier all round, for him and for me, if I wasn't around. When he got the freedom of the city a few weeks ago I went to City Hall for the occasion and probably spoiled it for him – the innocent decent Lord Mayor goes out of his way in his opening remarks to name me specially for being in the audience, and then Louis le Brocquy (also being freemanned) cites me in *his* remarks as a special friend. I could just imagine Kinsella thinking, what the fuck, am I to be haunted by him even here? So, damned if you do, damned if you don't. But then, as the jarvey on the Aran Islands said to Longley when told he came from Belfast, 'Sure no matter.' Though it's still a trouble, if not 'the troubling of my life'.

Said life in good order again. I'm walking half an hour a day about three to four days a week, and should be doing more. I'm on the warfarin and the Lipitor, but feel free to ingest the blude-red in sufficient quantities to keep me happy – not to mention the odd analeptic preprandial vodka or post p. Redbreast or Green Spot. But no 'binge drinking'. It just means I get to bed earlier when those Corkmen show up.

This, dear Matthew, is not a letter, just a wave across. I hope all goes well for you, and that *Black Moon* will rise full and darkly effulgent over Bloomsbury on July 5. I'm sorry to say I'll miss your launch, and the Faber party next day – headed just then for Devon where I'll be giving the Ted Hughes lecture at Dartington on the Friday. My first 'appearance' since the stroke. Enclosed also the first poem I wrote after that episode. I don't think you got a copy last Christmas.

Fondest wishes –
Seamus

The Donegal-born poet Matthew Sweeney was living in Berlin at the time; their mutual friend, the Irish poet Greg Delanty (b.1958), has a house in Derrynane, Co. Kerry.

In 1932, grand, Tudor-style Muckross House, in Killarney, had been bequeathed by the American business magnate William Bowers Bourn (1857–1936) and his son-in-law, the politician Arthur Rose Vincent (1876–1956), to the Irish state; A. W. B. ('Billy') Vincent (1919–2012) was Arthur's son.

Black Moon, Sweeney's latest collection, was published by Jonathan Cape, whose offices had been in London's Bloomsbury until their move to Vauxhall Bridge Road.

To Jane Feaver

MS Feaver

29 June 2007

Glanmore Cottage, Ashford,
Co. Wicklow

Dear Jane,

Four minutes ago I did what should have been done four, five, six months ago: I finished reading your novel. Which I read all at once, between 8 o'clock this morning and now – 2:30 . . . I'm a deadly slow-coach, a 30 pages an hour creature, but I was held fast line by line and page by page, as if guided by a beam. The book has the inner, inmost tuning of a poem, it sings and tingles and stings (musically, not malignantly) out from a perfectly located, perfectly secluded point of origin where – if you'll excuse me for the (self-) plagiarism – suffering and decision have pivoted themselves. I'm no good at talking about novels, in fact I rarely read one through, but I was like a fish on a line with Ruth. The *writing* is substantial and full of the joy of accuracy – I'll never forget that Scottish landlady *chopping* her way upstairs; but the comprehension and fairness of the narrative, the intimacy and adjudication of it at one and the same time, took things beyond lyric . . . plot and character, 'grief and reason' as Brodsky might have said (plus unreason, of course). The whole feel of the landscape was both solid, realistic, reliable *and* mythic, 'a prospect of the mind' – river, farmyard, graveyard, and so many scenes/images have a dreamforce worthy of Hardy or Lawrence – that drowned calf, those beaten rugs, the disposal of the hands in the river.

Of course, I am sorry not to have read the book and written to you sooner. But somehow I failed – paradoxically, because I did want to most definitely. The deadline had to be – of course – my Devon visit and I didn't want to be meeting next week and starting to murmur to you in both praise and mitigation. Better this too quick scribble. But I do look forward greatly to seeing you again. All the more so now because of the mystery of achieved work: the complex beautiful thing that has been delivered by our fond and lovely Jane.

With love to Esther too –
Seamus

PS. I apologize for not having written immediately to reassure you that the proof-copy/advance comment situation was *nothing* for you to worry about: I knew it wasn't Jane's style to say 'get one to Heaney pronto . . .' So. As C. Monteith is said to [have] written in a telegram to J. McGahern on some publication day or other: 'Torrential congratulations' – xxx

Jane Feaver (b.1964) had been Assistant Poetry Editor at Faber before moving to Devon; her first novel, written there, was *According to Ruth* (2007).

To Patrick Crotty

TS Crotty

29 July 2007

Glanmore Cottage, Ashford,
Co. Wicklow

Dear Patrick,

To-day you assemble for the opening of the School and in my mind's eye I see ye go by in twos and threes – your astonishing self, the indomitable Vendlery, that rutted man Dick Murph, the bould O'Donoghue, the unelementary Watson – so naturally I have my pangs at not being with y'all. Ye should be written out in a verse. Or should I say 'written in'?

All the same, there are compensations for having reneged on attendance, not least the leisure to read your Reception(s) chapter. I skimmed it first, in my usual anxiety for friends who are constrained to write about me: how free have they been to speak freely, to what extent have they been (as you say of Bro. Deane) 'in some respects . . . reserved', and so on. But whether from a developed self-regard on my part or an impeccable style on yours, I found myself happily in the swim of your estimations and in the pink of my demurely blushing self. So I went back and re-read with a pencil in my hand and an even deeper appreciation of your much tested friendship and your vigour and vigilance as a reader and writer.

The shape and organization of the chapter are masterful: for better or worse, there's so much 'reception' stuff out there it has to be taken on with pedagogical clarity as well as the occasional precise pounce on specific responses. Your lead-in with the invocation of the big canonical names both puffed and put the wind up me, but then the contextualization of things Irish, the immediately clear, cogent account of the Clarke/Kavanagh/Kinsella/Montague/Murphy fifties and sixties (much enlivened and illuminated by the report on the anthology situation) cleared the ground and established the original perspective. The fact that the story concentrated on the poetry itself rather than the acknowledged reality of other significant factors – Fabers, professorships, Troubles – moved me, and several specific observations and references (the reading of 'Funeral Rites', the comparison with Muir) had me bowing to myself and then remembering to bow to you as well. Anyhow, no need to follow on where you know you went in the pages that follow after that, felicity by felicity, book after book, article after article. What does need to be remarked on is the light swift touch that disguised so much deeply absorbed knowledge of those texts – everything, as it were from CRicks to Coughlin. Again I bow down in my deep littered abode.

Since I had the examiner's pencil in hand second time round, I made a few marks, so I hope you won't mind if I mention not only some of my favourite phrasings but also some of the places where I think you might think again, as much for your own sake as for mine. These latter observations stem from the un-get-roundable situation we are placed in, you of your courtesy not wishing to downplay and me in my unease anxious about overplay. For example, at line 3, you write of 'his increasing dominance of anglophone poetry' for which I thank you but wonder if it goes too far: what if you spoke of 'international attention' in the previous line and substituted 'ongoing prominence' for 'increasing dominance'? I realize that this is intrusive and presumptuous, but like Magnus on *Mastermind*, I have started so I'll go on. To wonder if it might be better if I 'participated in' rather than 'officiated at' the EU tumescence; whether the definitive 'forty honorary degrees' mightn't be made less certain ('up to forty'?), since I myself am truly not sure of the number; whether 'the by now almost standard practice of describing H. as BIPSWBY' couldn't be 'the much contested practice'. Whether you don't want to give more weight to the negative

commentary, around *North*, say, or from Edna (although again your being in between friends and in-fighting makes for a reticence) or even from Fennell. Don't think I'm asking to be immolated, but don't think I don't realize the difficult job you had on your hands.
[. . .]

SH writes as the Yeats Summer School, of which Crotty was director 2006–8, was assembling in Sligo; the essay he refers to is 'The Context of Heaney's Reception', contributed by Crotty to *The Cambridge Companion to Seamus Heaney*, edited by Bernard O'Donoghue (2009); 'BIPSWBY' stands for 'Best Irish Poet since W. B. Yeats'.

Two final paragraphs praising Crotty for heroic achievements in other areas have been cut.

To Patrick Crotty

TS Crotty

5 August 2007

The Old Schoolhouse,
Dunfermline Town, Scotia

Dear Professor Crotty,

A few years ago I wrote to you about one of your fellow countrymen who had taken it into his head to put my work into his (I suppose we must call it) English. Happily enough he appeared to run out of steam after doing *The Testament* and a couple of the fables. Now, however, he appears to be at it again, partly because his publisher gave him a push, and partly because he's determined to set up in earnest as a writer. Which for him, if you ask me, is just that wee bit late.

Still, as you'll see, he has indeed got started, apparently on a day when he was meant to go to Galway for a book launch by somebody called Fallon or Falloon – and has been free to keep scribbling ever since. How desirable this development is you can decide for yourself. I'm sending his most recent 'translation' – if that is the word – which he intends for a southron series called 'Poet to Poet', a page of mine fornenst a page of his. This, as they say, is what you're up against. Apparently he has versions as well of 'The Two Mice', 'The Fox, the Wolf and the Carter', 'The Cock and the Jasp' and 'The Paddock and the Mouse'. And a notion of doing 'The Lion and the Mouse' and maybe even 'The Fox, the Wolf and the Husbandman' – the one about the mooncheese in the well. *Parturiunt montes*, says I . . .

Since we were last in contact, I know you have moved to Scotland. This makes me even surer that you are the right person to consult about this appropriation, but nobody knows better than myself how unremitting work in the schools can be, so I truly do not expect you to reply. But when and if you see this canny clerk, just let him know I have my eye on him.

Yours sincerely,
Robert Henryson.

'A few years ago': on 13 June 2000, SH had written under similar guise to Crotty, who had begun his reply: 'It gart me grue tae see thon Irisch brybour bard file the Lawlan leid o your braw scrievans we his Sudroun – or Westroun! Ane Lawland erse wad hae made a better noyis.'

'parturiunt montes': 'mountains are in labour' and . . . *'nascetur ridiculus mus'*: 'a silly little mouse is born' (Horace, *Ars Poetica*).

To Dennis O'Driscoll — TS Emory

6 August 2007

Dear Dennis,

That chronology. I wince at the work you've put yourself to. And through. It is Keatsian, in that it surprises by a fine excess, Yeatsian in that it manifests the fascination of what's difficult, Hopkinsian in its conscientious thoroughness. But all in all, simply pure O'Driscoll.

But poor O'Driscoll, too, I think to myself. Doomed votary of the god of detail, prodigious in application, self-punished by high standards, unrewarded except by his own virtue . . . I am upset, in fact, to see how far you have gone to serve the purpose of this 'life reviewed'. I think you must relent. Your own life must be renewed. Loath as I am to object to anything you do, since it is all in pursuit of a final excellence, I find myself wondering if the apparatus – if it keeps at this pitch of precision – won't be an overfreighting of the book, an over-canonization of the subject, as it were. I'll not be able to supply anything like as full an account of what went on in my life year by year, and don't think I'd try to, even if I could. At the same time, I am utterly grateful to you for the fullness of the record and dismayed to be reminded of all that happened *in illo tempore*. Or maybe that should be *in hoc*. Or hock, like me to you.

We will speak further on all this. In the meantime I am abroad in the fields of medieval Scotland with Henryson's mice and birds and wolves and foxes. Got bogged into a good long fable last week and finished it yesterday. Virgil in abeyance. If I put in a surge over the next three weeks I think I can get the fables off my hands [. . .]

'That chronology': the one that prefaces *Stepping Stones*; I can attest to its value.
'*in illo tempore . . . in hoc*': in that time . . . in this.

To Christopher Reid

TS Reid

11 August 2007

Glanmore Cottage, Ashford,
Co. Wicklow

Dear Christopher,

Rachel Alexander sent me (contraband?) page proofs of Ted's letters and I am atremble and in awe. Have only read your introduction plus the first fifty or so pages (up to those letters to Sylvia) and then the last fifty or so, with a few swoops on other bits. I came down here last night and got stuck in, same again this morning, and now will follow your advice and read the whole thing as it comes. But already the intensity and abundance have tilted scales and changed perspectives. His mind and his hand went together, and farther than I ever anticipated – and I did anticipate great things. But the devotedness and exhaustiveness of the writing surprise by that old fine excess, generous, as you say, and every bit as spontaneous, sagacious, sudden, self-forgetful as Keats. The sweep is immense – the book doesn't just complement the poems, it gets out (as Frost might say) by getting through, through into a new order or ether of art-knowledge. Your perception of the artistic/musical score element in the actual written page is marvellous and points to the helplessly creative, truly Shakespearean nature of the whole barely credible effort. Although there is also an edge of Joycean steel, the self-determination and clarity of purpose, the strength of the early resolution to write and be his own man which you also take note of. Your introduction has perfect pitch – true to the friendship, to the editorial requirement, close, kind, grave, loyal and loving. (And the acknowledgements likewise an achievement – a written work, a discovered tone, instead of the usual hit and run, thumbs up, Bob's your uncle conventionality.) When I think of you transcribing those hundreds of pages, I bow down to you as gratefully as to the shade himself. You have magnificently recked your own rede, been virtuous in every possible sense of the word, *pius* beyond Aeneas . . . Founding the Roman race was snip *labor* compared with your transcriptions and collations and annotations. *Monumentum exegis*. Delivered a culture shock that will stay seismic and salubrious for ever. I just needed to whoop.

Love from us both –
Seamus

PS He would have deplored the wafting of these words into an iBook, but for a non-initiate, the screen is an aid of sorts to self-hypnosis – which he did approve of.

Rachel Alexander was Head of Publicity at Faber.

To Tim O'Neill

TS O'Neill

16 August 2007 191 Strand Road, Dublin 4

Dear Tim,

It's a long time since I got such rewards from a night at the books. Deeply instructive and fulfilling. I feel this electronic medium is an offence against the scriptorium intimacy, the hand-to-hand, hand-to-mouth word-ply we managed. But I just want to print up what I'd suggest as possible workable drafts of the two testers. I also enclose handwritten copies of what we ended up with last night, with various suggested alternatives/revisions.

I'll probably be scooting about all day to-morrow because of the ravening Norse, but maybe call on Saturday? I'll be in Wicklow later in the day [. . .] then home Sunday evening.

Brother Hugh was in with me this morning, and he and Jeananne are looking forward to seeing you in The Wood – the name of the farm we moved to after Mossbawn, left to my father by his great uncle Hughie. (Christopher had been killed on the Toome Road a year or two earlier and I think that encouraged the move.) Hugh, incidentally, is the dedicatee of a poem called 'Keeping Going' in *The Spirit Level* and the presence in 'Quitting Time' in the latest book.

For Bellaghy, watch out for a left turn as you pass the egregious Elk Bar, about a mile and [a] half after you cross the Bann at Toome. The old Toome Eel Fishery is still to be seen beside the old bridge – not Roddy's – so when you come to the big roundabouts turn left to get into the village itself.

Pat Brennan at the Bawn will give you an itinerary locally – I'd love you to see the strand at Lough Beg, for sure; and maybe Hugh will take you to 'the moss' – but even that has been re-configured . . . The Lagan's Road is about the only thing not altogether altered, and even there it's only for about twenty yards that you feel the old *fál* and fen-world. You could always meditate on mutability in the Poet's Corner in The Thatch, next to our old Mossbawn House, and The Tin Hut . . . and visit Barney Devlin's forge at the Hillhead.

But enough. Thank you again for the nonpareil 'Scribes', aureate and agog above the spine or – strictly speaking, I suppose – on the lettered rump. To be revered. And, yes too, framed.

Love to you all –
Seamus

PS 'Pent' may be a bit fancy, but it shelters and protects, if ever so slightly imprisons . . . I thought 'high' might give some credence to '*fál*'?

Could the blackbird 'sing for' him? Would that be more selfish/ self-engrossed?

SH and O'Neill had had the first of an intermittent series of collaborative translating sessions the previous night, the 'night of the books'. By 'testers', SH means first attempts: one of these contains the lines 'no ravening Norse / On course through quiet waters', and by chance SH was at that moment expecting Scandinavian visitors.

O'Neill, who had never previously visited SH's home territory, was to lead a small group around historical and archaeological sites in Ulster the following year. Some of the group had asked to see Bellaghy and its environs.

'*fál*': hedge; the first line of the poem about the blackbird translates as, 'A hedge of trees surrounds me'; this and other poems which O'Neill and SH translated together first appeared in O'Neill's *The Irish Hand: Scribes and Their Manuscripts from the Earliest Times* (2014).

In one of his versions of 'The Scribes', O'Neill had used gold leaf, and the trace of the animal's lower spine was clearly visible on the vellum.

An additional page of postscript concerns details of translations in progress.

To Michael Longley TS Longley

20 September 2007 191 Strand Road, Dublin 4

Dear Michael,

That was lovely on Saturday, and you and Edna carried the day in every sense – as well as the days before. There was something wonderful about the utter spontaneity and unstintedness of the applause for Edna at the end of the City Hall event: there was real and credible specific gravity to it, and it made me all the sorrier not to have been in attendance earlier – but in truth I was glad enough not to be 'on' for more than 24 hours. 'Pretending to be myself', as Larkin puts it, becomes more and more of a test.

I told you how much I loved 'The Lifeboat' in *Archipelago*. Now I have to tell you how thoroughly I responded to 'White Farmhouse'. You'll remember, I hope, the purplish grey landscape of Loughanure by Middleton that Marie and I bought – it may have been our first purchase – in either the Bell or the CEMA gallery: I'd just had it reframed when 'Farmhouse' appeared, so when Andrew McNeillie wrote asking for something for the next issue, I suddenly and unexpectedly got going. The thing flies crooked, but it wouldn't have got off the ground (does it?) had I not read yours. It may be too late, but I'm sending it off to *Archipelago* to-day, so I thought you too should see it.

'These images that yet / Fresh images beget . . .'

Our love to you both. Look out in the public prints for a dribbing if not a drubbing of my *Burial at Thebes* which begins this week in the Barbican (if it's even noticed, that is). I'm going over this afternoon to show that I can take it, come what may. Me that can't even say the first lines in Greek.

Be sure I have the Irish. *Slán go fóill.*

Seamus

The 'applause for Edna' had been given at the celebrations, both academic and civic, in Belfast for the centenary of the birth of Louis MacNeice.

Enclosed with this letter was a typescript of SH's poem 'Loughanure' – '*i.m. Colin Middleton*' – which was to be included with other 'in memoriam' poems in *Human Chain*. Middleton had been an early friend of Longley's, whose own poem after one of his paintings, 'White Farmhouse', is in *A Hundred Doors* (2011).

'*Slán go fóill*': goodbye for now.

To Tim O'Neill

TS O'Neill

10 November 2007 — 191 Strand Road, Dublin 4

Dear Tim,

Many thanks for your satchel of learning. No homework done yet – on that front, at any rate – but I've been running interference over all the nightwork so far. I append the villainous results: to my ear, the cadencing and sonic patterns are better: the rhyme with 'bell'/'gale' I am eager to keep – at the cost of the literal windy night; I think line 3 of 'Pent' is more cogent and assonantal ('ruled' and 'book' squaring off a bit more, though we do lose literal 'little'); 'feral' in 'Fierce wind' may be a bit fancy, but it alliterates punchily with afraid and its *er* sound echoes the *orse* and *ourse* and *ers* that follow. Kiss my ourse, says you.

I'm sorry I was so sluggish on Wednesday: I hope it won't dull your appetite for another session whenever we can manage it. If I had been 'at myself' I think I'd have come up with the second two lines of 'Derry' as they now appear – for your re-construing or indeed stricture . . .

I go away to London for the Ted Hughes letters launch on Monday. Think again about the Christmas card. If it suited you, I'd love to have you do something where the both of us are involved – you perhaps inscribing the Irish. Otherwise, I'd just print 'Fierce wind', maybe with the Irish in the same typeface, and either try for the Dublin Viking boat line drawing or have a simple Tim device/line drawing on the front. The translation would still be attributed to both of us. Privately published for the authors.

Can I allow P. Fallon to get in touch with you? I'll be seeing him on Wednesday night when I get back.

Seamus

PS Some previous cards enclosed also. The smaller format this time, I think.

The poems being worked on here appear in *The Translations of Seamus Heaney* as 'The Monk's Tryst', 'Pent under high tree canopy', 'Wind fierce to-night' and 'Colmcille's Derry'.

To Michael Longley

TS Longley

22 November 2007

191 Strand Road, Dublin 4

Dear Michael,

Next Monday is the Glen Dimplex Awards dinner and I see you are one of the judges and may well be in attendance at the event, so I thought I'd write to let you know that I cannot attend: it's Anna Rose's first birthday and we're long written into Christopher and Jenny's plans for her first party that evening. I'd have liked to be there for Cathal McCabe's sake and Jane Feaver's (whose excellent first novel is in with a chance, I hope); but I'd also like to have talked to you since I had this sudden worry a few weeks ago and should have rung you straight away and tried to clear it, instead of putting it laboriously on the record here: when I didn't hear from you after I sent the Middleton poem I began to wonder if you had taken it as some kind of trespass on your own white farmhouse ground and began to doubt my eagerness to share it and publish it. But I hope I'm wrong. I hope you could see that what was at work was gratitude for the grace of inspiration that I got from you – a way into that picture I'd been wanting to write about for years. In my more or less babyish joy at having done the thing I sent it off to Andrew and you, perhaps without enough forethought. If you afterthought it tactless, I'm sorry for that.

Other things have been weighing on my mind too, not least D. Hammond's ongoing dissolution. It's a long and dismaying and uncertain decline, and there's going to be no reversal. The specialist told him a couple of months ago that he was unlikely to see Christmas, but even there, there was nothing certain.

Love to Edna too –
Seamus

Neither Cathal McCabe nor Jane Feaver (see SH's letter to her of 29 June 2007) received the Glen Dimplex New Writer Award, which went to John Stubbs for his biography, *Donne: The Reformed Soul.*

David Hammond's 'ongoing dissolution' was from leukaemia.

To Eamon Duffy

TS Duffy

18 December 2007 191 Strand Road, Dublin 4

Dear Eamon,

Your letter managed to be at once grievous and gleeful, tingling and shingling, snoz-pimpled and unself-pitying. I can only hope that your Muslim pharmacist lady didn't inform the local *cumann* of the Legion of Mary about your disgraceful little secret, and that the affliction has cleared or at least been seriously ameliorated by her medicaments.

When we met in Dublin I knew you were stretched too far, doing more than was feasible, but that, like Beckett, you weren't interested in the feasible. Tumult of effort and inspiration from the extreme conditions can really work – and produce work – but some relapse, some respite is called for. You kept going with such high expectations from yourself, you were pitched, if not past pitch of grief, then into the more pang of the wilder shing. So I hope you will now repeat what the last malefactor to be hanged in Crumlin Road jail is reputed to have said to the chaplain as they approached the swinging rope: 'This, father, is going to be a lesson to me.' (Come to think of it, that's written in a gloss of sorts in *Electric Light* – I'm afraid I'm starting to cave in.)

And truth to tell, I *am* a little frazzled. Not shingled but still a bit shaky. All well physically, but worn down a bit by the long illness of friend Hammond in Belfast (acute leukaemia, prediction that he might be gone by Christmas, much phoning and up and downing to/from Belfast); by recurrent cancer problems after previous breastbothers suffered by wife of brother Hugh; by anxieties about the book-length interview – now handed in by Dennis O'Driscoll – wondering if there's not far too much information of a gossipy nature, too much self-conscious, for the record selfswank; suffering a general lassitude, uncharacteristically short of relish and resource. But please don't think this is deep or dangerous, I'm just (surprisingly, but because it's yourself that's in it, your honour) taking the opportunity to speak freely and truthfully – ventilating rather than hyperventilating.

And here's a more immediate cause of anxiety. Or hilarity. About three weeks ago I opened – by accident – a big special delivery package for Marie (I always assume without looking that such packages will be for me). It contained a missive with a promise of large sums of money, hundreds of thousands of dollars, and since I was in speed-read, open-and-throw-away mood, I assumed it was some kind of hoax or publicity stunt and simply dumped it. Then last night Marie tells me that the Pushkin Prizes trust, of which she is a trustee, had been expecting her to receive a cheque for tens if not hundreds of thousands (something to do with her having an address in the Republic) and I suddenly remembered what I had done with the special delivery. Yet couldn't even remember if there was a cheque in the package. So I had to telephone the Duchess of Abercorn in Baronscourt – she is the head and onlie begetter of the Trust – to report on my folly. Imagine, as the poet Mahon has it, my chagrin. But also my relief, when she tells me that a cheque had been posted from the States on December 12 and should be on its way. I await the courier with trepidation. Marie has gone out to lunch with a group of women who organized themselves years ago for weekly lectures and self-betterment, but who revel a little at Christmas. I pray to Christ that the courier arrives.

So, dearly beloved, that is the lesson for to-day. Given your beautiful elegy for the Norfolk coast, I should have been telling you about the dual carriageway they are going to cut past the strand at Lough Beg and Leitrim Moss, but another time. My love and Marie's to Jenny also. I hope that all goes well and that home and healing and happiness come dropping slow on you and yours as dew in Aprille –

Seamus

SH had learned that Duffy was undergoing a bout of shingles, which had affected him below the belt, a detail of some embarrassment to the sufferer when he had consulted the pharmacist. A *cumann* is a society – in this case a local branch; the Legion of Mary is a lay apostolic organisation of volunteers serving the Catholic Church.

'into the more pang of the wilder shing': SH is playing with the second line of Hopkins's sonnet, 'No worst, there is none. Pitched past pitch of grief', which goes, 'More pangs will, schooled at forepangs, wilder wring.'

Duffy's 'elegy for the Norfolk coast' was his rueful account in a letter to SH of the sea's encroachment on the coastal town of Cley; for the significance of SH's remark about the dual carriageway, see 'The Strand at Lough Beg' (*Field Work*).

2008

SH's fluctuating qualms about *Stepping Stones* appeared to increase as soon as the typescript was put into the hands of his publishers at Faber, not least because of their immediately expressed doubts about the unconventional format; but loyalty to the project's co-begetter, Dennis O'Driscoll, steadied and the book, more or less as presented to Faber, was carried through to publication later in the year.

Following an operation for breast cancer late in 2007, Marie Heaney underwent a course of treatment that included chemotherapy, lasted a year, and was ultimately successful.

To Desmond and Mary Kavanagh — PC Kavanagh

[January or February 2008] [St Lucia stamp, illegible postmark]

Here for a healing sun week, but our thoughts very much with the people at home – Hammond weakening, Michael's new baby girl burgeoning, Hugh grieving and your good selves – so kindly attentive to us all. Meanwhile, the Carib surf thunders, the coconut palms susurrate and the bride browns like a berry. Wish ye were here – *Le grá* –

Seamus
and M.

To Paul Keegan and Stephen Page — TS Faber

15 February 2008 191 Strand Road, Dublin 4

Dear Paul, Dear Stephen,

A week ago, just before Dennis set out for a different interview – with Eamon Grennan, at the Lannan Foundation in Santa Fe – we concluded the revision of what will be *Stepping Stones*. That revision makes it a more satisfactory production and was the result of a very helpful reading of the manuscript by Paul – a reading I had requested but which nevertheless had a dismaying effect on me. This was because Paul plainly and honestly stated things which had been whispering at the back of my own

mind – the question, especially, about whether there shouldn't be, have been, a memoir-type book in my own voice rather than the interview which had grown to such proportions over the years . . . It is no exaggeration to say that the raising of this question put me into a panic for weeks; I wondered if the whole enterprise hadn't been a mistake, and in the course of a phone conversation with Paul conceded that there could be a case for pulling the more 'writerly' chapters at the beginning in order to hold them for a different more inward book. Dennis's reaction to this was naturally one of hurt surprise and resistance, to put it mildly, and I soon came to my senses. What was done, what we had on our hands, was the book I had agreed and had enjoyed putting together, one conceived by Dennis and co-authored by me, one that I very deliberately opted for in the beginning precisely because it would preclude a certain kind of literariness, would be 'for the record'. In all justice and friendship, therefore, I could not see my way to cutting the two opening chapters, so set about nipping and tucking the rest in order to take account of many of Paul's local criticisms. And as I did so, going back over the material section by section, I got over the panic. It seems to me that the thing is still longer than it needs to be, but that's how it has emerged, and given that Dennis has moved from 'interviewer' to author, has done an unconscionable amount of work and has had my co-operation to this final point, that – if you agree – is what we go with.
[. . .]
I have to say it would be good to get back to writing poetry. That time will come again, I hope. And a time when we meet again in the environs of Queen Square. I could do with a revel . . .

Fondest wishes
Seamus

Stephen Page had been Chief Executive at Faber following Matthew Evans's departure to the House of Lords.

To Michael Longley MS Longley

25 February 2008 191 Strand Road, Dublin 4

Michael –

That was a triumph, all right: the work that went into the lecture immediately appreciated, the art well advocated, the hospitality deserved and immensely enjoyable. In the meantime, I saw Peter Fallon and reported our notion of a publication for J.M.'s 80th – since he has the poems on his list, he seems the man to do the job. Should he go ahead and get an editor? The idea that different poets would write – briefly, I'd suggest – on their favourite poems should make things easy enough all round.

Meanwhile, enjoy the gown – and fondest wishes from M. and me to you both –

Seamus

Longley had just delivered his inaugural lecture as Ireland Professor of Poetry, under the title *A Jovial Hullabaloo*.

An anthology very much as envisaged here, *Chosen Lights: Poets on Poems by John Montague*, was published by Peter Fallon's Gallery Books the following year, Fallon himself the editor.

To Paul Muldoon

MS Emory

25 February 2008 191 Strand Road, Dublin 4

Dear Paul,

For a good while – since around Christmas – I haven't been 'at myself' and have been most neglectful of friends, obligations, correspondence. But I'm back to the old self, through the anxieties, and in a position where I have to apologize to a score of people for not having been in touch. But most especially to you, who should have received whin-blossom wreaths and garlands of bog-furze for the grand tour from Egypt to Athens to Rasharkin to Toome. Brilliant, generous, binding, bettering . . . Late but in earnest, with love, I thank you for doing the honour.

See you in October, but probably before that: in this country?

Love to Jean and the young –

Seamus

Here, SH thanks Muldoon for the poem he had written in his honour on the Royal Irish Academy's award to him of the Cunningham Medal.

To Carol Hughes

MS Hughes

20 March 2008 — 191 Strand Road, Dublin 4

Dear Carol,

Oddly, paradoxically, perhaps mistakenly, what I liked from the start about the interview format was that it held things a bit out there, not at arm's length, but not as an inward accounting, which is something I don't know I can or could do. Maybe a shorter, different book, when the data is out for the record. I was a bit taken aback at the thought of it as 'appropriation' – though I see how it can look like that, being billed as Dennis's book. But in fact, again, I'm in favour of the screening effect of the attribution, and so, I think, is Paul K.

Naturally, I have my uneases – I'm not at all a teller of my things – but not to the point of a renege. Though I more than appreciate your impulse to protect . . . And wasn't free to reply until I had a big engagement concluded yesterday. Her Maj. is in NI these past couple of days along with the Dook, and yesterday she unveiled a 'centenary stone' at Queen's University in Belfast (my alma mater) – a stone on which is carved a 'centenary stanza' by me, which I read on the occasion, in the presence. Present also: Rev. Paisley, President McAleese (another QUB graduate) and multifarious distinguished personages. Worth doing, but anxiety-inducing, just because of the high exposure factor. (A bit like a book length interview, sez you.)

Marie out at present for her third chemo session. She has been wonderfully 'up', so I hope that can continue. But that may be expecting too much –

With love –
Seamus

Seeing *Stepping Stones* advertised in the Faber catalogue, Carol Hughes had expressed her worries about the personal exposure that publication would bring, as well as the attribution of authorship to Dennis O'Driscoll rather than SH.

To Thomas Lynch

MS Lynch

28 March 2008 — 191 Strand Road, Dublin 4

Dear Tom,

Your 'Ground Sense' – whose better – deserves more than this quick note, but your piece is so knowledgeable about both the quick and the dead I want to thank you for the care and commitment of your undertaking – and I have to say I was impressed with the Abbey for having thought of you as the man for the job. I'm also glad to report that this production is going to be first rate: I saw a rehearsal the day before yesterday and had the sweet experience of forgetting I had written the words the actors were speaking: they seemed just to discover themselves and discover the characters *super spotum*, as it were. So all is working together towards good, and I bow with gratitude – and not just for what you have done on this occasion, o good and gracious one –

Seamus

PS I enclose a photo cartoon done by my son, after Lizzie had unveiled a 100th anniversary stone at QUB, with my 'centenary stanza' carved into it. S

Lynch's 'Ground Sense', a professional undertaker's meditation on the significance of burial rites, was written as programme note for the Abbey Theatre's revival of *The Burial at Thebes*. In his final paragraph, he asserts: 'It is Heaney's ground sense, his lifelong digging in the layers of language, that recalls us to these gravities. In *The Burial at Thebes* he draws us nigh to Sophocles' old urgency, the sense of species obligation that informs Antigone's decision to bury her brother and the sadness that proceeds from Creon's ruinous decree.'

'*super spotum*': schoolboy Latin for 'on the spot'.

The cartoon is a photo of SH and the Queen meeting, to which Michael Heaney had added a speech balloon issuing from his father's mouth: 'And you are?'

To Alasdair Macrae

TS Macrae

17 May 2008 — Glanmore Cottage, Ashford, Co. Wicklow

Dear Friend,

There's something not right, I know – between friends – about this iBook way of doing business, but we're down in the cottage as usual for the weekend and I like accumulating what Beckett's Molloy would call 'a little store' for printing out on the Monday morning back in Strand Road – it provides a stopper in the time-sink, a feeling of at-least-that-much-got-done. So forgive me for not digging with it on this occasion.

And for not having answered sooner. You'll have done your New York and New England gad-about by now, will have seen the mighty Vendler, sampled the chowder and the swordfish, walked the Yard/Ya-ad, come home and mowed the lawn and be wondering if that craythur ever got your letter at all. And you'll not, alas, be the only one wondering if I'm still functioning. I've been sluggish these past weeks/months, a certain low barometerish period having been gone through, but now things look up again in this verdant *ver*. Still, I managed to let Helen's 75th birthday pass without sending even a greeting, and her the most attentive thoughtful generous present-sender and birthday-greeter in my life. But enough.

I was delighted to hear from you and to know about the reading of 'Postscript' at the wedding. That you chose to do so means a lot to me – and even more because the nuptials were in Nairn. I went there once with Marie and two friends (from Cambridge, MA, husband wishing to do the malt Scotch circuit) because I'd read David Thomson's *Nairn: In Darkness and Light* – and had known David. Went also to the Culloden site which was a sadder experience than I had anticipated – the space wide open, the sky high, an emptiness over earth and in the air; and went to Cawdor forbye. We arrived there after Skye and Talisker and a visit to Braes where Sorley managed by some stratagem to hang up the Yank's jacket and then put it on himself as we got ready to leave and he got ready to walk us out to the gate. Which is another reason for thinking very seriously about Norman G.'s invitation. But at the moment I'm reluctant to make a commitment, while still deeply attracted to the notion of assembling, especially if yourself and Elise might be there.
[. . .]
Meanwhile, we should have told you about Marie's wee bit of surgery (maybe we did?). A lumpectomy before Christmas, entirely successful, no lymph glands affected, but chemo being undergone as a precaution, five treatments over, one to go, side-effects so far not at all drastic, the braveheart lady lionhearted as ever; radiog. to start in a month or two, I guess, then Herceptin. Because of warnings about possible infection, plane travel and crowd-gathering have been advised against this past while, so that too has added to the hesitations. But it has not affected

her general health and happiness. Which retain a MacCaigish villainy. (I would enjoy seeing your Norman monograph, so I would.)

So. I'll maybe talk to you(se) soon on the telephone. You'll understand I hold off the Sabhal Mòr proposal without enthusiasm. I am also, I'm happy to report, through the cautious stage of the warfarin warnings and can manage three-quarters of a bottle of red without too much anxiety. As long as *she* thinks it's half a bottle. (I'll always remember your defiance of the rationing in The Oxford that night – and then I went home and got a stroke.)

Much love to you both. Grandchildren the best tonic that Granny could have had this year, given her condition. No. 2, another girl, this time to Michael and Emer, arrived on January 13. I told them it was the day Yeats wrote 'Cuchulain Comforted', but do they care? Maybe, just a little, to humour me.

Much love, and to Elise too, from both of us.
Seamus

Nairn in Darkness and Light is the title of David Thomson's 1987 memoir of his childhood in that Scottish coastal town.

'*ver*': Latin for 'spring'.

'Norman G.' was Professor Norman N. Gillies, who ran Sabhal Mòr Ostaig, Scotland's National Centre for Gaelic Language and Culture, on Skye; his retirement dinner took place in November 2008.

The 'Norman monograph' was Macrae's *Norman MacCaig*, in the OUP series 'Writers and their Work', which SH did not see until it was published in 2010.

The Oxford Bar is on Young Street, Edinburgh.

Accompanying this letter was a photograph of Marie and her granddaughter Anna Rose, with the caption, 'Tonic no. 1, to Christopher and Jenny, November 2006 (taken last year – the littl'un not as stern nowadays . . .)'.

To Edna Longley

MS Longley

9 June 2008

Dear Edna – The Thomas poems arrived this morning and I was whelmed to the point of over-. Not just because of the surge of recollection of Malone Avenue poetry-starts, but in genuine gratitude for the accumulated strength of the scholarship sustaining the book and the delicacy and stamina of the critical attention. It made me feel young again, but also as old as we all are. And, for once, the rewards of all that. The Paul Nash cover is also sweet and strong. Much love –

Seamus

SH acknowledges receipt of Edna Longley's *Edward Thomas: The Annotated Collected Poems* (Bloodaxe, 2008). The Longleys lived in a flat on Malone Avenue, Belfast, for three years after their marriage in December 1964. The cover of her book shows Paul Nash's *Spring in the Trenches, Ridge Wood, 1917*.

To Thomas McCarthy

TS Princeton

14 August 2008 191 Strand Road, Dublin 4

Dear Tom,

My cupboard is pretty bare just now – apart from a big hunk of classical cheese – a translation of the guts of *Aeneid* VI, a venture that I promised myself long years ago and which I have almost completed but whether or not it will be a book in itself I'm not sure.

'Palinurus' is one of my favourite bits, and I send you more of it than you need. It would probably be better to stop near the bottom of the first page here, at ' . . . loll me, roll me', rather than plunge forward into his pleas to Aeneas etc.

[. . .]

SH encloses two pages of typescript, from the lines 'And now there appears his helmsman, Palinurus' to 'The thought / Of the land in his name makes him happy'. McCarthy had requested a contribution to the *Stony Thursday Book* (Limerick Arts Centre) of which he was guest editor for number 7. He followed SH's advice about the length of the excerpt. SH also sent 'In Memory of Nancy Wynne-Jones', which was printed on the following page.

To Ciaran Carson

MS Emory

22 August 2008 191 Strand Road, Dublin 4

Dear Ciaran,

Your dedication of *On the Night Watch* and your letter are an honour and a reward – and for many reasons, but most immediately because of [the] gleam off the poems. It's as if you've been drilling steel or iron and spinning out those glittering little cuticles. I've only sped through the manuscript once, but the inner joys and links and chinks were registering even at that rate and wakened me up to things very deep in myself and very far out, at the edge of us all. It's another triumph for you, full of a newness auge(ur)ring old originality. Reading it made me want to write. I thank you for one of the best moments in my life of opening envelopes with manuscripts in them. Cannot, indeed, thank you enough – and look forward to seeing you again, and to a second reading . . . Rosin the bow / Take it away. *Le meas* –

Seamus

On the Night Watch, with 'for Seamus Heaney' on the dedication page, was published in 2009.

Carson was a talented folk musician, 'Rosin the Bow' an old Irish drinking song. '*Le meas*': respectfully.

To Marco Sonzogni

MS Sonzogni

2 October 2008

The Inn at Harvard,
1201 Massachusetts Avenue,
Cambridge, MA 02138

Dear Marco,

Your recent post-dream fax arrived just as Marie and I were gearing up for this first trip back to Harvard since 2004. I'm sorry as usual that the note is hasty but I just want to thank you for your kind thoughts and good wishes for the opera. I'm not at all sure that it will work – but we'll be there for the opening in The Globe.

I hope you will receive the enclosed without embarrassment. I was sorry to hear that TCD had been dilatory in sending expenses, but this is nothing but an ongoing part of the economy of Kindness. Years ago a friend who'd had a bit of a windfall sent me a gift just when I needed it – and it never needed to be spoken of or explained, except as part of the economy of amicability/*amitié*. I've just taken delivery of a Harvard fee, so no bother. And *no need to acknowledge. Pax.*

Nunc festino ad campum.

Love from Marie too (who is anxious about my boldness and fearful that you'll take umbrage at the *denarii*, but I tell her this is all easy, open exchange, and I hope you will agree) –

Seamus

In his dream, Sonzogni had been fishing with SH.

The opera, by the composer Dominique Le Gendre (b.1960), was her musical treatment of *The Burial of Thebes*; directed by Derek Walcott, it was performed both in Liverpool and at the Globe Theatre in London.

The 'enclosed' was a cheque for US$1,000, to help Sonzogni through difficulties, and which he used partly to finance a dual-language edition of SH's poem 'Eelworks', as a tribute to him on his seventieth birthday the following year. Sonzogni also persuaded SH to translate Eugenio Montale's (1896–1981) great poem 'L'anguilla' ('The Eel') for an anthology he was editing, which SH launched at the Istituto Italiano di Cultura in Dublin in June 2009.

'*Nunc festino ad campum*': 'Now I hurry to the campus'; '*denarii*': the smallest denomination in Ancient Roman currency.

To Bernard O'Donoghue — MS O'Donoghue

21 October 2008 [London]

Dear Bernard,

You'll be back from the chrysanthemum throne by now – many thanks for your card, and for your constant advocacy of the work, at home and beyant . . . I've no doubt you had a strange and beautiful experience of Japan, especially since it was so brief. And no doubt either that you will be invited back.

But chiefly I want to thank you for your kindness in writing like that in response to the 'writing block' situation. You said in your letter it was 'a bit of a whim' but it was a sign of unselfish care which meant everything to me. An actual grace, verging on the sanctifying. And all that as you were proofing more proof of that same unselfishness and care. Cambridge Companion it may be, but first and foremost it is Oxford Friend, fellow-*file*, brother in the mystery, shield-wall man, shoulder-companion . . . Full back, centre-field, full forward, linesman and umpire all in one.

Meanwhile, we have been much on the go since we saw you – twelve days in the States, around Harvard, BU and New York (with young Muldoon there); then a family wedding situation up north and two days at the ill-fated opera in London; a celebration of Zbigniew Herbert in Dublin, plus a swank night praising Kofi Annan to his face at a 'Concern' dinner in Dublin also; then back here to London for a Ted Hughes 10th anniversary event in the British Library. With the result, believe it or not, that instead of being exhausted I'm reanimated – in better form than when I set out. It may be that I relapsed into *too much* silence and withdrawal, although I may be driven back in when *Stepping Stones* comes out. Voices sing occasionally but insistently in my ear that it was folly to allow the thing to go on so long – over 400 pages . . . Yet other voices say, 'You were being yourself, so put up with yourself.' Or, as the *puncánaí* would have it, put up or shut up . . .

This, as usual, in too much haste, but as ever, with much love and gratitude to Heather and yourself –

Seamus

PS Saw Tom and Giti these last couple of nights, and sad to see Tom so unremittingly down and Giti so resolutely, unhopefully holding the emotional fort. Grievous, despairing times for them both. As much prayer time as therapy time. We are ourselves so lucky.

Blessings.

O'Donoghue had written to SH ('on a whim'), having heard that he was in low spirits. His own *Cambridge Companion to Seamus Heaney* was ready to be published in December 2008.

A *file* is a poet; the end of the same sentence employs phrases from *Beowulf*; and the following sentence refers to positions in a Gaelic football team.

'*puncánaí*': a play on *Poncáin*, Irish for 'Yanks'.

To Carol Hughes

MS Hughes

1 November 2008

Glanmore Cottage, Ashford,
Co. Wicklow

Dear Carol –

And All Souls' Night tonight . . . He'll be around. As Yeats says in the poem –

A ghost may come;
For it is a ghost's right,
His element so fine
Being sharpened by his death,
To drink from the wine breath
While our gross palates drink from the whole wine.

Ted would have known it by heart, but I had to look it up under ASN in the Yeats *Collected* . . .

Still, it was a rich experience, wholesome and strengthening, to drink from the whole wine of Ted's work in the British Library and to have the whole earth-axle voice on those CDs – for which many, many thanks. I've listened to the 'poems and stories' disc and will go back to my Belfast classroom in the early sixties when I get to 'Listening and Writing'/'Poetry in the Making'. (By the way, I found the fact of Sylvia's jealousy at the thought of Moira Doolan – whom I once met, a dumpy decent woman from, I think, Co. Down – quite funny: think I read about it in Elaine F.'s biography.)

Sorry, by the way, for the slight grubbiness of that previous page. The paper down here has been lying about for years, some of it.

You spoke with great sureness and freedom at the end of our evening, the valiant woman whom Ted had found now with her own well-founded 'achieve', as Hopkins might have called it, a high task performed, the stepping stones traversed – but still, I'm sure, with a feeling of loss in spite of all that is fulfilled. I'm not surprised that you felt the need to get home to the Orchard lands the next day: even though they now have to manage without your two 'hims' . . .

That *Stepping Stones* book got beyond what it should have been. Dennis is a civil servant of compulsive, exhaustive disposition, and over the years as we piled up the chapters, I simply did not realize how long the final thing would turn out to be. I actually enjoyed writing the answers when I was involved, but when it was all put together, I did balk. But the covenant with Dennis was years long and devotion deep on his part, so I went with it. I *did* want to get a lot of data on the record, but the whole book as it stands is probably far too much. But as they say in Scotland – and my own place – 'we'll pay for it'.

With love, until we meet again – Seamus

'under ASN': 'All Souls' Night' is the title of Yeats's poem.

Moira Doolan was a producer at the BBC and had been responsible for Ted Hughes's early radio broadcasts; the poet Elaine Feinstein (1930–2019) includes the episode of Sylvia Plath's jealousy in her *Ted Hughes: The Life of a Poet* (2001).

'Orchard lands': Carol Hughes's maiden name was Orchard, her father, Jack, a Devon farmer; for 'your two "hims"', see footnote to SH's pre-Christmas 1998 message to Valerie Eliot.

2009

It was never going to be that SH's seventieth birthday would pass without public celebration, and so, concealing his personal misgivings with good grace, he submitted to the jamboree. The private correspondence of this year, however, seems deliberately turned away from himself and in other directions, especially towards the praiseworthy achievements of SH's mainly American and Irish literary friends and associates.

His one major publication of the year was *The Testament of Cresseid and Other Fables*, his translations from the Scots of Robert Henryson – tellingly, more of an exercise in self-effacement than in self-expression.

To Sven Birkerts

TS Birkerts

1 January 2009

Glanmore Cottage, Ashford,
Co. Wicklow

Dear Sven,

Well, that stone shard has been in and out of the blue guitar alright (see Muldoon's 'Symposium' for stylistic prompt here: 'Make hay while you can still hit the nail on the head . . . Rome wasn't built between two stools.' etc.). I mean to say, by writing out the disappointment of the actual *après livre* experience of the Tower, you've re-dunked the whole place/event in the Forty Foot waters of memory so that it emerges with an entirely new dream-gleam, *le perdu retrouvé, hein*? Things as they were changed upon the snotgreen water . . . I was atremble with pleasure at the material purchase and meditative suppleness of the piece, envied you indeed the release and reward of it. Not to mention your other thirty look-and-tell, touchy-feely texts from pretexts. Sheer bloody genius, as Larkin would have said (but only if he himself [had] done them). Barks from a roadside Dothan-dog. Birk barks in fact (see enclosed – which I'm glad to say was written before I saw your shard piece: it appeared a few months ago in *Granta* 101, in a new series where they ask a scribe to dwell upon an *objet* that possesses some significance for him or her, however whimsical or private. Nice coincidence, what? But I only did the one.).

In fact, I've done hardly anything this last year. Something faltered in me around Christmas '07 when I had big doubts about the wisdom of having committed *Stepping Stones*; and then I think the fact that I had cadenced myself towards a conclusion in the last chapter of that book, allied to the fact that I'd let myself in for co-operation on that 70th birthday TV documentary – which felt a lot like a 'summing up' exercise – all combined to induce a not so subliminal sense of an ending. Which was overcome, I'm glad to report, by the visit to America in the autumn. All that swanning and swanking on podia revived bits of the old performing self, and the utterly credible joys of seeing you and Lynn and all the other friends that evening in Arlington lifted up my heart. So you should have heard from me before this.

I am grateful and not a little proud to be part of the *dramatis personae* in 'Stone Shard'; grateful too that it has stirred me to write this note on this day, and reawakened an urge to put pen to memory-paper once again. With love from both of us, and to Lynn and Mara and Liam also.

Seamus

'stone shard . . . blue guitar': Birkerts had shown SH prose pieces, meditations on objects, that would eventually be collected in his book of essays *The Other Walk* (2011). By alluding to Wallace Stevens's poem 'The Man with the Blue Guitar' – 'Things as they are / Are changed upon the blue guitar' – SH implies the transformations that Birkerts's writing brings about.

'experience of the Tower': taken by SH to see the Martello tower at Sandycove where the first scene of James Joyce's *Ulysses* is set, Birkerts had found it disappointing; Forty Foot is a nearby promontory, popular with swimmers.

'Dothan-dog': because Birkerts lived on Dothan Street, Arlington, Massachusetts.

SH's contribution to the series 'Subject+Object' in the UK magazine *Granta*, titled 'The Whisper of Love', was a prose account of finding a suggestively shaped, broken-off piece of birch sapling.

To Fred Marchant

MS Marchant

1 January 2009

Glanmore Cottage, Ashford,
Co. Wicklow

Dear Fred,

God only knows what is happening in Gaza to-day, but I've just re-read your letter of December 10 with new admiration for your moral and emotional stamina. It's like Chekhov going to Sakhalin: see and know and tell – yourself, at least, so that you are neither Yeats's rhetorician, deceiving others, nor his sentimentalist, deceiving yourself, but an initiate in the 'vision of reality'. Of which, of course, human kind cannot bear too much. But Fred Marchant, now, he takes the strain of it.

Please excuse, Fred, this mildewed notepaper – one of the last sheets of a cache we got as a present from Tom and Jean Flanagan the first Christmas we lived in the cottage here in 1972. Thirty-six years ago. I can hardly credit it. And me only 33 . . .

I've hardly written a poem this past year. I think the writing of *Stepping Stones* – putting a concluding cadence into the last chapter – and the participation in an RTÉ documentary film about myself (to go out on my 70th birthday) somehow induced a sense of an ending. Which I hereby vow, on 1.1.09, to outstrip.

And will be aided in that renewal by seeing you in March.

With love to Stefi too –
Seamus

Marchant had recently returned from a month in Israel and Palestine, where he had gone as member of a delegation from Interfaith Peace Builders, visiting non-violent activists and community organisers on both sides of the wall provocatively erected by Israel between itself and Palestinian lands. He had also intended to write about the visit, but found himself 'too rattled to write much'.

To Peter Sirr

TS Sirr

1 January 2009

Glanmore Cottage, Ashford,
Co. Wicklow

[. . .]
I have to apologize, therefore, for not having written earlier. But now that I've gone through the text again, I'm all the more grateful for your close, supportive responses to individual poems, for your conscientious yet entirely fresh and unfatigued survey of what is going on book by book, and for the way your insights as poet and reader into the verse are supplemented by familiarity with other stuff that has been published – interviews, lectures, etc., etc. I am also reassured not just by your admiring

remarks – about the likes of 'Oysters', for example, and 'Requiem for the Croppies' and 'The Mud Vision' (particularly glad to have these latter given a wee boost) – but I admire in turn your readiness to be silent about work that cannot be mentioned with honesty in the same critical breath.

Still, I was full of readerly glee – and, OK, a bit narcissistic – at the words you found to describe what you like. 'That lust for exactitude' which you attribute to me is one that I recognize in your own writing and feel rewarded by throughout the essay – when it is allied to a diagnosis of larger concerns it produces statements that 'strike me as a remembrance': for example, 'H. has had to bear the weight of public expectation – an expectation as ill-defined as it was pervasive' or 'H.'s imagination is to an extraordinary extent nourished by ritual . . . always reaching for a kind of sacral framework' or (really terrific, in a discussion of 'The Tollund Man' which does my heart good) 'the conflict is so internalized by those who live there . . . that any articulation of it, in journalism and poetry, strikes oddly'. In general, I appreciate your alertness to 'the shadow of the conflict' that hovers over the whole life and work for decades. Yet what I cherish most in the end are your final declarations of affection for the poems that convince because in poetry 'we are led by our ears, our instincts, and because of the way a particular configuration of language operates on mind, heart and body and won't let us go.' It means much to me that after that irrefutable statement you can adduce the lines you do.
[. . .]

RTÉ had brought out a set of CDs of SH reading his poems, for which Peter Sirr (b.1960), Irish poet and editor, had written an introductory essay. After the final statement quoted by SH, Sirr had drawn attention to lines from various poems, including the first two stanzas and final one of 'Mossbawn, 1: Sunlight' (*North*), the two concluding stanzas from the entire sequence 'Squarings' (*Spirit Level*), and the passage about the 'three-tongued glacier' from 'Höfn' (*District and Circle*).

To Andrew Motion

PC Motion

24 January 2009

Andrew –

These cards were a Christmas present but they're just the thing for the embarrassed man's 'thanks but sorry' message. I was on that jury the first time round and was at the presentation to Harold P.: and I like David C. and his wife. Even so. I couldn't make the September meeting, even if I wanted to, and I can't afford May 6. Glum old Heaney again. Ulster says no, there we go – keep going yourself –

Seamus

As chair of the judges for the David Cohen Prize, Motion had invited SH to join the panel; SH himself received the prize two months later.

The new card bears no postal address, but simply 'Seamus Heaney' top centre.

To Claire Tomalin

TS Tomalin

13 February 2009 191 Strand Road, Dublin 4

Dear Claire Tomalin,

It may be a while before you receive this, but I hope you'll get it before March 3, when a 'Portrait Gala' is to be held in the National Portrait Gallery – a fundraiser where they will be auctioning handwritten 'pen portraits' by contemporary scribblers – pieces about great ones whose painted portraits hang in the gallery. I chose to do Thomas Hardy, thinking of him as he was thirty years after the Strang portrait of 1896 – when he was still inhabited by the Bockhampton boy of the 1840s – but of course all the wonderful details of the old man's domestic circumstances in Max Gate come from your cherished biography. I ought to have written to you when it was published, it delighted and instructed me so thoroughly. And what I have written here should be footnoted with references to it and festooned with acknowledgements. I also took the liberty of quoting his remarks about the efficacy of the pen – which I know were not made in a letter, but I trust poetic licence can be pleaded in the circumstances. I enclose text of the handwritten thing they'll be auctioning, with gratitude for all the pleasure and profit I got and continue [to] get from *The Time-Torn Man*, he who smelt the stonework of Magdalene! That college is the one place where I can say I 'follow in his footsteps', since I was made an honorary fellow of the place some years ago, although the thing I usually sniff there is a malt Scotch from the cupboard in Professor Eamon Duffy's hospitable rooms.

Fondest wishes
Seamus Heaney

The biographer Claire Tomalin (b.1933) published her book *Thomas Hardy: The Time-torn Man* in 2006. She remembers meeting SH before a lecture on T. S. Eliot that he gave at University College London, when he confided, 'I wish I were speaking about Hardy rather than Eliot.' The description of Hardy in his pen sketch, titled 'Penman', depicts him 'in working clothes that would suit a stone mason', and departs entirely from what William Strang (1859–1921) showed in his oil painting.

To Donald Fanger

MS Fanger

2 March 2009 191 Strand Road, Dublin 4

Dear Don,

What is to be said? First of all, about my slowness to respond to Leonie's email, as it were? And now about your promptness to write that nonpareil response to *Stepping Stones*? The day your letter about the old Stalker having come out of its remission arrived was when I ought to have lifted the phone and spoken to you, standing on one slippy stone and waving to you on another. But of course even then I procrastinated . . . Then this morning, after a week when I was in England reading at Stephen Spender's centenary on Thursday and concelebrating Montague's eightieth on Tuesday, I came back to find a fax of a download from *Truthdig* (from the electronically-hyper O'Driscoll) and from Dan a mailed copy of the same life-enhancing review – but it's more than a review to me, more than advocacy, a laying on of trustworthy hands, a writer's benediction, a matter of beauty and love that is not – to quote W.B. – 'natural in an age like this'; it made me exult, not only because of the high terms of praise, the daring big words, but because of the intimacy of the reading, your palpable engagement with the stuff. To quote the gland old man again, 'Heart-smitten with emotion, I sink down' – only to rise up.

Your quotations from the book found the best that is in it, and so much of your commentary was balm and boost that I ought to have had more resistance, but all the time I could say to myself, 'This is Fanger you're reading, he's not into courtship, he has personal relations with the greatest and can wield the toledo blade as well as the magic wand.'

I ought, dear man, to go through the thing paragraph by paragraph, to rejoice in the perceptions, but that would be – to quote him a third time – to perfect the discipline of the mirror. Maybe later. For now

I apologize for this notepaper – the only stuff I have to hand in my brief-case, for it so happens I am not at home but in a private room in St Vincent's Hospital – admitted for a hernia procedure. A subtle hernia, the surgeon avers, when he felt it four or five weeks ago, but by to-morrow a sutured one, I hope. I came in a couple of hours ago, but I cannot give myself over to the torpor of the ward until I salute you.

Would that I could wave a wand that would be more efficacious than Lupron even, that would banish misfortune and make the *mortalia* non-tangent to the *mentem* and indeed the *corpus*. Instead, wafted towards you both comes the love of Catherine and Marie – who know I'm spending these first hours reading you and writing to you. And my own love and gratitude to a valiant, steadfast friend.

Seamus

PS When I told Brendan Kennelly that I was getting the hernia operated on he says, 'At least that's a stab in the front!' S.

The 'old Stalker' was cancer, affecting Donald Fanger's prostate; it is treated with injections of the synthetic hormone Lupron.

Truthdig is an online journal purveying, among other things, book reviews; writing there about *Stepping Stones*, Fanger declared of SH: 'His goal is to get things right, to make his presentations perfectly focused and suggestively resonant, and he is so supernaturally successful at that that you can't read him, whether in verse or prose, without a thrill of satisfaction and wonder akin to what he describes as his own experience of the way the writing takes shape. He makes the simplest words shine.'

'gland old man': because Yeats in old age underwent a treatment involving monkey gland injections to boost his virility.

'*mortalia . . . mentem . . . corpus*': see Virgil's *Aeneid*, Book 1, line 462.

To Robert Pinsky

TS Pinsky

14 March 2009 191 Strand Road, Dublin 4

Dear Robert,

The hour draws nigh . . . It must be close to thirty years since you came to Carysfort College and talked about William Carlos Williams and walked in the convent garden and had your embassy reception interrupted by the reports of the Reagan shooting. This time we have done our own shooting in the north ahead of time: the Real IRA at it again, shots like that cousin-shit in handfuls from the cage.

Still, it will be a sweetness to see you here, and Frank, and Venclova and all the rest. Susie will be sending out invitations by email on Monday, asking the visiting poets to the house here on the Saturday morning, for a coffee and/or something else to wet their whistle, so I'll get her to attach this note to the electronic messaging. It turns out that Frank will be doing a workshop at that time so I was wondering if you and he might be free to go for a spin in what some people call my brazen car, down to Glanmore in Wicklow, say, on the Friday morning – and maybe have lunch somewhere? I'm not sure when you're arriving, but even if you land on the Wednesday, I myself won't have clear walkabout/driveabout time till the Friday. A lot of things taken on earlier in the week so that the weekend can be kept clear.

In the meantime I have been back in the high wholesome enviable hullabulloo of *Gulf Music*. Kavanagh once defined technique as a method for getting at life and that is what you managed – with fury and finesse. The drunkenness of things being various, as MacNeice put it, but without canvassing those thing-thoughts underpinning and bowling over in a Pinsky poem. Experiment and exultation, the demarcation between avant-garde and accessible erased, poetic intelligence on a spree in the information age, a carnival in progress where the intimate and the remembered are every bit as present [as] the media, the news and the noosphere. Again you are working in utterly your own way and at the same time providing a way into the world we're all of us in. I'm jealous of the immense supply and contact in the poems, the strobe from line to line, the recurrent motifs which help you to let fly rather than tuck things up nice and tidy. We should have the banners and the streamers flying for you in Dún Laoghaire. Instead it will be crowded dinner benches and – probably – press interviews. Call me ahead if you like or email Susie.

Marie has laryngitis at the moment, but she still exhales her love and looks forward to seeing you soon.

Seamus

Robert Pinsky, with US poet Frank Bidart and Lithuanian Tomas Venclova, was a guest at the 2009 Poetry Now Festival in Dún Laoghaire. His outspokenly political poetry collection *Gulf Music* had been published in 2007.

'Reagan shooting': this places Pinsky's earlier visit in March 1981, when on the 30th of the month John Hinckley failed in his assassination attempt on the US President. On 7 March 2009, two off-duty British soldiers had been shot outside the Massereene Barracks in Antrim; two days later, the Continuity IRA murdered a Northern Irish police officer: these were the first such killings to take place in Northern Ireland since 1998. Pinsky's poem 'Stupid Meditation on Peace' (in *Gulf Music*) concludes: 'My mind resembles my restless, inferior cousin / Who fires his shit in handfuls from his cage.'

To Gerard Smyth

TS Smyth

24 March 2009 191 Strand Road, Dublin 4

Dear Gerry,

Forgive me for not having answered your earlier letters pronto. Now I can't lay my hand on the most recent one where you list the poems previously published in the paper, but I do remember 'Postscript' and a couple of others were mentioned. I'll call you or maybe see you tomorrow in Dún Laoghaire, but this is a last-minute attempt to atone for the neglect.

Partly I was held up because I wasn't sure which poems would be right on this particular occasion – I have several that depend on a sequencing of 'twelve-liners' and wouldn't be quite right for the one-offish kind of reading they'd get in the Saturday pages. However, I'm sending 'Miracle' which was printed as a Christmas card in 2006, but not I think in any other publication since then. Also 'The Door Was Open and the House Was Dark' which was written after a dream before David Hammond died, but which can now stand as a memorial – though if you were to use it, I'd prefer the 'in memory' bit to appear under the last line rather than under the title. But decide otherwise if you think otherwise. 'The Wood Road' I submit as a kind of post-peace process poem, nothing too spectacular. Three, I realize, is too many, but I want you to have a choice.

All your care, Gerry, now and heretofore, is deeply appreciated. There's going to be a lot of exposure in the days and weeks ahead – more plans for my birthday, I say, than there were for the Easter Rising – but the true attention of friends helps a fellow to survive.

See you soon, I hope –
Seamus

Gerard Smyth (b.1951), Managing Editor and Poetry Editor at the *Irish Times*, was gathering contributions to the special supplement titled 'Heaney at 70' that would appear in the paper's 24 April edition. The supplement included three of SH's poems – 'Miracle', 'The Wood Road' and 'Chanson d'Aventure' (one of the 'twelve-liners' mentioned above), as well as tributes and reminiscences by Helen Vendler, Paul Muldoon and others.

To Hughie O'Donoghue

MS H. O'Donoghue

15 April 2009 — 191 Strand Road, Dublin 4

Dear Hughie,

This morning I woke prostrated by the passage of the media juggernaut that bore down on me and drove over us all during the weekend, but when I lifted up my eyes to my *Inheritance* I felt some strength and pride return. The gift of that picture came at the start of the birthday boom, as it were, a work that will stand and stand to me always, a proof of the lines in another valued gift – Derek Mahon's poem in the *Irish Times* supplement – 'If a thing happens once / it happens once forever.' John Montague's old people were like dolmens round his childhood, but now those O'Donoghue ancestors are like caryatids around me and mine. Everything about the painting affects me deeply, intimately, mysteriously. It is utter work by someone whose artistry is second nature, the familiar defamiliarized and then – the mystery – refamiliarized. The tones and textures, the bold strokes, the foreverness of those figures in your affection and iconography, the rightness of all this both in itself and for somebody as ready as I am to be affected by it – I cannot thank you enough for helping the Dún Laoghaire people and for enriching this house and home.

To-day Marie and I are heading away with the family – down to the two grand-daughters – for three days of recuperation in London. Time to lick wounds to the self-composure caused by the unexpectedly drastic exposure, and lap up some wines . . .

When we get back, we'll have time to return again to dwell more leisurely and [with] more awed attention to the dimensions of your IMMA exhibition. It is a triumph. A great example of exfoliation as integrity, or integrity as exfoliation. Sublime stamina. Beauty (you make us free to say it) and daring. There is so much more to say, and yet not enough *can* be said. I thought of the medieval anchorite, Macoige of Lismore, who said – in Irish or Latin, I assume – that the best attribute of character was 'steadiness, for it is best when a man has set his hand to tasks, to persevere. I have never heard fault found with that.'

With love and renewed gratitude and respect – and to Clare too –
Seamus

Having been approached by Poetry Ireland, which wanted to offer a painting as a birthday gift to SH, O'Donoghue accepted the commission for a nominal fee and the painting that resulted, *Inheritance*, made with SH specifically in mind, was presented to him at an event in Dún Laoghaire.

To Marco Sonzogni

TS Sonzogni

9 May 2009

Glanmore Cottage, Ashford,
Co. Wicklow

Dear Marco,

Here in Wicklow, the May month, as T. Hardy so deliciously puts it, 'flaps its glad green leaves like wings, / Delicate-filmed as new-spun silk' and I only wish that my spirit frolicked as blithely, but it is anxious and full of self-rebuke. I am very sorry it has taken so long for you to hear from me about *Consider the Eel*. The birthday business began at the end of March at the Dún Laoghaire Poetry Now festival and went on without let until mid-April, after which I had to rise and go to Princeton to read at another festival organized by Paul Muldoon, then back to various pomps and travels here – an event in Queen's University, a hullabulloo called the Irish Book Awards where *Stepping Stones* got a gong in the Non Fiction Section and where I did the citation for Edna O'Brien's Lifetime Achievement Award. Only now, alas, am I starting to atone for my delays in relation to so much kindness and so many gifts, none more beautiful or cherished or devoted, Marco, than yours. Marie's breath was taken away too, she being the grand-daughter of the founder of the Devlin eel-export business (it lapsed in her father's time, but Grandfather Devlin started to export Lough Neagh eels to Billingsgate). And there was an extra delight for us, beyond the intrinsic joy of the writing and the exquisite paper and print and design of the physical book, in the fact that we had gone to an eel restaurant in Tokyo some ten or twelve years ago with our old friend Masazumi Toraiwa . . . So we were at home with more than the in-woven quotations and allusions. I am moved again every time I read the sequence by the *tendresse* and generosity of the *hommage*, not to mention the immense forethought and planning that went into the arrangement of the publication, including the so appropriate scroll/art work frontispiece. Above all, however, I am honoured by the quality of the imagining, the range and glee of the associations, the combination of quickness of connection (the lambent moves from Wellington to samurai in hot weather to Mozart to an eel's leap of faith and all the rest of the phantasmagoria) with such solidity of presence (those buckets, that table, that skinning, the guy with the stick) . . . If I am proud and given faith in myself by all this, you too must have got good reward from 'the achieve of it', as Hopkins might have said. 'Our poesy is as a gum which oozes / From whence 'tis nourished.' Yes, of course, but so too is our confidence. I look forward to seeing you soon in Dublin. With love from Marie too –

Seamus

In addition to the bilingual *Eelworks* (see letter to Marco Sonzogni of 2 October 2008), Sonzogni had presented his own poem *Consider the Eel*, also in both English and Italian, also in a limited edition printed by Joseph Weiss, as a birthday gift.

To Michael and Edna Longley PC Longley

15 May 2009 [Postmarked 'Roma Fiumicino']

Longley just misses imparting to Heaney the gift of the singing line? Still, great reports of the magnificent reading you gave the poems in Belfast on 30th April. Meanwhile, we're in withdrawal here, in sunshine and slackness, getting over the 70s extravaganza . . .

Love to you both –

Seamus

The postcard, sent from Rome, shows Michelangelo's painting of God creating Adam. A party celebrating SH's birthday had been held, in his absence, at the Seamus Heaney Centre for Poetry on 30 April.

To Jonathan Galassi TS NYPL

19 June 2009 191 Strand Road, Dublin 4

Dear Jonathan,

The Henryson book: I had an odd ambivalence about it. The last time we talked, *Aeneid* VI was at the top of the agenda and that seemed like the next project, but it wasn't quite ready when there was a Faber flurry and hurry to do something around birthday time, so Henryson jumped the queue. If we had been more in touch around that time, the subject might have come up, but I was preoccupied with the launch of *Stepping Stones* and the recording of all the published poems for a boxed set of 15 (!) CDs to be issued, again at birthday time – Easter Monday. More planning for that birthday, I maintain, than there was for the Easter Rising.

I wasn't sure if the book would have any real interest for American audiences. So I'm truly delighted that you take pleasure in it. I enjoyed doing every stanza – a hell of a lot more delight in letting slip the rhyme royal than unlocking the Anglo-Saxon word-hoard. And everyday life in fifteenth-century Scotland wasn't all that different from South Derry in the 1940s . . .

Meanwhile, I've written again to Henry Hart. I am most grateful for your alerting me to the circulation of that proposal and for your judgement and advice. I'll append my most recent letters to him, which must have knocked the stuffing out of the poor fellow. Though where we go from here I'm just not sure.

I look forward to the transatlantic *Testament* and *Fables*.

Fondest wishes
Seamus

Jonathan Galassi was now Editor-in-Chief at Farrar, Straus and Giroux and in charge of the poetry list there.

The US poet and academic Henry Hart (b.1954) had already published a critical study of SH: *Seamus Heaney: Poet of Contrary Progressions* (1992). Hearing that Hart now planned to write a biography of him and that the proposal for a book was being circulated among publishers by his agent, SH fired off a fax stating reasons for his objection, which included that he had already turned down proposals by other 'experienced and highly respected biographers' and that he would want any 'official biographer' to have 'more than a scholar's awareness of the Irish context'.

To Peter McDonald

MS McDonald

20 June 2009

Dear Peter,

To have the Henryson book assayed and approved by you was more than I could have hoped for: I took great pleasure in doing the work, stanza by stanza, and knew that my 1940s mid-Ulster self was closer to Henryson's fifteenth century than it is to many another's twenty-first, so felt I was on to the right material – odd as it might appear to others. But voices still cried in the ear that it was all folly. Now I feel safe and sound – at least in that particular regard. I also felt you had managed something at once focused and happily free in 'Country' – in *Archipelago* – and envied the way you found of giving 'power from well beneath the surface' – Seamus

The review by Peter McDonald (b.1962), Northern Irish poet and lecturer in English at Christ Church, Oxford, of *The Testament of Cresseid and Seven Fables* appeared in the *Guardian* of 13 June; his poem 'Country' was in *Archipelago*, the literary magazine edited by Andrew McNeillie, and was later included in his book *Torchlight* (2011).

To Greg Delanty

TS NLI

5 July 2009

Glanmore Cottage, Ashford,
Co. Wicklow

Dear Greg,

Very sorry to have kept you waiting for this 'Deor'. As it happens, kindly Michael Matto's gift of the Malone edition and your own gentle prod – can I say that? – came at exactly the right moment. The excellent package Michael sent a hundred years ago has been down here on my desk, sunk deep in the mail-midden, but I excavated the strata last night and spent a happy day getting to the enclosed version. It's a quick second/third draft, but who knows, more may be needed, especially if Michael has any queries or worries.

All the commentaries confess bafflement about the worms in line 1, so I played with the smith Weland's status as a metal worker and the coiling/worming of rods beaten into damascene swords and made him a metal-*wormer*, but that may be going too far. Still, I enjoyed it . . . And the lapping/lopping interpretation in that first stanza comes from reading about the background story of hamstringing. What a crowd!

Until this week I have been unable to relax or focus on anything – my whole worry was the 'opening address' at the first T. S. Eliot International Summer School – taken on because of my friendship with the director, Ron Schuchard. But when I began to face the reality of facing an audience of lifelong Eliot scholars and editors and biographers and critics – Denis Donoghue, Lyndall Gordon, Frank Kermode, Christopher Ricks and a host of others – I quailed and got blocked and was like a rabbit in the headlights. But, as the master himself put it, now that's done/and I'm glad it's over. Finally it worked out OK and our few days at the school were most enjoyable – went to Little Gidding, read the poem there with Robert Crawford (whose PhD/first book was on Eliot), met Christopher (who came after the opening, thank God) and Judith, etc. etc.

More when I see you. [. . .]

The poet Greg Delanty, a Cork man now living and teaching in the USA, was joint editor, with Michael Matto of Adelphi University, of the 2011 anthology *The Word Exchange: Anglo-Saxon Poems in Translations*.

SH types the current draft of his translation of 'Deor', which differs in many details from what would appear in *The Word Exchange*, immediately below his letter; at this stage, the first stanza read:

Weland the metal-wormer   suffered woe.
That steadfast man   knew misery.
Sorrow and longing   walked beside him,
wintered in him,   kept wearing him down
after Nithad   had him lopped and lapped,
sinew-bonds   on the better man.
That passed over,   and this will too.

The text of this and the following stanzas is garnished with queries and alternative wordings in Delanty's hand.

To Chris Hardy

MS Hardy

23 July 2009   191 Strand Road, Dublin 4

Dear Chris Hardy,

A while ago you wrote a good letter about Helicon and Osias

Loukas – where I did stop one clear and happy morning when we drove with friends from Delphi to Thebes (and found our parking spot there on Antigone Street) – but even though I read that you could get to Hesiod's farm by muleback I never got up the mountain.

The hotel in Pylos I loved: can't remember the name, but it was a couple or three hundred yards up from the harbour: put your back to the land, go round to the left of the water and turn left up the hill. The place was on the right, on the waterside – small, with little balconies.

'What is beneath / a few nailed planks is theirs' – I loved that, partly because it so immediately and intimately makes it *ours*. And of course I am entirely at home 'where stones and thistles grow / Straight through a wired-up gate . . .' I even remember a neighbour of ours who threshed in a barn where the machine was driven round a 'tight hippodrome' – though we thought then a hippodrome was a cinema in Belfast –

Sincerely
Seamus Heaney

Chris Hardy (b.1947) had sent SH his poem 'Purdah', about an ancient Greek well; Osias Loukas is a Byzantine monastery, standing beneath Mount Helicon, in countryside rich with literary associations, as is Pylos, where Homer's Nestor lived.

To Frank Ormsby

MS Ormsby

22 October 2009 — 191 Strand Road, Dublin 4

Dear Frank,

Fireflies is a first rate book. I began it with gratitude and admiration and ended – that 'Builder' – close to tears. There is a quality of inwardness and attention and constant mental alertness as well as wily word-joy. A great sense of a life lived devotedly and then repossessed imaginatively. Very coherent too, webbed and woven. And various – you do the meditative, discursive (and unexpected) longer lyric and then those kite-tails of haikus – I think the well level not changing would have made Bashō jealous, though he might have got angry when you keep bringing it off – that mud, that wiped window, that West Cork funeral. I thought the journals – Valhalla and City – a wonderful combination of American freedom and Ormsby fidelity.

I could go on, but need to get a taxi soon – heading for poetry conference in Kraków – just didn't want the first relish and trust to pass without telling you.

Marie and I were glad to see you in that foyer –
Love – Seamus

The 'haikus' in Frank Ormsby's book that SH picks out for special praise are discrete verses in his poem 'Small World'. The one that might have made Bashō jealous goes:

> Kneeling, we fill two buckets
> to the brim. The well-
> level does not change.

To Sean O'Brien

TS O'Brien

9 November 2009

Dear Sean,

Since I saw you, it's been more a case of on the road than on the toon: Kraków, the British Library, homework in Dublin with the Association of Secondary Teachers of Ireland, swank work in Belfast with fellow septuagenarian Longley, the pair of us dickey-bowed and bowing with the Ulster Orchestra; advocating Amnesty, book launching, fund raising . . . 'Events, dear boy, events!'

I finally got settled a while yesterday and got to read 'On the Toon' and absorb *Night Train*. Birtley and you made a lovely job of the latter, a real coallaboration, the black beauty of it growing page by page, the poems and the art as at home with each other as the thumb and the smudge. It's a book that has been waiting to be made, a lovely smoky extension to those songs for Birtley in *The Drowned Book*. And of course the undergroon toon, the visionary river and bridge has been implicit for years now – a sure strong note struck there, a totally athletic gait to the verse, a sense that you can do anything, go head on or get high, get anything in from drugs to Dante. It's genuine poetry indebted to the *Commedia* but dodging pastiche, full of appetite, subject matter and phantasmagoria, as W.B. would have said, and matters of fact. A triumph, as C. Monteith used to say. And so, as he once wrote to John McGahern in a telegram, torrential congratulations!

And many thanks for the extra 'Slack's, which arrived a while ago. As did Linda's generous note . . .

Love to Gerry too.

Seamus

The British poet Sean O'Brien (b.1952) is the author of many volumes of poetry, including *The Drowned Book* (2007), *Night Train* (2009), which has illustrations by Birtley Aris (1927–2021), and *Inferno* (2006), his 'verse version' of the first book of Dante's *Divina Commedia*; 'On the Toon' is the poem that concludes his 2011 collection, *November*. His partner is Gerry Wardle.

SH had read his own poems in Newcastle-upon-Tyne, where O'Brien was Professor of Creative Writing at the university, on 13 October; he had also written and donated his poem 'Slack' (*Human Chain*) to support the Newcastle Centre for Literary Arts, and prints of it were made and sold.

SH's quoting of 'Events, dear boy, events!', the words of Harold Macmillan (1894–1986), Conservative Prime Minister of Britain, when asked what were the biggest challenges a statesman had to face, were perhaps meant as a tease to the socialist O'Brien.

To Andrew Motion MS Motion

10 November 2009 191 Strand Road, Dublin 4

Dear Andrew,

You have been on my conscience for a while: at my Hibernian distance, I missed the news of your knighthood – and that of Christopher Ricks – and when I did hear, I thought, 'Christ, he'll think I'm not writing because my passport was green,' but still procrastinated. So, hats off. A sennet. A flourish. A doffing to you. And congratulations: no anxiety about that honour, fully earned and well deserved. You ought to have heard from me before now.

Mark Pigott? I'm not sure when/if we are to meet, but I'll certainly bear the Archive in mind when/if we do. Meanwhile, it seems only right that the President/Patron should throw in a few bob, especially in a year when the Poet Laureate handed over the David Cohen Prize. The bank here tells me I'd better not write a cheque, but if you sent the bank details necessary for a transfer from here to there, euro to sterling, I'd pitch in the one grand, in your currency.

This not to be mentioned, contested or noted in any despatches.

Meanwhile, as ever, we hurry. But to-day, at least, to go to the west of Ireland for 'a break' – which, as you know, means catching up on what should have been done long ago.

Love to Kyeong-Soo too, and from Marie. Hope the flat business proceeds satisfactorily –

Seamus

The Poetry Archive, which collects and generates recordings of poets reading their work, was an initiative of Andrew Motion's while he was UK Poet Laureate; the US businessman and philanthropist Mark Pigott (b.1954) helped fund it.

To Paul Keegan

EMAIL

14 November 2009

Dear Paul,

Ever since you sent me that wise saw of Eliot's – 'The point at which one has "enough" for a book (of verse) is not a quantitative matter alone. One only has not enough, when one feels that the poems written require the cooperation of certain poems not yet written, in order to be themselves quite' – I have been waiting for those unwritten necessary ones to arrive. And when I found a way of including the second grandchild – 'A Kite for Aibhín' – and 'The Conway Stewart' (to link to the parent poems early on and look forward to the Colmcille translations, 'Lick the Pencil' and 'Hermit Songs' in the latter part) I felt the book was near to being itself quite. So I'm sending it to you for a preliminary read, knowing that you may be over in Dublin before Christmas and that we might have a chance to mull and muse then. About if and when, as it were . . .

So! As the *hwaet*man says. Let's see how decided the thing turns out to be. In order to keep things provisional, I've not included a dedication or acknowledgements or – perhaps – a note or two. On *sidhe* as a fairy creature/fairy dwelling? On 'Sweeney Out Takes'? Can/should we assume/presume awareness of names and incidents in *Sweeney Astray*? Or mention the Book VI parallels for 'Route 110'? Or can that be done in the jacket copy? The luxury of these fusses . . .

All good wishes

Accompanying SH's presentation of the first full draft of *Human Chain*, which was published without notes of the kind he wonders about in his second paragraph.

The Eliot 'saw' is from Eliot's letter to Marianne Moore of 31 January 1934 (*Letters of T. S. Eliot*, 7, p. 54).

In his *Beowulf*, SH translates the original poem's first, declamatory word, *Hwaet*, as 'So!'

To Thomas McCarthy

MS Princeton

28 November 2009 191 Strand Road, Dublin 4

Dear Tom,

Many thanks for sending *The Last Geraldine Officer* and my apologies for the long delay in replying. I was waiting for a time when I could read the whole of the title poem and give the book the attention it deserves. The whole thing is beautifully of a piece and the *Officer* deeply imagined, strange and familiar at once, defamiliarized but not distanced, very present and envisaged, in fact, like that overture to light at the beginning. The pillars of meditative stanzaic narrative/reminiscence at the start and finish have a beautiful cello tone to them, but a cello that can play woodnotes and warnotes, as it were, can tune eros and Eire, and can stand like unbroken columns, with their rhyme and rumination. I love the way things are reprised, the recipes – so rich and juicy and joyful in themselves, a kind of folding in of Brueghel and Beeton – reappearing and replaying not just a motif but a history – that nettle soup, those silky, slurpy apricots . . . But then too the whole montage of the middle sections, the historico/political realism binding and bound by your own inwardness and lyricism and gifts *mar file i nGaeilge*. I loved the whole symbolic/authentic period life of Uncle Walter and the Usshers and O'Díreáin, and the appearances of MacLiammoir and Le Brocquy and (!) Lemass . . .You have surprised by a fine excess and paid something back not just to a noble cast(e) but to a suffered destiny and tested dignity. I am full of admiration for the scope and *tendresse* of your imagining, the way you can do the Audie Murphy in the tank bits as well as the Cappoquin interiors and the Templemaurice epiphanies.

Beavers aloft. Ringing cheers. Love to Catherine –

Seamus

PS And prophetic too . . . That 'flood plain by a tidal river'. We are so mindful of that biblical deluge . . . S.

The Last Geraldine Officer is the title of both McCarthy's Anvil Press collection of 2009, and of the long poem on historical themes, in verse and prose, in English and Irish, with which it concludes. A striking feature of the latter is the number of mouth-watering culinary recipes it gives in full.

'*mar file i nGaeilge*': 'as a poet in Irish'.

The exclamation mark preceding the name of Seán Lemass, Taoiseach from 1959 to 1966, signals SH's amusement that this politician should have found his way into artistic company.

'biblical deluge': of the great downpours and floods that afflicted both Britain and Ireland in November 2009, some of the most severe were in Co. Cork, where McCarthy lives.

To Greg Delanty

TS Cork

29 November 2009

Dear Greg,

When I got the manuscript I sent a text to your Irish mobile, but it may never have reached you. I was saying that my heart usually sinks when I hear the thump of a heavy envelope on the hall floor but it leapt up that morning when I discovered *Book XVII* and read those first fine, careless, confident, sagacious, rapturous lines. Never mind the feet of Mount Parnassus. You are well up the leg of ParnassA by now, maybe even at the mount stage. The book has freed and founded you at once – it gets in all of your voices, the extent of your knowledge, the intensity of your commitments, the delight of your scepticism, the weight, as Shauneen Keogh would say, of your passion, your rage for justice, your gumption and humour, your stylistic agility, the scope of your imagining. All of which reminds me, as I said to you before, of Berryman's *Dream Songs*, but also of Kavanagh's conviction about the strength of the comic vision. Your string is not slack – the poems have spring as well as fluency and flyness – but the true note gets played as if it were 'a moment's thought'. And when the spontaneity and the cultivation/learning/lyricism/irony get melded and modulated from voice to voice, there's a high readability quotient, a fulfilment of what Mahon and Longley once called 'the good crack' requirement – yet the poems aren't out to suck up to the reader, they are startles of wisdom rather than knowing winks, 'for wisdom is a butterfly / And not a gloomy bird of prey' (this, apparently was W.B.Y.'s favourite inscription from himself on his own books, and I commend it to you for future use).

Your Greek/Athenian visit and consequent familiarity with the classical ground deepens the imaginative purchase: the real and cod learning resonate all the more because contemporary tourist acropolis life is there also and the gods are going it as hard as ever in the synapses of the contemporary as they once did on the summit of Olympus. Especially that Eros and Aphrodite pair. And Hestia too, of course. I am very touched by the work of Seamius. In fact I'm inclined to repeat here words that Philip Larkin wrote to me about my essay on him in his 60th birthday festschrift: he was grateful, he said, that I could treat him as a 'poet' – and he put the inverted commas round the word – and not as some kind of versified John Osborne or cut-price Betjeman. Your tendresse and seriousness are gold bar, salt of earth treasure to me. I rejoice for you and hope this book will have a great glamorous success.

I know also, *a chara*, that you have been very busy – and send love from Marie as well to Patti and Dan – Seamus

Delanty's *The Greek Anthology Book XVII* is presented as an addition to the classical sixteen-volume *Greek Anthology*, and contains the short lyrics of numerous fictional poets, some of whose names – Montagus, Muldunus the Magister Grammaticorum, Bernardius Scholasticus, and so on – may remind readers of Delanty's Irish contemporaries. There is no poem by 'Seamius', though there are two by 'Heanius'.

'ParnassA' is not SH's feminisation of Parnassus, but rather his joke on the Cork City speech habit of adding a final 'a' or 'ah' to names.

2010

On 30 May, SH wrote to Seamus Deane: 'I have been in a doldrum for a good while now.' The heavy depression to which he referred hung over much of this year and the early part of the next and his creative output dropped, even while his public life continued in the same, driven and dutiful, international manner as before.

Few of the letters of this year retain the old outgoing animation, and a new, more nervous and guarded face at times seems presented to the world.

Human Chain, SH's final book of poems, was published in September.

To Rebecca Pearson

EMAIL Faber

25 March 2010

Dear Becky,

Sorry for the delay in responding to your note about the *Sunday Times* interview proposal. I agree with you about the good exposure that paper would provide and yes, I thought that Cathy Galvin's piece on Carol Ann Duffy was thorough, sprightly and honest work. Add to that the fact that my son Michael works on the *ST Culture* magazine in Ireland, and you have somebody perfectly well disposed to the paper.

But. And I'm sorry the 'but' is coming at this stage, though glad it's not later . . . This day last week I did a reading from the new book in St Andrews at that StAnza Festival. It was the first time I'd read some of those new poems in public, 'Album' and 'Chanson d'Aventure', for example – things that I like very much, but which arise from and are explicit about truly intimate experience. Afterwards it struck me that any interviewer is bound to ask again about my stroke and my parents and all that the 'Album' entails/contains, and that these are subjects that I do not want to address other than in the poems themselves. I think therefore that full press interviews had best be dropped. I'll be doing the reading in Aldeburgh in late August and I've taken on an engagement with the Aspects festival in Bangor, Co. Down on 22

September, so that will be a kind of Northern Irish launch, and no doubt there will be other readings and input on radio etc., where the exposure isn't quite so personal. After that 70th birthday last April and *Stepping Stones* and everything else that is on the record, I cannot bear to answer personal questions to another journalist or pose at home for another photographer. And I wonder if at this stage even the *Sunday Times* would make any great difference in the sales. Can we pull back and for the moment just say no all round?

Meanwhile, I'll send a copy of this letter to Stephen and Paul. I think I said something of the same sort to Paul when the manuscript was sent in.

All good wishes –

Seamus

Rebecca Pearson worked in the publicity department at Faber.

To Grey Gowrie

MS Gowrie

8 April 2010

Glanmore Cottage, Ashford,
Co. Wicklow

Dear Grey,

Yesterday morning – spring light, whins in blossom, uncrowded motorway – I drove from South Derry to South Dublin, on my own in the car, in what W.W. might have called 'that blessèd mood / In which the affections gently lead us on' – but I was lucky to be led on also by your voice and those poems on the CDs. It always takes me a while to know that I am aligned for poems: I used to have an appetite that was greedy for new work, but now I incline to go back to what I have known, and doubt my ability to take in the new and true; but in the case of *The Andrians* I needn't have worried. It came to me clearly and courageously – that last image of the squid-beating to make it tender! It traces 'truly though not ostentatiously the primary laws of our nature' (I've never got over W.W.'s *Preface*, still right on in so many respects), is utterly alert to the contemporary and irradiated at the same time by a generous sensibility, learned and loving. Mind-sweeping, as it were, as well as mood-invoking. I loved the way you used – if that is not too workmanlike a word – the Nolan and the man from Hartford, the way the metaphysical pining and the matters of fact and friendship filled the proud sail of verse and voice. And of course the *Third Day* disc had poems integrally linked to the line of courage and *tendresse* that's held in *The Andrians*. You managed the Lowell effect/ambition, to be heart-breaking. Hearing those particular poems read aloud made me think that books ought to be issued with CDs – but then I remembered that the voice I was hearing is preternaturally gifted and that listening to others is as likely to produce what Brother Friel calls 'a hash' as a high.

Anyhow, I won't ever forget my Derry/Dublin transport. With love to you and Neiti –

Seamus

Grey Gowrie, 2nd Earl of Gowrie (1939–2021), Scottish hereditary peer with family links to Ireland, had during his career as a Conservative politician served in the Northern Ireland Office; as a poet, he enjoyed a late blossoming and was the author of, among other works, a long, elegiac, allusive poem, *The Andrians* (2009); his *Third Day: New and Selected Poems* (2008) takes its title from a poem about his own heart transplant; Neiti was his wife.

The Wordsworth poem from which SH quotes is 'Lines Composed a Few Miles above Tintern Abbey'. 'Nolan' is Flann O'Brien; the 'man from Hartford', Wallace Stevens.

To Carol Hughes

GC Hughes

19 May 2010 [Ballymaloe House, Co. Cork]

Dear Carol,

Marie and I had a plan to go to Italy this week – Bologna for a couple of nights, then Rome for 3/4 – but what with the belching Vulcan to the north and a fortnight on the road in the States in April, we decided to stay at home – but to travel around a bit. Hence I find myself in Co. Cork, in a pleasure dome called Ballymaloe House, on a terrace by a lawn where the peahen struts and the peacock screams, the doves coo, the Mary month greens fuller and greener – and I'm at last writing a note. I was out of touch, maybe even out of the country, when news of the Abbey came through, but all that has a May-month plenitude and rightness to it – so here are Anne Yeats's *Eggs in a Basket* which delighted me when I saw them today in the Crawford Art Gallery: our first time in the place, and *about* time. Anyhow, just to send love from us both – and now the geese have begun to make their presence felt also. We must meet – maybe Cambridge?

Seamus xxx

The 'belching Vulcan' was Eyjafjallajökull, the Icelandic volcano that erupted intermittently between late March and late June 2010, causing, among other things, widespread disruption to air traffic.

Ballymaloe House in East Cork is a hotel with a celebrated restaurant.

'News of the Abbey': Ted Hughes was to be honoured with a memorial stone in Westminster Abbey's Poets' Corner.

The Crawford Gallery is the city of Cork's museum of visual arts.

To Saima Khan

TS Khan

28 May 2010 [Coleraine] Co. Derry

Dear Saima Khan,

My apologies for the delay in replying to your letter. There is always a backlog of mail requesting interviews and while I need to decline – my calendar is very full and there are already so many (too many?) interviews with me in print – I still hesitate to disoblige a research student. So I'll respond briefly to the questions you ask.

1. The title 'Redress of Poetry', etc. There's a good bit about this in my book of interviews with Dennis O'Driscoll, *Stepping Stones*, on page 431 and following. In some sense the lectures and the theme of redress are yet another attempt to answer the question 'What use is poetry? What does it make happen?' As I say in the poem 'Terminus' – and in 'Something to Write Home About' (in *Finders Keepers*) 'I grew up in between' – and for years I found myself between the somewhat journalistic expectation that a poet would intervene in politics in a *parti pris* fashion and the equal if not opposite orthodoxy that an artist's obligation is to honest, disinterested exploration and expression. But as I also say in the O'Driscoll interview, it took a while for me to get the theme into focus.
2. You are right about the access opened up by the word 'redress' – the dictionary definition allowed one to treat the poetry as an artistic entity in itself and also as a response to what Keats called 'a world of pain and troubles'. If you

want a more recent treatment of this you might want to get hold of a lecture I gave last year to the Irish Human Rights Commission entitled 'Writer and Righter' – it will be published by them this week, so you can probably access it on the internet.

3. The remark about poetry ending in self-consciousness is a rephrasing of Robert Frost's contention that poetry 'begins in delight and ends in wisdom'. I guess I was thinking more about the poet than poetry itself when I made the remark. But yes, a successful poem leads you to a better level of awareness, helps you to a clearer consciousness of what you didn't know you already knew. The starting point of a poem, I have often said, is an image or memory or some chance circumstance that awakens the sense of possibility in you – like a bleeper going off, wakening you up, asking you to find out what's behind it, or indeed ahead of it.

   'Markings', for example, which you mention, began with the wonderful memory of playing football as a child and continuing to be able to do so even in the dark, but as I re-entered the memory it opened up metaphorical possibility, analogies between seeing in the dark and 'seeing things' in imagination and so on. So you are entirely on the right track when you say the creative experience 'mysteriously leads the poet to spaces of meaning he is incapable of accessing without it'. Indeed the concluding sentence of your letter would make a fitting conclusion to this one of mine.

With every good wish

Sincerely
Seamus Heaney

PS The image I sometimes use to suggest how a good poem functions is that of reaching a landing on a staircase: the actual writing is like climbing the flight and the completion like finding yourself for a moment on a different plane with a more settled perspective – though you still have more stairs to climb.

Saima Khan, a graduate student at Ulster University, from Pakistan, had chosen as the subject of her thesis the concept of redress, both as advanced by SH in *The Redress of Poetry* and as exemplified by his poems. Told by a Heaney scholar that her understanding of the term 'redress' was faulty, she wrote straight to SH to check it against his own.

To Seamus Deane

MS Emory

30 May 2010

Glanmore Cottage, Ashford,
Co. Wicklow

Dear Seamus,

Many times since I saw you in Derry at that pre-par-ation for the St Columb's film I intended to write, having heard from B. Friel of your perilous surgery, but now Kevin Whelan gives me good reports of your health and has cajoled me into a reading on June 17 which will involve a happy birthday dedication at some point in the evening. I know you've been warned of this, because I wanted to know from Kevin if you were happy with the idea. If I had a chance to repeat my own 70th, I would certainly make sure to keep the head much, much farther down: I felt I put it spectacularly on the block last April. We live and don't learn.

Des Kavanagh had told me about meeting you at the Gate Theatre on that pivotal day when you were remembering and outliving your father and that too was a moment when I had an impulse to write. But, 'shying as usual'.

Nothing shy about your interview in the St Columb's book, all the same. Terrific scalding reading of the whole northern situation. It made me wish we could re-live those Field Day days and nights. Made me envy your passion and intellectual force. All the more so since I have been in a doldrum for a good while now. No writing. No confidence. Low barometer. So I look forward to tapping the glass at O'Connell House. Hope to see you then –

Seamus

The film SH mentions is *The Boys of St Columb's* (2009), a documentary, directed by Tom Collins, about the subsequent careers of ex-pupils of the school, who included the politicians John Hume and Eamonn McCann (b.1943), the songwriter Phil Coulter, and the historian James A. Sharkey, as well as SH and Deane.

To Michael Longley

TS Longley

11 July 2010 191 Strand Road, Dublin 4

Dear Michael,

It was good to see you and Edna at that gala on Tuesday – I had got myself into something of a state over it, the sheer public smiling aspect of the occasion, not to mention the unmentioned/unmentionable S.H. library buried into or under McClay. You had a lot of Heaneybop to listen to, and not only from me, so your generous stride to the top table and praisewords in the ear were all the more deeply appreciated.

I was saying that I have got myself overloaded with obligations and events and bits and pieces of writings that have me in a state – to the point this morning, for example, where I cannot find the letter and poems you sent last week, the one that crossed with my letter to you. They'll turn up, but I want to write to you now because for the next few days I'm crowded out of my own time, and the morning after I saw you something came up with Glenn Patterson that needs to be addressed pronto.

Glenn was interviewing me for the City Council's promotional video/film about writers in Belfast and their favourite places, etc., and when we finished he told me about his notion of doing a feature film, featuring you and me as young poets in the Belfast of the Sixties, covering the decade from The Group to Bloody Sunday, the years of the blue Volkswagen, as it were – not a documentary but a movie with actors being us and presumably a plot and background that would relate us to the Troubles and whatever lay behind them. This came out of the blue and dismayed, not to say distressed me. I could not bear to have such a thing happen in my lifetime and told Glenn that I was hyperventilating at the thought of it. And then I was even more upset to see how my response upset him. We parted uneasily at that point and there the thing hangs. But I wanted to let you know that I cannot give the proposal my blessing for several reasons.

First of all, it would enter the realm of biography and be taken as a matter of record, a first draft, as it were, of the material, a first strike, even, at the subject(s), and since I have been in the business of declining not to say forbidding biography proper, I could not condone the profiling and promotion that a biopic – demeaning word, but there would be a touch of that about the end product – would entail. And such a film would certainly have the effect of hotting up other would-be biographers, which is something I dread, especially now that I have turned into a kind of product already, as a result [of] that whole 70th birthday overkill and overfamiliarizing.

Glenn seems to have progressed as if the film were indeed a viable and agreed enterprise, which is a pity. I have no doubt, as I told him last Wednesday, about the purity of his motive in conceiving the project or his ability to give the story a true shape and no doubt about the care with which he would handle personal matters, yours and mine, his and ours. But the fact remains that I feel something is being intruded upon. I could not co-operate. My insides turn over at the thought of the publicity. Imagine versions of yourself/ourselves in the cinemas. The reviews, the previews, the launch, the undoable consequences . . . The irony is that *Stepping Stones*, which seems to some extent to have prompted Glenn in the matter, was meant to keep biographers at bay.

I am writing this in haste: since I saw you, I have been in Dublin for last Wednesday night, then back up for the Medbh do on Thursday, whence to Bellaghy for a day with my brother Pat, back from Canada, and all day yesterday at a nephew's wedding. I just need to send you this message, a holding action. And I need to write to Glenn also. With love to you both.

Seamus

PS Glad to say I've just retrieved your letter and poems – I envy your free access to what happens to you on the Italian paths and the family rooms, to the hurlygush and gait of your language, a sense of the poems presenting themselves and being welcomed . . . And I suddenly realize also that *Human Chain* does not include 'The City': I wish it had got itself into surer, stranger shape, but while I felt it was a fond salute for the festschrift, it didn't seem to me strong enough as a book-poem – as Plath might have said.

PPS To Glenn, I may just send paragraphs 3, 4 and 5 of the above, with a little note. S.

SH had officiated at the opening of Queen's University Belfast's McClay Library, into which the Seamus Heaney Library was subsumed.

Talking to SH on the steps of the Linen Hall Library in Belfast, Glenn

Patterson (b.1961), novelist and screenplay writer, had informally proposed an idea for the feature film about him and Michael Longley, and their experiences as young poets.

'undoable consequences': SH plainly means that the consequences would not be undoable, but no matter.

To Glenn Patterson

MS Patterson

11 July 2010 191 Strand Road, Dublin 4

Dear Glenn,

It strikes me that the postman may not be at full strength this week, but even so, I need to get a word to you after our mutually surprised chat last Wednesday. And I hope you won't mind if I approach you via a quick venting of the pent which I did a while ago in a letter to Michael. It blurts out what I feel at this crowded moment and am likely to feel as time goes on, but perhaps we could all pause for a few weeks? I'm up to my eyes in small jobs and duties and travels, feeling quite tensed up generally, so it would be good to let the stirred breast quieten – even [if] it quietens into the same attitude and reserve.

Marie was glad to speak to you on Thursday and I had too little that you would have wanted to hear said, so there we were, shy and uneasy. I'm sorry it was like that, but the following pages will let you know why –

Sincerely

Seamus

This was accompanied by extracts from SH's letter to Michael Longley of the same date. As SH's subsequent letter to Patterson, of 30 July, shows, the matter was resolved amicably.

To Eamon Duffy

MS Duffy

15 July 2010 191 Strand Road, Dublin 4

Dear Eamon,

Yesterday I came on an invitation that arrived here weeks ago for the Feast of St Mary Magdalene. I have to apologize for the discourtesy of not having answered in time. We couldn't have – I mean I couldn't have gone – since Marie and I are due to go to France on Monday as guests (and babysitters) with Christopher and Jenny and granddaughter Anna Rose. But still, it was a failing.

But not as grievous, really, as my having failed to keep in touch with you and *your* Jenny this past long while. I knew you had stresses and troubles and were taking the strain, and a friend ought to have been more mindful. I've drooped a bit since we last talked, I think in the end because of the 70th birthday last year – my having agreed to the public celebration left me feeling I had sold/lost a private part – the last bit of unpublic smiling man – feeling that I had agreed to be plundered. I don't know if you were aware of the extent of the exposure and commodification, but it left me oddly unconfident. Not oddly, come to think of it. Understandably and self-reproachfully.

All this is spilling out like a bottle bubbling and disgorging, without much forethought. I need to say that I'm sorry for not having written about so many things. That you and dear Jenny have been in my thoughts often but I've been too shy or distracted or in denial or bloody well busy with the itty-bitty to attend to the true and the good. I suppose it's a case of the old 'Bless me, father', brother –

Love –

Seamus

To Glenn Patterson

MS Patterson

30 July 2010 — 191 Strand Road, Dublin 4

Dear Glenn,

How am I to thank you for the grace and generosity of your letter? This is just an immediate note to say how deeply I appreciate the way you have responded to my perhaps too edgy reaction to the film proposal. It was not the most graceful of letters but it arose out of genuine anxiety. Maybe it's because I'm in the middle of stressful thoughts concerning the disposal of my papers/archive and trying to tidy up literary estate matters (something I gave scant thought to before now), but I find myself jumpy in a new way. But there is a candour and affection and a – dare I say – beauty in your reply that is balm to the spirit. I hope I shall write again, but I just want you to have my heartfelt gratitude for now –

Seamus

In the letter to SH of 25 July to which this is a reply, Patterson had written reassuring him that previous discussion of the film had 'all remained at the level of conversation not contract', that there was no script 'aside from a couple of pages of notes on my computer', and that he had 'now put all thought of the film out of [his] head'. He concluded: 'In friendship, in hopes of no awkwardness when next we meet, and, once again, with deep regret for the distress already caused . . .'

To Ciaran Carson

MS Emory

10 August 2010 191 Strand Road, Dublin 4

Dear Ciaran,

Filled and ready to go, and a lovely scrape and rustle attendant on every stroke and loop. These are the maiden sentences and I cannot thank you enough for the genius of the book and the bounty of Glandore Avenue – generous and ratifying. I had got started on *The Pen Friend* and was delighted with the early appearance of the Conway Stewart but there is something beyond expectation in that *Eine Kleine* chapter – the dismantling of the apparatus, the naming of parts, the exquisite operation, the meticulous reassembly, the paean to the casein – astonishing work, and that's only a few pages. My own few lines enclosed – my first day in St Columb's we drove over the border to Buncrana and got my own model – not sure exactly which one, in 1951 – but your gift pierces the heart. And the book is a Perseid shower of penlore.

Blessings on Deirdre too, and my deepest gratitude –

Seamus

Carson's novel of 2009, *The Pen Friend*, has as its protagonist a 'fountain-pen nerd', as Carson described him in an interview. SH's 'own few lines enclosed' must be his poem 'The Conway Stewart' (*Human Chain*).

To Eamon Duffy

MS Duffy

18 August 2010 191 Strand Road, Dublin 4

Dear Loving Man,

Some day I will tell you how much your letter means/meant to me. Just now I have been/am going through a period – my first ever – of shaken confidence and endeavouring to screw the courage to the sticking point. Which your generous copious words are helping me to do. I loved the shine off the wedding photographs but was sorry to hear that dear Jenny – like myself – is feeling fretful . . . Marie has to put up with that in me and I worry for her. But I rejoice in your holiday freedom – well, the latter regime curtails a lot of freedom, I know, but sooner or later I hope to answer as you deserve to be. For now, quick love and thanks from both of us to both of ye –

Blessings –
Seamus

In response to SH's letter to him of 15 July 2010 and his sending of an uncorrected proof of *Human Chain*, Duffy had written urging him not to 'brood too much on the underworld', adding, 'you have a lot of life and *lightenings* left in you'.

To John Montague

MS Cork

18 August 2010 191 Strand Road, Dublin 4

Amigo,

Many thanks for your letter – this is not so much an answer as a finger-fly-up-from-the-font sprinkle of the fictive water. I was sorry to hear about Elizabeth's pneumonia but glad of the antibiotic counter-attack, and the good prospect of citizenship. Glad too that you have those rills and refreshments of lyric that keep you convinced – I've done nought for months, although I am fond of stuff in the new book – maybe the most naked yet. For which reason I am a little more worried about the readings and reviews – not the artistic judgements, just the matter of the subject matter. You should be getting a copy – your name was on the list, at any rate. (I'm thinking of a sequence called 'Album' in particular.) (And the end of 'In the Attic', though I think, as Graves would say, 'That's all right.')

I liked that aquarium of *filí* –

Le meas –
Seamus

And, of course, yes, liked the gleam of 'Adam's Apple' – a true Montague poem, yours alone –
S.

The 'sprinkle of fictive water' alludes to the last lines of a poem by Montague,

'The Water Carrier', which SH admired: ' . . . half-imagined and half real / Pulses in the fictive water that I feel.'

Montague's US-born wife, Elizabeth Wassell, had applied for Irish nationality.

In the review of *Human Chain* that Montague wrote for the *Dublin Review of Books*, under the title 'The Big Splatter', he mentioned in passing that he had attended the fortieth anniversary celebration of Gallery Press, which he described in a six-line poem that likens the gathering of poets there to fish in an aquarium.

Filí (sing., *file*): poets. In ancient Ireland, *filí* were considered part of the elite class.

To Vona Groarke

TS Groarke

12 September 2010 Glanmore Cottage, Ashford,
Co. Wicklow

Dear Vona,

Your beautifully written, positively disposed, and entirely protective review of *Human Chain* has just appeared in the *Sunday Business Post* and I write to thank you for that and so much else, but also to let you know how badly I feel about the situation I am in now.

A year and more ago I wrote a preface for Patrick Crotty's *Penguin Book of Irish Poetry*, due out at the end of the month but you, dear Vona, and many other poets whose work I admire and whose friendship has been a sustenance and a sweetness to me are not included in Patrick's selection. I knew this when you wrote to ask me for a reference and didn't know what to say except yes, I am happy and still am to speak strongly on behalf of you and your work. Whether you will want me to do so in these new circumstances, I cannot say. But since I set out for a week in England tomorrow, I feel I must let you know how things stand.

When I wrote the original preface, the contemporary section was still undecided but when finally it was, I had to insert a disclaimer in the printed version.

I am distressed that we find ourselves in this painful situation.

Sincerely
Seamus

To Paul Durcan

MS NLI

5 October 2010 191 Strand Road, Dublin 4

Dear Paul,

Your letter and the news of your recovery from dungeon dark confinement lately means the world to me. The reviews of *Human Chain* have left me feeling more mortal than I had realized, but the utter attention that you devote word by word, poem by poem, to the thing itself is healing. Your generosity and stamina are a boon to us all, and as I prepare for the reception of the next book I'm associated with, I salute you with gratitude and *SALUTE*. Forgive the brevity. I'm off in half an hour to do national service, as it were, for Ambassador Ryan in Prague. Overdoing it again – Love from Marie too – Seamus

'*SALUTE*': i.e. the Italian for 'Health!'

To Wendy Cope and Lachlan Mackinnon

EMAIL Cope and Mackinnon

11 October 2010

Ah my dears, I would have wished for a different outcome. How kind of you to send that message. And you won't have received this one since you know I have no email and don't 'do' it. With love and in your debt for such grace.

Seamus

The British poet Wendy Cope (b.1945) had emailed to congratulate SH on winning the 2010 Forward Prize for Poetry with *Human Chain*; *Small Hours*, by her partner, the Scottish poet Lachlan Mackinnon (b.1956), had also been shortlisted. Cope told SH that his victory had, from their point of view, been 'the second best possible result'.

To John Montague

TS Cork

22 October 2010 191 Strand Road, Dublin 4

Dear John,

Great news about the Conferral of the Chevalier order of Honour. Herself and myself are delighted: nobody from our island deserves it more, so we're sorry not to be able to join the revels on 3rd November at the Embassy. Marie is in fact away with her sister for a couple of weeks and this old dog is tied into a charity appearance/obligation that same time. For the man who invented the Herceptin drug that Marie was treated with a couple of years ago.

Sorry not to be able to write a decent letter just now – feeling as old as the reviews of the recent book have been portraying me. Overwhelmed with mail and obligation, but elated that you are being celebrated in France. With love to Elizabeth, and regrets at missing the salute.

Keep going –
Seamus

Montague had been appointed Chevalier de la Légion d'honneur, and shortly afterwards, at another ceremony that SH was unable to attend, would receive an honorary degree from the Sorbonne Nouvelle.

2011

A number of the passages omitted from letters of this year rehearse, for the benefit of correspondents who had been out of touch, aspects of the depression of 2010 from which SH was now recovering, gradually and with the help of medication. In early May, however, while in Glasgow to receive an honorary degree from the University of Strathclyde, he underwent a minor, stroke-like episode that left him shaky; and this, along with other manifestations of bodily frailty, brought home to him – yet again – the need to slow down where public activities were concerned.

To John Montague

TS Cork

4 January 2011 191 Strand Road, Dublin 4

Dear John,

A couple of days ago I met Richard Ryan – in McCloskey's in Donnybrook – just before he went in to Blackrock Clinic where the sawbones are going to saw his hip bone, and he told me about your fine and honorific piece in the *Dublin Literary Review*, which he then sent me as a print-out. It is sprightly and generous: I value it highly and regard it as something more than a review – a salute, shall we say, or what you once said yourself in another context, one of those 'rope ladders across the abyss' – though 'abyss' would be overstating it, more an 'Epic' march drain. Anyhow, *cher poète*, it did me good.

It was also kind of you to telephone here a few weeks ago, when I was deep in the doldrums. I was also very sorry to renege on the Paris weekend, but I was in a state and not 'at myself', a condition which had grown over the previous few months. Had I been my usual self, I'd not only have gone to the Centre Culturel, but would have come earlier for at least one of your ennoblings. But that, alas, was not to be – nor was I in a state to go north to Queen's University early in December when Helen Vendler was getting an honorary degree – not sponsored by Edna Longley, as it turns out, but by an estimable fellow called Ed Larrissy, a Yeatsian whom I first met at the Sligo event, and who is now a Professor, maybe even *the* Professor in Belfast.

Anyhow, the good news is that all is well again, spirits have been restored, the dread depression has lifted and as the Reverend Herbert once put it, 'I once more smell the dew and rain' and would greatly 'relish versing', though I've been dry for the best part of a year. The only thing I'm relying on is a poem that was a counter truth to the one in *Human Chain* called 'Miracle' – which I think I'll send you, fornenst the aquarium full of Gallery poets. A niftily managed bit of music there: I look forward to the next book (yours, I mean).

Marie sends her love and to Elizabeth, as I do too. With all good wishes for 2011.

Le meas
Seamus

Not the *Dublin Literary Review* but the *Dublin Review of Books* had carried Montague's 'salute' to *Human Chain*, under the heading 'The Big Splatter', a phrase that Montague recalls SH using of his own work and which he takes the opportunity to return, after some outright praise, as a compliment with a spin on it.

For Montague's 'ennoblings', see letter of 22 October 2010.

Edward Larrissy (b.1950), whose surname SH misspells, was indeed Professor of English at Queen's University Belfast.

To Andrew Motion

TS Motion

11 January 2011 — 191 Strand Road, Dublin 4

Dear Andrew,

Just a note to wish you all good things in 2011 and to do something I promised myself I would do after the Forward Prize, which was to put it about, or rather put half of it about. It would probably be simpler if I were to send the enclosed to Richard but I cannot lay my hands on his address just now. And there will be other beneficiaries: there's a good magazine over here in Cork called *The Shop* – a kind of cousin to *Rialto* – and I intend sending a few shillings to them also. And there's an indigent scribe here in town, a kind of Eddie Linden understudy who was first in the queue with a letter mentioning his need and his suicidal impulses – just perhaps true, so – as my father used to say about a payout – I let the prisoner go.

You probably have one or two books gathering shape and substance

– certainly your reviews are a reminder of how thorough and gifted you are when considering the work of others, so I look forward to one of your own when it's ready to fly.

Perhaps I'll see you at the T. S. Eliot reading on Sunday week. I was going to miss it, having been down in the dumps and compelled to cancel several events on the home front and one in Paris before Christmas, but happily the pall dispersed just at the end of advent and Richard's himself again. Fondest wishes from Marie and me to Kyeong-Soo and you –

Seamus

The 'Richard' in the first paragraph was the sound engineer Richard Carrington, co-founder with Motion of the Poetry Archive; SH, who was president of the organisation from its beginning until his death, had volunteered a contribution to its funds of £1,000, the sum being a portion of his Forward Prize winnings.

THE SHOp was a poetry magazine, 'out of the wilds of West Cork', as its founder and editor John Wakeman (d.2018) put it, which flourished between 1999 and 2014; Wakeman had previously co-founded and edited the British poetry magazine *The Rialto*. SH is quoted as describing himself as 'a confirmed SHOp-lifter'.

The 'indigent scribe' was John McNamee (1946–2019), Dublin poet and organiser of the College Green 'Out to Lunch' poetry readings; Eddie S. Linden (b.1935) is a Scottish poet based in London, who published and edited the poetry magazine *Aquarius* until 2004, and whose style of life can best be understood from the book about him, *Who Is Eddie Linden?*, by Sebastian Barker (1945–2014), himself a poet.

'Richard's himself again': nothing to do with Richard Carrington, mentioned above, but proverbial for a return to health – after Shakespeare's *Richard III*.

To John F. Deane

TS J. F. Deane

11 January 2011 191 Strand Road, Dublin 4

Dear John F.,

Blather? I don't think so. The true voice of feeling. The way you cherished your brother and why you would do so aches through your clear, dear letter and your steeple-tall in-spired poem. I love the Keatsian sense of silence like a compost under the trees, the shared life implicit in the inhaled woodland earth and air; and then that ominous owl, and the way its dismaying presence opens up the poem again and permits, even conjures the roe-deer 'elegant and fearful' and the ballet-leaping buck. There is intimacy and a profoundly shared unspoken love, a forest-floor gentleness, a sacrament indeed.

Marie and I were very moved by the image of your brother keeping an all-night vigil at the gates of San Quentin, and glad that you had the chance of dwelling with him on those two final occasions: it seems indeed that you shared something hallowed and that it got into the poem. The 'dread devourer' was obviously a heartsore reality for him and you to bear, but given all you endowed him with, in life and the poem, it's no wonder that you feel 'calm and serene'.
[. . .]

John F. Deane (b.1943) had sent SH his poem 'Muir Woods, California', which tells of a sacramental experience among 'steeple-tall' redwoods while on a visit to his brother Declan, a priest in California, shortly before his death by cancer.

To Alasdair Macrae

TS Macrae

18 February 2011 — 191 Strand Road, Dublin 4

Dear Alasdair,

A week or so ago I read the MacCaig book through and should have written then, when the responses were fresh and glowing, but I'm still the better for having been instructed and delighted by that sweet and useful volume – sweet insofar as it dwells on scores of poems with close, informed, sensitive ear and a voice to match the old smoker's own intonations – sprightly yet with grave undertones; and useful in the amount of background information and serious philosophical concerns that you expound with the lightest of touches. I love the sustained insight and vitality of your writing, the way the wit is in the service of a critical mind: 'poems still stained with Apocalyptic murkiness', 'freed rather than free verse' and 'the orientation, or, rather, the occidentation' towards the Isle of Harris – all toe-curlers.

Your organization of the text was a real help. The chapter headings and the focus you derived from them saves you from a dutiful chronological account and the close readings considerably deepened my own sense of the seriousness of his endeavours – you remember that I once, as a retort to his taunt that he 'couldn't stand gloomy, ambitious poetry' (meaning, I was certain, *North*) I said, 'O yes, I suppose Herrick is the man for you.' It sufficed in the flyting game, but isn't right for the poet you bring to new attention with your commentary. I learnt with gratitude, for example, the sad background to 'The Sounds of the Day' and was relieved when you confessed to a puzzlement about its ending – a puzzlement I have always shared but was happy to live with. And I took serious note for the first time of 'On the Pier at Kinlochbervie' and 'Notations of Ten Summer Minutes'. I was glad also that 'Small Boy' got a mention – I chose to read it on the TV programme in spite of an awareness in my less merciful self that it probably sailed too close to the sentimental.

The book is bound to do good for the afterlife of Norman's poetry. You have raised the monument and done yourself proud – *and* your readers and the man himself (clearly enjoying it all on the cover). Throughout the book there is a love of poetry and a style of appreciation that should give criticism a good name.

Meanwhile the well here is dry. But a bit of serious divining may still give access to a jibble or two. Otherwise things are going fine. We were in St Lucia for 10 days as guests of D. Walcott and his Teutonic partner – had to go to London en route to line out with the T. S. Eliot Prize pack (D. Walcott, by a nice bit of timing, scooped the readies, but had stayed at home by the Carib surf and greeted us at the airport at romantically named Vieux Fort, the French and the British having fought over that ground repeatedly – or twice, at least). Marie lay in the sun, I out of the sun, on top of the bed, in our own little bothy, meaning to read but finding my cataract – and the heat – a problem, so nodding off rather than taking in.

With love to Elise too and hoping that spring works its wonders in your garden and your grounds,

Love again –
Seamus

PS The Rilke information was a real surprise and a happy one.

See letter to Macrae of 17 May 2008.

The poetry of Rainer Marie Rilke was an unexpected enthusiasm of MacCaig's, on whom, as Macrae writes in his book, the impact of *The Duino Elegies* – 'in their transcendent grandeur, very remote from MacCaig's poetry' – was nonetheless 'immediate and overwhelming'. SH shared that enthusiasm.

To Paul Durcan ᴛs NLI

12 April 2011 191 Strand Road, Dublin 4

Dear Paul,

What a birthday present. I was overcome, overjoyed, grateful, facing east, loving the running feet of young middle-aged women, loving the gait of the verse, so nimbly in step with 'Little Gidding' and Big Dante, and was pigeon-puff-chested, of course, by the marvellous exaggeration of being taken for a maestro. And the big glitter and sparkle of the bay as we trod the strand in springtime patrol.

There's something deeply enviable about your gift for transformation, how you can orchestrate and conduct the music of what happens into marvellous uplift. I could go on. But we're off this afternoon on a birthday romp down in Waterford – The Tannery in Dungarvan to start with and then rambles, or maybe spins in the rain.

Dear Paul, you made something flourish in this old breast and I only wish I could respond with a poem. But the better way, perhaps, is to keep responding to yours.

Love from Marie too –

Seamus

Durcan's 'birthday present' was his poem in terza rima, 'Sandymount Strand Keeping Going' (*Praise in which I Live and Move and Have My Being*, 2012).

To Rab Wilson ᴛs ᴀɴᴅ ᴍs Wilson

29 April 2011

EPISTLE TO RAB WILSON

Dear Rab, I write in English verse
In standard habbie, quick and terse,
To say that while I'm not averse
          To honouring Rabbie
Or taking Colia's Ayrshire airs
          And have been happy

Oftentimes to praise the bard,
The time has come when I must guard
What time I have, although it's hard
To just say no
To your brilliant invitation card –
It's virtuoso!

I'm honoured by that heartsome letter.
Could the man himself have done it better?
The Lallans word-hoard and the metre
Hand in glove
And rhyme a freedom, not a fetter –
On the move!

But even so, a new regime
Dictates a change of pace: I dream
Of a calendar unmarked and clean
And liberating.
(Which is to say, I'm out of steam
For talks and readings.)

Poets in the Burns Museum:
A noble and a proper aim.
I wish that I could let my name
Begin the rollbook.
But for now I must forgo that fame,
Step back a bit.

Dear Rab, That's a very handsome way to raise the question, but for various reasons I'm doing my best to take it easy, or easier. Dennis sent me the dossier a couple of days ago. You have a great base for an important series of readings. I hope you will excuse me –

Seamus

Rab Wilson (b.1960), Scottish poet writing mainly in Scots, had sent SH a rhymed invitation, in the Standard Habbie form SH employs here and that Burns favoured for epistolary extemporisation, to inaugurate a series of poetry readings at the Robert Burns Birthplace Museum in Alloway, Ayrshire.

To Patrick Crotty

TS Crotty

11 May 2011   191 Strand Road, Dublin 4

Dear Patrick,

You should have heard from me earlier. I'm very sorry that we didn't meet last week, especially after the long drive you had and the loss of your time at the desk – but perhaps a while in the salubrious Macrae company compensated for the longueurs of the graduation.

The whole episode was strange. First I was tilting to the left and feeling wobbly in the legs. Then Andy O'Hagan took the initiative (after I had staggered dangerously on the steps) and sent for a doctor who was on the spot very promptly, followed immediately by paramedics and their wheelie stretcher. In we go then to a little room where I was stripped of my garments (academic), had an ECG done and was conveyed by ambulance to the Glasgow Royal Infirmary. I was given a room there and a brain scan and went through all the regular procedures – blood pressure, blood-letting (once they had found a vein) and so on – then met with 1) a young doctor from Limerick called Fitzgerald and 2) a consultant called Stott whom I liked and trusted. He said it would be better if I stayed another night or two – which I was happy to do. Next day, Thursday, mid-afternoon, after examining the brain scan x-ray he declared I'd had a small stroke and presumed it had come from my irregular heartbeat. Anyhow, I was let out that evening and Marie and I shacked up in the Millennium Hotel and were driven in a university car to the airport next morning. The whole thing shook me and I took it very easy for a couple of days, but I'm back to myself again, trying to get the chain back on the sprocket . . .

It's a pity to have missed the chance to spend some time with you and Alasdair and Elise, but I was glad that you were over in their place that evening. Meanwhile, the Queen is here next week and shoneens that we are, Marie and I are going – on Mary Mac's invitation – to a state dinner for her in Dublin Castle. At least it won't be a buffet with the usual scrum and surge towards the smoked salmon. I'll keep you posted.

I hope all goes well for you and with you. Maybe we'll talk after Lizzie's feed on Wednesday.

Seamus

As SH was getting dressed and ready to receive his honorary doctorate from the University of Strathclyde, Marie noticed that he was listing to one side and unable to stand straight. After he stumbled on a flight of steps – though luckily caught and saved from a bad fall – an ambulance was called and took him to the hospital where treatment proceeded as described above. Andrew O'Hagan, who was with the party, read the speech that SH had been appointed to deliver on behalf of the other graduands.

'shoneen': disparaging term for an Anglophile snob; 'Mary Mac': Mary McAleese, Michael D. Higgins's predecessor as President of Ireland.

To Michael Alexander

TS Alexander

2 June 2011 191 Strand Road, Dublin 4

Dear Michael,

There's a shake in my hand from medication so I'm using the electronic script, but it <the hand i.e.> also shakes a little nervously because I've left this simple and pleasant task so late. I hope you will excuse me.

I've been doing my best to take things easier but have found the more time I have the less efficiently I operate. Maybe it has something to do with being 72. I wonder what age was Beowulf when he faced the dragon? If he was in his early twenties when he contended in Denmark, he must have been in his 70s. And how many children had Lady Macbeth, I hear you cry.

Pat McCall would no doubt regard the old warrior as a young fellow. I know 90 is an age when people remain sprightly, having recently sat beside a nonagenarian at a banquet here: I felt like a *scop* in Hrothgar's hall when I was placed at the top table at a state dinner during the recent royal visit. The other guests (only 9 in all) included the Queen, the Duke, David Cameron and Mary McAleese. I had the Duke on my left and David C. on my right. I got on very well with Philip – 90 or thereabouts – who did not live up to his reputation for being curmudgeonly but kept the small talk nicely alive. He turns out to be one of the tribe who think Shakespeare didn't write Shakespeare . . . Her Majesty was a bit too far round the board for any discourse, but she chatted happily to Enda Kenny, helmet of the Hibernians . . .

It was lovely to get your good letter, and your euros – which leaves me wondering which is the more indelicate – to keep them or to let you have them back. But since you'll not be able to use them in your realm . . .

Fondest wishes – until we meet and I can scatter my profit at some counter with you.

Seamus

The dramatically irrelevant question 'How Many Children Had Lady Macbeth?' was the title of an essay by the literary critic L. C. Knights (1906–97).

Pat McCall was the mother of Alexander's first wife; Pat's father had been a cattle importer from Co. Tyrone.

Scop is Old English for 'poet'; Hrothgar was King of the Danes in *Beowulf*.

David Cameron was British Prime Minister, and Enda Kenny Ireland's Taoiseach, at the time of the British monarch's unique visit to the Republic.

'your euros': sent because of little use to the sender.

To Iggy McGovern

MS McGovern

6 June 2011 — 191 Strand Road, Dublin 4

Dear Iggy,

Many thanks for sending Chaumes and Johnston copies. The former is ready to make the big affirmations about poetry – and as poet and scientist he probably has the authority to do so, while the latter isn't afraid of the big castigations. Maria is very bright and ready for the fray – didn't she have a go at Ms Boland a while ago? As they say around South Derry, her tongue would clip tin. I hope all goes well with Chaumes – whose name, according to my big dictionary, means 'stubble' or/and 'thatch'.

All good wishes to Eileen too –

Seamus

'Chaumes' is actually the Professor of Physics Jean Patrick Connerade (b.1943), who, under the non-de-plume 'Chaunes', writes poetry in French; he, McGovern and SH were to convene at 'Science Meets Poetry 3', part of the European Science Open Forum in Dublin. McGovern does not recall what of Connerade's he sent, but the other item was *Poetry Ireland Review 100*, edited by Paul Muldoon, to which the scholar Maria Johnston had contributed an unsparingly critical essay titled 'Reading Irish Poetry in the New Century: *Poetry Ireland Review* 2000–2009'.

To Edna O'Brien

TS O'Brien

25 June 2011 Glanmore Cottage, Ashford,
Co. Wicklow

Dear Edna,

When you urged me to take my time with *Saints and Sinners* you could hardly have meant take three months. But my general lassitude and slow pace as a reader mean that I'm behind with everything.

I love the book, so various and substantial in its different characters and settings, so exhilarating in its accurate detail, so ready to accommodate the suggestive and the strange. The joy is in the writing, of course, the sense of supply, as Frost called it; but it's also in what Auden called 'the knowledge of life'. Joseph Brodsky wrote that book called *Of Grief and Reason* which made me think yours could be subtitled 'Of Grief and Easing', insofar as articulation gives some order or relief, and many an ending has hurt in the story yet healing in the cadence. 'Shovel Kings' is a marvellous opener, history, hurt, homelessness sounding their grievous notes and acting as an overture for much that is to come. Other favourites: 'Inner Cowboy', 'Send My Roots Rain', 'Old Wounds' – and, in a different register, 'Black Flower'. But starting this favourites game is not the way to go for it leaves out the very different drama of something potent and understated like 'Green Georgette', not to mention the frolics of 'Sinners'. Words obey your call.

And you are probably still calling on them for your memoir, or perhaps you have finished it – a chapter in the moral history of our country, I am sure, as well as 'the growth of a poet's mind'.

Marie and I are down for the weekend in the Wicklow silence-shelter and send our love. And I am sorry about this electronically generated print, but lately my handwriting has gone to hell. Love –

Seamus

PS Sorry we missed you that last time.

Saints and Sinners: O'Brien's new volume of short stories.

When talking about 'sense of supply', SH may have in mind this passage from 'The Figure a Poem Makes', where Robert Frost meditates on the writing of poetry: 'For me, the initial delight is in remembering something I did not know I knew. [. . .] There is a glad recognition of the long lost and the rest follows. Step by step the wonder of unexpected supply keeps growing.'

'the knowledge of life': the phrase occurs in Auden's eight-line poem of 1937, 'Orpheus', from which SH quotes in his T. S. Eliot lecture 'Sounding Auden' (*The Government of the Tongue*) as the starting point of his discussion of 'the relative values we attach to poetic sense and poetic sound'.

It was James Joyce who said of his *Dubliners*: 'My intention was to write a chapter in the moral history of my country', while 'Growth of a Poet's Mind' was Wordsworth's alternative title for *The Prelude* – high expectations for O'Brien's memoir!

To Alasdair Macrae

TS Macrae

20 August 2011 191 Strand Road, Dublin 4

Dear Alasdair,

Many thanks for your letter about Sheena – and the compensatory account of Iain and the Brillo Pads. I can imagine his glee – that kind of thing makes you miss him more than reading the poems – which is a kind of presence.

Madeline McGuckin, as she was then, was at secondary school with Sheena and they were best friends for a good while, until they both got off into adult life. I'm glad she heard the news and that she passed it on.

Sheena was the one next to me in the family – seven more to follow, another girl after her, then the six boys – and at the start and then later on, towards the finish, I was close to her, first taking her by the hand to school and six decades later (that passed like six weeks) on the phone to her regularly just for the refreshment of her 'news', and staying with her and her country solicitor husband when I was up north. She went suddenly on a Sunday morning, an easy way for her to go, but shocking for friends and family. She was a great spirit, a good mother, a cherished character in the district, a giver, equally capable of sympathy and revelry. So again my thanks to you for writing.

The Dalmatian coast, no less. More than half a century on. It's the *Wanderings of Oisin*, the sequel, as he returns with his Niamh to the land of the ever young. Although that fancy has its perils, so mind your step when you get back.

I'm minding my own step these days, what with a wobble in the legs and a shaky sense of balance, but the form is good. Have a great time, you and Elise. All love from Marie 'n me –

Seamus

SH's sister Sheena, his closest sibling in age, had recently died, and the news of her death had been passed to the Macraes by Madeline McGuckin (whose name SH doubly misspells), wife of the novelist and short-story writer Bernard MacLaverty (b.1942).

The story of 'Iain [Crichton Smith] and the Brillo Pads' has been lost to memory.

To John Montague

TS Cork

22 November 2011 191 Strand Road, Dublin 4

Dear John,

The lullaby is right – the pathos of Michaela Harte's loss is in it and the trim little craft of its stanzas sails lightly in the wake of Glencull Water, flowing for more than 40 years now. I think the *Ulster Herald* or indeed the *Irish News* would be glad to publish it. (My own link-in to the first place came at a remove, when I had a poem in the All Ireland Final programme some time in the early Nineties when Derry was playing.)

I'm using this computer because my own hand is shaky and while the writing is legible enough, it strays a good bit. The shake, I'm told, comes from medication I'm taking, which also tends to make me what Hammond used to call 'dwammy' in the mornings – dozy, that is. So I tend to lie in till nine. And generally, it's low barometer time, though I'm in good enough order, body and spirit, and long over the dip that came last winter.

I had two cataract operations myself this year but I still need reading glasses. The only time I notice an improvement is when I'm driving at night – the lights of cars had begun to appear as a starry dazzle and I felt slightly panicky as I met them. What a catalogue of geriatric woe. I'm not even writing. So I greatly admire the spirit and stamina of your reviews in the *Irish Times*. And your ongoing affair with the muse.

And now we have Michael D. in the Park. A happy outcome, given that it could have been the martial arts and *The Apprentice* man – although the result was thanks in no small measure to Martin McGuinness ambushing Mr Gallagher on TV in the presidential debate. But it wasn't all plain sailing for Michael D. – you probably heard about the article Carol Rumens wrote in the *Guardian*, cutting hell out of one of his poems and worst of all quoting Longley quoting Frank Ormsby's definition of bad poetry: 'mad-dog-shite'. But 'that passed over, so will this'.

Michael was elated when I told him he was in your good books – and I too am delighted. I never worry about him – except financially, since he was laid off a year ago from the Culture Supplement staff of the *Sunday Times*. When it comes to delivering the stuff, however, he seems to be well able for the job. He has two wee girls, Aibhín and Síofra.

A level playing field in Garvaghy? What do you think yourself?

With love from Marie (who is all in favour of the poem and especially touched by what she called 'the impulse' – that brought it into being) and from me to Elizabeth and yourself.

Seamus

Michaela Harte, daughter of Mickey Harte, manager of the Co. Tyrone football team, was murdered on her honeymoon in January 2011, and Montague had written an elegy for her.

Among Michael D. Higgins's rivals for the presidency had been Seán Gallagher, black belt in both judo and karate, and TV celebrity. The presidential home is in Phoenix Park.

The British poet Carol Rumens (b.1944) writes a regular column on poetry for the *Guardian*: the one to which SH refers, dated 1 November 2011, is bluntly headlined 'Michael D. Higgins is no poet.'

2012

Seemingly throwaway references to the poetry of mortality and disappointment – Eliot's 'Journey of the Magi' and Dunbar's 'Lament for the Makars' in the letter to Alasdair Macrae of 13 April; 'The Love Song of J. Alfred Prufrock' and *The Waste Land* in the one to Nick Laird of 20 May; Yeats's 'Sailing to Byzantium' and Dunbar again, when writing to Matthew Sweeney on 27 June – are frequent enough to suggest SH's growing acknowledgement of the tribulations of age and the shadow of death.

To Alasdair Macrae

MS Macrae

13 April 2012 191 Strand Road, Dublin 4

Dear Alasdair,

That was a heartwarmer you sent and even though my handwriting has turned niggardly and jiggly, I still feel the pen and ink are called for.
[. . .]
We've been to Italia ourselves, a couple of weeks ago, to Bologna. The excuse was a conference marking the 100th anniversary of the death of a poet called Giovanni Pascoli: there's a trace element of him in the last poem of *Human Chain* and I've done other translations since. He was a sort of Italian Celtic Twilighter – *Crepusculari* I think may be the denomination. Anyhow, we met old friends and wined and dined and ambled in the arcades and it was, you may say, satisfactory.

This is my 73rd birthday. For decades birthdays were truly a matter of indifference to me, but not any more. I may not be at the *conturbat* stage but a chap has to brace himself, even so. Nothing untoward to report, all the same. [. . .]

A substantial booklet of SH's translations from the poems of Giovanni Pascoli (see letter to Dennis O'Driscoll of 25 November 2001) would be published by Gallery Press posthumously, in late 2013, under the title *The Last Walk*.

'*conturbat* stage': William Dunbar's (*c.*1459–*c.*1530) 'Lament for the Makars' has the refrain '*Timor mortis conturbat me*' ('Fear of death disquiets me'). Reference to the same poem in SH's letter to Matthew Sweeney of 27 June 2012 may suggest that Dunbar's theme – the deaths of fellow poets – was much on his mind.

To Nick Laird

MS Laird

20 May 2012

Dear Nick –

A wedding in Cullybackey. Reminds me of S. Deane's quip in the days of Field Day when there was talk that J. Simmons was at work on a certain play by Euripides: quoth Deane: 'That would be the Cully *Bacchae*.'

Thanks for the Sheekey album – Ardboe, verdant Tullyhogue, the long hungry one. My uncle by marriage, Jack Conway, he of the Belfast House years ago, used to tell about the two Ardboe men hesitating on the kerb who he heard say, 'We'll cross her here.' I'm beginning to sound like Ben Kiely.

Catherine told me you took her to dinner a couple of nights ago – it made her very happy to have your kindness and company. And now I'm wondering if perhaps you were at home to see your mother. I was sorry to hear she has her troubles these days and hope that things will change for the better. There are times when we wish we could use the word 'pray' without hesitation.

Meanwhile, you're a happily busy man. I envy you the charge you must get – and give – working on the novel, the translations, the TV job with Zadie, not to mention the November collection. I, on the other hand, wear the bottoms of my trousers rolled. On Sandymount Strand I just now can connect nothing with nothing.

I'm sorry you didn't get that job, but Princeton's not a bad fallback. In fact, a shot forrit . . .

Love to Zadie too – and to the crescent Kit –

Seamus

The 'Sheekey album' refers to a few old postcards of Ardboe and elsewhere that Laird had bought in Sheehy's newsagents in Cookstown and sent to SH; the town, Laird's birthplace, is known as 'long, hungry Cookstown' on account of its high street, the longest in Ireland.

Laird, whose mother was suffering from ovarian cancer, is married to the British novelist Zadie Smith and they were working on a TV script together; with a reference from SH, he had applied for a Cullman Center fellowship; at present, he was teaching poetry at Princeton. 'forrit': forward.

To Yvonne Reddick

TS Reddick

14 June 2012 191 Strand Road, Dublin 4

Dear Yvonne Reddick,

Your letter raises one of those old questions that keep turning up: do we trust the writer's intentions or the reader's understanding of what has been written?

For what it's worth, I didn't have in mind a contrast between Ted's ways with words and mine – the poem was dedicated to him because it was about fishing. And the Britain/Ireland/Irish Sea trope which you divine was not intended. Nor had I in mind the very interesting political reading you give that links Ted's royalism and nationalism with the political right. Which does not mean you aren't entitled to your own reading.

I think the clue to the poem might be found early on in a couple of essays – 'The Fire i' the Flint' and 'The Makings of a Music', in *Preoccupations* – which contrast two poetic dispositions. One 'masculine', work of will, and one 'feminine', work which is engendered. The distinction is too absolute but the question interested me – in a writer like Theodore Roethke, for example, who I dwelt with a good deal in the 60s, there are great swathes of Whitmanesque free verse but there are also poems of formal mastery where the swathe has been tied into sheaves, as it were, rhymed stanzas and even a villanelle. As someone doing the more and less formal kind of poem, the lush and the ratcheted as it were, I was basically saying (I thought) there is finally no contradiction between the caster and the gatherer, both inhere in the act.

River is a wonderful book and I am sure you will hook and net good things aplenty in your thesis. I'm just sorry I don't have a less 'contrary' reading for you.

With all good wishes, to you and David Morley –

Sincerely
Seamus Heaney

Yvonne Reddick, a PhD student at the University of Warwick, where the poet David Morley (b.1964) is Professor of Writing, had sent SH her interpretation of his poem 'Casting and Gathering', dedicated to Ted Hughes, from which she had inferred a contrast between SH's and Hughes's methods of poetic composition.

To Matthew Sweeney

TS Sweeney

27 June 2012 191 Strand Road, Dublin 4

Dear Matthew,

The executive style – address as above – is adopted because I want to keep a record of your whereabouts in Cork. And I'm using a laptop because my handwriting is a bit wobbly, as are my knees. Himself was right, an agèd man is but a paltry thing.

You're in full production: a new collection, a pamphlet, and a half of that satirical novel whose title is very promising. *Timor libri conturbat* them. I'd be delighted and honoured to have 'The Tunnel' dedicated to me and I apologize for not having written about it. These past months I've been on medication and my usually slow responses to letters have grown ever more sluggish – the compensation being, again thanks probably to the medication, that the guilt evaporates.

And you have a daughter getting married on the Feast of Peter and Paul . . . when I'll be up on my hind legs on Parnassus, in the Queen Elizabeth Hall. And you as father of the bride will have to be up on the hind legs too: so I'm sorry that this letter will get to you too late to look at Tom Brangwen's speech at the wedding of his daughter in Lawrence's *The Rainbow*. It's more than fifty years since I read it, but something of its power (then, at any rate) keeps in the memory.

Blessings. I'll check *The Moth*. Keep going –

Seamus

'The executive style' refers to SH's placing, unusual for him in friendly correspondence, of Sweeney's address at the top of his letter. Dunbar's poem – see letter to Alasdair Macrae of 13 April 2012 – presents a solemn roll-call of poets who have died, while Sweeney's novel, *Death Comes for the Poets*, written jointly with John Hartley Williams (1942–2014), has one poet after another being gruesomely murdered.

Timor libri: fear of the book.

To David-Antoine Williams

TS Williams

10 July 2012

Dear David Williams,

It's unlikely that I'll have answers to all of your questions, although I am grateful for the opportunity to respond in writing. So let's see how this goes.

1. I cannot remember the words of my mother's rhyme, but it was a chant that somehow incorporated the links to be found between Latin and English vocabularies. The first dictionary I remember was a red-backed old Chambers in the Mossbawn house. I must have been eleven or twelve when I used it – if I used it. The physical book and the authority that was lodged in and around it are what stay with me most.

2. What dictionaries etc.

As a student and young teacher, I had one of the standard issue single volume dictionaries available at the time. In my mid-twenties, however, I bought the third edition, two volume *Shorter OED* – which I still keep to hand, although for years I've also had the thirteen volumes and supplements of the full dictionary [. . .]. I don't have any dictionary online – not in order to resist the IT developments, rather a matter of sheer laziness and ineptitude. Nor do I use dictionaries 'as part of my compositional practice' – although I have been long aware of the Irish language as an underlay in Irish placenames. And undoubtedly my undergraduate work involving the history of the English language – and the language of Ulster as planted there by the English and the Scots – contributed to a sense of the layering of the tongue. Some poets are more ardently and obsessively dictionary prone, but my own use of them is mostly for traditional reasons – checking the meaning of words I half know (in order to make sure) and ones I don't know (in order to find out).

3. The adoption of a lexical taxonomy for rhetorical organization has been something of a habit. A few years ago in my tribute at the funeral of the late Benedict Kiely – novelist, broadcaster – I remember playing with the man himself as 'benedictus', playing with his reputation as a raconteur as 'bene dixit', of his love of a thing well said as 'bene dictum'.

Also recently, in the foreword to a book of Anglo-Saxon translations entitled *The Word Exchange* (Norton), I ended up suggesting that 'render' might be a better word for what poets do when they 'translate':

> Among the primary meanings for 'render', for example, the third edition of my *Shorter Oxford Dictionary* gives the following: to repeat (something learned); to say over; to give in return, give back, restore; to submit to, or lay before, another for consideration or approval; to obtain or extract by melting.

In cases like these, and in the case of 'redress', I don't begin with the idea of plundering the word for meanings; it's rather a discovery, a saving grace, something that clinches or copes. (I'm inclined to look up 'copes' here . . . It came to mind just now, no doubt via the alliteration, but I'm curious about the lexical meaning. I've a hunch it's worth looking up.)

4. In some cases a word is chosen because it carries a particular etymological or historical charge – 'telluric', for example, in 'Anything Can Happen' (*District and Circle*) and 'transported' – meaning borne up into a fantasy and borne off to a camp, both meanings at work in the last line of 'A Sofa in the Forties' (*The Spirit Level* and *Opened Ground*). But no, I hadn't noticed or intended a play with 'soft bog-pillows'.

The collection where language and its historical/political charge come into focus is *Wintering Out*. 'Fodder' pronounced 'fother' where I grew up, rhyming with mother, half-rhyming with father; 'Anahorish' being similarly caressed in the poem of that title, 'Ana' as the gradient, 'horish' the 'vowel meadow'. And 'Broagh' with its 'rigs' and 'docken', Scots and English traces in the local speech, their otherness from the Irish *bruach* which is Broagh which is 'riverbank'. The phonetic element was the primary relish in such writing but the reach was into history and relevant to politics in the Ulster of the late sixties, early seventies.

5,6,7 – Please excuse me here – nothing worthwhile to contribute.

8. I suppose the need that the 'etymological'/'word' poems arose from, which was to a large extent political, has been assuaged. Since *Field Work* (1979) the language, as I have often said, was wanting to be more like clear glass than stained glass – although I have just noticed a poem called 'Derry Derry Down' in *Human Chain* that ends with four of my dialect words in the emotional scales with their standard English equivalents. And in the same collection the ending of 'Slack'

uses 'catharsis' as much for its therapeutic effect as its phonetic match. But it's true that 'words alone' are less the subject at this stage.

9. I did not know of those citations and I can see why words like 'adoze', 'aftergrass', 'coolth', 'easter' (v.), 'moisting', 'murex', 'pash', 'rattle-bag', 'sogged' and 'wheep' might warrant inclusion, since they are dialect usages or extensions of a word's function – as in 'easter' as verb (which happens to occur in Hopkins). But 'chemotherapy', 'hell', 'Irishry' (utterly Yeats's), 'middle ground', 'plough' and so on – 'potato', for God's sake! – they're common currency. It's certainly a reward to have words like the first ones above cited in one's name: I remember an anecdote about an author – I think Thomas Hardy – looking up to check a word only to find that it occurred in his own work. Or perhaps I should say he found that it occurred only in his own work.

I hope this is of some help to you. I think it is more coherent than anything I'd have found to say 'live', as it were. And in Belfast you will no doubt have the opportunity to meet the dictionary master Ciaran Carson. A jubilant worker in many a word hoard.

All good wishes with your study.

Sincerely
Seamus Heaney

David-Antoine Williams, an associate professor at the University of Waterloo, Ontario, had sent SH a copy of his book *Defending Poetry: Art and Ethics in Joseph Brodsky, Seamus Heaney, and Geoffrey Hill* (2010). The questions he asked may be inferred by and large from SH's answers to them; the book that eventuated from his researches was *The Life of Words: Etymology and Modern Poetry* (2020).

To Yvonne Reddick

TS Reddick

16 August 2012 — 191 Strand Road, Dublin 4

Dear Yvonne,

You wrote your letter on June 27, but it arrived only this morning. And as you will see from the Royal Mail's sticker, they were being unexpectedly vengeful because you treated Dublin as 'domestic' rather than 'rest of the world'.

I must admit that the lines from *Orts* that you quote do have elements that would suggest a *Bog Poems* influence, but I'd still say 'influence' is too strong a word for what, if anything, was involved. The vocabulary is suggestive – oak, bog, goddess – as is the thematic content, the 'hope / Of being disinterred'. Perhaps we could call it an echo? Perhaps, as you say, a dialogue, although that might suggest more engagement on Ted's part than I think likely. Admittedly it is true that he liked those bog poems, otherwise I don't think Olwyn would have done the limited edition on her Rainbow Press. I just don't think of Ted being prone to sound like anybody but himself, so it pleases me to think of the possibility that once, as he cleared his throat, he uttered a bog-croak.

Sunningdale is a resonant name for those of us who were around in 1973/4 when it was the place where British, Irish, and Northern Irish Governments signed an agreement to put that set of relationships on a new footing, but it was wrecked by the Loyalist Workers' Strike. When an agreement was eventually reached – the 'Good Friday Agreement' of 1998, one SDLP politician called it 'Sunningdale for slow learners'.

Fond wishes –
Seamus Heaney

The lines from Ted Hughes's *Orts*, his privately printed collection of 1978, that Reddick had offered for SH's comment, are in Hughes's *Collected Poems* (2003).

Reddick had written from Sunningdale in Berkshire; it was Seamus Mallon (1936–2020), of the Social Democratic and Labour Party, who made the quip about slow learning.

To Pat Boran

MS Boran

21 September 2012 191 Strand Road, Dublin 4

Dear Pat,

Dare I say you have wormed your way into the muse's favour? For years I have loved Harry Martinson's 'Earthworm' poem but your opener – of the book, the earth, the imagination – means that Harry must step back a bit in the line. There's a plenitude and ease about the art of *The Next Life* – a nice equivalence between the emotional content and the formal means – I especially like the at homeness with rhyme.

I've not read it totally but enough to know I should lift the hat to you and it –

Seamus

Pat Boran (b.1963) is an Irish poet and the publisher of Dedalus Press; 'Worm Song' is the first poem in his 2012 collection *The Next Life*. Could it be that 'your opener – of the book, the earth, the imagination' is a conscious echo of Christopher Ricks's pronouncement on *Field Day*? See footnote to letter to Ricks of 13 November 1979.

Harry Martinson (1904–78) was a Swedish poet and joint winner, with Eyvind Johnson, of the Nobel Prize in Literature, 1974; his 'The Earthworm' is included with several other poems by him in *The Rattle Bag*.

To Justin Elliott

TS Hull

27 September 2012 191 Strand Road, Dublin 4

Dear Justin,

Many thanks for writing like that: we had in fact changed our phone number a couple of years ago since it seemed to have gone into general circulation. I'm very sorry, however, about the circumstances in which you tried to get through on it.

The photograph you attached was a sweet and potent reminder of that period in Harry's life and ours, all of us then being young scramblers on the lower slopes of Parnassus. The sight of Harry's smiling face, of the young Edna Longley, the bookcase, the cigarettes (I think they're cigarettes) on the arm of the sofa – all of that brought back the dawn of our Belfast naissance.

We were in fairly regular contact after he moved to Didsbury and I remember attending a teachers' conference at the College, and a reading or two on other occasions. And we met, if I'm not mistaken, in his old stamping ground in Liverpool, in the tavern called The Philharmonic. When he went to Cornwall (and I half the year to Harvard) we were less in touch, but we were all part of the same growth ring from those early days.

I suppose the main thing is that his life was lived with total dedication to one thing, serving poetry and poets – a man of the 'passionate serving kind', as Yeats might have said. He was kind and – again as Yeats might have said, 'merry / For the merry love the fiddle and the merry love to dance'. Not that I ever saw Harry footing it.

Please give Marie's sympathy and mine to Hannah and to her mother who was part of the Belfast experience also, and our regrets that we didn't make the funeral. And thank you again for writing.

Sincerely
Seamus Heaney

Harry Chambers had died on 14 September. Justin Elliott is married to Chambers's daughter, and executor, Hannah.

To Philip Coleman

TS Coleman

31 October 2012 — 191 Strand Road, Dublin 4

Dear Philip,

You wrote your letter on October 5 and by October 16 – when I set out for a read-around in the States – it had not arrived. But when I got back here on Monday, having caught the last Aer Lingus flight out of Boston on Sunday evening, your invitation to take part in the Milton programme was waiting.

To do a relay reading, as it were, of *Paradise Lost* is a grand, simple idea and also a bit of a test. Thunder in the thorax required, to say nothing of the breath control. Even so, I'll be happy to join the cast/chorus, but would like to do my bit earlier in the day since that Friday evening is marked up for other business.

Dartmouth is a congenial place and I have happy memories of visits there, so I'm sure you'll have enjoyed your term in Frostrovia and Eberhartia. It was very good to hear from you and I look forward to seeing you on December 15, though not 'on the night'.

All good wishes,
Seamus Heaney

SH duly played his part in the reading of Milton's *Paradise Lost* in its entirety that took place at Trinity College Dublin on 15 December – the date, in 1667, on which the poem was first published; SH read Book I, lines 1–83.

Dartmouth College, where Philip Coleman was Visiting Associate Professor in the English Department and which houses the Milton Reading Room, devoted to studies of Milton and his works, is in Hanover, New Hampshire. Robert Frost studied at the college, and the poet Richard Eberhart (1904–2005) spent his last years in Hanover.

To Niall MacMonagle

TS MacMonagle

24 November 2012

Glanmore Cottage, Ashford,
Co. Wicklow

Dear Niall,

Windharp is a great idea, a great title and is fortunate to have a great editor. I count myself lucky to be included in the 'more than one' category and am honoured to be invited to contribute a 'postscript'. Which I shall endeavour to do.

As a way of celebrating the centenary of the Rising, it seems to me perfect. You have the Pearse and the Plunkett and the Yeats to give pleasure and gain applause wherever green is worn, and then you have all the rest who, if they're not making love outside Áras an Uachtaráin, may well be assembled for the Sunday game. The plain people of Ireland will be well served by you, yet again.

At the moment, I'm in an Old Mother Hubbard phase and have very little in the cupboard, but your invitation stirs the pot, if you'll excuse a bit of metaphor-mix. The main thing to say is how much your trust in my capacity to deliver some class of goods means to me, and I'll try my best to do so.

With fondest wishes to Mary and yourself –
Seamus

Windharp: Poems of Ireland since 1916, edited by MacMonagle, appeared in 2015; its purpose, as MacMonagle himself puts it, was 'to tell the story of Ireland, its people and beliefs, its landscape, its passion and politics, and the extraordinary changes that have occurred since the Easter Rising, 1916, through its poetry'. SH's poems 'Churning Day', 'Thatcher', 'Orange Drums, Tyrone, 1966', 'Casualty', 'Clearances 3', 'Postscript' and 'St Kevin and the Blackbird' were included. The anthology carries the dedication: '*In memory of Seamus Heaney* / For his bounty / There was no winter in't . . .' – quoting Cleopatra's praise of Antony in Act 5 of Shakespeare's play.

'making love outside Áras an Uachtaráin': there is a poem by Paul Durcan with this title.

To Monica and Tomas Tranströmer

MS Tranströmer

25 November 2012 191 Strand Road, Dublin 4

Dear Monica and Tomas,

A hundred years ago you sent a lovely kind note, which our Irish postmen spurned and returned, so you had to send it again. Please forgive me for not writing to thank you before now: partly because I didn't want us to get into a *perpetuum mobile* of 'thank you' notes, partly because I was just procrastinating.

Yes, you were right to say the prize came early – too early – in my life. I suppose I was in denial about it for the first ten years or so, but it doesn't go away and nowadays I realize that most invitations to speak, read and/or travel have little to do with me or my work, everything to do with the magic of the N word – especially in a small country like ours, which is a sort of parish, really.

Still, there should be no complaints. Marie and I are in good spirits, we have three grandchildren, three girls, youngest two, eldest six, each an apple of our eyes, of course. I spend too much time saying no to invitations, not enough being indolent, being in what Wordsworth called 'a wise passiveness'.

But the news of Tomas's Nobel gave us all an occasion for joy and allowed us to reread work that we loved already. It wakened the young poet in all of us, reminding me in particular, who have not been writing much lately, that I am 'not empty, I am open'.

I hope you dear people keep well and keep going. We remember such happy times in your company –

Love from us both to both of you –

Seamus

If SH had been awarded his Nobel Prize 'too early', the same could not have been said of Tomas Tranströmer, whose merit was not recognised by his fellow citizens until his eighty-first year. In her own congratulatory note to the Tranströmers of 12 January 2013, Marie Heaney told them: 'Seamus once said that getting the prize was "like being hit by a *mostly* benign avalanche".'

To Edna O'Brien

TS O'Brien

8 December 2012 191 Strand Road, Dublin 4

Dear Edna,

The Feast of the Immaculate Conception: at St Columb's College we would get a free day and the boarders would be allowed out into the city, to be back by 5.00. In my senior years, when I was past Santa belief and being treated by my mother as the eldest, I would go to Woolworth's to purchase coloured paper decorations – little closed accordions that opened out into long flimsy garlands and semi-circular or semi-oval units that unfolded into beautifully honeycombed spheres and ovoids. All attractive and delightful in themselves but – thinking back – strangely at odds with [the] atmosphere of that long lived-in kitchen, not yet a living room.

Would I have permitted myself that paragraph if I had not been reading *Country Girl*? Highly unlikely. But for me the book, in the early Irish stages, was total immersion, recognition and amplification, page after page of sheer language joy, image-flowering. The world retrieved and renewed. I kept making notes – the laying hen's 'yodel', the 'copious, dipping sleeve' of the Sacred Heart on *The Messenger* (which passage reminded me that the red cover was often employed in our place as a filter paper that changed a flash-lamp into a tail-light). For me there were constant little sunbursts of vocabulary that made the sparks jump and illuminations to flare. Peggy's Leg. Sun-showers. Bumpsy-daisy. Salve. As P.K. put it, 'a world comes to life'.

On the last page, that little rhapsody in blue, the blue remembered from a mosque in Istanbul and the blue of Reckitt's dye, is a lovely, perfectly placed image for what has been happening throughout the book. The dye of the west – the dye of the land, so to speak – is in the fabric of the writing, indelibly, but the exit and exultation of 'the other' is the motif that is embroidered over it.

The griefs of your young days and your maturity, the loves and partings, the exhilarations of London and New York – it all constitutes a sensation of great plenitude, and come to think of it, those blue seals at the end are like the final seal of symbolic approval on your early blue road.

And of course it was a delight to find old friends in the pages, Roger and Joseph, Andy, Stephen Rea and Neil Martin, and an especially recognizable portrait of Patrick Magee whom I met only the once, but over a couple of days when we were rehearsing and then performing John Montague's *The Rough Field* at – where – The Round House? – I was very conscious of the lava in there, just ready . . .

But the perfect pitch of Beckett's response to the news that Marguerite Duras and Peter Brook had been to see you in your post LSD distress – 'Ah, that could do it to you' – that must surely go down in the classic literary anecdote category.

I have to apologize, Edna, for not having written until now. I am a damnably slow reader and an ill-organized worker, so I hope you will pardon the tardiness.

So. Anyhow. I hope you will take pleasure in the many accolades *Country Girl* has received. It has a wonderful drive and writerly glee to it, and as my brother would say, 'We're proud of you.'

With love from Marie and yours truly –
Seamus

Edna O'Brien's memoir, *Country Girl*, is what sparked both the first paragraph and those following: Peggy's Leg is an item of confectionery, described by O'Brien as 'sweet, cinnamon-coloured and sticky', in the chapter 'Carnero', concerning her family's wild farmhand; Roger Straus, Joseph Brodsky, Andrew O'Hagan – a 'steadfast friend' of O'Brien's – the Belfast-born composer and cellist Neil Martin, and Patrick Magee (1922–82), Northern Irish stage and screen actor, are the mutual 'old friends' who appear in the book.

'a world comes to life': see Patrick Kavanagh's poem about the emergence of distant memory, 'Kerr's Ass'.

To Dean Browne

MS Browne

12 December 2012 191 Strand Road, Dublin 4

Dear Mr Browne,

Months ago you wrote a highly appreciative letter – and credible to boot – and you deserve to have heard from me long ago. So I must apologize for my long delay in getting in touch, and for the brevity of this note.

Among other things, I greatly enjoyed the accuracy and brio of your report that in your place there exists 'a humorous philistinism towards such matters as poetry' – in which phrase I see a real resilience, as well, perhaps, as a regret that there isn't more kindred company, people with an interest in the art. But even if you were surrounded by congenial literati you would still have to repair to the solitary place in yourself in order to do your own work.

In a way, the poets you read with gratitude and conviction are your literary society and I am glad to figure in your good books, as it were.

So with renewed apologies for the delay in responding and best wishes to you and yours at Christmas –

Sincerely
Seamus Heaney

Dean Browne, whose name SH spells without the 'e', now a published poet, was a seventeen-year-old schoolboy when he wrote to SH, a year before receiving this (in his own words) 'unexpected and very encouraging' reply.

To Paul Casey

TS Casey

23 December 2012 191 Strand Road, Dublin 4

Dear Paul,

Enclosed please find an unfinished letter that could not rise to saying yes to your earlier invitation in February last year and yet could not descend to saying no.

I am glad therefore that you have given me the opportunity to do better this time, so let's consider 16th December 2013 settled. And a half of the fee you mention will be plenty – use the other half for another 'gig'.

And my apologies for that dumbness earlier. I'm glad you gave me the chance to atone.

Sincerely,
Seamus

Born in Cork, the poet Paul Casey (b.1968) travelled widely before returning to his native city and setting up Ó Bhéal, his reading series there. SH's 'unfinished letter', dated 6 May 2012, was a reply to Casey's invitation to do a reading:

'Months ago you wrote me a very friendly letter and shortly after that the indomitable Delanty spoke of you "in terms of praise" so I have to apologize for the bad mannered delay in responding to your invitation to read for Ó Bhéal.

'All that you told me about the series was corroborated by Greg and he encouraged me to make the journey south. So why didn't I respond? Reluctance to put another mark on the calendar, an increasing tendency to want to stay at home rather than go out – as Larkin says – "pretending to be myself [. . .]"'

2013

The letters of this final, curtailed year of SH's show little relaxation from either public duty or the loyal keeping-up of personal friendships.

To Eoghan O'Driscoll

TS E. O'Driscoll

17 January 2013

Dear Eoghan,

Thanks for sending your book and the copy of that typically attentive, insightful and – in retrospect – heartbreaking letter from Dennis. 'Running on low', all right, he might have been, but never low enough to stint on his care for other people. The attendance at the funeral was a magnificent testimony to the place he occupied in the culture of the nation. And obviously his place in the affections of the family will be ever harder to fill.

I Went to the River is a fine title for the book, the river being an image that's invoked in so many contexts, getting to its banks a symbol for so many crises and resolutions, and it is truly a symbol since the meaning is not pat and prepackaged but holds various emotional possibilities. There is a fine passionate impulse behind many of the poems, a solidarity with the strays and outsiders, and an alertness to the contemporary world that is all your own – the way the poems are voiced by a character/characters living between the most deprived condition of the city and the old sturdy ways of the country. They have a ring of truth. And I liked your little 'author's note' on the first page.

All good wishes
Seamus Heaney

Eoghan O'Driscoll is an artist and a nephew of Dennis O'Driscoll, who had died on Christmas Eve 2012. Reporting his death in a letter to Donald Fanger of 2 January, SH had written, 'The poetry community is bereft'; but Dennis was also well known for the diligent care he took of his family in spite of his own poor health and the weight of his professional and literary commitments.

I Went to the River is a self-published collection of poems by Eoghan O'Driscoll.

To Adolphe Haberer

TS Haberer

8 April 2013 191 Strand Road, Dublin 4

[. . .]

I myself have anxiety about this whole legacy/bequesting business. There are notebooks with unpublished early student work – useless stuff, really – and I'm not sure whether to deposit it for posterity or use it for kindling in the cottage. And there are boxes of what I label 'miscellaneous mail' – a hoarder's pointless hoard. And no place to put any more books. And I'm only 74 – well, will be by the time you get this.

As to weak legs and balance, I have the same problems. Going down steps without a bannister or rail, going up steps to a podium. Wobbly, I am, with this 'absurdity', as the Gland Old Man called old age, which is a term I find unsuitable, since old people *in illo tempore* tended to be much older than I am now. But you have the nine grandchildren: three times our three (girls). *Non omnis moriamur*.

And now there comes the news that Margaret Thatcher is on Charon's barge just now. We must prepare for a media avalanche.

Marie too sends her love and is moved by your generous intentions – as is your affectionate

Seamus

Haberer had written to SH asking if he thought the National Library of Ireland might accept some of his papers relating to Irish writers; they are there now.

'*Non omnis moriamur*': after Horace's *non omnis moriar*, 'I shall not wholly die', SH putting the verb into the first-person plural while keeping *omnis* singular.

Margaret Thatcher (1925–2013), Conservative politician and British Prime Minister from 1979 to 1990, had died that very day.

To Joe Broderick

TS Broderick

20 April 2013 Glanmore Cottage, Ashford, Co. Wicklow

Dear Joe,

The natural impulse is to begin whimpering excuses for not having written sooner but I hope you will take that as read. For the past couple

of months I have been on the go constantly – two weeks in the States, a while in Oxford, several writing tasks – and I've got to the stage where I can't sit down and write a human letter unless there's a clear few days ahead. So I've finally got here to the dacha and down to business.
[. . .]
In the end I didn't go to the opening night of *Lincoln*. The thought of all that celebrity splash and flash, the red carpets, the press, the photographers – and then a black tie dinner – I didn't think it was my place, among the glitterati, though as I told you I have a very high regard for Daniel Day-Lewis personally and as an actor. I saw the picture – archaic word by now in this context – and liked it well enough, but I agree that the real energy was in the Day-Lewis scenes. There was something dutiful about it overall. I also saw the much hyped *The King's Speech* which again I thought was, in that limiting Irish sense, 'grand', or as Beckett might have put it, a bit 'trim'. (You probably saw those other Day-Lewis gems, *Gangs of New York* and *My Left Foot*.)

Speaking of gangs in New York reminds me of gangs in Boston. Not Whitey Bulger or *The Departed*, but a conference where I 'appeared' at the end of our American trip. It was the annual gathering of the AWP, the Associated Writing Programs, involving it would seem every professor-poet in every state of the union, and their graduate students as well – 12,000 overall, of whom 4,000 turned up to hear a 'conversation' between myself and Derek Walcott, mediated by Rosanna Warren, a daughter of Robert Penn Warren, a poet, scholar and a dear woman. That all went off grand too, but the surging thousands were a revelation of the bewilderment the aspiring young must experience in the writing realm, as well as being an explanation of the myriad books of poetry emitted by university presses, small presses, big presses, self-published or online.
[. . .]
I was in Lisbon a couple of times, once to read in the Casa Pessoa, an event sponsored by the Irish Embassy, and I too enjoyed that waterside stretch with the full-sailed vessels sailing past in the imagination. But I also enjoyed visiting Pessoa's favourite café, the one with a sculpture of him outside, and eating fish in tiled restaurants and going up a street level in the lifts. And indeed the late-night fado. All more or less *fadó fadó, mar a deirfeá i nGaeilge*.

A week from today Marie and I set out for Rome – and what changes there have been in that place since we met. Still, our destination is not the Vatican but the American Academy in Rome. A former student from Harvard days, now in his last year as director (it's a five-year appointment) has been inviting me since he arrived, so I finally caved in. We have rooms for three weeks in a villa which is in their grounds, but my notion that it would be all *calme, luxe et volupté* turns out to have been very wide of the mark. While we are there I am included in a three-day conference on Ovid, must do a reading at The British School, read and go through with the reception at the Irish Embassy, read at an exhibition of a limited edition ($12,000) of poems of mine about classical subjects, chosen and introduced by Helen Vendler, but there I go, whimpering again. As my father would have said, 'It's a good, dry job,' which is to say indoors, 'out the wind and the rain's way'.

I too enjoyed our while in the Shelbourne and since you mention the tea, I should remind you of Elizabeth the First's welcome back to court of the courtier who had offended some years previously: 'We have forgot the fart.'

Thank you also for the rambling birthday card. And high marks to the Rwandan postal service.

Oh – and disgracefully late greetings and gratitude for Fernando included.

Keep going –
Seamus

Joe Broderick (b.1935), an Australian living in Colombia, is a freelance writer, a translator from Shakespeare's plays, and one of the translators into Spanish of SH's poetry. Among his works is the monograph *Samuel Beckett: La tragicomedia de la vida* (2005). In a recent letter to SH, he had reported finding the movie *Lincoln*, just released, long and boring, in spite of Daniel Day-Lewis's acting in the title role.

'Whitey' Bulger (1929–2018) was a crime boss in the Boston area; Martin Scorsese's 2006 film *The Departed* is about a Boston-Irish gang; the Associated Writing Programs Conference is an annual gathering of all sorts involved in the creative writing industry; Rosanna Warren (b.1953) is a poet and scholar, daughter of two writers, Robert Penn Warren and Eleanor Clark.

Casa Fernando Pessoa, in Lisbon, is where the great Portuguese poet Fernando Pessoa (1888–1935) lived for the last fifteen years of his life; '*fadó fadó, mar a deirfeá i nGaeilge*: 'once upon a time, as you would say in Irish'.

By 'changes' in Rome, SH means the recent election of Pope Francis to succeed the very different Benedict XVI; Karl Kirchwey, as Arts Director of the American Academy, had invited SH to speak there.

John Aubrey tells the story of the Earl of Oxford and his unforgotten fart in *Brief Lives*.

The birthday card that SH describes as 'rambling' had been sent by the Colombian postal service to Rwanda instead of 'Irlanda'.

To David Harsent

TS D. Harsent

27 April 2013 191 Strand Road, Dublin 4

Dear David,

Dismayed as I am by my tardiness in thanking you for the Ritsos book, you must be even more so, more like pissed off, in fact. It's not that I hadn't read it, just that – well, excuses are always limp.

Always when I go to Ritsos I want to write, so *In Secret* brought me alive again after a dormant spell. It's the combination of clarity and mystery, image and implication that opens the inner doors. And because of the cleanliness of your versions, it is possible to move from one scenario to the next buoyantly, to go through the collection more swiftly and thoroughly than one would usually be fit to with a book of poems. It's a whole thing, in many senses, fit to accommodate the political and the erotic, the men and women, the gunshot and the knock on the door, the mirror and the dangers.

It is substantial and utterly convincing, and your long immersion in Ritsos has resulted in a sure and swift voice for the translations. The contents page here is now full of ticks, but it's the constancy of each single success that is the impressive thing, each poem – to quote W.B. – like a new bud on an old bough, or perhaps we should say a new thorn on an old briar.

Your afterword is another gift to the reader and I have copied out the manifesto/apologia of the last paragraph: 'a poet's vocabulary isn't dictionary-definable.' Anyhow, I'm the better for having read and dwelt with the book and I thank you for the gift of it.

We also had a happy reunion with Simon – and then *from* him a copy of his magnificent iceberg book. Maybe the best book of photographs I've seen –

Seamus

The British poet David Harsent (b.1942) had published *In Secret: Versions of Yannis Ritsos* the year before; Ritsos (1909–90) spent many years of his life imprisoned or in detention under right-wing Greek governments.

'Simon' is Harsent's son (b.1965), a photographer who had taken SH's portrait (see letter to Simon Harsent of 31 May 2013) and whose book of photographs, *Melt: Portrait of an Iceberg* (2009), SH refers to here. The paragraph concerning him is in SH's hand.

To Conor O'Callaghan

MS O'Callaghan

22 May 2013 191 Strand Road, Dublin 4

Dear Conor,

For the past three weeks I've been on a 'residency', the first ever, at the American Academy in Rome. Busy, on show, but taking pleasure in it even so. Rome was reward enough.

But there was another reward waiting when I got back in the shape, indeed the shapes of *The Sun King*. Tremendous vigour and variety of registers – tender, rumbunctious, meditative, truthful. A great charge running in the language, a sense of work being done, matters being cleared, experiences got through and changed into free things, enjoying themselves. Your letter moved me greatly and is cherished for its forthrightness and generosity. I once wrote in similar vein – a once off, quick-quick semaphore to Ted Hughes.

More power to you. It's a terrific book – Seamus

The Sun King, recently published by Gallery Press, was the fourth collection of Conor O'Callaghan, born in Northern Ireland but brought up in the Republic.

The 'semaphore to Ted Hughes' would have been in this book if it had been traceable.

To Simon Harsent

MS S. Harsent

31 May 2013 191 Strand Road, Dublin 4

Dear Simon,

Marie and I have just come back from a while in Rome where we saw many great portraits of popes and princes, especially in a mighty Titian show, so it was exhilarating to arrive home and find the magnificent prints. I know from other occasions how difficult it is to 'get' so many things that need to be gotten – some sense of the sitter's being, the photographer's technical and artistic standards to be met to his own satisfaction, a certain otherness in the likeness – all triumphantly achieved. You are extremely generous to send so many, any one of which is outstanding – and in-dwelling, as it were. I have a sense, indeed, that I'm about to attain iceberg status.

Masterly work. I'm honoured by it and deeply grateful –

Blessings on the work –

Seamus

See letter of 27 April 2013 to David Harsent, Simon's father.

To Michael Alexander

TS Alexander

2 June 2013 191 Strand Road, Dublin 4

Dear Michael –

That's a handsome edition and a vivid, valuable renovation of the introduction. So much knowledge and insight – and true life confessions, as it were: an hour a line the rate you reckon . . . But I believe it as I read through your pages once again. You are so true to the otherness and the idiom, the metrical rule and the decided movement of the verse. So I could without exaggeration praise a mighty achievement. But still. It distresses me to have to decline the invitation to give a pre-publication quote. Given your generosity and blessings on my own go at the Geat, I would like to salute a master, but if I did it would look like betrayal of the many people I have already refused. Years ago I had to take the decision to say no to every request of this nature, otherwise it would end up being an agony of decision on each occasion, not to mention a toll on one's time. So many friends have been disobliged in this way that I cannot, as they say, make a liar of myself at this stage – and in fact after I write this I have to write to another poet friend with the same message. And I'll enclose to him also what I enclose here for you, a copy of the form letter that goes out often and always uneasily.

I am truly sorry that this needs to be such a niggardly response.

Exit, hangdog –

Seamus

In answer to a request for SH's endorsement of the revised edition of Alexander's verse translation of *Beowulf*. 'Exit, hangdog' is handwritten.

To Matthew Hollis

EMAIL Faber

9 June 2013

Dear Matthew,

You should have heard from me before this to thank you for those terrific minutes of our working lunch. It really lifted the heart. The day after I set to, ridding the attic, sorting through casefuls – four big casefuls – of papers and letters and keepsakes and scripts and press cuttings. Still one and a half cases to go, but the move signifies a new address to the days ahead.

My purpose now, however, is to mention a poet who submitted a manuscript to Faber in February. Truth to tell, I promised him I would tell you about the submission but failed to do so. But now that he is re-submitting, with my encouragement, for the New Poets series, I must mention Cathal McCabe. I did make it clear that he must not expect results just because I am letting you know about his entry, but feel in honour bound to fulfil my promise, late as it is. There now, why didn't you do that long ago, Seamus?

The Muldoon book is a nifty job, both cover and contents. Thank you for that also. We had dinner with him on Friday – on his way to London, to join up for another 'Semester at Sea', but round the Mediterranean this time. Quite a lad.

Seamus

SH and Matthew Hollis, who had become Poetry Editor at Faber in 2012, had met over lunch on 27 May at the Cliff Townhouse in Dublin, to discuss future projects.

Cathal McCabe's submission was not successful.

Paul Muldoon's new book was *Word on the Street*, a collection of his rock lyrics.

To Donald Fanger

EMAIL Fanger

10 June 2013

Dear Fanger,

Heap sorry for not getting back to you super dottum. Not to be taken as any symptom of unwelcome.

We look forward greatly to seeing you and hope this hold-up hasn't messed up your flight plans, since earlier usually means cheaper. Anyhow, the news is that we are both in good working order and good spirits, which will be lifted higher when we see you and Leonie.

The days that we are tied up are as follows: August 4, 5, 6, 7, at the Yeats Summer School in Sligo.

August 14, 15 – Reading in Derry City with Uilleann Piper, Liam O'Flynn.

August 16 – at Merriman School in Co. Clare – Brian Merriman, author of sexy dream vision poem in Irish, late 18th century.

We'll be in Dublin 1–3 August, 8–12 August, 19–31 August. So we could assemble in Strand Road or revel in some 'atin' house' as the poet Kavanagh called the higher rated restaurants in Dublin.

I'll be at home tomorrow but we're off to Paris on Wednesday and I'm so primitive when it comes to email that I can only do it from my machine here on the desk at home. But Susie will be keeping her eye on the messages.

It is very good to know you're on the move, that you have faced down the enemies and will ride in triumph through Hibernia.

Love from both of us to both of ye –

Seamus

SH's assistant Susie had been helping Donald and Leonie Fanger plan their 2013 trip to Ireland.

The 'enemies' Fanger had 'faced down' – in the spirit of Marlowe's Tamburlaine at Persepolis – were health problems.

To Joseph Woods

TS Woods

17 June 2013 — 191 Strand Road, Dublin 4

Dear Joe,

You know the way the Romans marked time by naming the consuls who were at the head of the operation that year – well, as far as poetry in Ireland is concerned, the opening years of the twenty-first century will be known as Consule Silvis.

Your constancy and care, you hand on the helm, your rein on the Hibernian Pegasus since 2001 – all that, and your sturdy presence at event after event, not to mention the preparation of introductions, the arrangement of programmes, the general availability – it has all been an inestimable service to the art, the artists and the audiences.

So I am sorry that Marie and I have to be in Oxford this Friday to attend a memorial service for Jon Stallworthy's wife Jill, who died a couple of months ago. The service is well outside the town, so Marie and I are booked on the 8.10 p.m. flight home – which means we can't attend either the earlier or the later celebration. A real pity, but there we are.

I know you and Sara are off to pastures new after this. We wish both of you all the best on the Burma adventure and will gratefully remember the readings and revels you treated us to.

Fondest wishes and bon voyage,
Seamus

Woods, who has been director of Poetry Ireland since 2001, was about to move with his wife to Yangon, Myanmar.

To Mary Clayton

EMAIL Clayton

23 July 2013

Dear Mary,

You make everything so easy and reassure the creature that all will be well. I am extremely grateful for your suggestions about poems to read and for arranging the travel with Niall.

Now that I have had a look at the programme, I realize what an enormous feat of organization you have been involved in this past couple of years, and from the look of what has been arranged you will have a happy squad of scholars and a memorable success on your steady hands.

The Lay of the Last Minstrel, certainly, and a couple of other extracts, definitely. 'St Kevin and the Blackbird' and the Clonmacnoise poem. Maybe that bit of the 'Voyage of Bran' where Manannán tells how Bran cannot see what he sees – a bit of the marvellous, as it were. Maybe at some point 'Deor', and a bardic poem – 15/16 century by date but culturally much much older – the question of craft and rivalry of poets arises in each case. (Attached.)

The Colmcille poems, definitely. Maybe a few early blackbirds . . . I appreciate the half-hour slot.

I'll be delighted to sign the Henrysons when Niall calls here. And I decided that he was a bit late in the day for the reading.

I'm looking forward to seeing Dan and Jack and – so near and yet so far – the stupendous Carrigan.

With thanks for all the care you've taken –

Seamus

Mary Clayton, Professor of Old and Middle English at UCD, was organiser of the 2013 International Society of Anglo-Saxonists Conference held at the National Museum, Dublin; SH's reading, the contents of which are under discussion here, was the opening event, on 28 July. 'Niall' is Clayton's husband, Niall MacMonagle.

To Matthew Hollis — EMAIL Faber

31 July 2013

Dear Matthew,

Thanks for keeping those ideas bobbing towards a perhaps landfall. And it so happens the latter part of August is when some time opens up for me too. So, to be continued, definitely.

Off now to Yeats summer school in Sligo.

Seamus

This followed a discussion between SH and Hollis of possible future books, which included translations of Sophocles's *Ajax* and Virgil's *Eclogues*, neither of which materialised, as well as the posthumously published *Aeneid Book VI* (2016), *New Selected Poems 1988–2013* (2014) and *100 Poems* (2018).

To Marco Sonzogni

EMAIL Sonzogni

8 August 2013

Dear Marco,

What scrupulous and painstaking work you are doing. I am very glad to give what guidance I can. Am a bit late since I'm just back from Sligo and the Yeats school.

1. The 'she' in 'Sloe Gin' is the spouse of sh . . . sh . . . sh.

2. 'Making Strange' was intending to have its academic cake and eat it along with its colloquial Irish usage, but that double meaning is probably not to be found in Italian. I suppose the immediate sense of the closing phrase is indeed 'began to go shy'. The speaker had in a sense betrayed the territory by 'selling' it in the telling, and so was a little shy in face of it. You express the subtleties and fine distinctions wonderfully well.

The school-leaver under the beech is being 'No-Good Boyo', as Dylan Thomas called an adolescent in *Under Milk Wood*. Experimenting with himself, as you so elegantly put it.

3. 'I want away to my father . . .' is a slightly altered quotation from my version of *Philoctetes*, *The Cure at Troy*, where the lines are spoken by the protagonist at a point where he is in dialogue with the chorus. In the Faber paperback it comes on page 64.

4. I have indeed changed the fountain pen poem to end as in the attached – and cut out 'to be', since whether I write or not, poems will not cease to be. Will attach new version – but I don't think there needs to be any change in the foreword – it's pens rather than spades that make the link in that paragraph. But tweak if you need to.

There have been no changes in 'Postscript' – perhaps a slip of the tongue was what the vigilant Piero heard in Rome.

5. I can see the logic of including 'Nostalgia . . .' but can hardly bear to think of it 'resurrected'. The earliest one I'd like is 'October Thought' which appeared in the QUB student magazine *Q* in 1959. Then perhaps 'McKenna's Saturday Night', published in the *Kilkenny Magazine*, Autumn/Winter 1963–64:17.

I realize 'October Thought' is untranslatable, so don't worry about that. Just go wild.

I wrote three poems with McKenna as protagonist – influenced by Kavanagh.

I'm not sure about a translation – if I get a Pascoli that's passable, it would save you the job of construing . . .

Fond wishes, Marco –

Seamus

Poesie Scelte, containing poems by SH translated into Italian by various hands, edited by Sonzogni and published by Mondadori, did not appear until 2016. Of the more obscure items mentioned here, 'October Thought' is a heavily Hopkins-influenced product of SH's 'Incertus' period, while 'McKenna's Saturday Night' – concerning the behaviour of an archetypal figure a little like Maguire in Patrick Kavanagh's *The Great Hunger* – had been in a 1963 issue of the *Kilkenny Magazine*.

To Marie Heaney — TEXT MESSAGE

[30 August 2013]

Noli timere.

SH died on the morning of 30 August as he was being taken to the operating theatre in Dublin's Blackrock Clinic, for an emergency procedure on a ruptured artery. His last, texted message to Marie Heaney, though in Latin – meaning 'Don't be afraid' – almost immediately achieved widespread circulation and proverbial status.

Quotation Acknowledgements

pp. 15–16: Letter from Ted Hughes to Charles Monteith, May 1966, taken from the Faber archive © Ted Hughes. Reproduced by permission of the Ted Hughes Estate p. 156: Ralph Hodgson, 'The Song of Honour', *The Song of Honour* (A. T. Stevens, 1913). p. 185: Robert Lowell, 'Waking Early Sunday Morning', *Near the Ocean* (Faber and Faber, 1967). p. 187: Philip Larkin, 'Afternoons', *The Whitsun Weddings* (Faber and Faber, 1964). p. 311: Letter from Ted Hughes to SH, 8 October 1989, in *Letters of Ted Hughes*, ed. Christopher Reid (Faber and Faber, 2007). p. 358: Anna Kamieńska, 'The Other World', in *Spoiling Cannibals' Fun: Polish Poetry of the Last Two Decades of Communist Rule*, ed. and trans. Stanisław Barańczak and Clare Cavanagh (North Western University Press, 1991). p. 365: Robert Bly, *Airmail*: *The Letters of Robert Bly and Tomas Tranströmer* (Graywolf, 2013). p. 428: Patrick Kavanagh, 'The Hospital', reprinted from *Collected Poems*, ed. Antoinette Quinn (Allen Lane, 2004), by kind permission of the Trustees of the Estate of the late Katherine B. Kavanagh, through the Jonathan Williams Literary Agency. pp. 481 and 549: T. S. Eliot, 'The Love Song of J. Alfred Prufrock', 'Fragment of an Agon', *Collected Poems 1909–1962* (Faber and Faber, 1963). p. 486: Letter from Ted Hughes to SH, 1 January 1998, in *Letters of Ted Hughes*, ed. Christopher Reid (Faber and Faber, 2007). p. 598: Hugh MacDiarmid, 'Perfect', *The Islands of Scotland*, 1939, *Selected Poems*, ed. Alan Riach and Michael Grieve (Carcanet 1992; Penguin 1994), who acknowledged that the wording of lines 2–8 were taken from Glyn Jones's 'Porth-y-Rhyd', *The Blue Bed*, Jonathan Cape, 1937, reproduced by the kind permission of the Estate of Glyn Jones and Llenyddiaeth Cymru/Literature Wales. pp. 615–16: Derek Mahon, 'Glengormley', *New Selected Poems* (Gallery/Faber and Faber, 2016). p. 647: Paul Durcan, 'A View of the Bridge', *The Laughter of Mothers* (Harvill Secker, 2007). p. 678: Simon Armitage, *Sir Gawain and the Green Knight* (Faber and Faber, 2007). p. 712: Thomas Lynch, 'Ground Sense' [Programme Note], *The Burial at Thebes*, Peacock Theatre (Abbey Theatre, 2008). p. 721: Wallace Stevens, 'The Man with the Blue Guitar', *Collected Poems* (Alfred Knopf, 1954; Faber and Faber, 1955). p. 728: Robert Pinsky, 'Stupid Meditation on Peace', *Gulf Music* (Farrar, Straus and Giroux, 2007). p. 736: Frank Ormsby, 'Small World', *Fireflies* (Carcanet, 2009).

Index

Index of Works

Index of Recipients